THAT DREAM SHALL HAVE A NAME

That Dream Shall Have a Name

NATIVE AMERICANS REWRITING AMERICA

David L. Moore

University of Nebraska Press
Lincoln and London

A portion of the proceeds from this book will be donated to the American Indian Higher Education Fund.

Library of Congress Cataloging-in-Publication Data

Moore, David L.

That dream shall have a name: native Americans rewriting America / David L. Moore.

pages cm

Includes bibliographical references and index.

ISBN 978-0-8032-1108-7 (pbk.: alk. paper)

1. American literature—Indian authors. 2. Indians in literature. I. Title.

PS508.I5M64 2014

810.9'897—dc23   2013034297

Set in Lyon Text by Laura Wellington.

Designed by J. Vadnais.

Dedicated to the land, the ancestors,
the children, the wounded, and the healing.

That dream
shall have a name
after all,
and it will not be vengeful
but wealthy with love
and compassion
and knowledge.
And it will rise
in this heart
which is our America.

—Simon Ortiz, *from Sand Creek*

CONTENTS

PREFACE

Over decades of trying to help college students of all backgrounds read Native American literatures, I gradually saw patterns in their questions. Thus I came to recognize five areas of understanding necessary for listening and responding to Native voices, and those five areas form the circle and the center of this book. Collecting and addressing the underlying questions as a set, I have chosen from time to time to engage classroom issues directly as an entrée into grounding thematic questions and as a link to those audiences in classrooms and communities. Native and non-Native students and their teachers are one intended audience, and I address scholarly readers as well, because I find that maintaining practical connections to classroom and community refines theoretical inquiry.

In that process the themes of this study emerge. Whether in high school and university classrooms, in Indigenous communities, or in professional conferences and publications, wherever conversations about Indians may turn on historical perspectives, cultural values, legal relationships, political dynamics, economic issues, or spiritual understanding, the following five underlying themes almost invariably come into play: authenticity, identity, community, sovereignty, and humor, or more generally irony.

A number of Native writers and scholars have shared with me how tiresome the persistence of elementary questions about Indians can get, questions that can sometimes mask an automatic posture of disrespect—"Are you a *real* Indian?" "Why don't you just become Americans?" "Why do Indians get special privileges?"—even while vital issues remain far from resolved.

Authenticity and the other terms come immediately into play in countless daily exchanges in Indian Country. Similarly when I mention to a non-Indian fellow traveler on an airplane or at a picnic that I teach in the field of Native American literature, I sometimes get the skeptical response, "Do Indians *have* literature?" Sometimes the question is delivered with distinct vitriol. If Indian America is not only under the radar but semiconsciously repressed and suppressed, how could the American mainstream pay any attention to any of the themes of this book? Indeed I argue that Indigenous issues are ignored for ironic reasons that remain central to America's often unrealized longings for its own true authenticity, identity, community, and sovereignty.

Especially when dominant bureaucracies get involved, there are profoundly different ways, Indian and white, of approaching each of these five broad issues, and America's discourse about Indians, whether casual or official, remains contested particularly around these terms. Scholars, Native and non-Native, eventually agree on some fundamental differences between Indigenous and Euro-American cultures, having to do with interconnection, complexity, and kinship. By such differences each of the five terms may be understood in reductive, either/or ways of thinking or in more complex, nuanced, even tricky ways. Native writers tend to move away from the either/or options that Euro-Americans find easier to manipulate and to drive relations with Indians. "Kill the Indian and save the man!" would be the ultimate expression of that kind of assimilationist policy. Pluralism would be its opposite. For both cultural and historical reasons, binary narrative structures tend to support stories as told by the invaders: winners versus losers; civilization versus wilderness; even Indian versus white. As Native American writers might think of sovereignty, community, identity, and authenticity in complex, often humorous or ironical ways, then America might gradually think beyond the binaries of history.

What I discovered further is that those five areas of social interaction also tend to define or map what the world thinks of generally as a national entity, a national identity. To be a nation, we collect our stories within those themes of authenticity, identity, community, and sovereignty, and within each of those areas we experience unresolved ironies that often generate a vital sense of humanity, of self-reflection and empathy, at times most vividly crystallized in humor.

The convergence of these two lines of thinking, where five key terms in

Native expression merge with five key terms constituting a nation, resulted in this book: a look at how Native American voices would rewrite the American nation, indeed how they have been rewriting it from the start. As the historian William E. Farr wrote at the turn of the millennium, "For the past twenty years, western revisionists have been saying that we in the region must 'rewrite our narrative,' tell a different story, change our values" (Farr and Bevis, *Fifty Years after* The Big Sky 4). That urge to "change our values" has not been limited to America's West. Clearly the pressure of "a different story" has been building in Indigenous voices for far longer than twenty years. Some Native authors have rewritten the story explicitly, some implicitly, and I try here to read how those literary efforts might speak to Native and non-Native readers alike.

Fundamentally this discussion arises from a deeper recognition that both the questions and the answers to a key issue of the modern age are pulsing in the veins of Native American literary expression. The modern, and now millennial question, from America to Bosnia to Sri Lanka, from Rwanda to Sudan to Venezuela, is ethnic difference within nation-states. It is a political question which translates into the philosophical and ethical problem of unity in diversity and which is the challenge of a now post-postcolonial and post-postmodern world. It is the originary American question of a "united states."

Native American voices have been speaking cogently in print to that question for centuries. One of the fundamental dynamics of Native American storytelling may be the vitality and practicality of this principle of unity in diversity, specifically that it refines the Latinate discourse of *e pluribus unum*, which is linear in its trajectory of moving from diversity toward unity as "*out of* many, one." Instead the unity in diversity suggested in such terms as the Lakota "Ho mitakuye oyasin!" (All my relatives!) or in the Iroquois "Akwe:kon" (All of us) balances unity *and* diversity in the dynamic of difference as the robust energy of community.

The material repression and oppression of Indigenous voices for over five hundred years by the oppositional forces of history are the denial of this principle. The dialectical materialism that would swallow up Native land stands in direct antagonism to unity in diversity by unity in uniformity, by the mercantile co-optation of otherness as resource and marketplace. By the turn of the twenty-first century, the self-destructive tendencies of that global system are becoming clearer to some, perhaps to many. Indigenous ways of knowing and being interconnected within ecosystems are emerging by default against the corruption and pollution of the dominating economic logic. Strategically, dialogue beyond dialectics seems to be the dynamic of that unity in diversity.

Of course, many Native communities and individuals have not always demonstrated such dialogue when confronted by the brutal dualities and dilemmas of colonial domination. Yet there remains a voice of dialogue in Native literature, and that is what I am listening to here. How it speaks both among Native voices and between the Indigenous and the invaders plays out in a variety of ways that I have factored into those five interweaving categories. By analyzing texts of some key Native American writers over three centuries in relation to those five themes of interrelationship, I hope to tease out a clearer understanding of the possibilities of unity in diversity for America today.

A note on terminology, which goes to the heart of this study: Like many of my colleagues discussing Native studies, I variously employ terms that are used both casually and formally in tribal and scholarly contexts, such as *Indian, American Indian, Native American*, and *Indigenous*, but I prefer tribally specific monikers whenever appropriate. Such flexibility actually matches the resilience, as well as the resistant autonomy, of Native discourse and expressed values. In referring to the invaders, I generally employ *Euro-American*, though I want to address a fascinating choice by the Cherokee scholar Daniel Heath Justice, who prefers the label *Eurowestern* over *Euro-American* because the latter, Justice says, is "another appropriation by the colonizers of Indigenous presence" (*Our Fire Survives the Storm* xvi). While I entirely agree with Justice's compelling and nuanced point in this discursive observation, I have important reasons for retaining more common terminology. This book is partly about Native self-expression as it bears on non-Native national identities, specifically how Indigenous writers would change Europeans into Americans. Indigenous writing often, though not always, bears the burden of this purpose. Thus I use *Euro-American* not as a colonizer's appropriation but, toward the indeed utopian undertones in much of Native writing, as a goal of mutuality and respect. (And I retain the capitalized first

A to maintain the continental and cultural distinctions.) I respect Justice's reasons for suspecting the term of insidious discursive theft. His own approach as "explicitly activist and to some degree polemical" (8) makes room for such revisionism. My own position as a "Eurowesterner" requires a different ethical approach. Trying to remain descriptive rather than prescriptive in foregrounding Native voices, this study is indeed an attempt to reenvision what Euro-Americans might become if they learn to listen to Native American approaches to America.

ACKNOWLEDGMENTS

Since writing is a dialogue, I'm grateful for so many conversations that clarified living facets of this research. First of all, to my wife, Kate Shanley, the deepest, loving thanks. To our sons, Jay and Caleb, thanks for all your open-hearted support. To my father, Richard O. Moore, and my late mother, Eleanor McKinney Sowande, I'm endlessly thankful, and I hope this text is worthy of your legacy. To all the rest of my family, friends, colleagues, and students, living and dead, our connections have made many insights possible. The shortcomings remain my own, and I continue gratefully to learn from you: Thomas Parkinson, Ariel Parkinson, Lewis Hill, Joy Hill, Fela Sowande, Ruth Moore, Flinn Moore Rauck, John Rauck, Jere McKinney, Christopher Cole Hill, Martha DeHart, Bill Owens, Sandy Frazier, Ellsworth LeBeau, Gloria Kaberna, Florence Swift Hawk, Phyllis Swift Hawk, Bryant High Horse, Frank Fools Crow, Bill Lone Hill, Vinson Brown, Barbara Brown, Keven Brown, Tamara Brown, Charlie Kills Enemy, John Halsey, Adam Sitting Crow, John R. Milton, Dennis Klein, Helen Fremstad, Gervase Hittle, Wayne Evans, Chuck Swick, Charlie Leucke, Mack Cash, Faith Spotted Eagle, Joseph Marshall III, Louis Moves Camp, Terry Culhane, Edwin Roberts, Dace Roberts, Ruhaniyyih Ruth Moffatt, Glenford Mitchell, Daniel Jordan, Dwight Allen, Francis Auld, Deanna Ellenwood, Francine Dupuis, Joe Dupuis, Leroy Black Jr., Paul Black, Josiah Black, Billie Thomas Black, Vivian Black, Leroy Black Sr., Willie Caye, Junior Caye, Gigi Caye, Rosemary Caye, Reuben Mathias, Phyllis Mathias, Alec Lefthand, Pat Lefthand, Naida Lefthand, Joseph Macdonald, Sherry Macdonald, Ron Therriault, Ginny Therriault, Roy Bigcrane, Frank Tyro, Bettina Escudero, Joyce Silverthorne, Ruth Silverthorne, Renée Roulier-Madrigal, Betty White, Germaine White, Greg Dumontier, Myrna Adams Dumontier, Joe Pablo, Johnny Arlee, Joan Arlee, Frances Vanderburg, Candace Fleming, Bearhead Swaney, Billy Swaney, Grace Musser-Sage, Max Sage, Thompson Smith, Karin Stallard, Robey Clark, Alexsandra Burt, Merle Yellow Kidney, Michael D. Wilson, Jose Barreiro, Katsi Cook, Ron LaFrance, A. LaVonne Brown Ruoff, Kim Blaeser, Simon Ortiz, Vine Deloria Jr., James Welch, Lois Welch, Bernadette Rigal-Cellard, Arnold Krupat, Robert Warrior, Jace Weaver, Craig Womack, Elizabeth Cook-Lynn, Ron Welburn, Susan Brill de Ramirez, David Abram, George Price, Christopher Preston, Gyda Swaney, Phil Condon, Celeste River, Don Birchfield, Adam Fortunate Eagle, Raso Hultgren, Martin Suda, Margaret Kingsland, Katie Kane, Linda Juneau, Rob Collier, Pat Weaselhead, Irvin Morris, William YellowRobe, Daniel Heath Justice, Deborah Madsen, Robert M. Nelson, Lawana Trout, Henry Dobyns, Frederick Hoxie, Duane Niatum, Kay WalkingStick, Dominick LaCapra, Ross Posnock, Robert Abrams, Hazard Adams, Charles Altieri, Joseph Cash, Herbert T. Hoover, Barry Maxwell, Shelley Wong, Lisa Brooks, Sean Teuton, Kay Yandell, Dylan Suagee, Sarah Pevar, Matthew Henry, July Cole, Nick Myers, Matthew Burkhardt, Ben Kuntz, Travis Burdick, Steven Hawley, Kerry Fine, Adrianna Ely, Michelle Brown, Ashby Kinch, Lynn Itagaki, Nancy Cook, Ken Egan, Roger Dunsmore, W. Jed Barry, Prageeta Sharma, and Dale Sherrard. Thanks to the Assiniboine family and community at Ft. Peck reservation that I married into, especially The Magnificent Seven, and Larry Wetsit, Kenny Ryan, Joe Miller, Robert Fourstar, Edna Wetsit, Jim Shanley, Claymore Shanley, J. D. Wetsit, Michael Shanley, Jack Shanley, Lois Steele, Cary Williams, Stacy Steele, George Redstone, Ron Jackson, Ruth Jackson, Dude Jackson, Bernadette Jackson, Doug Runs Through, Harold Bailey, Mark Turcotte, Oliver Archdale, Rosalee Archdale, Butch Bell, Patty McGeshick, Nathan Beaudry, J. R. Beauchamp, Colleen Clark, Tony Plummer-Alvernaz, Joe McGeshick, David Miller, Jim Johnson, Ron Dumont, Frank Dumont, and many others. Thanks to my editors at University of Nebraska Press, Matt Bokovoy, Gary Dunham, Ann Baker, and Judith Hoover. For fellowship support, thanks to the Cornell Society for the Humanities and the O'Connor Center for the Rocky Mountain West. Thanks to Cambridge University Press, publishers of my essay "Sherman Alexie" in *The Cambridge Companion to Native American Literature*, from which some of the passages in the humor chapter have been reworked. Pinamiya.

THAT DREAM SHALL HAVE A NAME

INTRODUCTION

Fool Soldiers

A True Story

Around 1860 in what is now South Dakota, Wanatan, or Martin Charger, a young mixed-blood member of the Lakota Sioux nation, lived in the Indian village across the Missouri River from the old Ft. Pierre trading post. Charger, a member of the Two Kettles band, was reputed to be the grandson of Meriwether Lewis. According to one Two Kettle Lakota oral tradition, Lewis had had a liaison in late September 1804 with the daughter of Buffalo Robe, a Lakota subchief along the Missouri trek where the Corps of Discovery had camped for four days of tense negotiations and conciliatory feasting at the mouth of the Teton River. The result of that union was Zomie, or Turkey Head, also known as Long House, who in turn was the father of Martin Charger. Another story makes Charger the grandson of an early trader named Reuben Lewis.[1] Whichever story is real, it is clear that this young man grew up with a unique perspective as a mixed-blood, yet traditional, Lakota.

Just prior to 1862, Charger, along with his *kola* (beloved friend) Kills Game and Returns Triumphant, had organized a band of *akicita*, a soldier society. Their uncomplicated mandate, "to help others," had come from Kills Game's vision of ten black deer. In the dream, one among the black stags who spoke to Kills Game had said simply and forcefully, "Do good for the people." Charger and Kills Game felt their lives were lined up together in this vision. They joined with a small number of companions, among them Swift Bird and Four Bears, to respond to frontier events in the spirit of traditional Lakota values of courage, fortitude, generosity, and respect for wisdom, to be a peaceful center in the growing storm.

The late summer and fall of 1862 brought the full force of that storm down upon them. Just east of Dakota Territory, their woodland cousins the Santee Sioux had been squeezed for decades by white settlements into a narrow corridor along the Minnesota River. The Santees' treaty rights to annuity supplies had been trampled by corrupt agents from the Bureau of Indian Affairs. They were starving, and the now famous retort by the agent had been, "Let them eat grass." After a violent incident over a settler's cow in July, the Santees finally ransacked the settlements in Minnesota, more populous than the Dakotas, killing more than eight hundred men, women, and children and driving off the other settlers. To put down the so-called Minnesota Uprising, a local militia, backed by the U.S. Army in the midst of its own war farther east and south, retaliated and defeated the Santees, imprisoning around two thousand warriors. But many Santees escaped and scattered, both to Canada and to the Dakotas along the Missouri River.

One starving Santee band of fugitives, led by White Lodge, arrived that fall near the trading post called Ft. Pierre on the Missouri, where Charger, his family and friends, and their akicita society made their home in the permanent Sans Arc and Two Kettles camp. Though the Santees were defeated and bedraggled, they still were looking for allies to fight the whites. White Lodge's band paraded their secret weapon: white hostages, two women and four children. Saying the whites wouldn't fire on them as long as they held captives, White Lodge challenged the Two Kettles and Sans Arcs to join them in war against the whites so that what had happened in Minnesota would not happen in the Dakotas. Many older Two Kettles wanted to join White Lodge, but some of the warrior youths were against it, partly because the Santees had previously encroached on their hunting grounds. So the Two Kettles said no thanks to the prospect of war and sent the disappointed Santees and their hostages upriver with some provisions.

Charger's young akicita society saw here an opportunity to fulfill their vision. They spoke in council to rally their people to join them in freeing the white hostages from the Santees. Yet their words did not move their fellow Lakotas. Unsuccessful in persuading the rest of the skeptical camp to support them, they loaded up goods donated from Charlie Primeau's trading post at Ft. Pierre and headed upriver on horseback, about ten days behind the Santees. They found White Lodge's band camped on the cottonwood flats across from the mouth of the Grand River. The camp was in bad shape, having been joined by more Santee stragglers from the Minnesota fighting. It was October, with winter coming on, and there was little food. Charger's group of warriors, barely ten strong including some of their wives to mark them as a peace delegation, considered attacking but knew they could not fight that many Santees. They were in a position only to barter for what they wanted, but the ground they stood upon served their purposes.

White Lodge and his followers were starving. They took the ransom goods and more. Although one member of Charger's group refused to give up his horse, White Lodge traded the hostages for nearly everything else the *akicitas* had: horses, blankets, dried meat, even moccasins.

As Charger and his friends headed back south with the captives, the early snows began. They walked and carried the children on their backs or on their one horse, stopping to wait out the icy storms in an abandoned cabin. When they finally reached Ft. Pierre after a grueling trek of wintry weeks, the trader Charlie Primeau provided a wagon and horses, and they hauled the captives farther south along the Missouri, two or three days, to Ft. Randall, where the bluecoat troops could return the freed hostages to remnants of their Minnesota families.

But Charger's *akicitas* were not prepared for the greeting they got from the U.S. Army troops under Colonel Pattee, in charge of the Ft. Randall garrison. Ever since the Minnesota war that fall, the whites all over Dakota country had been trigger-happy. Aggravating the tensions, President Lincoln had issued an order that those involved in the massacres should be executed. Pattee received the hostages, heard nothing of their friendship with their rescuers, and promptly threw Charger, Kills Game, and their companions into the stockade jail. They watched two members of their soldier society die there of exposure. After weeks of imprisonment, the rest were sent back to Ft. Pierre with Colonel Pattee's bizarre warning: Let this harsh treatment be an object lesson to any Indian who crosses the whites.

Ironies mounted on ironies. When Charger and his exhausted, grieving group drove Primeau's wagon back into the Two Kettles camp, they were not welcomed home. In the confused distress of 1862–63, the rest of the Two Kettles met them with the mocking epithet by which history now knows them: *Akicita wacintonsni*, "Fool Soldiers."

Though the wind-driven snows had covered the plains and the river breaks, the small group of warriors and their wives soon left the shame of that camp and moved to a new site upriver, a corner of the later Cheyenne River Sioux Reservation, where for decades they lived out their lives. Until recently Lakota descendants of the Fool Soldiers remained ashamed of their family heritage, though several among them claimed into the later twentieth century that their own ancestor had been the leader, whether Swift Bird, Four Bears, or Charger. Charger died around the turn of the twentieth century, after congressional hearings and reparations had recognized his efforts at reconciliation as "a friend of the white man," always a dubious distinction.[2]

The Imaginary Frontier

Beyond language, beyond limiting labels that divide and conquer lives on the land, the earth itself exemplifies a way to behave, a way to think without borders, in cycles, a way to live, serve, die. The powerfully silent earth finds voice in Indigenous lifeways. The Fool Soldiers, not unlike Indian activists a century later at Alcatraz in 1969 or at Wounded Knee in 1973, were advocating essentially what Native storytellers and writers have been saying from the beginning, like the earth itself: We are here. We are alive. We are not leaving.

These are some radical ideas I hear in this story. Since first hearing of Martin Charger and his akicita band during my days as an undergraduate at the University of South Dakota, I've come to understand how resolutely Indian activists and writers have been trying to rewrite history, the "vanishing" narrative of Indians in America, from the beginning of the colonial era, since long before the 1960s or 1970s.[3] With an activist agenda, Native writers have struggled to redefine America from the start, because America is built on the vanishing of Indians.[4] Indeed among the grievances in the Declaration of Independence was the standard view that King George III "endeavoured to bring on the inhabitants of our frontiers, the merciless Indian Savages, whose known rule of warfare, is an undistinguished destruction, of all ages, sexes and conditions." "Merciless Indian Savages" don't fit into the body politic.

Listening to Native American voices, this book considers that misfit, that missed fit, and that body politic, the ways those "merciless Indian Savages" have been speaking and writing to America's ideals of freedom. This introduction contextualizes the book's five themes and five authors in light of America's national narrative. A brief conceptual map for the sections of this introduction will be useful.

In the first section, "A True Story," we have read the Fool Soldiers' story, where a set of key concepts emerges, forecasting dynamics of the literature. For historical and ideological context, this section, "The Imaginary Frontier," maps American self-contradictions as fertile ground for Native American irony, where the Fool Soldiers drama took place. Thus we begin with America's founding binary of civilization and wilderness, culture and nature, white and Indian, and that overview turns us to alternatives in the next section.

Toward the specific chapters, the short section titled "Circle of Five Themes and Five Authors" forecasts the five key concepts of Native American nationhood emerging from the Fool Soldiers' narrative that have spoken directly to contradictions in American nationhood: sovereignty, community, identity, authenticity, and irony. By unraveling or complicating America's frontier, Native activists and writers suggest the chapters of this study.

I read the five themes across five major authors: William Apess, Sarah Winnemucca, D'Arcy McNickle, Leslie Marmon Silko, and Sherman Alexie. Each chapter of the book focuses on one theme and applies that theme to one of the authors, with additional examples from the others. Thus the chapters on each theme linger with one author before drawing the others into the conversation. They all speak to the five issues in the story of America, reshaping modern notions of nationhood.

Because this study focuses on the themes and not on the authors, a biographical appendix must suffice for each of these remarkable voices. Other biographical and critical studies have covered their lives, and I will offer more biographical perspective where appropriate for the discussion of each theme as well.

After introducing the themes, we begin to mark their significance in "Rewriting Nationhood, Rewriting Sovereignty," previewing a vision of American nationhood suggested by these writers. Understanding Indigenous approaches especially to "sovereignty" will lead us briefly to "Ground Theory," a multifaceted lens that focuses the five themes for analysis of Indigenous texts. Through ground theory, we try to keep listening in specific ways to voices of the earth that cross America's ideological borders.

We will read Indigenous approaches to each theme as a facet of nation-hood, and further how these writers thus strategically complicate America's reductive and exclusionary binary of the frontier.[5]

Let's begin with America's originary contradiction, that potent frontier men-tality, a fissure where America's outsiders have found both inequality and opportunity. One of the many intriguing dynamics of the ongoing process of revision by Native American writers hinges on the irony in America's vision. Not only has America always been at war with Indians, but it has always been at war with itself. The Civil War was only the most dramatic moment of this. From the start of Christian colonization, the inequities of race, class, and gender have remained the parallel, if repressed, history. At the founding of the republic, a clash between American ideals and Ameri-can oppression was clear to many, and Indigenous writers, like other "oth-ers," have exploited that fissure, that crack in the Liberty Bell. Maureen Konkle measures that crack as "a contradictory discourse on Indians" (*Writing Indian Nations* 9). Inherited from the colonial Doctrine of Discovery, standard discourse of U.S. federal Indian policy mixed the ideology of racial difference, where whites were necessarily superior and Indians inferior, with the practicality of treaty making, where whites and Indians were necessar-ily equal signatories. If America's right hand had to sign for legal title to aboriginal lands, its left hand held the Bowie knife. Such a contradiction equaled a denial of Indian nationhood—in favor of American nationhood—where, as Konkle explains, "A modernizing Indian nation—an autonomous Indian nation in time—is inconceivable within the theory of Indian differ-ence; the only civilized society possible is that of EuroAmericans" (10). The subjection of the antebellum Cherokee nation in America's South to the reactive, illegal executive and legislative policy of Jackson's Indian Removal Act of 1830 is one of the most famous cases of America's fatal contradictions, among hundreds, thousands, even millions of other examples. The sorrow and irony of that representative history are only intensified by the analysis of nationhood by the Cherokee scholar Daniel Heath Justice: "Indigenous nationhood is distinguished from Eurowestern nationalism by its concern for respectful relational connection" (*Our Fire Survives the Storm* 152).

Unable to conceive of such "relational connection" with Indigenous nations, America's story of itself relegated Indians to a timeless past—and to an "Indian Territory"—to avoid facing the contradictions in its own founding ideologies. If the Civil War was the loudest explosion of those contradictions, Sand Creek, Wounded Knee, and the Oklahoma Land Rush were among countless others. Across this history and into the twenty-first century, Native writers have been exhorting, warning, joking, pleading, grieving, reconciling, rebelling, and revising. From the beginning they have offered their own people a story to live by, and they have offered America a way to conceive of potential American healing in the ultimate ironic reversal: modern Indian nations.[6]

The politics of Indigenous nationalism took a global step recently with the 2007 UN Declaration on the Rights of Indigenous Peoples, in which Article 5 both affirms the right to existence for Indigenous nations and subsumes them under modern nation-states: "Indigenous peoples have the right to maintain and strengthen their distinct political, legal, economic, social and cultural institutions, while retaining their right to participate fully, if they so choose, in the political, economic, social and cultural life of the State." Not only has Indigenous "choice" been conflicted historically in the phrase "if they so choose [to participate]," but definitions of the term *state*, in which Indigenous institutions "participate," remain quite open as well.[7] The erasure of Indian nationhood, the "right to maintain and strengthen their distinct political, legal, economic, social and cultural institutions," has been the real agenda of American history and its textbooks.

Concisely summarizing this long-running discursive battle over whose story to tell—whose freedom to celebrate—the late Tewa anthropologist Alfonso Ortiz lists eight errors of the standard historiography.[8] In "Indian/White Relations: A View from the Other Side of the 'Frontier,'" Ortiz claims that the first concept "that historians of Indian/white relations have used in their efforts to interpret Indian experiences" has been "the celebration of Western civilization" (2). This a priori notion in "the old way of doing history" "has bred a relentless linearity of thought and, sometimes, cultural arrogance" (2). Ortiz continues, worth quoting at length:

> A related notion, that of the frontier has been much more actively harmful to the cause of Indian survival and to the writing of meaningful histories of Indian/white relations, let alone of Indian tribes themselves. As long as the white frontier was alive and well, Indian people had to

fight a desperate rearguard action to survive its advance, so they had neither the time nor the means to tell their stories, to relate their own experiences. The notion of the frontier has fallen into disfavor as both an assumption and a research tool, so I will avoid flaying it yet again. However, because it has been around so long and is so pervasive in our lives and language, it may be a long time, if ever, before the concept of frontier is expunged from our everyday consciousness. (3)

Ortiz is offering a radical revision that requires jettisoning the persistent frontier paradigm, so that "Indian people" may "tell their stories" and "relate their own experiences." (We shall see echoes of this precise dynamic in the views of another pueblo writer and scholar, Simon Ortiz, in his seminal statements on authenticity as nationalism.)

Alfonso Ortiz continues, "I would propose that we dispense with the notion of frontier altogether when talking about historical encounters between peoples, both for the reasons I have already indicated and because it is possible to make so much mischief with this notion. In our everyday life, the concept of frontier is too deeply entrenched for there to be any hope of expunging it soon; but since historians put it there to begin with, historians and their students should work to root it out" (9). If historians did "put it there to begin with," Native writers, as we shall see, have been working "to root it out" from the beginning as well.

This study is essentially a look at both the "mischief" in this binary notion and at some of the efforts to rewrite the record without the frontier defining the dynamics. Since he published "A View from the Other Side of the 'Frontier'" a generation ago, this suggestion by Ortiz has been gathering momentum. For instance, Joshua David Bellin, in *Demon of the Continent: Indians and the Shaping of America*, explains the historical content of this shift in perspective, that "cultures in contact are *intercultural*, consisting of the complex, intricate, and even indeterminate interrelationships among their diverse members" (5). The a priori fact of interrelationship leads to the logic of this fundamental shift in historiographic discourse: "What cultural encounter illustrates is the inadequacy not only of fixed frontiers but of fixed cultures" (5). A certain mode of postmodernism might claim the relativism, indeterminacy, or impurity of culture, but throughout the modern era of colonial "frontiers," and long prior, according to Bellin, the fixed duality of cultural identity is doubtful. The Fool Soldiers embodied and acted upon that more fluid version of cultural identity that melted the rigid frontier of the American mind. Thus my choice in this study is to reject the term as unhelpful to critique the dynamics of Native—and non-Native— American narratives, because, as Bellin, Ortiz, and others insist, "frontier history" is too loaded with dualistic filters that blur the stories of more complex lives. (I return to a discussion of "frontier" terminology in the chapter on identity, which is so often split by that imaginary line.)[9]

If the classic text of the American historical mentality of opposition was articulated by the Harvard historian Frederick Jackson Turner in his famous 1893 essay, "The Significance of the Frontier in American History," its racial markers were clear from the start.[10] Although it defines America's self-concept, the frontier is more of a myth than race itself. The frontier is a fantasy built upon a fantasy. Turner's description of the frontier as the basis of American character is full of the language of freedom for whites that assumes dispossession of Indians, even as it obscures disenfranchisement for blacks: "opportunity," "movement," "free land," "unrestraint," "escape from the bondage of the past," "ever retreating frontier," "discovery." Turner's founding discourse fails to recognize humanity across the "frontier." To borrow from Rennard Strickland, an Osage/Cherokee scholar, professor, and former dean at the University of Oregon School of Law, this is a historiography of justification ("The Eagle's Empire" 261).

Other historians have summarized Turner's thesis as they critiqued it: "Euro-America's frontier expansion into 'free land' explained the development of American democracy" (Klein, *Frontiers of Historical Imagination* 13), and "the frontier experience had a lasting if not permanent impact on the American character and society" (Ridge, "Turner" 1090). The "Turner thesis" soon "became the organizing principle of American historical studies and a subject of continuing controversy" (1090). William Cronon writes, "Turner believed that the encounter with 'free land' had transformed the American character, making it restless, inventive, acquisitive, individualist, egalitarian, democratic. The frontier, in other words . . . had forged American nationalism and democracy" ("Turner" 692).

The crux of the controversy is whether the "frontier" strengthened or split the American psyche, whether it charted the vision or the blindness of America—or both. Patricia Limerick identifies the fundamental dichotomy in Turner: "Turner said that the frontier was the most important factor in American history. . . . Perhaps his most memorable suggestion was this one: 'the frontier is the outer edge of the wave [of settlement], the meeting point between savagery and civilization'" ("Frontier" 255). The problem is that there never was such an "outer edge." Instead both "savagery and civilization" abounded across the reductive racial divide. Clearly America built itself on its own apprehensions of the violent divide between wilderness and civilization. It was hampered by the fear dwelling in the heart of its inventive and democratic faith. The historical misreadings of land and peoples triggered by the dominant discourse of savagery and civilization remain the tragic flaw of America. As the years saw extensive scholarship toward abandoning or tweaking Turner's frontier thesis of American history, the significance of the Fool Soldiers story has grown.[11]

Yes, the problem has been that Turner was too right: Americans do see their world as a frontier. That is the metaphor by which the nation fantasizes and constitutes itself on this continent.[12] Without material facts, Turner was describing an ideology rather than an intellectual history, much less a documented, historical reality. He expressed an ideology that claimed history for itself and denied history to what Hegel described as a "voiceless past."

As Kerwin Klein says of a Euro-American frontier mentality: "The frontier was not just the place where civilization and wilderness made American democracy, it was the ragged edge of history itself, where historical and nonhistorical defied and defined each other" (*Frontiers of Historical Imagination* 7). Like the unpopulated, inhospitable, and therefore liberal or free fantasy space of the "Great American desert," America assumes an ahistorical time of its disembodied Indian projection. Indeed one reason that "the Indian" has always been vanishing in the Euro-American mind is that Natives have never been seen to have a history. Ideologically they have always been not-here, not-now, perhaps to directly offset the material reality that they were and are so very much here now in their embodied presence on this land, and ultimately that the land itself is embodied in their humanity. Thus merely by speaking or writing, by voicing that grounded, embodied humanity, Native artists try to offset their ideological erasure. The Anishinaabe poet and scholar Kim Blaeser writes of the challenge, "Indeed, any discussion of the literary representation of history in the Americas finds its center in the notion of possession" ("The New 'Frontier'" 38).

The ideology of American "possession of the land and its resources" built a settlement culture upon a fantasy of the evaporating Indian that has permeated American courthouses, statehouses, and jailhouses. Rennard Strickland writes of a "jurisprudence of justification" carried out by the U.S. Supreme Court "that rationalized legal grounds for the conquest and the conquerors' will" ("The Eagle's Empire" 261). Because resistance to colonialism and manifest destiny has been seen by European and other immigrants to be so pointless in what Strickland describes as "a nation of the future" (260), there was no real story to tell on the other side of the frontier.

Against such a unilateral history, the Native writers we study here show us from across that frontier imaginary a narrative different from Euro-American domination. They guide us toward a more complex paradigm of individual and national identity that resists the reductions of Turner's binary frontier.[13] Thus when we read of the Fool Soldiers, it raises questions widely unrecognized by "history." The tale is too complex, too elusive for conquest, with its double fold of resistant difference within the Indian community apart from any resistance across the colonial frontier. Instead the colonial drone, with its tired binary of civilization and wilderness, is still educating and entertaining America.

A further, more specific reason that America fails to recognize the ongoing presence of Native America as a de facto part of itself is its refusal to recognize the reality of tribal sovereignty in its own history. If this sounds tautological, that's because it is. America is built on a tautology: Indians must have disappeared because we're here now; we're here now because Indians must have disappeared. The cyclic reasoning of this racist formulation overlooks the facts of Indian presence and American pluralism—because of a contradiction prior to the tautology: American history is unique among modern nations, following on the Iroquois model, in the Constitution's originary claim, if not its achievement, of uniting diverse states and, by extension—by incremental legislation—uniting diverse immigrants, freed slaves, and original Indigenous inhabitants of this land. The disjunctions between American ideals and realities in forging that union measure against that claim of unity across difference.

In this context, one may say that Euro-American national identity has molded itself around denial of tribal sovereignty. That absent presence defines the nation, from its legal codes to its literature. As a number of scholars (whom we will discuss further in the "Rewriting Nationhood" section) have established, America's conflicted notions of Indianness have indeed shaped American identity, community, nationalism, and empire.[14] Roy Harvey Pearce explains, "In its origins the American's need to compare himself with the Indians whom he knew is as deep and basic as humanity. . . . Even as all American thinking about the Indian was based, at the very least, on an implicit comparison of savage and civilized life, a great deal of his thinking about himself was based on explicit comparison of the two" (*Savagism and Civilization* 135). An internal frontier reflected the external, and vice versa. Amplifying Turner, Pearce points to "the westward course of empire" as the exterior consequence of that projection. Because that "American mind" remained locked in the binary projection of "a good devoutly to be wished for" in savagism, the "civilized man face to face with savages" (135) must miss the independent realities of those "savages."

Thus if America built itself around "the Indian," this mold, like the negative space in and around a sculpture, has taken the negative cast of projection, erasure, and self-definition that denies the positive presence of tribal sovereignty in the so-called American Other. The canonized James Fenimore Cooper, author of some of the first American, early nineteenth-century "best-sellers," is perhaps the archetypal American writer for precisely these reasons: he both affirms and mourns the Native presence only as negative and terminal, as the *last* of the Mohicans. This American literary prototype does not acknowledge that an Indigenous presence remains after Leatherstockings, or Shane, or the Lone Ranger, or he who "Dances with Wolves" rides off into the sunset.

Beginning from a different story of Indigenous continuance, the point in so much writing by Native Americans is that Native survivance is not a retrospective, after-the-fact, postmodern event, not a recapturing of agency *after* revised history, but that it remains an ongoing, multifaceted set of facts that have always been in play.[15] The Spokane scholar and poet Gloria Bird offers such a challenge: "When we change our focus to a native readership and what is being represented *to* us and *about* us, a very different set of relationships must be examined" ("The Exaggeration of Despair" 48). The potential dynamics of internalized oppression as well as cultural and political reaffirmation emerge where Bird refocuses questions of Native American literature on behalf of "a native readership." Indeed such a complex role for Indigenous writers hearkens in the quiet of print on paper to the more dramatic role of the Fool Soldiers and their bare footprints in the snow. As a mediating force, the Fool Soldiers strove to "satisfy the epistemological expectations of both audiences," as James Ruppert characterizes contemporary Native American writers who "insist on their freedom to use the forms and expectations of both Native and Western cultural codes to achieve the goals of each" (*Mediation* 7). Could Native and Western goals ultimately merge? We shall see what some Native writers have to say on this fundamental question.

Resistance runs deep against multiple perspectives. The past generation has seen various efforts at revising history textbooks to give more recognition to the experiences and contributions of women, people of color, and labor classes. However, a 1995 Senate resolution against such revised "history standards" advocates "a decent respect for the contributions of Western civilization" (Nash et al., *History on Trial* 235).[16] The entrenched domination by race, class, and gender digs as deep as the civilization-wilderness divide in the frontier imagination of America's leadership and its populace.[17]

An argument of revisionary historians, as well as Native writers since the beginning of this nation, is not to inflict mere guilt on whites for the past but to foster informed responsibility for the inherited present and future. A central piece of that information is the ideological rather than factual basis of the frontier. The Native American writers in this study have maintained as one of their primary purposes the peeling back of dominant American blindness to their own people's ongoing humanity. Reading their narratives and their pronouncements, we may begin to understand the historical mismatch of consciousness.

Circle of Five Themes and Five Authors

Replacing the linear notion of a frontier, the story of the Fool Soldiers embodies four concepts in a circle, plus a fifth at the center as an animating principle. Readers of any background must begin to grasp this set of ideas in order to read American Indian literatures with critical simpatico. A grasp of these key dynamics helps listeners listen to Native American texts. With the help of the Fool Soldiers and five selected Native authors, plus a number of other Indian writers, this study looks at Indigenous views of sovereignty, community, identity, and authenticity—each and all pivoting round a fifth dynamic, humor, a fundamentally humane Native irony that so often animates and undergirds the other four concepts. Conceptual and etymological links between *humor*, *humus*, and *human* suggest the grounded humanity that is the life of these stories, enacting the historical irony that Indigenous humanity remains on the ground of America.

Although easily read in a tragic mode, the Fool Soldiers' story indeed embodies the irony that is at the heart of Native humor, the complexity of Indigeneity that will not be reduced to existential or historical predictability. A full spectrum of stories, from "tragic" to "comic," emerges from this circle of five concepts, and the full set constitutes what may be called a "nation." The project of this volume is to complicate the definitions of these key terms in Indian studies, and thereby in American studies. It is precisely the limited definitions imposed on these terms by "frontier" history that has limited Americans' readings of Native literature and lives, and by reflection has limited Americans' readings of themselves.

The point is to read authenticity, identity, community, sovereignty, and humor beyond the frontier in dialogue with each other, both within communities and between them. To understand a tribe's national identity, we cannot discuss Indian identity without discussing sovereignty and vice versa; nor can we discuss community or sovereignty without a redefinition of authenticity; and so on.[18] Where appropriate, I intersperse comparisons and conversations with mainstream American approaches to these terms. All the spokes of the wheel are necessary for the national narrative to roll forward.

Between the isolating death of tragedy and the animating life of comedy the conceptual sphere of these terms offers various positions for Native voices in history. Each writer is unique in complex context. Some speak more to sovereignty, some more to identity, some more to community. Critical perspectives generated by the interaction of these dynamics in Native stories emphasize revisionary notions that play out in countless ways in Native American literature. These dynamics suggest, for example, that authenticity is not defined by time; identity is not defined by a single center; community is not defined by a circumference; and sovereignty is not defined by domination. Humor is the surprise in each of these redefinitions, a play of interrelationship as the operative term inside each and among these ideas. Such a dynamic replaces the stoic and static.

As the chapters focused on each term explain, Indigenous sovereignty becomes the dynamic of sacrifice. Community becomes animism. Identity functions paradoxically as change. Authenticity works as translation. The ironies of humor work to humanize Indigenous subjects. Effectively each of the five terms becomes a verb instead of a noun. Sovereignty sacrifices. Community animates. Identity changes. Authenticity translates. Humor humanizes.

Although they intricately entwine, each lens, as a mode of reading, asks separate questions. Native and non-Native readers looking for authenticity tend toward the anthropological; students and critics analyzing identity lean toward the psychological; readers focusing on community frequently tend toward the historical; and those looking for sovereignty tend toward the political or legal issues in a text. While most scholarly readers draw on the mythical, they often end up interpreting Native narratives from their various disciplines in ways that continue to miss the stories' own purposes for Native survivance. Seeking authenticity, readers often reify the "vanishing Indian" by an anthropological focus on static ethnic purity in the past. Seeking identity as a psychological focus they reify a story's unsustainable dilemmas of cultural mixing in the present, following an oppositional dualism. Even seeking sovereignty as a political or historical focus in a text may overstate the dreams of community for the future. Each overreading will then produce a certain romantic and static nostalgia. A more precarious but perhaps more accurate and dynamic mix of these four terms, each vivified by humor, is necessary for a fairer reading of Native literary expression.

All of these are the questions of national identity. Each lens brings up different textual and contextual dynamics, which I explore selectively. For example, in the sovereignty chapter, I map the discourse of "three sovereigns" deriving from the U.S. Constitution. Similarly in the authenticity chapter and the conclusion, I briefly explore some general issues of America's own anxiety over authenticity, questions of settler colonialism longing to become authentically at home in what is still described as "the New World." Such contexts mold the national identities of Native texts and their readership.

The contextual cycle of these five terms establishes what it means to live in an Indigenous precolonial world, but it has served to strengthen a sense of struggle, hope, and humor that enables survival in a colonial world of invasion and alienation. As we shall see, tribal sovereignty grows on a sacrificial depth of commitment to interrelationships or kinship between matter and spirit, human and nonhuman. Native peoples continue to conceive of their tribal sovereignty as the spiritual, historical, legal, and political essence of nation and community that in turn serves as the ground for individual identity. As this cycle constitutes the set of criteria for authenticity, the circle goes round and round.

To explore these central ideas, we will look to writers who, like the Fool Soldiers, have striven to speak across the cultures. They each have suffered some of the same misreadings as the Fool Soldiers as well: William Apess in the 1830s, Sarah Winnemucca in the 1880s, D'Arcy McNickle focusing on the pre-1930s, Leslie Marmon Silko launching from the 1960s and 1970s, and Sherman Alexie at the turn of the current century.

My rationale for choosing these five writers is both historical and thematic, both diachronic and synchronic. Each writer speaks to and from his or her time to ours and to each other. Each is both representative and unique. Apess and Winnemucca bracket the nineteenth century. McNickle and Silko bracket the twentieth, though the lines begin to blur as McNickle also moves chronologically into the later twentieth and Silko crosses into the twenty-first century, and both write of earlier periods as well. Alexie helps us to define the late twentieth and the beginnings of the twenty-first century in new directions for Native literatures. All five writers concern themselves with persistent issues of land dispossession and cultural repression. Each is deeply in conversation with the experiences of Indians across America in their own and previous periods, sometimes addressing the future as well. Each tackles intimate questions of identity, community, authenticity, and sovereignty in critically ironic, sometimes humorous ways that additionally bear on America's own emerging self-definitions.

For the sake of length, each thematic chapter focuses more on one of these writers, with generally shorter treatment of the others. Since the focus of this study is thematic analysis rather than critical biography, the chapters allow for varied emphasis from each author's examples. Of course, different aspects of each author organically lend themselves to explicating different aspects of the five themes. While they all address each of the themes, one author's work may lend itself more to a discussion of identity or community, for example, than another. (For salient details about each writer, see the biographical appendix.)

All five of these writers, like the Fool Soldiers, are somewhat liminal figures in their own Indian communities, a pattern true of many writers, Native and otherwise. For example, Louis Owens, a Choctaw, Cherokee, Scots Irish scholar and novelist places his own work, "like that of many other writers identified as Native American," as an outside-inside observer to Native communities: "I do not write from the heart of a reservation site or community and was not raised within a traditional culture. It would not be incorrect to say, in fact, that today in the U.S., urban centers and academic institutions have come to constitute a kind of diaspora for Native Americans who through many generations of displacement and orchestrated ethnocide are often far from their traditional homelands and cultural communities" ("As If" 171). It may be safe to say that all but Winnemucca, among the writers in this study, would fit Owens's description of displacement in their various ways.

Rewriting Nationhood, Rewriting Sovereignty

By listening to how they address American audiences, this becomes a study of how these five Indian writers, among many others, have rewritten American national identity in ways that don't exclude Indians. The set of five concepts derived from Indigenous expression combines aspects of nationalism as a sense of internal solidarity, distinct from an external history of imperial nation-building. We shall see how the dialectic of domestic and imperial nationalism comes into play, however, especially as Native writers from the beginning have questioned the Euro-American ideology of manifest destiny.[19] At the experiential level, authenticity, identity, community, and sovereignty interlace as a set of ideas that shape the image, often turned ironically, that a people or a nation has of itself. Here it is that writers from Indigenous nations find both self-irony and plenty to ridicule in these aspects of America's self-image.

The idea of a nation may take the sociohistorical form of an ideology, an "imagined community" or "a deep horizontal comradeship," as Benedict Anderson suggests in his classic study, *Imagined Communities: Reflections on the Origin and Spread of Nationalism*. Or it may take an even more subconscious form, also grounded in material circumstances, of a "national fantasy," as Lauren Berlant suggests in her literary study, *Anatomy of National Fantasy: Hawthorne, Utopia, and Everyday Life*. In either formulation, nationalism functions as just that, an idea, an *imagined* reality or a projected *fantasy* of community defined in the modern era by increasingly arbitrary borders (such as the 49th parallel). As Daniel Heath Justice writes, "Nationhood is woven in large part from the lives, dreams, and challenges of the people who compose the body politic" (*Our Fire Survives the Storm* 7). The American dream is just that.

Often eclipsing common qualities and quotidian activities shared across the globe, or eclipsing watersheds, mountain ranges, rivers, or other "natural" borders in favor of cultural and political ones, nationalism begins and ends as an abstraction. At times the ideology of nationhood rises up from the grassroots. At other times the "nation" is an ideological imposition constructed from above by the state to maintain the most efficient rule by oligarchs. The state remains a legal entity, while the nation, yet more abstract, remains a political and cultural one.[20] This distinction clarifies the peculiar modern dynamic of a single state dominating multiple nationalities within its borders, often simply a legalization of economic empire in other terms.

Yet for all its erasures, a "nation" itself rarely remains distinct from a particular, bordered geography, a beloved homeland. Whatever economic, cultural, and other social forces meld into nationhood, and whatever precedence Marxist analysis might give to economic over ideological forces— whether we set Hegel or Marx on his head—we still often think of a nation as a natural rather than a cultural force. Manifest destiny as a nationalistic rationale—naturalizing cultural definitions of *destiny* as "manifest" on a particular geography—would be the quintessential case in point.

In this discussion of Native perspectives, we can get at different ideas of nationalism—colonial ideas and pluralistic ones—as contending forces through competing histories of this nation. Unilateral versus multilateral definitions of America continue to play out in literature and legislation, precisely in terms of American versus Native American definitions of sovereignty, community, identity, and authenticity. Thus in a fundamental irony, these Native authors are able to reenvision America by their Indigenous perspectives on the five dynamics. The logic here is that even given unequal power relations, a Native "opposite" of Euro-American conquest and genocide is not Indian domination of whites. Justice proposes an ethical pendulum swing in his own tribal perspective on revising history: "It's an open assertion of the liberating potential of our Indigenous histories and experiences, not a blanket rejection of Eurowestern ideas and traditions" (*Our Fire Survives the Storm* 8). Amid the countless battles and miscommunications, a pattern of pluralism can be seen historically from Apess's 1830s characterization of the Wampanoag king Philip's seventeenth-century negotiations with the Puritans to the Confederated Salish and Kootenai tribal council's twenty-first-century negotiations with the U.S. Fish and Wildlife Service for tribal management of the National Bison Range. Today, amid some reactionary non-Indian rhetoric opposed to mutual management, the Flathead tribes affirm neighborly relations with the white majority on the rez. "We have worked together on many projects with both the Bison Range staff and the U.S. Fish & Wildlife Service," said Fred Matt, recent chairman of the Confederated Salish and Kootenai Tribal Council. "We believe this new partnership will help us all as stewards of the land."[21]

Following the logic of these voices, I try to trace a literary trail of tribal sovereignty politics as they are eclipsed and illuminated by American identity issues. That politics, like the land itself and its original peoples, continues to push on America's sense of itself as a nation opposed to Indian presence. The study thus starts from the perspective that American literature cannot be mapped without tracing the spaces, both geographic and ideological, of tribal sovereignty in its midst. The point here is not to absorb Native into American literature but to read how a complex insistence on difference in Native literature maintains and sustains both Indigenous dynamics and potential American pluralism as its original principle.

To round out this preliminary introduction to the ways Native writers are rewriting the nation, we have to more fully acknowledge the obstacles to reading Native self-representation, which range across dominant culture from the mining industry to the film industry and the academy. Academic culture also varies in its ways of reading Indigenous voices. Popular American notions still expect to absorb otherness, to erase difference. "The white people would shake their heads, more proud than sad that it took a white man to survive in their world and that these Indians couldn't seem to make it," Silko writes (*Ceremony* 265–66). Even in the twenty-first century, the land must be cleared. When Indian nations proclaim their tribal sovereignty, and then express it, for instance, in economic development through gaming revenues, their de facto reversals of manifest destiny fly in the face of

American legal, cultural, and psychological understandings. When Native writers publish, they pose the fundamental question of what would change if America were to accept the fact that Indians never vanished and never will. Equally, what would happen if American audiences listened to Native writers? As the Dakota scholar Vine Deloria Jr. wrote in his best-seller, *Custer Died for Your Sins* (1969), "Indian people today have a chance to re-create a type of society for themselves that can defy, mystify, and educate the rest of American society" (262). Deloria made that challenge in the same year that the Kiowa writer N. Scott Momaday won the Pulitzer Prize for his novel *House Made of Dawn*. Especially since 1969, a flood of Indian voices has been writing "to re-create" that "type of society."

Indeed against ideological and material obstacles, a thread of utopianism or, perhaps more simply, faith weaves through these narratives. As James A. Banks writes, "The margins of U.S. Society, to which people of color have often been confined, have usually been the sites for preserving and defending the freedoms and rights stated in the founding documents of the United States when they were most severely challenged" (*Multicultural Education* vii). This long history has seen many developments of Indian and other intellectuals' takes on community in America, and the writers that are the focus of this study are in deep dialogue with many other voices, Native and non-Native, as they try to set America on a course of justice.

A previous generation of twentieth-century scholars has made some progress in the slow and fitful unraveling of colonial and patriarchal power dynamics that have defined America. However, studies by non-Natives of Native American literature have often become self-reflexive studies of Euro-Americans and of how they gaze at Native American expression and experience. That work needed to be done, but it was not actually listening to Native American authors. Across the second half of the twentieth century, some valuable cultural and historical analyses in this long process of peeling back have yielded such classic works as Roy Harvey Pearce's *Savagism and Civilization: A Study of the Indian and the American Mind* (1953/1988), Leslie Fiedler's *Return of the Vanishing American* (1968), Robert Berkhofer's *The White Man's Indian: Images of the American Indian from Columbus to the Present* (1978), and Richard Drinnon's *Facing West: The Metaphysics of Indian-Hating and Empire-Building* (1980/1997). Each of these studies reverts to a focus on the male Euro-American psyche and ideology as it both projects and eclipses American Indians, who unfortunately continue to vanish beneath these meditations on *the white man's* Indian.

In fact the Pearce-Fiedler-Berkhofer-Drinnon tradition of studies of Euro-American projections onto the Indian unintentionally perpetuates a certain myopia of colonial ideologies. Even in doing the necessary work of uncovering the racialist project of American expansion, they had yet to look at Native American experience eclipsed by racial ideologies. It remained for the "other side of the frontier" to speak. America's colonial mind has remained blind not only to the rich complexity but also to the potential of reciprocity and exchange with Native cultures. Thus, because of a prerequisite focus on colonial domination, a remarkable if inadvertent feature of this broad critique of American ideology is that these scholars managed to map white projections with minimum reference to Indian views. Their necessary exposure of Euro-American images of "the Indian"—and hence of American self-definitions—laid the groundwork for revision, but Indians' voices remained unheard. Indeed as in many of the latest Hollywood projections, from *Dances with Wolves* to *Pocahontas* and *Apocalypto*, Indian lives and rights continue to disappear behind that screen.

Maureen Konkle offers important perspective on the gaps in scholarly criticism of Native nationalism in her careful discourse analysis, *Writing Indian Nations: Native Intellectuals and the Politics of Historiography, 1827-1863*. She identifies problems with a "culturalist criticism" that not only misses the foundational political and legal aspects of antebellum Indigenous publications but that even complicitly "downplays violence and conflict" (32). Like problems with "traditional" versus "individual" categories, Konkle shows how readers' preoccupation with issues of cultural authenticity (traditional focus) and ensuing psychological identity (individual focus) crises tend unfortunately to reinforce "the theory of Indian difference." She explains America's theory, "that Native peoples would disappear—but they did not," in the face of U.S. government jurisdiction and the ideology of manifest destiny. The racist extension of that theory of racial difference, once confronted by the fact of Native survivance, was the assimilation policy to "kill the Indian and save the man." Konkle's nuanced analysis shows how "both the hypothetical civilization of Indians and the hypothetical extinction of Indians are part of the same discursive field. They both ultimately lead to the same thing: the denial of Native political autonomy, the naturalizing of the incorporation of Native land under U.S. jurisdiction, and the reinforcement of white superiority and Native subordination" (34). Assumptions of white supremacy and of the "noble but doomed" Indian remain deeply ingrained.

While she does not attribute such racist repercussions to "culturalist" critics, Konkle's map is compelling. A cultural criticism tends toward the erasures of a new, co-optive multiculturalism that replays the "same discursive field" of assimilation and extinction of Indians. She suggests that the tendency of some non-Native scholars to focus nostalgically on cultural change can eclipse the more enduring legal, political, and economic realities of tribal survivance and tribal sovereignty. By stirring Native writing into the melting pot, such critics dilute the potency of Indigenous political critique that would rewrite the nation.

Among these efforts to sharpen the critique of Native literary nationalism, I observe a tendency of many critics who fail to question the dependent aspect of America's founding federal Indian policy: "domestic dependent nations." Konkle's preferred focus instead is on the discourse of *in*dependence in Native writers of the formative decades of the United States. She notes the reification of limits on Indigenous nationhood: "It is sometimes objected that an 'Indian nation'—a phrase that became common in Anglo-American legal discourse by the mid-eighteenth century—is not really 'Indian' because it is a product of colonization and settlement, an argument that reifies culture as the only real freedom for Native peoples" (*Writing Indian Nations* 6). Certainly freedom is the underlying issue, and Native writers have been calling for political as well as cultural freedom, where both fall under the discourse of sovereignty. Konkle's work thus helps me to focus on that larger set of terms that constitute Native nationhood and on how that Indigenous design might affect U.S. national evolution.

Konkle and other critics, both Native and non-Native, would emphasize the political and legal dimensions. Many others would emphasize cultural aspects of Indigenous narratives. Of course, both are necessary and relevant, and both speak to each other. Without dialogue among those parts, the network that is Native discourse remains not only incomplete and erasable but ineffective and dismissible. As this study looks at conversation among the larger set of five dynamics, sovereignty especially, but the other key terms as well, resonate politically, spiritually, and culturally.

After the work of Fiedler, Pearce, Berkhofer, and Drinnon, scholars like Konkle have begun the task of critiquing Native voices on their own terms, cultural and political, and in their own community contexts, not primarily as subjects of the United States but as citizens of their own Indigenous nations. Addressing those quite different dynamics is the heart of an ethics of a new criticism and a new pedagogy by a growing presence of writers and scholars, Native and non-Native.[22] They are steering critics and student readers away from recycling the colonial gaze. At this critical stage, scholars do well simply to foreground Native voices, to put often humorous but always serious affirmations of sovereignty, community, identity, and changing authenticity—as well as Native "wrongs and claims"—before a wider readership in ways that speak to rising Indian generations. Robert Dale Parker's phrasing is concise on this point: "Some critics persist in misreading the project of writing about a people or its literature as writing for that people, in effect as speaking for them. Speaking for Indians is the furthest thing from my mind" (*The Invention of Native American Literature* 16). By entering the conversation about both autonomy and inclusion, this study offers an exchange across and around the exclusive cultural frontier that Fiedler et al. have shown is a colonial construct at the heart of American consciousness.

Thus we rediscover the emerging but ancient notion that underneath the many narratives of identity politics in Native American literatures, a driving energy that animates those stories and poems, either by its presence or its absence, is tribal sovereignty. Contemporary criticism and pedagogy around Native literatures have reached a saturation point in focusing so much on secondary identity issues that finally the prior sovereignty issues that have shaped Indigenous identity are crystallizing out of the mix. Reasons why colonial issues in the literature are secondary and Indigenous sovereignty issues are primary emerge when Native stories suggest narrative dynamics of plot, character, and symbol that do not merely reflect or deflect colonial power.

The trick, as always, is power, not to privilege colonial perspectives in the telling of America's story, thus not to misread Indigenous perspectives as somehow nostalgic nor as powerlessness grasping for lost power. A driving dynamic in this rereading of Native rewriting is then how the "question" of Native identity, key to so much of contemporary Native literature, leads to sovereignty or community. We shall find sovereignty not as an answer in the literature but as a process. The five terms of nationhood map different modes of reading Native texts, each looking for and recognizing a different narrative and each with its own political resonances. Most critics emphasize one or two among these terms, and most leave out humor altogether.

E pluribus unum

After looking at the obstacles, let's focus briefly on the goals of a redefined *e pluribus unum* to further clarify the introductory context. In his retrospective preface to a 2000 edition of *from Sand Creek*, Simon Ortiz writes, "Even though most times we were not acknowledged to be a part of history, we knew innately that we were a part of the times and circumstances that human societies and cultures were experiencing" (6). Indian communities have identified in many ways with "America." Among many reasons for this sense of linkage are these three: a common sense of humanity, shared territoriality, and a warrior ethic that translates to patriotism. Following the logic of such values, Indian writers have portrayed Indian nations as potentially viable within or beside the American nation.

Such a vision of the American nation affirms the *pluribus* in the nation's motto, against dominant, conformist modes of the *unum*. James A. Banks reflects a twenty-first-century perspective on this question: "The changing ethnic texture of the United States intensifies the challenge of educating citizens and creating an authentic *unum* that has moral authority. An *authentic unum* reflects the experiences, hopes, and dreams of all the nation's citizens" (*Educating Citizens* xii). Banks contrasts such an authentic *unum* with the "imposed *unum*" reflecting "one dominant cultural group" "throughout most of the nation's history."

Many artists of marginalized groups continue to try to imagine what such an "authentic *unum*" means. Native communities working to affirm sovereignty are not focused as much on inclusion as they are on equity. Quite directly Native writers have often pursued an educational agenda with their American readership, inculcating equity. That agenda certainly focuses further on a political curriculum, addressing Banks's "challenge of educating citizens and creating an authentic *unum* that has moral authority." By humanizing Native experiences and perspectives on history, writers of Indian literature attempt to generate the moral authority of an authentic *pluribus* within American society.

Against the imperial projection of bloodthirsty savages, a Native vision of plurality, if not mutuality, has been lost on America's phobias and philias. Indians upholding the founding American principle of equality have quietly confounded the prevailing American aberration of manifest destiny. By not vanishing, by denying America's erasure of themselves, Native voices have called America to its own principles of inclusion, even as they earned its founding exclusions. Their centuries-long claims to natural justice have reminded America of both its wrongs and its ideals. As Banks explains, "A major ethical inconsistency exists in U.S. society" (*Multicultural Education: Issues and Perspectives* 10). Each of the writers we will look at in this study strategizes by speaking to Native readers of hope in such ideals and to non-Native readers of the gap between those ideals and American social practices.

The revisionary historian's and critic's job, including that of many Native writers, has been precisely to show how actual relations and possibilities on the ground were made invisible by the narrative expectations of that split ideology of colonialism and its frontier legacies. Over generations it is conceivable that northern California farmers and Klamath Indians, or Montana settlers and Crows, Cheyennes, Salish, Kootenais, or others might have imagined ways to balance their needs if their respective narratives had not been imagined and institutionalized as completely polarized. The work of self-defense leaves little energy for compromise. The pragmatic facts of an inextricable mutuality can trigger either celebration or mourning, but they remain after erasure of otherness fails.[23] Justice points out that the mode of "accommodation and cooperation," what his Cherokee tradition calls the "Beloved Path," "requires a greater conceptual leap" than the warlike "Chickamauga consciousness," "for the actively peaceful resistance of this perspective is accorded a much lower status in U.S. contexts" (*Our Fire Survives the Storm* 16). According to Justice, "a Eurowestern fascination with an assumed oppositional dualism" between traditional white/peace and red/war misreads both Cherokee culture and Indian-white relations. Such cross-cultural misinterpretation persists because "warriors who advocate the shedding of blood have far more cultural capital in the United states" (156). It seems easier just to erase the Indian.

The Native literary storyteller's job has been to undo that erasure in the dominant narrative. Instead of a center erasing the margins, stories by American Indian authors show an undercurrent of ongoing life, the broader cultures of the land on which frontiers have been imagined and overlaid, so often with tragic consequences. Moreover these so-called marginal stories accumulate to redefine the so-called center, that is, to decenter the national narrative, if not the national centers of power. As they show the material relations of colonial history wherein Native individuals can see their way to act for their people, they also show where non-Natives can build toward America's potential democratic society, America's own dream, "wealthy with . . . compassion and knowledge," in the words of Simon Ortiz. A collective humanity and agency in Native stories complicates the neat oppositional lines in Hollywood and in American history textbooks.

The static or dynamic qualities of culture and the permeability of cultural boundaries emerge as larger questions that govern authenticity, identity, and community. Can cultures and individuals change and yet remain themselves? The Fool Soldiers negotiated precisely this ground. They presaged Simon Ortiz's generous lines around such historic events as the Sand Creek massacre of 1864. Ortiz represents that Colorado tragedy, of the same decade as the Fool Soldiers affair, as survivable within this cyclic process:

That dream
shall have a name
after all,
and it will not be vengeful
but wealthy with love
and compassion
and knowledge.
And it will rise
in this heart
which is our America. (*from Sand Creek* 95)

With such a vision, Ortiz and other Native writers are clear about America: at the heart of that dream is tribal sovereignty, an extreme test of the plural in America's goal of *e pluribus unum*.

Ground Theory

If the American ethic is a redefined *e pluribus unum*, ground theory maps those redefinitions in texts. It applies aesthetics to that ethic by reading Indigenous values of expression and representation. It is that five-faceted lens. It helps make visible how any or all of the five principles might change or evolve in a text as it tells stories of ethical relations with the living ground. Thus it is a theory of both analysis and advocacy. The ground is always already spherical and in motion, three- and four-dimensional, a solid and a fluid, breathing space linked in time with the sky through rain, rivers, sun, roots, leaves, lightning, clouds, as water, atomic energy, and other life forces circulating through the system that is the earth. Each of the five principles circulates by those natural laws.[24]

Beneath the tragedies of oppositional dualism, beneath the "frontier thinking" that so misreads the Fool Soldiers, the ground of these five discursive fields in both oral and written Native traditions remains a way of knowing and a way of analyzing texts that recognizes survivance beyond tragedy. The more comic mode of that narrative ground encourages qualities of systems thinking, field orientation, dialogics. The very openness of such thinking calls not for a lack of rigor but for an honest, we might say good-humored or at least ironic refusal to pretend final definitions. A ground theory looks at narrative structures of lives linked to stories of the soil, where ideas of nationhood play out, often in monologic, tragic terms.

Contemporary Indigenous intellectuals remain alert to the material repressions of frontier thinking as ideological oversimplification. For example, Daniel Heath Justice identifies the repercussions of "an oppositional dualism based on old ideas of 'savagism vs. civilization'": "Simplification is just another word for genocide, and that philosophy is fundamentally antithetical to relational principles of kinship, respect, and mutual accountability" (*Our Fire Survives the Storm* 157). Efforts to structure an alternative American history have always required rethinking the frontier precisely because the frontier operates by a reductive binary formulation. By focusing on "relational principles" of survivance and exchange, of "mutual accountability" rather than fantasies of erasure and domination, Native storytellers and a theory built on their dynamics make visible the often dialogic realities working on that ground. Those dynamic processes factor into our five themes.[25]

In "Decolonializing Criticism" (1994), I analyzed a politics of epistemology wherein Indigenous dialogics contrast with an invasive dialectics of the frontier. Dialogic ways of looking at the world lead to narrative perspectives and choices more agile and able to circumvent or subvert violent dialectics of colonial mentalities.[26] Allowing for historical exceptions, here is that politics of epistemology in a nutshell. Interconnectedness activates more channels for agency around and through reductive binaries. Stories and identities build differently on those different mental structures.[27] When one's way of knowing is structured by the reciprocal economy of the world as natural, spiritual, and social, by the comic complexity of Indigenous reality, then one's political choices and judgments expand into those interconnected relations toward a more democratic pluralism. Alternatively, when one's way of knowing is structured by the extractive economy of the industrial, financial, colonial world, by the perceived simplicity of imperial fantasy, then one's political choices and judgments follow those relations of dominance toward a more hierarchical politics. The former, a dialogical model, conceives a culture of mutuality and integration of difference. The latter, described well as "dialectical materialism," exploits race, class, gender, and other pluralities, including the diversity of earth's resources, to maintain its hierarchical nightmares.

While the hierarchical model writes history, this distinction between a dream of dominance and the reality of pluralism is one of Native America's clearest literary gifts to America. Of course, in a winner-take-all society, political pluralism is also a dream, however actual the plural realities of the body politic may remain. Tim Schouls explores possibilities for aboriginal pluralism as "a public arrangement in which distinct groups live side by side in conditions of mutual recognition and affirmation" (*Shifting Boundaries* x).[28] The dream stays alive because the reality is plural. Such writing moves at the heart of the American experiment, and because it is yet to be realized, Native writers, in their unique ways, have been working among others across the centuries to make it real. A ground theory reflects those ways of knowing in order to make those narrative structures more visible to readers schooled in binary thinking.

Robin DeRosa describes theoretical steps that move in this less binary direction, in her introduction to *Assimilation and Subversion in Earlier American Literature*. DeRosa refers to controversies among "students, professors, and literary critics alike" about the enslaved Phyllis Wheatley, one of the first African American poets, and whether she was "fully assimilated into her new American culture" or her poetry expressed "a veiled but tangible statement against her own oppression" (1). DeRosa offers "a different paradigm" for analyzing Wheatley, instead of the reductive dialectic that would "polarize 'assimilation' and 'subversion.'" Instead the critics in her collection "give readers useful models for approaching texts by nondominant subjects, models that consider the polyphonic flow of power and the possibility of simultaneous multiple, conflicting, and even oppositional effects of oppression" (1). Applying a more nuanced, perhaps deconstructive approach, the essays in her collection "offer new ways to think about dialectic itself" (1), as these illuminate works by marginalized writers such as Wheatley and Native American Christians such as Samson Occom and William Apess.

On Native ground, I find indeed a system of thinking that moves beyond dialectic readings and realities. Thus I read in many Native texts a fundamental pattern—with exceptions—of dialogic approaches to modern dialectics. The dialogics of Indigenous narrative structures tend to deconstruct and sometimes even transcend historical binaries. Their deconstructive strategy reveals how opposites, such as white and Indian, civilization and wilderness, actually share qualities across the apparent divide. Their transcendent strategy resists domination by representing Indigenous lands and lifeways as central to a wider narrative, in contrast to Euro-Americans as culturally impoverished and therefore less connected to the strength of the land.[29] We can see these dynamics specifically in those five key questions of modern national self-definition. As the Choctaw poet Joy Harjo puts it, "We exist together in a sacred field of meaning" (Harjo, *This I Believe*). And as the Cherokee scholar Jace Weaver puts it, "Unlike any other racial or ethnic minority, Native American tribes are separate sovereign nations. As flawed as it was, the treaty process confirmed this status" (Weaver et al., *American Indian Literary Nationalism* 46). That flawed sovereign status on "a sacred field of meaning" invites a ground theory to map its dynamics.

Susan Berry Brill de Ramírez offers a valuable "conversive" critique of dialogics that helps to refine this ground theory. She prefers the "co-" of what she calls a conversive model of literary scholarship to the remnants of duality inherent in the "di-" of dialogics. The positive direction of her rationale is clarifying: "Here relationality is intersubjective and takes the form of a circular conversivity (as distinct from the linear oppositionality of dialectic, discursive, and dialogic models). Such a model provides a strategy in which peoples, cultures, persons, and texts interrelationally inform and reform literary scholarship, thereby leading to new readings and insights otherwise not possible" (*Contemporary American Indian Literatures* 37). Brill de Ramírez envisions a democratic, nonhierarchical theory of reading "interrelationally" that derives from a larger set balancing unity and diversity: "Difference is not, thereby, lost; on the contrary, difference is affirmed through the intersubjectivity of conversive relations that recognizes the subjective status of oneself *and* of others" (110). Her analysis is explicitly, and etymologically, true to the conceptual linkages and differences, that is, binaries versus commonalities, in these theoretical terms. Where her conversive communications might "co-create and transform their own stories and each other" (73) we might envision Native writers and both Native and non-Native readers rewriting the story of America.[30]

An adequate term for this theory of reading, or this way of knowing, will then have to be *ground*, where all the voices standing on and under and over that ground may speak and be heard. Ground theory invokes the comic ecologic of reciprocal interrelations between subject and object, self and other, human and nature, and, in ongoing colonial history, of interconnections between Indian and white. The social and psychological dynamics are planted in a larger ground of culture and nature, where humanity and environment, nature and culture are inextricable.

Ground theory, then, reaffirms the primary challenge in Indian-white relations: the land, its creatures and its people interrelated and always seeking balance. To protect creatures of that land, such as the salmon, a Klamath tribal member invokes such social and psychological ground—as a defense against the frontier mentality—when he claims to understand the farmer irrigators' plight: "This is simply a battle over limited resources. We live on those fish. We understand what those farmers are going through. They've been strangling our water for generations."[31] Similarly when a Crow tribal chairman pronounces the obvious, "People in Montana need to know that Indian tribes are part of Montana,"[32] he is returning the discussion to fundamental human ground that has been overlooked even while expropriated.

Invitations to dialogue frequently are dismissed as naïve. To apply ground theory, to focus on a matrix of narrative factors, is not to deny the powerful oppositional stance that many Native nations and tribal individuals have adopted against the cultural, economic, and military forces of a sustained colonial project. The warrior mode, the arrow, the coup stick, the trigger, the war club, the critical or satirical pen, certainly invoke nuanced values of opposition, even to the ultimately lethal violence of the dialectic.

That force of direct Native resistance to colonialism is the stuff of American history. Powhatan and his Confederacy in the late 1500s; King Philip and Po'Pay in the 1600s; Brant and the Iroquois Confederacy and Tecumseh in the 1700s and early 1800s; Blackhawk again in the early 1800s; Crazy Horse, Red Cloud, Sitting Bull, and Geronimo in the late 1800s—these are only a few leaders among thousands, who are in turn only the vanguard of hundreds of thousands, indeed millions of Native warriors who defended their homelands. Yet it is not only because that history is written mostly by the victors that an alternative history needs to be unearthed. As scholars of the "white man's Indian" have pointed out, America needed a noble savage, a worthy but dispensable enemy, to ennoble their own ignoble and illegal conquest of a continent.[33] An alternative history grows out of Native storytelling, and it offers America not only a human enemy but a regrounded, humane America.

Invoking sacred ground in their persuasive narratives, Native writers often aim the rhetoric of their texts, their "wordarrows," to quote the Ojibwa writer Gerald Vizenor, at a non-Native audience. As soon as Native writers set pen to paper or fingertips to keyboard, they recognize the enormous challenges for what I call dialogics to elude, deconstruct, and transcend layers of American investments in dialectical thinking. The very colonial relations that launched Columbus's mercantilism in the "New World" and that gave Colonel Pattee his mandate to jail the Fool Soldiers on the "frontier" still make it difficult for non-Native readers to see dialogic ground, the pluralist possibilities for American society. Indigenous narratives shore up legal, political, cultural, spiritual, and ecological ground against the linear torrent of mainstream dominance.

If the ground, the homeland functions as a network for the action of these stories, the fact that humans share the earth does not mean that anyone can come along and claim it. Native communities fiercely defend their aboriginal land rights and all the associated rights that come with their sovereignty on that land. A ground theory that recognizes Native voices thus moves beyond multiculturalism to pluralism, not a melting pot but a matrix. As Elizabeth Cook-Lynn warns critics of Native literatures, to read Native voices only for what they can offer to white audiences or to imagine that Native writers merely want entry into the American literary canon is to misread the dynamics of their community-based narratives.[34] Sacred ground never was for sale.

Cook-Lynn's vital 1993 publication on "cosmopolitanism and nationalism," "The American Indian Fiction Writer," triggered the literary nationalism of Craig Womack, Jace Weaver, Robert Warrior, Lisa Brooks, and other Native American scholars.[35] The pluralism of ground theory grows from her propositions as well. Cook-Lynn outlines the power issues of cultural integration for "the nativist" scholar, her term for those who dedicate themselves to a community-based approach. She raises "the question of whether or not 'opening up the American literary canon' to include Native literary traditions and contemporary works will have much relevance within its own set of unique aims, i.e., the interest in establishing the myths and metaphors of sovereign nationalism which have always fueled the literary canon of tribal peoples, their literary lives" (29-30). Opening the American canon to "others" promises neither freedom from co-optation nor freedom for self-representation. Elucidating narratives of tribal sovereignty, Cook-Lynn suggests, is the responsibility of both writers and critics of Native literatures. Literary sovereignty resists the melting pot.

What emerges here is a fundamental direction in the Native value of tribal sovereignty that underlies many narratives of Indian community and disintegration. That direction remains not only to resist the melting pot but further to remap America toward a genuine culture of diversity, a conceivable matrix of autonomous cultural centers. James Ruppert's analysis of "the mythic mode of identity production" and "the greater self in the communal" (*Mediation* 27-28) in Native literatures of "mediation" goes far toward clarifying dynamics of identity and community in these texts, while here we add both the mythical and political dimensions of sovereignty.

Thus a balanced nationalism of tribal voices can and does confront the dominating, co-optive cosmopolitanism of a globalized readership, especially as non-Indian readers have so often constituted the target audience for Indian writers. Cook-Lynn's renowned criticism is sweeping, worth quoting at length to contextualize and contrast a ground theory:

> What may be important to conclude here, then, is that much of what is called Contemporary American Indian Fiction is sustained as such by non-Indian publishers and editors, critics and scholars for Euro-Anglo canonical reasons (some might even suggest imperialistic reasons) rather than for either the continuation of Indigenous literary traditions and development of nationalistic critical apparatuses or for the sake of simple intellectual curiosity. Because of flaws in pedagogy, much modern fiction written in English by American Indians is being utilized to provide the basis for the cynical absorption into the "melting pot," pragmatic inclusion in the canon and involuntary unification of an "American National Literary Voice." Ironically, much criticism as it is being published today contributes to the further domination of first-world nations and individualism all the while failing in its own implied search for Sovereignty and Tribalism. ("The American Indian Fiction Writer" 35)

Cook-Lynn depicts the corporate world of publishing Native literature as it is linked to the corporate academy, marking not only collisions but collusions between cosmopolitanism and capitalism that by definition would co-opt otherwise autonomous cultural centers as new markets in which to expand.[36] The massive problem that Cook-Lynn and other scholars are responding to has been the de facto Euro-American co-optation, assimilation, and destruction of so many Native lands and cultures. That absorption and assimilation are part of what Cook-Lynn identifies as cosmopolitanism, an economic engine of aggrandizement that generalizes cultural differences into commodities for its ever-expanding markets. *Cosmopolitanism*, as I understand her use of it, is a twentieth-century term for "manifest destiny" in the academy. Her nationalism is a resistance against that co-optive universalism.

Cook-Lynn also is describing here the antipluralistic dangers in the academy parallel to corporate multiculturalism in business, where ostensible diversity becomes merely another American term for the melting pot. The established economic powers welcome a "multicultural" version of otherness that would provide more markets for its products without challenging the economic structures, built on colonized land, that bolster their bottom line. An entrenched academy, and its editors often linked to the corporate world of global publishing, welcome multicultural diversity as the ground for academic careers, intellectual curiosity, and sales of classroom texts.

By Cook-Lynn's account, we may see how American Indian literatures do not ask to be absorbed into American literature like Indigenous corn, squash, beans, tomatoes, and potatoes melting into a pot of America's literary soup. Instead the inverse has occurred, as we will discuss; Native cultural production evidently has long been acculturating Euro-Americans, even transforming them (and the rest of the world) on fundamental cultural and institutional levels. One grounded example is how applications of Indigenous agronomy now account for two-thirds of the modern world's food products.[37]

The land has voices. Assertions of Native American writers become the assertions of the land. Cook-Lynn focuses a grounded critique on a connection between Indigenous literature, the land, and the nation. Implicit in her charge is the suggestion that Euro-American scholars, following the lead of Native scholars, might enter a discussion of how land issues of tribal sovereignty shape the narratives of Native writers and their vision for twenty-first-century relations.[38]

The point here is to enter a conversation, not to appropriate or represent Indian voices. The ground speaks dialogically, requiring listening, inviting conversation. Instead of a wannabe, co-optive universalism that projects and then helps itself to its own cultural smorgasbord, a ground theory tries to listen to the ways those songs and that drum speak to me and to others, to what literary celebration and grief over Indian lives and cultures have said to both Native America and non-Native America about issues that matter to them, including diversity and community. Justice offers both a measure and a kind of resolution: "Native spiritual and intellectual traditions have a long history of inclusive flexibility. A world that's imbued with innumerable spirits has room for the different entities and the worldviews of other peoples. This flexibility is marked by an attention to relationships, which require sensitivity and engagement to stay healthy" (*Our Fire Survives the Storm* 49). That "inclusive flexibility" invites conversation.

Over the centuries Native writers have insisted on humanity, dignity, and autonomy, and again tribal sovereignty, as a realignment of America's power relations. Such insistence only reaffirms the *pluribus* in America's own promise. As Cook-Lynn explains, "The idea of decolonization is not new to tribal peoples" ("The American Indian Fiction Writer" 214). Readers and writers of Native American literature thus return to fundamentals, to the ground. Simon Ortiz describes the poignant invitation of that animate American earth, even under contestation:

> Like a soul, the land
> was open to them, like a child's heart.
> There was no paradise,
> but it would have gently and willingly
> and longingly given them food and air
> and substance for every comfort.
> If they had only acknowledged
> even their smallest conceit. (*from Sand Creek* 79)

1

KNOWING IT WAS TO COME
Sovereignty as Sacrifice

"A boy had to have a good feeling about himself and about his people, or the fire would go out of his life," Bull muses on his grandson's primary needs in D'Arcy McNickle's *Wind from an Enemy Sky* (239). The brief phrase speaks to the complexity of reciprocal relations that is "tribal sovereignty." The Choctaw Cherokee scholar and novelist Louis Owens speaks to the link between community and identity, describing Native writers working at the "rearticulation of an identity, a process dependent upon a rediscovered sense of place as well as community" (*Other Destinies* 5). The critic James Ruppert similarly speaks of a "greater self in the communal" as an Indigenous value that bridges the conceptual divide between individual and group. "This path to identity is an active one where the individual works with others to define a place and existence for himself or herself," Ruppert asserts.[1] That place is active as well, participating in the story of communal existence. The communal individual is woven always with the history of that geographical space as a social place, and in Indian Country that history is woven into the cycles of what current discourse describes as tribal sovereignty. This process of rebuilding grounded, communal identity in Native literature therefore leads us to further discussion of sovereignty as the underlying term, for which a first working definition might be Bull's phrase for the coming generation: "a good feeling about himself and about his people."

"This Conception of Land as Holding the Bodies of the Tribe"

I use *sovereignty* in two contexts: its current political and legal meaning as a force for sustaining Indian community on the local level and its literary deployment in Native texts as "the fire . . . of his life," the will of the people. This chapter traces the threads between legal discourse of "inherent powers" and literary discourse of "stories in the blood."[2] Where courts and Congress debate aboriginal land rights and inherent powers of self-government, Native authors and citizens affirm parallel stories in the blood of communal selfhood. Apart from etymological European roots of sovereignty in courtly power, Indigenous discourses of sovereignty arise today from ancient practices of autonomy and agency on the part of clans and kinship systems. The spirit that holds together a people on common ground works its way through history. A fuller pattern of sovereignty emerges across this weaving of the social and the spiritual.

Beneath a pragmatic definition of sovereignty as "self-government," the term carries diverse usages but generally conveys a value of *the people first*. Again, I am looking at a functional, active, indeed flexible definition for this key term rather than a static codification. In its many expressions, sovereignty is a spirit of sacrifice that tribal people feel for their nation. It is enshrined in legal, political, economic, and cultural traditions, and it animates individual and institutional commitments to Native community and identity. Indeed tribal sovereignty is also a cross-cultural term. shaping not only federal Indian policy but America's own self-definitions. In October 2006 then Montana senator Conrad Burns spoke of tribal sovereignty as "good for them," referring to Montana's twelve Indian tribes.[3] My point, as I have gleaned it from Indian writers in this study and elsewhere, is that tribal sovereignty is good for America. It codifies the fundamental value of *e pluribus unum* by structurally democratizing power relations, not only in the government-to-government relations advocated by federal and tribal policymakers but also by institutionalizing the affirmation of cultural difference.

However, a nation that founded itself, against its own ideals, on the erasure of Natives still can hardly imagine Native Americans having their own autonomous nations beyond "domestic dependent" ones. Tribal sovereignty is regarded by marginalizing reflex as only "good for them." The Supreme Court's 1831 formulation of "domestic dependent nations" in *Cherokee Nation v. Georgia* has itself seemed to American policymakers only a legal fiction, a temporary appeasement of conscience, a brief interruption of empire. In 1832 President Andrew Jackson openly dismissed and defied the Supreme Court and Chief Justice Marshall's acknowledgment of limited sovereignty of the Cherokee Nation in the related decision of *Worcester v. Georgia*. Jackson stated, "Marshall has made his law, now let him enforce it," as Congress and the state of Georgia proceeded to seize Cherokee lands.[4] By forcing his policies of dispossession and then Indian Removal against the opinion of the Supreme Court, Jackson was in fact precipitating a constitutional crisis between the executive and judicial branches. Yet eager popular indifference and covetous opposition to Indian land rights ignored that tear in the American constitutional fabric.

Legally and literally the language of *Cherokee Nation v. Georgia* affirms the Native fiat, "until that right shall be extinguished by a voluntary cession to our government." Yet the ideas of tribal sovereignty and Native nationhood remain anathema to American national identity not only because of de facto power relations whereby non-Indians continue to desire to possess and control the land and resources but also because of the invisible ways power constructs nationhood and citizenship, a public identity, an American self-definition: American identity requires the vanishing Indian.[5]

The land must be cleared. While Henry David Thoreau proclaimed, in his 1862 essay *Walking*, that "in wildness is the preservation of the world," he also celebrated the (white) farmer draining and *redeeming* the meadow as he becomes "more natural" than "the Indian": "I think that the farmer displaces the Indian even because he redeems the meadow, and so makes himself stronger and in some respects more natural" (101). The remarkable contradictions in Thoreau's statement mark the American ideology of erasure—erasing first the Indian, then any immigrant's difference as well.

For all its legal, political, and ideological history, in Native literary usage sovereignty becomes a feeling, a spirit, a quality of good humor, open-heartedness, and generosity combined with courage to sacrifice for the community. Indeed "living in two worlds," as the phrase is so often used, while maintaining a traditional ceremonial life, inculcating Native values in one's children, or holding on to hope of cultural survivance, can be a sacrifice in itself. *Sovereignty* as a term thus carries connection to community, ancestry, spirit, and land. As Vine Deloria Jr. explains, "This conception of land as holding the bodies of the tribe in a basic sense pervaded tribal religions across the country. It testified in a stronger sense to the underlying unity of the Indian conception of the universe as a system in which everything had its part" (*God Is Red* 173). The dancers in a ceremonial lodge today are willing to sacrifice their pain because of that connection and that conception. That is who they are. It is not a wannabe realm. Young Native lawyers, men and women, who return to their communities to develop tribal justice systems are equally willing to sacrifice their corporate careers. Tribal members who bring unique perspectives to their corporate professions might do so by sacrificing the assurance of career safety. It is "stories in the blood." Sovereignty thus forms a logic of sacrifice for the people in their place on the land, a logic that means Native individuals often give everything so that their families and communities may struggle to maintain "a good feeling" about themselves and about their people. When McNickle's Bull tries to protect that "good feeling," he is striving to affirm generational connections between his grandson and a physical and conceptual space peopled with ancestors. As Crazy Horse is reputed to have said, "My land is where my dead lie buried."[6] Their sacrifice makes sovereignty sacred.

In the dawning light of "inherent powers" and "stories in the blood," the balance between authenticity, identity, and community appears to operate as a cyclic return to the ground of sovereignty that exists prior to the field of relations between Europeans and Native Americans. That is one reason I set sovereignty in this first chapter, although each of the other terms could occupy the primary or central position. If authenticity questions are about Native roots and identity questions are about the turmoil of those roots being laid bare, then questions of community and sovereignty remain the ground in which to replant that tree and to try to balance that turmoil. Irony and humor are the inherent, flexible life of that tree buffeted by history.

Black Elk's prophecy of the replanting of the sacred tree, part of the spiritual discourse that provided so much impetus for Native American political and cultural resurgence in the second half of the twentieth century, continues to resonate: "I know not what this meant, that the bison were the gift of a good spirit and were our strength, but we should lose them, and from the same good spirit we must find another strength. . . . And suddenly the flowering tree was there again at the center of the nation's hoop where the four-rayed herb had blossomed" (Neihardt, *Black Elk Speaks* 32–33). Native writers before and after *Black Elk Speaks* have shown how tribal sovereignty "from the same good spirit" may flower as "another strength." (Black Elk's manuscript in *The Sixth Grandfather* suggested the military medicine power of another "soldier weed of destruction," which, in the name of peace, he refused to employ.)[7] In Native stories sovereignty undergoes the kind of losses and transformations mapped in Black Elk's vision of the tree at the center of the nation's hoop. Sovereignty also maps the community politic from which Native narratives of roots and turmoil have drawn life.

Thus scholarly polemics about Native stories, if the literati focus on colonial relations of authenticity or identity as the "meaning" of the narrative, can remain suspended between the horns of a colonial dilemma. Locked in the limiting logic of either/or narration that has structured discussions of authenticity and identity, marching to the death beat of dualism, such critiques often miss the narrative energy that survives the terminal creeds. Even "multicultural" efforts to celebrate Native literature in the classroom can become ground for subtle but pervasive erasure of Native voices when this limiting logic relegates them to a static past. As ethnic commodities in an educational marketplace, Indians continue to fall into the prehistory of America. However, when scholarship and classroom begin to address sovereignty issues, "teaching the conflicts" can generate ways to move through limiting colonial oppositions of past and present to more complex issues of internal American struggles or the specific dynamics of diverse cultures.[8] Constructing a theory about the ironic ways in Native stories that authenticity, identity, and community unfold together on the ground of sovereignty is part of a process of retrieving a usable past and future for both Native and non-Native readers.

To underscore this fuller spectrum of sovereignty issues is not to underestimate careful analyses of identity questions or community dynamics in the fiction, poetry, autobiography, other nonfiction, or criticism of Native literatures. Instead it is to recognize a unique Indigenous value that shapes literary issues of authenticity, identity, and community as much as colonial history shapes them. If authenticity was the nineteenth-century focus of colonizing anthropology, and if identity was the twentieth-century focus of the social psychology of colonialism, perhaps a twenty-first-century crosscultural focus on sovereignty and community may clarify the legal and spiritual foundations of these stories.

Sovereignty as Peoplehood

Due to the primary importance of the term, I will review notions of tribal sovereignty for those readers of Native literatures who are less familiar with this cultural, political, legal, and historical issue. I recognize the Osage scholar Robert Warrior's approach, to "use the term 'sovereignty' in a rather undefined way" because "a definition of sovereignty should emerge from the experience of communities rather than in academic discourse" ("Temporary Visibility" 51). The Creek scholar Craig Womack echoes Warrior's point, affirming theoretically and practically that the meaning of sovereignty "is defined within the tribe rather than by external sources" (*Red on Red* 14). Warrior's challenge for the academy is to respond to rather than impose definitions of sovereignty expressed in the literature, as many writers and activists in Indian Country certainly do work with more concrete functions of sovereignty than anything "undefined." He derives this flexibility from what he calls, in *Tribal Secrets: Recovering American Indian Intellectual Traditions*, a "process-centered definition of sovereignty" (91) in the work of Vine Deloria Jr. Such discussions affirm that sovereignty is not a defensive or colonized reaction but is, as Deloria puts it, "oriented primarily toward the existence and continuance of the group" (Deloria et al., *We Talk* 123). Thus scholars patently need to pay attention to grassroots notions of sovereignty coming from Native communities themselves. The key here, not unlike the issue of authenticity, is a certain radical experientialism in the expression and application of Native sovereignty.[9]

Further, I recognize the rejection of the term *sovereignty* by the Mohawk Kanien'kehaka political scientist Taiaiake Alfred.[10] He does a convincing job of analyzing reasons for jettisoning the term, both because of its inappropriate discursive roots in a European history of monarchical state power and because of its historical erosions under the dominance of modern states.[11] Alfred's arguments are sound and compelling, and I will return to them, but I address sovereignty as a pivotal principle because the term is not going away. His argument is parallel to my rejection in the introduction of the word *frontier* as irrecoverable. Yet both terms continue to be used, and it is crucial to engage those conversations here. The term *sovereignty* is so much a part of the current discourse that I use it in a descriptive, critical way, not by way of advocating for the term itself. I leave the necessary prescriptions to those Native scholars and activists who may claim the right to issue a manifesto.

Indeed Kevin Bruyneel, another political scientist, reads Indigenous sovereignty as not necessarily co-opted in the ways that Alfred claims. In his book, *The Third Space of Sovereignty: The Postcolonial Politics of U.S.-Indigenous Relations*, Bruyneel describes "postcolonial nationhood," which "located itself across the boundaries and through the gaps of colonial imposition, in the third space, where Indigenous political life fights to claim its modern status on its own terms" (124). The assertion of "its own terms" is precisely the question that Alfred raises, and that question reverberates with my discussion, thanks to Simon Ortiz, of authenticity as the translation of colonial experience into Indigenous terms. In entering this discussion, I thus foreground the fact that usage of the term *sovereignty* is indeed conflicted. Wherever it may lead and whichever term survives, the political energy of sovereignty is gaining momentum, while its complexity, and perhaps its indefinability, may be part of its sustaining power.

I don't pretend in this short space to give a full evolutionary chronology of the term *sovereignty*; instead I offer a summary of key concepts. Vine Deloria Jr. and others have written usefully on the topic that cannot be exhausted.[12] Deloria attributes the rise of Native sovereignty discourse specifically to the activism of tribes in Washington state who, starting in the 1950s, reaffirmed their fishing rights by treaty. That movement, which resulted in the landmark Boldt Decision of 1974 that recognized reserved aboriginal fishing rights, arose out of nationwide community strategies against the federal policy of "termination" that held sway from the mid-1940s through the mid-1960s.[13] Later in the chapter, after mapping some of the key directions for the term, I will discuss some of the implications of tribal sovereignty for changing American concepts of community and nationhood as those concepts are reshaped by Native American voices, especially in the work of Apess, Winnemucca, McNickle, Silko, and Alexie. We will find that Native communities redefine the term *sovereignty* as time and conditions change, yet it connects to something enduring, resilient, and dynamic. Such Indigenous resilience challenges the American community to live with its own diversity by default.

Sovereignty, or peoplehood, a term we read in Alfred as well as in Deloria and Lytle, can be both a cause and an effect of the people's solidarity, their sense of themselves as a people and their commitment to their national identity. Sovereignty comes out of solidarity, and vice versa. The Cherokee scholar Daniel Heath Justice describes a "relational peoplehood" as the "terrain of Cherokee nationhood," "the system of relationships between the People and the rest of Creation" (*Our Fire Survives the Storm* 20). The reemergence of the politics of tribal sovereignty in the late twentieth century might suggest how intra- and intercultural relations are cycling into sharper focus. Solidarity and sovereignty are codefinitive.

The legal historian Rennard Strickland, of Osage and Cherokee heritage, offers a useful metaphor for contemporary tribal sovereignty: "Imagine the eagle as the sovereign and each arrow held in the claws as the embodiment of the attributes of sovereignty. . . . What arrows does it still hold? . . . We see the tribal eagle with few of the arrows of sovereignty in place, but nonetheless still a sovereign, free-flying and powerful" ("The Eagle's Empire" 247). Strickland's metaphor affirms a "free-flying" principle of sovereignty even when many, if not most of its literal and legal "attributes" are gone. He goes on to discuss the history and legal concepts: "The roots of Native Americans' sovereignty and the laws of her sovereign nations stretch back long before the black robes or the blue coats came and built their courthouses and guardhouses" (251). Strickland gives us a vivid picture: "The constitutional and legal history of America's sovereign Indian tribes demonstrates that law is more—much more—than powdered wigs, black robes, leather-bound statutes, silver stars, and blindfolded ladies with balanced scales. . . . In fact, a command from the spirit world can have greater force as law than the most elaborate decision devised by the highest and most honored of court judges" (250–51). Strickland puts sovereignty into perspective not only in terms of pre-Columbian time and space but equally in terms of a certain timelessness. Sovereignty in his rendering becomes both an individual and a communal force for clarity of purpose in service to a society, a nation. A Cherokee priest and a Cheyenne warrior do their work to uphold ethical laws of people and place that give sovereignty a force of "the spirit world." The logic of animism that we will discuss as a foundation of Native community thus emerges by that reasoning at the heart of sovereignty as well.

In contrast, Joseph P. Kalt and Joseph W. Singer see the issue of sovereignty through a practical perspective in a 2004 publication of the Harvard Project on American Indian Economic Development. They maintain a traditional Western usage as the political and legal basis of self-rule: "The sources, meanings, consequences, limits, propriety, and other fine points of 'sovereignty' seem destined to be widely and vigorously discussed, dissected, and debated for years to come. This is no less true when it comes to Indian sovereignty. But here we adopt the most straightforward of definitions of 'sovereignty.' *Sovereignty is self-rule*" (*Myths and Realities of Tribal Sovereignty* 5). For Kalt and Singer, self-government functions as both cause and effect of multifarious historical, legal, political, economic, cultural, psychological, and spiritual dynamics. We may see this practical cycle, for instance, in the functioning of the Confederated Salish and Kootenai Tribes on the Flathead Reservation in Montana, like many across the nation over the past generation, where the tribes have negotiated for "retrocession" of the administration of hydroelectric power, forest resources, water rights, law enforcement, courts, health, social welfare, education, and numerous other exercises of civic authority.

However practical such a functional definition may be, Kalt and Singer also trace its renaissance and profound resonance:

> The last three decades have witnessed a remarkable resurgence of the Indian nations in the United States. After centuries of turmoil, oppression, attempted subjugation, and economic deprivation, the Indian nations have asserted their rights and identities, have built and rebuilt political systems in order to implement self-rule, and have begun to overcome what once seemed to be insurmountable problems of poverty and social disarray. The foundation of this resurgence has been the exercise of self-government by the more than 560 federally-recognized tribes in the U.S. (*Myths and Realities of Tribal Sovereignty* 1)

Although Kalt and Singer set self-government as the foundation of this political and cultural resurgence, the question remains whether such historic revitalization is founded on less definitive events in Indian communities, such as sacrificial efforts to maintain cultural identity. Leaving the elusive—or, more likely, circular—dimensions of that question aside, there is no historical doubt that the new politics of what some call tribal sovereignty has grown volcanically in the past generation, a shift codified especially in the pivotal Indian Self-Determination and Education Assistance Act of 1975.

Focused efforts by Native intellectuals and activists throughout the 1960s

Knowing It Was to Come   45

eventually maneuvered the Nixon and Ford administrations through Congress to finalize that Act in the mid-1970s. These efforts followed generations of Indian leadership working persistently in this direction. (The 1934 Indian Reorganization Act had been a major step, only to be eroded by the ensuing federal policy of "termination.") The Self-Determination Act not only reversed federal termination policy that would have eradicated—in scores of cases did eradicate—Indigenous treaty rights and federal responsibilities, but it went further to encourage "maximum Indian participation in the Government and education of the Indian people." The Act fundamentally reaffirmed the federal government's fiscal and fiduciary treaty responsibilities to Indian Country, while at the same time it reaffirmed tribal sovereignty. It launched the discourse, now common in political circles, of a "government-to-government relationship" between federal and tribal leadership. The legislation set up specific processes for federal educational and social services to be contracted to individual nations, that is, a step toward self-rule; it established grants to tribes for such programs; and it fostered educational reform by legislating Indian parents' participation on school boards. Over the decades since 1975, amendments to the Self-Determination Act further reestablished self-governance through contracts and block grants for social services across Indian Country.

Although legislators might not have envisioned the depth and breadth of tribal sovereignty that continues to reemerge, the Indian Self-Determination and Education Assistance Act was a major step in the political, cultural, and literary resurgence launched in the 1960s in the wake of the civil rights movement. Indeed nearly two hundred years of Indian activism was affirmed in 1975 by this Act, not unlike the affirmation of women's rights after a century and more of the women's suffrage movement in 1920 by the Nineteenth Amendment. In both cases, the social victories were long in coming, and the turning point marked only a gradual change, with future slippage requiring further activist sacrifices.

So before Kalt and Singer's "last three decades," where did tribal sovereignty come from? What is the origin of this power of Native nations and voices to define—represent—and govern themselves?

Legally and historically, but seldom militarily, tribal sovereignty has been subjected to "conquest," as America struggles to suppress the very model of its confederated potential. The Marshall Supreme Court decisions of the late 1820s and early 1830s explicitly claimed such concrete and abstract historical conquest in "the actual state of things" as the rationale for establishing tribes as "domestic dependent nations." Writing of the federal "tribalizing" process of Indian peoples, the law professor Raymond Cross (Mandan-Hidatsa) explains that through Chief Justice Marshall's writings, "hundreds of linguistically, culturally and economically distinct Indigenous peoples were assimilated as tribes into the American domestic sphere of control" ("Tribes as Rich Nations" 1). Following on the work of Morton Fried in *The Notion of the Tribe* that positions the word *tribe* within the modern discourse of states, Cross writes that this policy of reducing Indian peoples to tribes from nation status has a more than two-hundred-year history. He describes Marshall's abstract conquest: "Chief Justice Marshall, in his famed Trilogy of Indian Law opinions [*Johnson v. M'Intosh, Cherokee Nation v. Georgia, Worcester v. Georgia*], birthed the tribe out of a primal source that he called 'the actual state of things.' This pastiche of historical, cultural, economic and geographic circumstances was orchestrated by Marshall so as to define an exclusive, bi-lateral relationship between the federal government and those Indigenous peoples who were resident in America at the time of European Discovery" ("Tribes as Rich Nations" 2–3).

Because Georgia wanted Cherokee land, they also wanted prior power, a legal abstraction, over Cherokees to take that land. Marshall's decisions arrogated that prior power to the federal government instead of to Georgia or the other states. In so doing, Marshall was also drawing on a prior legal logic, invoking the even more abstracted "doctrine of discovery" issued by a fifteenth-century pope, Nicholas V, in 1452, that became the "legal" foundation of colonization over the centuries (and continues today, for instance, in Russia's recent claims to the seabed of the Arctic Ocean).[14] That unilateral Eurocentric doctrine not only consolidated power, it homogenized the diversity of Native nations in the eyes of colonial and then U.S. governments, and in so doing set up the bureaucratic reductionism that then could "administer" to the tribes. By this legal legacy from papal decree, federal sovereignty over Native nations under the Marshall Court in the 1820s and 1830s became a direct expression of colonial relations from centuries before. It is no accident that the Indian Bureau (later to become the Bureau of Indian Affairs) was established in Marshall's time, first in the War Department in 1824, and later moved to the Department of the Interior in 1849.

Cross continues by emphasizing the arbitrary but strategic logic of Marshall's discursive formulation: "Once fully sovereign peoples, by the operation of the 'actual state of things,' these Indigenous peoples were reduced to the legal status of 'domestic dependent nations.' This new status under American law, intermediate between that of a foreign nation and that of a purely voluntary association of individuals, Marshall denominated a 'tribe'" ("Tribes as Rich Nations" 2–3). The rhetorical reduction from "nation" to "tribe" achieved precisely the erasure necessary to establish the legal foundations of federal legitimacy on the land.[15]

Cross uses the term *bilateral* to describe what was neither an equitable policy nor a balanced exchange between the federal and Native nations. Instead, by this federal maneuver to limit state power, Marshall could more readily control a bilateral relationship hierarchically between the U.S. government and Indian tribes than allow an obstinate third party such as Georgia to hold sway. That hierarchy of federal over tribal governments was important to Marshall in the structural exclusion of separate states' rights. Georgia wanted to claim conquest over the Cherokees, but Marshall reserved that "sovereignty" for the United States. (Andrew Jackson and his political debts to Georgia also played a part.) However, only the external powers of Indian nations were restricted by that jurisprudential conquest, limiting only the "tribes'" disposition of lands and their relations with foreign governments. Their own internal affairs remained at that point under their sovereignty.

Horizontal, bilateral systems of power tend to become vertical.[16] A discourse that insisted on federal sovereignty drove the founding rhetoric of the Marshall decisions. In the double context of states' rights and dispossession of Indian lands, it was precisely this assumption of a vertical hierarchy in federal over state power that motivated the Marshall Court to insist on the subordinate status of "domestic dependent nations." Indian governmental structures were the original prize in the battle over states' rights, as they were made dependent on the federal government to block state power from becoming equal or superior to federal power. States would have had to claim sovereignty over *independent* Native nations in order for those states to have risen to a level of sovereignty equal to the federal government's. By claiming that Native nations were dependent on the federal government, Marshall thus required states to go through the federal system in their relations with those Native nations. Thus states' rights were relegated subordinate to federal power. Because federalist hierarchy cannot conceive, much less concede, plural sovereignties, its solution was to reduce Native nations to dependent ones, to the same level it was insisting on for states over which it was trying to extend federal power.

Over the decades until 1871, when Congress straightforwardly abrogated the widespread and ostensibly more reciprocal treaty procedure in favor of its own unilateral "plenary power," treaty law continued as an uneven process with different stipulations on land tenure mandated by different local histories. Land disposition and foreign relations certainly remain important legal gaps in "tribal" sovereignty, "but otherwise," as Arthur Lazarus Jr., counsel for the Association of American Indian Affairs, states, "in every other respect, the internal sovereignty of the tribe, its power over domestic affairs, remained unchanged" (Swagerty, *Indian Sovereignty* 30–31). Over the years there have been various further erosions, from congressional abrogation of treaty relations in the 1870s and the 1885 Major Crimes Act to Supreme Court cases such as *Ex Parte Crow Dog* of 1883 and cases restricting Native American religious freedom near the turn of the twenty-first century. Again there have been federal policies that fortified tribal sovereignty as well, especially the 1975 Indian Self-Determination Act and the 1980 Native American Graves Protection and Repatriation Act. Yet as Vine Deloria Jr. has explained, such domestic sovereignty remains the simple and direct goal of Indian communities.

Looking back two generations in *The Nations Within: The Past and Future of American Indian Sovereignty*, Deloria and Clifford M. Lytle discuss crucial legal discourse in "a vast reservoir of inherent powers" as they became clear in the legislative unfolding of the 1934 Indian Reorganization Act (IRA):

> "Powers of Indian Tribes" was issued on October 25, 1934, and was some thirty-two pages in length, hardly a casual commentary on the wording of the statute. The opinion adopted the theory that "those powers which are lawfully vested in an Indian tribe are not, in general, delegated powers granted by express acts of Congress, but rather inherent powers of a limited sovereignty which has never been extinguished." The theory of tribal political powers was that Indian tribes had at one time been fully sovereign and that in embracing a relationship with the

United States they had, from time to time, allowed some of those powers to be changed, modified, or surrendered. They had, however, a vast reservoir of inherent powers, which any political entity had. (158)

This legal formulation of "inherent powers" summons up humanistic, even metaphysical values of the Enlightenment that evoke both Emerson's Transcendentalism and Jefferson's inalienable rights. It is a Platonic, certainly abstract foundation of Western law extending concretely across colonial history and applied to Indian law.

Most Americans would be surprised to learn what has been going on in Indian Country according to these inherent powers. Few Indian folks, however, would be surprised by a list of "reserved" powers of "reservation" governments like the following that Deloria and Lytle list from the 1934 legislation:

Among the "inherent" sovereign powers . . . were the right to adopt a form of government; to create various offices and prescribe their duties; to prescribe the procedures and forms through which the will of the tribe was to be expressed; to define conditions of membership; to provide or withhold suffrage; to regulate domestic relations; to prescribe rules of inheritance; to levy fees, dues, and taxes; to remove or exclude nonmembers; to regulate the use of property; to administer justice; and to describe the duties of federal employees insofar as such powers were delegated by the Interior Department. . . . Some of these powers were undoubtedly of historical origin, and some of these powers can be found in treaty provisions or negotiations. (*The Nations Within* 158–59)

Although the presence of such tribal powers within the larger geographic space called America is invisible to the general public, it shapes the law of the land on and off reservations.

Prior to its political and legal meanings in Indian Country, sovereignty conveys a set of qualities of sacrifice in community, identity, and authenticity: sacrifice precisely for an authentically communal identity. Looking back before the twentieth-century generations described by Deloria and Lytle, long prior to this recent resurgence, what has come to be called tribal sovereignty, whether in celebration or under siege, has always been the ground of American Indian stories, both oral and written. The concept of sacrifice expresses a rich spectrum of narrative traits that may have a dramatic or quiet expression in stories, spanning loyalty, memory, dedication, perseverance, generosity, courage, confidence, humor, hope, reverence, respect, humility, and more.

The dramatics of narrative play also on the human tendency to refuse to sacrifice one's own pain. Sometimes it is most difficult to let go of one's own suffering, and such complications may play out in stories of internalized oppression. Like any notion, tribal sovereignty can also be corrupted, and some plots and ironies in Native writing have to do with the misuse of this key value in Indian Country, precisely when sacrifice is removed from the term. Qualities of sovereignty give Indian people a reason to live, a reason to be strong beyond their individual selves, a wider, deeper fulfillment of self in service to the whole.[17] The group potential for negotiating change is of course the key issue.

Recastings

Most discussions of the word *sovereignty* in Indian Country stagger under the weight of the Euro-American word's etymological history in feudal notions of the power of monarchy. Vine Deloria Jr. is as helpful in defining the European and Middle Eastern roots of the term as he is in redefining contemporary Indigenous usage: "Sovereignty is an ancient idea, once used to describe both the power and arbitrary nature of the deity by peoples in the Near East. Although originally a theological term it was appropriated by European political thinkers in the centuries following the Reformation to characterize the person of the King as head of state" ("Self-Determination and the Concept of Sovereignty" 22). Apart from Indigenous politics, and sometimes spilling over into Indigenous usage, the hierarchical and individualistic resonances of European history drown out much cross-cultural potential in the term. Native and non-Native thinkers in the previous generation have redescribed the function, if not the definition of tribal sovereignty as the spiritual, cultural, and legal foundation of Indian communities. More than self-government, it becomes the combined legal and spiritual protections of Indian community. By this trajectory, I see it residing ultimately in the will of the people to sacrifice for the group. On that broad foundation, the conversation builds in various directions.

The Lenape scholar Joanne Barker's conclusion to her essay, "For Whom Sovereignty Matters," helps to map the moving ground: "Sovereignty is historically contingent. What it has meant and what it currently means belong to the political subjects who have deployed and are deploying it to do the work of defining their relationships with one another, their political agendas, and their strategies for decolonization and social justice. . . . Sovereignty carries the horrible stench of colonialism. It is incomplete, inaccurate, and troubled. But it has also been rearticulated to mean altogether different things by Indigenous peoples" (*Sovereignty Matters* 26). Those differences range from political to intellectual to spiritual claims.

James Youngblood Henderson (Cheyenne and Chickasaw), a Harvard-educated lawyer and the coauthor of *The Road: Indian Tribes and Political Liberty*, spoke of the difficulty of definitions during a 1979 Newberry Library conference on American Indian sovereignty. I quote his transcript at some length to convey his sense of the complexity, and perhaps the simplicity, of *sovereignty* the word, quite in contrast to Kalt and Singer above:

> Basically, I don't think we've heard anything about sovereignty. I think we've heard a lot about land claims, and we've heard a lot about tribal governments, but I don't think we've heard anything about sovereignty. And I don't even like to use the word because I don't [know] what it means, and neither does anyone else in the world. . . . Sovereignty varies from tribe to tribe so I don't speak in generalizations. . . . I guess what I dislike personally most about the word "sovereignty" is that it is devoid of any spiritual connotations because it comes out of Western political history at a time when they were looking for something other than religion and found legitimate powers in society. . . . But when I talk about sovereignty, to me *it's a mystical assumption. No one has it; no one possesses it.* But no one really knows what it means anymore. Everyone keeps confusing governmental sovereignty, but sovereignty is *the people* who consented to the compact of the Constitution. . . . When we talk about political power, we're also talking about spiritual power, because if we don't have a spiritual, a cultural base to our power, to be legitimate, then we don't have the right to exercise the power. (Barsh and Henderson, *The Road* 56–57, emphasis added)

Henderson sees sovereignty mystically embodied in the body politic, "the people." By this reasoning, the Native community as a spiritual basis for sovereignty contrasts with a historically Western focus on the individualistic divine right of kings in the archaic roots of governmental sovereignty. Henderson's primary insistence on spiritual dimensions need not be read as a mystification, a cynical dismissal, nor a frustrated denial of discussion. It renders a rough translation of sovereignty, an attempt to move from Euro-American discourse that first sees sovereign rulers in their monarchical and feudal forms, to a Native discourse that sees sovereign human bodies and communities as simultaneously spiritual and political.

If sovereignty is peoplehood, following Henderson one might say it is the embodied spirit of the people, requiring the body politic to survive, while it is the motivating energy of that survivance itself. Native American sovereignty, like other aspects of various Indigenous cultures, must operate with what we have seen as less of a conceptual divide between body and spirit. That mystery, a paradox of interpenetrating matter and energy, generates unique dynamics in Native cultural traditions. Deloria affirms such dynamics: "Ceremonial and ritual knowledge is possessed by everyone in the Indian community, although only a few people may actually be chosen to perform these acts. Authorization to perform ceremonies comes from higher spiritual powers and not by certification through an institution or any formal organization" (*God Is Red* 271). Deloria suggests linkage between the spirit and the body politic.

Such a blurring of material and ethereal becomes more complicated by comparison with trans-Atlantic echoes in the European doctrines of the divine right of kings, from feudal patterns through the seventeenth century, culminating in the proclamation by Louis XIV, "L'état c'est moi!" (The state is me or I am the state) The etymologies of *sovereignty* that so irritated Henderson meander through usages far from Native American ones. Yet it is worth pointing to a parallel, that from the Holy Roman Empire through the papal monarchy across the centuries, the papacy itself derived through Christianity from the theocracies of the Near East, religious purposes were not divorced from governmental ones. Deloria's "ancient idea" alludes to usage that conflated government power with deity. Feudal and courtly lords came to represent the biblical Lord, and vice versa.

Post-Athenian European versions of a political philosophy that would merge state and church were decidedly aristocratic, often autocratic, at times despotic compared with Native American versions that often were more democratic, a governance by open council, frequently of men and women. For example, Sarah Winnemucca discusses the Paiutes' council tent in the nineteenth century: "The chiefs do not rule like tyrants; they discuss everything with their people, as a father would in his family. . . . The council-tent is our Congress, and anybody can speak who has anything to say, women and all" (*Life Among the Piutes* 52–53). Among many tribal governmental systems in current practice, we must note the ongoing history of the Iroquois Confederacy, where the Grand Council continues to meet, the clanmothers continue to install the chiefs, and dialogue is comparatively democratic.[18] Certainly there are corrupt and despotic exceptions in Native American history as well as contemporary examples of political controversies wherein Native constituencies compete in unprincipled ways for power. Yet the crux of this difference between European and Native American sovereignty is in patterns of hierarchical versus reciprocal structures of "divine" authority. Both traditions have invoked spiritual dimensions of governance.

A comment by the Meskwaki poet and novelist Ray A. Young Bear suggests the subtlety of different Indigenous approaches to nonhierarchical leadership still considered to be in touch with the divine. In the afterword to his cross-genre novel, *Black Eagle Child: The Facepaint Narratives*, Young Bear refers to changes in the distribution of power in his community that came about when "suzerainty," his archaic synonym for modern "sovereignty," replaced "divine leadership." Those changes in the Meskwaki Settlement at Tama, Iowa, arose when the Indian New Deal offered the Indian Reorganization Act of 1934. In many Indian communities, the IRA replaced traditional leadership by merit and inheritance in clan structures with constitutionalized elections, corruptible by manipulating campaigns. Young Bear writes, "Historically, there was equality in the First-Named systems, but materialism and greed spawned novel methods by which to manipulate others. The day divine leadership was deemed unimportant was when the sacred myths began to crumble under the wheels of suzerainty" (260). With his usage of the archaic term *suzerainty*, Young Bear, who is always discriminating in his choice of words, evokes feudal European and colonial Euro-American notions of absolute individual power that contrast with the more traditional reciprocity of community structures connoted by Meskwaki "divine leadership." Such "inherent" sovereign forces at the state and tribal levels continue to exercise their yearning for authority. Thus the United States remains an open question of how to unite its ongoing diversity, its states, a question continually raised by Native nations and Native writers.

Henderson's explicit notion of power as both political and spiritual and his notion of community as the focus of sovereignty resonate further with Deloria on the subject of the divine. Deloria wrote in the *New York Times*, "The message of the traditionals is simple. They demand a return to basic Indian philosophy, establishment of ancient methods of government by open council instead of elected officials, a revival of Indian religions and the replacement of white laws with Indian customs" (qtd. in Warrior, *Tribal Secrets* 33.) Philosophy, open council, religions, and customs: these bonds of Indian community break any boundary lines of politics and spirituality in Deloria's lexicon.

Deloria's "message of the traditionals" implies a dialogue which itself is the fulfillment of its own purposes, a democratic validation of the people themselves. Such a process of dialogue that circulates in the heart of sovereignty emerges in infinite ways: in a reservation school parent committee's opposition to a demeaning sports mascot; in tribal efforts at preventing alcohol abuse by teenagers; in powwows and more private ceremonies; in poems, stories, songs, essays, and plays by Native writers.

In the Eagle's Claws

Taiaiake Alfred gives a nuanced perspective on sovereignty in two books, *Heeding the Voices of Our Ancestors: Kahnawake Mohawk Politics and the Rise of Native Nationalism* and *Peace, Power, Righteousness: An Indigenous Manifesto*. Outlining three major divisions within his Mohawk community in Quebec, Alfred describes in the first text a spectrum of community emphases in sovereignty from the spiritual through the cultural to the political. Some groups emphasize one aspect more than another, but "most of the general [Kahnawake Mohawk] population have managed to integrate rediscovered traditional principles into a modern interpretation serving as a philosophy of government in the modern age" (*Heeding* 87). Affirming the adaptability of communities built on changing definitions of sovereignty, Alfred explains, "Mohawks see the consideration of self-government arrangements as part of the inevitable process of divesting themselves from colonized status and regaining the status of an independent sovereign nation. Thus self-government means simply regaining control over the processes and powers of governance as an interim measure to the eventual objective of autonomy" (102). We can only speculate how, after that "interim," self-governing tribes will decide to shape their systems of governance. Yet according to Alfred, while other Canadians looking at the Mohawk community consider "community control over its internal organization, expanded jurisdictional powers, and more flexible external relationships" as "ultimate objectives[,] Mohawks assuredly do not" (103). Again other dimensions of sovereignty, beyond governmental control, remain on the mind of Mohawks: "Thus Mohawk sovereignty is conceived of not only in terms of interests and boundaries, but in terms of land, relationships and spirituality. . . . The idea of balance among people and communities is pervasive in Mohawk culture and spirituality; the achievement of balanced relationship based upon respect for differences, whether among individuals or communities, is valued as the achievement of a harmonious ideal state of affairs. The essence of Mohawk sovereignty is harmony" (102–3). Balance, spirituality, harmony: these principles from an ancient Haudenosaunee tradition again carry notions of sovereignty into realms other than partisan politics, perhaps other than governance. Such language echoes Henderson's "mystical assumption" and Deloria's "revival of Indian religions."

In his second book, Alfred emphasizes the difference between this harmonious sense of sovereignty and prevailing Western notions, adopted by many Native leaders, as what he calls "an inappropriate concept" (*Peace* 55). He explains, "Traditional Indigenous nationhood stands in sharp contrast to the dominant understanding of 'the state': there is no absolute authority, no coercive enforcement of decisions, no hierarchy, and no separate ruling entity" (56). If we move this far from the seventeenth- and eighteenth-century absolutism of Louis XIV, or from the nineteenth century's and today's plenary power of Congress over tribal relations, or from today's executive power in the secretary of the interior over all decisions by Native domestic dependent nations, how can we have sovereignty without hierarchy?

Alfred describes a radically democratic form of government that does not comport with the hierarchical tendencies of Western states. "What do traditionalists hope to protect? What have the co-opted ones forsaken? In both cases, the answer is the heart and soul of Indigenous nations: a set of values that challenge the destructive and homogenizing force of Western liberalism and free-market capitalism; that honour the autonomy of individual conscience, non-coercive authority, and the deep interconnection between human beings and the other elements of creation" (*Peace* 60). According to Alfred, Western cultural hegemony prevails in the name of Western economic freedom. Certainly more Jeffersonian political traditions in the West might agree with him. Regarding an eighteenth-century historian whom Jefferson opposed on several grounds,[19] Alfred makes this cultural critique in the earlier text as well, when he contrasts the Kahnawake Mohawks' "reformulation" with the Euro-American conception of sovereignty described in the eighteenth century by William Blackstone in *Commentaries on English Law* as "a supreme, irresistible, absolute, and uncontrolled authority" over territory (*Peace* 102). Alfred's Mohawk reformulation moves sovereignty into a territory outside the British codes that became—in spite of Jefferson's opposition—a foundation of the American legal system. Perhaps the American Revolution is not over. We may say, with Alfred's prompting, that Native American writers in the tradition of William Apess have been trying to release America itself from European forms of sovereignty. For more than two hundred years, Native voices have asked the United States to understand Iroquois and other Indigenous forms of sovereignty as more dialogic.[20]

Here, then, the U.S. legal code and Native cultural perspectives on sovereignty might find some common ground, if Native nations are indeed recognized as sovereign over their own domestic affairs and if autonomous domestic affairs are recast in terms of expanded jurisdictional authority. Alfred's "autonomy" might be a further step, but oversight by the secretary of the interior and congressional plenary power—two key institutional structures of domestic dependency in U.S. federal Indian law—might be made advisory instead of supervisory without undermining federal treaty obligations of fiduciary and fiscal responsibilities to Native nations. At the same 1979 session with Henderson and others, the historian Francis Jennings clarifies the distinction: "What Indians mean by sovereignty is different from what courts mean by it. Indians want the power to rule themselves in their own way in their own territories. They want political independence for their tribes. Courts have much more elaborate definitions that have developed out of many centuries of history in England and America. . . . They seem to me to be only different faces of the same historical problem" (Swagerty, *Indian*

Sovereignty 2). The issue of power may factor down generally to the question of autonomy, while the issue of law may factor down specifically to treaty obligations and the fiduciary and fiscal responsibilities of the federal government to Native nations. Certainly in Indian communities there are many rhetorical gestures to sovereignty as well. Community members who may have little experience with their own treaties, or with the legalities of treaties in general, may invoke sovereignty to affirm national pride. While inextricably tied, power and law might be distinguished by different functions. Legal recognition of domestic sovereignty in Indian nations remains a first step toward common ground. However, clarifying internal, domestic sovereignty cannot be separated from issues of autonomy in tribal relations in a modern market society built on a global ecosystem. To round out this introductory context, let's look at a contemporary example of such relations.

Three Sovereigns

One recent expression of the autonomy of Native nations emerged in the Northwest, where discourse of common ground moved haltingly toward official policy under a Columbia River Basin planning initiative called the Three Sovereigns Forum.[21] This intergovernmental group, working in the late 1990s, would coordinate "federal, state, and tribal governments in collaborative decision-making."[22] Oregon's governor John Kitzhaber, who launched the group in June 1997, refers to it as "a new regional governance structure for the Columbia Basin."[23] In February 1998 the Affiliated Tribes of Northwest Indians, citing their "rights secured under Indian Treaties and benefits to which we are entitled under the laws and constitution of the United States and several states" and "the sovereign rights and authorities of tribal governments," endorsed this "comprehensive reform of current federal and state ecosystem management."[24] Focused on endangered salmon recovery, the Three Sovereigns Forum implicates the Columbia River's hydropower and irrigation systems for four states and thirteen Columbia Basin tribes.

These are not new legal relations. Indeed in the Three Sovereigns model, "no existing law is changed and no legislation is required." It simply improves "working relationships between governments with fish and wildlife responsibility."[25] In the name of the salmon, tribal sovereignty would realize another level of official recognition.

Not surprisingly, there has been opposition. "Farmers, ranchers and other of the river's economic stakeholders" on a local level have raised fears that they will be left out of the process, and Governor Phil Batt of Idaho declared, "It flies in the face of Idaho's sovereignty. . . . It flies in the face of the tribes' sovereignty."[26] (Perhaps Batt's latter, rather incongruous point relates to tribes' historical government-to-government relations with the federal and not state governments.) As a press release declared on February 27, 1998, "Congressman Bob Smith (R-OR), Chairman of the House Committee on Agriculture, and three key northwest lawmakers today criticized the Three Sovereigns Forum for failing to clearly define its authority over Columbia Basin Water use issues and for excluding a broad range of river use interests from its decision making process."[27] An editorial in the *Seattle Times* stated, "No, a Three Sovereigns Forum won't bring peace to the Basin salmon wars. River governance reform won't revise philosophies, ideologies and self interest. What it could do, however, is put the debate in one place, at one table, for all to see."[28] Whatever the politics, this process is historically, culturally, and spiritually significant as the People of the Salmon now sit at that table in the effort save the salmon themselves.[29]

These developments, however incremental, suggest how a dominant narrative of American history is gradually being revised as American political leadership intermittently listens to Native voices. Governor Kitzhaber asks, "Will we, as a region, meet our sacred obligations—the treaties between the people of the United States and the sovereign Indian tribes of the Northwest?"[30] This certainly is a different discourse from manifest destiny. Similarly each U.S. executive in the past three decades has reaffirmed the aforementioned "government-to-government relations" that President Nixon's administration articulated toward the Indian Self-Determination Act of 1975. However delayed and often politically motivated such executive and legislative gestures might be, Native nations are finding ways to use them to reaffirm sovereignty in their own terms.[31]

In the years preceding the Three Sovereigns Forum, the poet Elizabeth Woody (Yakama, Warm Springs, Wasco, and Navajo), from Warm Springs Reservation in Oregon, wrote of the return of the salmon: "Abalone swinging on the ears of Salmon Woman signals / the time to witness. . . . Salmon Mother at the head of stream, speaks. . . . The passage absorbs the deep voice of her renewal song. / The woman's mouth breaks through the surface of tranquility" (*Seven Hands* 41). Woody alerts us to the voice of the Salmon Mother, a voice of "renewal." Such visionary poetry takes on a prophetic rhetorical strength as the compelling emergence of green economics begins to take seriously the social value of free-running rivers. Simultaneously that material emergence of riparian economic necessity moves on the river of principle, the "time to witness" a "renewal" of an authentic American justice in recognition of Indigenous sovereignty.

"Justice and Humanity": Sovereignty in Apess

In the name of justice for American Indians as full-fledged members of "humanity," William Apess (1798–1839; see biographical appendix) was an explicit advocate for Indian communities to exercise powers of what today would be referred to as tribal sovereignty. Like other Native writers in this study, Apess launched a literary appeal to the humanity of his white readers for a fellow feeling that might protect the humanity of his own people. "And do you believe that Indians cannot feel and see, as well as white people?" (*Eulogy* 285).[32]

As he argued for Indian rights in Jacksonian-era New England, Apess appealed to an Enlightenment notion of universal human value. Through what David J. Carlson calls "Indian liberalism," Apess evidently adopts "the dominant American legal model of subjectivity to provide the necessary grounding for his autobiographical act of self-definition" (*Sovereign Selves* 96). If he appropriates the discourse of "the transformation of the Indian subject into a generic, possessive individual" along a "basically Lockean model" of "republican ideology" (96), Apess does so strategically. His rhetorical strategies connect America's own sense of authentic humanity to Indigenous claims about sovereignty. We read this logic, for instance, in his *Eulogy on King Philip*, where we find this formulation: "Justice and humanity for the remaining few prompt me to vindicate the character of him [Philip] who yet lives in their hearts and, if possible, melt the prejudice that exists in the hearts of those who are in the possession of his soil, and only by the right of conquest" (277). Apess asks not only for Indian rights based on universal values of the Enlightenment, "justice and humanity," but also for non-Indians to open their hearts. Further, by reference to Philip's "soil," especially by retaining the possessive pronoun "his," Apess offers the humane principle of sovereignty over the inhumane practice of conquest.

Philip was humane; Philip owned the soil; therefore a humane America will return that soil—or rights to a portion of that soil—to Philip and his people. Justice respects humanity; humanity has a right to its own land; therefore a just America will respect Indian land rights, their sovereignty. He builds that prior principle of sovereignty on the value of humanity itself.[33]

Thus Apess's activism and advocacy animate his writing specifically to affirm sovereignty. He builds on Enlightenment principles in the American Declaration of Independence and the Constitution to claim that sovereignty as self-government is an inherent human right. More fundamentally he affirms that Indians are human, with "rights and feelings." Further, he asserts that the Mashpee and other Indians have the right not only to claim but to enforce their inherent rights of self-government and control of their own property.

Yet because of his nuanced thought and because of his resonance in if not direct influence on Native literary expression across the centuries, we must look for context in Apess beyond his appeal to the universal humanity of the modern Enlightenment. For there are elements of his prescription of Indigenous rights that forecast postmodern dynamics of culture, specifically the decentering of colonial authority. It is especially useful to discuss his linkages to postmodernism in the context of sovereignty because it helps to clarify an Indigenous notion of decentralized sovereign political power.

What is postmodern about Apess? In his and other Native writers' vision, sovereignty may shed its absolutist baggage from the modern European rise of nation states—as they culminated in the Enlightenment through the United States of America—and move toward a pluralist model quite explicitly suggested by Apess and other modern Indigenous intellectuals. This theme of Indigenous sovereignty in Apess forecasts a positive, strategic application of postmodern indeterminacy, where ultimately a central nation-state may be decentered by pluralities of Indigenous nationhood.

Thus to launch this historical healing process, Apess, in *Eulogy on King Philip*, first rewrites Puritan New England, mythologized by Daniel Webster as "the republic in embryo,"[34] by recasting American history and nationhood as oppressive. As Maureen Konkle explains, "The rise of the pilgrim-republican narrative . . . can be seen . . . as politically necessary for U.S. intellectuals to justify and explain the existence of a state the actions of which are in deep conflict with its professed ideals—as antislavery and antiremoval writes pointed out at the time, over and over again" (*Writing Indian Nations* 135). The decentering of America's manifest narrative first required retelling the story with the brutal facts. The context of America's historical actions in "deep conflict with its professed ideals" remained the focus of writers such as Apess. Rewriting the "history of heroes" to include Native leaders such as King Philip, archenemy of the Puritans, called for a fundamental change in validation, a recentering of the core of American value. If this strategy to decenter history presaged the postcolonial and postmodern rhetorics of a later century, it still shows how some postmodern strategies have long been the purview of the dispossessed.

To mark these strategies, Philip Brian Harper writes, in *Framing the Margins: The Social Logic of Postmodern Culture*, of a postmodern fascination with "the psyche's fundamentally incoherent and fragmentary, or 'decentered,' nature" (3). He focuses further on a "similar decenteredness" among "the socially marginalized and politically disenfranchised": "To the extent that such populations have experienced psychic decenteredness long prior to its generalization throughout the culture during the late twentieth century, one might say that the postmodern era's preoccupation with fragmented subjectivity represents the 'recentering' of the culture's focus on issues that have always concerned marginalized constituencies" (3–4). Long before the postmodern era, those who were excluded by centralized, racialized, genderized power felt, and sometimes fought, the decentering and fragmentation of their aspirations, their humanity. Apess's writings, such as "An Indian's Looking-Glass for the White Man," are remarkable precisely for his early American insistence that whites should "focus on issues that have always concerned marginalized constituencies." Because it is less difficult from the margins to see the socially constructed nature of the center, Apess was not alone in his position to recognize the imbalance, but he was remarkable in his forceful Native articulation of that imbalance at the heart of American society.

This dynamic of visibility and invisibility operates by the reflexive mechanism of specular colonialism, by which colonial desires and fears project onto the colonized. Those who receive those projections are in a better position to mark their absurdities, inaccuracies, and brutalities than are those who cast and are convinced by their own projections. Congruent with Harper's claim that "the experiences of socially marginalized groups implicitly inform the 'general' postmodern condition" (*Framing the Margins* 4), such relative fragmentation can be turned, in complex negotiations, to a site for agency. Apess's contribution to the literature of sovereignty lies in his artic- ulation of this kind of agency. He expresses an enthusiastic and energetic recognition of marginalized alternatives to an ideology of manifest destiny.

We may read Apess's arguments for individual and tribal sovereignty in his penultimate publication (with the fashionably verbose title), *Indian Nullifi- cation of the Unconstitutional Laws of Massachusetts Relative to the Marshpee Tribe; or, The Pretended Riot Explained*.[35] Along with his final work, *Eulogy on King Philip*, this *Nullification* is most explicit among his writings on issues of sovereignty. As a Connecticut Pequot adopted into the Mashpee tribe, he wrote and organized on behalf of the Mashpees of "Indian Town" near Plymouth, Massachusetts. Under his leadership, they asserted the right to self-government in the form of their own religious leadership and control of their woodlots against exploitation by overseers (appointed by a govern- ing board at Harvard University). In addition to a succession of exploitative white ministers who had long ignored the Mashpee congregations, genera- tions of non-Mashpees had been expropriating Mashpee property and resources, including their woodlot, for the benefit of their own non-Indian families. Taking direct action, Apess and his Mashpee relatives quietly unloaded the overseer's wagon of stolen firewood.

Cresting the flood of public hysteria and legalese that washed over "the pretended riot," Apess gave his remarkable document the sweeping title that does more than place him inside the discourse of American law as it emphatically encapsulates his argument. By asserting nullification of laws that he labeled unconstitutional, Apess employed contemporary discourse in antebellum questions of states' rights, especially southern states' rights, that would nullify suggested U.S. constitutional amendments to outlaw slav- ery. In this treatise, he defended his own reputation and documented how he and the Mashpees were able to gain land rights to their woodlot and a measure of sovereignty for the tribe through the Massachusetts legislature. That they accomplished this feat during the height of the Jacksonian Indian Removal period testifies both to Massachusetts's progressive tradition and to Apess's rhetorical power. They accomplished this remarkable reversal, a small, nonviolent revolution, by the energy of his uniquely righteous, cross-racial inclusiveness and by his articulate expression of an ethical standard that challenged the nation.

John J. Kucich, in an essay on Apess, Samson Occom, and Jonathan Edwards, marks the historic significance of Apess's activism: "That his formative act of civil disobedience sought to reclaim the traditional rights of the Mashpees to gather wood is no accident—Apess forges at the beginning of the 19th century a new ethic in which the forest and its inhabitants are inextricable. His act, at once religious, political and environmental, may well have inspired Thoreau; it undoubtedly established a standard of social and environmental justice that America has barely begun to realize" ("Sons of the Forest" 6). That "new ethic" is an ancient one, woven deeply in the discourse Apess uses to connect legal, political, and cultural Indigenous identity with the "soil" of America.

For instance, he laid out five specifics of tribal sovereignty in the "Petition of the Marshpee Tribe of Indians" to the Massachusetts House of Representatives, published in *Nullification* from the newspaper record:

Yesterday morning, in the House, Mr. Cushing of Dorchester, presented the petition of the Proprietors and inhabitants of the Marshpee Plantation . . . in all 287: praying for the privilege to manage their own property; for the abolition of the overseership, that they may be incorporated as the town of Marshpee, with the right to make municipal regulations; that one or more Magistrates may be appointed among them; and for a repeal of the existing laws relating to their tribe, with the exception of the law preventing their selling of their lands, which they pray may be retained; and for a redress of grievances. (206)

These points outline their vision of sovereignty: self-management or self-government, municipal incorporation, judicial presence, repeals, and redress. The context for local justice at Indian Town was Apess's broader vision of equality as universal justice.

This political work focused a religious faith, invoking Christ's promises of a Kingdom of God on earth, in a vigorous activism that he viewed as ongoing creation: "But the work of God rolled on, like an overwhelming flood," he writes of his early experience with Methodism (*Experiences of Five Christian Indians* 126). As Barry O'Connell writes of Apess's reappropriation of Christian discourse, "'Conversion,' which for most white readers would conventionally have read [*sic*] as a synonym for assimilation, becomes the medium, instead, for an affirmation of Indian pride and autonomy. And whites, not Indians, become those in need of conversion" (Introductions 118). Apess used the discourse of Christian conversion to persuade whites to convert their own political conscience, which had erased Indians and Indian sovereignty. In a realistic view of contemporary power, he saw such conversion of America's conscience as a necessary step to reestablishing Native sovereignty.

Linguistic and Legal Parallelism

In his written descriptions we thus may read a balanced juxtaposition in the way Apess structures his historical moment. As a public speaker and writer, his exercise of a balanced sovereignty between Indian and non-Indian social structures is tied to the expression of parallelism in his rhetorical structures. Clearly his ardent study of Christian scripture shaped his thinking in fundamental ways. Where language structures both theology and history, Apess is trying to rewrite and rebalance history according to the balanced structures of his biblical discourse. By the shaping force of discursive equilibrium, he would have others do unto him as he would do unto them. His logic of equality is rooted in biblical ethics and aesthetics.

Reflecting his larger Christian context for thinking through reform, his prose echoes especially a biblical rhetoric of parallelism, matching a linguistic symmetry of eloquence to his arguments for the racial symmetry of equality. In "An Indian's Looking-Glass for the White Man," for instance, he cites epigrammatic and parallel biblical phrases to set up a neat contrast to the hypocrisy of white racial prejudice against Indians: "Again, John in his Epistles says, 'He who loveth God loveth his brother also' (1 John 4:21). 'Let us not love in word but in deed' (1 John 3:18)'" (157). Similarly in *Nullification* he invokes "the words of the Savior" to condemn the crimes of the Mashpee missionary: "It is written that my house shall be called the house of prayer, but ye have made it a den of thieves" (171). The linguistic reflection emphasizes the political reversal, another "looking-glass."

Indeed parallelism functions as a syntactic mirror of social ironies throughout his prose. That frequent stylistic device—which he may have adopted as much from the oral traditions of religious meetings or from Native oratory as from the text of the Bible—suggests a deep discursive imprint of dialectics. It impresses Apess with an ideal balance and fairness in human relations, along with an equally strong sense of injustice. Certainly his own physical and emotional injuries impressed him at the start. Yet his parallel language usage inscribes a world of balanced equilibrium often in sharp contrast with the stumbling pain of his own experience. By inverse logic, this symmetry also structures the irony that so systematically punctuates his prose. Irony indicates a discursive reflection of the oppressive potential of a dialectic, the lordsman-bondsman social relations, that structured his experience so early as an indenture.

Here is another notable example from *Nullification* among myriad passages of parallelism. Apess is denouncing the two missionaries appointed in sequence by Harvard College to minister to the Mashpees over later decades of the late eighteenth and early decades of the nineteenth centuries:

> Neither of the reverend gentlemen [Mr. Hawley or Mr. Fish] set up schools, and when the Marshpee children were put out to service, it was with the express understanding, as their parents all agree, that they should not be schooled. Many of those who held them in servitude used them more like dogs than human beings, feeding them scantily, lodging them hard, and clothing them with rags. Such, I believe, has always been the case about Indian reservations. I had a sister who was slavishly used and half starved; and I have not forgotten, nor can I ever forget, the abuse I received myself. (187)

Two parallel constructions flow in these few lines, punctuated and intensified by other basic musical devices such as rhythm, sentence variety, and intense, imagistic diction. In the first, more elaborate instance, "feeding them scantily, lodging them hard, and clothing them with rags," a triple repetition of participles each precedes direct repetition of the pronoun "them" that in turn precedes an adverbial word or phrase, "scantily," "hard," ending vividly "with rags." This list of multiple parallels not only accumulates a catalogue of crimes; the structured nature of a parallel pattern itself argues implicitly that a pattern of abuse, a systematic crime, exists. If that oppressive catalogue of signifiers lines up in irrefutable parallel formation, then such an oppressive experience must exist just as irrefutably. Explicitly the abuse experienced by Apess's own family in another state—as a microcosm of historical mistreatment of American Indians that he has been cataloguing as "always . . . the case about Indian reservations"—becomes the logic for change. The rhetorical system provides evidence against an oppressive social system.

The comparative brevity and simplicity of the second parallel structure, "I have not forgotten, nor can I ever forget," merely repeating different declensions of the verb *forget* at the ends of two conjoined clauses, builds on the effects of the longer example and drives its rhythm into the incendiary word choice of "abuse" for dramatic emphasis. This syntactic dimension underscores the thrilling brutality in images of "dogs," "rags," "slavishly," and "starved." The drama is further aggravated by the intricate understatement midway in the passage, in the first person to establish a certain objective and thus convincing third-person distance on the "Indian" question, "Such, I believe, has always been the case about Indian reservations"—all in preparation for the intimate and ultimate punch line: "the abuse I received myself." His rhetoric thus draws on parallel linguistic power to open a door for his readers to the incontrovertible logic of justice and injustice. As an explicit claim for sovereignty here in the context of *Nullification*, an argument for reform and redress makes sovereignty itself incontrovertible.

The Sacrificial Logic of Rights

Apess's rhetorical acuity and complexity build such linguistic traps and doors for his audiences and readers in every paragraph. What is fundamental to these structures is the dialectical symmetry of his thinking. It drives his prose either to the irony of hypocritical reality in symmetrical contrast to the ideal or to the sympathy of humanity in symmetrical communication with that ideal.

Such sympathy, as recognition of humanity, translates in Apess to an American inclusivity. An inclusive code animates *Eulogy on King Philip*, where he rewrites the American pantheon of patriots and founding fathers to include *both* George Washington and Metacomet, who led King Philip's war in the 1670s. While he describes Philip's decades of generous and savvy negotiations with the settlers, eventually thwarted by harassment, siege, and murder by the Puritans, Apess is articulate about the implications on the ground of an ideological shift that would recognize a humane King Philip. That shift would rebalance history according to the symmetry that characterizes Apess's discursive universe, returning Indian soil to Indians.

Thus, in what at first may seem contradictory in Apess's thinking, the principle of shared humanity becomes a principle of sovereignty. Applying to Native rights an antebellum discourse of Christian transcendentalism for which he was perhaps a preeminent orator, Apess affirms recognition of the humanity in others as the recognition of their inherent sovereignty as children of the Lord. He invokes a divine principle beyond race, "that God who is the maker and preserver both of the white man and the Indian, whose abilities are the same and who are to be judged by one God, who will show no favor to outward appearances but will judge righteousness" ("Looking-Glass" 155). Such individual sovereignty, "whose abilities are the same," translates into social rights. Humane social values translate into material political values.

Indeed, according to Apess, sovereignty as a principle of justice is also a set of legal codes. A century before Indians were "given" the vote in 1924, Apess was explicit in *Eulogy* about America's shift toward tribal sovereignty requiring legal restructuring: "I say, then, a different course must be pursued, and different laws must be enacted, and all men must operate under one general law. And while you ask yourselves, 'What do they, the Indians, want?' you have only to look at the unjust laws made for them and say, 'They want what I want,' in order to make men of them, good and wholesome citizens" (310). While Apess clearly envisions Indians as American citizens, his "different laws" are predicated on a universal human desire for autonomy, "They want what I want." They want what any human wants: a measure of sovereignty for themselves and their communities.

Crucially Apess equates the natural ability to feel such suffering with the authority of natural rights: "In the meanwhile I went to Falmouth, nine miles distant, where I held forth upon the civil and religious rights of the Indians. Some, who apparently thought that charity was due to themselves but not to the red men, did not relish the discourse; but such as knew that all men have rights and feelings, and wished those of others to be respected as well as their own, spoke favorably of it" (*Nullification* 173). He sets "rights and feelings" in the same constellation. The logic of his juxtaposition here suggests that a criterion of rights becomes feelings, a gesture to the principle of animism underlying, as we shall see, a Native sense of community, here a community of "the civil and religious rights of Indians."

The *Nullification* document does not so much equate feelings with rights as it links them in an inextricable pair, a logical sequence: "These resolutions were adopted by the tribe and put in force, as will be seen hereafter. It was hoped that, though the whites had done all they could to extinguish all sense of right among the Indians, they would now see that they had feelings as well as other men" (175). Invoking feelings that cover the spectrum of human emotions, Apess expresses a faith in human sympathy or empathy that will follow a logic from shared feelings to shared entitlement. Indeed he forecasts the political strategies of Gandhi and King, whose nonviolent action across lines of domination was designed to evoke that sympathy in the oppressor to effect eventually an official reversal of inequity.

In Apess's logic, suffering, as a measure of feelings deprived of their rights, itself becomes the negative proof of those rights: "All men have rights and feelings." That is, according to Apess's couplet, if feelings prove rights, and suffering produces feelings, then suffering proves rights. This syllogism actually honors those who suffer oppression, the deprivation of their rights, by marking them as the negative measure of their own and every observer's human rights. That mark of suffering for justice then becomes the logic of sacrifice. With echoes of Christ on the Cross, this reasoning registers one level of sacrifice that is tribal sovereignty, the suffering of the ancestors.

Thus the linkage between human suffering, human rights, economic opportunity (a woodlot), and self-governance, so fundamental to the American experiment, becomes irrefutable in Apess's appeal to his American readers. Rejecting the overseers and the oppressive missionary who had reigned for a generation, Apess declares, "We were never consulted as to his settlement over us, as a people. We never gave our vote or voice, as a tribe, and we fully believe that we are capable of choosing for ourselves, and have the right to do so" (*Nullification* 176). Apess and the Mashpee are asserting their political sovereignty as spiritual sovereignty and vice versa.

"An Investigation of the Whole Ground": Apess's Nonviolence and National Identity

In a set of telling passages in *Nullification*, Apess turns these specific petitions to the larger issue of whites reducing people of color to some subhuman species. By confronting the reactionary prejudices of his oppressors, Apess illuminates connections between individual sovereignty of persons and collective sovereignty of Native nations. Further, he not only speaks about such relations; he embodies a reciprocally sovereign self through nonviolent action.

Speaking for Mashpee sovereignty, "to provide for our own wants," he, like Sarah Winnemucca, underlines the importance of education as another affirmation of Mashpee humanity: "If the white man desired the welfare of his red brethren, why did he not give them schools? . . . We have now a house respectable enough for even a white teacher to lodge in comfortably, and we are in strong hopes that we shall one day soon be able to provide for our own wants, if the whites will only permit us to do so, as they never have done yet. *If they can but be convinced that we are human beings*, I trust they will be our hindrance no longer" (212, emphasis added). If they recognized Native humanity, he reasons, whites and their power structures would recognize Native sovereignty: "they will be our hindrance no longer." Apess was clear on this fundamental error in American thinking that blinded its citizens to diverse humanity, and he evidently knew how his claims to sovereignty for the Mashpee confronted America's national identity, as those power structures are built on white supremacy, and vice versa. The burden of this ideological consciousness is part of his historical importance.

Apess and the Mashpee were committed to enforcing their right to choose for themselves. This Mashpee claim was no nebulous invocation of abstract principle but a specific assertion of the sovereign right to act. To grasp the internal logic of Apess's early insistence on their right to enforce their inherent sovereignty, it is illuminating to look at his external methods, especially as they forecast the techniques of nonviolent civil disobedience of Gandhi and King. Apess's nonviolence functions by a different definition of American national identity, with its colonial logic of violence in slavery and conquest.[36]

Gandhi's *satyagraha* is commonly translated as "nonviolence," but the literal translation would be closer to "grasping (*graha*) truth (*satya*)," thus "holding on to the truth" or "upholding truth." It functions by the same appeal to the common truth of humanity that is Apess's key strategy and belief. By keeping faith in the (God-given) humanity of even one's oppressors, and thus not invoking violence against them while standing up for one's just claims, the self-sacrificing discipline of *satyagraha* can wield real political power while not sacrificing principle.[37] Apess envisions a sovereignty that is dialogical rather than adversarial.

Upon the sheriff's serving "a warrant for [his] apprehension," Apess remained civil. The following passage is remarkable for his self-abnegation as he put his body peacefully into the hands of the police in order "to have the truth appear," to prove that the Indian people he serves are peaceful, thus to make a point directed to and in faith with his accusers' better nature: "The fact is I was in no wise unwilling to go with him, or to have my conduct brought to the test of investigation, or to give all the satisfaction that might be required, had it appeared that I had done wrong. I was also very desirous to have the truth appear, viz., that it was not the intention or wish of the Marshpees to do violence or shed blood" (*Nullification* 184). Apess had reasoned that the clarity of their civilized petition could stand for all to see when not clouded by violence or clamorous protestation.

Because this account is in his own hand, we might assume some selective description of his own tone and behavior, but rhetorically his focus certainly is on humane nonviolence. While still in jail he writes, "I said to the gentlemen, who were rejoicing over my supposed downfall, that I was glad they had taken me into custody, as it would lead to an investigation of the whole ground in dispute" (189). That self-sacrifice is itself given on the larger altar of expected—and threatened—violence by the whites, all the way to the governor's office. Indeed the governor of Massachusetts resorted to saber rattling, threatening full militia attacks against the Mashpee. Apess apparently was willing to lay his body down for a clear statement of human rights.

Yet the clarity of his voice for the Mashpee also emphasizes the urgency of their cause. His equanimity does not relax the passion of their "praying" to the Massachusetts legislature for redress of their grievances. Apess's nonviolent approach to institutional violence insists that now is the time for change: "I believe that neither I nor any of my brethren went fast enough. I think there is no white man, Christian or infidel, who would have shown half so much forbearance as we did in the like circumstances" (184–85). This combination of an eloquent recital of their wrongs and claims, backed up by forbearance in the face of grinding injustice, is the engine of the Mashpees' relatively successful campaign for relative sovereignty as designed by Apess in consultation with the tribal elders. Their nonviolent expression made their human feelings visible to whites in power; in turn, their feelings made their humanity visible as a basis for a small change in an inhumane system. However unremarked, the eventual vote of the Massachusetts legislature may be seen as one beginning of American redefinitions: Native Americans have sovereign rights. Again, Apess achieved this success as the Indian Removal era hit hardest in the East and even as the "Indian wars" were continuing and growing in the Midwest and Far West.

In organizing the details of the "revolt," Apess augurs the language of a future century: "I then, having previously cautioned the Indians to do no bodily injury to any man, unless in their own defense, but to stand for their rights and nothing else, desired them to unload the teams, which they did very promptly" (181). By way of linkage to future historical movements, it is important to note that this strategy of admitting self-defense in a non-violent demonstration is more in line with Frederick Douglass of the 1840s than with Gandhi of the 1940s or King of the 1950s and 1960s. Douglass celebrated his own ferocious wrestling match with the slave-breaker Covey and marked it as a "glorious resurrection" in his quest for freedom: "The battle with Mr. Covey was the turning-point in my career as a slave. It rekindled the few expiring embers of freedom, and revived within me a sense of my own manhood. . . . He only can understand the deep satisfaction which I experienced, who has himself repelled by force the bloody arm of slavery" (*Narrative* 113). Douglass is not exactly advocating violence, though he grants it legitimacy in personal defense against the brutalities of the "peculiar institution." In avoiding "bodily injury" "except in their own defense," Apess aligns his strategy more with Douglass and John Brown (and especially Henry David Thoreau's *A Plea for John Brown*), than with the pure pacifism of the twentieth century. Gandhi's principle of *satyagraha*, applied in King's movement, encouraged and honored the sacrifice of those who submitted non-violently to violent treatment in the effort to kindle human empathy in the perpetrators. If somewhat different in their methods, their aim was the same: to kindle that fellow feeling in the tormenters.

Apess was spared the physical confrontation that Douglass and Brown embraced. The citizens of Massachusetts, initially up in arms under the bellicose leadership of a reactionary governor, backed down and considered the Mashpee petition through deliberations in the legislative venue. Had Apess not restrained himself and his Mashpee compadres, violence probably would have broken out, and this "pretended riot" might never have had such an eloquent voice to "explain" it.

In these complex ways, Apess and the Mashpee, consulting with sympathetic lawyers, were able to mount a direct challenge to the law of the land. Imagine the heady atmosphere of revolutionary reason in the Mashpee meetinghouse as they proclaimed their new resolve in the "Notice": "And now we would say to our white friends, we are wanting nothing but our rights betwixt man and man. And now, rest assured that said resolutions will be enforced after the first day of July, 1833. Done at the National Assembly of the Marshpee Tribe, and by the authority of the same" (*Nullification* 180). At the heart of their national sovereignty is their authority, as authentic human beings, to make these claims.

"Rightful Lords of the Soil"

By foregrounding non-Native voices struggling through the irritations of Indigenous nations within the United States, Apess structured *Nullification* to make his readers face their own crimes against humanity in the dispossession and oppression of Native Americans. Yet a thread of utopianism weaves through the account, if only by its absence, so that reflection on culpability may mirror a possibility of change. One of the more compelling non-Native voices is that of legal counsel B. B. Hallett, Esq., hired by the Mashpees to work with Apess. His far-seeing presentations to the legislature are included in the dialogic collage of voices for and against Mashpee rights that is the *Nullification* publication. In Hallett's long section delineating the illegality of Reverend Fish's presence on the parsonage, the missionary appointed by the Harvard overseers, he offers numerous arguments for a kind of sovereignty at Mashpee to match that of other municipalities, including this: "Have not the Indians a right to their own property? Has the Legislature and Harvard College a right to establish a religion by law in Marshpee, and take the property of the Indians to support a minister they will not hear? Where did the General Court get any power to give away the property of the Indians, any more than the lands of white men, held in common?" (263). This comparison to property rights of white men now extends that prior assumption of Indian humanity into the most American of values: property itself. The reasonableness of these rhetorical questions tries to smooth the way for the radical, utopian redistribution of power over property.

This radical logic of *Nullification* is evidence of how Apess reasoned that his serious readers were likely to work for their own ideals, to become a diverse America, to fulfill their purported identity as a nation of freedom and inclusion. He quotes, for example, the local William Penn, who voices not only classic liberal guilt but also an American discourse of tragic-romantic phraseology resonant of James Fenimore Cooper, here in a letter to the *Boston Advocate*: "I do not know much about the remnants of a once noble and hospitable race, and yet I know enough to make me grieve for them, and ashamed of the State" (215). "I know enough to make me grieve": this white sympathy is Apess's first rhetorical goal, as a step in rebalancing race relations and in redressing specific wrongs against the Mashpee. Penn's phrase "ashamed of the State" moves toward the second step in Apess's strategy: legislative reform of oppressive laws.

Hallett summed up the circumstances in explicit terms of liberal reform, in contrast with Georgia and other southern states: "Is there, then, any danger in giving the Indians an opportunity to try a liberal experiment for self-government? They ask you for a grant of the liberties of the constitution; to be incorporated and to have a government useful to them as a people.... Is there anything unreasonable in their requests? Can you censure other States for severity to the Indians within their limits, if you do not exercise an enlightened liberality toward the Indians of Massachusetts?" (238). Certainly such a reasonable course of action against the objections of "clergymen, lawyers, physicians, counselors, governor, senators, and representatives . . . arrayed against us" would consummate an American aim, as Apess explains: "We Marshpees account all who opposed our freedom, as Tories, hostile to the Constitution and the liberties of the country" (204). In this heady and patriotic discourse, looking back on their limited success with the Massachusetts legislature, Apess slips in a radical redefinition of "the country" itself: "We thank the majority of the controllers of public affairs, that they had more sense than to think of holding the rightful lords of the soil in bondage any longer, for the gratification of selfish and unjust men" (205). Those "rightful lords of the soil" were not finished in their claims for tribal sovereignty.

"We Lived That Way in Peace": Sovereignty in Winnemucca

Such claims are the stuff of Indian literature. Sarah Winnemucca (1844–91; see biographical appendix), perhaps at the practical opposite of Apess's idealism as she is at the opposite end of the devastating nineteenth century, wrote in her *Life Among the Piutes* of an even more desperate accommodation of tribal sovereignty to American ideology. In her public speeches touring the Northeast, as well as in her private conference with the reform-minded Senator Henry Dawes in Washington DC in 1883, she petitioned for allotment and "land in severalty" on behalf of her people, who had been dispossessed of their Nevada homelands. Dawes was the senator infamous today for the 1887 Allotment Act. The politics of her moment determined the limited practicalities of sovereignty for the Paiutes, with devastating implications for all other tribes. It is not unreasonable to assume that her conversations with Dawes helped to fuel his interest in finalizing the Allotment Act four years later. In the 1880s the Paiutes were landless refugees, pushed off their lands at Pyramid Lake, Nevada, and some of her nation had been "arbitrarily removed" after the Bannock War to the Yakima Reservation in Washington Territory. They now were trying to procure other land on the Malheur Reservation in southeastern Oregon.

> I, Sarah Winnemucca Hopkins, grand-daughter of Captain Truckee
> ... together with the undersigned friends who sympathize in the cause
> of my people,—do petition the Honorable Congress of the United States
> to restore to them said Malheur Reservation ... where they can enjoy
> lands in severalty without losing their tribal relations, so essential to
> their happiness and good character, and where their citizenship, implied
> in this distribution of land, will defend them from the encroachments
> of the white settlers, so detrimental to their interests and their virtues.
> (*Life Among the Piutes* 247)

Invoking Paiute "severalty without losing their tribal relations" or their "happiness and good character" and emphasizing their "citizenship," Winnemucca envisioned a different frontier from the standard history of binary relations that was to be reified by Frederick Jackson Turner in the next decade. Indeed invoking any of "their interests and their virtues" when applied to Indians was an affront to America's self-narrative. By endowing her Paiutes with American citizenship and land ownership, she hoped to establish a legal foundation for civil relations, to "defend them from the encroachments of the white settlers." Like Apess, she evidently saw the United States as a potential community of difference, allowing both settlers and Indians, both George Washington and King Philip, both Fremont and Truckee, to affirm their Americanness in balanced relations by mutual law.

It is particularly significant that Winnemucca also envisioned this Americanization "without losing their tribal relations, so essential to their happiness and good character." Such a phrase as "tribal relations" resonates with Deloria's language of "the people" and with the domestic sovereignty which even at that time was the Paiutes' legal standing, if not their material and human condition. These relations as she envisioned them continue to be worked out in the courts today.

The sovereignty that we see invoked in Winnemucca's prose, written during such desperate times for the Paiutes, is primarily the affirmation of peoplehood, of their natural need and right to stay together on the land. It is thus at times a sovereignty in retreat, even in flight, yet always in awareness that the current sacrifices, under grievous circumstances, are for the people to survive. For instance, early on in her narrative, when the Paiutes were first faced with marauding white settlers, she writes, "My father got up very early one morning, and told the people the time had come,—that we could no longer be happy as of old, as the white people we called our brothers had brought a great trouble and sorrow among us already. . . . 'I fear we will suffer greatly by their coming to our country; they come for no good to us, although my father said they were our brothers, but they do not seem to think we are like them'" (*Life Among the Piutes* 14).

At this moment in her narrative, Winnemucca makes the severe comment, "Now comes the end of our merrymaking." It is difficult not to consider the romantic simplification with which she paints the "merrymaking" of her precontact community, yet her rhetorical purposes are clear: to enlist the sympathy of her white readership in support of Paiute land claims. Because she cannot let them "vanish," she proclaims not the end of her people but the beginning of that "great trouble and sorrow." Clearly her father's sad decision, wishing he were wrong in expecting the worst of the whites, is to protect the people's sovereignty on the land, with the gifts of the land, in pine nuts and dried fish: "And to avoid bloodshed, we must all go to the mountains during the summer. . . . Let us keep away from the emigrant roads. . . . In that way we can live in the mountains all summer and all winter too" (*Life Among the Piutes* 14–15).

By conveying the sorrow of her father, Old Winnemucca, and of her grandfather, Truckee, at their "white brothers'" denial of their common bond, she speaks to the basic principle of respect animating Paiute culture that is at the heart of the sovereignty issue. We may refer back to Taiaiake Alfred's description of Mohawk sovereignty embodying fundamentals of respect, balance, spirituality, harmony as "the achievement of balanced relationship based upon respect for differences, whether among individuals or communities." The anguish of the Paiutes is in their trampled vision of such a balanced relationship of reciprocal sovereignty. In its reflexive prefix, the English word "*re*spect" invokes reciprocity: looking again and seeing the outward in the humane terms of the inward. When Winnemucca writes plainly, "So my father told all his people to go into the mountains and hunt and lay up food for the coming winter. Then we all went into the mountains" (*Life Among the Piutes* 11), she understates the difficulty, the sorrow, the sacrifice, of such a move. Not only do her people have to "move camp," they also have to bow to the profoundest disrespect and brutal treatment of white settlers, a prejudice that opens to the most violent sexual outrages on Paiute women and girls, sparking wars and smaller conflicts.

Indeed that historical spark—raping Indian women—as a fundamental crime against personal sovereignty, ignited the larger imperial conflagration that engulfed the Northern Paiutes. The social and political blaze originated in the spark of sexual domination.[38] Things got so bad for Paiute women that they began to doubt even their own will to carry on, questioning their own biological choices: "My people have been so unhappy for a long time they wish now to *disincrease*, instead of multiply. The mothers are afraid to have more children, for fear they shall have daughters, who are not safe even in their mother's presence" (*Life Among the Piutes* 48, emphasis in original). Winnemucca recognized that basic immorality reflected the institutionalized disrespect that Paiutes received across the racial divide. Yet even the connection she draws between Indian women's bodies and the Indigenous body politic reaffirms tribal sovereignty, as she asserts her people's right to survive white incursions. Those depraved causes of war mark the negative space of tribal sovereignty under siege.

"When We Were a Free People": Sovereignty in McNickle

D'Arcy McNickle's fiction similarly dramatizes the drastic erosion of tribal sovereignty. Here there seem to be almost no arrows left in the eagle's claws. If Apess claims it, if Winnemucca pleads for it, if Silko prophecies it, and if Alexie assumes it, McNickle weeps for it. While his nonfiction, like Apess's, charts the slow yet hopeful process of cleaving to and regaining sovereignty, McNickle's fiction shows only a glimmer of hope. *The Surrounded* and *Wind from an Enemy Sky* and the short fiction constitute an extended narrative critique of the American frontier project to erase Native sovereignty. Like Winnemucca, McNickle (1904–77; see biographical appendix) forges a link between individual bodies and the body politic. At the end of *The Surrounded*, handcuffs surround Archilde's wrists just as white domination surrounds his people. At the end of *Wind*, Bull sacrifices his life in a final personal statement of violence for the survival of his grandson and their people. There is also a parallel to Winnemucca's and Apess's writing in McNickle's emphasis on respect as a fundamental value of social order. As Bull in *Wind* puts it in the negative, "But the white man means, 'You'll be a strong man when you become a white man.' It's his way of offering me friendship. He looks, but doesn't see me" (93). Respect not granted becomes in McNickle respect demanded. If reciprocal respect is fundamental to his Native society, then sovereignty evidently entails the ultimate expression of respect, that is, sacrifice for others. As we see in McNickle's characterizations, this sacrifice of self for the sovereignty of the people moves in a cycle that strengthens both.

Bull in *Wind* often expresses McNickle's historical view on sovereignty by tracing the negative: "It was that way when we were a free people and had to hunt in country where others came to hunt. Sometimes we had to fight, and somebody would get hurt, maybe killed. We learned to bear our losses by ourselves. No one else would be troubled by what happened to us" (90). In "by ourselves," the sense of solidarity sustains the people "to bear our losses." Further, the flip side of sovereignty and self-government here is a kind of self-sufficiency that does not look for pity from others. As Bull discusses the contemporary murder of a white man in the context of old intertribal warfare, he is modeling—and suggesting for white characters in the novel—both the solidarity and the sovereignty that moves on from "our losses." The sustaining principle remains the people themselves.

Bull asserts this value of peoplehood even over a central artifact, the Feather Boy bundle, of the traditional culture itself. By his hard-headed, unsentimental logic, the sovereignty of community stands prior even to their sacred medicine bundle. As he advises against trusting the white men's courts to deal justly with one of his people, he comments, "Somewhere there is a trap. . . . I say, if we give up one of ours, the good feeling we buy will be the trap that finishes us. Just hear me out. The government man will be pleased if we do that. He will open his arms to us. He will even help to bring back our medicine bundle. But maybe the power will be gone from it" (*Wind* 92-93). He speaks of the ceremonial medicine bundle as a transitory power compared to the primary solidarity that he would preserve by refusing to "give up one of ours." He is open to change, even to recognizing the loss of the medicine bundle, as long as the people may elude "the trap that finishes us." Bull is savvy, reasoning that their community solidarity and sovereignty take priority over ceremonial losses and even over worrying about cultural consistency.

McNickle's depiction of stern pragmatism about the Feather Boy bundle resonates with Silko's understanding of the "hard-headed" elders at her own Laguna pueblo who value the community itself even more than the evolving stories that the community generates, because while community and culture are intertwined, it all begins with peoplehood.

According to McNickle, the people know how to adapt to change. Bull's grandson, Antoine, for example, even after four traumatic years in boarding school, can return to savor that "time of pleasure, to be riding in the early morning air." We see Antoine's strength in community, his solidarity: "To be one among his people, to grow up in their respect, to be his grandfather's kinsman—this was a power in itself" (*Wind* 106). The power in these passages, whether the rhapsodically hopeful grandson or the skeptically distrustful grandfather, is survivance of the nation before all else, "to be one among his people."

Wind from an Enemy Sky, especially in the dramatized difference between Bull and his older brother, Henry Jim, is principally about this binary tension between community and cultural change. The binary is always false, as McNickle makes clear by suggesting that the real question is sovereignty. As most social issues come down to questions of power, McNickle shows that the issue is not whether the people should follow Henry Jim into assimilation or Bull into the mountains; it is who decides. Why should the "government men" decide how the fictionalized Salish people should live their lives? Who but the people has the power to make such decisions in a way that can make them work? As Winnemucca shows in the Paiutes' relations with the evenhanded Agent Parrish, when the people's power is respected, they can make any decision work. If respect is the personal manifestation of this principle, sovereignty is the social and legal manifestation. It is the democratic principle that Indians have been trying to persuade America to uphold on Indian lands. The "Indian problem" detailed in McNickle is America's own failure to fulfill its own pluralistic principles of democracy. Tribal sovereignty would be, for America, an ultimate expression of democracy, whereby the people decide.

Because of the democratic value of peoplehood, McNickle is not committed to despair. The balance of continuity and change, of culture and history, of identity and reciprocity keeps surfacing in *Wind from an Enemy Sky*. The sovereignty of peoplehood rises especially in the next generation, in Antoine. Whereas Archilde in *The Surrounded* only gradually achieves his commitment to the people, confirmed by his sacrifice in the finale, Antoine in *Wind* stands committed from the start: "When the people saw Bull and his grandson walking in the woods or riding their horses side by side, large man and growing boy, they realized that it had been a long time coming. When Bull put his hand on the boy's shoulder at the midsummer dance, a bad time ended" (200). Something deep is working through the camp. It's a renewed sense of continuity, of the sovereignty that keeps the changing people who they are.

If the complexity of issues leading to Bull's cross-cultural murder-suicide comes down to the simple issue of power, and if power in its complexity is the heart of sovereignty, we may read also in McNickle's texts how sovereignty translates into the simple issue of jurisdiction over resources. Like the silence that surrounds the fact of "stolen land" in America's larger historical narrative, a pall of denial meets claims to Indigenous jurisdiction, as noted in contemporary negotiations over jurisdiction of the National Bison Range on McNickle's home reservation. This issue, the land, lies at such a fundamental level in American law and consciousness that it becomes difficult to grasp, because it must be repressed by both the colonizer and the colonized.

McNickle maps the links between jurisdiction over their own lives and jurisdiction over their own land, for instance, through the speech of old Iron Child in *Wind*, where the repressed truth of fundamental loss comes to the surface: "White men were coming in to our country, taking our land, killing the game, and sending our children away" (84). He registers the consequent erosion of the solidarity and sovereignty of peoplehood: "So we began to fight among ourselves." And he punctuates this collapse with the theft of their ceremonial culture: "We lost the Feather Boy bundle." In passing, he gestures at the unifying principle that could save them: "That was wrong, since we are kinsmen."

Further, sovereignty as sacrifice in McNickle is what makes *Wind*'s Feather Boy bundle sacred. There is a sacred connection between the people and the bundle that only the experiences of sacrifice can sanctify. That same principle also makes it possible for Bull to consider that "maybe the power will be gone from it," because he accepts this dire possibility as no worse than giving up "one of ours." The people sacrifice ultimately for the people, so to break up the people by giving "one of ours" over to the whites would be worse sacrilege than trading solidarity for the bundle. The Feather Boy bundle is sacred only so long as the solidarity of the people is sovereign. If that inner sovereignty is shattered, "the power will be gone" from the medicine bundle anyway.

This set of nurturing premises underneath Bull's protective logic lies at the heart of the old man's character and at the heart of the novel itself. It is the communal logic of a sincere warrior. He ponders "how such a thing could happen and how the people could no longer protect themselves or their own children" (*Wind* 203). Here a consistent gentleness and sacrifice of self for others in the community is the personal commitment that is tribal solidarity and, ultimately, sovereignty.

Sacrifice in McNickle's fiction is about the generations. In recognition of ancestors and future children who seem to be elsewhere but who are present in an animate earth and sky, such sacrifice maintains the sovereignty of the people by giving up whatever is required, even life. Old Two Sleeps offers up himself as proxy for the young man, Pock Face, to turn himself in to the white "government men" for the murder, saying, "He is young. He has a young wife to lie with. . . . I am the one who will stand up and tell how I shot the man on the dam. . . . What can they do to an old man that hasn't already happened?" (*Wind* 92) The gaze of his kinsmen marks their modest wonder at his willingness to sacrifice.

Yet Bull refuses to "give up one of our own." As he says, "My kinsmen, it is too much to pay. What if we give up this boy, or this old man—or what if I show them where my gun is hiding? One of us will be taken, and we will be one less" (*Wind* 92). The very purpose of the principle is to keep the camp circle intact. As Bull says of camp wariness in the old days, "Death always waited beyond the camp circle" (93). Eventually McNickle's ironic plot unfolds so that Bull himself, who knows this threatening presence of death, becomes that "one less." He sacrifices himself.

What remains in both *The Surrounded* and *Wind from an Enemy Sky* is the next generation. Like any future, the next generation is hidden in both novels, off the page in understatement. Archilde, "shackled," seems headed for prison, while his nephews ride off in uncertain rebellion. Antoine, contrasted with Archilde by a lack of alienation, grows so close to his grandfather that he likely will become a leader of the people, and thereby a source of hope: "Bull sat at the head of the circle, opposite the entrance, where recently he had made a place at his side for his grandson, home from school. He said nothing to the camp, but everybody talked about it and it pleased them. The boy would grow up to be a leader" (*Wind* 10–11).

What little confidence McNickle does make visible in *Wind* is focused through plot and character on Antoine as the future. Behind the humor and the tragedy, McNickle's lament carves out the negative space of Indigenous sovereignty in America. Through Antoine's elders, the author clearly voices the values of peoplehood, self-government, and sacrifice that constitute sovereign nationhood. Through Antoine's surviving presence, McNickle envisions a future for those values and that America.

While his own deeply informed historical perspective sets the grim tone of losing Native American jurisdiction over their own resources in his novels, his nonfiction history and commentary, *Native American Tribalism: Indian Survivals and Renewals*, expresses McNickle's sense of possibility for renewed sovereignty. The book offers a sequence of both the historical trajectory and the author's hope. He charts first the "colonial antecedents," then "the formative years" of eighteenth- and nineteenth-century legal structures of governmental Indian policy, then the "years of attrition" through the nineteenth century's corrosive policies of Removal and assimilation; then the "time of reassessment" in the early twentieth-century Indian New Deal, the "return to negation" in the seesaw policy of mid-twentieth-century termination, and finally "the tribal world" of gradual renewal of sovereignty. His last chapters focus on the 1975 Indian Self-Determination Act, the Native American literary renaissance, cultural resurgence in Indian communities on and off the reservations nationwide, and the emerging force of educated

Indian professionals. If McNickle saw the end of the twentieth century as a time of renewal for "Native American tribalism," he was one of the first to recognize the emerging politics of renewed tribal sovereignty.

"Inherent Powers": Sovereignty in Silko

The explicit animism in Leslie Marmon Silko's (1948–; again see biographical appendix) literary universe, as we shall see it functioning at the heart of her sense of community, helps to clarify and summarize the dynamics of sovereignty in this study. For consideration of space, I will let Silko's animism serve as a lens on four summary points in understanding the narrative dynamics of sovereignty. Her communal animism clarifies these perspectives on the topic of sovereignty: inherent powers, sacrifice, peoplehood, and storytelling.

The inherent powers recognized legally as the precolonial foundation of sovereignty, as we saw in Deloria and Lytle, resonate with Silko's description of "what the earth's spirits wanted." In her sense of animistic purpose in *Almanac of the Dead*, we read a vision for those inherent powers: "Tribal people would retake ancestral land all over the world" (712). Whether or not this fiction is prophetic in political and economic reality, Silko articulates the principle of inherent sovereignty still working its way back through Native nationhood into the fabric of modern America. The achievement of Tayo in *Ceremony*, with communal help from Ku'oosh, Night Swan, Betonie, Ts'eh, and Grandma, offers another affirmation of the inherent power of the people on the land, like the end of a drought: "But this time the grass along the road was green and thick, and to the east, south, and west, as far as he could see, the land was green again.... The valley was enclosing this totality, like the mind holding all thoughts together in a single moment. The strength came from here, from this feeling. It had always been there. He stood there with the sun on his face, and he thought maybe he might make it after all" (246, 249).

Similarly the workings of sacrifice, drawing in uncountable ways on Native lives dedicated to community and sovereignty, come into imagistic clarity in Silko's focus on "the spirits." As we shall see in "All the spirits ate blood that was offered to them" (*Almanac* 512), there is a covenant in her animistic world between spirits and human beings: "The spirits of the mountains had to have their share; if people did not sacrifice to the mountains willingly, then the mountains trembled and shook with hurt and anger" (512). It is not necessarily that Silko, or her characters such as Tacho here, insist on a linear, cause-and-effect relationship between blood offerings and the relative calm or agitation of geologic faults and tectonic plates, but her text asserts that in consciously sacrificing for the mountain, the people recommit to their reflexive relationship with the land. Further, that commitment, that sacrifice in its multiple forms, maintains long-term balance of the people in their particular place on the earth. Their peoplehood grows from that soil, so their sovereignty protects it by sacrificing for it in whatever ways that land and that peoplehood require. They are open to a reciprocal relationship with their home.

Another aspect of the balance that a sacrificial relationship cultivates is perspective on the macrocosm and microcosm, blurring the boundaries between the communal and the individual. Tayo's journey in *Ceremony*, for instance, through the alienation of war and shellshock to gradual, ceremonial reintegration with the land, follows a road of sacrifice to return the rain to the land: "His sickness was only part of something larger, and his cure would be found only in something great and inclusive of everything" (132). The sacrifices he makes to follow the spotted cattle, honoring his uncle Josiah, reconnect Tayo to "something larger." Ultimately his decision to give up his own destructive and megalomaniacal desire to fight with the destroyer works by interdependence, not domination. That reaffirmation of kinship, that balance of his individuality with "something great and inclusive," is itself the sacrificial cure for his own sickness and for the larger disease of drought.

By reconnecting with the land, as we shall see in the discussion of identity in Silko, the individual joins the people of the earth as well. Tayo grows in loving his own people, moving from adolescent self-doubts to mature reciprocity. The spirit of this bond is the sovereignty of peoplehood, but for Tayo the intensity of a love for the people, a love for which he will "sacrifice willingly," conveys some of this meaning that animates sovereignty: "The mountain could not be lost to them, because it was in their bones; Josiah and Rocky were not far away. . . . The damage that had been done had never reached this feeling. This feeling was their life, vitality locked deep in blood memory, and the people were strong, and the fifth world endured, and nothing was ever lost as long as the love remained" (*Ceremony* 230). The gravity that is Indigenous identity is a "vitality locked deep in blood memory," so "the mountain could not be lost to them." Flowing with that vitality, they retain "this feeling" of sacrificial sovereignty on and in and for the land and its people in spite of the historical "damage that had been done." Tayo's task has been to reach inside and outside, where "this feeling was their life." Where the gravity of identity in Silko's ground translates into love, there "the people were strong" and willing to sacrifice for sovereignty.

Here we return to storytelling, its power to maintain the sovereignty of peoplehood, and its affirmations against dominant history. The story of sacrificing for sovereignty is the story of escaping that history. Thus Silko returns us to the dynamic of sovereignty to rewrite America. As in her short story, "The Storyteller's Escape," when Native storytellers depict an animate universe, they elude death and redefine the history of suffering as sacred. Here is a direct expression of this principle from *Almanac*: "The white man hated to hear anything about spirits because spirits were already dead and could not be tortured and butchered or shot, the only way the white man knew how to deal with the world. Spirits were immune to the white man's threats and to his bribes of money and food. The white man only knew one way to control himself or others and that was with brute force. Against the spirits, the white man was impotent" (581). What is the key issue underneath such torturing and butchering and shooting by the white man? It is the land, as property. Conquest requires reductive judgments. Yet those who tell the stories of a land alive with spirits, of an animistic world, are able to declare the white man "impotent" against that different reality.

Thus Silko's project, as with all these Native writers, has been to animate the Native world, in Alfonso Ortiz's terms, as " fully sentient and multidimensional beings" ("Indian/White Relations" 10), because, "against the spirits, the white man was impotent." According to Silko's texts, because of those sovereign "inherent powers" on the ground of Native America, the United States of America itself must change, will change, is changing.

"The Weight of Those Stories": Sovereignty in Alexie

If another word for sovereignty is freedom, and another word for freedom is agency, and another word for agency is poetry, then Sherman Alexie's literary formula, "poetry = anger x imagination," affirms sovereignty as a fundamental principle of Native American cultures. Poetry claims the ability to tell one's own story, a creative kind of sovereignty in the writer's realm, and when a Native American writer claims it, by extension it becomes, for good or ill, the representative purview of American Indians. Alexie's project is indeed centered on sovereignty as both means and end. For example, in his novel *Reservation Blues*, Thomas Builds-the-Fire, narrator and protagonist who is constructed as "the misfit storyteller of the Spokane Tribe" (5), shows us dimensions of the sacrificial dynamics of sovereignty, as we are coming to understand them in this study. He devotes himself to telling the stories of his people: "He'd caught some disease in the womb that forced him to tell stories. The weight of those stories bowed his legs and bent his spine a bit" (6).

Further, Thomas accepts the ridicule and even the violence directed at him by tribal members who don't understand how to survive with stories. Indeed he sacrifices primarily to heal the internalized oppression within his own community. For example, near the beginning of *Reservation Blues* we meet the characters Victor Joseph and Junior Polatkin, "two of the most accomplished bullies of recent Native American history," as Alexie's tone of quotidian hyperbole elevates the meanness of everyday experience to historic levels and conjures the colonial weight of modern Indigenous experience. Resonating within that context, the grueling daily history of Thomas's sacrifices becomes apparent in an episode where Victor and Joseph smash Thomas's face into wet cement on a rare sidewalk project: "The doctors at Sacred Heart Hospital in Spokane removed the cement from his skin, but the scars remained on his face. The sidewalk belonged to Thomas because of that pain" (13–14). What is quietly surprising, without fanfare, is Thomas's apparent equanimity, even his understanding, in the face of his own hurts.

Similarly Thomas's pain in the next sequence is the conscious receptacle of the people's pain, even of the despicable bully Victor: "Thomas was not surprised by Victor's sudden violence. These little wars were intimate affairs for those who dreamed in childhood of fishing for salmon but woke up as adults to shop at the Trading Post and stand in line for U.S.D.A. commodity food instead. They savagely, repeatedly, opened up cans of commodities and wept over the rancid meat, forced to eat what stray dogs ignored. Indian men like Victor roared from place to place, set fires, broke windows, and picked on the weaker members of the Tribe" (*Reservation Blues* 14).

As the smallest and most vulnerable, Thomas is the most conscious of the causes of reservation violence and ennui. The point of view in this narration positions Thomas as so insightful, and essentially so compassionate, that he takes on the pain of his people, precisely the sacrifice that maintains sovereignty of the people. When Victor is threatening and again playing out his bullying tactics, "Thomas didn't say a word, didn't struggle, but thought *It's a good day to die. It's a good day to get my ass kicked*" (*Reservation Blues* 14). The classic warrior line, now a cliché, now even Indian camp, ironizes Thomas's willingness to be the target of oppressed frustration.

In another instance, when Victor has smashed Thomas's prized guitar, "Thomas looked around at the little country he was trying to save, this reservation hidden away in the corner of the world. He knew that Victor and Junior were fragile as eggs, despite their warrior disguises. He held that cracked guitar tenderly, strummed the first chord, and sang that Patsy Cline song about falling to pieces" (*Reservation Blues* 16). The poignancy of Thomas's sacrifice pushes the irony to humor.

There are moments when this quiet theme of sacrifice is linked in the novel explicitly to the Catholic messiah and to a Christian pattern of redemption. For instance, after thinking about the misery of growing up poor, a friend of Thomas's, the young Indian woman named Checkers, walks into a church: "A small church. Four walls, a few pews, an altar. Jesus crucified on the wall. Mary weeping in a corner. It felt like home" (*Reservation Blues* 137). Her observations link messianic sacrifice to everyday Indian existence, "like home." The presence of an unassuming yet potent character like Thomas Builds-the-Fire, whose sacred name indicates the vivifying light and heat in the heart of the people, indeed reflects a strangely postindian, messianic sacrifice.[39]

Thomas even sacrifices his own social status both inside and outside his community, as he tries to live traditional values: "For thousands of years, the Spokanes feasted, danced, conducted conversations, and courted each other in certain ways. Most Indians don't follow those rules anymore, but Thomas made the attempt" (*Reservation Blues* 4–5). However, lest Alexie let his narrative fall into the nostalgia of the White Man's Indian, he moves the narrative and the characterization along with this pronouncement: "More than anything, he wanted a story to heal the wounds, but he knew that his stories never healed anything" (6). Hope is not automatic when Alexie invokes "stories." Yet his narration here uses the padding of that cynical statement to introduce the most mystical and powerful character in the novel, Big Mom, who lives across centuries and witnesses all that suffering: "'I know somebody who might be able to help you,' Thomas said" to a mythical Robert Johnson seeking healing on the rez (7). Even more than Thomas's, Big Mom's sacrifices are millennial:

> Big Mom wept as the soldiers rode away on their own pale ponies and heard their trumpets long after. She walked to the clearing where the horses had fallen, walked from corpse to corpse, and searched for any sign of life. After she counted the dead, she sang a mourning song for forty days and nights, then wiped the tears away, and buried the bodies. But she saved the bones of the most beautiful horse she found and built a flute from its ribs. Big Mom played a new flute song every morning to remind everybody that music created and recreated the world daily. (10)

Her sacrifice translates into song, and those songs keep the world and the people going. For Alexie, that community for which Big Mom sacrifices is a global one:

> In 1992, Big Mom still watched for the return of those slaughtered horses and listened to their songs. With each successive generation, the horses arrived in different forms and with different songs, called themselves Janis Joplin, Jimi Hendrix, Marvin Gaye, and so many other names. Those horses rose from everywhere and turned to Big Mom for rescue, but they all fell back into the earth again.
>
> For seven generations, Big Mom had received those horses and held them in her arms. (10)

Thus Alexie lays out the mythical context at the beginning of his narrative. It raises the pointed question precisely on this theme: What will all this sacrifice add up to? Will the people and their sovereignty survive? What, then, is the dynamic, what are the fruits, the results of all this sacrifice?

"Sovereignty Is Neither Fence nor Feathers"

Gerald Vizenor (Ojibwa) translates a positively postmodern sovereignty: "The notion of tribal sovereignty is not confiscable, or earth bound; sovereignty is neither fence nor feathers. The essence of sovereignty is imaginative, an original tribal trope, communal and spiritual, and the idea that is more than metes and bounds in treaties" (*Heirs of Columbus* 7). If there is a politics in "an original tribal trope," it is a pluralism built around the relative sovereignty of disparate communities, a community of difference. Where sovereignty is built on sacrifice, where it is "neither fence nor feathers," a ground theory must recognize the "communal and spiritual" dimensions of Native American literary dynamics. These "imaginative" tribal tropes are what make sovereignty inherent and "not confiscable."

The U.S. Constitution has been described as a system of dual sovereignty between federal and state powers, with separate realms of sovereignty: commerce regulation and international diplomacy for the feds; crime and welfare for the states. Indeed the recent Supreme Court has seemed dedicated to realigning states' rights in that dual-sovereignty system, "a trend that is causing a basic rearrangement of the powers of modern government at all levels," as Lyle Denniston of the *Baltimore Sun* describes it.[40] Yet, as we saw, the Constitution also recognizes a third sovereignty—Indian nations—although the Marshall decisions relegated them to "domestic dependent nations," even while protecting a measure of inherent sovereignty. Movements such as the Three Sovereigns Forum suggest that we are going further, to recognize the constitutional (commerce clause) establishment of "triple sovereignty" between federal, state, and tribal units, each with its own, mutually viable jurisdictions. Such a legal recognition, built on the economics of watershed ecology and other systems, might forecast a political healing which this country has always set as its own ideal in *e pluribus unum*.

The material reality mapped by these five themes bears its own historical momentum in a tortoise-and-hare race for America's future. Historians have been impressed by the hare's speed, its manifest destiny, while the tortoise continues steadily onward. As the legal scholar Charles Wilkinson writes in *Blood Struggle: The Rise of Modern Indian Nations*, "For more than 500 years, white society on this continent has discussed how long it would be before Indian people finally disappeared into the general society. Not if, but when. In a generation? Three? Five?" (383). At the end of his nearly four-hundred-page history of the reemergence of tribal sovereignty, Wilkinson concludes, "But now we have data: five centuries of survival under the most excruciating pressure of killing diseases, wars, land expropriation, and official government policy—forced assimilation, then outright termination. Yet the tribes are now the strongest they have been in a century and a half. Never has this land seen such staying power" (383).

Through Indian activism and diplomacy since the 1960s, official government policy is still shifting from termination to self-determination. That changing politics reflects cultural resurgence in the body politic of Native America. Ethics reflects aesthetics, life imitates art, as Native voices keep the songs alive and find new songs. The restrengthening of the tribes, now "the strongest they have been in a century and a half," coincides with the strengthening of Native literary voices since the 1960s, an artistic movement that resonates with Native writers throughout the modern history of the Americas.

Those echoes include screams as well as songs. The American pluralism that would recognize reciprocal sovereignty envisioned by Apess, Winnemucca, McNickle, Silko, and Alexie is a discursive weapon against the violence that underlies colonial conquest and slave economies. Such violence is first and last a denial of bodily commonality and thereby an authorization of invisibility. Disappearance is the story such power prefers.

That disappearance became bizarre with the Fool Soldiers. At Ft. Randall, Dakota Territory, in 1863, Colonel Pattee could not "see" even the Native rescuers who delivered white captives into his hands. So he threw the Fool Soldiers into the stockade. With racial marking, those visionaries were on the "other" side of his mental divide, however eloquently their actions and even the protestations of the rescued captives expressed otherwise. Neither could the Lakota Two Kettles later "see" their returning youths as anything but naïve against the insurmountable evidence of frontier oppositional violence. Thus they were *akicita wacintonsni*, Fool Soldiers. The fact that Charger and his friends were willing to risk their lives for peaceful dialogue, reconciliation, and mutual accountability, to affirm the commonality of their Indian bodies and the white hostages' bodies, must have seemed to the Two Kettles to be merely a false idealism wreaking more death among their own people, already plagued by oppression and confusion.

Indeed the doubly defeated Santees of White Lodge's band also held the

Fool Soldiers in a contempt that mirrored Colonel Pattee's. In 1864, a year following the Fool Soldiers incident, one of White Lodge's wandering fugitive warriors fired a lead ball of revenge into the back of Kills Game and Returns Triumphant's head. The visionary of the ten black stags lay dying for weeks, finally leaving Charger without his *kola*, his ritual brother.

2

A PLETHORA OF ANIMISTIC FACTORS
IMMERSED IN ETHEREAL REALITIES

Community as Animism

In scholarly efforts at mapping Indigenous identity, from Owens to Vizenor to Clifford, the term *community* recurs as the ground of identity on which the map is laid. Louis Owens marks "the recovering or rearticulation of an identity" as crucially "dependent upon a rediscovered sense of place as well as community" (*Other Destinies* 5). Similarly Gerald Vizenor's "invitation to tribal survivance" envisions survivance as a communal achievement ("Ruins"), and James Clifford's description of Mashpee dynamics places a nexus identity in a wider system of community as exchange. Following on such analyses, the Cherokee critic Jace Weaver affirms community as *the* key to Native literature, in complementary contrast to Owens's assertion that novels by American Indian authors are "defined primarily by a quest for identity." In his 1997 study, *That the People Might Live: Native American Literature and Native American Community*, Weaver throws down his theoretical gauntlet: "I would contend that the single thing that most defines Indian literatures relates to this sense of community and commitment to it" (43). It is instructive to look at both the stark contrast between Weaver's and Owens's opposing claims about "the single thing that most defines Indian literatures"—identity or community—and negotiations between those not necessarily opposite positions.

Identity or community? Certainly they interweave, and by reading how Native voices balance those values we may read for notions of national identity. Weaver concocts a neologism, *communitism*, combining *community* and *activism*, to describe literature that "has a proactive commitment to Native community, including what I term the 'wider community' of Creation itself" (*That the People Might Live* xiii). Weaver sees Indian writers' rhetorical activism on behalf on Indian community as that defining feature of the literature: "In communities that have too often been fractured and rendered dysfunctional by the effects of more than 500 years of colonialism, to promote communitist values means to participate in the healing of the grief and sense of exile felt by Native communities and the pained individuals in them" (43). Weaver gets at an undergirding politics and worldview in Native literatures through "this sense of community and commitment to it." It is difficult to summon any Indian writer whose impulse for writing does not engage "the healing of the grief and sense of exile felt by Native communities" over "more than 500 years of colonialism." The agonies of authenticity and identity take place on this often uncertain and slippery stage of Native community.

"Actual Experience" of Animism

Elsewhere I have suggested that not only is healing of Indian community a goal and a context of Indian writing but that dialogical dynamics of Indian community form the very method, content, and structure of many Native narratives.[1] The texts themselves incorporate reader, content, context, and writer into a process that advances a value of community in general and Native community in particular. From Apess to Alexie, discursive elaborations of community values permeate the meaning and the manner of narration. If there is a key dynamic, it is not only commitment to community but a kind of commitment *of* community in the way stories are told. As may be true of literary endeavors in general, Native texts strive to generate fellow feeling through communication. The very manner of writing Native stories creates community across disjunctive frontier boundaries that have tried to limit Indian lives.

Silko notes an angle of this dynamic in *Almanac of the Dead*: "Narrative as analogue for the actual experience, which no longer exists; a mosaic of memory and imagination" (574). This cryptic fragment, as it focuses on "actual experience," gestures at the "crisis of representation" that Gerald Vizenor negotiates through postmodernism's agonies of the sign. How can language convey or represent experience? Especially after the unspeakable, inconceivable losses of the Jewish Holocaust, even as that reflects the Indigenous Holocaust, this question remains the writer's and the storyteller's quandary. Yet there remains further a dialogic reality in the process of signification that eludes such linguistic impasses: the very act of communication, especially as it modulates into narration, fundamentally assumes an animate universe, a community of listeners. Narration is about animation. In spite of its abstract disconnection and its linguistic emptiness, narration cognitively and practically connects actors and audiences, characters and listeners, funneling a system of exchange through the storyteller. Storytelling is an expression, an operation, of animism.

Thus the discussion of community translates into animism through the etymological links between community and communication, especially as communication becomes narration. If narration is animation, it functions as a circulation, a translation between language and reality as well. Narration enacts the animate universe not only in the story's content but also in its context, including its readership. The very "reciprocal participatory perception" that registers an animate world becomes the act of reading or listening to stories.[2]

Thus we clarify the *place* of animation and narration, where we find that storytelling places us in the reciprocal perception of animism. Yet Silko in *Almanac* applies this animate dimension of narration to *time* as well. She accounts for memory as not relegated to past representations, but as applicable to present and even future events: "An experience termed *past* may actually return if the influences have the same balances or proportions as before. Details may vary, but the essence does not change" (574). Just as stories reciprocate with the witness in an animate universe of space, so they reciprocate in a universe of time as well. Or rather the space-time continuum becomes subject to the reciprocal perception of animism. The "essence" that "does not change" animates experiences and may continue in past-present-future. Thus the acute reciprocal perceptiveness of memory would be able to register a "future" essence that "does not change." This suggests the mechanism of prophecy as a kind of broad perception.

In these Native writers' attempts to revision history and indeed reshape America's future, their essential appeal to humanity and to the animate essence of their readership aspires to prophetic force. We may see such force most directly in Apess and Silko, at two far ends of confidence in their futures among Native communities and tribal nations. Winnemucca and McNickle were less sanguine, in immediate witness to devastations of Indian sovereignty. Alexie seems darkly comfortable with clowning the future into being, as an open question. As federal Indian policies recovered at the end of the twentieth century some essential default levels of respect for Native humanity, for instance in the 1975 Indian Self-Determination Act or the 1990 Native American Graves Protection and Repatriation Act, that Native humanity, amid rigorous activism and legal struggles, may perceive America's future as a "compassionate heart," again in the terms of Simon Ortiz. As Silko writes in *Almanac*, a utopian Native future does not mean the disappearance of Euro-Americans but a transformation of their cultures by the American land itself and by its Indigenous cultures into one that is more harmonious with the earth: "All ideas and beliefs of the Europeans would gradually wither and drop away" (511). In a sense, she envisions a communal solution, an Indigenous embrace so strong that European "ideas and beliefs" would find no room on this land.

Thus contours of thought generated by landed Indigenous kinship values build stories of alternative possibility that many American Indians tell themselves and the invaders. This very storytelling is a form of survivance. As I have argued, readers of Native literatures need to follow the lead of Native writers into the dialogical structures of Native stories. Readers then would take a community-based approach if they are to do justice to Native texts, since those texts are so woven with community dynamics and needs. Drawing on Clifford's discussion of "identity in Mashpee," characterized by a "nexus of relations," I distinguished between dialectics and dialogics as ways of reading Native literatures.

A less technical and more direct explanation of dialogics might point simply to animism. The animistic perspective is a compelling direction, moving positively beyond my 1994 discussion of decolonializing criticism and into traditional perspectives. On a dialogical field, as on an animistic field, everything has a voice. Everything participates mutually in perception and communication. As Neil Evernden writes of animism, "For once we engage in the extension of the boundary of the self into the 'environment,' then of course we imbue it with life and can quite properly regard it as animate—it is animate because we are a part of it" ("Beyond Ecology" 101).

Beyond Evernden's sketch of a self-projected animism, in a fully animistic world, objects are subjects. Trees, stones, animals, places may have their own consciousness, their participatory awareness of their circumstances. As Vine Deloria Jr. explains, "In the religious world of most tribes, birds, animals, and plants compose the 'other peoples' of creation" (*God Is Red* 274). That consciousness of "other peoples" is at the core of Indigenous links to the land. The Meskwaki poet and novelist Ray A. Young Bear writes of an animistic value of the ground:

> My maternal grandmother used to say it was crucial we have a place of our own. Listening intently, I learned that our lives were dependent upon a plethora of animistic factors immersed in ethereal realities. Basically, she instructed that the very ground on which we all stood, Grandmother Earth, was the embodiment of a former Supernatural being. She was all of nature, this Grandmother: She was the foundation for rivers, lakes, fields and forests; she provided homes and sustenance for insects, birds, reptiles, fish, animals, and human beings. She held everything together, including the clouds, stars, sun, and moon. Our sole obligation, my grandmother instructed, in having been created in the first place by the Holy Grandfather, is to maintain the Principal Religion of the Earthlodge clans. (*Remnants of the First Earth* xii)

Young Bear indicates this value at the core of having "a place of our own," a tribal community. That community includes " a plethora of animistic factors immersed in ethereal realities." Near the core of kinship, of community, in the heart of a Native epistemology is what Young Bear calls animism, "the tribal domain where animism and supernaturalism prevailed" (*Remnants* 250). "Listening intently" to what Young Bear prefers to call "ethereal realities," whether or not that dimension is explicable, is what animates his Native redefinition of community on the land, and hence of tribal sovereignty.

Young Bear's emphasis on animism is not unique to his Meskwaki culture. An early twentieth-century ethnography of the Ojibwa looks at a similar "cognitive orientation" toward "listening intently" to voices in nature. Irving A. Hallowell's "Ojibwa Ontology, Behavior and World View" tries to take a serious look at Ojibwa views on animism: "If we wish to understand the cognitive orientation of the Ojibwa, there is an ethno-linguistic problem to be considered: What is the meaning of animate in Ojibwa thinking? Are such generic properties of objects as responsiveness to outer stimulation—sentience, mobility, self-movement, or even reproduction—primary characteristics attributed to all objects of the animate classes irrespective of their categories as physical subjects in our thinking?" (25). Hallowell is trying to see if the English word *animate* translates into Ojibwa experience and related linguistic structures. His definition, "responsiveness to outer stimulation," applies to "sentience, mobility, self-movement, or even reproduction" in ways that might be read as various modes of communication. He continues with a particularly relevant focus of the question:

> Since stones are grammatically animate [in Ojibwa language], I once asked an old man: Are all the stones we see about us here alive? He reflected a long while and then replied, "No! But some are." This qualified answer made a lasting impression on me. And it is thoroughly consistent with the other data that indicate that the Ojibwa are not animists in the sense that they dogmatically attribute living souls to inanimate objects such as stones. The hypothesis which suggests itself to me is that the allocation of stones to an animate grammatical category is part of a culturally constituted grammatic set. It does not involve a consciously formulated theory about the nature of stones. It leaves a door open that our orientation on dogmatic grounds keeps shut tight. (25)

Hallowell contrasts the mechanistic Euro-American view in "our orientation" as "dogmatic" to Ojibwa usage, which does not "dogmatically attribute living souls to inanimate objects." His Western projections are problematic here: he begs the question of "*inanimate* objects" in a question about animism, and he ignores the further question that it might be possible to "attribute living souls" to rocks without being dogmatic at all. Yet through his own linguistic and cultural filters, he points, with the help of the "old man," to something clear. It is interesting that Hallowell evidently did not ask a medicine man or a shaman, but merely "an old man" who carries the culture of the Ojibwa people. That culture bearer points the ethnographer to living stones. We might wonder how other questions—that do not assume dogmatic absolutes about "all stones"—might have been answered.

However, Hallowell's scientific restraint in the analysis is especially useful here. Although his distinction between Ojibwa animism as a "grammatic

set" rather than "a consciously formulated theory" harkens to an unfortunate, condescending paternalism—indeed he de-animates the Ojibwa by
denying them consciousness of these questions—his minimalist reading of
animism offers precisely the notion of dialogics that Young Bear suggests.
"It leaves a door open," describing that very attention to other voices, that
"listening intently," that is one key to animism.

The notion of dialogism may thus be simply "listening intently," an attention, a sense that others might speak and listen—that they can be animate
and conscious. Dialectics tends to reduce "the other" to either a passive,
inanimate object that cannot speak or a projection, a reaction, an antithesis
to the self as thesis. Thesis against antithesis becomes self against nonself,
and any synthesis reverts reductively to further dualistic hierarchies. (This
is a fundamental weakness in historical analysis in both Hegel's spiritual
phenomenology and Marx and Engel's dialectical materialism. They can
miss the third, fourth, and more factors on a strategic field. We shall see
Silko's take on this weakness of Marx later in this chapter.) In contrast, animism tends to see and to listen to the other as a self in its own right, as an
alterity, on a field of selfhood. As Evernden puts it from an ecocritical perspective, "There is no such thing as an individual, only an individual-in-
context, individual as a component of place, defined by place" ("Beyond
Ecology" 103). The individual in a system of authenticity-identity-commu-
nity-sovereignty becomes the relatively insignificant but necessary nexus
in a system of relations, all animated by what Young Bear might call ethereal significance.[3]

Thus the founding two-dimensional frontier dialectics of white/Indian,
civilization/wilderness, culture/nature, and even mind/matter—built on
dualisms deep in the linguistic and ideological structures of Western cultures—are all the more inadequate to tell the stories of the past five hundred
years, precisely because they miss the dynamics of animate community.
They de-animate the "other." Although many on "both sides" of the racial
divide have been tragically persuaded by those dualistic reductions imposed
by colonial imperatives, dialogical reading opens up generations of conversations, sometimes brutally cut off, sometimes ignored, sometimes quietly
prevalent, sometimes comically surprising, that have crossed the colonial
divide from so many animate angles, always from the ground up.

Co-optation versus Community

There is a peculiar obstacle that Native writers confront in applying Indigenous animism to the process of transforming American national identity. Because animism today is generally considered a "primitive" worldview, understanding animism in new ways is necessary if redefinitions of Native America will redefine America. Although non-Native readers often sentimentalize and lament a single sense of Native community as some naïve, pantheistic kinship system, they rarely register how such a reduction to a prelapsarian paradise serves America's need to infantilize the Indian. Even as national bookstore chains now feature literature, history, and social science sections on Native America, Indian oral stories still are often catalogued and thus reduced as children's literature. Missing Winnemucca's Paiute respect in usage of the paternal honorific, the "Great White Father" continues to patronize and infantilize the Indian body on disputed land, more so now that racist demonizing has become unpolitic. In fact Native communities, built on ancient stories even as they build new stories, have always been complex, often conflicted systems of tradition and innovation, poverty and vitality, vision and shortsightedness, wisdom and corruption, dispossession and renovation. Out of this social matrix spring the gossip and legends, the jokes and the literature that reaffirm implicitly and explicitly an underlying tribal community characterized by internal tensions and connections.

Thus those communities and their cultures are always changing, and authenticity develops and changes with community. As Silko suggests in an interview, in reference to cultural change, "I tend to align myself with the tougher-minded people. The folks at home will say, 'If it's important, if it has relevance, it will stay regardless of whether it's on video tape, taped, or written down.' It's only the western Europeans who have this inflated pompous notion that every word, everything that's said or done is real important, and it's got to live on and on forever. . . . The people at home who say the story will either live or die are just being honest and truthful" (Barnes, "Leslie Marmon Silko Interview" 89). According to Silko, attachment to purity, "everything that's said or done is real important," derives from an illogic that equates authenticity to the past, "and it's got to live on and on forever." Instead a certain tough human humility in the face of larger-than-human forces finds ways to survive beyond expected change. It is neither fatalism nor resignation that sees change coming, but a resilient realism of community facing change together. Authenticity serves community in a cycle of animated change.

Clifford offers a dramatic metaphor to describe this cultural resilience: "Groups negotiating their identity in contexts of domination and exchange persist, patch themselves together in ways different from a living organism. A community, unlike a body, can lose a central 'organ' and not die. All the critical elements of identity are in specific conditions replaceable: language, land, blood, leadership, religion. Recognized, viable tribes exist in which any one or even most of these elements are missing, replaced, or largely transformed" (*The Predicament of Culture* 338). The ability of communities to replace "critical elements of identity"—not only "in contexts of domination" but in equitable processes of "exchange"—confounds the romance of nostalgia and cultural purity. While the atavistic equation of authenticity and past history implicates discussions of identity, the community is there in the very embrace of those questions. Community remains, and community remains the value, the purpose of the very stories themselves. Stories are the means to the end that is community.

We saw how Weaver's focus on communitism registers how Native texts serve to sustain and heal the community contexts out of which they emerge. Similarly Robert Allen Warrior in *Tribal Secrets* says of Native writing, "A generational view . . . invites us to see contemporary work as belonging to a process centuries long, rather than decades long, of engaging the future contours of Indian America" (2). The focus on Native community is unquestionably primary in Native texts. However, I hope to make clear that many Native writers—for the survival of their own communities—are and were conceiving and even striving to heal not only Native community but American national identity, American community, as well. Indeed Native writers as part of communities and cultures have entered centuries of cross-cultural conversations, both by their own choice and by historical pressures. Out of their own ways of knowing and surviving, these writers tend to address issues of American community from an animistic, dialogic, nondualistic, nonfrontier worldview, because eluding or changing that frontier worldview is vital for the well-being of Native communities. In fact, extending Weaver's communitism, we will see how Native writers have sometimes linked their Native national communities to the American nation—not always in desperate, co-opted terms of passively being engulfed or assimilated by the mainstream but in resistantly affirmative terms of both actively exchanging cultural strengths and reinventing American community. This affirmation grows out of Indigenous animism, calling for listeners across the human and more-than-human community. As redefinitions of authenticity and identity interacting with community constitute key moments in the cycles of resistance, absorption, and exchange that play out in Native stories, it is the dynamic principle of animism that indeed drives those cycles.

Community Praxis

Before reading moments of animistic community in Apess, Winnemucca, McNickle, Silko, and Alexie, there are popular notions of community that need addressing. The language of community and kinship and animism carries baggage. These are "nice" terms carrying expectations of naïveté and, more darkly, incompetence, that eclipse the pragmatics of difference. Specific practices of Indian writers and their communities confront notions of community versus nostalgia, naïveté, assimilation, and co-optation in their various cultural and political forms. I will list nine community practices out of which these stories emerge.

Praxis 1: Tribal membership. Strategies of Indigenous writers to form larger communities need be neither a sentimental retreat to romantic homogenization nor a naïve surrender to co-optation. They extend community exchange into a pluralistic society as both a pragmatic and a visionary prospect, where vision and practicality often interweave. In the current practical politics of tribal sovereignty, this larger principle of community translates into constitutional clauses that determine enrollment and membership criteria, among many other issues. For example, the Mandan-Hidatsa journalist Jodi Rave writes of relevant membership controversies among the Montana Chippewa Cree in the contemporary context of recent Cherokee and Seminole votes limiting membership: "The disenrolled families of the Chippewa-Cree aren't seeking $20,000 monthly payments. Nor are they being questioned of their blood line. Most of all, they represent a classic example of tribes' historic willingness to accept—or reject—people in their community."[4] Leaving for another discussion the complexities of eight decades of "disenrollment" of many Chippewa families from the Rocky

Boy's Reservation, the point here is that the principle of sovereignty as sacrifice regulates the principle of community as animism. Self-governmental aspects of tribal sovereignty shape real Indian communities.

Praxis 2: Exchange. Historical examples abound of a vision to extend community strategically beyond traditional limits. In the eighteenth century the Iroquois suggested to the colonists that they join themselves together in a "covenant chain" to be a more efficient trading partner with the ancient Iroquois Confederacy. This Haudenosaunee diplomacy offered a simple vision of extending community without surrendering identity, and that vision was built on centuries of practice among the Six Nations of the Confederacy.[5] In the nineteenth century the Fool Soldiers sacrificed themselves for such a vision of exchange across lines of difference, effectively invoking a more inclusive community from "both sides."

Another nineteenth-century literary example of cross-community exchange lies in an autobiographical account of the Omaha anthropologist Francis La Flesche, written in 1900, of his mid-1860s boarding school experiences, *The Middle Five: Indian Schoolboys of the Omaha Tribe*, in which he intends "to reveal the true nature and character of the Indian boy." In his preface he is explicit about focusing on his Omaha schoolfellows instead of his other young "friends who knew only the aboriginal life." He is clear about the ability of those Indian boys, himself among them, to maintain their identity within that extended, cross-cultural school community. Although the missionaries running the school intended to dominate and erase "the Indian" in their students, the boys, according to La Flesche, managed remarkably to navigate relations with their white teachers on a basis of mutual exchange. Addressing his non-Indian readership, La Flesche explains why he is not writing about Indian boys in their own traditional communities:

> I have made this choice [to write the story of my schoolfellows] not because the influences of the school alter the qualities of the boys, but that they might appear under conditions and in an attire familiar to the reader. The paint, feathers, robes, and other articles that make up the dress of the Indian, are marks of savagery to the European, and he who wears them, however appropriate or significant they might be to himself, finds it difficult to lay claim to a share in common human nature.

So while the school uniform *did not change* those who wore it, in this instance, it may help these little Indians to be judged, as are other boys, by what they say and do. (xv, emphasis added)

La Flesche claims that "the influence of the school" run by white missionaries did not fundamentally alter "the qualities of the boys." Patently he sees no contradiction between revealing "the true nature and character of the Indian boy" and showing how such a boy might "share in common human nature." He must be affirming common human nature as that which "did not change" by attending the boarding school, while he also equates that human quality with "the true nature and character of the Indian boy." A spirit or quality of human nature animates the race. He thus reflects a certain ease with human communities outside of Omaha territory, even as he refers to his non-Indian readers as "European" rather than "American." Indeed La Flesche himself, a scholar and ethnologist with a degree from the School of Law at National University in 1893, bridged a traditional culture of the High Plains with a profession in the exotic wilds of the Bureau of American Ethnology in Washington DC. Without surrendering the Osage identity of the schoolchildren against their brutal missionary teachers, he manages to write of their membership in the human community of his Euro-American readers.

Praxis 3: Kinship rules. To point out Native offers of forging community with the American nation is not to blur the various and specific kinship rules by which Native communities define themselves as sometimes fiercely distinct from others. Native nations frequently view themselves as collections of smaller clans. When Winnemucca writes, "My people were scattered at that time over nearly all the territory now known as Nevada" (*Life Among the Piutes* 5), she is mapping a community built of clans. Winnemucca's biographer, Sally Zanjani, explains, "In the aboriginal period, they [the Northern Paiutes] seem to have had little sense of themselves as a single people, an Indian nation of Paiutes. . . . Because life depended on the joint efforts of a group working together cooperatively, the family was the essential unit, and families often shifted their allegiance from one band to another. . . . Thus the bands remained loose clusters of families, perhaps one hundred to two hundred individuals, that followed seasonal food supplies" (*Sarah Winnemucca* 7–8). Whether or not speculations by historians and ethnologists about Paiute national identity are valid, the necessary intimacy of living in such close communities clearly welded generational kinship ties, expressed throughout Winnemucca's narrative. Those kin were even skeptical of the cross-cultural overtures of their own elder, Truckee, to his "white brothers."

For a High Plains example of kinship rules, the Dakota scholar Ella Deloria, writing in 1944, underlines this dynamic among her people:

> Kinship was the all-important matter. Its demands and dictates for all phases of social life were relentless and exact; but, on the other hand, its privileges and honorings and rewarding prestige were not only tolerable but downright pleasant and desirable for all who conformed. By kinship all Dakota people were held together in a great relationship that was theoretically all-inclusive and coextensive with the Dakota domain. Everyone who was born a Dakota belonged in it; nobody need be left outside. . . . I can safely say that the ultimate aim of Dakota life, stripped of accessories, was quite simple: One must obey kinship rules; one must be a good relative. No Dakota who has participated in that life will dispute that. ("Kinship Was the All-Important Matter" 10)

Deloria sets kinship and community in the forefront of Dakota values. Built explicitly on the ground, "coextensive with the Dakota domain," kinship generates its "demands and dictates" as well as "privileges and honorings," ultimately in reference to that ground.

One wonders how much of America's fluctuating fascination with Indians, for all its stereotypes, may be driven by a modern, industrial culture's alienated longing for such community, a "relationship that was theoretically all-inclusive." Certainly mainstream imagery of tribal life paints its own projections and erasures more than community linkages across the colonial divide. Berkhofer's *The White Man's Indian* establishes ways that Europeans and Euro-Americans make use of their own projections onto Native America in order to gauge their own European ideals. This projection becomes the basis of co-optation, the erasure of difference, the opposite of community:

> Many commentators on the history of White Indian imagery see Europeans and Americans as using counterimages of themselves to describe

Indians and the counterimages of Indians to describe themselves. Such a negative reference group could be used to define White identity or to prove White superiority over the worst fears of their own depravity. . . . Since White views of Indians are inextricably bound up with the evaluation of their own society and culture, then ambivalence of Europeans and Americans over the worth of their own customs and civilization would show up in their appraisal of Indian life. (27)

By this formulation, when whites look at Indians, they see their own "counterimages." Thus in trying to read Native American literature, non-Indian readers looking for community, like authenticity, find it difficult to avoid co-opting Native experience to fill mainstream cultural gaps.

Yet Native writers address and even manipulate this Euro-American longing for community in specific ways. As we shall see, Apess and Winnemucca call for humane treatment. McNickle underlines the economic and cultural incursions of Euro-American dispossession. Silko ultimately directs Euro-Americans to their own cultural roots in the name of community built on authentic identity. Alexie traces Native navigations of modern American culture. All of these writers call explicitly for a cross-cultural community of diverse ethnicities that would enact America's ideal principles.

Praxis 4: Respect. Against a too easy pseudo-reconciliation that merely replays Euro-American domination of things Indian in the name of co-optive kinship, Native writers look for equity in community, for Winnemucca's "respect." The Lakota invocation, "Ho, mitakuye oyasin!" (All my relatives!), made popular in *Black Elk Speaks* and other venues, is not an invitation to co-optation.

For instance, the Dakota writer and scholar Elizabeth Cook-Lynn warns against romanticizing, and then co-opting, a Native sense of community. Grounding her critique, she takes to task the scholars Raymond DeMallie and Julian Rice for blurring Lakota and Dakota kinship lines in their parallel assertions that behavior, or "social usages" (DeMallie, "Kinship" 323), and not blood is the currency of kinship.[6] DeMallie analyzes Native American kinship terminologies in general as "sometimes strongly contrasting with those of mainstream American culture": "Although they involve genealogical connections, kin terminologies usually classify persons and phenomena beyond actual webs of biological relatedness, and genealogy may not be the defining criterion of kinship in any Native American culture" (322). Cook-Lynn suggests that DeMallie swings the nature-versus-nurture pendulum too far toward the social side and away from the biological. She affirms instead, "One cannot be a Lakota unless one is related by lineage rules of the tiyospaye [clan]. While it is true that the 'narrow definition of biology' was not accepted by the Lakotas, since they are also related to the animal world, spirit world and everything else in the world, biology is *never* dismissed categorically" ("The American Indian Fiction Writer" 35). Her distinction—that kinship societies can be *both* biological and spiritual, even that those are not necessarily two separate spheres—is important partly because it suggests that Sioux writers such as Charles Eastman, Zitkala-Sa, and Cook-Lynn herself, who have addressed an American audience, can do so with clarity about boundaries.

For a broad cultural example of respect across boundaries between the American nation and America's first nations, witness generations of Native veterans' pride in their U.S. military service. This is a profound gesture, as old as the nation itself, toward a multiform American dialogue, protecting this *land*. Native men have enlisted to serve in the American military during all of America's eighteenth-, nineteenth-, twentieth-, and twenty-first-century wars at a higher rate proportionally than any other ethnic group. Although non-Indian observers often see this as co-optation or assimilation—liberals finding it bizarre and conservatives finding it patriotic—Native veterans reaffirm their warrior status in their own cultures, while claiming their own and an American identity redefined as diverse.[7] The logic of respect is concise and reciprocal: warrior authenticity becomes identity, drawing on Native community, enlarging American community, validating tribal sovereignty, re-creating authenticity.

Praxis 5: Dialogue. For all the de facto exchange, those who openly advocate dialogue between the races incur the same suspicion of foolishness as did Martin Charger and his companions. In nineteenth-century Dakota Territory, a mixed-blood was cursed as "half Indian, half white, and half devil." The wisecrack entrenches a negative view of interrelations as miscegenation. Reducing each multiple position—Indian or white, devil or (tacitly) angel—to an oppositional polarity, the joke expresses a dialectical suspicion of dialogical realities. The frontier mentality cannot read the pluralist body. Colonialism cannot read transculturalism. The productive irony of more than two halves is lost on the castigator of the epithet by demonizing the third term as evil itself, as "half devil." Actual, practical human experience beyond the racial divide would engage the third term as a plural reality, a multiplicity, not as anathema. But anathema it remains to a divided mind.

Those who step into the perceived no-man's land of interpreter or mediator can still be viewed as half-devil. Frances Karttunen characterizes Sarah Winnemucca as a gifted interpreter among others "between two worlds," who sometimes "fled for their lives, or lost them in violent encounters when negotiations failed" (*Between Worlds* xi). Winnemucca's mediating role led to heartbreak. Yet Karttunen points out that we live in a world "where we are dependent on interpreters" (xii). The drama, however, is not the act of storytelling itself. Narrative structures, like language itself, might mediate experience into comprehensible, and survivable, forms. In this vein James Ruppert suggests, "In working toward an understanding of Native American writers' texts, it is more useful to see them not as between two cultures (a romantic and victimist perspective) but as participants in two rich cultural traditions" (*Mediation* 3). Native literature then becomes "a dynamic that brings differing cultural codes into confluence to reinforce and re-create the structures of human life: the self, community, spirit, and the world we perceive" (3). This generous and affirmative view is not idealistic. Ruppert is among many scholars, Native and non-Native, who affirm the strength of Native storytelling. Yet this view, like the literature itself, does stand in stark contrast with prevailing prejudices. Ancient dualistic boundaries, essentially of miscegenation, still prevail in Clifford's description of a "Puritan taboo on the mixing of beliefs and bodies." Certainly the racial divide is reinforced by elements on both sides of the color line, to the effect that "the white man" remains the disconnected intruder while "the Indian" remains the dispossessed Native. That mutual denial and its negative dialectic are the dark energy of American history. The efforts of American Indian writers function to shed a light of humanity into those shadows. They try to animate the wooden Indian.

Implicit in American Indians' literary striving is a burdensome recognition that for Indians to heal, the white man has to heal as well. Vine Deloria Jr. thus calls for that national "maturity" instead of an America dazzled by its own insecure fantasies. Many Native writers have tried through dialogue to instruct their enemy to reconnect on this land. The devilish difficulty of imagining such a future of transformation is part of the load that mediators carry. Winnemucca's narrative begins with her grandfather Truckee's pathetic attempts to welcome his incorrigibly belligerent "white brothers" to Paiute lands in the 1840s. While that open ethic extended definitions of community even across colonial history, it was not necessarily shared by all Paiutes. Zanjani mentions Paiute bands other than Winnemucca's who "resented the growing prominence" of her family leaders "above their head-man," and who indeed "ridiculed . . . the old man's naivety" (*Sarah Winnemucca* 16). Whether political infighting or external suspicions prompted such derision, we shall see also in Truckee's own band a growing disagreement with his broad trust of "our white brothers." Open-hearted-ness, as always, risks brokenheartedness.

If dialogue is the currency of community, it is always risky, and those who try dialogue still are called fools. Some of my own students and some scholars, both Indian and non-Indian, accuse Apess of being a sellout as a Christian. Winnemucca was dismissed by some of her own people in her own time as a self-promoting opportunist and apologist for the U.S. govern-ment's deceitful intrusions. McNickle, a Métis enrolled as a child into the Salish tribe, was never Indian enough for some. Silko at times is dismissed as a peripheral figure raised outside of Laguna ceremonial circles and sub-stituting her own mythopoetics. Alexie has been under fire for ostensibly exaggerating the despair of his people for his own literary profit. Perhaps Simon Ortiz is the only writer in this study who has not endured such a crossfire of public criticism, but his turn may come.

Praxis 6: Horseshoe curve. While each writer sees the possibilities for peace or war with the intruders differently from within their own time and place in history, we may map larger patterns as well. In terms of Native con-cepts of community across racial borders, there is an upside-down bell curve, a U, thus a dish or horseshoe curve, from the early nineteenth century, drop-ping to its nadir at the turn of the twentieth, and then rising again in the later twentieth century, each stage in long generational increments.

First Apess around 1830, although he was witnessing the draconian Indian Removal policy, is still energized by America's millennial and revolution-ary idealism—toward a reversal of colonial dispossession and repression of New England Natives. Then Winnemucca around 1880 is driven to desper-ation by the convincing nineteenth-century pattern of continued dispossession and repression in America's westward push. Her courage and despair follow the downward pressure of federal Indian policies of conquest, annihilation, and assimilation. Out of the bottom of that pit, McNickle then begins writing around 1930, although he was witnessing the emerging Indian Reorganization Act and, a generation later, the renewed talk of Indian self-determination. Knowing the fatalism that tinged those political efforts, his fictional perspective is duly dark. Silko, beginning to write in the 1960s, inherited a renewed momentum toward sovereignty that was codified in the Indian Self-Determination Act of 1975, and her prose reflects a certain optimism on a mythical level. Alexie, inheriting all that despair and all that hope, plays the contemporary field with inventive duende. In terms of America's racial identities, following this trajectory across two centuries, we can see both consistency and change on this question of community among these Native voices.

They all affirm pluralism, a sense of difference as a value within American community. Within those parameters, Apess envisioned the possibility of a cross-racial Christian community. Winnemucca, in the years after publication of her dramatically pained autobiography, envisioned and worked for the possibility of a cross-cultural educational model for Paiute children. McNickle, in his fiction and unlike his nonfiction, envisioned very little possibility of cross-racial community. Silko again forecasts a world of cross-racial and cross-cultural interaction on Native terms. Alexie affirms "political" Indians living in postmodern America. Each of these writers struggles with the possibility of Indian community within and with American society. Against the material history of conquest, the energy and imagination that each applies to such questions speak to the power of Native community.

Two more introductory perspectives on Indigenous practice will suffice briefly to draw parameters of Indian community in America before we look at working definitions in these writers.

Praxis 7: Urban Indians. The next point comes from demographic census data: more than half of the tribal members of most Native nations today live in urban centers off their reservations. This current reality was boosted by the mid-twentieth-century federal policy of relocation that tried to drain Indian communities of their populations and to relocate them geographically, economically, and culturally. Relocation worked in tandem with the different and subsequent policy of termination. However, following the policy shift to the 1975 Indian Self-Determination Act and with concurrent cultural rejuvenation, plus with the erratic rise of gaming revenues since the Indian Gaming Act of 1988, economic development on some, not all, reservations has begun to reverse the downward population trend. Birth rates are also higher on average. Certainly the land-based aspects of Indigenous communities are given over partly to familial and cultural ties in a more mobile, modern context. It is striking indeed, as studies have shown, that Indigenous values persist across generations of even such geographical change.[8] Again, as is often true elsewhere, kinship ties, both biological and social, sustain Indian community.

Praxis 8: Indian time. Different from urban Indian life, there remains another perspective on grounded Indian reservation community that links kinship values with both a sense of place and a sense of time, as these entwine. In Frank Waters's 1942 novel, *The Man Who Killed the Deer*, we get a remarkable passage that suggests how space and time combine to shape pueblo cultures and communities. Describing a traditional southwestern pueblo as it stirs awake in the morning, Waters locates "Indian time" in "Indian space," even after centuries of colonial contact:

> As the first beam of light struck across the well of darkness, all emptied their hands of corn meal and spoke their prayers to the sun coming out standing to his sacred place. Jets of pale blue smoke began to spout from a hundred and fifty chimneys.
>
> The plaza below awoke with life. Women waddling down to the stream balancing water jars and tin buckets on their blue-black heads. Children, naked and shivering, running after more faggots. Men returning from the corrals to stand in front of ovens or against the sunny walls. Wrapped to eyes in cheap cotton blankets, rolling corn-husk cigarettes, saying nothing, seeing all. It was the rhythm of Indian life: an unvarying, age-old pattern whose mutations changed regularly and simultaneously with the patterns of day and night. (5)

As Waters identifies "the rhythm of Indian life" in sync with "the patterns of day and night," he locates those cyclic measures of time in a place, "the plaza" and its surrounding canyons. A few pages later, Waters is explicit on the significance of these place-centered rhythms that readers might construe as measurements of time:

Who knew what o'clock it was? There were no battered clocks, no dollar Ingersolls that kept time. The people likely couldn't read them anyway. They had no sense of time, these people. To them time was no moving flow to be measured, ticked out and struck at funny intervals. Time was all one, ever-present and indestructible. It was they who moved through it. There was only the consciousness of the moment for right action. No one knew how it came. But when it came they obeyed. (9)

Waters is describing a worldview built through millennia in a single place. His description echoes English-language overtones for the ancient Anglo-Norman and Old French word *présent*, which still conveys being both in this place and/or this moment, being here and/or being now (OED). For Pueblo time to be "ever-present," it is "present" in a place. In Waters's description time and place are inextricable, indeed "all-one." His choice of language is more transcendental, perhaps more romantic than Vine Deloria Jr.'s, who identifies "place" as central to a Native sense of time, religion, and reality in his chapter "Thinking in Time and Space" in *God Is Red*: "The vast majority of Indian tribal religions, therefore, have a sacred center at a particular place, be it a river, a mountain, a plateau, valley, or other natural feature. This center enables the people to look out along the four dimensions and locate their lands, to relate all historical events within the confines of this particular land, and to accept responsibility for it" (67). A nonlinear sense of time can influence a contemporary Indigenous sense of authenticity, and identity as well. As we move further into discussions of various perspectives on community in Native literature, the interactions of cyclic time and landed place will influence those dynamics also.

Praxis 9: Communication as community. Finally, by way of introduction to community dynamics in these Native narratives, we must remember language itself and the reciprocal exchange of storytelling as a language act. In *Sacred Water*, her contemplative work of desert photography and spare text, Silko writes of "the communal, collaborative spirit which informs the old storytelling tradition" (83). She suggests that the very act of hearing and telling a story affirms the dialogic nature of language. Embedded within a "collaborative spirit," Native narration is animated by generations of voices, agreeing and disagreeing, listening and refining the stories on the ground of community. Native writers and their readers enter into that animate spirit in varying degrees as a communal act. These writers present to their readership critical community responsibilities that are part of literary extensions of that tradition.

Those responsibilities carry the sometimes earnest, sometimes ironic weight of authenticity, identity, community, and sovereignty, and it is often only the irony of Indian humor that makes that weight bearable. Responsibility here includes its etymological links to *respondability* or *responsiveness*, which is at the generous heart of taking on the burdens of responsibility. To shape language around and through such a system of experience, the Native writers in this study, like many others, translate traditional mythologies, complex psychological matrices, intimate and sweeping maps of animate relations, and revisionary perspectives on history, economy, policy, and politics. Irony is built into those reversals and complications of mainstream binary perspectives.

By way of a brief example, and to complete this introduction to literary community dynamics, let's look at one small piece by a community poet from South Dakota. In a 1982 poem by Sandy Frazier, who later returned from urban life to work as a counselor and to raise her family on her Cheyenne River Sioux Reservation, she offers an insightful view of those responsibilities. Beneath the screech and rush of subway wheels, the quiet emotions are poignant:

New York

I didn't recognize you at first,
standing there in your old raincoat.
You looked so different, even your face—
You could have been anyone in the city!
Waiting in the subway, your reflection
Flashed on passing windows—
The image was a broken holograph.
I wanted to peer around the corner
to see your missing parts—children
tagging on your clothes, the shadow
of ancestors across your face.
Your eyes spoke softly as they met mine,
"I am alone, I could disappear!

My footsteps would not track
This concrete maze—Hawks fly free
in the canyons of this city."
The promise hung in the air for a second,
then shaking my head silently
at my reflection, I caught the train.

In spite of the temptations of urban anonymity, this Lakota poet sees her own image rooted in family and community history. Far from the impersonalized Imagist distance of Ezra Pound's faces of subway commuters as "petals on a wet, black bough" in "In a Station of the Metro," Frazier lives too near her blood to allow urban abstractions to keep her from her own responsibilities to home. In both text and context, she moves from "a broken holograph" to a more complete picture of "children / tagging on your clothes, the shadow / of ancestors." Family and community are things she cannot abandon "around the corner" of her own "old raincoat" or the subway station. Although there is a "promise" of release in losing her name, where "Hawks fly free / in the canyons of this city," and where her reservation responsibilities could be ignored as "My footsteps would not track / This concrete maze," she only shakes her head at the idea that "I am alone, I could disappear!" Tempted to remain a broken holograph, she instead gathers her communal selfhood and steps decisively onto the train of ambiguity, but not of anonymity.

This complex poem's flirtation with anonymity brings us back to animism and its relation to communication and community. What's in a name? A story? Anonymity, meaning no-name, means no story, no history, no connections with the people who make up a community. (American exceptionalism is the colonialist's dream of anonymity, of detachment from European and our own American history and community, out here in the urban wilds of New York, where "Hawks fly free / in the canyons of this city." The fantasy is as tempting as the investments in its unreality are large.) If she can become anonymous, she can step away from community. When one has a name—given only by community and not by oneself—that name carries the stories of interconnection and animation that are the responsibilities and privileges of participation in community. A name is a nexus. A name is reciprocal and thereby holds a story. Communication is the telling of those community stories, and what enlivens them all is the sense of animate spirit that recognizes the name of one's own and others' peoplehood in the world.

The opposite of community is thus anonymity; the opposite of communication is not having a name, a nexus. Animism means having a name to communicate with, a story, as both subject and object, again a nexus. Thus animism is inherent in storytelling. Animism and communication become different aspects of the same thing. They intertwine, where communication is the exchange of animism. Frazier's poem enacts a gesture of responsibility to that exchange.

Let's look now in more detail at how five writers each present those community responsibilities to their community of readers. Not only is Winnemucca next in chronological order, but I will foreground her work in this chapter because of ways that her animist expression of community dynamics extends explicitly to American audiences as well.

"For God and for Humanity": Community in Winnemucca

Sarah Winnemucca develops her rhetorical standards of community cross-culturally, drawing on traditional Paiute and American humanitarian principles. Through a remarkable set of performative and narrative strategies, she reveals animate peoplehood on all sides of the American racial divide, and she does so especially by leveraging issues of gender.

In the company of publisher and Boston Brahmin Elizabeth Peabody on her lecture tours, in rousing and nuanced speeches from which the manuscript of *Life Among the Piutes: Their Wrongs and Claims* was developed, and with the editorship of Mary Peabody Mann, wife of the educator Horace Mann, she pays particular attention to Victorian American values of womanhood. Winnemucca tried to connect with what has been called the "cult of domesticity" for women of nineteenth-century America. In Euro-American terms, this was the cultural tendency to place woman at the moral center of society, and it worked cross-culturally in Winnemucca's favor. With the gradual erosion of the status of the Christian church in the wake of the eighteenth-century Enlightenment and the scientific revolution, the ethics of feminine domesticity began to stand in for orthodox authority. Susan Conrad discusses the nineteenth-century feminine ideal as "the cult of true womanhood" in *Perish the Thought: Intellectual Women in Romantic America, 1830-1860*: "This particular interpretation of woman's nature and social role grew out of a complex of then-current attitudes, beliefs, and conventional wisdom in which the virtues considered truly feminine were submissiveness, piety, purity, and domesticity" (8). These Victorian and American values continued throughout the century, when "the cult of true womanhood" was the keeper of the moral sanctity of the family. The pure woman in the home, for Winnemucca's audiences, was thus the heart of order and community in American society, and that ideal became the target of Winnemucca's rhetorical strategies, precisely as a counterbalance to masculine intrusions and perversions on the frontier.

On the broad basis of parallel Paiute and Victorian values, Winnemucca thus advances notions of domestic community as Native tradition against the colonial depredations of America's official and default Indian policies. She drives home this contrast by associating the morality of Paiute order against the rapacity of frontier chaos. If, as we shall see, community in Winnemucca means a sense of domestic equilibrium built on reciprocity, it extends across layers of relations—land, plant, animal, human, male and female, parent and child, Indian and white—where all are granted tacit animate standing. We will return to a discussion of her treatment of colonial frontier gender issues in building community especially with her female American audiences.

"They Wish Now to Disincrease"

Winnemucca recognized that brutal immorality of frontier rapists reflected the institutionalized disrespect that Paiutes received across the racial divide. As we read, "My people have been so unhappy for a long time they wish now to *disincrease*, instead of multiply" (*Life Among the Piutes* 48, emphasis in original). Such despair over racialized and sexual affronts is in direct contrast to traditional Paiute codes of sexual and personal conduct.[9] Here we may see directly how personal sovereignty translates into tribal sovereignty, while the narrative context uses that principle as an appeal to cross-cultural community.

As Winnemucca describes young Paiute women's coming of age, she points out the autonomy and respect built into their role: "She is never forced by her parents to marry against her wishes. When she knows her own mind, she makes a confidant of her grandmother, and then the young man is summoned by the father of the girl, who asks him in her presence, if he really loves his daughter, and reminds him, if he says he does, of all the duties of a husband" (*Life Among the Piutes* 49). The contrast with white settlers' abduction and rape of Paiute girls could not be more stark.

Indeed Winnemucca claims in her chapter "Wars and Their Causes," and throughout, that it is the rapacity of white settlers that caused so much fighting and loss of land and life. She explains that the War of 1860 in her homeland was triggered by two traders who abducted two twelve-year-old girls, keeping them hidden in bondage in their shack's basement as sex slaves. The peace treaty terminating the ensuing conflict established for generations to come the long-to-be-contested Pyramid Lake Reservation (*Life Among the Piutes* 73). Individual sovereignty as an issue in rape extended to the militant defense of Paiute tribal sovereignty in Winnemucca's Nevada. The imperial effects of Euro-American immorality were clear to her people, and she uses the shock of such immorality as rhetorical leverage to recruit American community to her Indigenous cause.[10] It is an extraordinary moment.

To make these political linkages for the reader between individual and social levels of sovereignty and community, Winnemucca strategically shaped the book so that in chapters 1 and 2 she first constructs Paiute authenticity, identity, and community, where a new sense of community is offered, though unrequited, even to their "white brothers." Her rhetorical purpose for starting with ethnographic detail is to authorize her individual voice before discussing her social agenda for America, in "Wars and Their Causes" from chapter 3 onward: "I will now stop writing about myself and family and tribe customs, and tell about the wars, and the causes of the wars" (*Life Among the Piutes* 58). Her clear purpose from that point onward is to advocate, by negative example, an American peace that will no longer jeopardize her people's basic right to survive on the land. By narrating white atrocities, she both affirms wounded Paiute sovereignty and ironizes her Paiute impulse to community with the whites, who flout that offered community. Community self-preservation against denied cross-cultural community reaffirms a claim of sovereignty at the basic level of maintaining her people. Underneath that level lies in turn a basic principle of animate, humane respect. It is not only her grandfather Truckee's and others' leadership that unites them but a sense of respect for each other in a Paiute way of life.

This concept of respect is fundamental to understanding Winnemucca's sense of community, as it is the door to understanding animism. As respect in its Latin etymology means "look again," respect conveys a self-reflexive dimension to perception, where the self sees a self in the other. Respect for trees, for creosote bushes, for fish, for clouds, for "our white brothers," and for fellow Paiutes suggests a recognition of the selfhood, call it spirit, if you will, that animates Paiute being in her text. That is the principle of animism animating a Paiute sense of community across difference. This quality of respect for their shared peoplehood animates Winnemucca's sense of sovereignty and community.

In the context of her community, Winnemucca's own commitment to her grandfather's legacy of leadership remains her rhetorical focus: "When I think of my past life, and the bitter trials I have endured, I can scarcely believe I live, and yet I do; and, with the help of Him who notes the sparrow's fall, I mean to fight for my down-trodden race while life lasts" (*Life Among the Piutes* 6). Here in her introductory pages, the Christian allusion (Matthew 10:29) to an overseeing Father is one of the few in *Life Among the Piutes*. Winnemucca is clearly appealing to her white readership by invoking their biblical deity's support for her own and her people's cause.

Her frequent allusions to the Paiutes' "white brothers" explicitly appeals to her readers for a wider sense of community, embracing both the Indigenous and the invading populations, yet we can follow in her usage the growing disillusion and despair of cross-racial community that bore down on her frontier Paiutes. It begins early in the text with her grandfather Truckee's loving exclamation, "My white brothers,—my long-looked for white brothers have come at last!" (*Life Among the Piutes* 5). This enthusiasm derives from an origin story, which Truckee shares after he eventually and sadly understands that the first white travelers into Northern Paiute country would not trust him. They rebuffed his friendly advances with guns raised.

> He immediately gathered some of his leading men, and went to the place where the party had gone into camp. Arriving near them, he was commanded to halt in a manner that was readily understood without an interpreter. Grandpa at once made signs of friendship by throwing down his robe and throwing up his arms to show them he had no weapons; but in vain,—they kept him at a distance. He knew not what to do. He had expected so much pleasure in welcoming his white brothers to the best in the land, that after looking at them sorrowfully for a little

while, he came away quite unhappy. But he would not give them up so easily. He took some of his most trustworthy men and followed them day after day, camping near them at night, and travelling in sight of them by day, hoping in this way to gain their confidence. But he was disappointed, poor dear old soul! (5–6)

The "First Meeting of Piutes and Whites," as Winnemucca entitled chapter 1, tends to conflate the historical and the mythical, as is true of so many such moments across colonial history—but here with particular resonance and poignancy because of explicit Paiute prophecies and immigrant pugnaciousness.

"Then he summoned his whole people, and told them this tradition: 'In the beginning of the world there were only four, two girls and two boys. Our forefather and mother were only two, and we are their children. You all know that a great while ago there was a happy family in this world. One girl and one boy were dark and the others were white. For a time they got along together without quarrelling, but soon they disagreed, and there was trouble'" (*Life Among the Piutes* 6). Truckee explains that the story of separation "across the mighty ocean" (7) promises a day of reunion, which he thought was upon them.

"And by-and-by the dark children grew into a large nation; and we believe it is the one we belong to, and that the nation that sprung from the white children will some time send some one [*sic*] to meet us and heal all the old trouble. Now, the white people we saw a few days ago must certainly be our white brothers, and I want to welcome them. I want to love them as I love all of you. But they would not let me; they were afraid. But they will come again, and I want you one and all to promise that, should I not live to welcome them myself, you will not hurt a hair on their heads, but welcome them as I tried to do." (7)

Winnemucca's own skepticism shows immediately, as she comments on her grandfather's story, "How good of him to try and heal the wound, and how vain were his efforts!"

Thus her own usage of "white brothers" gradually takes on a distinctly ironic and increasingly tragic tone, while the phrase is fraught with apprehension early on as well. After the infamous Donner Party travels through

Paiute country toward their demise in the mountains, she writes, "My people talked fearfully that winter about those they called our white brothers. My people said they had something like awful thunder and lightning, and with that they killed everything that came in their way" (*Life Among the Piutes* 12–13). Describing an early massacre at Muddy Lake, she patiently catalogues the crimes: "In 1865 we had another trouble with our white brothers. . . . Yet my people kept peaceful" (77). Further on, she grows plaintive: "Dear reader, I must tell a little more about my poor people, and what we suffer at the hands of our white brothers" (89). She delivers the growing irony both directly—"Dear reader"—and indirectly, quoting other Paiute leaders such as her uncle, Captain John: "My dear people, I have lived many years with white people. Yes, it is over thirty years, and I know a great many of them. I have never known one of them to do what they promised. . . . These are your white brothers' ways, and they are a weak people" (225).

These references to "white brothers" become accounts of betrayal and brutality by "white *people*" (emphasis added), as when chiefs Leggins and Egan respond to the threat of settlers and militia in Canyon City who typically want to have part of the reservation for themselves: "Another thing, we do not want to have white people near us. We do not want to go where they are, and we don't want them to come near us. We know what they are, and what they would do to our women and our daughters" (*Life Among the Piutes* 116).

Paiute efforts at building community across racial lines with their "white brothers" were trampled into the desert soil. In the midst of the Bannock War, a sympathetic army captain tells Winnemucca "that the citizens were very angry with the soldiers because they would not kill all the Indians they could find" (*Life Among the Piutes* 196). It is difficult to extend the hand of community friendship across racist battle lines.

Winnemucca is careful to distinguish between these two views of community, one universal, one racial. Contrast her accounts of the earliest contacts. She describes how generous and hospitable her people were when the emigrants traveled too late in the season and had to winter over with the Paiutes: "That same fall, very late, the emigrants kept coming. It was this time that our white brothers first came amongst us. They could not get over the mountains so they had to live with us. It was on Carson River, where the great Carson City stands now. You call my people bloodseeking. My people did not seek to kill them, nor did they steal their horses,—no, no, far from it. During the winter my people helped them. They gave them such as they had to eat" (*Life Among the Piutes* 10).

The point concerning community here is not only that Winnemucca's approaches were not based on race. Neither was Paiute community extended only as far as limited resources on the land might allow. Was it naïve of Truckee to imagine sharing Nevada with the white settlers whom he welcomed to his homeland? Fully cognizant that his people traditionally "scattered" across the sparse Nevada countryside, he certainly knew intimately the limits of his land's resources, if not the full extent of the looming white emigration. Yet he welcomed them to his humble abode. In Marxist terms, the superstructure of Truckee's mythology, not the base economy, was driving his attempt at social relations with whites. Truckee's Paiute values in fact invert a standard Marxist analysis that would put the motivating force in the economic base: so little land, so little welcome. Instead: so little land, so generous a welcome.

When her sister Mattie says to Winnemucca, speaking of their own skills as translators, "We have to work for them [the soldiers] and if they get our people not to love us, by telling what is not true to them, what can we do?" (*Life Among the Piutes* 204), she is responding both to economic realities and to ideological changes among her people brought by the frontier mentality of "our white brothers." Driven away from Truckee's mythological community, Winnemucca's fugitive people have indeed become defined by the dialectical materialism of the American Empire. This historic shift causes a further shift in Winnemucca's own pronominal identifications; now her actual community fades as she watches her nation dissolve into sorrow and alienation: "I thought to myself, 'My poor, poor people, you will be happy to-day; to-morrow or next week your happiness will be turned to weeping.' Oh, how sad I was for them! I could not sleep at night, for the sad thing that had come" (204). What they have lost is a sense of order and assurance in Paiute community. What Winnemucca has lost is a first-person identification with her own Paiutes, who now become "you" or even "them."

"They Do Not Seem to Think We Are Like Them"

Along that historical trajectory, however arbitrary it may have been (rather than destined or inevitable), let's look more closely at the contours of

Winnemucca's Paiute animate sense of fellowship. Echoing the biblical Fall, she invokes traditional Paiute community in an idyllic moral order to contrast with the invaders' rapacity and sexual conquest along the frontier divide. From the start of her first paragraph, Winnemucca refers to an originary, precontact Paiute community joined together by culture if not by proximity: "My people were scattered at that time over nearly all the territory now known as Nevada. My grandfather was chief of the entire Piute nation" (*Life Among the Piutes* 5). The sparse nature of resources in the Humboldt Sink meant that families, clans, and the nation itself must spread across a broad topography. Her term *scattered* both tests and reinforces a sense of Paiute community, stretching it until absence highlights the presence of communal bonds. In fact the word argues against the reductive ethnographic judgment, cited in Zanjani's biography, that the Northern Paiute were more "unorganized" than most Indigenous societies worldwide. Strictly ethnographically, the political structure of Northern Paiutes was evidently a much looser confederation of bands than any Euro-American monarchical model of an Indian "chief" over his "braves." The structure was more democratic than despotic. Zanjani explains that cooperative hunting and gathering meant that "families often shifted their allegiance from one band to another" (*Sarah Winnemucca* 8). She cites anthropologists who observed that "there are few native people in the world who were so unorganized as the Northern Paiute," and she writes, "Scholars agree that the concept of chieftainship was alien to the Paiutes, only developing when whites demanded a central authority they could deal with" (9). If Winnemucca invented and exploited her family's reigning role, she did so as part of a broad pattern of intercultural strategies. More than that, the ability of Native people to translate colonial experience into terms like *chief* and *princess* that work in their own community contexts *is* authenticity.[11] Strictures of static authenticity shape anthropological pronouncements on what was or was not "alien to the Paiutes, only developing when whites" arrived on the scene with their demands. The assumptions of imbalanced power in such analysis both erases the Paiutes and relegates any authentic Paiute experience to the past.

Winnemucca certainly does play on her white readership's assumptions about authentic Indian community as a prelapsarian past. Her first two chapters, in addition to setting up her authenticity and identity as a Paiute woman with the authority to speak to American audiences on these issues, also set up a dialectic of faith and grief, a communal, peaceful contrast with colonial conflict later in her text. Thus in the two opening chapters, "First Meeting of Piutes and Whites" and "Domestic and Social Moralities," she establishes the parameters of community that the third chapter, "Wars and Their Causes," will violate.

During her childhood, her father, Old Winnemucca, took her people to the mountains for a final celebration of their way of life before announcing the "end of our merrymaking," as we saw, due to the incursions of the whites. As he proceeds to prophesy, Old Winnemucca bases the fundamental problem in the shaken ground of mutual respect. We return to the old man's words in this context of animistic respect rebuffed: "I fear we will suffer greatly by their coming to our country; they come for no good to us, although my father said they were our brothers, but they do not seem to think we are like them" (*Life Among the Piutes* 14). Further exercising Paiute respect not only for his tribal interlocutors but also for the whites of whom he speaks, Old Winnemucca models democratic principles of Paiute communal leadership: "What do you all think about it? Maybe I am wrong. My dear children, there is something telling me that I am not wrong, because I am sure they have minds like us, and think as we do; and I know that they were doing wrong when they set fire to our winter supplies. They surely knew it was our food" (14). He is describing the incongruity of conscious immorality in a Paiute ethos. In Winnemucca's account, the colonial choices that clearly led to genocide were inconceivable to a Paiute way of life, though her community was both witness to and victim of such ethical outrages. In this context of conflict, where moral health confronts immoral disease, Old Winnemucca then tells his people of his "fearful dream, as he called it" (14):

> I dreamt this same thing three nights,—the very same. I saw the greatest emigration that has yet been through our country. I looked North and South and East and West, and saw nothing but dust, and I heard a great weeping. I saw women crying, and I also saw my men shot down by the white people. They were killing my people with something that made a great noise like thunder and lightning, and I saw the blood streaming from the mouths of my men that lay all around me. I saw it as if it was real. Oh, my dear children! You may all think it is only a dream,—nevertheless, I feel that it will come to pass." (14)

This early in her text, Winnemucca shows her white audiences the snake in the garden, summoning all their Christian apprehension of the Fall from the Garden of Eden, and turning it on themselves. Like Apess, Winnemucca offers her audiences their own mirror image in the horrified faces of her own people.

Thus she does not dwell on a Paiute prelapsarian paradise, nor is the sense of moral order that she propounds relegated to an unattainable past. Instead she locates it quite pragmatically in the military and political present, as, for instance, when she advocates U.S. Army jurisdiction rather than Bureau of Indian Affairs (BIA) jurisdiction over Paiute affairs: "It is this generosity and this kind care and order and discipline that make me like the care of the army for my people" (*Life Among the Piutes* 92). Effectively she connects an orderly Paiute set of customs with the moral-ethical relations of military discipline, not a difficult stretch given the mendacity and manipulative avarice of agents Rinehart at Malheur and Father Wilbur at Yakima reservations. After a parsimonious issue of government clothing at Yakima was completed, Winnemucca writes, like Apess, of the agent's officious cupidity as Christian hypocrisy: "My people talked and said,—'Another Reinhard! [*sic*]—don't you see he is the same? He looks up into the sky and says something, just like Reinhard.' They said, 'All white people like that are bad.' Every night some of them would come and take blankets off from sleeping men and women until all were gone. All this was told to the agent, but he would not help my poor people, and Father Wilbur's civilized Indians would say most shameful things about my people" (212). Not only are the foxes in charge of the henhouse, but some of the flock have joined the foxes now. The insult added to injury is that the community is under lethal pressure not only from without but from within as well. She shows now neocolonialism and internalized oppression grow hand in hand with American empire and Christian hypocrisy.

While she confronts colonial evil, Winnemucca strategically avoids painting an imbalanced portrait of colonial greed in order to maintain a communal link with her audience through objective reportage. Of course, she does not entirely demonize the whites—precisely as she appeals to the feminine and even feminist contingent in her white readership. Instead she writes extensively of communal values, of her people's thirst for community as moral order, as when she recounts their one positive experience of a BIA agent, Samuel Parrish. This contrast only serves to show the preponderant colonial crimes in sharper relief. Essentially Parrish showed them Paiute respect, along with his own self-effacing humor and humility. When he sets about teaching them how to work the fields in the white man's agrarian model, he starts by modestly downplaying his own nonsectarian, even non-Christian orientation: "I am a bad man; but I will try and do my duty, and teach you all how to work, so you can do for yourselves by-and-by. We must work while the government is helping us, and learn to help ourselves" (*Life Among the Piutes* 106). Note how even his pronouns bridge the racial divide to establish a communal order in "we must work." The predictable Paiute response, filtered through Winnemucca's anti-BIA politics, is immediate: "So my people went to work with good heart, both old men and young women and children. We were as happy as could be" (108). They set about building a cross-cultural, cross-racial community with enthusiasm and disciplined effort when their own human spirit, the animistic reciprocity that they bring to relations and perceptions, is respected.

The Parrish episode is a poignant period of hope in the Paiutes' relations with the whites and their institutions, and it sets Winnemucca's discussion of more shadowy "wars and their causes" against the light of other real possibilities. For a couple of years at Pyramid Lake, prior to the federal imposition of Christian missionary agents under President Grant's post–Civil War Peace Policy, Parrish and his wife worked with the Paiutes to build a thriving community. The new policy replaced governmental and military agents with sectarian ones, allocating to each reservation a Christian denomination, ostensibly moving toward the policy of assimilation and away from annihilation, effectively replacing conquering with a practical policy of rationing. By a logic explicable only to bureaucrats, when Grant's policy decided to appoint missionary denominations to run the reservations, Parrish was replaced by the draconian Christian agent William V. Rinehart. Clear success at a modicum of autonomy in agricultural development was replaced by clear failure, brutal autocracy, and corruption.

Although Parrish spoke in the discourse of imperious paternalism that characterized official white relations with Indians, he clearly afforded them a measure of respect, and that quality clearly bore different results. A quality of mutual recognition in his character may have contributed to his contrasting policies as well. Unlike other agents, he did not steal from the Paiutes. In late twentieth- and early twenty-first-century terms, his respect for persons and property might be called a small recognition of tribal sovereignty. In terms of Indigenous understanding of community, he saw Paiutes as simply animate: "All my people say that you won't work; but I will show them that you can work as well as anybody, and if you go on as we have started, maybe the Big Father at Washington will now give us a mill to grind our corn. Do all you can, and I know the government will help you. I will do all I can while I am with you. I am going to have a school-house put up right away, so that your children can go to school, and, after you have cut your hay, you can go out hunting a little while and get some buckskins; I know you would like that" (*Life Among the Piutes* 109). The paternalism that Parrish brings into play starts in the third person, describing "the Big Father" and "the government" that "will help you." By his even slightly distancing himself from "all my people" who "say that you won't work," Parrish won the confidence and cooperation of the Paiutes. We see their appreciation in Winnemucca's description of their response to Parrish's plan:

> My father said to his people, "Now, don't you think this is the best father we ever had in all our lives?" One and all of them said: "Yes, and we are all ready to do what he wants us to." So they all went to him and shook his hands, and his brother's hands, too, Charley Parrish, and he has a lovely wife. Mrs. Parrish is dearly beloved by my people and myself. She is a beautiful lady as well as a good one. Oh, if they had staid with us for five or six years, my poor people would not have suffered so much, and those who have been frozen to death would be living to-day. (109)

The Paiute discourse of respect includes "father" as community leader. Unfortunately this tribal respect could easily fall subject to manipulation by Indian agents. Parrish's paternalism contrasts with the neglect and corruption of other BIA agents and with settler hatred. However compromised, as Winnemucca's commentary suggests, his simple respect for sovereignty, personal and political, even while it fosters community, becomes a matter of life and death for the Paiutes, who "have suffered so much."

After Parrish is peremptorily relieved of his duty and Rinehart is installed, the contrast in her narrative is stark in terms of community dynamics across the lines of race and hierarchy. Subchief Egan is explicit about respect as a factor in community, so lacking since Parrish left: "The white folk have to work very hard and we must do the same. Our good agent never had any trouble with us, because we would do everything we could to please him, and he did the same by us. . . . He treated us as if [we] were his children, and we returned his kindness by doing everything he set us to do" (*Life Among the Piutes* 145). Egan characteristically recognizes the common value across the color line by acknowledging how hard "the white folk have to work" to develop their farms and ranches. On the basis of that common humanity, he and his fellow Paiutes are willing to cooperate and work hard as well.

Yet when the fruits of their labor are seized by the new, corrupt agent, that official thievery changes the terms of mutual community. The simple respect intrinsic to reciprocal relations is replaced by disregard on the one hand and resentment on the other. Again through the lens offered by classic Marxist analysis, we might consider briefly the shift of dynamics away from Winnemucca's sense of order in Paiute community in this historical and economic turn. In terms of labor's ownership of the means of production and of the products themselves, we may contrast the tribal community's approach versus Agent Rinehart's. In cooperation with Agent Parrish across lines of race, a Paiute order would cycle labor's ownership of the land and its products in an animistic field of respect. Profit sharing respects labor. Labor (people) and land all are served in a reciprocal system of exchange. In self-serving opposition to Paiute community, Rinehart imposed a one-directional, linear sense of order as capitalist extraction or mercantile colonialism. In so doing he created the classic clash between capital, as management, and labor. He insisted that Paiute land and the fruits of Paiute labor on the land "belong to the government," meaning himself as agent of that government. He would then distribute the harvest to his nepotistic network of family, friends, and Native sycophants.

The conspicuous injustice led Egan to complain about the agricultural storage: "My children are dying with hunger. I want what I and my people have worked for; that is, we want the wheat. We ask for nothing else, but our agent Parrish told us that would be ours." Rinehart's rigid response is breathtaking: "Nothing here is yours. It is all the government's. If Parrish told you so, he told you lies. . . . Why, if you take the government wheat, you rob the government" (*Life Among the Piutes* 133). Subchief Egan replies with questions based on fundamental respect for humanity—that become questions of community and sovereignty on the land: "Did the government tell you to come here and drive us off this reservation? Did the Big Father say, go and kill us all off, so you can have our land? Did he tell you to pull our children's ears off, and put handcuffs on them, and carry a pistol to shoot us with? We want to know how the government came by this land. Is the government mightier than our Spirit-Father, or is he our Spirit-Father?" (133–34). The offense against principles of community is complete, as an exclusive caste of whites tries to squeeze out a segregated, and now truly "scattered," group of Paiutes.

To dramatize her strategic analysis of the Paiutes' "wrongs and claims," the causes of wars that have wounded her people, Winnemucca focuses on their damaged humanity, and thus on personal and tribal sovereignty, through a catalogue of heartrending contrary examples of brutish intrusions. The effect, like portraying the corpses of victims, is to insist on their animate nature by negative contrast. Community becomes an agonizingly elusive standard, dramatized by catharsis of tragedy in ways that McNickle echoes by his literary strategies two generations later.

"I Scarcely Can Believe I Live"

It is against this desperate pressure on her community that Winnemucca set out to travel to California, Washington DC, and the Northeast to try to establish community linkages with common Americans and those in power. Her performance strategies on those multistop lecture tours tell us much about Winnemucca and her white audiences, raising questions about whether her efforts at reaching across the cultural and racial divides were indeed communal or "merely" performative and rhetorical. In the foundational links between communication and community, the distinction may be meaningless for Winnemucca. Essentially she sought to animate her Paiute people in the eyes, ears, hearts, and minds of her audiences. To do so, she used the tools of theater and literature. Even in the face of her historical failure to change legislation, she might claim that her success at swaying American public opinion did communicate an American community. Ultimately she performed community by appealing to humanity, and her articulate sincerity embodied the communal force of her cause. The animating effects on her American audiences were complex. Aspects of late twentieth-century postcolonial, feminist, and performance theories are just beginning to clarify the dynamics of Winnemucca's nineteenth-century strategies. As we shall see, she was entirely aware of her audience and their subconscious expectations. Indeed, unlike Apess, she "performs" the role—Indian princess, in her case—that they expect in order to win their respect and political leverage.

A study of the autobiographical and romanticized performances of Winnemucca on stage and in print can look at how she negotiated some of the hurdles she faced in making her story known. Indeed her particular performative relation to her audience foregrounds that entirely non-Native audience's role, along with her manipulation of it, in constructing her performative narratives. Yet the polyphonic dynamic in her multiple strategies necessarily frees her voice and constrains her at the same time. Let's examine performative dynamics in Winnemucca's work as they are shaped by orality and literacy, interacting with gender and ethnicity. Tribal sovereignty, however violently contested, remains the ground, and the stage, on which Winnemucca's life was played out as she strove for community with her audiences.

Margo Lukens's essay "Her 'Wrongs and Claims': Sarah Winnemucca's Strategic Narratives of Abuse" surveys the literature on Winnemucca and carefully maps the sentimental and dramatic strategies by which she presents the "wrongs and claims" of her Paiutes before her audiences: "Her strategy for touching her readers and moving them to action was to forge links between the sociopolitical abuses suffered by the Piutes as a group and the abuses she or individuals she had known had suffered" (94). Lukens links the aesthetics and the ethics of Winnemucca's self-presentation: "Her rhetorical purpose was to convince her readers not of the differences but of the similarities between the Piutes and their white 'brothers'" (95). Winnemucca's desperate and utopian cry for community, echoing her deeply disappointed grandfather, is at the heart of her politics, her plea for justice.

For all the historic seriousness of her cause, Winnemucca indulged in carnivalesque manipulations of Indian images. Drawing on the dime novels of her era and prefiguring Hollywood's pan-Indian costume imagery, Winnemucca constructed for her stage performances an "Indian Princess" outfit that had nothing to do with Paiute traditions and everything to do with white projections. As one of her biographers writes, "She enjoyed creating a dramatic impression, dressed in fringed buckskin and beads, with armlets and bracelets adorning her arms and wrists. She even included the affectation of a gold crown on her head and a wampum bag of velvet, decorated with an embroidered cupid, hanging from her waist" (Canfield, *Sarah Winnemucca* 201). Brigitte Georgi-Findlay carries the analysis of Winnemucca's carnivalesque performative strategies into gender territory: "The reports on Sarah Winnemucca's public appearance support the idea that she was aware of the effect she had on her public in the romantic role of the 'Indian Princess,' a role certainly not entirely of her own making. . . . As some abstract, noble Princess tied to 'America' and to sacrificial zeal, she has power as a symbol. As the Squaw, a depersonalized object of scornful convenience, she is powerless" ("The Frontiers of Native American Women's Writing" 228). "For the purpose of winning her audience's sympathy for her tribe," a tribe in pitiful conditions, Winnemucca was willing to find virtually any means, including a certain parody of herself, a first layer of self-erasure that precedes more performative paradoxes and invisibilities of gender. Her openness to eclectic representation matches her dedication "to fight for my down-trodden race while life lasts" (*Life Among the Piutes* 6). It would be misleading to describe this as an emphasis on community over identity or individuality, because her Paiute worldview might not operate by that binary. Her identity moves in more multifaceted exchange between her "down-trodden race" and their "white brothers."

Indeed this coalescing—rather than subsuming—of self into the people's cause represents a form of feminism that Kathryn Shanley finds characteristic of Native American women. She writes that in light of "the importance Indian people place on tribal sovereignty . . . equality for Indian women within tribal communities, therefore, holds more significance than equality in terms of the general rubric 'American'" ("Thoughts on Indian Feminism" 215).[12] According to Shanley, the boundary between gender and ethnicity appears to be relatively malleable among American Indian women. If a Native feminist identity is focused on tribal community as much as on female community, that description would go a long way toward mapping Winnemucca's identity as a warrior woman in the cause of her people. It might also account for her facility with the complex dynamics of projection, erasure, and self-expression built into any Native performance on a Euro-American stage.

Both her writings and her stage lectures remain a remarkable performance, always managing delicate negotiations between the specular male gaze of the colonizer and the desperate politics of her people. She and her audience had remarkably different perceptions of her presence staged before them, but, as is generally true of the insights of the colonized into the mind of the colonizer, she was keenly aware of their perceptions while they remained quite unaware of hers.

Yet part of her longevity lies in her ability to embody and reflect back the humanity in her audiences, to which she appealed in spite of their erasures. Focusing on humanity as community was her grandfather's animating strategy, and it is a key dynamic in twenty-first-century issues of Indigenous sovereignty as well. Her father praised her for her sacrifice to this greater humanity: "Oh! how thankful I feel that it is my own child who has saved so many lives, not only mine, but a great many, both whites and her own people" (*Life Among the Piutes* 193). Perhaps that is another reason—both sad and affirmative—her voice continues to speak.

"Bury . . . Plymouth Rock": Community in Apess

Let's turn to some of these same issues of community from William Apess's perspective in another homeland at the earlier end of Winnemucca's century. Apess developed his voice syncretically, interweaving Christian and tribal community values, striving against the dialectics of dominance to make one community in difference out of two in domination. For Apess in Connecticut and Massachusetts in 1830, definitions of community echoed John Winthrop's 1630 Christian vision of community "A Modell of Christan Charitie" and its "citty on a hill," "knit together" in "the unity of the spirit in the bond of peace"—with the crucial difference of added inclusiveness across the racial frontier. Apess's own devotional path was directed toward social justice, as he carried forward and expanded that vision of the Pilgrims for America in his own rhetoric of an American Zion. Toward that vision, Apess attempted to animate the Native population in the mind of America. To rehumanize the demonized Indian in the American psyche, he tried every rhetorical device he could muster to probe and reignite a sense of reciprocal humanity in his readers' and his detractors' view of the Native American communities in their midst.

Expansion and redefinition of American community were Apess's fundamental strategy, even across the boundaries of pitched battle. His *Eulogy* on *King Philip*, as a prime example, directly challenged America's racial boundaries of national identity. "An Indian's Looking-Glass for the White Man" attempted to show whites that genuine Christianity is beyond racial prejudice. It remains a dialectic, mirror-image exposure of the Euro-American orientation, throwing monstrosities and hypocrisies back in their own face. The *Eulogy on King Philip*, however, opens up more of a dialogic strategy, reflecting Christian virtues in an Indian face across the racial divide. In it Apess calls for a historical Indian hero to join the pantheon of American patriots with George Washington.

Humanizing the demonized enemy of the Massachusetts Puritans, Metacomet or King Philip, explicitly on a level with Washington, Apess foresees a day of reciprocal rather than hierarchical history: "As the immortal Washington lives endeared and engraven on the hearts of every white in America, never to be forgotten in time—even such is the immortal Philip honored, as held in memory by the degraded but yet grateful descendants who appreciate his character. . . . Where, then, shall we place the hero of the wilderness?" (*On Our Own Ground* 277). An "immortal Philip" is supremely an animate Philip rather than the centuries-old inanimate image of the king's head on a pike in a Puritan town for decades after the war. If decapitation is de-animation at its bloodiest, then Apess's revisionary history is indeed reanimation.

Yet Apess's method of reanimating Philip, of rehumanizing the demonized other, is communal, not personal or individualistic. His rhetorical logic has a directly social sense. Legal issues of property follow closely on the reanimation of a historical figure who, with his people, was deprived of "his soil." Just as he hints at his own identification with Philip as a "son of the forest," Apess's suggestion in his rhetorical question "Where shall we place the hero of the wilderness?" is to replant Philip—and his descendents—in a reshaped America: "Justice and humanity for the remaining few prompt me to vindicate the character of him who yet lives in their hearts and, if possible, melt the prejudice that exists in the hearts of those who are in the possession of his soil, and only by the right of conquest" (*On Our Own Ground* 277). That New England soil remains "his," Philip's, while Apess calls for a mutual American humanity rebuilt on justice.

These grounded terms are central to Apess's rebuilding project, and we may say central to the other writers in this study. Deborah Gussman, in her essay "'O Savage, Where Art Thou?' Rhetorics of Reform in William Apess's

Eulogy on King Philip," points out that "Apess's project of revising history from a Native American perspective returns to the very beginnings of the colonization of New England" (453). She suggests that Apess was one of the first in the United States to assert in print a Native American version of history.

Mastering the master's discourse, Apess in *Eulogy*, as we have seen, invokes eighteenth-century Enlightenment language in "justice and humanity." Such language moderates earlier ideals of Puritan discourse of the seventeenth century in principles of "justice and mercy" or Winthrop's call to "work, as one man . . . in brotherly affection." Certainly Apess also wields Christian discourse rooted in American Puritanism, as he writes elsewhere of a future for Indians in America as a kind of Second Coming: "Let us pray for Zion—and let us remember her scattered and peeled people in their sorrowful season of desertion. The lamp of Israel shall burn again, and the star of Judah shall rise again, never to go down, for it will shine over Bethlehem" (*The Increase of the Kingdom of Christ: A Sermon* in *On Our Own Ground* 107). Apess is naming a future America that no longer causes Indians such sorrow. He tries to focus a kind of humane animism on "the Indian" in his white readers' eyes, so colored by the romanticization or demonization, the "noble savage," of popular novels and plays of the early nineteenth century.[13]

Later in the *Eulogy*, and in accord with his exertions toward building American cross-racial community, Apess directs that realignment of history and ideology directly to a realignment of his contemporary society: "What, then, shall we do? Shall we cease crying and say it is all wrong, or shall we bury the hatchet and those unjust laws and Plymouth Rock together and become friends? And will the sons of the Pilgrims aid in putting out the fire and destroying the canker that will ruin all that their fathers left behind them to destroy?" (*On Our Own Ground* 306). Apess suggests that Americans bury Plymouth Rock in order to become fully American. Like Winnemucca in her chapter "Wars and Their Causes," he lays America's intrinsic problems on predatory white dispossession of Indian lands and the oppression of Indian bodies. He regards this foundational crime as more than an ethical lapse. Along with slavery, it is the crack in the Liberty Bell.

After a scathing critique of the Jacksonian Removal policy, "as if he had said to them, 'We want your land for our use to speculate upon; it aids us in paying off our national debt and supporting us in Congress to drive you off'"

(*On Our Own Ground* 307), he lays the blame for violent history on Euro-American spiritual corruption, translated into colonialism: "Now, while we sum up this subject, does it not appear that the cause of all wars from beginning to end was and is for the want of good usage? That the whites have always been the aggressors, and the wars, cruelties, and bloodshed is a job of their own seeking, and not the Indians'? Did you ever know of Indians hurting those who was kind to them? No. We have a thousand witnesses to the contrary" (307). Yet Apess does not stop there. As he damns a Euro-American history of hypocrisy, he trumpets a transformative future: "What, then, is to be done? Let every friend of the Indians now seize the mantle of Liberty and throw it over those burning elements that has spread with such fearful rapidity, and at once extinguish them forever. . . . Let us have principles that will give everyone his due; and then shall wars cease, and the weary find rest. Give the Indian his rights, and you may be assured war will cease" (307). If you want peace, work for justice. If the opposite of war is community, Apess details the options for his American readership.

As O'Connell puts it succinctly, Apess in *Eulogy* is "refusing to see the conflict between Europeans and Native Americans as that between two tragically irreconcilable races and ways of life. Apess's Indians are not doomed to fade away. His Philip and his Indians suffer and are diminished, but in the *Eulogy* he insists upon connecting the past to the current treatment of Native Americans and calls for their full citizenship in a republic of equals" (introduction xx). The principle of national community in Apess derives from his deepest identification with Indian ancestry, with the blood of King Philip. He establishes equal respectability by rewriting history and profiling Philip as a model for Washington himself, outdoing the Puritans in Christian, and by implication American, virtues: "Shall we not do right to say that Philip, with his one talent, outstrips them all with their ten thousand? No warrior, of any age, was ever known to pursue such plans as Philip did. . . . And as to his benevolence, it was very great; no one in history can accuse Philip of being cruel to his conquered foes; that he used them with more hospitality than they, the Pilgrims, did cannot be denied; and that he had knowledge and forethought" (*On Our Own Ground* 306). A revised history becomes an irrefutable rhetoric of a reenvisioned American community.

Toward the end of his account of Philip's beneficence and the colonists' betrayals (allied with other Indians), Apess rallies all his rhetorical powers to widen the spectrum of historical validation, of Americanness, across the racial divide: "But by this time you have been enabled to see that Philip's prophecy [that the white people would not only cut down their groves but would enslave them] has come to pass; therefore, as a man of natural abilities, I shall pronounce him the greatest man that was ever in America; and so it will stand, until he is proved to the contrary, to the everlasting disgrace of the Pilgrims' fathers" (*On Our Own Ground* 301–8). Although he excoriates the hypocrisy of the Puritans, Apess affirms Philip and the Pequots without invalidating Washington and his achievements.

Indeed the community that Apess strives to engender through his prose speaks at the conclusion of the *Eulogy* in his pronouns. The first-person plural "we" sums up his efforts: "Having now given historical facts, and an exposition in relation to ancient times, by which we have been enabled to discover the foundation which destroyed our common fathers in their struggle together; it was indeed nothing more than the spirit of avarice and usurpation of power that has brought people in all ages to hate and devour each other" (*On Our Own Ground* 308). Buried in the bloody soil of this language is the animating seed of American national community: "our common fathers." Apess offers up both white and Indian ancestors as common victims of devilish power. We shall see a more specific but similar mythology in the work of Leslie Silko at the end of the next century. Apess's phrase "the spirit of avarice and usurpation of power" presages Silko's witchery, especially in Apess's description, "that has brought people in all ages to hate and devour each other."

Further, Apess sets up a fine ambivalence under "our common fathers" by appending the phrase "in their struggle together." The phrase is rich with complex connection even during conflict, united in mutual affliction, so to speak. Are they struggling against each other or together against "the spirit of avarice"? Where he clearly separates whites and Indians in other passages, for example, setting up "the sons of the Pilgrims" against "us, poor Indians" (*On Our Own Ground* 284), he here invokes a hint if not a hope of reconciliation both in "our fathers" and in "together," even if in "struggle."

Clearly Apess's American community would be multiracial, although, as we shall see, he affirms difference and what we may call pluralism against "amalgamation." He folds the arms of God around a global vision of racial pluralism, in which whites remain a minority and Indians retain their soil.

As his animating principle is the divinity of creation, he positions America's race politics of slavery and conquest in a larger, transcendental map of divine decree where "black or red skins or any other skin of color" (*On Our Own Ground* 157) not only outnumber Europeans but affirm their differences under one creator.

"Beloved Images of God"

In "An Indian's Looking-Glass for the White Man," Apess's God is not "a respecter of persons" but is the one who created differences of race: "Or have you the folly to think that the white man, being one in fifteen or sixteen, are the only beloved images of God?" (*On Our Own Ground* 157). Holding such an umbrella of divine authentication instead of reaching out to whites, Apess even basks in Indian community. He writes of the traditional communities in Canada, where he traveled as a young man, "through the wilderness, and saw many of my brethren, who ornamented the wood with their camps and chanted the wild beast of prey with their songs" (151). In parallel, he writes of the Methodist communities in New England, of "home and those kindred friends," where he "strove to walk with them in the way to heaven, and can say that I spent many happy hours with them in the worship of God" (132). His cradle of comfort in Indian community, however, is disturbed directly by white racism, as he begins to feel the call of his Christian vocation. Indeed the intense pressure of prejudice grinds directly against his joy of conversion: "I began to be exercised more abundantly about the salvation of precious souls and began to have a desire to call sinners to repentance in a public way; and it appeared I could not rest in any other way. But I knew that I was weak and ignorant as to the letter; and not only so, I was already a hissing-stock and a byword in the world, merely because I was a child of the forest; and to add any more occasion to the weak and scornful family of the whites was more than I wished to do; but there was no peace for me, either by day or night" (132). Characterizing his white detractors as serpents in the garden is Apess's rhetorical response to bigotry.

He is exacting in his perception of white estrangement: "And although I can say that I have some dear, good friends among white people, yet I eye them with a jealous eye, for fear they will betray me. Having been deceived so much by them, how can I help it?" (*On Our Own Ground* 310). Even gestures of friendship Apess recognizes as specular and alienating, as "only to satisfy curiosity." Against a lifetime of mistreatment, both subtle and crude, and precisely because he looks at the humanity underneath the differences, "whether Christian or not," he yet holds to his vision of an America where "this tree of distinction shall be leveled to the earth, and the mantle of prejudice torn from every American heart" (161). Apess implies that only then shall he freely join hands with whites.

We must note in the context of his cross-racial vision that Apess could envisage extending his hand to non-Indian community on the basis of his strong ties to Indian communities across New England and southeastern Canada. He knew he stood on Indian ground, those "once delightful plains and homes of their peaceful habitations" now "taken from them." Further, he knew what supportive Indian community in his Christian manner could feel like. Fulfilling Winthrop's prayer for the Pilgrims within Indigenous congregations, Apess experiences even the ecstatic brotherhood of communion: "My Christian friends were around me singing the sweet songs of heaven; and I thought I was in the suburbs of glory. And when I saw them, they looked like angels, for they were praising God. I felt the love of God like a river flowing into my soul" (*On Our Own Ground* 142). One can only wonder what Winthrop would have thought to see Indian meetinghouses so full of the spirit, finding "delight in each other . . . as members of the same body."

If both nostalgia and rapture characterized Apess's sense of Indian fellowship, his equally acute sense of the validity of difference and the invalidity of hypocrisy kept him further distant from whites. A moment in *Nullification* suggests the weariness that he and other Indians felt against daily—and centuries-long—depredations by whites. Apess writes of the Mashpee guarding their woodlot: "The Indians now made it part of their business to watch their property, being determined to disappoint the rapacity of the whites. They soon learned that the governor had sent an envoy to deal with them, and the news cheered their hearts not a little; for they earnestly wished for peace and quietness" (*On Our Own Ground* 182). The respite sought by Apess and his Indian community is so edged by racial boundaries that it must hearken through history and geography back again to those "peaceful habitations" now "taken from them." Even refuge is delineated by invasion and near despair.

Such a context of colonial pressures on community informs Apess's remarkable discussions of "amalgamation" and intermarriage. Without directly conflating the social and the sexual, he allows the latter to intensify his radical discussion of the former. In his insistence on the legitimacy of racial difference, that is, the authenticity, identity, and humanity of people of color, he argues for separate community as well. This principle of separation or nonamalgamation weaves with his presumptions about sovereignty. An astonishing aside in *Nullification* makes this point with his characteristic flourish, wielding his rapier ironies on the same subject of sexual conquest as in "Looking-Glass." Again leaning longingly and ironically toward peace rather than interracial distress, he writes of sexual depredations similar to those Winnemucca addressed: "My advice to the white man is to let the colored race alone. It will considerably diminish the annual amount of sin committed. Or else let them even *marry* our daughters, and no more ado about amalgamation. We desire none of their connection in that way. All we ask of them is peace and our rights. We can find wives enough without asking any favors of them" (*On Our Own Ground* 230–31). One can only imagine the mixed puritanical prurience glowing in the eyes of bewhiskered hecklers and sympathizers alike as they accost Apess after his sermons, when he refers to this unwelcome subject that has been "rung in my ears by almost every white lecturer I ever had the misfortune to meet" (231). He wearies as they lecture him on race relations according to their own obscene prejudices. Who would want amalgamation with such Yankees as he has had "the misfortune to meet"? Tired of racist rhetoric when he sees through it to racist lust, Apess brings into focus the long history of sexual conquest, the carnal body of colonialism, as he accounts for the historical burdens of bigotry. He further underlines the centuries-old mixed-race reality that already was the American *pluribus* in the 1830s.

Yet for all his verbal jostling, for what one may call his manly and good-humored translation of his own weariness with the erotics of racial prejudice, Apess's view of intermarriage is built on careful consideration of the history of social interaction. In one of his published sermons, *Increase of the Kingdom of Christ*, he reflects further on amalgamation through his biblical discourse on an ancient pattern of cultural contact in the Jewish diaspora. As he envisions true American community emerging with millennial design, he comes out in favor of differentiation and against assimilation of Indians by invoking the Jewish model of cultural and ethnic differences retained across their spread through various "strange nations." Identifying Indians with the biblical chosen people, the wandering Hebrews—"as many eminent men . . . believe, the Indians of the American continent are a part of the long lost ten tribes of Israel" (*On Our Own Ground* 106)—Apess writes of the coming return of Christ's spirit, remarkably as a step toward the eventual triumph of racial difference: "The great stumbling block before the chariot of Christianity shall then be removed. The ancient chosen people shall then be no more a scorn and a hissing among men. . . . Earth and hell are not able to accomplish their extermination, or to amalgamate these dispersed people with strange nations" (106).

Amalgamation is extermination. Dispersed Jews have maintained their own distinct identities and communities across history within "strange nations" as a measure of their being chosen by God. His method of animating otherness does not mean homogenizing. Humanity does not mean uniformity by this logic.

He indeed affirms ethnic difference, as he affirms the parallel between the Jews and "the Indians of the American continent." Apess clearly does not want to see Indian community diluted and melted into the hypocritical artificiality and inequity of America. He even invokes divine providence for the preservation of racial difference, as he continues: "Has not one reason [for America's failure to amalgamate the red man] been that it was not the purpose of God that it should be done—for lo, the blood of Israel flowed in the veins of these unshackled, freeborn men?" (*On Our Own Ground* 107). The logic is concise: Indians as free spirits remain separate from corrupt America in their racial difference because they are God's chosen. When America rises to its own dream of freedom, Indians will again stand as "unshackled, freeborn men" because they have been preserved by God in their difference; that is, "it was not the purpose of God" that "the red man of the woods" should amalgamate into "the artificial, cultivated ranks of social life." Apess ratifies difference of both class and race while critiquing and inspiring America to its highest ideals. Such a system of understanding offered him a strategic context larger and an anchoring point deeper than the daily struggles of race and class in early nineteenth-century New England.

"Earth Power Coming": Community in McNickle

D'Arcy McNickle's fiction invokes no Christian vision of biblical community, as in Apess, yet his writings a century later go directly to the animate spirit of humanity in nature that flows through Indigenous community in Apess as well. Pressed by the weight of history, the layers of irony and ambiguity in McNickle's narrative voice are perhaps ultimately impenetrable, and his hope for community, either within or across cultures, remains ambiguous at best. Indeed McNickle's aesthetic of tragic modernism dictates that his ethics of Native cultural resurgence remain uncertain. As modernism's ambiguities must embrace his historical ironies of unvanishing Indians, the challenge to the reader is to understand a Native paradox of continuity as fully as possible. That continuity of community moves in McNickle's quiet but steady affirmation of animism.

To introduce examples, let's review a remarkable tale within a tale in McNickle's *The Surrounded*, not only for his rigorous spirit of openness to both continuity and change but for his clear warning of the violence that grows from simple lack of animate respect. What is telling about the Big Paul episode are the parallels with and differences from our foundational Fool Soldiers story. Both relate strategic attempts at communication across racial and cultural—colonial—boundaries, both with tragic consequences, yet both with a residue of hope. However, with McNickle's aesthetic appetite for violent tragedy, the Big Paul story plays out to an even more brutal conclusion than the Fool Soldiers', amplifying through blood the ironic lack of "co-" in failed communication and failed community across the frontier.

Here is a synopsis, told in the journal of an unreliable narrator, Father Grepilloux, an aged, almost ancient missionary, harking back to the first contacts of the Salish and the Black Robes in the mid-nineteenth century. Some of the names are actual historical figures. Big Paul was one of the sons of old "Nine-Pipe, who was called the Judge, because for many years he had acted as peacemaker in the tribe" (*The Surrounded* 52–53). The missionary calls this second-youngest son "the brightest boy I ever taught in any Indian tribe. It was more than sharpness. His quick mind was only one side of a superior nature" (53). This quality of character apparently shows up in Big Paul's magnanimity and self-sacrifice in dealing with frontier conflicts. Grepilloux goes on to describe the fiasco in which old Nine-Pipe is murdered by drunken whites in reflex revenge for the killing of one of their own disruptive group in an Indian camp. Grepilloux then explains, in his condescending tone, how increasing levels of miscommunication trigger increasing levels of violence.

When his brothers want "to avenge the murder," Big Paul refuses to join in. "When he saw that it was useless to reason, he refused to take part in the affair. 'I tell you this,' he said. 'If you are killed, I will not carry on this foolishness. You will have to die by your own stubbornness. I will help you catch these men and give them to the Indian Agent, but I will not put my own neck in a rope.' The brothers cursed him and made their plans without him" (*The Surrounded* 54–55). Clearly Big Paul's choice for more peaceful reconciliation is not due to timidity, although the "hotbloods . . . called Big Paul and his friends cowards" (56).

What ensues is the dialectically predictable bloodbath, with a particularly unpredictable poignancy to the finale. First, another of Big Paul's brothers ambushes and kills some the remaining white murderers and then hides in the mountains. Eventually Big Paul himself, still standing for the principle of communication, that is, perceiving and respecting the animate consciousness and conscience of the whites, "went to the mining camp, unarmed, alone, and offered himself as a hostage. If his brother were not found and brought to trial, then they could try him instead" (*The Surrounded* 57).

Big Paul's self-sacrifice for cross-racial justice, and for a stop to the killing of his own people, is not unlike that of Martin Charger and the Fool Soldiers, who not only avoided war but ransomed everything they owned and risked their lives in the winter trek to return the white hostages to the soldiers' fort. The bitterness of his own people turning against Big Paul is also not unlike the bitterness of the Lakota Sans Arcs and Two Kettles who ostracized the ones they taunted as "Fool Soldiers." In Grepilloux's account, when Big Paul's culpable brother was caught by "sheer coincidence" and his "own carelessness" and "his battered body" was left "just outside the Indian village," "Big Paul's friends deserted him. He was accused of betraying his brother and his friends were afraid to defend him any longer." Others in the tribe, led by Big Paul's younger brother, "organized to go after him" (*The Surrounded* 56). Here is where the brutality in McNickle's story outpaces the finale of the Fool Soldiers, many of whom lived out their long lives in a separate community. We thus see the absence of community, both within and between cultures, most starkly in McNickle's rendition.

With the whites and his own people gunning for him, Big Paul valiantly fights his way out of a saloon brawl staged by the white miners to kill him, where "he plunged in among them and fought like a madman." As proof that he is no coward, the narrative continues, "Big Paul enjoyed the fight. He was smiling through it. He began to taunt them because they could not overpower him. He cleared a path through the mob and sang his war song as he went singing. He was bleeding from many wounds but he stayed on his feet" (*The Surrounded* 58). Yet when he breaks a window and escapes, still shooting back at his white assailants with one of their revolvers, his younger brother's revenge party arrives outside. "Big Paul staggered toward them through the snow, and without stopping to ask a single question, they fell upon him and stabbed him to death. It is said that every man in the party drove a knife into his wounded body. . . . The feud ended at that" (58).

The Messianic overtones are clear, with Big Paul dying for the sins of others on both sides of the racial divide. The attractiveness of this story to Father Grepilloux is immediately recognizable, although the narrative denouement dismisses the old priest's story of Big Paul as "battered . . . pages in which he had recorded the lost life of a primitive world" (*The Surrounded* 59). We can only speculate, by contrast to the priest's dismissive and patronizing understatement, that the author characterizing this sympathetic but prototypically flawed Black Robe sees more significance in the story of Big Paul. McNickle must include it for thematic resonance, and indeed it dramatizes the dangers, perhaps the foolishness of trying to bridge the cultural communication gap in McNickle's time.

For many readers, that tone of futility structures the violent finales of both of McNickle's novels. They seem to offer either a grim object lesson or a grim prognosis, or both. For McNickle, such a tragic story line measures either the absolute limits or the relative dangers of colonial relations. Both interpretations make a good story.

Yet by looking more closely at some of his other richly layered representations of community and its violent absence, both within Salish society and between Salish and non-Native worlds, it becomes apparent that McNickle avoided such absolutes in favor of relative possibilities. The violence of the Big Paul episode sets those possibilities in clearest contrast.

Horse and Rider

In any attempt at communication and community, the animating principle is precisely animism itself: a speaker assumes a listener, an animate interlocutor. Further, the affirmations of connection in the comic mode of narration, in contrast with the isolation of the tragic mode, assume a certain empathy in that animate consciousness, a responsiveness that will not be an immediate threat. The comic intention of communication is precisely that a conversation should ensue rather than a confrontation. A communicator must expect a responsive exchange of ideas. Because of McNickle's tragic mode, that assumption of communication is what gets characters like Big Paul, Henry Jim, and Archilde in trouble.

Yet in spite of his tragic aesthetic, McNickle uses his own authorial role as storyteller to perpetuate the effects of a comic mode, a mode of survival rather than termination. Thus John Purdy writes of McNickle, "As a storyteller in the written medium of the novel, he felt his voice, and his voice had power to bridge the abyss between cultures" (*Word Ways* 85). To bridge that abyss is ultimately an act of animation, a certain register of animism, the perception of a self in others. In the terms of this discussion, McNickle in that bridging role not only appeals to or invokes the animate consciousness of his non-Native readers; he also effectively animates Native Americans for non-Native readers—while he carefully maps the consciousness of Indians for his Indian readers as a first focus. Thus he generates a literary ecology of speakers and listeners. Some have called this literary process creating one's own audience. Yet the process is more circular. As we saw earlier, the linkage between communication and community on the one hand and narration and animism on the other makes storytelling, even in the catharsis of tragedy, a communal event that affirms an animate universe.

The narrative act by a poet, novelist, or storyteller of building a character, of personifying a voice in a human being, in a tree, in a coyote, in wind, animates the sign system of words and their referents. Animism animates. When McNickle writes Two Sleeps onto the mountain seeking a vision for his people, he not only gives us the old man's consciousness, but he hints at the mind of the mountain and the wind as well: "The winter night came quickly, the storm bringing it on, but he moved even so. Old men who have lived a long time with their own thoughts know how to be at ease with the night. And storms are filled with the voices they wish to hear" (*Wind* 195). Although the world is full of interlocutors, we find as the plot unfolds that those voices don't necessarily say *what* the old man wishes to hear. That autonomy of natural voices only reaffirms their spirited being as perhaps something other than a projection or an anthropocentric mirror. Again, the cognitive act of narrative communication generates animation.

Thus whatever an animistic community consciousness may be in McNickle's view of Native cultures, it is neither sentimental nor anthropocentric. As we see in Two Sleeps's warning, success at connecting with the animate spirits can wreak grievous insight: "I wanted to know everything, to be inside of everything—I thought. But my brothers, that is a terrible thing to want. My heart is already dead" (*Wind* 220). Part of the poignancy of McNickle's prose is that he penetrates into the animistic world of communal consciousness, only to find it shut off from its comic possibilities by the tragedy of colonial closures. Pushing relentlessly against Indian community and its assumptions of animism, historical prejudices de-animate and deny conscious selfhood in the other.

Still, McNickle does give the reader a full sense, however under siege, of that animistic universe, especially amply in *Wind from an Enemy Sky*. In each case, tactile description via a flood of the five senses fulfills a suitable prose technique of vivid detail. Yet we may read in his texts other layers in McNickle's descriptions, layers through the senses of memory, vitality, consciousness, animated spirit, as in this simplest of passages: "These were the men who had ridden with Henry Jim. The fragrance of many campfires, of smoked buckskin, of sage winds filled the room" (83). Here we are in the narrative point of view of The Boy, who straddles uncomfortably the gap between Indian and white worlds and thus may translate. "Jerome, Frank Charley, Iron Child, Baptiste, Tom John, Little Man, Old Charles, Quis-Quis, and Antoine Beauchamp, called Tony . . . came in, one at a time, lifting off their big hats as they crossed the threshold" of the agent's office (83). After the list of names, the "fragrance of many campfires," breathes their presence as an animistic reality to the reader.

One particular animistic epiphany with community resonance for young Antoine occurs on horseback—we may say *because* it is on horseback. It is worth citing not only for its sense of animism and community, but also for the dramatic contrast when McNickle, after affirming that community, lets the horse and rider cross the ideological frontier into the sphere of white intruders. Animism meets intolerance. The phrase "earth power coming" is particularly evocative as it focuses McNickle's animistic understanding of the land:[14] "It was a time of pleasure, to be riding in the early morning air, to feel the drumming earth come upward through the pony's legs and enter his own flesh. Yes, the earth power coming into him as he moved over it" (*Wind* 106). All of the elements of this study are present in this passage and its surrounding lines, crystallized again in that notion of respect. We may read Antoine's authenticity in translating the experience of his body, "to feel the drumming earth come upward through the pony's legs and enter his own flesh," into language that means and reaffirms something culturally to himself, "earth power coming." We may read an identity in change, where he has "already lived among such people and knew the fear," yet he rediscovers himself as "one among his people" in a system of exchange holding both "danger" and "a healing warmth." We may read community, both as "his grandfather's kinsman" and as "a being in flight," "riding in the early morning air" in communion with an animistic earth. And here is sovereignty, a peoplehood, "a power in itself, the power that flows between people and makes them one." Yet all that animated experience might be challenged by a historical irony as he rides into the settlement: "this country of government buildings and government kind of people" who overpower others' voices by their "loud voices" and who de-animate others and isolate them from their community. "They could lock you up in a room and leave you by yourself" (106).

This boy on horseback is riding to face all of his history in the ironies of this moment. He wonders if the authentic identity that he feels in his flesh will be denied as his community's sovereignty continues to be denied. As he wonders whether he will be reduced to "a small body swept into a corner," he registers exactly how thoroughly "his own flesh" that could "feel the drumming earth" might be denied, how his own attunement to the animate forces of the earth can be overwhelmed by other forces deaf to that earth. In the opposite of community, isolated again where "they could lock you up in a room and leave you by yourself," he would be cut off from his animate world.

It is noteworthy also that in the dramatic structure of Antoine's characterization, McNickle has represented the boy just a page earlier as somewhat of an isolated outsider: "He said aloud, but in English, in the manner of a returned student: 'Those Indians don't know what's going on, so it's up to us to find out so I can tell them what to do'" (*Wind* 105). In fact he speaks these alienating words to his horse, "the little mare" that was "his grandfather's gift, to celebrate his coming home from school. She was a trim animal, with black tail and mane, and a forelock that fell forward across the white blaze between her eyes. Her winter coat was coming on and the thickening hair was soft and warm where he ran his hand over her neck and shoulder" (105). The sensuous description of the special horse launches the chapter and will lead to the epiphany on horseback a page later. The fact that his grandmother overhears his outsider's words only serves to begin the process of transforming the outsider status that his upcoming communion will more fully erase. Through the ride on horseback, he comes to feel himself as a first-person Indian instead of setting "those Indians" in third person. He does so by connecting with the animated world through which the horse carries him.

Details of horsemanship throughout *Wind*, some for comic relief, are not mere local color or verisimilitude; they speak to the animate life that is the point of the novel: "The pony preferred not to leave the other horses and she started off at a stiff-legged trot, but Antoine coaxed her, kicked at her ribs and pulled up her head, until at last she blew the frost out of her nostrils and settled into an easy loping stride" (105). The next paragraph then begins with the complex passage cited earlier, "It was a time of pleasure." Through the spirited body of the horse, the boy is coming out of himself into his own communal world.

The horse in McNickle is thus a prevalent expression of his sense of animism. A potent animal symbol of freedom, strength, and reciprocity, especially evocative of a Salish hunter-warrior ethos and culture, the horse receives full play in McNickle's fiction. There are a number of scenes where horses further animate the sense of community in nature that McNickle grieves. The "old mare" episode in *The Surrounded* neatly reverses and complicates the animism and autonomy of horses in an allegory of colonial oppression. Partly because of the symbiotic relationship of horse and rider, this particular vehicle serves well to animate McNickle's fictional world. The intelligence and responsiveness of horses, as well as their will and autonomy, extend beyond their flowing mane and muscles to animate the natural and cultural worlds they have shared so closely with humans.

John Purdy places McNickle, who grew up just as the open range was being fenced by white homesteaders on the Flathead Reservation, at "a focal point where the two ways met", between "two opposing systems of order: one Euramerican and one Native American. One culture vests its power in written, standardized documents that dictate policy. The other exercises its power through traditions of spoken words. . . . Each has its own history, its own ways of perceiving events, and its methods for solving problems" (*Word Ways* 85). This focal point is a useful image for describing not only McNickle but other Native American writers who share his position as translator between cultures. In McNickle's pivotal moment in history, his imagery of the horse works to focus the animate natural world sustaining his people's experience.

Animism in "the Voices They Wish to Hear"

If horses in McNickle offer one of the most direct invocations of animism in the text, there are many other signs in his fiction that open his characters and his readers to a more animate world. The very fictionalized name of McNickle's Salish people, the "Little Elk" nation, near "Elk City," hints at a connection with the animal, the animate, and animism. Two Sleeps contemplates an animate universe during his quest in the mountain snows for a vision: "He had to reach with his mind into all things, the things that grew from small beginnings and the things that stayed firmly placed and enduring" (*Wind* 197–98). The novel even begins with a challenge to animism, in Bull's seemingly naïve assertion that the white man cannot dam the water: "They can't stop water. Water just swallows everything and waits for more. That's the way with water. . . . The big machines will just fall into the water and the water will still be hungry" (1). The elemental substance of water has desire and hunger, even patience and its own "way" for Bull. This passage on the opening page poses the key dramatic principle, the tragic opposition, the question of the novel: Can an animate universe of spirit be destroyed by the de-animating and dehumanizing forces of modern culture?

McNickle's representations in *Wind* of an animate world become quite explicit in the dialogue of some key characters, notably Bull, Two Sleeps, Henry Jim, and Dr. Edwards. Let's look at the foregrounded juxtaposition that McNickle sets up between Bull and Henry Jim. We will find in their conflict and reconciliation some more clarity from McNickle about community and animism.

Henry Jim, trying to set right his lifelong mistakes before he dies, articulates some of the most explicit theory of community in McNickle's fiction, although his views are always tinged dramatically and ironically in the novel by his former failures as "the 'runaway' kinsman" (*Wind* 112). He speaks in the lodge with his brother Bull of his own error in relation to the community. We hear a group vision restrengthened through loss: "In those days I had the foolish thought that a man stands by himself, that his kinsmen are no part of him. I did not go first to my uncles and my brothers and talk it over with them. The government man said how it should be, and I listened to him. . . . It went that way for a long time. I didn't notice it at first, but one day I could see that I was all alone" (117). The old man comes to realize that the strategic choice for colonial resistance and survival is not between the new or the old ways, but between staying together or not.

Later he explains the value that his people sustained: "I didn't understand that at first; I thought the people were just spiteful because they would not follow. Now I see why they were afraid and why they held back. They knew it would split us up; some could do it and some could not, and those that refused to go would be left behind with nothing—no game, no wheat. In their hearts they were saying, 'We'll just all starve together.' Today, I'm glad it went that way. The people stayed together—I was the only one who left the camp" (*Wind* 126). The point remains community. James Clifford uses the term *exchange* for Indigenous interactions that make solitary "identity" more flexible, where "stories of contact, resistance, and assimilation appear from the standpoint of groups in which exchange rather than identity is the fundamental value to be sustained" (*The Predicament of Culture* 344). Henry Jim's error was not so much his trying to farm as his leaving the camp, his failure to sustain that fundamental value: "The people stayed together."

Climbing toward death, Henry Jim is learning Two Sleeps's lesson from the mountain, as the visionary says: "But a man learned much in a lifetime, including one special thing. Above all else, a man learned to be strong in support of his kinsmen. A man by himself was nothing, a shout in the wind. But men together, each acting for each other and as one—even a strong wind from an enemy sky had to respect their power" (*Wind* 197). Here is Two Sleeps's positive spin on the ominous title. The "strong wind from an enemy sky" is not overwhelming; it "had to respect their power" if they dedicated themselves to each other, each "in support of his kinsmen." Life-and-death moments bring the value of such support into sharpest focus.

Vine Deloria Jr. writes even of "the communal nature of death in the tribal context": "Again we see the fundamental conception of life as a continuing unity involving land and people. One might be tempted to suggest that as land is held by the community, the psychic unity of all the worlds is made real. We are not faced with formless and homeless spirits in this idea but with an ordered and purposeful creation in which death merely marks a passage from one form of experience to another. Rather than fearing death, tribal religions see it as an affirmation of life's reality" (*God Is Red* 174). Henry Jim's communal passing is indeed "an affirmation of life's reality," of his return before the end of the story to the culture of the beginning. Through his kinsmen's supportive singing, "the psychic unity of all the worlds is made real" by marking his "passage from one form of experience to another." His spirit regains its purpose as he reconnects with his "land and people," and certainly he does not fear death. He is "held by the community" that holds the land in their hearts, and his death finds his place in "an ordered and purposeful creation." We looked at Two Sleeps's evocative lines of being "strong in support of his kinsmen" in the discussion of sovereignty, of peoplehood, and it is clear here that Henry Jim has learned his communal lesson, the hard way, to dedicate himself to his people.

For all his faith in an animistic world, Bull is clear even about his own disengagement from it. In fact his anger and alienation serve only to reinforce by absence the force of those voices, partly because he knows how the intruders deny those voices in his own people. In his own humility, he sees clearly how colonialism denies an animate reciprocity across the racial divide of the frontier:

> That was when the anger settled and turned into rock. It had come first when these men from across the world, from he knew not where, had told him that he could not have his own country, that he no longer belonged in it. They would make it into a better country and let him have just a small piece of it. He wouldn't need a big piece because it would be easier to live in the new country. These mountains, trees, streams, the earth and the grass, from which his people learned the language of respect—all of it would pass into the hands of strangers, who would dig into it, chop it down, burn it up. . . . They were a people without respect, but they managed to get what they wanted. (*Wind* 130–31)

These "men from across the world" respect nothing not their own and therefore have never learned the language of respect, the language of listening. They lack the reciprocity to hear "these mountains, trees, streams, the earth and the grass." Here again Bull echoes Winnemucca's Paiute respect, that foundational value of community that looks again, re-spects another in animate perception.

Yet Bull knows that his own anger interferes with these values, for it essentially denies animism as it denies respect. What one respects is the value of animating spirit. As Bull says of himself to Henry Jim, his older brother, who hurt him by leading the people away from their ways, "But visions never come to an angry man" (*Wind* 21). In anger one denies the humanity, the selfhood of the rock, the tree, the water, the other. Yet Bull's anticolonial anger at the dam's builders is a reflection of their seeing him as inhuman. After he fires his rifle impotently at the dam, he proclaims these words of anger at inhumanity itself: "Then the angry words came, almost shouted: 'I am a man walking this earth! Who is the creature who built that thing of rock and stopped the water? Is he two-legged like other men? Or is he a monster first-man, who decides things in his own way? Why should he do this to me? I have not offended him. How could I, when I don't know his name?'" (7). The anger is at being treated as a nonhuman, at having to reassert the fundamental fact of respect, that "I am a man walking this earth!"[15]

Bull's pronouncement follows a number of contextual passages about communal animism as the grandfather and Antoine approach the dam: "It had been a holy place, this mountain-locked meadow. 'Be careful what you do here,' the boy had been told by his relatives. 'This is a place of power. Be careful what you think. Keep your thoughts good.' He was just old enough to walk by himself on that first visit, and it was important that he begin to understand the proper way to behave. 'Don't have angry thoughts here,' he was told" (*Wind* 5–6). The very thoughts that animate the place must be full of respect. Yet the grandson witnesses his grandfather's shame: "The boy Antoine saw this happen in bright sunshine, and while he could not understand all of it, he knew how terrible it was. A man alone, with bare hands and a gun. And the man was his grandfather. . . . What would happen? In this place, where one had been told not to have angry thoughts?" (7). The animate voices themselves cannot connect with angry thoughts because such thoughts deny the animate validity of others. The fact that Antoine in Bull's tepee was able to connect with Henry Jim's humanity, despite the angry thoughts of the grown men of camp, bodes well for a future of this community.

Fittingly Bull's self-reflection is able to recognize and protect the potential in his grandson, protecting Antoine even from the grandfather's anger. After his own outburst, Bull's gentle guidance to his grandson remembers the future: "Just the same, you will remember what happened today. After a while, you will understand it. The white man makes us forget our holy places. He makes us small" (*Wind* 9). He makes us small by not respecting our humanity, our agency, our animate spirit.

In a more provisional expression of animism, Bull has another poignant comment that poses one of the few expressions of his slight hopefulness in the novel. After an exchange of condolences with Geneva and Thomas Cooke, newly arrived from the East to retrieve the body of their slain son, Bull says in Salish to The Boy, "These people are polite. Maybe in that country they come from they make a different kind of white people" (*Wind* 161). Here is the faintest glimmer of community through a glimmer of reciprocal, animate respect.

"What the Earth's Spirits Wanted": Community in Silko

The spirit of animism that flows as an undercurrent in the writings of McNickle, Winnemucca, and Apess rises to the surface in Silko's work to writhe and strike like a water snake. Her animistic world is present with an immediacy of myth that implicates every narrative action and idea: "A giant water snake named 'Ma'sh'ra'tru'ee' lived in the beautiful lake which was connected to the four worlds below and which allowed the gentle snake to travel down below. Down there, clear streams run all year round, and flowers are everywhere because Mother Creator is there. The snake was a messenger who carried the prayers of the people to the Mother Creator below" (*Sacred Water* 23–24). Silko's literary sense of animism embodied in snakes, other creatures, in the very land and sky, even in machines like guns and knives made from the earth, can be benign or fierce, or both. "The forces were harsh. A great many people would suffer and die. . . . All the spirits ate blood that was offered to them" (*Almanac* 511–12). In comparison with the writers we looked at earlier, Silko's representations of this animate power move from active background to active foreground. Apess invoked "justice and humanity" to "melt the prejudice" of American hearts; Winnemucca tried "pleading for God and for humanity"; and McNickle tentatively followed the visions of an old man in "the voices they wish to hear" for a sense of community survivance. Silko, however, openly proclaims an animistic view. Following Native writers of generations before, she makes clear that the survival of Indian community builds on a fundamental sense of animism. El Feo muses in *Almanac*, "The Spirits of the Night and the Spirits of the Day would take care of the people" (523). These animistic spirits are the essence of Indian community, "the people," in Silko's work.

Such a mythic presence in Silko's world takes many forms, functionally animating the world by providing a common denominator that translates mythic potency to material beings: "Rattlesnakes sense the approach of summer rainstorms, and they emerge to join the horned lizards, tortoises, tarantulas and the red-spotted toads—all of them waiting for the rain. The coyotes have a particular ecstatic howl they give for the rain; the curved-beak thrashers and cactus wrens also have special rain songs. The red-spotted toads carry on with their singing all night after a summer rain storm" (*Sacred Water* 30). Her picture of "all of them waiting for the rain" presents an image of shared, conscious attention that is the heart of Silko's sense of community, human and other-than-human. "Tribal clans acknowledge the kinship between human beings and other beings" (58).

To register this kinship, her animate system has several salient aspects in the passage of "waiting for the rain." The various creatures unite in waiting for what in Silko's Laguna terms would be a spiritual gift of rain in material form. In an expressive world those creatures are active and animated: they "emerge," they "join" each other, "they *give*" their howls and songs "*for* the rain," and they actively wait. Further, any perception of this animistic sphere comes through precise observations of that material world: "a particular ecstatic howl" of coyotes, the "special rain songs" of curved-beak thrashers and cactus wrens. This attention in the observer matches attention in the observed, both "waiting for the rain" of life-giving reciprocity. To apply David Abram's terms, which we will explore further below, the circle of reciprocal perception and intricate participation is a paradigm of natural animism.

"The 'Electricity' of a Being's Spirit"

Mother Creator imagery animates Silko's chapbook *Sacred Water*, self-published in 1993 when she "was tired of the big publishers after the book tours"

(80) for *Almanac of the Dead* (1991). This small collection of photographs and journal entries resonates with the gentle, almost idyllic tone of some passages in her subsequent novel, *Gardens in the Dunes* (1999). Silko presents the Mother Destroyer as well. What unites their different manifestations is the same principle that unites the coyotes, wrens, and red-spotted toads: "The energy or 'electricity' of a being's spirit was not extinguished by death; it was set free from the flesh. Dust to dust or as a meal for pack rats, the energy of the spirit was never lost. Out of the dust grew the plants; the plants were consumed and became muscle and bone; and all the time the energy had only been changing form, nothing had been lost or destroyed" (*Almanac* 719). The changing forms of energy animate "a being's spirit." In Silko's cosmos, in both fiction and memoir, the focus on that "energy of the spirit" moves her narratives beyond imbalances of tragedy to the larger equilibrium where "nothing had been lost or destroyed." The austere faith in community survivance that drives Silko's work arises out of this animistic alternating current, this cycle of electricity. It is stern and tough-minded because electricity is not personal.

As explicit as she is about that force that drives the body electric, her prose returns repeatedly to the reassurance of its life-giving power, wherever it must be respected, as Tacho ponders in *Almanac*: "Knives, guns, even automobiles, possessed 'energies' that craved blood from time to time.... Even fire had to be fed the first bit of dough or fat; otherwise, sooner or later, the fire would burn the cook or flare up and catch the kitchen on fire. Airplanes, jets, and rockets were already malfunctioning, crashing and exploding. Electricity no longer obeyed the white man. The macaw spirits said the great serpent was in charge of electricity. The macaws were in charge of fire" (512). Evidently the white man fails to respect the energy living in the natural resources of a technological age: "They failed to recognize the earth was their mother" (258). If "the snake was a messenger who carried the prayers of the people to the Mother Creator below," it appears to be the translator of prayers because of the common "energy of the spirit" or electricity in the prayerful words themselves. In Silko's context here, prayer, a verbal, emotional, spiritual gesture of communion or communication, like physical gestures of blood sacrifice or of feeding "the first bit of dough or fat" to the fire, is a reflexive mark of attention, of re-spect, a reciprocal indication that one recognizes an animate presence outside oneself.

From *The Spell of the Sensuous: Perception and Language in the More-than-Human World*, here is David Abram's take on such a process growing out of oral language use:

> In the untamed world of direct sensory experience *no* phenomenon presents itself as utterly passive or inert. To the sensing body *all* phenomena are animate, actively soliciting the participation of our senses, or else withdrawing from our focus and repelling our involvement. Things disclose themselves to our immediate perception as vectors, as styles of unfolding—not as finished chunks of matter given once and for all, but as dynamic ways of engaging the senses and modulating the body. Each thing, each phenomenon, has the power to reach us and to influence us. Every phenomenon, in other words, is potentially expressive. (81)

In the animated perceptual world of oral expression, everything speaks, and one listens to everything for its mutual message, whether rain, friend, enemy, food, or song. Abram explains this reciprocal perception to a readerly audience who might still see the world as dead text: "It is by a complementary shift of attention that one may suddenly come to hear the familiar song of a blackbird or a thrush in a surprisingly new manner—not just as a pleasant melody repeated mechanically, as on a tape player in the background, but as active, meaningful speech" (*The Spell of the Sensuous* 81). A world that speaks is a world one cannot afford to ignore. The resulting "shift of attention" allows animate consciousness not only to the beholder but to the beauty and terror of the world as well.

Yet in Silko the register of animate consciousness, as it expands across historical and mythical time and across planetary geographies, remains grounded in specific community, again in clans. Her first book, *Laguna Woman*, invokes her own clan's place and local stories from its title to its last line of poetry. Her first novel, *Ceremony*, traces the agonies of a young half-breed to find his place in his small, contested family unit on southwestern desert land, as that clan is buffeted by the global violence of World War II and by the American legacies of conquest. Her autobiographical cross-genre collection, *Storyteller*, is a celebration of her particular family links to Laguna pueblo and its images in photography and story. Her magnum opus, *Almanac of the Dead*, traces a clan of keepers of the Almanac across generations and centuries. Her later novel, *Gardens in the Dunes*, follows the opposite and interpenetrating journeys of two women, one Native American and the other Euro-American, to reconnect with their clan sisters on their respective Indigenous myth-lands, precolonial America and pre-Christian Europe. Her memoir, *Turquoise Ledge*, walks the ground of her southwestern home. Silko writes with that sense, as Abram put it, wherein "every phenomenon . . . is potentially expressive," or, as Silko put it, less benignly, everything "possessed 'energies' that craved blood from time to time."

Silko's descriptions of spirits in an animate universe gradually do take on a more benign presence, as here in *Sacred Water*, continuing her description of Laguna: "On All Souls Day, November 2, the people take oven bread and red chile stew to the graves to feed the spirits of the dead. All these feedings of the spirits were conducted with such tenderness and love, that as a child, I learned there is nothing to fear from the dead. They love us and they bless us when they return as rain clouds" (17). Rain cloud ancestors are one of many notable expressions of animism throughout pueblo and other Native cultures, from the Hopi rain gods to the Assiniboine *oyate mahpiya* (cloud people). As animism gains center stage, Silko's affirmation of community knows, again, "no boundaries, only transitions through all distances and time." Although that resonant line from *Ceremony* occurs in the context of witchery's master plan of destruction, Silko's animism evidently moves from "tenderness and love" through the witchery, and eventually toward a more sanguine sense of "nothing to fear from the dead."

The connections Silko draws between human beings and the spirits function to enlarge human possibility as they enlarge human community. When we identify with the land and sky, we draw on power. Calabazas explains this sense of empowerment across the Sonoran desert:

We don't believe in boundaries. Borders. Nothing like that. We are here thousands of years before the first whites. We are here before maps or quit claims. We know where we belong on this earth. We have always moved freely. North-south. East-west. We pay no attention to what isn't real. Imaginary lines. . . . We have always had the advantage because this country is ours—it's our backyard. We know it in the black of night. We know it in the July heat of hell. The gringos come in and the going for us gets rough. But we just get tougher. That's how it's always been. (*Almanac* 218)

What isn't real to Calabazas are the gringos' imaginary frontiers: "imaginary lines." According to his Indigenous values, if "we know where we belong on this earth," then "we have always had the advantage." Because the land and the people are a single animate community, "no one stops us."

Further, according to Silko, if humans do fail to identify with the land, that power nonetheless remains for people to reidentify with: "But human beings desecrate only themselves; the Mother Earth is inviolable" (*Sacred Water* 76). In this direct echo from *Almanac of the Dead*, we see how the affirmation of an animate earth sustains Silko's thinking about Indian community. In a radical identification with an animate earth, it is collective animism itself that survives, whether or not in individual human form: "One human lifetime wasn't much; it was over in a flash. Conjunctions and convergences of global proportions might require six or seven hundred years to develop" (*Almanac* 618). If animate community is the reality, it offers an acute hope, a sense of power: "Despite all of Yoeme's lying and boasting, the 'almanac' was truly a great legacy. Yoeme and others believed the almanac had living power within it, a power that would bring all the tribal people of the Americas together to retake the land" (569). The animate earth itself holds the people's highest hopes.

Thus "waiting for the rain," as an image of the prayerful communion of animate life in the desert, translates passive waiting through a hopeful sense of community survivance into a radical redefinition of activism. The body politic of activist community then takes a new shape as well. When time itself is animate, when the days are gods, waiting through those days and years and centuries is a communal balancing act to "retake the land." Silko is quite explicit about the interlinking of time and space, of years and the land itself. This equation adds up to her Indian community's feeling that the land is on their side, that change will eventually come round their way: "The only true gods were all the days in the Long Count, and no single epoch or time of a world was vast enough or deep enough to call itself God alone. All the ancestors had understood nothing stayed fixed in the universe" (*Almanac* 257–58). Thus the Almanac has to do with recounting the activities of these gods who were the days, whereby "nothing stayed fixed." The patience of the old ones is a patience of counting those days, without assuming one can count them all. In keeping track of the days, in "waiting for the rain," one is performing the most efficacious action available until the cycle comes round again. "Politics didn't add up. In the end only the Earth remained, and they'd all return to her as dust. . . . El Feo himself did not worry. History was unstoppable. The days, years, and centuries were spirit beings who traveled the universe, returning endlessly. The Spirits of the Night and the Spirits of the Day would take care of the people" (*Almanac* 523).[16]

Another key expression of Silko's explicit description of a communal faith in animism arises in *Almanac*'s focus on dreams: "The battle would be won or lost in the realm of dreams" (475). Here again is a realm animated by imagery and sound, by expressive ethereal being, and it is here where "history was unstoppable": "Tacho recalled the arguments people in villages had had over the eventual disappearance of the white man. Old prophets were adamant; the disappearance would not be caused by military action, necessarily, or by military action alone. The white man would someday disappear all by himself. The disappearance had already begun at the spiritual level" (511). Once it is in motion "at the spiritual level," the outcome seems "unstoppable."

In a quite Hegelian view of a dialectic of spiritual and material history, Silko's *Almanac* foregrounds the "realm of dreams," the spiritual, as the initiator, the thesis, to which the material workings of the world respond as antithesis: "The Barefoot Hopi's entire philosophy was to wait; a day would come as had not been seen in five thousand years. On this day, a conjunction would occur; everywhere at once, spontaneously, the prisoners, the slaves, and the dispossessed would rise up. The urge to rise up would come to them through their dreams. All at once, all over the world, police and soldiers would be outnumbered" (617). *Almanac* hinges on this view of dreams, the realm of animated pure expression, as the energy, the electricity of history. The reassurance for Indian community is imperturbable: "It made no difference because what was coming was relentless and inevitable; it might require five or ten years of great violence and conflict. It might require a hundred years of spirit voices and simple population growth, but the result would be the same: tribal people would retake the Americas; tribal people would retake ancestral land all over the world. This was what the earth's spirits wanted: her Indigenous children who loved her and did not harm her" (712). This dream will be "won or lost in the realm of dreams."

Whether or not Silko is committed to a particular scenario wherein "the prisoners, the slaves, and the dispossessed would rise up" or to revolution by "simple population growth," her manifesto of Indian survivance through animism builds toward a remarkable community mixing Indians, Mexicans, blacks, Koreans, and many others, even whites. "Nothing could be black only or brown only or white only anymore. The ancient prophecies had foretold a time when the destruction by man had left the earth desolate, and the human race was itself endangered. This was the last chance the people had against the Destroyers, and they would never prevail if they did not work together as a common force. . . . A day was coming when each human being, man, woman, and child, could do something, and each contribution no matter how small would generate great momentum because they would be acting together" (*Almanac* 747). In her work the prime factor of animistic respect for the earth and for each other generates such a community that would foster a society of "Indigenous children who loved" and "did not harm" the land.

The revolutionary community she envisions goes beyond the communism of the past century and a half precisely in this animistic difference: "Poor Engels and Marx! . . . They had been close, but they hadn't quite got it. They had been on the right track with their readings on Native American communal economies and cultures. For Europeans, they had been far ahead of their time; they had been close, but they still hadn't got it quite right. They had not understood that the earth was mother to all beings, and they had not understood anything about the spirit beings" (*Almanac* 749). The larger dialogics of the earth, the ground, transcends the dialectics of classic Marxist analysis. Her explicit inward focus on "the spirit beings" animates Silko's outward focus on a community that understands that the earth is in fact "mother to all beings," even Marxists.

"Tribal Ties": Community in Alexie

"Whatever happened to the tribal ties, the sense of community?" is an explicit question in Alexie's short story "This Is What It Means to Say Phoenix, Arizona" (in *The Lone Ranger and Tonto* 74) As the germ of Alexie's popular film, *Smoke Signals*, the story introduces the conflicted characters

Thomas and Victor and poignantly resolves that central question—and their conflict—through Victor's recognition that "he owed Thomas something, anything" (74). Between these same characters, and adding others from the Spokane Reservation, the principle of community as animist field becomes a matter for endless play in the novel *Reservation Blues*. Not only are wannabes and more-Indian-than-thou's ironized across and within racial boundaries, but identities dead and alive play across time, with nineteenth-century bluecoats of the Indian wars in confessional dialogue with twentieth-century Native shamans and storytellers, who also are in dialogue with rock stars, with the classic Delta Blues man Robert Johnson, and with quite animate contemporary ghosts in comically grotesque cameos. The effect is a mythic, or virtual, community of animate souls struggling to extricate themselves from the oppressive limits of global history.

Big Mom wields maternal and mythic influences on modern music in the novel, and thereby on the modern psyche. Her presence and witness at America's atrocities regenerate and rewrite history, where slaughtered horses scream in the heart of American blues and rock and roll. In the textual trajectory of plot and characterization, that poignant, animist universe, as context, embraces a more conflicted pragmatics, we may say dramatics, of community building. Conflicted questions of community drive the narrative among the members of the rock band Coyote Springs, between that young group and its Spokane Reservation population, and between Indians and whites as clergy, bureaucrats, music producers, townspeople, and wider audience. Interplay around the question of community indeed generates the plot of the novel, and we may trace those dynamics through the same two sets of community relations that map Native humor itself: outgroup and ingroup.

A continual sense of outgroup animism emerges mythopoetically in the timeless relations of Big Mom within the musical heartbeat of America and also within the confessional agonies of the nineteenth-century general who repressed the Spokane people and slaughtered their horses. The contemporary New York City music producer George Wright from Cavalry Records morphs across time with U.S. cavalry general George Wright of the nineteenth century. Eventually and appropriately that cavalry cannot come to the rescue of the Indian band from their own dysfunction. However, a deeper connection emerges along the way as General Wright confesses and is shriven by a maternal figure who also blurs the distinction between the general's wife and Big Mom:

> She patted his head as he wept and remembered all those horses who had screamed in that field so long ago. He remembered shooting that last colt while Big Mom watched from the rise.
>
> "I was the one," Wright said to his wife. "I was the one. I was the one who killed them all. I gave the orders."
>
> The horses screamed in his head.
>
> "Shh," Margaret whispered. "It's okay. I forgive you. . . . You've come home. . . . You're home now." (*Reservation Blues* 270–71)

By narrating the violent white oppressor's recognition of culpability and his remorse across the centuries, the novel effectively animates all of the parties on "both sides" of the Indian wars, old and new. The frontier melts into the ground of "home," a place of humanity and community. It is quite a tall order for an almost farcical tale, but that is the dynamic Alexie achieves here.

A complex example of ingroup community building occurs when the rock band Coyote Springs, the microcosm of Indian community in the novel, first drives into Seattle for a gig. Their ingroup solidarity is crystallized against the outgroup environment, generating an effective dialectic tension across racial divisions to be transcended in the plot by the more mythic threads of the narrative:

> The van drove into downtown and found a Super 8 Motel right next to the Pink Elephant Car Wash. Coyote Springs all strained their necks to look at everything: the Space Needle, the Olympic and Cascade mountains, the ocean. None of them had ever visited Seattle before, so the sheer number of people frightened them. Especially the number of white people.
>
> "Jeez," Victor said, "no wonder the Indians lost. Look at all these whites." (*Reservation Blues* 133)

Against the alienations of history, even their vehicle, "the van," plays an animate role in the narrative, perhaps like the car-as-Indian-pony in *Smoke Signals*, as it seems to drive itself. Across the small-town history of their personality conflicts, and especially of Victor's and Junior's lifelong harassment of Thomas, their common musical purpose, proving themselves to both their Indian and non-Indian worlds, is bringing their small community together. The plot registers this emerging internal solidarity in dialogue directly following the passage above, when they wonder if their promoters will be paying for the Super 8:

> "Shit," Victor said, "shouldn't those guys at the Backboard be paying for all of this anyway?"
>
> "Yeah, they probably should," Chess said, forced to agree with Victor for the very first time. (*Reservation Blues* 133)

This gradual resolution of internal conflicts again toggles back and forth with a focus on the outgroup race relations, as the band members move through a farcical set of miscues with the clerk behind the motel desk: "Up to that point, how many desk clerks had seen a group of long-haired Indians carrying guitar cases?" (*Reservation Blues* 133) "'Cash then,' Victor said. 'What Indian has a goddamn credit card?' 'Are you guys in a band?' 'Damn right,' Victor said. 'What do you think we have in these cases? Machine guns? Bows and arrows?'" (134).

The ironic repartee generates humor, thus a sense of animate intelligence, thus humanity, even in Victor, whose prickly temper in fact speaks for all of the band in this situation. Yet the blistering ironies in this dialectic also have the ironic effect of humanizing the clerk, "a white guy in his twenties, a part-time business student at the University of Washington," mainly by exposing his vulnerability, a kind of innocent ignorance in the face of Victor's instantly incisive ideological critique. Alexie steers away from sentimentality in this briefly animist glimpse of the pitiful clerk by then having him mouth a line echoing the refrain of a running joke in the novel. This is at least the third instance in which a white official asks, "Which one of you is the lead singer?" (*Reservation Blues* 134), a classic projection by whites of hierarchical individuality onto a Native dynamic of community. Here it throws into relief the increased sense of ingroup cohesion, an animist community, that has been developing within the band.

The final scene of *Reservation Blues*, however, carefully complicates the questions of community by refusing closure while assuming a finale. A close look may see the animist community still in play, as some of the central characters explicitly affirm their survivance—after Junior's suicide and with Victor now "trying to drink himself to death" (305). Under "a song of mourning that would become a song of celebration: we have survived, we have survived" (306), even the slaughtered horses live on as shadows: "In the blue van, Thomas, Chess, and Checkers sang together. They were alive; they'd keep living. They sang together with the shadow horses: we are alive, we'll keep living. Songs were waiting for them up there in the dark. Songs were waiting for them in the city. Thomas drove the car through the dark. He drove. Checkers and Chess reached out of their windows and held tightly to the manes of those shadow horses running alongside the blue van" (306).

As the former band members drive off the reservation for good, the living spirits of the dead ponies "were following, leading Indians toward the city, while other Indians were traditional dancing in the Longhouse after the feast, while drunk Indians stood outside the Trading Post, drinking and laughing" (*Reservation Blues* 306). Thomas and his friends evidently do not lose that primary connection to the shadow horses on Native ground. Is it a nostalgic fantasy or an animist reality? Alexie leaves such questions to resonate in the reader's mind and heart.

"Justice and Humanity"

Our study of animism in Native American stories of community ultimately erases the divide between nature and culture to reveal a community that makes the two terms one.[17] This dynamic is most explicit in our writers' relations to "the land," the "setting," where ground theory reveals how stories of Native American "cultural" community are rooted in or struggling to recover a "natural" community—that is, the land's language. That new space of nature *and* culture resonates with all the binaries of American history and identity: civilization and wilderness, white and colored, and so on. The animistic deconstruction of these two linguistic constructs, revealing their interpenetrations and fluid borders, plays through many other fictional and nonfictional literary features as well, in point of view, characterization, plot, symbol, or diction.

Thus as Apess argued for Indigenous rights to the land, he not only shifted his point of view animistically through all the available pronominal voices, but he made those identity linkages while appealing to a larger community of principle: "Justice and humanity for the remaining few." His radical politics of nullification, built on the affirmation of Native humanity, as in *Eulogy on King Philip*, still pushes toward tribal sovereignty against American principles of hierarchy in community. Because of his political purpose, Apess's Christian individualism and personal responsibility return his analysis to public qualities of character. Thus again his critical phrase "the spirit of avarice and usurpation of power" presages Silko's witchery, especially in Apess's description, "that has brought people in all ages to hate and devour each other." The tragedy of lost community in Apess is indeed the cultural sin of lovelessness.

Similarly Winnemucca's desperate appeal bridges and blends numerous discursive communities of the late nineteenth century: the domestic feminine, the frontier military, the Western journalistic, the federal bureaucratic, the ideal democratic. Her autobiographical narrative recounts the agonies of American imperialism in their moment, as the westward wagon trail rolled directly through her homeland. Against the sexual brutalities of renegade frontiersmen, she appealed to the purity of "womanhood" to leverage political support for her tribal rights. Against the corruptions of "the Indian Ring" she rallied righteous reinforcement through the newspapers and her lecture tours. Against the patent injustices of land-grabbers, she lobbied for democratic distribution of land for the Paiute people. Her fundamental invocation of mutual respect demanded a recognition of animate presence across the frontier. All of these efforts expressed both an equation of personal and tribal sovereignty, while they reached across America's racial divide to establish the solidarity of community in an animate humanity. The simultaneously sad and enthusiastic echoes of her grandfather Truckee could not help but reverberate among their "white brothers."

What is equally sad in Winnemucca's personal story is her own eventual alienation and isolation from her Paiute people. Her narrative ends with the failure of community and the tragic success of racial polarity. Betrayed by her "white brothers," for whom she worked as an Army interpreter, she is identified by the Paiutes as one of the betrayers, in a classic example of killing the messenger. The Fool Soldiers are always sent away. Yet Winnemucca's strategic narration of the positive experience of that one BIA agent, Samuel Parrish, points to the arbitrary, willful nature of racial polarization rather than any historical inevitability. Thus in spite of her own and her people's losses, her narrative holds the door open to American community.

If the imagery of horses in McNickle offers one of his most visible invocations of animism, there are many other signs in his fiction that open his characters and his readers to a more animate world, thus to a wider community. McNickle drives a verbal road through early twentieth-century American community with his complex characterizations of Native and non-Native Americans. By offering the nuanced humanity of so many primary and secondary characters in his novels from both "sides" of the racial divide, and by revealing the full array of their weaknesses and strengths, McNickle dramatizes the lack of community in America even while he helps the reader envision a new possibility. As American Indians became American citizens, McNickle built on that political franchise to flesh out their humanity, thus potentially strengthening the American body politic.

Indeed in this look at the community dynamics of animism, a first reading of McNickle senses its opposite: the violent denial of common humanity, both across and within racial groups. It is noteworthy that Apess and Winnemucca, both writing while wars and pitched battles still raged between whites and Indians in America, each downplayed violence in their nonfiction, while McNickle, writing decades after the Indian wars had moved from the battlefields to the courts and Congress, built his fictional narratives around moments of violence between Indians and whites. Silko follows McNickle in this focus on violence. In their nineteenth-century nonfiction, both Apess and Winnemucca avoided dramatizing direct violence. Their narratives placed violence at the far end of a spectrum of miscommunication between the races. McNickle, inheriting a world where white imperial violence had even more thoroughly institutionalized that miscommunication and dominance, dramatized that violent undercurrent in his fiction as the narrative core of race relations.

Thus McNickle's narratives are caught to some extent in the oppositional frontier paradigm of which violence is the ultimate expression. As opposition becomes hierarchy, and as hierarchy becomes dispossession and oppression, violence becomes its narrative beginning and end. Appropriately *The Surrounded* ends in the violence of shackles: "Archilde, saying nothing, extended his hands to be shackled" (297). *Wind from an Enemy Sky* begins with the violence done to a river—"They stopped the water"—then proliferates into a single, murderous rifle shot, and eventually explodes into a not quite classic western shootout, with a martyr's sacrifice at the finale. After the point-blank bullet to the heart, the novel ends with a Yeatsian mythic song: "No meadowlarks sang, and the world fell apart." In McNickle, unlike writers of the western genre, this is not a regeneration through violence.

Writing at the opposite end of a century filled with the global violence of the corporate war machine, Silko, like McNickle, locates violence at the heart of the problem. Yet she universalizes and mythologizes it as the bloody oppositionality of witchery behind both whites and Indians. Unlike McNickle, Silko envisions in her fiction a wider alternative that returns to a kind of communication, a solidarity of witness, keeping the Almanac, against self-destructive violence itself. Once the explosive pattern that McNickle recounted expands to a global scale, the insanity of its mutually assured destruction comes clearer in Silko's narratives. In the post–World War II context of The Bomb, her rhetorical approach to the five principles of national identity takes another turn not available to McNickle, Winnemucca, or Apess. United by affliction on a planetary scale that could threaten life itself, the cross-cultural community logic of the Fool Soldiers begins to come more clearly into focus.

Alexie's driving ironies push that sense of deterritorialized community further still, toward the urban, but it remains communal, appropriately conflicted, and animist nonetheless. As the shadow horses run beside the van leaving the reservation (and its blues), the narration provides neutral observations of two factions, remaining traditionals and drunks, dancing and laughing separately. Differences within the Indian community play out here, just as they did for the Fool Soldiers, and the narrative voice itself unites them in their various afflictions. The ground of their spirits never leaves, wherever they go on the outstretched land. "They sang together with the shadow horses: we are alive, we'll keep living. Songs were waiting for them in the city."

3

THE SOUL OF THE INDIAN IS IMMORTAL

Identity as Change

If the question of identity must involve the ever changing cycles of selfhood and otherness, of interaction between the body and the world, those cycles may seem to represent broad enough categories for analysis of identity to extend in those terms across cultures. Yet immediately different cultural meanings come into play among such categories and distinctions as self and other, body and world, individual and group.

Identity studies across cultures become themselves a cycle of changing boundaries of analysis and projection. If *group* and *individual* are terms for analysis, we must acknowledge how, in a "group-oriented" versus in an "individually oriented" society, the term *individual* partakes of *group* dynamics differently, and vice versa. Discussing these terms, my students often overlook the critical point that the same "individual" is not participating in the same "group" across the spectrum. The terms beg for definition, perhaps to the extent that *group* and *individual*, even *self* and *other*, are no longer workable terms.

Given such revolving constraints, we may proceed incrementally to understand identity comparatively across cultures, but it is this very circular dynamic of group and individual, other and self, balanced differently in different cultures, that makes the question of identity both so necessary and so difficult to handle as to become hackneyed and even banal. Ground theory offers what remains, what is always there for identity to stand on, the humus that makes the human, the circle that gives life.

Let us say, simply, that identity is elusive by definition. It emerges from desire and curiosity, fear and insecurity, nudging cycles of interaction between "self and other" toward a sense of integrity or coherence, or pathologically as disintegration and incoherence, all within cultural forms. To survive and thrive, the self must have developed a perceiving eye; it must have accumulated a symbolic vocabulary to describe its perceptions; and, crucially, it must have decided on a set of values by which to discriminate among those symbols to match its perceptions to the world as closely as it can. That set could be called identity, closely tied, by the translation of perception, to authenticity. Layers of psychological research apply terminology like *ego, id, superego, cognition, intuition, the imaginary, neurophysiology,* and so forth to various aspects of this process. To whatever extent necessary or possible, a self strives by default to become author of its world. In that authorship is the act of translation, acknowledged and authenticated by self and society.

Thus we return to basic questions driving Indigenous literature. Following closely the common binary logic of authenticity as temporal and racial—past or present, Indian or white—a mode of reading for identity asks, as the Choctaw Cherokee scholar and writer Louis Owens opens his study of the Native American novel, "What is an Indian?" (*Other Destinies* 3). As we have seen, he even places this question "at the center of American Indian fiction": "the recovering or rearticulation of an identity, a process dependent upon a rediscovered sense of place as well as community" (5). Owens claims that identity issues are the fundamental focus of Native literary efforts, a declaration that this and other studies have found useful but ultimately limiting. Even with his "rediscovered sense . . . of community," Owens's focus on identity leads in turn to his description of "the dilemma of the mixedblood, the liminal 'breed' seemingly trapped between Indian and white worlds" as "the dominant theme in novels by Indian authors" (40). He explains, "In spite of the fact that Indian authors write from very diverse tribal and cultural backgrounds, there is to a remarkable degree a shared consciousness and identifiable worldview reflected in novels by American Indian authors, a consciousness and worldview defined primarily by a quest for identity: What does it mean to be 'Indian'—or mixedblood—in contemporary America?" (20). As he equates "Indian" here with "mixedblood," the full weight of history leans on his dualistic critical construction, wherein the binary logic of power in colonial and capitalistic dichotomies traps both narrative and critique, writer and reader, in this dilemma of the mixed-blood. By this logic, the descriptive force of dialectical materialism comes to bear most intimately on the bodies, indeed the genetic codes, the "blood," of Indian characters. This focus becomes a narrative vortex that swallows Indian lives.

Native writers since the beginning of colonialism have offered a counternarrative to Owens's dominant theme: if identity is the dialectical question, tribal sovereignty, through tribal community, remains a dialogical answer. Innumerable Indigenous stories have told this tale in innumerable ways. Yet the analysis that Owens offers is tragically mesmerized by the dialectical trap, the continuous back-and-forth between only two options. For example, in *Mixedblood Messages*, when he has described James Welch's research for the historical novel *Fools Crow*, Owens writes that authenticity questions are enough to drive a critic or novelist crazy: "Are we not caught up in a Borges-like maze of contradictory signifiers when an Indian author must go to white writings about Indians to find out who he or she is or where he or she comes from and then 'write back' against the dominant culture? To write 'authentically' the 'Indian' author must consult constructions of 'Indianness' by the dominant non-Indian culture that has always controlled printed discourse. It is enough to drive one mad" (19). This is the madness of material dialectics, the ceaseless swinging of the pendulum of duality between Indian and white, strictly aligned, respectively, with past and present. What a number of authors do imaginatively with this reductive formulation around identity is to relax the racial and temporal boundaries, at times to elude them altogether in redefinitions of what it means to "write 'authentically.'" Painfully, authenticity in Owens must be equated with antiquity, if, when only written records remain, the maddening turnstile to authentic Indian selfhood spins only by efforts of non-Indian writers of those records of the past.

Yet Native writers, including Owens elsewhere, raise other strategic questions of aesthetics, ethics, and politics: whether art and experience can elude, transcend, deconstruct, ignore, resist, or revise such material history. Detached from the past by history, can authentic identity find itself in the present? When issues on the Indian streets of reservations and cities are reduced to a competition between tradition and methamphetamines, or only slightly more benignly between Grandma's storytelling and the seductive violence of video games, the literary efforts of Indian writers seem far from turning the tide of Indian teen suicides. The patterns of resilience and survivance documented in Native literature remain far from political leverage, but they are part of a cultural resurgence, and they echo a drumbeat toward pluralism continuing in recent political and legal discourses of tribal sovereignty.

Because he wrote the book on "understanding the American Indian novel," Owens's further discussion of identity is crucial here for its strengths and weaknesses. Although he describes writers moving beyond "ethnonostalgia," the temporal structure of his binary analysis tends to reify that yearning for the past. Owens refers with compelling clarity to "the dilemma of identity and authenticity which, while common to inhabitants of the modern Western world, is particularly intense for Native Americans and, especially, mixedbloods" (*Other Destinies* 11). His own conflicted experience as a novelist and critic surfaces in his subtle analysis. He marks "the oral tradition—the reality of myth and ceremony—an authorless 'original' literature" as the goal of "Native American writing" in its "attempt to recover identity and authenticity." Thus he also defines the "immediate tension" of "the Indian writer" who must necessarily inscribe "an authorial signature" (11) against that "communal, authorless, and identity-conferring source" (11) in the tradition.

Yet he finds his way beyond the trap of that "faint trace of 'Rousseauist' ethnonostalgia." Native American novelists, according to Owens, may instead work toward, and encourage their readers to work toward, "an affirmation of a syncretic, dynamic, adaptive identity in contemporary America" (*Other Destinies* 11–12). According to Owens, the very act of writing alienates a Native writer from the "identity-conferring source" of her Native culture. He thus frames the key question of Native identity in terms of a dilemma between oral and literary traditions, while he gestures toward a wider field wherein an "adaptive identity" might find "syncretic, dynamic" possibilities for survivance.

In that direction, Owens contrasts Native American fiction with the postmodern and deconstructionist focus on a fragmented self. Against the strictures of history that might "drive one mad," and against postmodernism's celebration of "the fragmentation and chaos of experience" (*Other Destinies* 19–20), Owens, like others, also sees in Native literary efforts an affirmation of traditional, cyclic, "'eternal and immutable' elements." Thus, in a description particularly apt for Silko's mythopoesis—yet seemingly contradictory to the later emergence of Alexie's comic aesthetic—Owens provides a metaphysical corollary to colonial history, setting cosmic "eternal and immutable elements" or philosophical negotiations of history across the binary from modern chaos. His map of the literary conflict bears a resemblance to the historical conflict zone known as the frontier, a historical trope that he endorses as a theoretical lens. Because of his dichotomous analysis, one effect, in spite of his description of novels moving beyond ethnonostalgia, is to reify nostalgia by polarizing the cultural past.

However, Owens's study moves on to invoke Gerald Vizenor's trickster survivance in a wider field of possibilities, linking trickster discourse to those "eternal and immutable" values. Again Owens insists problematically on "the frontier" as a useful descriptor against postmodern chaos in his dual system of an oral past against a literary present: "In today's classrooms it is a commonplace that discourse exists within what Mikhail Bakhtin defined as 'dialogically agitated space' and that communication between cultures takes place within what Mary Louise Pratt calls those 'social spaces where disparate cultures meet, clash, and grapple with each other.' Such seams constitute what I prefer to call 'frontier' space, wherein discourse is multidirectional and hybridized" (*Mixedblood Messages* 25–26).

Owens tries to recuperate and nuance the term *frontier*, calling it "this deadly cliché of colonialism," but I fear that he chose a terminal trajectory in the identity wars. He tries to make it "multidirectional and hybridized," but "the frontier" is entrenched ideologically—it *is* the ideological trench—between the two Euro-American foundational fantasies of civilization and wilderness. As Mary Louise Pratt explains in *Imperial Eyes: Travel Writing and Transculturation*, following on her seminal article "Arts of the Contact Zone," the frontier is "grounded within a European expansionist perspective" (6–7). She maps the frontier as irretrievably embedded in the discourse of European colonialism. Because of this colonial entrenchment, I consider the term *frontier* beyond recuperation, as I suggested in the introduction, and so it is crucial to retire the term for analyzing alternative identity structures precisely because American identities are built on the frontier. Again, a binary always reads complexity in reductive dualistic terms. Attempts to remake the frontier as multidirectional are always already reoriented by the frontier's magnetic force, aligning any critical iron filings between its dualistic polarities.

Toward a wider field of choices for young American Indians, and perhaps for other Americans, let's revisit James Clifford's description of a more fluid Indigenous identity as "a nexus of relations and transactions" (*The Predicament of Culture* 344) that offer strategic options unavailable to Owens's maddening dualisms. Looking at different structures for narrating identity under colonial history, Clifford tries to explain the elder Mashpees' insistence that history has not erased their Indian identity. Part of the potency of Clifford's "nexus of relations" is that it does not naïvely dream away dualisms; it encircles them. It makes visible some alternatives to tragic oppositionality. Certainly the colonial experience, like much of historical narration, has been driven largely by oppressive dualities and hierarchies. Certainly various Native orators, writers, and storytellers, like non-Native writers and historians, act and react, speak and respond in both dualistic and multifaceted, dialogical forms. Although the factual dualities of day and night, life and death, male and female, white and Indian usually drive the way we all experience the world, Indian writers, by my reading, tend to try for stories with dialogical potential. Not all and not always, Native narratives tend to avoid Manichaean dualisms and reductive dialectics in favor of wider complexities that offer more strategies for survival.

The material forces of oppositionality remain on Clifford's map, and they often launch the plot of Native narratives, both oral and literary. As Daniel Heath Justice affirms of adaptive identity among his own Cherokee people, "Our long history of intermarriage, adaptation, and innovative accommodation has brought a wide range of physical features, cultural practices, languages, and ideas into our varied understandings of what it is to be Cherokee, and we thrive as a result. Our history as a people is one marked by cycles of change, trauma, regeneration, and growth" (*Our Fire Survives* 6). "Innovative accommodation" suggests the ironic agency exercised in these cycles of identity, authenticity, community, and sovereignty.

Even though hierarchies of race, class, and gender tend to manipulate standard histories, yet strategies for political action, for identity construction, and thus for narration in a wider system of exchange are not limited to what Clifford describes as "absorption or resistance." Instead the actual triangulations of each oppositional moment offer relations and exchanges that redefine the possibilities for survival. Identity as mobility on a field of relations can both change and remain the same.

Other discussions focused on Native American autobiography and Indigenous constructions of the self have clarified some of these dynamics. Notably Arnold Krupat argues that selfhood represented in Native autobiographies "most typically is not constituted by the achievement of a distinctive, special voice that separates it from others, but, rather, by the achievement of a particular placement in relation to the many voices without which it could not exist. . . . Indian autobiographies are quite literally dialogic" (*Voice* 133). Such cultural constructions of personal interrelationships and "a particular placement" in a system of interpellations eventually navigate across cultural contacts and conflicts as well.

Where the ingrained frontier dualisms would erect barriers between white and Indian as between educated and uneducated, many American Indian writers, such as Apess, Winnemucca, McNickle, Silko, and Alexie, have triangulated those options simply by being both Indian and educated (and some as both Indian and white). Less obvious examples might be a twentieth- or twenty-first-century Inuit choice of a snowmobile over a dog sled, or a Lakota dancer's choice of an RV camper trailer over a tipi on the summer powwow circuit, or a Makah whaler's selection of a high-powered rifle instead of a harpoon. Such choices still routinely receive criticism, both privately and publicly, as "un-Indian." Although binary thinking must identify Indian with the primitive and white with the technological, an Inuit hunter, Lakota dancer, or Makah whaler sees a way to triangulate those false oppositional categories, to sustain a distinct culture and community while adopting technological innovations of the modern industrial economy. In the 1820s steel pots and tomahawks exchanged in the fur trade did not make Cheyenne women or men question their own Cheyenne identity. In the sixteenth, seventeenth, and eighteenth centuries the reintroduction of the horse along the length of the Western Hemisphere did not make Indians any less Indian in anyone's eyes. Indeed the historical return of the horse converged in numerous cases with mythical roots of some tribal stories that date back to the glacial era of *equus*. Many tribal mythologies incorporate the horse into the origin stories of their communal identity.

For some, less comfortable examples of exchange today might include Native American individuals, tribes, or corporations that do not live up to the "noble" side of a noble savage stereotype: when some go to court in land disputes and do not fulfill idealized roles as communal ecologists; when some invite hazardous industrial waste sites and technologies onto the reservation to boost their local economy; when some develop high-tech tribal businesses with federal defense contracts in the military-industrial complex; certainly when tribes engage in high-stakes gaming. When binary thinking still lumps racial others with lower classes, thus Indians with poverty, the new economy of gaming casinos or defense contracts on a few luckily situated reservations, and the enormous wealth they sometimes provide, again confuses dualistic categories that would relegate Indians to second- or third-class citizenship by way of mythical prelapsarianism. Multiple frontier-boundary crossings and triangulations such as these few examples begin to map a more complex field of relations than the "Puritan taboo on mixing beliefs and bodies" would allow (Clifford, *The Predicament of Culture* 344). Eventually they evoke a different body politic, a new individual and national identity.

This subversive refusal of dialogism to fit into the linguistic categories of the dominant dialectic invokes different ways of knowing the world, of using language, of perceiving and relating across cultures, different identity structures. A dialogical ethics translates into an aesthetics. The very exchange processes of identity formation that Native Americans have developed in infinite ways over thousands of generations, and polished over the past five hundred years, turn into flexible narrative structures. We thus find in mapping identity a link between Indigenous ethics and aesthetics. The ways that Native narratives structure identity on a field of irony, authenticity, community, and tribal sovereignty authorize an aesthetics with ethical ramifications for readers of that literature. Expression of a different aesthetic becomes survival for those traumatized by the abusive effects of others' inability to think, see, or act beyond dualisms.

Especially in the past two generations of Native writers, a variable Native aesthetic resonates with various modernist and postmodernist projects. For more perspective on the changeable dynamics of Indigenous identity, it is worth taking another angle on this postmodern fascination and its modernist roots. Gerald Vizenor, as a prime example, invokes Jean-François

Lyotard's definition of postmodernism "as incredulity toward metanarratives" (*The Postmodern Condition* xxiv) when he affirms his own literary endeavors: "The postmodern turn in literature and cultural studies is an invitation to the ruins of representation; the invitation uncovers traces of tribal survivance, trickster discourse, and the remanence of intransitive shadows" ("Ruins" 7). Among the rubble of postmodern ruins of colonial history, there are "traces of tribal survivance" and other shadows of possibility. Prevailing historical and anthropological representations of Indians, as Vizenor famously asserts, are "terminal creeds" (*Bearheart* 185) that project only the end of Indians that were always already European projections anyway. Those representations therefore are "ruins." Vizenor's skepticism of "the aesthetic remains of reason in the literature of dominance" (7) and of "the paracolonial pretensions that precede a tribal referent" (7) casts off those ruins of representation in favor of "an invitation to tribal survivance" (8). "Incredulity toward metanarratives" of manifest destiny and tribal erasure uncovers tribal survivance.

Vizenor's affirmations resonate further back in literary history with the modernist projects of revisionism, as Native writers have often sought entry into the literary project dubbed by Gertrude Stein "the making of Americans." Indeed Whitman's claim that "the United States themselves are essentially the greatest poem" maps the now more than two-hundred-year literary history of an effort to forge the narrative of this nation, an effort that Native writers have been working to influence. Within that larger project, Native writers echo or presage some of the forms as well as content of modernism. Certainly the Indigenous arts of Africa and the Americas showed Picasso and others how to reenvision an aesthetics of reality, and a similar process was happening in literature. For instance, Robert Baker in *The Extravagant: Crossings of Modern Poetry and Modern Philosophy* writes of the "adventures" of modern Euro-American poetry as focused not only on reworking literary traditions but on exploring the edges of expression, the unspeakable, "the extravagant." He describes a modernism fascinated by the forces of "responding, searching, thinking, inventing, and writing that remain inadequately addressed in other disciplines of knowledge, above all because such forces are irreducible to clear and distinct representation" (26). Baker cites Emily Dickinson, the Impressionism of French painting and poetry, the Imagism of early Ezra Pound, and the mythical eclecticism of T. S. Eliot, among others, as modern attempts to address such irreducible forces at the edges of history. There stands an elusive and changeable Native American identity that plays directly with such forces.

Thus part of the popularity of contemporary American Indian writing among its wide non-Indian readership is attributable to this parallel across such vastly different roots of similar expression as modernist, postmodernist, and ethnic literatures. That celebratory modernist skepticism of "clear and distinct representation" echoes Marilyn Notah Verney's Diné philosophy of language that we shall discuss in relation to authenticity, where "this process of writing separates our being in the world, and we can lose touch and become isolated from all our relations" ("On Authenticity" 138). When centuries of mainstream representations of Indians would reduce them to "the vanishing American," Native artists become directly invested in "responding, searching, thinking, inventing, and writing" in ways that make visible Indigenous forces of survivance that are not reducible to definitive Euro-American erasures. Indian identity affirms process. The material ethics of cultural survival trigger a grounded aesthetics, as Owens puts it, "toward an affirmation of a syncretic, dynamic, adaptive identity in contemporary America." Artistic creation maps identity formation and vice versa. Native aesthetics, drawing on the ethical ground of authenticity, identity, community, and sovereignty, generate ironic narrative structures in poetry and fiction that drive the modernist aesthetic into the "irreducible" field where both myth and history begin. Identity on that wider field is not released from history, but history reshaped by alternate myths no longer restricts Native or American identity to exclusive classes.

"To Be Born Was Not Enough": Identity in McNickle

If McNickle maps the low point in American Indian social conditions, it is all the more significant how deeply he reaffirms Indian identity (and thus community and sovereignty) as the way to heal those conditions. It is remarkable further how thoroughly he analyzes the ideology of American community and identity through his fictional characterizations of whites in *Wind from an Enemy Sky*. In his literary effort to map the imbalance of power relations in which Indian communities and identities find themselves, McNickle suggests by contrast the severe need to rebalance. Thus in addition to describing the issues inside Indian lives he lays out the cognitive pitfalls and ethical requirements that white America must consider if it is to reach its own ideals by supporting Indian community in its midst. Such an ethos of community would mean an expansion of American identity.

Because McNickle was raised at the nadir of western American Indian economic and cultural life, his tragic representations indeed required a different rhetorical approach from that of other writers in this study. With encouragement from publishers, he gave up the desperate hopefulness of Apess and Winnemucca from the century before. His fiction, unlike his nonfiction, does not envision Silko's later tough but healing perspective through the cultural and economic resurgence in Indian Country at the other end of their shared century. Silko's narratives have the benefit of cautious optimism after the Indian activism of the 1960s and 1970s, codified in the Indian Self-Determination Act of 1975, on top of a resurgence in Indian populations rising back to several million nationwide. McNickle, although he lived through some of those later decades, directly felt and portrayed the dwindling numbers, barely 250,000, in the early twentieth century. He knew directly the claustrophobic trauma of continental dispossession, the fencing of their lands. For all his hints of generational survivance in Archilde's nephews or in Archilde's own renewed commitment in *The Surrounded*, or in Antoine's cultural grounding in *Wind from an Enemy Sky*, McNickle's honest approach required tragedy. In the harsh, realistic voice of a jeremiad, he built fictions without the prophetic promise of Silko's mythopoetics.

It is significant for understanding his fiction and his nonfiction that he lived past the 1975 Indian Self-Determination Act before he died in 1977, the year that Silko published her pivotal novel, *Ceremony*. While Silko began writing her lyrical prose in the more idealistic 1960s, McNickle at the end of his days was still modeling his fiction on the spare precision of the Lost Generation of writers with whom he had shared New York, London, and Paris in the 1920s. That style fit his astute dramatizations of the nadir of Indian identity and sovereignty and the devastating effects of federal Indian policy on Indian community in the early twentieth century.

Indeed his tragic tone may have been influenced further by the economic fact that his publishers in the 1930s and 1940s were not interested in Native survivance. In manuscript, his fiction tended toward brighter prospects, which his nonfiction eventually articulated. The publisher of his first novel, the venerable New York house Dodd, Mead & Company, rejected early drafts of his second novel, "explaining to the author," as McNickle's biographer, Dorothy R. Parker, writes, "that the story 'lacked interest for a broad reading public'" (*Singing an Indian Song* 114). Catching the difference, Parker describes the manuscript thus, in sharp contrast to the stark final product: "He wrote of a utopian world where love and good will eventually triumphed, where men of different races learned to communicate with mutual understanding, and where the damage inflicted by a century of insensitivity and greed was undone and forgotten" (113-14). Evidently, during wartime most publishers were even less interested in reconciliation between Indians and whites than they were in Indians themselves. However, as Parker points out, that period did see the emergence of a market in nonfiction books on Indians, for example, from Oliver La Farge, John Collier, and indeed McNickle himself, with his first historical study, *They Came Here First*, published in 1949.

The two major novels dramatize calamitous results of affirming Native ways, while McNickle's histories and ethnographies hold open the door to cultural perseverance. Silko adopts this dual theme as well, but in a more optimistic mode, as McNickle's fictional stories of catastrophe must be the ashes from which Silko's bird of hope rises later in the century. Perhaps it is because of this historical phoenix effect that McNickle's prose, taken as a whole, carries a sense of assurance rather than the evident doom of his novels. Alfonso Ortiz, in an obituary for his friend in *American Anthropologist*, points out that McNickle "observed that, despite what seemed on the surface to be massive and rapid breakdown in Indian cultures across the continent, an essential core of cultural integrity was being maintained" (636). Similarly Dr. Joseph McDonald, a prominent Indian educator and founding president of Salish Kootenai College on McNickle's own Flathead Reservation in Montana (a college that was established the year of McNickle's death and that now includes the D'Arcy McNickle Library), points to McNickle as one of the first historians to claim that Indians are not vanishing.[1]

"New Conception of America"

The circumstances of McNickle's emergence as a historian and essayist on Native American issues, coincident with his early publications in fiction and poetry, shed some light on the darker themes of his fiction as they shadow his Indian identity questions. As a participant in John Collier's New Deal for Indians since the mid-1930s, he had emerged as a skillful organizer and administrator in the Bureau of Indian Affairs on behalf of Native rights and community economic development, as well as a writer for the Bureau's newsletter *Indians at Work*. After an article for the newsletter was also published in the progressive journal *Common Ground*, McNickle contributed a few more pieces for that publication during the 1940s. His connection with its editor, Louis Adamic, who was also an editor at J. P. Lippincott Company, another New York publishing house, led to that first book of history, *They Came Here First*.

His connections with Adamic's progressive agenda put McNickle's publications into a political light and reveal the larger agenda for his narrations of early twentieth-century Indian identity issues. Michael Denning describes Adamic's project, in which McNickle was clearly a primary, if rare, Native American presence, during the social upheavals of the Depression and its ensuing years: "*Common Ground* was a journal founded by Louis Adamic and M. Margaret Anderson in 1940 to explore 'the racial-cultural situation' in the U.S. Looked at a half-century later, it seems the very embodiment of the cautious, semi-official 'cultural pluralism' of the time" (*The Cultural Front* 447). Denning goes on to list the "mainstream liberal" corporations and individuals, from the Carnegie Foundation to Eleanor Roosevelt, who sponsored the journal, as well as the "younger black and ethnic writers" who found it a crucial platform for their work, including Langston Hughes, Zora Neale Hurston, Ralph Ellison, Gwendolyn Brooks, Toshio Mori, Carlos Bulosan, and George Sanchez. McNickle was in good company, as these writers expressed themselves in various directions toward "Adamic's project to create a 'new conception of America'" (448). Certainly a small "market" in America was willing to read voices of "diversity," including McNickle's—even if only to reflect their own mythology of the vanishing Indian. As Denning elucidates this midcentury progressive movement under FDR, we may read McNickle's postcolonial logic of Native revisions of the American story emerging across ethnic and racial lines.

However, Adamic seems to have pushed the conversation further. In the introduction, I discussed the pitfalls of the term *multicultural*, which was co-opted in the decades following *Common Ground*. Adamic's recognition of "a nation of nations" resonates not only with ethnic pluralism but also with the ongoing and reemerging legal codes of tribal sovereignty at the heart of McNickle's work. Evidently the social and political context for the reemergence of self-determination and tribal sovereignty in the late twentieth century was built by this set of voices, including McNickle's.

Denning writes further of "racial and ethnic transformations" after the late nineteenth century's "racialized legal codes" (*The Cultural Front* 451) of Jim Crow and immigration controls. By Denning's account, the momentum of a new story for America seems to have been irresistible. What he does not mention is that those "racialized legal codes" were established at the height of the nineteenth-century "Indian Wars" out West, as well as during Reconstruction in the South, with reverberations north and east. Those racialized legal codes were both reinforced and subverted by the prior fact of tribal sovereignty. In Indian Country the further unraveling of those codes continued in the postwar period as the GI Bill sent a later generation of Indian warriors—who had fought *for* the United States—into the growing ranks of Indigenous citizens educated in both worlds. Thus McNickle's pivotal position in a "pre–Civil Rights," left-wing, interracial social justice movement underlines his critique of America, if not his utopian aspirations.

Casting an insider's perspective on progressives' "new conception of America," McNickle documents the dark days of Indian decline in both numbers and cultural vitality after the turn of the twentieth century. His novels dramatize a downward spiral of scarred optimism over failed attempts to bridge Indian and white cultures. Like Apess and Winnemucca before him, there is an anxious faith in Indigenous people's ability to survive, and there are instances of promise in American ideals. In his nonfiction McNickle affirmed from an anthropological perspective that Indians "accepted change as a normal process of nature" and that "the attitude of acceptance" became in Indian cultures a process of harmony with natural change that allowed Indian identity to become "highly adaptive." The resilience and flexibility that developed in "the extremes of climate and terrain to which the people shaped their lives" strengthened them to meet "the coming of Europeans in the 16th and 17th centuries" (cited in Purdy, *Word Ways* 108). Radically different from an urban and pastoral view of nature as stable and unchanging, McNickle's sense of nature, like culture, is ever in flux. Colonialism is the de facto process of changing the land, as the fences in *The Surrounded* and the dam in *Wind from an Enemy Sky* attest.[2] By his reckoning Indigenous people have learned to be always alert to changes on the land. From millennial changes in glacial and temperate climate to earthquakes, floods, and simple seasonal transformations, daily shifts in weather, animal migrations, and other sights and smells, the changing land establishes a changeable identity and culture for the people of the land.

However, in McNickle's fiction, as in the works of all the writers of this study, these qualities are darkened by an "enemy sky." One of the central brothers, for instance, in *Wind from an Enemy Sky* matches some of Winnemucca's experience as a frustrated translator: "Henry Jim knew the talk. He had heard it many times. . . . So many times when the understanding fell apart afterward. And the people in the camps laughed at him or were angry. How would it be this time?" (28). McNickle's stark tragedies caution against expecting change from the dominant, white side of the frontier. Instead, as his nonfiction does explicitly, his fiction looks to tribal communities for the strength to adapt and survive.

McNickle does not offer easy answers. As the story of *Wind from an Enemy Sky* unfolds, the Little Elk community slips deeper into a sense of heaviness, not only in the historic rift between the competing leadership of brothers Henry Jim and Bull but in smaller ways, as when the women are going down to the valley to check on their men, in Antoine's narration: "It was puzzling, but it just seemed that everybody was mixed up" (100). Yet there are moments of solidarity, as at Antoine's boarding school: "When the strangeness wore off and they learned they were all Indians, wherever they came from, they found ways to work together against the common enemy. In spite of what the Long-Armed-Man [bearing a whip] said, they had no desire to forget where they came from" (107). A cultural connection to changing identity, as it affirms new connections here through opposition, authorizes and grounds them to forge a united resistance. Flexible identity continues to serve the people under duress.

To discuss identity issues in McNickle's fiction, we need to consider two of his perspectives that, as shorthand, I call the philosophical and the political. They could as easily be termed the spiritual and the historical or the ideological and the material. In *Wind from an Enemy Sky* we see in McNickle's contrast between the characters Two Sleeps and Bull his view of the identity challenge in Indian communities. They wrestle differently with the question of how to combine a Native philosophy with specific colonial politics, that is, a dialogic worldview with a dialectical history. The novel's more foregrounded, plot-driving juxtaposition of brothers Henry Jim and Bull neatly sets absorption against resistance, respectively, in Clifford's terms. Neither of their answers works, neither absorption by Henry Jim nor resistance by Bull. Yet McNickle's crucial construction of the identity of Two Sleeps, in contrast with both Bull and Henry Jim, offers an elusive alternative narrative that matches Clifford's nexus of exchange. In fact Two Sleeps is the one at the fatal finale who keeps the songs singing beyond Henry Jim's natural death and Bull's unnatural death. Although Two Sleeps and Bull share each other's goals for their people, the spiritual philosophy of animism in the older mystic directs his view, while the practical politics of exclusion in the tribal leader directs his. And the mystic survives.

A closely related set of issues arose in discussion of community principles in McNickle's work, where in chapter 2 we looked at the other major narrative juxtaposition of Bull and Henry Jim in *Wind from an Enemy Sky*. As the characterizations of Bull and Two Sleeps bear on alternate structures of Indian identity, dramatically matching the political and the philosophical approaches, they will offer much of the focus of this section.

Old Two Sleeps lives with a different sense of boundaries, a wider sense of inclusiveness, than does Bull. The older man's background is intertribal, having been a wounded amnesiac taken in by Bull's forebears after being left for dead in a remote battle. Indeed McNickle's choice of a name for the old dreamer suggests that he contemplates his way through more than one world, even across the divide between life and death in the following key passages, a quietly eloquent deconstruction of polarizations between identity and animistic community.

We followed his thoughts when Two Sleeps is back in the winter mountains desperately seeking a dream for his people's future. Here is more of that quotation, where we see not only animistic perception but the internal experience of it, a "reaching with his mind," as something different from a linear projection between a separate self and other. In a stream of consciousness energized by the blowing snow, McNickle shows us a grounded identity. Two Sleeps has learned to build his sense of self on a delicate balance between change and continuity, "the things that grew from small beginnings and the things that stayed firmly placed and enduring." Thus he must grow in consciousness and understanding. Merely "to be born was not enough. To live in the world was not enough." The assurance he seeks, to "know certainly," requires a dissolving of self and other, "reaching with his mind," until he identifies with both change, "the small seed from which the pine tree would grow," and permanence, "the mountain that endured forever." He does this on animistic ground "until he himself dissolved and became part of everything else" (*Wind* 197–98).

This impressionistic mental susceptibility, this "reaching with his mind," resonates in McNickle's characterization of Two Sleeps with David Abram's description of Indigenous shamans of oral cultures. Not entirely unlike the aesthetic discernment described by Keats as negative capability, shamans, in Abram's description, reside on the edges of human perception of the "more-than-human" world (*The Spell of the Sensuous* 15). Two Sleeps "emerged from the heavy timber and skirted an open face of the mountain, where a sharp-edged wind swept fiercely up from the black depths of the valley and lashed the snow into a fury of whirling ice clouds" (*Wind* 197). Shamans often work their insights on the edges of human society in more remote regions of the nature-culture interface. Abram refers to this value of perception as "the shaman's allegiance to nonhuman nature" and as "long and sustained exposure to wild nature, to its patterns and vicissitudes" (*The Spell of the Sensuous* 21). Abram explains, "The traditional or tribal shaman . . . acts as an intermediary between the human community and the larger ecological field, ensuring that there is an appropriate flow of nourishment, not just from the landscape to the human inhabitants, but from the human community back to the local earth" (7, 10). Within a material universe of reciprocal "solicitations" and perceptions, Abram depicts a permeable mind and identity in the shaman that includes an "intimate relationship with nonhuman nature" (11). Two Sleeps disciplines himself for this relationship, although, by exposing the old man's weaknesses as well, McNickle's characterization is careful to avoid romanticizing such a spiritual role. The effect is a quite accessible identity that keeps the balance while he holds a mystery.

Although this philosophical and imaginative reach of the mind seems to extend here to an ideal prospect, McNickle places that vision politically in his novel, farther up in the mountains above the old camps and not down on "the flats," as Bull describes the valley, "where they could have had government wagons and teams, flour and coffee, fence posts." McNickle never reveals to the reader the dream that followed on Two Sleeps's struggles in that mountain storm, only its unspeakable, untranslatable pain, the ultimate pain of "reaching with his mind." Bull, the most in need of Two Sleeps's guidance—because he is incapable of "reaching with his mind"—can only say to himself, "As the days passed and the old one stayed behind his closed eyes, the silence began to speak for itself. The mountain had given no answer, or the answer was something the old one found too disturbing to report" (*Wind* 199–200). Ultimately the vision of Two Sleeps is affirmed in its negative power. Yet unlike a Cassandra whose announced prophecy of doom won her ostracism from her community, Two Sleeps's own silence about his prophetic vision helps him sustain the community beyond the vision's tragic fulfillment. In silence he is able to maintain the more pliable "reaching with his mind" that remains alert to change and survival for his community and the next generation in Antoine.

McNickle's choice of a name for Bull suggests a character and identity just the opposite of Two Sleeps's. The author spells out how the dynamics of the name "never pass from one language to another without some loss," explaining that the name Bull conveys to Indians more than standard cowboy- and-lariat connotations of bull-headed: "To the people who lived with him in his camp, and to others who encountered him, he had always been this man who 'lives inside,' as they said" (*Wind* 2). This insularity as it extends to stubbornness may be why he is incapable, either as a personality or as a leader, of Two Sleeps's imaginative "reaching" into other perspectives. Bull's boundaries are firm, and they are reinforced by anger, as he muses, again, "That was when the anger settled and turned into rock. It had come first when these men from across the world, from he knew not where, had told him that he could not have his own country, that he no longer belonged in it" (130).

Bull himself understands how his own mind-set excludes him from Two Sleeps's intuitions. Here his frustrations are notable not only for his contrast with Two Sleeps but also for the colonial dynamics, sometimes genteel but ultimately violent, that so enrage Bull. Although McNickle rounds out this characterization through poignant personal interchanges within his family, Bull, for good reasons, is not interested in exchange across material borders.

We see his political logic as he counsels with his headmen over the question of working with the new, more humane Agent Rafferty: "How can a white man help us? When he looks at us, the way we live, the way we pray, what can he see? If his heart is good, maybe he will smile, put his hand on my head. . . . But the white man means, 'You'll be a strong man when you become a white man.' It's his way of offering me friendship. He looks, but doesn't see me" (*Wind* 93-94). The focus of Bull's skepticism—he even concludes by saying, "The white man has only destroyed us"—evidently becomes the horror of Two Sleeps's dream in the mountains, as political violence pushes on spiritual philosophy.

Two Sleeps hints toward the end, "I wanted to know everything, to be inside of everything—I thought. But my brothers, that is a terrible thing to want. My heart is already dead" (*Wind* 220). Whatever Two Sleeps in the mountains saw of human suffering in the valleys was enough to end his storytelling on his return, as it seems at some level to end the narrative of this novel, inscribing a seeming fatalism that critics have been unraveling ever since.

The mountains in McNickle's earlier novel, *The Surrounded*, promise a similar island of potential natural identity apart from the white man's world, only to be invaded by that world as in *Wind*. For many readers contemplating such invasions, McNickle's first novel seems to encourage the reductive dilemmas of certain identity studies that so limit recognition of human agency. Many see *The Surrounded* as McNickle's novel of divided identity, with its autobiographical protagonist, Archilde (a fitting pun), quietly locked and shackled between the antagonistic cultures pumping in his own mixed blood. Archilde's split heritage, Indian and white, certainly seems to trace the narrative path that Owens defined for the American Indian novel: "the dilemma of the mixedblood, the liminal 'breed' seemingly trapped between Indian and white worlds" (*Other Destinies* 40). Indeed Owens describes the trajectory of *The Surrounded* as a map simply of the "tragic, incomprehensible fate of Indians" (65). However reductive the effect of this earlier novel, we could trace an affirmative pattern through both of McNickle's major fictions (with the young adult novel *Runner in the Sun* more explicitly affirmative as well). The final, insulating choices that Archilde makes to stake his identity with his traditions are indeed worked out further in *Wind*, where young Antoine and his grandfather pursue the apparent resistant logic of authentic tradition, guided by Two Sleeps, against American colonialism.

Yet, as usual, closer reading finds things more complicated. In the distinct fictionalized world of *The Surrounded* and *Wind from an Enemy Sky*, the former novel is set somewhat earlier than the latter in the actual history of the renamed Flathead Reservation.[3] Although they both take place after turn-of-the-century allotment, *The Surrounded* unfolds before the Flathead Irrigation Project—still controversial today—was constructed by the federal government in the 1930s, while the plot of *Wind* begins with that project's completion. Chapter 19 of *Wind* fictionalizes a construction project that conflates two actual histories: the hydroelectric Kerr Dam on the reservation's Flathead River, flooding the sacred Place of Falling Waters, and the valley-wide canal system of the Flathead Irrigation Project, damming key mountain streams.

In *The Surrounded* the historical impacts of allotment and cultural erosion bear directly on Archilde's blood mixture. Is he to bow to assimilation, or will he make a stand for Native cultural continuity? McNickle skillfully maneuvers the social forces of family, community, religion, tradition, and understated romantic liaison to help Archilde make that choice of identity for continuity. Purdy describes a process of gradual identity construction, explaining, "At first [Archilde] too seems limited by the fatalistic misconception of the doomed Indian that permeates the popular literature of the time, but he is also actively engaged in a reinitiation into tribal life. This builds a tension between a popular stereotype and evidence that it is baseless, and this tension takes the reader far beyond the conventional 'clash between two civilizations' that was the basis of most popular fiction about Native peoples in McNickle's time and since" (*Word Ways* 66–68). Accepting Purdy's optimistic, nondualistic reading, we must also acknowledge that McNickle dramatizes Archilde's choices as precisely between "two civilizations," tracing the bloody divide that is the frontier. Owens reads the novel on those grimmer terms: "Apparently there can be no merger of paths; the maps point in different directions and a choice must be made. Archilde opts ultimately for the Indian road and tragic consequences" (Afterword 258–59). Yet Purdy does a detailed job of clarifying how the novel works to affirm "a reinitiation into tribal life," however conflicted that life might be. Nonetheless what McNickle and his historical circumstances elucidate through that reinitiation is how real was Owens's mixed-blood dilemma for McNickle's time. Native choices had to be made if Native culture would survive. Archilde makes that choice for culture, and thus his hands are shackled by history.

One particularly remarkable chapter in *The Surrounded*, the painful episode of the old mare, provides a striking passage to compare that novel's identity dynamics with the juxtaposition of Bull and Two Sleeps in *Wind from an Enemy Sky*. This chapter is also rich as a dramatic example of McNickle's rhetorical power, his vivid prose, his allegorical imagination, his social critique, his narrative fluency. Chapter 27 reveals further what is missing thematically in the earlier novel in comparison with his final fiction. Although *The Surrounded* features elders such as Baptiste and Catherine, its narrative lacks the presence of a dialogical figure like Two Sleeps in *Wind* to offer an alternative to the shackles of dialectics. The old mare chapter is a dialectical nightmare, like the novel itself.

While the plot of *The Surrounded* simmers toward its conclusion after the violent confrontation in the mountains (based on the historical Swan Valley Massacre),[4] this inserted chapter weaves a colonial allegory of Archilde's and his people's circumstances in a gruesome anecdote. As he considers his decision to leave the reservation and his Indian life forever, the protagonist is "spending much of his time alone" on horseback in "the Badlands" on "the open range along the Big River" (236). He comes across "an aged bay mare and her spring colt" (238), the mare barely surviving on the scant, drought-parched forage, "occasionally nipping at a shriveled spike of grass" (238), while the colt frolics around her. Shocked at the skeletal condition of the mare and repulsed by her bedraggled tail, "a tangled mass of hair and mud," Archilde decides "to put a rope on her, feed her, trim her tail. It was the least thing a creature of feeling could do" (238). However, when he advances "with his hat full of oats . . . the mare would not be caught" (238). What ensues is hours of tragicomic frustration, mutual stubbornness, and petty impatience that lead ultimately to the brutal and hopelessly pathetic death of the mare, to Archilde's helpless culpability, and to a clear analogy for McNickle's view of the complications of colonialism.

Pursuing this foolishness, Archilde, the archetypal mixed-blood character, takes on the dominating characteristics of a colonizer, with dramatically ineffectual and destructive results. McNickle thereby unmasks the ultimate violence of the good intentions, "the least thing a creature of feeling could do," in whites trying to assimilate Indians. Over the larger trajectory of the novel, this incident, running the ideology of domination to its cruel conclusion, is the tragic catharsis that energizes Archilde to embrace his Native identity.

In the short space of a few pages, McNickle outlines colonial dynamics with gendered and sexualized undertones, playing the scene back and forth across the dialectic of domination toward death and moral defeat. The chapter thus portrays the inner torment of Archilde's own split identity: "The tormentor had become the tormented" (*The Surrounded* 241). The ironies are painfully clear, especially as the scene draws to its agonized conclusion. For the pursued mare is not yet dead. The colonizer must face the consequences of colonialism. As he tries through the moonless night to save the barely breathing object of his desire and despair from scavenging coyotes, he plays out the perverse logic of domination. Because she was always already his own projection, and because her ethically inconvenient body now mocks his self-righteous interference, he must snuff her out to complete the score:

> Finally, in a rage that was partly resentment at the unfairness of the whole episode and partly interrupted sleep, he went out to her, placed his rifle against her head, and blasted her into eternity.
>
> Then, in a confusion of feeling, he sat down and spent the rest of the night guarding her worthless carcass. (242)

As in the shocking finales of both of his novels, here McNickle reveals a narrative preference for facing the worst possible outcome.

The low point must be the only place of honest regeneration. Where else can survival prove itself? What other fictional world could match the grim reality of his people in the 1930s? McNickle thus concludes this chapter with a protagonist as pathetic as the object of his destruction. The dialectic has played out incessantly and maddeningly, oscillating within the mixed-blood Archilde. This chapter, which stands quite alone in the narrative, is thus a cautionary tale against not only domination but oscillation as well, advocating instead for the firm choice that Archilde ultimately makes to support his culture from the inside. Instead of repeating such external, colonizing, patronizing, and destructive "support" of a culture, like Adam Pell in *Wind*, Archilde will step back within the communal embrace of his people.

The grotesque absurdity of this scene (McNickle uses the word *grotesque* twice in the chapter) marks the late turning point in Archilde's decision-making process. Although his shift does not rise to the articulate surface of the narrative, it is clear once he has killed the mare that following the dominating colonialist in his own blood is not the way he wants to live his life. The ethical divide comes into focus by his ethical overreaching. He no longer identifies with the colonist, the white man in himself. As the end of the next chapter subtly suggests, he actually learns from his mistakes with the old mare how to elude colonial domination. Thinking of his rebellious nephews, Archilde understands that the mare's strength is like the strength of Indian people to go their own way: "Mike and Narcisse taught him something—it did no good to make a fuss about things; just go ahead and do what you liked, and ask only to be let alone. They had that in common with the mare in the Badlands" (*The Surrounded* 248).

Further toward some value beyond the brutal absurdity of the mare's death, we cannot overlook what is certainly the most understated aspect of the old mare episode. The survival of her "spring colt" is barely mentioned after the initial description: "Her colt, who was drawing the life substance out of her, was plump and frisky. It was always outrunning its dam and waiting for her to catch up" (*The Surrounded* 238). Like Antoine surviving at the edges of the fatal finale of *Wind from an Enemy Sky*, this colt is held in abeyance for McNickle simultaneously to highlight the historical tragedy and to hold out some hope for cultural survival.

The old mare episode can serve as an allegorical cautionary tale against reductive thinking in the later novel as well. Underneath all of the polarized confrontations that McNickle unravels in *Wind*, he traces such complexities and interpenetrations as Adam Pell's fatal entanglements, Rafferty's involuntary complicity, Dr. Edwards's compassion, Bull's resentments, The Boy's ambivalences, Louis's wounded bitterness, and Two Sleeps's ironic efforts at transcendence. The double effect on identity structures in his calamitous narrative is both to reduce fields of wider influence to either/or choices and to explain severe either/or positions by their more complex layers. The story of Indian versus white distills out of the mix, yet here it remains different from the relative simplicity of *The Surrounded*, where the narrative explores the process of choice. In *Wind* the choice for culture has been made already at the start—by Bull and his grandson, Antoine—and the narrative follows instead the repercussions of such a hard choice. His two novels thus follow a Bildungsroman logic of radical innocence, a knowledge beyond loss in how to survive, a severe sense of hope for strength through experience—surrounded by a wind from an enemy sky.

In both novels the drama of social disturbance nearly eclipses the personal search, only thereby reinforcing the principle of communal identity, as both Archilde and Antoine reconnect their selves to their culture. In each case the individual blends with community through the dramatic events of resistant solidarity. Archilde takes the rap for his mother's lethal defense of her family: "Archilde, saying nothing, extended his hands to be shackled" (*The Surrounded* 297). Antoine identifies with his grandfather's rifle shots that struggle to retake power from white intruders: "His grandfather would feel strong again, and the boy was proud for him" (*Wind* 255). McNickle's plots highlight the system of exchange that is Native identity by reuniting both youthful protagonists with their struggling communities, their kin. Thus Archilde, to his own surprise, reinvests in his culture after boarding school, only to end the novel shackled by the colonial white forces that would erase that culture. And Antoine, who eagerly reembraces his culture after boarding school, at the end of the novel similarly, though not on center stage, watches as his grandfather Bull is gunned down. Yet in the latter novel, the songs continue, thanks to Two Sleeps, and, "despite the hasty actions of individuals, . . . the people survive" (*Word Ways* 133), as Purdy argues. The design of McNickle's narrative structures, where identity moves as a nexus in a larger system of exchange, is not individual triumph but survival of the people. As Two Sleeps says, "It is not enough to be born." One must choose to connect.

By the mapping in his nonfiction history, *Native American Tribalism: Indian Survivals and Renewals*, McNickle's two major novels are set during the transition from "Years of Attrition" to "Time of Reassessment," and thus they dramatize the human costs of that transition through tragedy. In his last decade, while he was polishing the manuscript for *Wind from an Enemy Sky*, McNickle also was revising and expanding *The Indian Tribes of the United States* into *Native American Tribalism: Indian Survivals and Renewals*, whose subtitle hints at hope. The balanced affirmation in the revised title shows up, for instance, in a passage from his final chapter, "A Closing View": "The Indian political voice as well as their creative expression reject the values of the dominant society and turn inward for individual and group support. Indian nationalism, pan-Indianism, Red Power—terms used with some degree of common meaning—indicate a growing sense of shared problems, shared goals, and a shared heritage. . . . It is this certainty of self which the young proclaim, sometimes loudly. There is no such certainty for them in the white man's affluent society" (*Native American Tribalism* 170). Here McNickle comments on the rising American Indian Movement of the 1970s, among other activist groups. With plenty of Bull's resistant "No" to "the dominant society," McNickle, as both a political and a creative voice, advocates solidarity, as does Bull: that his Indian readers "turn inward for individual and group support." If he also is advocating a position for his non-Indian readers here, McNickle calls not only for the tolerance that a pluralistic society promises but also for the legal recognition of tribal sovereignty required for Indian generations to reclaim "this certainty of self," a communal Indian identity.

"The Mantle of Prejudice Torn from Every American Heart": Identity in Apess

William Apess moves quite freely in his rhetorical postures among "contradictory signifiers" of orality and literacy, of Indian and white identities that become so maddening to Owens a century and a half later. Undoubtedly Apess agonized in private over the same issues plaguing Native writers for generations after he died, but his writing persona, bolstered by his stage presence at the pulpit and the podium, finesses a stunning array of positions for an American Indian in Jacksonian America. His own mobility among these identity poses shapes his potent verbal arguments for a flexible, inclusive American national identity.

What, then, are identity structures in the writings of Apess, and how are they reflected in narrative structures and other aesthetic features of his prose? Following his rhetorical and ethical purposes, how do those structures bear on notions of America's definitions of itself? Let's begin by making a distinction between the voices in Apess's autobiographical writings and his other essays. Although his uniquely ironic discursive force carries across his various works, he identifies himself with quite different roles in a full spectrum of agency and identity, from the pitiable sinner of *Son of the Forest* to the polemical prophet in *Eulogy of King Philip*, from the hagiographic historian of *The Experiences of Five Christian Indians* to the legal historian of *Nullification*. Never self-righteous but always full of righteous indignation at American Christian hypocrisy, Apess sets about to tutor his white audiences and readers in the ideals of American civilization.

"An Indian's Looking-Glass for the White Man" might serve as a pivot point between his identity positions. Appended as a sermon to follow his shorter autobiography among the others in *Five Christian Indians*, "Looking-Glass" reflects the clear trajectory of his publications, what he refers to as his "holy work" (*Son* 43; all Apess citations are to *On Our Own Ground*): Indian autobiography as an impetus for reforming American identity. Thus Apess's notion of "an Indian's looking-glass for the white man" charts a path for American Indian literatures, addressing non-Indians to give them an Indian perspective on themselves, on Indians, and on a vision for America. Each of the writers in this study picks up that mirror to shine it on their white readership and/or to encourage their Indian readership in affirming the resilience of their identity.

Thus the energy fortifying his project that Apess saw fundamentally as spiritual was also polemical and political—explicitly to reinscribe Indians as human against America's inhumane treatment. With such millennial purposes, a rhetorical didacticism permeates his prose: "Is it right to hold and promote prejudices? If not, why not put them all away? I mean here, among many of those who are civilized" ("Looking-Glass" 155). He achieves his purpose by alternating between or sometimes playing simultaneously the roles of powerlessness and power, between Indian as victim of America reduced to history and Indian as voice of America redeemed. When he writes of Indians as "the most ingenious people," whom Americans have tried "to distress and murder . . . by inches" ("Looking-Glass" 156), or when he summons his biblical discourse to write of Indians as "a tribe of Israelites suffering under the rod of despotic pharaohs" (*Nullification* 179), he represents them and himself as casualties of history. However, when he writes, "I am not talking about the skin but about principles" ("Looking-Glass" 156), he identifies and authorizes himself with the values on which America was founded. And he identifies those American principles with the Gospel when he writes, "I will refer you to St. Peter's precepts (Acts 10): 'God is no respecter of persons,' etc. Now if this is the case, my white brother, what better are you than God? And if no better, why do you, who profess his Gospel and to have his spirit, act so contrary to it? Let me ask why the men of a different skin are so despised" ("Looking-Glass" 159). By these equations, his rhetorical questions become irrefutable declarations of mutual identity.

Framing this spectrum of identities, with Apess's own characteristically confident distinctions, is his Christian theological identification of power with the Creator and powerlessness with the creation: "I believe that it is assumed as a fact among divines that the Spirit of Divine Truth, in the boundless diversity of its operations, visits the mind of every intelligent being born into the world—but the time when is only fully known to the Almighty and the soul which is the object of the Holy Spirit's enlightening influence" (*Son* 8). Apess draws on this metaphysics of spiritual influence in the discourse of his own double identity as author of *Son of the Forest*: "When I think of what I am, and how wonderfully the Lord has led me, I am dumb before him. . . . I stand before you as a monument of his unfailing goodness" (52). By this construction, he represents himself to his "dear reader" as simultaneously pitiful and powerful, as both "dumb before him" and "a monument to his unfailing goodness." Through a singular reflexive logic of the religious, he invokes a certain spiritual absent presence where the believer, here "dumb," functions as an adequate "monument." This very absence in the believer stands as a verification of the presence of divine power.

Such theological contemplations are illustrative of Apess's identity questions of agency, especially in the exceptions that he also makes to certain doctrine. Identity issues for Apess appear as much religious as racial. Indeed religious power stands in as racial recognition, measured by the importance of his eventual ordination in the Methodist Church. Thus his ability to serve the church and to sermonize, as a confirmation of his agency, becomes a validation of his Native voice to America as well as to American Indians. For example, in the last chapter of *Son of the Forest*, while recounting his inner pilgrimage in the Methodist community—"I was now very constant in attending meetings"—he makes a brief but telling commentary on a doctrinal debate: "They agreed in all points of doctrine but one, and that related to perfect love—some said it was inconsistent, and another said it was not. I could not see wherein this inconsistency manifested itself, as we were commanded to love God with all our hearts, and contend for that faith once delivered to the saints" (43). Barry O'Connell offers a useful footnote explaining the debate: "The 'inconsistency' speaks to the fact that as creatures of the Fall, of original sin, we are by definition incapable of such love," the "perfect love" to which Christ enjoins us (*On Our Own Ground* 43). Apess refuses to see that inconsistency, because he is confident in his own ability to love selflessly and confident that he is both commanded and enabled by divine power so to love. Indeed his work on behalf of Indian communities, especially at Mashpee, emerges out of such communal love as he felt early on in the Methodist meetings. He introduces the debate above with these sanguine words: "I cast in my lot with this little band and had many precious seasons" (*On Our Own Ground* 43).

Accordingly the paragraph following that debate launches with an affirmation of his calling, his link to divine power: "While in Colrain the Lord moved upon my heart in a peculiarly powerful manner, and by it I was led to believe that I was called to preach the Gospel of our Lord and Savior Jesus Christ" (*Son* 43). Here his call to preach, around 1820 at the age of twenty-two, comes at home in the Native community of his father's town. It is an affirmation of his Indian identity as part of that community of believers, especially as he considers "the holy work" of raising up Indian rights on the basis of Christian principles: "In the present day, a great variety of opinion prevails respecting the holy work. We read in the Bible that in former days holy men spoke as they were moved by the Holy Ghost" (43). Apess is moved to affirm and strengthen Indian lives, and it is his ability to fulfill that work, his agency linked to his racial identity, that concerns him, as he relies again on the metaphysics of power and powerlessness: "My exercises were great— my soul was pained when the Lord placed before me the depravity of human nature. I commenced searching the Scriptures more diligently, and the more I read, the more they opened to my understanding; and something said to me, 'Go now and warn the people to flee from the wrath to come!'. . . I was nothing but a poor ignorant Indian and thought the people would not hear me" (44).

His oscillation between identity constructs, between absence and presence of power, continues until he takes as a sign an accidental advertisement that sets him up to preach a sermon to one of the meetings, launching his vocation. Under the discursive cloak of sin and redemption, he proceeds to build his themes of American reconstruction. Throughout his work, the divine agency that he accepts in himself he then identifies with the divine purpose of America's founding principles, as indeed the Kingdom of God on earth: "May author and reader be preserved until the perfect day and dwell forever in the paradise of God" (*Son* 52). "The Lord will reward you, and pray you stop not till this tree of distinction be leveled to the earth, and the mantle of prejudice torn from every American heart—then shall peace pervade the Union" ("Looking-Glass" 161).

Within the parameters of this religious and democratic discourse, Apess projects a voice that identifies himself with and indeed embodies American multiplicities as a Christian Indian and as a mixed-blood. His identity is literally all over the map. He represents himself, with however many historical inaccuracies,[5] as a blend of Europe and America: "My grandfather was a white man and married a female attached to the royal family of Philip, king of the Pequot tribe of Indians" (*Son* 3). His own being, as both invader and invaded, prompts him to try to transcend American colonial history. O'Connell usefully describes the resulting discursive challenge of reading Apess: "How complex and intriguing a thinker and writer William Apess was . . . one who struggles to find language with which to play out the elements of several cultural heritages: Pequot, Native American, Anglo-American, and, very possibly, African-American" (introduction xxiv). The thrust of this history embodied in his voice drives toward a unity in diversity, another *e pluribus unum*. Apess was thus in a position to consciously use his own identity, his autobiography, and his ministry to try to change America toward its own ideals. Indeed he spoke variously, and sometimes simultaneously, from each of these vantage points. Whether addressing Native congregations or a non-Native reading public, he was always in dialogue with himself, because he was himself a dialogue.

Perhaps this internal dialogue is a reason for a certain rhetorical distance early in his writing. While his affirmations are millennial and the groanings of his soul are Dantesque, there frequently occurs a speculative or interrogative edge to his religious assertions or an ironic framing of direct rhetorical questioning of Christian hypocrisy. Such subjunctive bracketing reflects an ironic distance in his voice from the direct assertion of such belief, even while it affirms his familiarity with doctrine in his bid for ordination in *Son of the Forest*. The tragic edge of disappointed idealism, his distance from religious authority that appears in his diction and syntax equals his racial distance from the centers of material power. It takes the form of constant interrogatives and of irony most notably, but there is a considered intellectual space between Apess and much of his own affirmations. Looking again at his allusion, quoted in full earlier, to St. Peter's precept, "God is no respecter of persons," note how Apess then invokes that authority through the distance and ambiguity of a hypothetical "if": "Now if this is the case, my white brother." And he follows not with declarations but with a string of interrogations: "What better are you than God? And if no better, why do you, who profess his Gospel and to have his spirit, act so contrary to it? Let me ask why the men of a different skin are so despised" ("Looking-Glass" 159). If this and if that, then thus, or failing thus, then why not? The rhetorical distance in "if" here certainly builds on the authority of a philosophical discursive tradition of logical syllogisms, but it also serves in his unique historical and personal circumstances to elevate his prose and himself above the error and ignorance of Christian hypocrisy that directs itself at prejudice against himself and his race. His interrogative distance not only deflects defensive reactions from his white audience, but it also reflects his outsider's role as an Indian in both American and Christian categories.

A generation ahead of the author of *Benito Cereno*, these circumlocutions are not unlike Melville's multilayered sentences. Unless such rhetorical strata are merely an exercise in mastering the master's discourse, which certainly they are as well, they point to Apess as a speaker standing apart from the church powers that wield such discourse. He eludes while he alludes to their authority. Drawing on the intimate discursive authority of third-person narration, Apess does break away from rhetorical questions to declare "that the soul of the Indian is immortal" ("The Indians: The Ten Lost Tribes" 113) against centuries of colonial denial. He never seems to doubt himself or his people in that primary avowal.

"Then Shall Peace Pervade the Union": Shifting Pronouns

Others have explored poignant psychological issues in Apess's writing that may have confronted and perhaps even undermined his identity.[6] Rather than focusing on his presumed biographical struggles, I will look more closely here into the texts at ways that Apess manipulated his multiple identities rhetorically for his singular aim, to inscribe an alternative America. A principal example of his alternative strategies embodied in his discursive identity drives both the logic and the rhetoric of "An Indian's Looking-Glass for the White Man." Close reading of his tactical use of pronouns in critical terms of what Vizenor calls "pronounance" illustrates Apess's focus not on identity as separateness but on what Clifford suggested as an exchange of difference. Similarly Mark Taylor's notion of "altarity" provides a lens to understand Apess's rhetorical gymnastics in "Looking-Glass." Taylor defines altarity as difference demanding its own identity instead of mere otherness. Instead of the nonself of otherness, altarity insists on mutual selfhood. Accordingly Apess's narrative voice in "Looking-Glass" claims a pluralist identity, occupying and accumulating through a dance of pronouns the full spectrum of potential positions of speakers and listeners in the rhetorical map of his America of 1833. Indeed he goes beyond his own time.

If the effect of Apess's pronominal shifts is to emphasize exchange rather than boundaries between American identities, we will see in his "Looking-Glass" that this is not an easy exchange but more of an ambush, a reappropriation of dominant discourse, a battle of carefully placed volleys. More, he shields his readers from the critical impact of some of his volleys by inspiring in them and joining their own sense of righteous indignation and by attributing those volleys to divine justice. His readers thus become his allies in the struggle against racial prejudices: "Why not put them all away[?]" (155). He is constantly rushing in and out of the national fantasy as a participant and a critic, alternating across a dialectic between subject and object, author and audience of the dramatic national narrative in ways that set him always and already as transcendent in the agency of critique if not in the despondency of colonial victimhood. This manipulation of alternate voices within himself and of his various subject positions within the national narrative generates a dizzying polyvocality, a virtuoso performance of dialogism that runs circles around the monologism of racial and colonial discourses.

Apess's pronominal feats prefigure some of Vizenor's postmodern discussion of pronouns in Native autobiography, where identities do not align themselves with Western categories of self and other. Citing "the heard" as Native storytelling rooted in the oral tradition, Vizenor strikes a neologism in "pronounance" to underline the flexibility of identity in Native writing against dominance: "We must need new pronouns that would misconstrue gender binaries, that would combine the want of a presence in the absence of the heard, a shadow pronoun to pronounce memories in silence, in the absence of cotribal names and nouns" ("Ruins" 23–24). Vizenor has been discussing colonial pronouns as false representation, as a split between

I and we, false since we is always present in I and vice versa: "First person pronouns have no referent" (22).

His context is the history in which social science interpretations of Native literature are overly concerned with alienation of mixed-blood Indian characters from their communities—when the point of those narratives is to show the intermixing, the dialogics, between the two: "The suspicion seems to be that there are essential communal, but not universal, memories that cannot be heard in certain pronouns; the translations of unheard pronouns have never been the sources of tribal consciousness" ("Ruins" 22). A Native autobiographer's worldview, according to Vizenor, cannot help but be based in the direct experience of oral traditions rather than in the social science translations that remove and isolate identities into defined pronominal positions. The mature Apess spoke from Native oral traditions, not only as an exhorter in the oratorical traditions of the Native church but also in the storytelling cultures of his home Indian communities and those of his extensive travels in Indian Country across New England and southeastern Canada. The effect politically of his own pronounance that aspires to pronounce Native experience of injustice while claiming equal rights is to redefine national identity without racial markers. Racial exclusions of "we" would reify rhetorical separation by first-person pronouns. With that ethical rhetorical strategy as his safety net, he then performs political pronominal acrobatics in "Looking-Glass."

O'Connell touches on this politics of pronouns in his introduction to the complete works of Apess: "'Our' history and culture would no longer in its pronouns simultaneously make invisible the history and culture of Native Americans and disguise its own exclusivity. The advantages of such a new history, as Apess wonderfully grasped, are that contradictions could not be hidden and no single narrative could suffice . . . [in] the construction of a less exclusionary American culture" (xviii). O'Connell identifies strategies here that modernists and postmodernists after Apess would enlist in the structural and poststructural recognition of interpenetrating opposites, where "contradictions could not be hidden," and in skepticism of dominating ideological metanarratives, where "no single narrative could suffice." Against such contradictions and metanarratives, Apess levies accusations of hypocrisy and aggrandizement, of oppression and dispossession. His works pour across the American ideological landscape like a flood of reproach. Further, his language tries to water that land with new layers of American idealism.

In "Looking-Glass," Apess's facile movement among several relations of alliance and opposition, invoked by first-, second-, and third-person singular and plural pronouns, creates a radical continuum between object and subject: victimizer, victim; citizen, enemy; patriot, critic; white, Indian. His larger strategy in the short "Looking-Glass" is evident in his choice to append it to *The Experiences of Five Christian Indians of the Pequot Tribe*: to outdo the whites at their own game by describing exemplary Christian Indian experiences and to shame whites into change by seeing their own failures against virtuous Native Christians as in a reverse looking-glass. The piece becomes both his jeremiad and his prayer to the American spirit. As in his later *Eulogy on King Philip*, where patriotism is the reflective focus, here he tries to show transformative Christian behavior and to reflect it back at "the White Man" for social transformation. In the stories of *Five Christian Indians* his white readers can see not only their own oppressive shadows but also the fulfillment of their own Christian values and of the Christian American colonial mission, triumphing in the lives of the oppressed through a love achieved beyond those oppressions. Apess is explicit in showing how those values move across lines of race that prejudice would impose. As he writes of his renowned Aunt Sally George awaiting Judgment Day in her grave, "Her friends were many, both natives and whites. . . . But while she sleeps in dust below, she bathes her weary soul in seas of heavenly rest, and not a wave of trouble rolls across her peaceful breast—Oh reader, strive to meet her there" (151).

Driven by such biblical rhetoric, his method in "Looking-Glass" is polemical narrative history. Against a backdrop of universal mortality rather than universal colonialism, he calls for a change of heart. The opening sentences (and fragment) of the first paragraph set a pensive tone to offset and prepare for the luminous crescendo of the finale. Here note how the pronouns (emphasis added) begin to serve his larger purpose by moving his own voice across America: "Having a desire to place a few things before *my* fellow creatures *who* are traveling with *me* to the grave, and to that God *who* is the maker and preserver both of the white man and the Indian, *whose* abilities are the same and *who* are to be judged by one God, *who* will show no favor to outward appearances but will judge righteousness. Now *I* ask if degradation has not been heaped long enough upon the Indians?" (155). Ironical as Apess always is, here in "long enough" his argument is simple against prejudice and "degradation" "heaped" "upon the Indians." In fact it is so simple that he poses it not in a too obvious declarative sentence but in the long opening fragment, in subordinate clauses, and then in the rhetorical question. The slippery form supports the slippery content. His ingenious twists and turns continue as the syntax of multiple referents provides a valuable expression of what is American pluralism.

By the finale, after battering his readers with the forceful rhetoric and the gruesome reflected image of Euro-American injustices, he can elude their defenses and finish by stepping out of the arena. In the finale, his first-person voice drops away, avoiding any vulnerability of monologism. All that remains is the dialogical field, the community of voices driving toward his conclusions, which are communal, pluralistic ones. The disappearance of a personal voice in his finale points us again to his vision for America itself, in Clifford's terms, where "exchange rather than identity is the fundamental value to be sustained." Thus Apess ends "Looking-Glass" with no self-referential pronouns in this millennial exhortation. It's all up to "ye" and "you" compassionate Americans: "Do not get tired, *ye* noble-hearted—only think how many poor Indians want *their* wounds done up daily; the Lord will reward *you*, and pray *you* stop not till this tree of distinction shall be leveled to the earth, and the mantle of prejudice torn from every American heart—then shall peace pervade the union" (161, emphasis added).

"I Shall Be Beautiful while the Earth Lasts" and "My People Will Never Believe Me Again": Identity in Winnemucca

In Winnemucca's career as a vigorous advocate for the Northern Paiute people, her textual identity performs a clear example—with differences—of non-Euro-American selfhood as mapped by the scholar James Ruppert in a "greater self in the communal" (*Mediation* 28) or Clifford's "nexus of relations." Her autobiography embodies Jace Weaver's "communitist" aesthetic. Through dramatic monologue and dialogue on the stage and on the page, she lived a public self for her people. In the process she seized her own limited freedom in her people's name, fighting for their freedom. She herself stood and spoke as the linking point of an otherwise invisible cluster of relations between the Great Basin's Humboldt Sink, Boston, and Washington

DC. By tracing those ties she became a target especially of "the Indian ring" that she exposed and that was invested in maintaining the invisibility of those connections between federal appropriations and Indian Country.

Whatever her private self may have kept private, her various public names mark distinct roles on that complex field of identity: princess, flower, spouse, and author. As Winnemucca, she is the daughter of Old Winnemucca and granddaughter, on her mother's side, of Truckee, two arbiters of power on the Nevada, California, and Oregon frontiers, a position that she exploits to leverage her advocacy for Paiute rights. As Thocmetony, she is the Indigenous "Shell Flower" of Paiute land and language, following a gendered naming custom that links to her people and their place. As Sarah Winnemucca Hopkins, she is wedded literally to the "white brothers" of the Paiutes as well, both as spouse to Lewis H. Hopkins, among a series of husbands, and as translator in official employ of the U.S. Army. Further, as author of *Life Among the Piutes*, claiming all these names, she is shaper of her own complex persona and of Paiute representation as well. Each of these interpellations drew her identity into being, and no "death of the author" critique can do justice to the vitality she brought to each of her "callings."[7]

Yet if she represents a communal self, communal clearly does not mean comfortable. Each of her identity roles in such a field of energies brings her both enthusiastic pleasures and sustained agonies. As the "princess" daughter of chiefs, she was an easy target for enemies both Indian and white. As Shell Flower, Thocmetony, she was witness to dispossession of her ancestral lands. As Sarah she was an exploited, neglected, or betrayed wife more than once, herself a target of sexual colonization.

Each of these roles is draped in cross-cultural garments. Her princess persona was concocted on stage in her performance costume that reflected her white audiences' expectations and projections more than any tribally specific Paiute tradition of regalia. Her Shell Flower identity in her textual manipulation of this role indeed rises out of Paiute cultural soil in order to turn its lovely face to those white audiences and win their sympathy. Her wifely roles clearly tried to bridge the cultural divide as well.

If she is the most culturally "traditional" of the five writers in this study, and if somehow her voice is therefore the most communal, she also is an example of the phenomenon whereby a communal identity achieves radical individuality—and where individuality achieves community. Such a dynamic is paradoxical only to the binary model of cultural contact that Clifford describes as "a Puritan taboo on the mixing of beliefs and bodies." She demonstrates how a communal voice does not exclude a unique and forceful individual voice, and vice versa.

Whoever a changeable Sarah Winnemucca is, her bold language marks her identity. She bore the brunt of losses as fully as her names proclaimed her strengths. Her account of her people's history is animated by the individuality and originality of her own commanding speech, energized by suffering, drawing on Paiute oratorical traditions, and honed by experience with stage performance. As she waves to the crowds, there is never a question of losing sight of her roots. Yet although her Paiute purposes drive her travels and public performances, her efforts to speak for her people proved tragic for her personally, because they also required her to speak for her "white brothers" back to her Paiute people. The unreliable reversals and ironies of those white representations eventually led to her feeling of failure. Her communal self lost its two communities.

In fact her mediating role as army interpreter seems to have been the wedge that drove her people's losses most painfully into her own rambunctious and sad heart. She worked from a perspective bridging both sides of frontier history, yet without power enough to effect change on either side of the divide. Instead she herself was that change. Her family's position of both cultural and bicultural leadership itself prompted her professional role, and we may see the squeeze it put her in, for example, through two exchanges in her position as translator. In the first, she showcases integrity and dedication to her people's cause; in the second, she fears they will turn against her, as eventually many did. In "The Malheur Agency" chapter in *Life Among the Piutes*, where she begins to recount the machinations of the diabolical agent Rinehart, her cousin Jarry, a competing interpreter, gives a glimpse of the Winnemucca family's alienation from the tribe in a conversation with Sarah, entreating her to restrain herself from insisting that the agent deliver the Indians' supplies. In their neocolonial role, Jarry and his group plan to identify themselves as allies of Rinehart, not advocating for the rest of the tribe, and thus manipulating the agent into supplying Jarry's small contingent with grain. "What do we care," Jarry says to Sarah, entreating her not to make trouble, "whether he gives our people anything or not, so long as he gives us something to live on? What do you think our people care for us?

Let them go wherever they like." Jarry is cynically resigned to his estrangement as a bilingual Paiute, but Sarah's response emphasizes both her ethics and a wider sense of relational possibilities: "I said, 'Dear brother, I am ashamed of you, you talk so heartlessly. I am going to see my people dealt rightly by, and to stand by them, and I am going to talk for them just as long as I live. If you want to see your people starve, that is your own business'" (129). Whether or not the published shape of this exchange serves to set up Winnemucca as the heroine, her affirmation of both her people and her mediating role offers a different story from the oppositional limits her cousin-brother imagines. The narrative she advocates is a communal one, a relational foundation for her own identity: "and I am going to talk for them just as long as I live."

Yet that foundation can crumble in colonial times. Later in the narrative, in "The Yakima Affair," Sarah's sensible idealism is buffeted by what seem to be the malicious winds of history but are indeed the machinations of corrupt individuals. As her biographer Sally Zanjani writes, "[Agent] Rinehart may have had reasons for ridding himself of Sarah beyond her insubordination. He plainly saw her great influence among the Paiutes at Malheur—where she was known as 'the princess'—as a challenge to his authority. Moreover, Rinehart's poisonous hatred of her father may have further disposed him against her" (*Sarah Winnemucca* 140). While a band of her people are waiting at Camp Harney to go to Malheur Reservation nearby in Oregon—and hoping to see Rinehart leave there before they have to go—word comes from Washington DC that this group of Paiutes and Bannocks at Camp Harney must trek instead much farther through the snow to Yakima Reservation in Washington Territory.

Historians presume that Rinehart manipulated this relocation for his own convenience, so he would not have to deal with more Paiutes or with Sarah. Because she had been encouraging the people to trust the army instead of Rinehart's BIA bureaucracy, she now rightly fears that they will blame her for the white men's duplicity. Her nexus of relations has been threaded into a line along the frontier boundary of race and now become a noose: "Oh, Major! my people will never believe me again" (*Life Among the Piutes* 204). Her sister Mattie then speaks of the old Paiute economy as defunct. Where now translation is their only livelihood, they are privileged to be educated, yet torn: "We can't help it. We have to work for them [the whites] and if they get our people not to love us, by telling what is not true to them, what can we do? It is they, not us." Sarah's response laments her mediating role: "Our people won't think so because they will never know that it was they [the whites] who told the lie. Oh! I know all our people will say we are working against them and are getting money for all this." As she and Mattie walk down to the "happy" camp, before telling the people the bad news about the forced march to Yakima ahead of them, Sarah grieves, holding her people apart from herself, again in second- and third-person pronouns: "I thought to myself, 'My poor, poor people, you will be happy to-day; to-morrow or next week your happiness will be turned to weeping.' Oh, how sad I was for them! I could not sleep at night, for the sad thing that had come" (204). If Apess was able to bridge those pronominal roles, Winnemucca finds her own bridge as translator collapsing into the flood waters of history.

If her attempts to negotiate dialogue across the frontier boundary were frustrated repeatedly by dialectical oppositions, she yet insisted on her identity as a dialogical actor, especially as author of a dialogical text. She effectively embraced change, and thus her identity persists. A bronze statue of Sarah Winnemucca has recently been installed in the National Statuary Hall of the U.S. Capitol, an official gesture by the state of Nevada and the U.S. government to recognize her voice.[8] Belatedly, more than a century after her death, dialectical history slouches toward dialogism. Her more pluralistic narrative is still alive. We may understand Winnemucca more directly as a force in the direction of American pluralism if we look more closely at those four identities—princess, flower, spouse, and author—as they grow and weave on her pages. In the flower princess we may see her celebrating and mourning her mature Paiute culture. In the author and Mrs. Hopkins we may see her wedded to an adolescent nation. Yet her own mode of marriage, like her cultural and historical positionality, affirms her communal and political Paiute identity to authorize a new American identity.

As I mentioned in the discussion of community, Winnemucca's first two chapters establish her cultural authority to recount this history. They do so by authorizing her identity as the flower princess. The daughter of royalty steps forth immediately in the first paragraph: "My people were scattered at that time over nearly all the territory now known as Nevada. My grandfather [Truckee] was chief of the entire Piute nation, and was camped near

Humboldt Lake, with a small portion of his tribe, when a party travelling eastward from California was seen coming" (*Life Among the Piutes* 5). At the start her Paiute princess identity is complicated across racial lines—and with a peculiar poignancy by her blood connection to the chiefdom—by Truckee's attempt to embrace his "white brothers." When he receives only suspicion, "he knew not what to do. He had expected so much pleasure in welcoming his white brothers to the best in the land, that after looking at them sorrowfully for a little while, he came away quite unhappy" (6). Citing Grandfather Truckee, Winnemucca's many references to "our white brothers" include her ironic usage implying that "our white brothers" are the cause of wars as well. She writes of the painful Washoe incident, "their own white brothers had killed the [white] men for their money" (66) and then blamed the Indians. Thocmetony's mother is the most explicit critic, as she complains of white men's sexual assaults during their California travels: "Oh, if your father only knew how his children were suffering, I know he would kill that white man who tried to take your sister. I cannot see for my life why my father [Truckee] calls them his white brothers. They are not people; they have no thought, no mind, no love" (37). By the contrast between Truckee's warm expectations and their white brothers' depredations, Thocmetony presents her people and herself as battered flowers longing from the first for something far different from the frontier: a cross-racial family in mythic time to match their creation story.

Winnemucca's resulting childhood terror of whites mirrors Apess's childhood terror of Indians. Eventually she reached across that initial divide to work with whites, just as Apess reached through his early fears to work with and for Indians. Sarah not only overcomes her childhood terror of her grandfather's "white brothers"; she, like her grandfather, tries unsuccessfully to embrace them. In her narrative she sets up a contrast to Truckee's vision by linking other Paiutes' apprehension of racial boundaries in the text with sinister troublemakers, especially the corrosively ambitious subchief, Oytes. In one of Oytes's earlier discourses, he claimed to have brought a sickness to the people and extorted payment from them because of it (*Life Among the Piutes* 111). In his selfish scheme he is quite explicit about his racial identity, as he wants Sarah to speak to Agent Parrish: "I want you to talk to your father, as you call him. Tell him I and my men are going to live with our brothers; that is, the Columbia River Indians. I cannot call that white man my father. My father was black, like myself, and you are all white but me, and therefore, tell him I quit my country" (112–13). This opaque quotation suggests that Oytes associates Paiutes who collaborate with whites as racially identified with them as well. Winnemucca explains elsewhere, concerning "father" or "mother" as a mode of greeting to convey fundamental Paiute respect, "This is the way our people address any one who is their superior. If a woman, it is their mother; if a man, it is their father" (143). She does not measure superior and inferior by racial markers but by power. Oytes, however, uses racial distinctions to mark the limit of any "superior" rank in his world. Eventually in the narrative he returns in disgrace after repeatedly breaking ranks with his own people, failing to respect anyone, and thus his racial boundaries are associated with values that are not Paiute. Tragically appropriate to Winnemucca's ethical map, he even turns violently against some of his people, killing Subchief Egan (whose respectful discourse was the occasion for Winnemucca's explanation of "father" and "mother"). Oytes's lack of Paiute ethics thus is associated with his emphasis on racial distinctions. Winnemucca's equanimity across racial divides indeed is one of the remarkable dynamics of her text, especially as it claims traditional roots. Undoubtedly it accounts for some of her recognition today, but it points to the particular way she wielded her powers as a princess to clear a way toward pluralism for her people. It is important not to sentimentalize the phrase "white brothers," yet the brutalities of frontier relations cannot eclipse the depth of interaction, the openness to respectful exchange rather than naïve vulnerability residing in Truckee's high expectations, even as dialogics was again rebuffed by dialectics.

In contrast with the initial princess persona, Winnemucca's more subtle flower identity unfolds gradually, in the chapter "Domestic and Social Moralities," as she identifies her voice with wholesome traditions of gender relations. Indeed it is a chapter designed to win the support of nineteenth-century American womanhood for the Paiute cause by establishing the modesty of Paiute womanhood. She wants her audience to identify with her people and her cause. Thus the flower blooms demurely, as we may see in a detailed ethnographic passage from her text: "We [girls] would all go in company to see if the flowers we were named for were yet in bloom, for almost all the girls are named for flowers. . . . I will repeat what we say of ourselves [at the Flower Festival]. . . . 'My name is Thocmetony. I am so beautiful! Who will come and dance with me while I am so beautiful? Oh come and be happy with me! I shall be beautiful while the earth lasts.' The young men sing with us as they dance beside us" (*Life Among the Piutes* 46–47). "I shall be beautiful while the earth lasts." This gendered identification with flowers is rooted in ancient and intimate Paiute connections to their land. The lightness of this youthful enthusiasm sings against the weighted sorrow of her narrative. The complex power of those flowers, fertile and vulnerable, the power of the land, here intensifies her political appeal.

That power is indeed gendered in her account. Appropriate to respect in Paiute culture, based on an animistic sense of environment, this identification with a delicate flower does not deprive her of recognition for her own intelligence and will, as we saw in her account of parental guidance: "She is never forced by her parents to marry against her wishes" (*Life Among the Piutes* 49). This equitable relationship with parents and grandparents establishes a fundamental mutual self-respect. Here Thocmetony's identity as shell flower would in fact intensify her political position as princess, planted as it is in such a generational network of supporting female and male roles.

The esteem for daughters and the nurturing and protecting force of Paiute fatherhood that we see in this custom arises elsewhere in her text, especially in her gentle childhood relations with her adoring grandfather Truckee. This Paiute flower is raised as royalty, linking again her princess and her flower identities. At one point, when, very young, she cries for fear of white men's guns, Truckee calls her "the young lady" and his "dearest" and himself "her sweetheart." Even while he is trying to convince his people of the white man's good intentions, Truckee is extravagantly patient with her fearful and eventually willful tears, teasing, "Well, I shall not live if she does not come and tell me she loves me" (*Life Among the Piutes* 17). The affectionate side of his masculinity mirrors her later tough role as female leader. She in turn refers later to "his dear old face" and calls him "the great light" of the world. When she describes his death, she writes tenderly, "I think if he had put out his hands and asked me to go with him, I would gladly have folded myself in his arms" (68). As a child she clearly found her own strength of will growing in a nourishing parental embrace, a specific balance of personhood and peoplehood.

The masculine nurturing role in her identity construction was not unique to her grandfather. In her heroic adulthood, when she was in her mid-thirties, her father Old Winnemucca greeted her with similar solicitude when she arrived in Camp McDermitt after an all-night ride during the 1878 Bannock War: "My poor papa was the first one who came up. He ran up and took me in his arms and said, 'Oh, my poor child! I thought I never would see you, for the papers said you were killed by the Bannocks. We have all mourned for you, my child. Oh, when I heard you, my darling, who saved my life for a little while longer, had gone first, I thought my heart would break!' I put my face down on his bosom" (*Life Among the Piutes* 189). This shell flower is rooted in Paiute soil.

She would need that emotional self-assurance of a royal daughter to fulfill the destiny that her grandfather laid out for her by having her educated in the white man's tongue and pen. Standing between the worlds, straddling the frontier, she exercises bilingual fluency and bicultural facility as multiple layers of translation. Yet she always does so from the vantage point of her Paiute identity. Indeed her role as intermediary sets up self-reflection that consolidates her Indian identity against the colonial gaze. For example, again during the Bannock War, when she is riding with the soldiers in search of her people, she asserts her Indian identity against the whites in affirming her cultural knowledge against their ignorance of "signal fires" on the high ridges above their trail. Earlier, one of Old Winnemucca's sons had lit a "son's signal fire" to notify the traveling camp that he was approaching, and now here is a different message in a different form of fire: "We had travelled from the Malheur Agency one hundred and forty-four miles. The first night we camped there sister Mattie and I saw a signal-fire of distress and loneliness, and for help also. All the officers came to me and asked me the meaning of it. I told them it was the signal-fire of one Indian. They asked me how I knew. I said, 'I am an Indian woman and understand all kinds of signal-fires'" (*Life Among the Piutes* 186). The understanding that comes with being "an Indian woman" is the certificate of her power, while it positions her cross-culturally both inside and outside that identity, speaking across to communicate from within.

Another dramatic scene from "The Bannock War" chapter will suffice to recap the changing complexity of her multiple identity roles. She is standing at Battle Creek beside the commander of the cavalry at the beginning of a battle, even while she looks across the literal frontier and identifies herself with the Indians facing down the army guns. "Oh, what a feeling I had just before the fight came on! Every drop of blood in my veins went out. I said to sister, 'We will see a great many of our people killed to-day, and soldiers, too.' Then the bugle sounded 'Fire!' I heard the chiefs singing as they ran up and down the front line as if it was only a play, and on our side was nothing but the reports of the great guns. All my feeling was gone. I wanted to go to them" (*Life Among the Piutes* 175). Her afterthought, "and soldiers, too," locates her attention first on "our people," while acknowledging her secondary identification with her employers. As she stands there, her torn identity as Sarah, the army employee, agonizes for Thocmetony, the shell flower princess. The circulation of her dialogical identity is stunned and paralyzed by a dialectical war: "Every drop of blood in my veins went out."

"The Center that Pulled Him Down Closer": Identity in Silko

If Native literatures show America how identity is the ground of change, Leslie Silko's narratives focus on that ground as a way of processing change in particularly affirmative ways, where endings are seen as beginnings, as transitions, in natural, mythical, not necessarily benevolent but balanced cycles. Here is such a place in time near the climax of *Ceremony*: "A transition was about to be completed: the sun was crossing the zenith to a winter place in the sky, a place where prayers of long winter nights would call out their long summer days of new growth. Tonight the old priests would be praying for the force to continue the relentless motion of the stars" (258). In a place of prayer, winter and summer overlap in time. In time of prayer, summer and winter overlap in a place of prayer. Prayer here is an act of translating space into time, endings into beginnings. The prime markers of earthly time remain the solar positions in space at solstice and equinox. Time and space overlap. Identity in Silko, as here for Tayo, strives to tune itself to those cycles on that spinning ground: "His protection was there in the sky, in the position of the sun, in the pattern of the stars" (259).

Similarly we find in *Almanac of the Dead* that her stories of resilient identity on Native ground grow from a linkage of ground as space and change as time. Identity enlarges to recognize itself in that cyclic process. Especially through the ruminations of old Calabazas, the narration offers an ancient notion, akin to now somewhat popular perspectives derived from quantum physics, of space and time as interchangeable, here as two aspects of a larger "living organism": "Each location, each place, was a living organism with time running inside it like blood, time that was unique to that place alone" (629). That living organism becomes specific places on the earth itself, and those who keep in touch with the cycles of the earth in those places can thereby survive, even celebrate change. The affirmation in *Almanac* pivots on this circulation of space and time, as Old Pancakes asserts: "Guns and knives would not resolve the struggle. He had reminded the people of the prophecies different tribes had. In each version one fact was clear: the world that the whites brought with them would not last. It would be swept away in a giant gust of wind. All they had to do was to wait. It would be only a matter of time" (235). If time is the place, the land will come back around. The giant gust of wind may be time itself, the process of change that moves on and in the ground. "Because he had seen a lot of changes throughout those years of struggle," and because Old Pancakes remains in synch with the land of his people, he can travel Europe with the Wild West shows, he can be mistaken for Geronimo as a white projection, he can listen to the prophecies that draw on those cycles of time and space, and he can wait on—or in—that ground through the changes.

The "giant gust of wind" does not operate as an allegorical or even symbolic relation between wind and time, just as Silko's linkage between ground and space is something other than symbolic in the Euro-American literary sense. Paula Gunn Allen's elucidation of "symbolism in American Indian ceremonial literature" is key here, as she states that it "is not symbolic in the usual sense; that is, the four mountains in the Mountain Chant do not stand for something else. They are those exact mountains perceived psychically, as it were, or mystically. The color red, as used by the Lakota, doesn't stand for sacred or earth, but is the quality of a being, the earth itself" ("Sacred Hoop" 16). Interior and exterior are not distinguished. As Abram describes Indigenous discourse, there is a "subtle dependence of various 'interior,' mental phenomena upon certain easily overlooked or taken-for-granted aspects of the surrounding sensuous world. . . . The presumably interior, mental awareness of the 'past' and the 'future' [is] dependent upon our sensory experience of that which is hidden beneath the ground and concealed beyond the horizon" (*The Spell of the Sensuous* 261–62). If the linguistic signs by which humans mark their own awareness are indeed "dependent upon our sensory experience," Abram is describing this intricate relationship between cognition and physical perception as latent beneath human language across cultures. Even those cultures that take pride in their literate mental gymnastics as rational may repress or "easily overlook" their linguistic dependence on the earth. The changing wind *is* the change of time.

Silko is celebrating earth-based identity because it becomes as resilient as the earth itself, not merely symbolically. Thus the affirmation in this human-nature reciprocity for Calabazas and Old Pancakes is that such a direct relationship with the earth cannot but prevail, because the earth is bigger, we might say, with its geologic cycles, than a white culture's mental constructs that would separate us from it: "The world that the whites brought with them would not last." Because time and space are interchangeable, "all they had to do was to wait" where they are. Native ground in Silko is both symbol and reality, both signifier and signified, a single sign system whereby identity moves in her stories. Because Old Pancakes and Calabazas identify with that Native ground, they can change with the seasons: "It would be only a matter of time."

Toward the end of *Almanac*, Silko writes of an ultimate identification with the earth through the "giant stone snake" that had reappeared at Laguna: "The snake didn't care if people were believers or not; the work of the spirits and prophecies went on regardless. . . . The snake didn't care about the uranium tailings; humans had desecrated only themselves with the mine, not the earth. . . . Man was too insignificant to desecrate her" (762). This radical identification of the story of identity with the earth itself can even write, "With all humans dead, the earth would still be sacred" (762). This is the relentless detachment in *Almanac* from all but identity as earth, the ground itself. Humans can either hold on to that sacred connection or be lost.

Similarly in *Ceremony*, Tayo gradually experiences the trust of a reconnection to the cycles of identity on the ground, as in an evocative passage celebrating the process of his reuniting with the land and thereby with himself:

> He stood on the edge of the rimrock and looked down below: the canyons and valleys were thick powdery black; their variations of height and depth were marked by a thinner black color. He remembered the black of the sand paintings on the floor of the hogan; the hills and

mountains were the mountains and hills they had painted in sand. He took a deep breath of cold mountain air: there were no boundaries; the world below and the sand paintings inside became the same that night. The mountains from all the directions had been gathered there that night. (152)

Not only does the ground prevail in her narratives, but here Silko's text is explicit about the interchangeability of symbol and symbolized, of the sand painting and the mountainous ground it invokes, of earth as identity. Again Allen's articulation of Native symbolism is useful here as well. Just as the sand painting and the mountain are interchangeable, so the mountain and its meaning are one: "There were no boundaries; the world below and the sand paintings inside became the same that night."

The ground of identity in Silko thus works like gravity, keeping us in motion yet on our feet on the earth's crust, keeping selfhood both changing and the same, as in Tayo's perhaps most eloquent prayer in *Ceremony*: "When the mountain lion stopped in front of him, it was not hesitation, but a chance for the moonlight to catch up with him. Tayo got to his knees slowly and held out his hand. 'Mountain lion,' he whispered, 'mountain lion, becoming what you are with each breath, your substance changing with the earth and the sky'" (204). The invocative focus on being and substance, becoming and change is the lyrical expression of Silko's fascination with these ancient existential questions.

As Tayo recovers on his back from a fall from his horse, Silko's narration takes this notion of land as identity further still. She recounts his meditation that neatly clarifies identity in gravity itself, in the immanent energy of the ground, of mass, of physical presence. Because it so vividly expresses the principle of identity as the ground of change, I cite her passage at some length:

Black pebbles and the ancient cinders the mountain had thrown poked into his backbone. He closed his eyes but did not sleep. He felt cold gusts of wind scattering dry oak leaves in the grass. . . . He was aware of the center beneath him; it soaked into his body from the ground through the torn skin on his hands, covered with powdery black dirt. The magnetism of the center spread over him smoothly like rainwater down his neck and shoulders; the vacant cool sensation glided over the pain like feather-down wings. It was pulling him back, close to the earth, where the core was cool and silent as mountain stone, and even with the noise and pain in his head he knew how it would be: a returning rather than a separation. He was relieved because he feared leaving people he loved. But lying above the center that pulled him down closer felt more familiar to him than any embrace he could remember; and he was sinking into the elemental arms of mountain silence. (*Ceremony* 210)

With clear sensation, the phrase "lying above the center that pulled him down closer" maps a relation to the land that is precartographic. It is gravitational. It is an identity so elemental, so mineral that it approximates death.

This identity in Silko's description lies continuously beneath the boundaries of nations and states, just as identity functions beneath systems of selfhood and otherness. Where there are "no boundaries," there must be no cultural, historical constructs operating within limited time frames, no wins or losses of an oppositional history. Again, she is not jettisoning specific tribal difference or identity in favor of homogeneity in "no boundaries." Instead she is transcending the limits of colonial history that would erase those differences: "The dreams had been terror at loss, at something lost forever; but nothing was lost; all was retained between the sky and the earth, and within himself. He had lost nothing. The snow-covered mountain remained, without regard to titles of ownership or the white ranchers who thought they possessed it. . . . The mountain outdistanced their destruction, just as love had outdistanced death. The mountain could not be lost to them, because it was in their bones" (*Ceremony* 230). Tribal identity "remained" with the "snow-covered mountain" that Tayo stands upon.

While Silko builds Tayo's identity on this ground, he has a choice: either to remain in the surface world of "separation" and opposition or to opt for "returning": "He could secure the thresholds with molten pain and remain; or he could let go and flow back. It was up to him" (*Ceremony* 211). Out of fear generated by the witchery of opposition, he could choose resistance, or he could return to "the center, where the voice of the silence was familiar and the density of the dark earth loved him" (211).

As we saw in the introduction to this discussion of identity in Native American literatures, Owens asserted that mixed-blood identity is "the dominant theme in novels by Indian authors" (*Other Destinies* 40). Certainly the plots and characterizations in some of Silko's longer works would support Owens's view. *Ceremony* is "about" the mixed-blood dilemmas of Tayo; *Storyteller* is "about" Silko's own mixed-blood heritage in her relation to the stories of her Laguna pueblo community; *Almanac of the Dead* is "about" mestizo as well as full-blood characters negotiating the dark forces of colonialism; *Gardens in the Dunes* is "about" the question of mixing bloods and cultures while holding onto home, whether Native or Euro-American. *Turquoise Ledge* is "about" such liminal space. And certainly her attention to the mixed-blood theme develops from book to book as well. For instance, in contrast to *Ceremony*, where the "half-breed" Tayo represents a future through healing, in *Almanac* the mestizo Menardo is doomed by his assimilation to white material, indeed mercenary values.[9] Again, it is not race, and certainly not the "separation" of oppositional racial marking, that constitutes a stable identity in Silko but "returning" to the ground of identity, to Indian land, to the stories and communities that live across time in and on that land.

Thus on literary dimensions built through plot and characterization in Silko's works, Owens's mixed-blood theme, with all its psychological and political richness, is only part of Silko's more abstract theme and pragmatic strategy of negotiation, one might say translation, that occupies her work in philosophical, metaphysical, or spiritual terms. She addresses a question: In a world of "surprises" and "sheer wonder," including the witchery that drives *Ceremony*, *Storyteller*, *Almanac*, and *Gardens*, how to negotiate the oppositions, the binaries of existence, ultimately the dichotomy of death and life? Evidently for Silko, such a poetic question underlies political and psychological questions of race and legal questions of land.

Another way to translate between Owens and Silko is to suggest that she is talking about something different from the "hybridity" that Owens foregrounds as the mixed-blood identity issue (*Mixedblood Messages* 52). Indeed Silko moves in the direction of the Creek scholar Craig Womack, whose chapter "The Integrity of American Indian Claims" in *American Indian Literary Nationalism* (Weaver et al.) bears the tongue-in-cheek subtitle "Or, How I Learned to Stop Worrying and Love My Hybridity." Amid detailed intellectual exploration of the problems of the "hybrid" label, Womack makes the positive claim "that exploring Indian realities (whatever their degree of purity or impurity) was just as legitimate as confessing European influences" (131). Whatever theoretical "hybridity" might inform Native discourse, Womack validates a focus on Indigenous sources and "realities." As Justice puts it succinctly, "Hybridity is all the rage, but the political expression of *peoplehood* remains the central principle of Indian literatures" (*Our Fire Survives* 214).

I invoke the academically popular, but unfortunate, dehumanizing discourse of hybridity only because I want to deflect this term. Precisely because of the opportunity to register its colonialist, hence racist connotations, I would contrast Silko's resistant discursive strategies, especially to show how she reinvents the meaning of hybrids in *Gardens in the Dunes*. Silko's "ghost dance" mythopoetics specifically contrast with hybridization's linear colonial narrative strictures. All of her novels take the radical step of claiming what could be called precolonial hybridity. She invokes alliances and spiritual sources that not only precede the colonial era but preempt history itself. The "witchery" in *Ceremony* and *Storyteller*, the "almanac" itself in *Almanac of the Dead*, and the "ghost dance messiah" in *Gardens in the Dunes* all conceive a mythic substrate that transcends history. Perhaps a term such as Vizenor's "paracolonial" (*Manifest Manners* 77) might suit Silko, meaning beside or parallel with colonial history, except that Vizenor's term actually emphasizes "colonial" as the determining force, in "the simulations and cruelties of paracolonial history," that is, history written as the voice of colonialism. Silko's narratives suggest instead that there is an entirely different yet forceful story that constitutes our experience apart from that history. The almanac in *Almanac of the Dead* and the homing quest in *Gardens in the Dunes* focus on that different story, that "Day of Deliverance," to clarify the suffering of the innocent. By way of the intercontinental ghost dancers of *Gardens*, Silko makes visible an alternative chronos and thus an alternate cosmos.

Beyond history, Silko's is an extreme question of identity: not only "Who is an Indian?" but "Who is an Indian after death?"

> She keeps the stories for those who return
>> but more important
>> for the dear ones who do not come back
>> so that we may remember them
>> and cry for them with the stories. (*Storyteller* 247)

While this line from "The Storyteller's Escape" summons another of Silko's motifs, the power of story, it indeed affirms a tribal identity beyond the body, at a gravitational level, out on southwestern lava beds.

Much has been made of Silko's affirmation of the power of stories to keep the people alive. Her texts and her interviews are explicit on this point. Yet beneath a stern and lyrical insistence on the power of stories lies this sorrow, "for the dear ones who do not come back." To understand this power, one must understand this sorrow.

Certainly the spiritual question of Indian identity beyond death, of ultimate human identity, is shaped by the social pressures of history. Silko's concern with surviving death must link to any Indian writer's concern with surviving history—a history of genocide. Is there any escape from the manifest destiny of death? That becomes the question of Indian identity in Silko. Yet in a pattern of Indigenous ceremony, her answer is to walk through death itself, not to avoid or deny it. Indeed, as in the passage of Tayo contemplating the earth's center, the embrace of gravity that is identity links imagistically to death and decay. Rational resistance and self-defense only postpone the inevitable embrace: "He knew if he left his skull unguarded, if he let himself sleep, it would happen: the resistance would leak out and take with it all barriers, all boundaries. . . . He would seep into the earth and rest with the center, where the voice of the silence was familiar and the density of the dark earth loved him" (*Ceremony* 211). That "unguarded" return of apparent decay is the ground of identity. Where "the dark earth loved him" is where he can be sure of himself, where he knows by the pull of gravity that his identity resides. Whether that pull is life or death remains secondary to the choice to be loved, as in his musing on the Elk Woman, Ts'eh: "Their days together had a gravity emanating from the mesas and arroyos, and it replaced the rhythm that had been interrupted so long ago. . . . The breaking and crushing were gone, and the love pushed inside his chest, and when he cried now, it was because she loved him so much" (238). Gravity, the cosmological force of attraction, is the energy of identity in Silko's ground, here as it translates into human love.

"The Storyteller's Escape," positioned near the end of *Storyteller*, is one of Silko's most direct treatments of this "postmorbid" level of the question of identity. Yet for all this verse narrative's clarity, it resonates, appropriately, with ambiguity, even mystery. Where the enemy could be tribal or colonial, stories here are equated with escape, both from the enemy and from death.

> The storyteller keeps the stories
>> all the escape stories
>>> she says "With these stories of ours
>>>> we can escape almost anything
>>>> with these stories we will survive." (247)

If identity is the ground that witnesses and experiences change, these stories, built into the places of the people, the "storied ground" of Native land, help them to escape enemies and "almost anything," even death. "With these stories we will survive," because the stories hold onto that ground, the land, the witness.

> "In this way
> we hold them
> and keep them with us forever
> and in this way
> we continue."

Not only is the boundary overcome between life and death—"and keep them with us forever"—but the principle of opposition is overcome as well, "and in this way / we continue" beyond the fighting. In the light of this brief story, Betonie's advice and Tayo's decision to fight no more with the destroyers (*Ceremony* 134, 265) is not only a savvy strategy for living, but a transcendence of death.

The story line of this verse narrative in *Storyteller* dramatizes the identity principle of boundarylessness, leaving only the land and its people. Identity becomes the ground itself. An old storyteller is with "the people" as they "leave the village / and hurry into the lava flows / where they waited until the enemy had gone." Although in years past she had been the one who would look back at the incapacitated to tell their story of death—

> "Always before
> it was me
> turning around
> for the last look

at the pregnant woman
the crippled boy
old man Shio'see
    slowing up
    lying down
    never getting up again . . .
so I could tell where these dear ones stopped" (248)

—now the storyteller knows it is her turn to drop behind and die. She cannot expect the people to sacrifice for her. The sacrifice must be hers for the people. Death itself she does not fear, only the possibility that no one else will witness and tell the story, that her sacrifice might not register for the people's strength, that her oneness with the ground might be overlooked:

The only thing was
    this time
    she couldn't be sure
    if there would be anyone
    to look back
    and later tell the others. . . .
She was thinking
    I could die peacefully
    if there was just someone to tell
    how I finally stopped
    and where. (249–50)

The ground of her death, "how I finally stopped / and where," would become her identity beyond this life, if someone tells the tale. So, lacking a physical observer, she makes up a story of a witness, a child looking back, and of herself telling the child, "Don't wait! / Go on without me! / Tell them I said that— / Tell them I'm too old too tired." The power of story itself is affirmed as a story of an old storyteller making up a story of a young storyteller: "the child looked back." Storytelling becomes her "escape" as a story told. If consciousness is the gravity of self-reflection, she lives on because now there is "someone to tell / how I finally stopped / and where" on the land. This becomes a story of her identity surviving death by becoming a story of a place, a particular ground.

Yet when she dies of the heat after no enemies find her, or does not die—the metaphorical ambiguity is unlockable in the text: "About this time / the sun lifted off from her shoulders like a butterfly"—her spirit or her body returns to live on in the village.

> And it was the best escape story she had come up with yet
> > How four days later when the people came back
> > from their hide-outs in the lava flow
> > there she was
> > > sitting in front of her house
> > > waiting for them. (253)

The mystery of her sitting back at home nudges toward death in the last stanza, where she reviews "her getaway story" with reference to "the last day":

> > how they remembered her
> > and cried for her
> > Because she always had a way with stories
> > even on the last day
> > when she stopped in the shade
> > on the north side of Dough Mountain. (253)

The double entendre in the story line matches the uncertainty in questions of life and death. Where the power of the story carries her—as a story—further than death, the effect of this complexity is simply to affirm an identity that survives, again as ground, "on the north side of Dough Mountain." This last image of the land then returns us to identity as the matrix of the earth, where changes, even passages between life and death, continue.

Further, identities can choose their changes through storytelling itself in Silko. In escape, in the storyteller's ultimate ability to weave an alternative to death, lies Silko's aesthetic and ethic of witnessing as storytelling. In the keepers of the notebooks, as she reiterates in *Almanac of the Dead*, "Yoeme had believed power resides within the stories; this power ensures the story to be retold, and with each retelling a slight but permanent shift took place. . . . Where such miraculous escape stories are greatly prized and rapidly circulated, miraculous escapes from death gradually increase" (581). Essentially Silko is laying out the mechanism or the energetic field that explains how witnessing becomes retelling becomes rewriting history. Rewriting history means defeating the witchery that would tell only the story of domination and opposition, of the life of white America versus the death of Indian America.

Thus the mixing in Silko is more cosmological than racial. If mixed-blood identity is her topic according to Owens's analysis, that identity becomes potentially transcendent when it links to tribal ground. Indeed if it fails to make that link to the earth, identity, whether mixed blood or full blood, in Silko's narratives fails to survive as Native. Emo in *Ceremony* is a full-blood who revels and disappears in the witchery and thus is ostracized by the community, a fate worse than death as an exclusion from the ground of identity itself. "'After all the trouble he made for us . . . they told him to never come back around here. The old man said that. They told him.' Auntie paused. 'I heard he went to California,' she said. 'California,' Tayo repeated softly, 'that's a good place for him'" (273), as though the West Coast must be hell. It certainly is not Laguna. Emo is like those lost we see in *Almanac*: "The snake didn't care about the uranium tailings; humans had desecrated only themselves with the mine, not the earth." Yet in contrast to Emo, it is not Tayo's mixed blood that is the key to his survival. It is his identification with "no boundaries" on the earth, in essence his relaxation of the separate but "mixed" boundaries in his own blood.

To underline identification in Silko with earth energies beyond blood, we may finish by looking briefly in *Almanac* at the mestizo Menardo. Unlike Tayo in *Ceremony*, this mixed-blood is not the future, while those who live with the land, "the people," regardless of race, march for renewal. Menardo occupies himself only with accumulating wealth and the paranoia that follows: "Gamblers who got lucky numbers lived short lives. . . . Now Menardo had his mansion of white marble and his pool of water lily blossoms; on the ironed linens of his king-size bed, Menardo, the mestizo, savored the luscious fruit of a skinny white woman. . . . But Menardo's dreams were the dreams of a man soon to die" (472–73). In contrast to the border-crossing dealings of Calabazas, Menardo's capitalism is not communal; he does not share his wealth. In wise Tacho's Mayan point of view, we get the sense of doomed identity for Menardo, his boss: "The boss's dreams had been the worst dreams; even the slow-witted boss had understood that his days were numbered. Tacho traced Menardo's decline to the visit by the norteamericano who had given the boss the bulletproof vest" (472). If the mixed-blood Tayo survives in *Ceremony*, it is not because of his mixed blood but because of his reconnection with his identity on Native ground. Menardo misses that step. He is doomed because he misses the gravitational center, the earth logic, the ground under Silko's literary world.

"The Address Will Keep Changing": Identity in Alexie

The principle of identity in Alexie as the ground on which change unfolds plays out even in the title of *Reservation Blues*. The reservation itself experiences the blues of modern existence, as do its inhabitants, new and ancient. Alexie's early mixed reception in Indian Country might have been due not only to an "exaggeration of despair" and not only to the classic problem of writers airing dirty laundry but also his tendency toward what at first glance seems like postmodernist identity. As Owens distinguishes "literature by Native American authors" that "tends to seek transcendence" of the "ephemerality" of postmodernism, Alexie's comic mode seems willing to identify with Owens's description of postmodernism's "fragmentation and chaos of experience." Indeed Alexie's meteoric growth in popularity may be due to the courage of his narrators to find Owens's "ordered cosmos" and the "delicate equilibrium" of Native storytelling in the intense heart of change.

Let's look at one of Alexie's shorter texts for details of this dynamic of changing identities. His pivotal poem with the dead-pan title "Introduction to Native American Literature" is saturated in irony. It plays out his Poetry = Anger x Imagination formula through intimate confrontations as it toys with clichés of academic objectification of Indian lives and stories. We can trace the strength of identity to change through ironic agency in these lines.

As the first entry in the first section of *Old Shirts and New Skins*, published in 1993 on the momentum of his initial double-barreled success with *The Business of Fancydancing* and *I Would Steal Horses*, the poem directly proclaims a didactic, revisionary project that Alexie shares with so many American Indian writers who labor to retell history against the triumphalism of manifest destiny. "Introduction to Native American Literature" epitomizes Alexie's early voice, mixing in-your-face polemics with small dreamings of myth. The effect is at once cinematic and sermonic. The poem directly challenges the reader by flashing acute details of poverty and dispossession against fragments of reverie that briefly elevate misery to mythic proportions.

For starters, the poem lays down a foundational yet elusive principle of both identity and community, in the ultimate unknowability, rather than uncertainty, of shifting identity across difference. Here the ineffable becomes acceptable: "Send it a letter: the address will keep changing. / . . . Knock on its door: you'll hear voices" (*Old Shirts* 3–5). As the address keeps changing, so does identity. If no definition of another human is adequate, certainly the label of neither victim nor victimizer will suffice. According to the poem, America, in facing history, cannot recolonize Indians through sympathy. By empathy, however, with the consciousness that Alexie presents in these stories and poems, non-Native readers may feel not only the humanity but also the radical difference of Indian lives, a difference that itself must be a component of humanity.[10] To know is to know you cannot know.

Further, the poem's epigraph, "must I give you / the last words to the story too," quoting a lament by Alex Kuo, Alexie's mentor at Washington State University, slaps the reader. Standing inside the allusion are the author's attitude, his mixed literary traditions, and his accusation of the audience's historical and literary failures. Kuo's public exhaustion with cross-culturally ignorant readers is followed directly by the voice of Alexie's persona echoing the weariness of that task as he addresses his irresponsible audience invested in its own ignorance: "& here you are again (again) / asking me to explain broken glass." That shattered glass follows the drama of the first line of the poem: "Somewhere in America a television explodes." Such an opening, asserting its own condescending fatigue, immediately takes on the American audience and its media stereotypes of Indians. An angrily weary Indian is not a vanished Indian, and if not vanished, then he himself, not some manifest destiny, is an agent of change—if not already debilitated.

Alexie's textual persona, as a shifting identity itself, is thus explicitly and reflexively conscious of the traditions of Euro-American literature, the Native American literary renaissance, the painful colonial history and politics that continue to shape such literary outpourings, and of his own emerging leadership in that process. This mixed literary consciousness—itself a function of changing identity structures—takes many narrative forms, not the least of which is his early persona that may be characterized by a tough attitude of confrontation and provocation against a complacent white America and a rallying voice of anger and righteousness for despondent Native youth. His voice exemplifies the shifting ground of identity. This confrontative attitude is his claim to the agency of expression, the power of the word in both oral traditional and biblical senses that N. Scott Momaday and so many other Indian writers invoke.[11]

Relying on both print and film in a visual video age, Alexie's in-your-face approach to the not-so-dear reader reflects his urgent project to reshape Euro-American audiences' awareness of their liability for history. Thus he reshapes American identity from cowboy to colonialist.[12] It's not only Indian identities that are changing. The enlightened though exhausted voice of an American Indian bard in the poem reads the broken shards of American self-representation like a seer, telling an American readership to clean up after itself, to take responsibility for its brutal inheritance: "Am I the garbageman of your dreams?" That garbage may be the fetishized objects of the voyeuristic colonial gaze: "You scour the reservation landfill / through the debris of so many lives," where white readers, like grave robbers, look to Indian stories to fulfill their dreams. For Indians, the effect of white men's curiosity is further erasure and dispossession, as manifest destiny pursues New Age appropriations of Native cultures. Thus the section finishes in a solitary line: "All you bring me is an empty bottle."

If strong writers create their audiences,[13] Alexie is doing so by educating non-Natives to their own complicity in colonialism, as a sort of Indigenous shriver. By affirming his own bardic role to instruct readers through anger and imagination, intimacy and irony, he reshapes white readers' ability to face themselves, America, and American Indians.

Alexie thus dramatizes an individualistic literary attitude, laying claim to one's own voice and refusing to be defined by others. That refusal has taken on philosophical dimensions, opening creative agency to an existential randomness that affirms this key narrative structure of identity as change. In a preface, "What I've Learned as a Filmmaker," to *The Business of Fancydancing: The Screenplay*, Alexie explains, "We've all been trained to make movies in three-act structures, as if Aristotle could have somehow predicted how artistically conservative all of these liberal-filmmakers were going to become. 'Resolution! There must be resolution!' Fuck resolutions, fuck closure, fuck the idea of story arc. Embrace the incomplete, embrace ambiguity, and embrace the magical and painful randomness of life" (7–8). It takes a certain courage of identity to embrace incompletion and ambiguity as both magical and painful. Perhaps a good word for such an identity is *open*. Alexie spurns "resolution and redemption" because of the narrative weight of terminal creeds associated with such finales, but does he miss Vizenor's mediating compassion? Although he is less explicit than Vizenor, I do think Alexie dramatizes compassion in the poignancy of his characterizations.

Flexible identity structures are not only surprising or humorous; they know how to survive in the comic mode of ecosocial adaptation. Thus, in addition to literary realism as ambiguity, there are, again, other reasons for Alexie's aversion to narrative closure in standard plot patterns. As Vizenor's "terminal creeds" most directly indicate, colonial closure means tragedy for Indians. Oral storytelling patterns are often open-ended, even interactive. Sit-coms and prequel/sequel movies are open-ended in a more manipulative mode. Experience, for Alexie, tends to be random, magical, and painful; so why not art? He says in an interview, "I always want to be a moving target" (Spencer, "What It Means to Be Sherman Alexie" 6). The extent to which Alexie accomplishes an antiresolution narrative structure to match his proclaimed anti-Aristotelian poetics is certainly a question. Yet there is no unmediated resolution in his work. He invariably tinges, or sometimes loads, affirmations with characteristic irony of painful incompletion, doubly strengthening the affirmation by making it "a moving target" as well. His humorous effort to elude the effects of colonial mourning is in fact the flip side of what one Spokane critic has called his "exaggeration of despair" (Bird, "The Exaggeration of Despair"). "A song of mourning that would become a song of celebration" raises complex questions of an author's representation of his own community, amid the questions of changing identity.

"Miraculous Escape Stories"

Where the ground lies in works by Apess, Winnemucca, McNickle, Silko, and Alexie, it is more than the substratum. It is the horizon and the air, the breath itself in their words. Past. Present. Future. Or as the Hopi language would have it, manifest and unmanifest.[14] As "land" in politics and economics, as "home" in history and culture, as "mother" in body and spirit, the changing ground remains the substance of Indigenous identity. In Apess the focus is on "red soil," the Mashpee woodlot, and the "deep brown wilderness." In Winnemucca it is on the Paiutes' Pyramid Lake or the Malheur Reservation as a place for her people's national identity. McNickle fictionalizes the mountains, rivers, and sage flats of the Flathead Reservation as not only the stage but the stakes of Salish identity. Silko wanders the red plateaus and mountains of Laguna and the Southwest with the Stone Snake, then she wanders among ancient stones across the globe, to find this ground in the dynamics of Indigenous and American identity. Alexie offers an "introduction to Native American Literature" that ironizes America's uncomfortable ignorance of its own ground, historical and spiritual.

As the ground changes yet remains the same earth, these writers tell stories of Native identity finding ways to adapt while remaining connected to place and to principle. When "ownership" of the land changes hands through invasion and colonization, Indigenous hands try to hold onto ancestral soil and the cultural connections embodied there. That identity struggle changes with the balance of flexibility and continuity told differently in countless stories.

Thus Alexie represents Indian voices as they bend and break and heal and bend again with contemporary American pressures. Spurning "resolution and redemption," he keeps the possibilities open and flexible. Where he advocates embracing "the magical and painful randomness of life," his growing body of work riffs on the affirmations and uncertainties of that open ground.

Thus Silko sets Tayo on a circular path in *Ceremony* through mountains and desert to reconnect with his own sustaining cultural values, to affirm who he is. She extends that path through *Almanac*, where Indigenous peoples march along the spine of the Americas to reaffirm themselves on the land. In *Gardens in the Dunes*, she extends that march globally to the shores of the Mediterranean.

Thus McNickle's characters take their stand on the land, in shackles and in death. Yet the personal identities of Archilde and Bull both expand by their sacrifice into a communal, cultural identity, enacted by Antoine and Two Sleeps. By validating their connection in living and dying on the land, they validate their commitment to the ongoing life of their people and to the culture that sustains them in their unique identities.

By a similar fierce value of grounded identity, Winnemucca petitioned the U.S. government for "land in severalty." Her entire life's work, from the tableaux vivants of her early years on stage in Virginia City and San Francisco, through her later jobs as translator, her letter-writing campaigns, her lecture circuits on the West and East Coasts, her book, and the petitions that accompanied her public presentations—all were focused on securing a land base for her people. That focus in turn was a strategy to assure that "Piute" national or communal identity would not melt away. As she tried to win the hearts of Victorian women in her audiences by linking her cultural traditions to nineteenth-century virtues of womanhood, as she invoked fairness and equality in exposing the corruption of the Indian Ring, and as she strummed American chords of adventure with her own heroic exploits in the Wild West, she steadily offered a story of Indian identity gaining strength to face change in its connections to the land.

Apess set the pattern. His ironic and passionate discourse, from his autobiography to his *Eulogy on King Philip*, devotes itself to Indian rights to the land. No one is more aware than he of the changing ground of Indian identity. His own story testifies both to the changes and to the ground. No one was more successful in regaining local rights for an Indian nation to their own natural resources, at heart an affirmation of the cyclic relations of land and Mashpee identity. That cycle takes many forms—political, legal, cultural, economic, spiritual—each spiral a layer of Mashpee identity, as of other Native nations, and of the American nation now on this land.

How can we ground American identity? By Chief Justice John Marshall's "actual state of things"—illegal conquest—American identity has claimed the same territory that grounds Native identity by much longer tenure. To confront and perhaps gradually begin to rebalance countless inequities in that history of conquest, we can try now to understand Native American concepts of authentic translation of time and place. By listening to these stories, American identity might reconnect with our mutual ground and might reconnect with American ideals.

4

THE CREATIVE ABILITY
OF INDIAN PEOPLE

Authenticity as Translation

Understanding authenticity as translation is key to all the retranslated terms of this study and to the underlying irony of these slippery signifiers. A fundamental redefinition of authenticity as dynamic translation underlines the transformative dynamic of each of the other redefinitions. To negotiate identities between and within sovereign communities requires the authority to translate and register historical and existential ironies.

Instead of a dull and tiresome topic, authenticity—as it actually functions in many Indigenous narratives—works toward a summary of the discussion. It goes to the heart of America's binary thinking in space (manifest) and time (destiny), which would set "authentic Indians" as past and vanished from *the land*. Instead they remain present in America, with the authority to tell their own stories and to retell America's story. As Native writers work against the atavistic equation of authenticity with past history, they translate identity into systems of relations that become community. Rather than a static state, authenticity becomes a verb of motion in *doing* translation between various positions that imagine themselves to be immobile. Authenticity becomes the verb that moves in identity as the very process of change on an animistic ground of community, each stage serving, sacrificing for, sovereignty.[1]

"How Indian Are You?"

As I read active redefinitions of authenticity through Simon Ortiz in these five Native writers, I am not trying to redeem the term, much less advocate for "authenticity" to remain in the discourse of Indigenous studies. Instead I am trying to get at the way Native voices move cross-culturally inside and outside dominant discourse. Thus I aim to contextualize the term because of its persistent usage. It won't go away. Like *the frontier* and other dominant terms, *authenticity* might be so layered with colonial misreading that it becomes ultimately unredeemable. However, because of its persistence and dominance, it calls for attention and redefinition.

The fact is, readers from many backgrounds read Indian literatures for authenticity—sometimes only for authenticity—asking, quite sensibly, "What is Indian about this text?" The author? The narrator? The setting? The characters? Plot? Symbolism? Themes? The simple question quickly becomes complicated by contested definitions of the term *Indian* itself. As Jack Utter writes, "Before first European contact, the answer to 'Who is an Indian?' was easy. Nobody was. 'Indian' is a European-derived word and concept" (*American Indians* 25). Euro-American projections continue to burden the word. Utter goes on to describe dozens of competing definitions among tribal, state, and federal agencies. Beneath those definitions lie battlefields of Indigenous experience fighting against colonial ideology to establish the term *authenticity* itself. Who is to decide, declare, delineate what is authentically "Indian"? The self or the community? The text or the context? The colonized or the colonizer? The performer or the spectator? Such questions become a matter of survival when the dominant definition of authenticity is temporal, placing Native Americans in the past and eclipsing their presence by eclipsing their present in American public life.

In artistic contexts it is the performative character of authenticity that generates the problem. The puzzle lies in the audience, or more precisely in the disconnect between audience and performer. This disjunction is especially complicated by colonial relations, when dominant texts by non-Natives represent the "authentic" performer as an "object" and the observer as a "subject." Because of the performative nature of authenticity, where the audience, a reader, an ethnographer, or a critic plays a key role in defining what authentic is, that interactive dynamic leaves authenticity open to infinite misreadings, fluctuations, projections, arrogations, oppressions. As usual, it comes down to power, particularly the power to perform, to represent or misrepresent.

This question of authenticity has long felt tiresome to Native writers weary of performing for audiences ignorant of Indigenous realities. By standard, still colonial definitions, authenticity becomes an irritation, a non-question that keeps insisting on itself. Some, not all, non-Native critics of Native literatures have recognized an essentialist, static, past- oriented formulation in the authenticity question as a dead end. The Choctaw scholar Michael D. Wilson offers the useful term *strategic authenticity* (rephrasing Gayatri Spivak) to describe a dynamic in Native literary voices that attempts "to respond to destructive public policies." Wilson warns, "As a practical matter, however, such an approach is as dangerous as it is unavoidable, for sometimes those using strategic approaches forget that the strategy is not the game" (*Writing Home* 24). Clarifying the stakes of the authenticity game, Wilson explains, "The very desire to locate a kind of truth in the opposition between authenticity and inauthenticity guarantees its own failure, for the terms themselves do not provide any positive ground, only their differences (or *différances*)" (24). The circular chain of meaning for the noun, for static authenticity, only continues to spin and bind.

Many Native literary texts directly address the ironies of the issue. For instance, artistic impatience with this nonquestion is exemplified in one of the founding texts of the Native American literary upsurge of the late twentieth century, Gerald Vizenor's first novel, *Bearheart*, which ironically and probingly repeats the refrain, "What is Indian?" Pressing on the impossible question, the puzzle is shown to be impenetrable, or complex enough to elude definition. In the next generation, Sherman Alexie is dismissive: "The whole idea of authenticity—'How Indian are you?'—is the most direct result of the fact that we don't know what an American Indian identity is. There is no measure anymore, if there ever was one" (Nygren, "A World of Story-Smoke" 157). Yet Alexie, Vizenor, and other Native authors have always tried and continue to try to represent "real" Indians. To undo the force of historical misreadings, many Indigenous writers make the tedious topic of authenticity a central target.

In a very different view of authenticity, the Diné philosopher Marilyn Notah Verney writes of a continuing "authentic being" of her cultural lifeways in contrast to "the inauthentic ways of the dominant society" ("On Authenticity" 137). This comparative turn, resonating with Owens's "the remaining constant," pushes authenticity toward something beyond descriptions of ethnographic and psychological, or group and individual, authenticity. She identifies an ethical principle underlying the various forms authenticity may take. Writing of a "metaphysics of respect" (135), Verney affirms a processual, active dynamic of authenticity in its conversational, interactive ground. Resonating with David Abram's analysis of orality and literacy, Verney writes, "Once ideas are written down, in black and white, those ideas become objects, something to be studied and taken apart. This process of writing separates our being in the world, and we can lose touch and become isolated from all our relations. To be effectively taught in an academic classroom, American Indian philosophy must be taught orally. . . . Our philosophy can retain its meaning by making connection with those who are willing to listen to our oral teachings" (138).

For Verney, authenticity is neither bound by nor set in time, thus not in text. Authenticity in her Diné context is relational and alive, indeed communal, and thus ongoing in Indian communities, as well as in Indian classrooms. It does not reside in language printed on a page nor in other cultural practices frozen in time. Authentic relationality and vitality are built originally on relations between the speaker and his or her own language as oral, not written. Verney's theory calls to mind the "conversive literary theory" proposed by Susan Berry Brill de Ramirez on reciprocal principles of orality, which I cited in the introduction to ground theory. Brill describes a conversation in which "difference is affirmed through the intersubjectivity of conversive relations that recognizes the subjective status of oneself *and* of others" (*Contemporary American Indian Literatures* 110). In Verney, the language of respect that keeps us from becoming "isolated from all our relations" is affirmed as an oral pedagogy, embodied in the mouth and ear rather than projected permanently onto a page.

Through Sarah Winnemucca and other Native writers, we intensify Verney's focus on respect as a narrative dynamic. If Winnemucca's white enemies in the corrupt "Indian Ring" had succeeded even more than they did in silencing her, their slanderous and libelous portrayals in newspapers and in secret memos to the Department of Interior and the Bureau of Indian Affairs might have landed her in jail, like the disproportionate number of

Indian women in prisons today.[2] Disrespect is institutionalized across America's frontiers. The social cycle drained of respect becomes a cross-cultural trap.

Thus a reformulation of the question of authenticity proves fruitful as the authors in this study rework it, plucking it from the lips of social science discourse, indeed translating it. Instead of "How Indian are you?" or "What is Indian?" or is it "really Indian," they ask, "How many ways of being Indian are there?" Instead of claiming an essential Indian center that would only reaffirm colonial projections, Native writers more often speak to the multiplicities, the individual and tribally specific lives that build Native discourses. As Owens describes late twentieth-century fiction, "The American Indian novel shows its ability to appropriate the discourse of the privileged center and make it bear an other world view" (*Other Destinies* 92). This reappropriation is concerned centrally with redefining authentic representation. Indigenous writers remake the discourse of authenticity, of being "real Indians," into something immensely interesting, and often ironic, by opening a door to sovereignty, community, identity—that is, to the diverse humanity and tribal specificity—at the core of the literature.

"The Epistemology of Imperialism"

Historically *authenticity* in its common modern usage is an axiomatic colonial idea that the "real" ab*original* can only be precolonial. If it is not original, it is not authentic. The formulation has tried to erase Indigenous survival from the start. It is a reflexive projection, a mirror image by which the colonizer defines himself as present and future against the colonized as past. This conveniently self-serving projection forms the basis of an ideology of dispossession. By the central, though unspoken active presence of the American land, common authenticity remains linked to the soil for both Natives and Euro-Americans. This crucial ideology links the notion of authenticity to national identity in a peculiarly potent way. To be "authentically" Native, one must be of the land.[3] Next, by the Lockean Euro-American ethos, to be of the land means laboring on the land that one possesses. Once dispossessed of the land, one can no longer be of the land; thus, if landless, one cannot be authentic. Further, the reverse stands in as truth: the real possessors of the land become the real Americans. As Thoreau writes in *Walking*, the (white) farmer displaces the Indian even as he "redeems" the meadow. Indians become no longer real or authentic because they no longer possess the land. They were only authentic Indians before they were colonized and dispossessed. Hence authentic American national identity becomes built on dispossession of Indian land, a process that always already renders postcolonial Indians as inauthentic. Of course, this founding ideology works continually to erase the fact that many Native communities and individuals remain linked to the land in many dimensions, historical, economic, cultural, spiritual, legal.

For some historical perspective on the colonial dynamics of authenticity and national identity, and for concepts to disagree with in remapping Indigenous uses of authenticity, we may turn to Edward Said's outline in his essay "The Politics of Knowledge." Describing the long colonial era, "when the great modern Western imperial expansion took place all across the world," as background to identity politics of the 1990s, he observes that "a fantastic emphasis is placed upon a politics of national identity." Said suggests that this insistence on authentic national self-definition arises in reaction to colonial or imperial exclusion of otherness. Such exclusions would historicize Benedict Anderson's and Lauren Berlant's discussions of nationalism, which I referred to in the introduction, by mapping the imperial project onto the national one. Said's observation also resonates with Ronald Niezen's later analysis of *The Origins of Indigenism: Human Rights and the Politics of Identity*. According to Said, in order to claim "national identity," one must be authentically not-other. By "the epistemology of imperialism," the antagonistic colonial project categorized groups of people by race that "cannot ever be assimilated to or accepted by others": "Thus came into being such invented essences as the Oriental or Englishness, as Frenchness, Africanness, or American exceptionalism, as if each of those had a Platonic idea behind it that guaranteed it as pure and unchanging from the beginning to the end of time" (192). The "epistemology of imperialism" constructs a mental map built across centuries on "this mostly antagonistic interaction." Again, I'd like to emphasize that the real—or one might say authentic—issue is the land.

Where European powers in service of dispossession so thoroughly deny the humanity and economy of Indigenous cultures, Native peoples must resist by insisting on their own unique "race or category." Authentic national identity must become not only valid but ultimately "pure and unchanging," as an "idea" so "fantastic" and irreducible that it is "guaranteed" beyond "imperial experience." Thousands of different North American cultures and languages become "Indian." Because it has always already seemed to exist "from the beginning to the end of time," the label becomes "authentic." Further, the Native insistence on a "pure" and authentic national identity, according to Said, plays into the imperial project. Discourse of a pure past is as unreal as the language of a sure future in treaties: "as long as the grass shall grow and the rivers flow."

Built on colonial dispossession, such erasures and denials structure the production and reception of Native literatures, as many Indian writers try to deconstruct this dialectic, this "antagonistic interaction." Within the mind of the settler, beneath the boosterism of corporate colonial growth across the centuries, lies the dark side of that antagonistic projection of authenticity onto the colonial other. Even as the Euro-American self refuses to admit this, the colonizer's own gothic obsession secretly believes itself to be a destroyer of innocence. The imperial discovery of the Garden of Eden, from Shangri La to Yellowstone, must by this repressed logic of culpability lead to the Fall. The dilemma of innocence and experience remains entirely inside the colonial mind, masking perceptions of an exterior world that it overruns. Such destruction and such innocence remain first a colonial fantasy. By reducing the colonized both to a prelapsarian ideal and to a romantic victim of colonial power, a "noble savage," this dark side doubly denies the agency of the colonized. Gazing only into its own mirror image, the colonial definition of authenticity misses the Haudenosaunee or Lakota or Tlingit person standing here. Overlooking the Native people on the land, such an originary erasure conveniently proclaims it virgin territory.

Tied to an extensive network of cultural and religious ideologies, most notably that belief in the Fall from the Garden of Eden, this European projection, again the "white man's Indian," requires a poorly informed sense of cultural interaction and a further ideological assumption that colonial influence flows only from the colonizer to the colonized, not vice versa. Largely because of the force of this set of assumptions, various Native writers have labored to elude the colonial mind-set whereby authenticity resides only in the precolonial past. As Owens puts it, "For Native Americans . . . authenticity must somehow be forged out of resistance to the 'authentic' representation" (*Mixedblood Messages* 13).

The Grammar of Authenticity

There are useful linguistic perspectives to add to the historical and ideological processes of authenticity. Forged in this complex of competing definitions, the general grammar of authenticity becomes first-person narrative, auto-, either singular or plural. *I/we tell the story.* This grammar blends the first-person authority of authorship with the knowledge, the content, a sense of the "real" that is narrated, in the ability to recount or relate *the story*. This authority of authenticity, positioned however far along the spectrum of simulacra, locates itself in the voice or voices that speak of self and group, that represent their story, even silently.

Inside this grammar, etymological roots grow into a linked structure between authenticity and knowledge. In addition to the more obvious roots of authentic selfhood in the authorial auto-, to which I will return, the links between authenticity and narrativity, the ability to tell the story, emerge also through the roots of the verb *narrate*. The Oxford English Dictionary connects that storytelling ability, through eighteenth-century Spanish and Scottish usage, to the (Greek, then) Latin "*gnarare*, related to *gnarus*, knowing, skilled, and thus ultimately allied to KNOW *v.*" An author *knows* the narrative. Narrative and knowledge are etymologically synonymous, and, cyclically, the one who authors the story is authentic because of that knowledge. Authenticity *knows* what it's talking about. Further, narration resonates with a gnostic, special knowledge that generates mystery, even inaccessibility—the forbidden fruit, in Euro-American terms. That elusive quality is part of authenticity's modern nostalgic currency, its cachet, its magnetism.

Minimally authenticity is thus the ability to tell the story that comes from knowing experience. Through the Acoma writer Simon Ortiz and others who set the terms of this study, we see how authenticity *is* storytelling, the skillful use of language to recount experience to others. In a key statement, Ortiz writes that Indigenous authenticity emerges when Native writers and other artists "have taken the languages of the colonialists and used them for their own purposes" ("Towards a National Indian Literature" 10). Not a purity of a Native past, but a purity of Native purpose—to serve their "national" and cultural interests—energizes authenticity. In a larger aesthetic context, Paul Zumthor, in *Oral Poetry*, offers a summary of the "poetic function" that underlies storytelling itself as "a mythification of lived experience" (100). Such a basic formulation incorporates the voice, communal or individual, that creates an authentic narration or mythic structure for experience. Insofar as storytelling is itself a kind of translation of experience and imagination into language, authenticity thus becomes translation of experience into one's own terms, one's own language. If authenticity is translation, this is a functional definition that does not pretend to define the "humanity" itself, the voice or voices, behind the act.

This functional rather than exhaustive definition also uses translation not in a common meaning, where the translator is a discrete catalyst who facilitates the transfer of language's form but does not participate in language's content. Instead I am looking at translation in precisely the opposite of, for instance, common usage in David Cole's 2006 article in the *Nation*, "Lost in Translation." Commenting on the case of a translator for lawyer Lynne Stewart (who herself was convicted of "providing material support" to terrorists for relaying her terrorist client's message to his followers), Cole writes, "Translation is the art of erasing oneself in order to speak in another's voice. Good translators speak for others, not for themselves." Cole uses translation as the specific profession of taking others' words in one language and conveying them to still others in another language. The translator here is supposedly a neutral third party. However, when Ortiz describes Native writers using the languages of the colonizers "for their own purposes," their translations are anything but neutral.

Certainly the very act of using language is another form of translation, a linguistic third term between the perceiver and the perceived, between self and other, between consciousness and experience. Laura Beard, in an article on the Meskwaki writer Ray Young Bear, offers a similar definition "of translation as a kind of transformation or metamorphosis." The very act of naming, of language use, becomes an act of translation, to "include not just the change from one language to another that we normally think of when thinking of translation but also the changes from one place, position, or condition to another; changes in medium or form" ("A Society Based on Names" 131). Shifting physical and bodily movements underlie linguistic shifts as translation. Recognizing that prior dynamic of language, we may see in Native literatures how good translators, in order to be authentic, must indeed speak for themselves, for who they are, not for others.

Thus, following Ortiz, I'm using *translation* as a prior communicative and symbolic system of registering experience and then conveying it to one-self and others in one's language. This means translating both nonverbal and verbal experience into new verbal form. "And because in every case where European culture was cast upon Indian people of this nation there was similar creative response and development, it can be observed that this was the primary element of a nationalistic impulse to make use of foreign ritual, ideas, and material in their own—Indian—terms" ("Towards a National Indian Literature" 8). Such translation, according to Ortiz, renders experience verbally one's own, making it authentic. It accepts Said's nation-alist dialectic as authentic. We will look at Ortiz's affirmations further, but for now it is clear that the catalyst cannot help but get in on the act, taking the language content into the self and finding language content there as well. Authenticity as translation underlines this peculiar ability to speak for oneself or one's people.

Yet, as old Grandma says in Silko's *Ceremony*, "It isn't easy. It never has been easy" (272). Martha Cutter measures the difficulties: "Translation as trope often signifies a process of continual negotiation and renegotiation between language and an ongoing struggle between conflicting and often clashing cultures and ideologies" (*Lost and Found* 6). The "ongoing strug-gle" mapped here is the "often clashing" definitions of what is an authentic Indian and what is an authentic American.

Alterity Instead?

In the productive void that is authenticity, its force, weight, and currency lie, like "race," in its historical and ideological baggage. To shrug off some of that baggage, the term *alterity* might offer a useful alternative. Of course, authenticity likely will remain the—authentic—object of desire in cultural and personal formations, but notions of alterity can help to redefine and clarify some reasons for the authority of authenticity. If authenticity tends toward static selfhood, alterity flies from any predictable position as it tends toward dynamic otherness. Postcolonial and colonial identities long for both, for a position inside and a path away from the center. Alterity, like authenticity, is essentially a process of translation between self and other, but it offers a fuller translation of mutual selfhood.

This tension between selfhood and otherness remains a key modern and postmodern crisis both psychologically and politically, and it remains originally a crisis of authenticity. Mark C. Taylor writes of the larger perspectives in *Altarities*, "The history of society and culture is, in large measure, a history of the struggle with the endlessly complex problems of difference and otherness" (xxi). Quoting Heidegger, he goes on to explain traditional Western philosophy's failure, in its focus on unity of being, to conceptualize difference. He claims that difference, as such, is unthinkable to the Western theological codes: "What [Western metaphysics] cannot think—*cannot* think because metaphysics constitutes itself by the very act of excluding this unthinkable—is 'Being as difference,' 'Being thought in terms of the difference.' In other words, what Western philosophy leaves unthought is 'difference as such'" (xxvii). By focusing through Plato's lens on "oneness" and "unity," many Western philosophers have tended to eclipse the very "difference" and diversity that constitute the stuff of oneness. Lost in the semantic abyss of trying to conceive of "non-Being," seekers after "Being" have erased otherness. The *unum* subsumes the *pluribus*.

Alterity, or "altarity," as Taylor prefers to pun, offers a category of thinking that allows otherness to possess or retain being or presence instead of nonbeing or absence. Taylor compares efforts by twentieth-century philosophers from Heidegger to Derrida to conceive of this otherness that is more than an absence of self: "'Altarity' is a slippery word whose meaning can be neither stated clearly nor fixed firmly. Though never completely decidable, the field of the word 'altarity' can be approached through the network of its associations: altar, alter, alternate, alternative, alternation, alterity" (*Altarity* xxviii). Not only does difference find validation among these associations, but altarity (with no "e") suggests both a sacredness of otherness per se and the history of sacrifice that imperial selfhood has required on the altar of otherness. Either way, altarity or alterity makes visible a *being* who is other, no longer a *nonbeing* who is other.[4] Authenticity, although the colonial weight of anthropology has squeezed it into an artifact of nonbeing, strives for being, and alterity offers that.

Yet these processes of resolving being and nonbeing, of self and other, remain inconclusive, which for some is the point. The claim to difference must remain different to remain different. Brill maps the disjunctions neatly in her theory of "conversive" intersubjectivity. Problematizing "a recognition of the 'integrity' of the other," she explains, "Even in the desire to equalize the relations between a self and other, between the subjective scholar and the subjective other, the other is still viewed as 'other'—even if that other takes on subjective status through the self/other, scholar/subject relationship. Alterity raised up from the subaltern is alterity nonetheless" (*Contemporary American Indian Literatures* 37). Brill underlines the polarities inherent in the language itself, in any discourse of "self and other." The alterity that she dismisses does not carry the specialized definition of Taylor's altarity, with its potential recognition of integrity, but the clarity of Brill's critique is crucial: that an essential duality persists in the discourse of self and other that reifies opposition psychologically and historically. Alterity only heightens the stakes of otherness.

To find strategic tricks through the minefield of authenticity and alterity, Native writers often create texts that work to establish and select aspects of alterity rather than authenticity as a means of validation, a reclaimed—translated—otherness that affirms its sacred self. Such strategies might be inevitable on a field of adversarial history. For instance, as we have seen, Apess in "An Indian's Looking-Glass for the White Man" claims divine one-upmanship in God's having created larger populations of colored races "in His image" than of whites. Apess spells out a moment when America's Native Other claims alterity as divine creation. In a very different instance, McNickle in *The Surrounded* dramatizes the cultural gap that yawns between traditional Salish Indians and their white guardians on the Flathead Reservation, affirming their mutual alterity if not reciprocity. Both Apess and McNickle insist on the alternative being, the alterity, of the so-called other.

I retain the term *authenticity* for literary study because, like the nonreferential term *race*, it *matters*.[5] Susan Bernardin, speaking of real problems of pseudo-Indian authorship, puts it concisely: "The political stakes of authenticity, most especially for Native Americans, are far from 'trivial.' It is precisely because of the dominant culture's pervasive and deeply entrenched pattern of what Philip Deloria calls 'playing Indian'—by taking ownership of Native land, history, culture, and now spiritual traditions—that such literary fakes are so insidious" ("The Authenticity Game" 161). Whether in authorship or in content, authenticity remains a key criterion in publication, "most especially for Native Americans." It remains a key criterion in many other realms of Native American life as well, notably the legal status of federal recognition, from which entire economic and cultural constellations spin. Indeed authenticity, with its ancient Greek etymology, matters largely because of its historical linkages to colonial racism and to the legal, political, and physical violence spread from those racist patterns of exploitation and annihilation.

In the broader picture, authenticity vibrates with the material forces of the real and the unreal, the powerful and the powerless, in the momentum of modern societies as they struggle to hold onto meaning, a future, through the past. In spite of postmodern denials, where bricolage and celebrations of randomness actually do continue to draw on precedent, a future built on the past is an authentic future, especially when your future has ostensibly "vanished" into that past.

In addition to its historical magnetism, authenticity matters to both Native and non-Native American writers and readers because of those etymological echoes of *author* and *authority*. In both its Greek etymology and its contemporary usage, *authenticity* embodies the forces of selfhood in auto-, where the author has the authority to create a truth, a reality, thus an artistic original. Through its connotations of creativity and agency, *authenticity* conveys the primary potency of the linguistically fundamental Greek [poew], *poew*, "to make," thence the poetry and potency of *the maker*, the poet, even in the pluralistic literary universe of Native publications. For example, Sherman Alexie, as noted, explicitly leverages this particular agency of poetry.

Thus rather than throwing it out, many Native writers work to reappropriate authenticity, with affirmations of alterity, in both their texts and their positions as authors, in the what and why of their authoring. They summon literary and cultural authority to represent human selves in alterity, a kind of autochthonous rising up from the ashes of genocide. For instance, Elizabeth Cook-Lynn and Alexie defend authenticity against "cosmopolitanism" or "generic cultural touchstones," respectively. As Bernardin explains, "In one of the more controversial critical moves in recent years, both Cook-Lynn and Alexie have voiced acerbic criticisms of mixed-blood writers, whom they have claimed are wedded to narratives of invention that reinforce dominant culture's romantic-ethnographic assumptions about American Indians" ("The Authenticity Game" 162). Clearly such a critique is complicated by undertones that seem based on notions of cultural purity and impurity, yet a prior argument in both Cook-Lynn's and Alexie's positions is an affirmation of difference, of tribal specificity, and, especially important for this discussion, of authenticity as a form of difference. Perhaps we can say that they offer alterity against colonial hegemony, against some imagined mainstream center. As we shall see, redefinitions of authenticity by Native authors generally move the discussion away from essentialist and racial requirements.

Full Circle

To reflect the term's stubbornness, I must ask one more time: If authenticity is such a contested term, why focus on it? Why not abandon it? There are two compelling reasons: first, as we have seen, because it remains a persistent issue in the production and reception of Native literatures; second, because the ways that Indigenous writers negotiate, elude, deconstruct, or transform authenticity bear directly on understanding both Indigenous literature and American national identity. Authenticity and sovereignty form two multicolored bands at opposite ends of a single spectrum, populated by identity, community, and irony. To understand the dynamics of authenticity in Native American literary discourse is to travel that spectrum through the other key terms. When critics address authenticity, they might do so most productively in ways that question the question. Accordingly we will read how five Native authors have questioned ethnographic and romantic authenticity as a colonial ideology and how they redefine authenticity as translation.

Echoing his own book-length poem, *from Sand Creek*, published in the same year, Ortiz's 1981 essay, "Towards a National Indian Literature: Cultural Authenticity in Nationalism," identifies what now might be called "sovereignty" as "nationalism" underneath the authenticity of identity narratives. His essay was written as the recent discourse of "tribal sovereignty" was emerging, and I read Ortiz's term *nationalism* as an early version of (still contested) sovereignty discourse, which continues to evolve. The link he makes between authenticity and nationalism or sovereignty is key to the five terms of this study. For Ortiz invokes what can be called an authentic humanism, like Apess and Winnemucca in the former century. He roots authenticity in honest history via the voices of this land. He suggests that for America to achieve its own authenticity it needs to come to terms with the nation's full spectrum of those stories on the land.

Beginning by defining an authentic American Indian history as interactive with colonialism, Ortiz offers an authentic American history in dialogue with American Indians, and by extension other minorities misused in and misrepresented by America's hegemonic versions of history:

> It is not the oral tradition as transmitted from ages past alone which is the inspiration and source for contemporary Indian literature. It is also because of the acknowledgment by Indian writers of a responsibility to advocate for their people's self-government, sovereignty, and control of land and natural resources; and to look also at racism, political and economic oppression, sexism, supremacism, and the needless and wasteful exploitation of land and people, especially in the U.S., that Indian literature is developing a character of nationalism which indeed it should have. ("Towards a National Indian Literature" 12)

Ortiz juxtaposes a catalogue of ongoing historical crimes against Indigenous people's ongoing affirmations of rights. This juxtaposition sets up the act of translation in "a responsibility" of Indian writers "to advocate" for their people and "to look also" squarely at the catalogue of crimes. The courage and character of that responsibility of Native voices to speak to what Winnemucca called her people's "wrongs and claims" then becomes, in Ortiz, the basis of America's redefined, authentic identity: "It is this character which will prove to be the heart and fibre and story of an America which has heretofore too often feared its deepest and most honest emotions of love and compassion. It is this story, wealthy in being without an illusion of dominant power and capitalistic abundance, that is the most authentic" ("Towards a National Indian Literature" 12). Ortiz links authenticity with authority, with the expressive power to speak, sing, write, and perform one's genuine interactions. Indeed this authenticity is structural and social, an interpellation by contested relations, calling on Indian voices to dance their story on the plaza or put their story on the page. Deconstructing Said's dialectics and the epistemology of imperialism, the authority to translate, in Ortiz, becomes an authentic response to history.

Further, addressing those supremacist invaders with disarming probity and insight, Ortiz suggests that ongoing colonial dominance is a self-negating mask that fears its own "deepest and most honest emotions of love and compassion." Such a latent humane spirit in America would at least listen to his argument, by which authenticity is sovereignty and sovereignty is authenticity. The authenticity that claims authority to translate colonial experience into its own terms finds those terms on the ground of tribal sovereignty. Ortiz writes from this ground to that American subconscious.

The complex dynamics in his phrase "being without an illusion of dominant power" simultaneously subvert and divert American centralizing forces to recognize multiple centers of power beyond the standard story of center and margin. Precisely appropriate to his affirmations of authentic nationalism, or sovereignty, as the power to translate history into one's own cultural terms, Ortiz is suggesting that America's dream of domination is an illusion because Indian peoples have reserved their own rights and powers on the land. Indeed this vision of authentically expressive Indigenous sovereignty moves paradoxically but pragmatically toward an American federation to include Native "people's self-government, sovereignty, and control of land and natural resources," what we might call domestic *in*dependent nations. Or simply a United States of America.

Owens elucidates the delicate power relations of colonial and anticolonial discourse that point from such authentic expression to intellectual sovereignty: "Rather than merely reflecting back to him the master's own voice, we can . . . learn to make it bear the burden of our own experience. We can use the colonizer's language . . . to articulate our own worlds and find ourselves whole. This has been the project of Native American writers for a long time" (*Mixedblood Messages* xiii.) To articulate their own worlds, Native American writers have striven to remain "whole," perhaps another word for "sovereign" and "authentic," to tell their own stories. By telling their stories they remain authentic. They consciously represent themselves. According to Ortiz, the impulse to nationalism and sovereignty is itself authenticity, and thus Native storytelling embodies that impulse.

In the ongoing dialogue among the people between "tradition" and "the future," Ortiz merges dynamic rather than static authenticity with the dialogic act of translation into the discourses of First Nations. To be authentically Native is thus to exercise "the creative ability of Indian people to gather in many forms of the socio-political-colonizing force which beset them and to make those forms meaningful in their own terms" ("Towards a National Indian Literature" 8). The processes of "self"-expression in both ritual and contemporary Native art and literature become an affirmation of Native nationhood.

Here we may see the full circle of our key terms of literary practice. As humor breathes a lively spirit into the mix, sovereignty as sacrifice equals a right of self-expression. Community as animism equals reciprocal expression. Identity as change equals freedom of expression. And authenticity as translation equals power of expression. If expression is a form of survivance, and if expression is poetry, then poetry and writing pulse at the heart of cultural survivance. Ortiz's translating work of Native writers becomes central to survivance. His notion of authenticity as nationalism completes the circle from authenticity to sovereignty through identity and community by affirming the sovereign right of self-definition and self-representation as the foundation of self-determination, an authenticity of translation that itself invokes the full spectrum of sovereignty in the individual and in the nation. The work of readers of this literature is then to find ways of tracking that translation and expression to tribal sovereignty at its heart.

Whether or not Ortiz's vision of a compassionate heart of America will ever flower into realigned political and economic realities for American Indians and their invaders is not his question. Although the tone is utopian, he is not describing a necessarily linear, utopian future but instead a cycling, less visible, subterranean process that exists parallel—in past, present, and future—with the more visible narrative of "history." That process does exist in the literature of Native nations and in the communities that literature describes, amid oppression, violence, and moments of justice and reform. Native writers, in the very act of expressing and advocating for "their people's self-government, sovereignty, and control of land and natural resources," as Ortiz puts it, in looking "also at racism, political and economic oppression, sexism, supremacism, and the needless and wasteful exploitation of land and people, especially in the U.S.," are able to invoke the "deepest and most honest emotions of love and compassion" at the "heart and fibre and story" of America. He is setting American history on the ground of Native American sovereignty.

"For Their Own Purposes"

A recent example of authenticity as translation might be a musical track by the popular, Grammy-award-winning Black Lodge Singers, a drumming and singing group from the Blackfeet Reservation in Montana. In a children's powwow song, the lyrics, sung over a driving drumbeat, begin and repeat, "Is it a bird? No! Is it a plane? No! Oh my gosh it's Mighty Mouse—

hey hey ya hey ya!" Authenticity is not an issue here for the Black Lodge Singers.

Authentic translation into Native and tribal terms remains the goal, but Ortiz does not depict that goal as facile. In an interview published two decades after his 1981 essay, he confronts the difficulty of cross-cultural terminology and language use throughout the colonial era. He defines "a real dilemma, sort of a forced choice about what to do in terms of the language to use," and he goes on to affirm yet again the authentic expression of Indigenous thought in colonial languages: "Not that there isn't a way in which one can still be whole and express oneself in terms of one's integrity—cultural, spiritual, or physical integrity—with this other language. But it's got to be a real choice; it's got to be a real choice" (Purdy and Hausman, "A Conversation with Simon Ortiz" 3). Once a choice is made, the chosen language becomes "meaningful in their own terms" for Native speakers and writers within the specific history of conquest.

Bakhtinian terminology clarifies the dangerous dynamics of that difficult choice, whereby we recognize that Ortiz is affirming Native entry into the precarious heteroglossia of European languages. For Ortiz, the historical fact that European tongues formulated a particular language use, with its dominating linguistic paradigms, does not eclipse the historical fact that Native tongues have reformulated that language use and those paradigms as well. The Bakhtinian theory of polyglossia, for all its carnivalesque confusion and European projections of darkness, clarifies how language is dialogical, or layered with the mixed discourses of generations. Indeed this dynamic structure of language itself marks an opening, if not an invitation, for a new perspective, a different angle of light, for more voices to join and alter the chorus, to make the choice that Ortiz describes. The polyglossic and permeable structures of language itself open those doors to authentic translation, as Native writers and their communities often make the strategic choice to enter. Ortiz thus allows for a level of agency and invention, of flexibility and adaptation in his literary approach to authentic Indigenous national identity and individual expression.

This Indigenous redefinition of adaptive authenticity then bears on definitions of American nationhood and its roots. Cutter's study, *Lost and Found in Translation: Contemporary Ethnic American Writing and the Politics of Language Diversity*, carries this sense of discursive adaptation from literary texts to governmental statehouses. Against the current tide of "English-Only" legislation, Cutter describes another movement, "English Plus" (223). Native and other ethnic novels and autobiographies, voices of ethnic authenticity, as they themselves advocate diversity, challenge the center from more angles than it can defend against. We may say further that from Ortiz's perspective, this argument takes a reflexive turn since the ultimate challenge is from within the heart of the center itself, in what Ortiz sees as America's own dream of compassion. Redefining American roots, Cutter writes of "the translated, multilinguistic tongue that is the true voice of the United States" (241). In this context, an insistence on diversity is the external expression of an internal claim to authenticity, one that in such advocacy sets authenticity in a field of exchange rather than erasure or dominance.

Such a robust definition of authenticity introduces a different sense of temporality that contrasts with both a prevalent static view of Native cultures and the dominant view of "progress" in American culture. In the static view, a singular Native culture, in order to remain authentic, must camp forever in the eighteenth, seventeenth, or sixteenth century, or even leap back to the Stone Age, the ultimate petrified source of the stereotypically unperturbable yet perturbing "stoic Indian." Again, the real Indian must be the precolonial Indian. Nineteenth-century "salvage" anthropology, which assumed that "the authentic Indian" is a thing of the past, contributed to this temporal definition of Indigeneity, thus contributing to the view of colonial projects as "progress." Eventually this static view of one Indian past, as dramatically exciting as a diorama or tableau vivant, is necessary to reinforce the liberal sense of perpetual progress in "American culture" that must appear ever changing, ever youthful, ever individualistic, liberated and "free" of the past, ever free of responsibility to community, ever committed to an economy of "growth," and ready to light out for the territories.

Although America does not view its authentic self as contemporary with Benjamin Franklin, it views "authentic" American Indians just so. True Americans need not wear powdered wigs like Benjamin Franklin's contemporaries, yet true Indians must wear feathers. America still insists on looking at Indians with Franklin's eyes, or James Fenimore Cooper's. Colonial eyes, open only to religious conversion or later ethnographic objectification of Native subjects, have denied Ortiz's translation dynamic by ossifying authenticity into a time-bound past. You are either Indian or modern. In the mid-1990s one of my own close friends in New York City said to me over lunch on the Upper West Side, "Why don't they just give up that Indian stuff and become Americans?"

Apparently you can't be both. You are either Indian or American. Indian or educated. You can't be both. You are either Indian or Christian, or Indian or white. You can't be both. Unfortunately many Indian youth, against the material realities of exchange in their own Indian families, are warped into believing these either/or expectations for Indian authenticity. They thus feel that to succeed they have to reject "the past"—as their own Indian-ness—in order to live in the white man's world or the global media world, or they have to remain losers as uneducated Indians.[6] Identity becomes linked to victimhood, to a wooden authenticity, a dead past, and the ensu-ing identity crisis leads to reservations' highest teen suicide rates in the country. Vanishing sometimes seems like the only way. If Indian youth are to unlearn the impossible authenticity-as-past imposed on them by a dom-inant culture that would fantasize and thus engineer their "vanishment," it is Native writers who show them how through laughter and perseverance.

In an intriguing reversal of the indefatigable vanishing Indian stereotype, some Native writers have argued that Americans already have become more Native than they care to admit. *Non-Native* Americans are the vanishing breed! Authentic America is Native today! Indeed this reversal becomes the ironic fold structuring much of Native literary laughter. Individual whites might "play Indian" to fulfill their romantic quest for authenticity, but mean-while, back at the ranch, their political economy and their body politic have already been shaped inexorably by the original cultures of this land. America is great, according to this narrative of interactive authenticity, because of its Indian heritage, because of what Indians gave and are giving America today.

The idea of a redefined authenticity, that acculturation works both ways and that the colonials have been and can be influenced if not transformed, is a notion with much wider circulation among the colonized than the colo-nizers. The Choctaw author and playwright Leanne Howe, for instance, in "The Story of America: A Tribalography," writes, "Native stories are power. They create people. They author tribes. America is a tribal creation story, a tribalography. . . . Our stories made the immigrants Americans neverthe-less" (29). She goes on to explain that through the northeastern story of the Three Sisters, "Natives told stories of how to plant their crops, corn, beans and pumpkins (squash), which sustained the newcomers and taught them how to experiment with their daily diet by adding variety. As a result, Native foods were traded internationally and changed the food cultures of the entire world" (29). She adds recent statistics from the National Corn Growers Association to point out that "corn is grown in more countries in the world than any other crop, and the United States produces and exports more corn than any other country in the world" (30). As she continues, Howe revises authentic American history on another level in the influence of the Iroquois Confederacy and of their narrative *The White Roots of Peace* on the American Constitution:[7] "But the most important story the immigrants would hear from Natives was how to make a united nation by combining people from various tribes. It is this eloquent act of unification that explains how America was created from a story" (30). What, then, is authentic America if not an Indian story?

Such respect for the transformative power of the story and of language is at the heart of oral traditions that in turn form the bedrock of contemporary Native literary expression. If Howe and others assert that America itself is a Native story, this transformative power of language is the choice of translation that Ortiz invokes in his redefinition of authenticity, "to make those forms meaningful in their own terms."

It is worth pointing out in this context that even an old-school historian as venerable as Frederick Jackson Turner himself recognized some of what Howe describes in her tribalography. The source of "the Turner thesis" acknowledges this direction, whereby "the frontier" transforms the European into something not Indian and not European, something new. In his 1893 treatise, Turner speaks of the transformation of the European into the American via the "Indian fashion": "Little by little he transforms the wilderness, but the outcome is not the old Europe. . . . The fact is that here is a new product that is American" ("The Significance of the Frontier").

Of course, Turner's prospect becomes more appropriation of "free land" than reversed acculturation. Vine Deloria Jr., always in his characteristic tone of irony, underlines this distinction. With a twist on this redirected acculturation, on an America redefined by Native translations of authenticity, Deloria ponders the New Age "wholesale appropriation of American Indian rituals, symbols, and beliefs by the non-Indian public" (*For This Land* 261). He lets himself speculate, doubtfully: "Ecologists of all stripes including the self-appointed 'Deep Ecologists' claim a kinship with traditional Indian beliefs so that one would wonder whether the tribes did not in fact win the Indian wars and expel the hated invaders from their homelands" (261). By Howe's logic, if the "hated invaders" have found "kinship with traditional Indian beliefs," then they have been effectively expelled, and history has been reversed.

Deloria's sarcasm resonates with Leslie Silko's equally serious prophetic promise that "all things European will disappear" from the Americas. Always a discriminating observer and analyst, Deloria goes on to say with compelling hope, "What we can do is respect religious traditions and allow them to take us forward into the future. That is all the old ways ever promised they would do" (*For This Land* 268). He even invokes "the ancient prophecies of profound and universal planetary destruction" (267) and remarkably looks beyond them toward a renewed Indigeneity: "Thus it might not be a bad thing that ancient truths are understood by a large number of people who after having survived massive earthquakes and tidal waves might be inclined to believe that Mother Earth is indeed more powerful than human science and technology. The survivors might have a little humility and respect for the natural world" (267). Deloria here is understating a potential radical shift in American ideology. A "little humility and respect for the natural world" would constitute a complete reversal from what Deloria decries: "The non-Indian appropriator conveys the message that Indians are indeed a conquered people and that there is nothing that Indians possess, *absolutely nothing*—pipes, dances, land, water, feathers, drums, and even prayers—that non-Indians cannot take whenever and wherever they wish" (265). It is "the superior attitude which non-Indians project," Deloria states, that is why appropriation upsets Indians so much (265). "Our problem really has to do with the manner in which non-Indians receive traditional practices and beliefs and what they do with them" (265). He suggests that if natural disasters foster some "little humility and respect for the natural world" that would reverse non-Indians' "superior attitude," then the transformation might be working. Humility is akin to that "maturity" that Deloria prescribes elsewhere for his American readers (and which I discuss in the conclusion). "We can now pull together what is left and hope that it demonstrates the viability of what was given us long ago and that may be sufficient for our lifetimes" (267). The need for reversals could not be clearer.

To conclude this introduction to redefined authenticity for a reborn Indigenous America, let's return to Ortiz's less ironic phrasing, where the Native focus of retelling, of translating the stories to reshape history becomes "this heart which is our America." As mentioned, in Ortiz's book-length poem on one of the most brutal and desperate moments in American history, *from Sand Creek*, he remarkably expresses ragged hope for a recovered American heart. Here is the full stanza that we have seen in fragments:

That dream
shall have a name
after all,
and it will not be vengeful
but wealthy with love
and compassion
and knowledge.
And it will rise
in this heart
which is our America. (95)

Ortiz reclaims Indigenous land as "our" America, even as he again links "love / and compassion / and knowledge" to a future America's vivifying rather than dominating ethos. This stanza echoes his parallel prose gesture of intimate mediation in that essay describing "an America which has heretofore too often feared its deepest and most honest emotions of love and compassion" ("Towards a National Indian Literature" 12). Ortiz sees an America authentic in its ideals. Yet that America must face its brutal imperial past—a past true but inauthentic by Verney's standard of "respect," because disconnected from humanity. This honesty requires a readership—and a federal Indian policy—to shift its persistent paradigms. It requires retranslating the American story.

Cornel West uses the term *tragicomic hope* as necessary for people of color to survive and even win "the fight against imperialism" (*Democracy Matters*), and the term neatly triangulates the field of agency, where active affirmation in hope might emerge beyond the dialectic of tragedy and comedy. Native writers, so often functioning like the pre-twentieth-century translators who sat in council between our cultures, and like the Fool Soldiers rescuing American hostages abducted by history, have held out a tragicomic hope for the American heart, both Indian and white. Because readers have been raided by frontier ideology, Indigenous writers try to rescue the surviving hostages of split history on both sides of these Indian wars. If readers keep locking these rescuers in the stockade jail or jeering at them or, more likely, ignoring and ostracizing them as literary Fool Soldiers, it remains for history—and Native literature—to tell the story of translators who can see possibilities on "both sides" as the common ground.

"Whatever an American Is": Authenticity in Silko

More centrally than in any of the other writers in this study, authenticity in Silko's work becomes translation. As she participates in the processes set by Apess, Winnemucca, and McNickle, her juxtaposition with McNickle's fiction is again especially illuminating on this point. For all their underlying thematic consistency, the contrasts in tone between McNickle's modernist realism and Silko's mythopoetics reinforce critical differences in their narratives. McNickle hones his prose to Hemingwayesque simplicity, "how to translate from one man's life to another" (*Wind* 26). Silko expands her prose like a sand painting "through all distances and time" (*Ceremony* 258). Yet if McNickle chooses the tragic mode of dramatizing oppositionality and if Silko chooses the comic mode of transcending oppositionality, they both focus on similar dynamics of authenticity, identity, and sovereignty in the pulse of their Indian communities. McNickle stirred the ashes from which the phoenix of Indian survivance must rise; Silko writes in a time when that bird is beginning to test its wings. In the terms of Black Elk's vision, if McNickle told the story of the breaking of the circle, Silko tells the story of how that circle is beginning to take form again.[8]

One of the most remarkable characters in Silko's oeuvre provides a paradigmatic example of her open approach to authenticity as translation. Old man Betonie, although not the protagonist in *Ceremony*, is a particularly memorable figure in Native American literature for reasons directly tied to this dynamic of authenticity. He resounds with the authority of McNickle's Bull, but with a quite different song to modern history. The distinction lies in Betonie's strategy of cultural translation, which he models. Where Bull's characterization adds up to the tragic impossibility of adaptation and communication across cultures, leaving room only for the next generation to try, Betonie's characterization as a Navajo medicine man reinforces the ceremonial force of cross-cultural healing. Bull says of himself, "But visions never come to an angry man" (*Wind* 21), while Betonie in his compassionate role to "keep track of the people" (*Ceremony* 122) operates out of something evidently more efficacious than anger. Betonie has more in common with McNickle's old dreamer, Two Sleeps in *Wind from an Enemy Sky*, who sees the bigger picture and who does survive.

Silko's first detailed description hints at Betonie's physical connection to the medicine energy that is his life: "The old man was tall and his chest was wide; at one time he had been heavier, but old age was consuming everything but the bones. He kept his hair tied back neatly with red yarn in a chongo knot, like the oldtimers wore. He was sitting on an old tin bucket turned upside down by the doorway to his hogan. When he stood up and extended his hand to Robert and Tayo, his motions were strong and unhesitating, as if they belonged to a younger man" (*Ceremony* 122). The eccentric old Navajo seems to translate between age and youth as he translates between worlds. These touches of uniqueness add to Silko's sense of descriptive authenticity, even while they provide concrete cues to an air of mystery or inaccessibility in Betonie that enhances the realism.

Ceremony's protagonist, Tayo, is Betonie's mixed-blood palette for the sand painting of translation, as Betonie carries that mixture in his own blood: "Then Tayo looked at his eyes. They were hazel like his own. 'My grandmother was a remarkable Mexican with green eyes,' Betonie said, reading Tayo's surprise" (124). Betonie has traveled the middle path that Tayo is struggling to find. The healing that Tayo undergoes, and that the novel narrates, reaches precisely toward the authenticity of translation as a mixed-blood that Betonie has achieved.

Silko's characterization of Betonie is thus necessarily vivid, marking his central presence in the plot of *Ceremony*. In this paragraph at their first meeting that concludes with the green eyes, the accretion of verbal specifics adds to the sensuous impression of embodied authenticity:

All along there had been something familiar about the old man. Tayo turned around then to figure out what it was. He looked at his clothes: the old moccasins with splayed-out elkhide soles, the leather stained dark with mud and grease; the gray wool trousers were baggy and worn thin at the knees, and the old man's elbows made brown points through the sleeves of the blue cotton work shirt. He looked at his face. The cheekbones were like the wings of a hawk soaring away from his broad nose; he wore a drooping thick mustache; the hairs were steel gray. Then Tayo looked at his eyes. (124)

This animated portrait, however picturesque, functions in Silko's text not only to rescue the medicine man from any stoic stereotype but to carry the reader, and Tayo, "through the low doorway" of Betonie's hogan that "was here first" (124), before the town of Gallup "spread out below" (122). The hogan itself feels animate, looking down on "this filthy town" (123–24), where Betonie can "keep track of the people" (122).

The round building with its eclectic contents conveys Betonie's remarkable achievements of an authenticity in quite deliberate translation. The dark interior launches a dozen or so paragraphs of close description: "Currents of cool air streamed toward the door, and even before his eyes adjusted to the dimness of the room, [Tayo] could smell its contents; a great variety of herb and root odors were almost hidden by the smell of mountain sage and something as ordinary as curry powder. Behind the smell of dried desert tea he smelled heavier objects: the salty cured smell of old hides sewn into boxes bound in brass; the odor of old newspapers and cardboard, their dust smelling of the years they had taken to decay" (*Ceremony* 124–25). Through Tayo's traditional pueblo apprehension of witchery and through his shell-shocked-veteran's paranoia, the reader takes in an archive of the world, both natural and cultural, Native and non-Native. Clothing, catalogues, roots, tobacco, wool, newspapers, and "piles of telephone books" from St. Louis, Seattle, New York, Oakland, and other cities are introduced as Tayo "began to feel another dimension to the old man's room" (125). The concatenation of so many elements of the ancient and modern worlds is overwhelming to Tayo, just as the challenge of contemporary Indigenous living must be: "His heart beat faster, and he felt the blood draining from his legs" (125). Translation of such a cacophony of cultural artifacts can be daunting, if not frightening. Yet when Betonie recognizes the young man's apprehension, he speaks to that challenge, referring to the work of spiritual accounting and cultural translation that his own family line of medicine men and women have undertaken over generations: "The old man smiled. His teeth were big and white. 'Take it easy,' he said, 'don't try to see everything all at once.' He laughed. 'We've been gathering these things for a long time—hundreds of years. She was doing it before I was born, and he was working before she came. And on and on back down in time.' He stopped, smiling" (126). Betonie is at ease with this process, the daily and generational operation of authenticity: taking in experience, including colonial experience, and translating it into his people's terms. As part of the ceremonial procedures, Betonie is healing Tayo by example, laughing and smiling.

Within Betonie's authentic confidence, there is a dynamic that speaks to the authority of the healer. It is especially significant to clarify this process in order to distinguish Betonie's—and Silko's—sense of authenticity from Said's potent notion of resistant Native identity as an imperial construct. We see that Betonie's dynamic energy of healing for Indian people, drawing not only on natural medicines but also on catalogues, newspapers, and phone books from all around the country, seeks to integrate the outer world— as a margin—into the center of his healing circle: "We've been gathering these things for a long time—hundreds of years." His hogan integrates the world into itself, not vice versa. Betonie prompts Tayo to perceive the healing power in the room: "'You can feel it, can't you?' Tayo nodded. He was standing with his feet in the bright circle of sunlight below the center of the log ceiling open for smoke" (*Ceremony* 125). Worldly center and margin are reversed where Betonie draws the world as margin into the center of the hogan, "the bright circle of sunlight," and Tayo finds himself first healing there.

Betonie's integration of the world into a Native center poses a direct contrast with Said's postcolonial map of what he calls "worldliness." Said describes as worthwhile, as "necessary," the important work of colonized writers in reaffirming their unique history and humanity. Yet he calls on such writers to step from their unique history into compelling terms of universal suffering: "To testify to a history of oppression is necessary, but it is not sufficient unless that history is redirected into intellectual process and universalized to include all sufferers" ("Politics of Knowledge" 197). Said's goal is a kind of abstract reintegration, Indigenous expression "redirected into intellectual process and universalized." The local and provincial, according to Said's cosmopolitan terminology, must return to the larger and universal: "The point I am trying to make can be summed up in the useful notion of worldliness. By linking works to each other we bring them out of the neglect and secondariness to which for all kinds of political and ideological reasons they had previously been condemned. What I am talking about therefore is the opposite of separatism, and also the reverse of exclusivism. It is only through the scrutiny of these works as literature, as style, as pleasure and illumination, that they can be brought in, so to speak, and kept in" (196). Said's stated goal is restoration of postcolonial literary works into "the global setting." Clearly, in the context of his life work, whatever cosmopolitan values we may read here are part of his struggle to establish a decentered cosmopolis.

Yet Said's specific articulation misses Betonie's and Silko's Indigenous dynamic for aesthetic and ethical healing of colonial history. When Said calls for bringing nationalist or Indigenous literatures out of "neglect," we must ask: Neglect by which central authority? And when he refers to the "secondariness" of nationalist work, we must ask: "Secondary" by whose measure? Similarly when he describes such works as problematically "condemned," we must ask: By whom? Finally, when he calls for "these works as literature" to be "brought in, so to speak, and kept in," we must ask: Into which inner circle, which center, into whose canon, by what authority? He seems to miss Indigenous alterity.

If authentic writers have their own nationalist audiences, what is the imperative to expand that audience into "the global setting"? Many choose to do so, as this study finds, yet not because they see themselves as marginal or "secondary." Quite the opposite. If Navajo poets like Rex Jim choose to publish in Navajo, what is lacking? Said writes, "It seems to me absolutely essential that we engage with cultural works in this unprovincial, interested manner while maintaining a strong sense of the contest for forms and values which any decent cultural work embodies, realizes, and contains" ("The Politics of Knowledge" 196–97). Perhaps the material, economic reality of globalized colonial centers and margins—in so many realms, from publishing to foreign aid—compels Said's perspective to retain the province and the metropole, the standard colonial paradigm. Yet if it may be "absolutely essential" to become "unprovincial," it must be so only to the cosmopolis—which forms its own provincial insularities—not to those "cultural works" themselves as they affirm themselves elsewhere.

Aesthetically and ethically Betonie's project for himself, for "the people," and for Tayo is not to be "brought in" nor "kept in" anyone else's circle. He has his own hogan, his own center, his own circle. Still he is engaging in neither "separatism" nor "exclusivism," which, as Said suggests, is the only other course available. Instead Betonie collects and draws those outer circles into the hogan. Neither the agency, autonomy, authority, nor authenticity of "Others," as Said refers to them ironically, must be dependent necessarily on the imperial center for their identity construction in the literature of which Silko is a part. Betonie's hogan insists on being one of many centers—an insistence that itself is the healing process of authentic translation, drawing other centers, translated as margins, into his people's own. He does not need to seek Said's "place in the global setting, a restoration that can only be accomplished by an appreciation not of some tiny, defensively constituted corner of the world" ("The Politics of Knowledge" 196), because Betonie's healing process is not defensive but incongruously affirmative. Betonie is not caught in the dialectic of defensiveness. He does not seek that prescribed Other place because, in Said's description, the brokers of that global setting retain the agency to choose whether the so-called provincial Native voice is "brought in" and "kept in." The Navajo healer does not see his family's hogan as a far "corner of the world" but as another center of the world.

He explains to Tayo this feeling of awesome power and authority recognized by Navajo people in the authenticity generated by his translating the world into his "circle of sunlight":

> "There are stories about me," Betonie began in a quiet round voice. "Maybe you have heard some of them. They say I'm crazy. Sometimes they say worse things. But whatever they say, they don't forget me, even when I'm not here." Tayo was wary of his eyes. "That's right," Betonie said, "when I am gone off on the train, a hundred miles from here, those Navajos won't come near this hogan." He smoked for a while and stared at the circle of sunlight on the floor between them. What Tayo could feel was powerful, but there was no way to be sure what it was. (*Ceremony* 129–30)

As Tayo grows to understand, the power generated in the hogan is not Betonie's braggadocio but the authentic fearlessness of translation, transforming the world one Indian at a time through the spiritual power of a strong center.

Thus Said's useful notion of worldliness misses a key step beyond Eurocentrism that Silko makes clear through Betonie. The direction of authenticity as translation is not an attempt to move oneself from anyone else's margin into his or her center, neither to be "brought in" nor "kept in." Instead it is more faithfully to decenter the field of relations by multiplying and overlapping centers in translation. That is an insistence on authenticity that needs no external "integration" from margin to center. Such integration happens by affirmative default, when the integrity of the cultural and communal self is healed into authenticity.

"There Was Nothing Anyone Could Do"

Although Said misses this Indigenous dynamic of authenticity that claims the centered authority to translate, there is at the beating core of his notion of worldliness a moving respect for "all sufferers." It is the universality of "all sufferers" that directs him to invoke compassionately "the global setting." Perhaps it is suffering that bears the ultimate weight of authenticity, what Said refers to as "national identity." Suffering is unquestionably authentic. Suffering is why Indian communities, like other communities, so honor their war veterans.

> Screaming, with mud in his mouth and in his eyes, screaming until the others dragged him away before the Japs killed him too. He fought them, trying to lie down in the ditch beside the blanket already partially buried in the mud. He had never planned to go any farther than Rocky went. They tried to help him. The corporal who had helped carry Rocky for so long put his arm around Tayo and kept him on his feet. "Easy, easy, it's okay. Don't cry. Your brother was already dead. I heard them say it. Jap talk for dead. He was already gone anyway. There was nothing anyone could do." (*Ceremony* 45–46)

For all his own suffering on the Bataan Death March, Tayo is further connected to "all sufferers" in his recognition of the Japanese as genetic cousins, as he recounts to Betonie how they looked like his uncle: "My uncle Josiah was there that day. Yet I know he couldn't have been there. He was thousands of miles away, at home in Laguna. We were in the Philippine jungles. I understand that. . . . I feel like he was there with those Japanese soldiers who died" (130). Betonie's confirmation of Tayo's feelings of connection carries this sense of universal suffering across epochs: "'You've been doing something all along. All this time, and now you are at an important place in this story.' He paused. 'The Japanese,' the medicine man went on, as though he were trying to remember something. 'It isn't surprising you saw him with them. You saw who they were. Thirty thousand years ago they were not strangers'" (130). Betonie underlines the absurdity of warring against a world of enemies who "were not strangers."

Yet stories of battle, that is, of authentic suffering, have always been the stuff of national identity construction as they are translated after the battle and "recollected in tranquility." Betonie, as usual, stretches such constructs by expanding identity across oceans and ages, again multiplying and linking centers, here between Laguna, Navajoland, and Japan, between the twentieth century and preglacial times. We have looked at suffering in terms of sacrifice at the heart of tribal sovereignty. In our current context, suffering is the ultimately untranslatable experience that only authenticity can try to convey, or, to put it another way, authenticity becomes authenticity by trying to translate suffering. Tayo's efforts to speak to the medicine man are an effort to translate his experience of suffering in order to reach a measure of his own authenticity.

A lesser-known but moving work, *The Delicacy and Strength of Lace*, the collected letters between Silko and the poet James Wright, is built on this precise dynamic of translating suffering during Wright's ordeal of dying from cancer, as Silko's parallel storytelling translates empathy. The slim epistolary volume thus carries a tremendous potency of authenticity, and it may help us understand what is authentic in Silko's fiction. Her last letter, dated March 24, 1980, arrived after Wright's death. She had been writing to him of how much she missed his letters and of how he and she shared "this other present time and place." Her last paragraph reads, "Anyway, I treasure the words you write—your name most of all. But no matter if written words are seldom because we know, Jim, we know" (105). The poignancy in this exchange moves directly out of that paradox of the necessity to express the inexpressibility of suffering. Jean-François Lyotard in *Le Differend* puts the ineffability of suffering at the heart of postmodernism's postholocaust crisis of representation, where language can only fail. Yet as Silko assures Wright and herself that "we know, Jim, we know," she is making the claim to authenticity, that even "if written words are seldom," the translation is achieved. That is, she and his other friends reciprocally know Wright's suf-fering, his pain, and his desire to express, to translate his experience to his friends in poems and letters. That is why Silko can say "I treasure the words you write," because she loves the sufferer.

Of course, Silko being Silko and Wright being Wright, their letters explore these very limits of authentic expression quite self-reflexively. She wrote him two years before his death about the explicit artistic process of transla-tion: "In a strange sort of way, the film project is an experiment in transla-tion—bringing the land—the hills, the arroyos, the boulders, the cottonwoods in October—to people unfamiliar with it, because after all, the stories grow out of this land as much as we see ourselves as having emerged from the land there. Translations of Laguna stories seem terribly bleak on the printed page" (*The Delicacy and Strength of Lace* 25-26).

The storied physical context that Silko wants to convey with film, as she says, "a context, a place within which the narratives reside" (*The Delicacy and Strength of Lace* 25), is as integral to the stories as the spoken or written words. Authentic translation, to get beyond the "very lean" text of the nar-ratives themselves, according to Silko, must extend through the reader and the writer into context, into the land itself, "the hills, the arroyos, the boul-ders," that is alive with the experience of the people.

Robert M. Nelson's grounded, detailed analysis of Silko's novel *Ceremony* offers a deconstruction where land and human resolve: "The consciousness that returns to the Pueblo . . . is a shared one" (*Place and Vision* 37). Both land and humanity feel conscious of each other, as Nelson puts it, on "a particular landscape that contains, within itself, the power to heal and make whole and sustain life" (39). This contextual presence of land in Silko, in order to do its translation work of authenticity in her texts, thus functions as more than "local color" in both the fiction and the film. A presence of the land, "an experiment in translation—bringing the land—the hills, the arroyos, the boulders, the cottonwoods in October—to people unfamiliar with it," becomes an experience for writer and reader. There emerges a feeling, a principle of peoplehood, that the context conveys by visualizing the land. If the context is the land, and if her "experiment in translation" equals "bringing the land" to her audiences and readers, "to people unfamiliar with it," this context of translation invokes the very peoplehood that is Laguna life. The people on the land have undergone millennia of seasons, both natural and political. There is no precultural land, just as there is no prenatural humanity. Authenticity translates by this context into the identity, community, and sovereignty of a people: "We see ourselves as having emerged from the land."

A couple of juxtaposed passages from *Ceremony* will suffice to illustrate the dynamics of this contextual authenticity in the ground of Silko's stories. In her depiction of Tayo's first tentative interactions with the old Navajo medicine man, we get this primary principle, here in the author's careful handling of the words *comfortable* and *comfort* in relation to the people and the land itself:

> He turned and pointed to the city dump east of the Ceremonial grounds and rodeo chutes. "They keep us on the north side of the railroad tracks, next to the river and their dump. Where none of them want to live." He laughed. "They don't understand. We know these hills, and we are comfortable here." There was something about the way the old man said the word "comfortable." It had a different meaning—not the comfort of big houses or rich food or even clean streets, but the comfort of belonging with the land, and the peace of being with these hills. (122–23)

Betonie is comfortable because he possesses authentic knowledge that he belongs "with the land." His life is at peace here, where he has translated all his worldly travels into "these hills." Thus he is comfortable with "good English" also, as he describes his position in time and space prior to the arrival of the whites, sitting in his center, "where none of them want to live." The "different meaning," as Silko's narration explains, that "the old man had given to the English word," contrasts in this passage with her use of *comfort* ten pages later, when Tayo is struggling with his faith, when his anger and paranoia want to reject Betonie's hogan, its unkempt and dusty artifacts as merely "the leftover things the whites didn't want": "All of it seemed suddenly so pitiful and small compared to the world he knew the white people had—a world of comfort in the sprawling houses he'd seen in California, a world of plenty in the food he had carried from the officers' mess to dump into garbage cans. . . . All Betonie owned in the world was in this room. What kind of healing power was in this?" (133). The contrast is direct. The whites' "world of comfort" has nothing to do with "the comfort of belonging with the land, and the peace of being with these hills." "A world of plenty" juxtaposes a particular contextual relation to land as resource, as a set of extractable commodities, as "sprawling houses" of atomized individuals within nuclear families against Betonie's authentic comfort keeping track of the people. Such a world of plenty has nothing to do with the "belonging" that grows an Indian community "with the land." Silko's translation of this difference is a contrast between the "healing power" of authenticity and the "garbage cans" of commodification.

In Betonie's earlier passage, Silko is further contrasting Gallup's tourist-oriented "Ceremonial grounds" with the healer's ceremony for Tayo that is the center and circumference of the novel itself. As Tayo struggles between these contrasting worlds, the reader is given the dialectic of ambivalence in his thoughts: "He wanted to believe old Betonie. He wanted to keep the feeling of his words alive inside himself so that he could believe that he might get well. But when the old man left, he was suddenly aware of the old hogan . . . the leftover things the whites didn't want" (*Ceremony* 133). Again, "to keep the feeling of his words alive inside himself," Tayo is trying to reach Betonie's feeling of authenticity, his ability to translate the experiences of an oppressive world into his own circle of sunlight, not to be drawn out of his center into the periphery of another center. Tayo thinks bitterly, "This was where the white people and their promises had left the Indians" (133), as though, in focusing on the whites' "world of comfort," he has forgotten Betonie's claims that Indians are "comfortable" in these hills. There is plenty of evidence in Silko's story that, unlike Tayo's bitter recital, it is not whites' promises that have "left the Indians" these hills. According to Betonie, Gallup was theirs long before "all the promises" that Tayo so laments were broken. Indian authenticity precedes and supersedes white intrusions. Because Tayo buys into the whites' story of broken promises, he has not yet achieved the authenticity to translate his suffering into his own and his people's central place on the land.

This same preemptive principle under siege animates Silko's other novels. For instance, the elaborate structure of *Almanac of the Dead* is built on there being keepers of the Almanac, like Betonie's ancestral medicine family, over generations. Thus *Almanac* features old Yoeme and the sisters Lecha and Zeta, whose specific task is recording and translating events—keeping the Almanac alive, "Yoeme's old notebooks"—in cycles of history that transcend the colonial era: "Now Lecha had returned with the notebooks and claimed she was ready to begin the work Yoeme had entrusted to her years ago" (178). "Zeta had already completed the pages of the notebook Yoeme had given her. Zeta did not believe it was an accident Lecha had returned just as Zeta had finished typing the transcriptions of the pages into the computer" (136). Like Betonie's family of healers and like his hogan as a spiritual catalogue of history, the Almanac requires keepers who can bridge the worlds of living stories and electronic computers, Indians and whites, lives and deaths. Thus, not surprisingly, their work of "typing the transcriptions" is an outgrowth, for instance, quite exactly of Lecha's power of translation: "The power Lecha had seemed to be as an intermediary, the way the snakes were messengers from the spirit beings in the other worlds below" (138).

Similarly in *Gardens in the Dunes* the task of the young sisters, Salt and Indigo, is to go through the changes wrought by modern history—one in the mining camps of the West, the other in the hills of ancient Europe—and then to translate that experience back to their southwestern desert home, their garden in the dunes. Onboard ship, Indigo prays: "Tears filled her eyes and she cried softly into her pillow: Please help me, Ocean! Send your rainy wind to my sister with this message: I took the long way home, but I'm on my way" (226). In Corsica she understands the translation of suffering: "The rocky dry hills and their people were poor; their lives were a struggle here; that was why the Blessed Mother showed herself here; the people here needed her. . . . Indigo was much heartened; all who are lost will be found, a voice inside her said" (322). As in *Almanac*, the Indian characters in *Gardens* maintain their struggle for survivance with this faith that the outcome will be an authentic translation of their lives: "We will outlast them. We always have" (464). According to Silko's narratives, they do not become someone else in order to survive; they survive authentically, as themselves, because they are able to translate their experience home, back to Indian Country, as they transport themselves to their homeland in the story line.

Gardens is pertinent to this study also for Silko's explicit application of this theme of authenticity as translation to non-Indian Americans as well. Through her characterizations of Hattie and her feminist mentors, Silko reenvisions an America no longer groping for authenticity by "playing Indian," as Philip Deloria puts it, but translating their authentic, pre- and early Christian, mother goddess, European roots into modern life. Hattie's quest, through Aunt Bronwyn in Britain and others in Italy and elsewhere, plays on Aunt Bronwyn's teasing question, "Whatever an American is" (244):

> "This is a very special place," Hattie said. "I understand why you stay here."
>
> Aunt Bronwyn nodded her head with a merry expression on her face. Yes, the family did not understand her reasons for remaining in England after her husband died; after all, she was an American— "Whatever an American is," Aunt Bronwyn said with a wink at Indigo. She'd fallen under the spell of the old cloister, which was nearly in ruins when she leased it from an English family. (244–45)

Aunt Bronwyn is "under the spell of the old cloister" enough to live with the crowding tourists and the "odors of the baths." By connecting to her earthly roots, she has found a way to render her humanity in this place. Her "wink at Indigo" carries the full weight of this novel's themes in the land: an expatriate American, who has reconnected with ancient European stones and thus realigned her ethical relation to the American land, winks at a Native American on the topic of authenticity, "whatever an American is." Young Indigo's Native authenticity, by her own indissoluble linkage to "home" translating Aunt Bronwyn's wink, gets the joke.

Hattie later gets the principle as well: "Hattie had anticipated a joyous arrival and expected Indigo to be in good spirits now she was in her homeland. The return of the child to her family had become the primary focus of Hattie's attention. . . . Perhaps she would return to England or Italy—she dreamed about the gardens often. Aunt Bronwyn's old stones danced in one of her dreams" (*Gardens* 394). Hattie has become connected to something authentic that translates into "homeland." Against the full force of manifest destiny, she recognizes the ethics of returning an American Indian child to her homeland, because Hattie is beginning to recognize her own connection to the spirits of the earth.

In the spiritual climax at the end of *Gardens*, when a band from the Ghost Dance is interrupted by the police—an allegory for both broad and specific histories of intrusion—Hattie, Sister Salt, and Indigo celebrate "the soft yellow glow" (470) that unites ancient cultures of the earth. This is Silko's mythic, land-based reality at the authentic heart of humanity that can catalyze translation of difference:

The light she saw was the morning star, who came to comfort her, Sister explained. How could she have seen the same light in the garden in England and in a dream on board the ship? Oh the Messiah and his family traveled the earth—they might be seen anywhere. Tomorrow he would come as the Messiah with the others and speak to them.

But on the morning of the fourth day, three white soldiers and two Apache policemen rode up. . . . The policemen were polite, even friendly when they spoke to the dancers, but they let them know they must break up the gathering at once or be arrested. (471)

Silko here constructs yet another moment, softened by racial complications in comparison to the historic massacre at Wounded Knee, when Indigenous authenticity is refused permission to translate between worlds. The presence of "Apache cops" (471) among the small police squadron reflects McNickle's narrative twist on the complexities of history when Son Child, or The Boy, as chief of police, wields the revolver that takes down Bull.

In this passage and elsewhere in Silko there is something authentic beneath race translating human affairs, whether in the luminous "soft yellow glow" of unity or in witchery's violence of opposition, as the dancers curse the cops, "Your hands are full of blood!" (*Gardens* 471). Silko writes of the failures, successes, and tangles of that translation, as here in *Ceremony*, across layers of authorial irony, the army recruiter propagandizes to Tayo and Rocky over a fundamental truth: "'Anyone can fight for America,' he began, giving special emphasis to 'America,' 'even you boys. In a time of need, anyone can fight for her. . . . Now I know you boys love America as much as we do, but this is your big chance to *show* it!'" (66). Against Silko's buried thesis, the recruiter assumes, unlike Aunt Bronwyn, that somehow Indian men, "even you boys," are not the authentic Americans. Whether by negative or positive example, Silko, like Alexie, McNickle, Winnemucca, and Apess, suggests that an authentic America would translate back and forth between the *pluribus* and the *unum*.

"Son of the Forest": Authenticity in Apess

Apess offers a peculiarly suitable voice to discuss adaptive authenticity as translation. In fact I'm giving him as much space as Silko in this chapter because of the clarity he brings to this question and to mark its persistence across the centuries. Modern readers immediately note how thoroughly Apess's early nineteenth-century Native American polemics on the most American of issues—dominant racial projections onto the land and its peoples—were saturated in Christian terminology. Many thus question his authenticity. My students often ask, "How could *he* be Indian if he's *so Christian?*" Professional readers often remain perplexed also, as Maureen Konkle describes the assumptions brought to readings of Apess: "As Apess never equivocates about being a Pequot Native person, this leads to certain mental gymnastics on the part of his critics" (*Writing Indian Nations* 107), who persist in their "culturalist" critique without reference to political and legal issues. Because Apess fits neither standard cultural category of authentic or inauthentic, his writings challenge readers to redefine authenticity, citizenship, nationhood. The questions, carrying all the weight of colonial history, go to the heart of authenticity.

For example, when he writes, "But when I acknowledged myself a sinner before the people and confessed what a sinner I had been, then the light of God's countenance broke into my soul, and I felt as if I were on the wings of angels and ready to leave this world" (*The Experiences of Five Christian Indians* in *On Our Own Ground* 132), a reader even with the acuity of the scholar Arnold Krupat, may write that Apess "proclaims a sense of self . . . deriving entirely from Christian culture" (*The Voice in the Margin* 145). The implication in Krupat's context is that Apess, being Christian, is not authentically Indian. Against an authentic aboriginal dialogism, what he defines as "the dialogic or collective constitution of both Native self and autobiographical text" (134), Krupat reads Apess's autobiography as a "relentless monologue" (148) in the dominating mode of colonial discourse. Krupat not only assumes an absolute dichotomy between Christian and Indigenous discourse; he also strictly attributes only the Christian discourse and values of colonizing "salvationism" to Apess as a writer. Referring to Apess's conversion and vocation as a Methodist preacher, Krupat explains, "Indeed, inasmuch as Apess's autobiography is constructed in terms of its author's progress to full permission to speak the language of salvationism, we may see it as documenting a struggle for monologism" (147–48). He portrays Apess's efforts to master the master's discourse as entirely co-opted by the master's purposes. David J. Carlson responds to Krupat, "In the end, the argument he is making . . . is basically one about Apess's lack of cultural authenticity. In Krupat's view, Apess's adoption of religious discourse marks him as fully interpellated by the hegemonic colonial order" because of "the rhetorical dominance of colonial norms" (*Sovereign Selves* 92). In this formulation, Christianity equals assimilation equals inauthenticity. Carlson reads through that formulation to make visible how Apess develops instead "an opposition rhetoric of Indian identity in the wake of colonial contact." Thus Apess's strategies of Indigenous sovereignty are intricately linked to his strategies of authenticity.

To begin a further response to the prevalent notions of authenticity that Krupat and many others assume, I must remind readers that Apess himself was acute in observing the antebellum incongruity between professed Christian ideals and American actions toward Indians. That is to say, like Frederick Douglass, who, in his appendix to his *Narrative*, is careful to distinguish a genuine Christianity from "the *slaveholding religion* of this land" (153), Apess distinguished hypocritical from harmonizing Christianity, just as he distinguished injustice and oppression from compassion: "I am no sectarian whatever, but boldly declare that I have preached for all that would open their doors" (*On Our Own Ground* 133). Following an admixture of Old and New Testament discourses, Apess locates the oppressed victims of injustice as the Christian chosen against the prejudiced oppressors as non-Christian. Thus his early nineteenth-century mental map of whiteness, Indianness, and Christianity was quite different, for historical and rhetorical reasons unique to his moment, from a late twentieth- or early twenty-first-century map of ethnicity, race, and religion.

Following his particular terminology, Apess uses even Christian conversion as a strategy to offset white prejudice against Indians. His rhetorical structures indicate that he employs this approach not to prove that Indians are capable of assimilation but that they are worthy of admiration, not that they are *like* whites—who fail to live up to Christianity—but that his people are living *more* Christian lives than the whites who oppress them. For example, in 1833, while waiting for the Massachusetts legislature to meet on his Mashpees' historic petition for self-government and affirmation of their land rights, Apess participated in a four-day religious revival meeting, and he uses that event to mark the contrast. While the whites railed in the newspapers and in the legislature against their own projections of hostile Indians, Apess and his compadres proved them not only wrong but childish, petulant, and ignorant, as the Indians waited "patiently and remained quiet, according to our promise" (*On Our Own Ground* 190).

To cap off the holier-than-thou logic of Apess's critique, he affirms that during the meeting, "twelve Indians were redeemed from sin, and during the eighteen months that I have known them, the power of God has been manifested in the conversion of some thirty" (*On Our Own Ground* 190). He sets up the simple historical irony of these complex events and then articulates the reversal quite clearly: "God forbid that I should glorify myself; I only mention the circumstance to show that the Marshpees [*sic*] are not incapable of improvement, as their enemies would have the world suppose. . . . I do think that the result of this meeting was in no wise pleasing to our white enemies" (190). Far from a tool of assimilation, Christian conversion here becomes a tool of resistance "to our white enemies." These are the terms of his time and place, when he recognized that the real issue was not religion but an ideology of race and racial domination of land and property. Christianity was so far from the point in the minds of their oppressors that he could grasp onto it as a strategy against white power over Indian lives, as a reclaimed center not unlike Betonie's circle of translation.

Specific questions of authenticity in Apess are governed, as are so many discussions of Indian concerns, by the dualistic paradigms of the colonial era: wilderness versus civilization, Indian versus European, Indigenous tradition versus Christianity, each "side" conceived as singular and insular. The operative term is *versus*, determining the underlying oppositional paradigm. The question of authenticity is a prime arena where these larger questions of binary opposition play out or are negotiated. As usual, any hint of resolution in those negotiations tends toward deconstruction of the binaries.[9] Because some benefit from the hierarchies built on such supposed opposition, there is hegemonic resistance throughout the social binary against resolution. The story remains lopsided.

Thus a predominant view of authenticity, confounding racial and religious categories, judges that Apess cannot be Indian because he is Christian. If we begin to question not only such a judgment but even those a priori binaries that would be syncretized, then Apess's forest "wilderness" becomes redefined as a projected shadow of "civilization," each "side" implicated in a self-reflexive mutual construction. Similarly "Indian" becomes redefined as a flexible ethnicity no more demarcated by biologically racial boundaries than "white." Indigenous "traditions" and "Christianity" become redefined in mutually overarching and interpenetrating ways that, despite the rhetoric of dogmatic distinctions, include profound commonalities as well as important differences. (Again, those who hold to the preponderance of difference would disagree with any characterization of profound commonalities.)

Whether or not one can be both Christian and Indian theologically, the fact of blending such categories historically across Apess's New England and southeastern Canada bears today on questions of American and Native American authenticity. It is not necessary here, nor is it enough, to advocate for or against his authenticity. Nor is it necessary to argue ultimately whether Apess was syncretic or assimilated. The implication by those who resist his Christian terminology is that he is not only assimilated but a sellout. Those reflex readings would oversimplify his autobiography and his polemical essays. Instead we may start with the exhilarating fact that his was an eloquent and effective voice arising out of his peculiar circumstances. Tracing those circumstances leads to the logic of his voice and to a uniquely compelling logic for redefinitions of America itself. As Robert Warrior writes, "Apess turned a corner, and by the time of the *Eulogy*, he envisioned his history and his experiences as illuminating a path toward the future" ("Eulogy on William Apess" 8).

"Deep Brown Wilderness"

Thus there is a clear historical perspective on Indian authenticity and Christianity for Apess in the nineteenth century, as for the Mohegan preacher Samson Occom and the "praying Indians" of the eighteenth century, and for so many others caught in the colonial project. By their thinking, Christianity could not be assimilation for Indians *because* Euro-America, with its rum-runners hiding behind the black robes of its missionaries, *was not a Christian society*. Apess spoke against the secular violence of white America, and, like Occom in the generation before him, envisioned building a separate Christian Indian society with millennial implications. Occom had recruited New England Indians to his "Indiantown" Christian settlement at Mashantucket, Connecticut, in the second half of the eighteenth century. Under intense white settler pressure, these had moved farther west among the Oneida to "Brothertown" in New York State in 1769, and later to Wisconsin with a group of Oneidas in the 1830s. Apess was active among their root Indian communities in Connecticut and Massachusetts. These migrations were driven by an effort to build self-sufficient Indian Christian towns apart from secular white society and its corrupting, rum-pushing trade. Apess's own turn to political activism at Mashpee was a pragmatic, and successful, application of that millennial zeal to overcome hypocritical whites' corruption and exploitation of Indian communities.

Clearly by a peculiar but tight logic in Apess's texts, Christianity was not assimilation because he did not regard the United States as a Christian nation. Barry O'Connell points to a positive side of this different narrative: "For a Pequot to convert to Christianity is not, in this understanding, to take on white ways but only to claim one of her rights as a human being. . . . White people had to see that they were responsible for the history Indians were living. Christianity was a faith that could be offered to Indians because it affirmed their equality with all other humans" (Introduction lxvii). This connection of Christianity with social equality is not only part of what drove Apess and other Indian converts to Christianity; it reinforced their communal vision for America as well. Apess essentially saw Christianity as a step to freedom.

To consider this question of authenticity from another of Apess's own perspectives, it is crucial to recognize that he adopted and promoted the belief in Indians as the Lost Tribes of Israel, as in the appendix to his *Son of the Forest*. He regarded Christ's Kingdom as the spiritual fulfillment of the Native nations returning to their religious roots. Being one among the "ancient people of God" in Israel and having been "cast out of their inheritance by reason of their stubborn and haughty spirit of unbelief," American Indians, as Apess charts the theological history, "have not yet been gathered into the fullness of the Gentiles. . . . But . . . they shall rise again in the grandeur of holy affections, having repented of their great sins, and looked on him whom they pierced and mourn, then shall unspeakable glory from heaven baptize all nations" (*On Our Own Ground* 106). The key phrase here is "rise again," as it assumes an earlier link. The "holy affections" of Christian love, when pouring through Indian hearts, would transform "all nations," particularly his own America.

Indeed if Apess needed a reason, a divine purpose for the historical subjugation of the Indians from which they might emerge spiritually cleansed and triumphant, he found it in this myth of the Lost Tribes and their punishments by God. In *Nullification* he refers to the Mashpee community and their constitution in comforting, Old Testament terms, mixed with Enlightenment values of human rights: "We now, in our synagogue, for the first time, concerted the form of a government, suited to the spirit and capacity of freeborn sons of the forest, after the pattern set us by our white brethren. There was but one exception, viz., that *all* who dwelt in our precincts were to be held free and equal, *in truth*, as well as in letter" (*On Our Own Ground* 179). Again, the faith of his Indian brethren contrasts with the faithlessness of Americans.

Although Apess may have needed no biblical structures to reinforce his recognition of prejudice, those structures, and his ordination as a minister to that social apparatus, certainly sustained him. If the Lost Tribes provided some mythical meaning to his life's suffering, the emotional and autobiographical basis for this belief lay in his experiences as the direct victim of racism. His "mythification of lived experience," his translation, reinforced his authority and authenticity and vice versa. His was a childhood of abuse, neglect, and exploitation rooted in his racial identity as an Indian. The patent injustices and hypocrisies of his own treatment by Christian whites, and by Indians, family members, whose internalized colonialism and alcoholism victimized him as a young child, propelled him to develop alternative strategies of cultural exchange: "While sinners mourn, saints may rejoice. The windows of heaven are opening in blessings above the heads of devoted Christians" (*On Our Own Ground* 111). He describes Christ's Kingdom of spirit as one of unity and justice and peace, in contrast with the colonial world: "Come, then, child of the promises. . . . Revivals follow revivals, and the deep brown wilderness is vocal with the shouting and songs of the delivered tribes, long slaves to error but now emancipated and brought out of the wilderness of sin into the Canaan of Gospel liberty. Would not your hearts, my beloved friends, rejoice to hear the anthems of praise bursting from the hearts of twelve hundred church members in the woods of Canada?" (111). Where "Gospel liberty" equates freedom with equality through Christianity, yet that "deep brown wilderness" brings together an early modern global set of mythologies, celebrating a Native reappropriation of "wilderness versus civilization" as Christianity. The phrase rings with pre-echoes of twentieth-century affirmations in "Black is Beautiful!" and "Red Power."

For, as we have seen, fundamentally Apess does not regard Christ as white: "Did you ever hear or read of Christ teaching his disciples that they ought to despise one because his skin was different from theirs? Jesus Christ being a Jew, and those of his Apostles certainly were not whites—and did not he who completed the plan of salvation complete it for the whites as well as for the Jews, and others?" (*On Our Own Ground* 158). Apess in fact is at pains to disengage Christianity from Euro-American racist hegemony, and more, to rally what he sees as the egalitarian spirit of religion against the oppressive forces of colonization.

That "deep brown wilderness" is an underground network of Indigenous communities across the Northeast and Ontario, even during the Jacksonian era of Indian Removal. "Authentic" Native communities and identities populated his world, and whether or not Indians were Christians, he saw them as Pequot or Mississauga or Mashpee—as who they themselves knew they were.

"Their Wrongs and Claims": Authenticity in Winnemucca

If Apess is the most polemical of these writers, enlisting explicit theological and legal discourses of debate, Winnemucca is certainly the most traditional of the voices in this study. She conveys her equally direct political message primarily through narrative discourse of "their wrongs and claims," bolstered like Apess's claims by published affidavits of white approval. Apess's narrative passages in his later works like *Eulogy* and *Indian Nullification* are more documentary evidence than the storytelling of *Son of the Forest* and *Five Christian Indians*. Yet throughout his work he performs his personal style of Indianness for his white audiences as he invokes communal Indian rights to the land. Winnemucca's single autobiographical work follows Apess's genre of communal narration, while her similar moral appeals to the reader are more pathetic and less ironic in tone than those of Apess. Her urgent tone reflects the moment of desperation of her people, measured in decades, compared with the longer history of oppression endured by Apess's Pequot and Mashpee, measured in centuries.

For all her comparatively traditional upbringing, however, Winnemucca's education in the English language—following her grandfather Truckee's designs for her as a cultural mediator—placed her in a lifelong liminal position. Like the Fool Soldiers, her default role as both leader and interpreter straddled tragically the so-called frontier. Under brutal pressure on the Northern Paiutes from the Indian Ring in the Bureau of Indian Affairs, she inherited her family's precarious position as failed leaders of a stressed community, and they bestowed on her a role as translator-mediator to the less than trustworthy whites.[10]

Differences in Winnemucca's discourse from Apess's are further marked by their different religious worldviews. If Apess called for a transcendent religion of oneness under the name of Christianity, Winnemucca called for a transcendent respect for difference under the name of humanity. Winnemucca does not identify herself with Christianity. Instead she always speaks of Christians in the third person, frequently, like Apess, pointing out their peculiar hypocrisies.

Her narrative positionality outside Christian civilization structures the four-part rhetorical formula of her authentic appeal to her white audiences and readers: Indian *solidarity* and *irony* calling on *pity* in an outraged appeal to universal *humanity*. While she builds narratives to support these human qualities against the inhumane treatment by Indian agents under Grant's Peace Policy of missionary rather than military administration of the reservations, she advocates expressly for her people:

> This kind of thing goes on, on all the reservations; and if any white man writes to Washington in our behalf, the agent goes to work with letters and gets his men, and his aunts and cousins to help him, and they get any kind of Indians to sign the letters, and they are sent on to Washington. . . . And the agent is believed, because he is a Christian. So it goes on year after year. Oh, when will it stop? I pray of you, I implore of you, I beseech of you, hear our pitiful cry to you, sweep away the agency system; give us homes to live in, for God's sake and for humanity's sake. (*Life Among the Piutes* 242–43)

Here is her sincere, though not always guileless four-part strategy in a nutshell: all the Indians (solidarity) are oppressed by hypocritical Christian agents (irony); please (pity) change the system "for God's sake and for humanity's sake" (humanity). In resonances with the five larger terms of this study, Winnemucca's reciprocal rhetorical strategy speaks to the central concerns of national identity in both Native and Euro-American populations.

The title of her text, presumably influenced by her editor, Mary Mann, alludes to a broad popular literary tradition of "authentic" tales—*Life Among* accounts—that promised a Euro-American middle- and upper-class readership the dual reading pleasure of an outsider's look at the inside of the other. She is clearly addressing, and manipulating, expectations around authenticity carried by her settler-colonial audience. A small sampling of such titles in the nineteenth century includes the following, minus various paragraphic subtitles: *Life among the Indians* by Royal B. Stratton, 1857; *Life among the Indians* by George Catlin, 1870; *Life among the Indians* by James Bradley Finley, 1880; *Life among the Choctaw* by Henry Clark Benson, 1860; *Life among the Apaches* by John Cremony Carey, 1868; *Life among the Mormons* by William Elkanah Waters, 1868; *Capture and Escape; or, Life among the Sioux* by Sarah Larimer Luse, 1870. Preceding all of these titles and establishing a political paradigm upon which Winnemucca builds is, of course, *Uncle Tom's Cabin; or Life among the Lowly* by Harriet Beecher Stowe, 1851. The sense of authenticity built upon this tradition of *Life Among* publications lends further credence to Winnemucca's own subtitle regarding her people: *Their Wrongs and Claims*. Because that subtitle expresses the political focus of her literary project, she gives it all the weight of the literary tradition of authentic tales of "life among the Indians." On the basis of her realistic and authentic narration of recent history, their wrongs and claims might ring true.

Winnemucca intensifies that strategy of authenticity for her white readers, first, by bracketing the text with documents and testimonials by her white supporters: her editor's preface; her petition to return the Malheur Reservation to her people for audiences and readers to sign; then the appendix, with letters of support from prominent whites such as a brevet major general of the U.S. Army; the aide-de-camp and adjutant-general of troops in the field, Bannock and Piute campaign, 1878; a lieutenant colonel of the Office of Inspector of Cavalry, Headquarters, Military Division of the Missouri; the retired major-general of the Division of the Pacific and the Department of California; the acting secretary of war; the secretary of the interior; the commissioner of Indian affairs; and many others. This blizzard of published documents as testimonial to her veracity continues the colonial tradition of her grandfather Truckee's dramatic "rag friend," a prized letter of validation from the explorer John Charles Frémont. That text so inspired

Truckee with the protective power of the written word that he prepared his granddaughter for the adventures and sorrows of her literate career as a translator and writer by ensuring her education in English.

"Our Young Women"

There are so many fascinating aspects of Winnemucca's rhetorical control of authenticity in her text, as where she affirms her speaking role based on gender equity in Paiute culture, where she affirms her own authority to translate between material and dream worlds, and where she affirms democratic principles in Paiute governance. However, I will focus further here on her appeal to American womanhood, as it resonates with her other strategies. We can approach it through her rhetorical self-positioning of solidarity, irony, pity, and humanity.

Among Winnemucca's discursive strategies of translating the authenticity of pathos there is the direct lament, with its myriad layers: "Many years ago, when my people were happier than they are now, they used to celebrate the Festival of Flowers in the spring" (*Life Among the Piutes* 46). She speaks to Americans' own colonial guilt and to their teleological notions of the Fall from the Garden, with its associated dreams of a New Zion. The power of that nostalgia for lost innocence is driven deeper by a romantic sense of human emotion in a line that soon follows: "Oh, with what eagerness we girls used to watch every spring for the time when we could meet with our hearts' delight, the young men, whom in civilized life you call beaux" (46). In this direct translation, deciphering youthful, erotic eagerness across cultures, she employs a certain neutral irony in the rhetoric of identifying "civilized life" with "you" when the plain message is that Paiute life is equally civilized, here meaning equally heartfelt and authentically human. The savvy use of the French plural in *beaux*, employing a savoir faire, only heightens the erotic connotations in her translation. (We note her editor's possible influences more below.) The effect, again, is authenticity, here intensified by intimacy.

Toward her larger purposes, however, she is careful also to make distinctions, contrasts as well as comparisons, not so much to render her people exotic to her audiences as to render them superior in morals. By establishing their moral stature, she establishes their worthiness for political support, especially by upstanding white women.[11] Indeed, as noted, the tactic of

chapter 2, "Domestic and Social Moralities," is to summon pity for lost innocence due to white incursion, a picture of purity under attack: "Our children
are very carefully taught to be good" (*Life Among the Piutes* 45). She launches
the chapter with that affirmation, followed by an ethnographic catalogue
mentioning traditions, love stories, stories of giants, and fables. Describing
Coyote as "a mean, crafty little animal, half wolf, half dog," who "stands for
everything low," she sets up a primary juxtaposition against white frontier
abuses of language: "[Coyote] is the greatest term of reproach one Indian
has for another. Indians do not swear,—they have no words for swearing till
they learn them of white men." Instead, according to the text, Indians are
"very sincere with one another": "We are taught to love everybody" (45).

In this context of universal love, Winnemucca proceeds through her
polemic narrative to establish authenticity as sexual purity. This unique
moment of authenticity, translating Victorian morality into Indigenous moral
authority, lays the foundation for her later critique of "wars and their causes,"
where white male sexual depredations turn the tragic wheel of history. She
proceeds in chapter 2 to recount a story of comparative authenticity, literally translating nineteenth-century codes of morality into Paiute codes and
vice versa in an effort to validate Paiute lives in the translation. Whatever
may be there of pure or authentic Paiute life—and apparently much is there—
is translated always already by the writer's purpose and her complex relation to her white audience.

In the following passage, the effect is to represent *authentic* Paiute men
and women as chaste and virtuous, against the corrupting influences of
unchaste and unvirtuous white civilization. Compare Apess's depiction in
"An Indian's Looking-Glass for the White Man" of New England reservations as "a complete place of prodigality and prostitution" (*On Our Own
Ground* 155) under white rule. Winnemucca writes of traditional sexual purity
in Paiute culture: "Our young women are not allowed to talk to any young
man that is not their cousin, except at the festive dances, when both are
dressed in their best clothes, adorned with beads, feathers or shells, and
stand alternately in the ring and take hold of hands. These are very pleasant occasions to all the young people" (*Life Among the Piutes* 45–46). Ending
on a hint of the erotic pleasure in the exchange, Winnemucca's focus on
"our young women" emphasizes her own pivotal role of purity, both as the
narrator/translator herself and as an exemplar of Paiute womanhood in

general. Thus she is addressing especially the women in her audience, for whom she even arranged special, women-only sessions in her public lecture tours. As the dowager Elizabeth Peabody, Winnemucca's sponsor and "devoted admirer" (Zanjani, *Sarah Winnemucca* 245), writes, "All this . . . prepared me to appreciate and understand the first lecture I heard from her, which she addressed 'exclusively to women,' in which she unfolded the domestic education given by the grandmothers of the Piute tribe to the youth of both sexes, with respect to their relations with each other both before and after marriage—a lecture which never failed to excite the moral enthusiasm of every woman that heard it, and seal their confidence in her own purity of character and purpose" (*Sarah Winnemucca's Practical Solution of the Indian Problem* 27–28).

It is noteworthy that this innocence was "sealed" for Winnemucca herself, the public speaker, for whom, in an age of "the cult of domesticity," a woman with a public life was a woman under suspicion. In fact the corrupt agents back at the Malheur and Yakima agencies in today's states of Oregon and Washington had instituted campaigns of slander against her through correspondence with officials in the Bureau of Indian Affairs, the Department of the Interior, eastern newspapers, and elsewhere. They were effective in thus undercutting her lobbying efforts back east. This potent campaign further clarifies the logic of her literary equation between authenticity and moral purity.

In Zanjani's biography of Winnemucca, she contextualizes Peabody's superlatives:

> Like any effective speaker, Sarah tailored her lectures to suit the interest of her audience, while always asserting her fundamental themes. Not unaware of the eastern reformers' interest in woman suffrage and the prevailing belief in the superior morality of women, she argued on some occasions that if the agent system must be continued, the agents should be women. When speaking to an audience of women, she stressed, perhaps a little fancifully, the virtue of Paiute courtship and marital practices and the role of the grandmothers in caring for the marriageable young. (*Sarah Winnemucca* 245)

For all the emphasis on "the superior morality of women," Winnemucca's discussion of morality carries the frisson of eroticism, precisely because here the "dirty little secret" of Victorianism has been supplanted by her clean little secret of indigeneity. Such a strategy, as Peabody's account suggests, was immensely attractive. I suggest that it drives the political efficacy of her Indian princess persona. Winnemucca writes, "But the courting is very different from the courting of the white people. He never speaks to her, or visits the family, but endeavors to attract her attention by showing his horsemanship, etc." (*Life Among the Piutes* 48). To this strict Romance of the Rose, Winnemucca adds the remarkable account that the suitor may sit at his beloved's feet in her lodge at night in the presence of her grandmother, an intensely romantic image of nearness and distance, of desire and restraint that invokes chivalric dreams in her Euro-American readers.

She further offers to fulfill her readers' voyeuristic desires as imperial tourists where a detailed paragraph lays out the ritual festival of womanhood: "The grandmothers have the special care of the daughters just before and after they come to womanhood. . . . That period is recognized as a very sacred thing, and is the subject of a festival and has peculiar customs," some of which the text then elucidates (*Life Among the Piutes* 48). Here we have the erotics of storytelling itself, or the inverse, in the storytelling techniques of erotics, revealing just enough and not too much to keep her readers interested.[12]

During a lengthy description of matrimony, emphasizing the young woman's autonomy, as we have seen, Winnemucca scores more points of comparison: "She is never forced by her parents to marry against her wishes. When she knows her own mind, she makes a confidant of her grandmother" (*Life Among the Piutes* 49). In a remarkable dialectic, the wedding vow within the family merges the gender identities: "She promises to 'be himself,' and she fulfills her promise" (49). Later, when she is describing women's role in the council tent—"Our Congress, and anybody can speak who has anything to say, women and all"—she articulates that dialectic of marriage with a different pronoun that sparks the mutuality of the exchange. Out of matrimonial reciprocity, she then projects a revised interracial dialectic on her theme:

> They are always interested in what their husbands are doing and thinking about. And they take some part even in the wars. They are always near at hand when fighting is going on, ready to snatch their husbands up and carry them off if wounded or killed. . . . It means something

when the women promise their fathers to make their husbands *themselves*. They faithfully keep with them in all the dangers they can share. . . . Marriage is a sweet thing when people love each other. If women could go into your Congress I think justice would soon be done to the Indians. (*Life Among the Piutes* 53)

Her cross-cultural translation is ever ready to speak for her political purposes. She makes the personal political in this instantaneous leap from the "sweet thing" of marriage into advice on "your Congress."

Strategically balancing gender representation in order to establish a contrast with corrupt frontiersmen, the narration segues eventually to a description of manhood hunting ceremonies. Thus a similar refrain of social justice versus injustice follows on her description of Paiute manhood rites that proceeds from her account of the wedding feast: "Our boys are introduced to manhood by their hunting of deer and mountain-sheep," ritually, after each boy has "been faithful to his parent's command not to eat what he has killed before" (*Life Among the Piutes* 50–51). Careful monitoring of the growing boy's strength instills respect for their game. When he is strong enough to hunt with respect for the dignity of the kill, "he can now do whatever he likes, for now he is a man, and no longer considered a boy" (51). Immediately the translation ethos surfaces again in Winnemucca's text, as she compares the relatively peaceful Paiutes with their mercenary invaders: "If there is a war he can go to it; but the Piutes, and other tribes west of the Rocky Mountains, are not fond of going to war. I never saw a wardance but once. It is always the whites that begin the wars, for their own selfish purposes" (51).

She follows these assertions with a litany of authentic Paiute virtues in contrast with the shameful behavior of "our white brothers":

My people teach their children never to make fun of anyone, no matter how they look. If you see your brother or sister doing something wrong, look away, or go away from them. . . . Be kind to all poor and rich, and feed all that come to your wigwam. . . . Be kind both to bad and good, for you don't know your own heart. This is the way my people teach their children. It was handed down from father to son for many generations. I never in my life saw our children rude as I have seen white children and grown people in the streets. (*Life Among the Piutes* 51)

These are the streets of Winnemucca's travels in Boston and Brattleboro and Baltimore, as well as Virginia City, San Jose, and San Francisco. Winnemucca catches her audience by juxtaposing herself incongruously as an Indian princess in the streets of America, mapping and dramatizing the further incongruity of a savage teaching whites how to be civilized.

This momentary irony "in the streets" intensifies the deeper irony of her focus on women, in clear contrast with American inequality and a long-frustrated politics for women's suffrage. Enlisting her connections with the famous and well-placed sisters Mary Peabody Mann and Elizabeth Peabody, she returns to her Indian perspective on a need for reform of American government. The intensity of Winnemucca's message to women at this point prompts Mann to offer one of her few editorial footnotes, this one her longest, where she rhapsodizes on "other refinements and manners that the Indian mother teaches her children; and it is worthy the imitation of the whites" (*Life Among the Piutes* 51). Mann then launches into a discussion of education and the benefits that whites may glean from Native cultures: "When something like a human communication is established between the Indians and whites, it may prove a fair exchange, and the knowledge of nature which has accumulated, for we know not how long, may enrich our early education as much as reading and writing will enrich theirs." From there she levels a diatribe against "the Christian bigots who peopled America" (52). Mann may have missed her own point: that Indians have as much *culture* as *nature* to offer whites, yet, considering the times, she may have been Winnemucca's greatest convert or, one might say, human translation. The author and the editor converse in realms of high discourse, comparing morality and domestic practicality across cultures. Winnemucca insists on the golden rule of humility and respect, "for you don't know your own heart," as the core of Native education, and Mann responds by affirming the need for education as *mutual* learning across cultures; then she branches off into wholesale history and condemnation, citing *A Century of Dishonor* and other American self-critiques. Together they transform authenticity as translation into a new sense of American community, inventing a language of reciprocity.

Thus Winnemucca struggled to maintain a utopian appeal to solidarity, irony, pity, and humanity toward the end of the nineteenth century, during the climactic decades of the Indian Wars. Her principles fit into a reciprocal rhetoric that had taken different form in Apess toward the beginning of her century and that were translated further by McNickle, Silko, Alexie, and many others in the twentieth. As she exposed the colonial oppression of her people, she articulated a desperate optimism that saw beyond her people's pathos to a different American ideal.

"Who Would Put the Sun Back in the Sky": Authenticity in McNickle

Any optimism for authentic survivance in D'Arcy McNickle is buried in his fiction, while he expresses it clearly in his nonfiction. His dramatic purpose was clearly to expose the desperate, downward spiral of Indigenous communities after the turn of the twentieth century, while his critical purpose was also to envision and serve the dim possibilities for agency. He took as his setting the early decades on his reservation during the lowest ebb of Native American sovereignty, as he sought ways in his own career to protect Native communities against the domination of non-Indian society.

In redefining authenticity through American Indian voices, McNickle's fiction is the exception that proves the rule. If Indian stories suggest how authenticity is translation in Native American and American history, McNickle's novels tend to do so by charting the failure to translate. Because his narratives take the tragic view, because he consciously constructed them along the disastrous oppositions of real frontier mentalities, his fictions function more as solemn cautionary tales than the inspirational calls to action of Apess, Winnemucca, or even Silko. In his measured perspective, he perhaps presages Alexie's unromantic skepticism. Although his stories wind through moments of confidence and expectation, they finish as lamentations. As Doc Edwards says in *Wind from an Enemy Sky*, "The real loser was the country itself. . . . The land was the loser, but of course the Indians were part of the land" (230). It is such authentic insight that McNickle wishes for his American readers, a direct recognition of Indian losses, a willingness to face the brutal culpability of modern America for dispossession of Indian land. Because of his tragic take on that historical era, because his and his mother's generation met face-to-face the full tragic force of cultural and territorial losses on the western frontier, we shall see how authentic Indianness in McNickle does seem to vanish into the past tense.

Because of his dramatic fascination with polarized frontier oppositions,

McNickle's fictional treatments remind us of key structural and poststructural dialectics in Native American literature: how authenticity requires inauthenticity. By a deconstructive interplay, authenticity is always a measure, a comparison, a dialectical difference set against and within the inauthentic and vice versa. For instance, the plot of McNickle's last novel, *Wind from an Enemy Sky*, is built on representative characterizations that dramatize direct opposition of authenticity and inauthenticity, setting up internecine politics of one versus the other. First, the Little Elk people as a whole are set against the "wind from an enemy sky" of an invasive and oppressive white settler culture. Second, Bull and his elder brother, Henry Jim, stand as authenticity and inauthenticity, respectively, set against each other in the plot precisely along the question of how to act as a member of their tribe in response to those colonial pressures. In Said's discussion of "an epistemology of imperialism," this historical pressure translates authenticity into a "fantastic emphasis" on "a politics of national identity" under siege. Bull and his band embody such an emphatic fantasy, with tragic consequences. McNickle's brilliance as a fiction writer lies largely in dramatizing the personal stakes of historic, public issues, translating between the authentic individual and the authentic cultural struggle for survival.

Wind from an Enemy Sky was written over the span of four decades and is structured around questions driving the development of McNickle's thinking on survivance. Through a fictional conflation of two historical events, the construction of Kerr Dam and the Flathead Irrigation Project on the reservation of the Confederated Salish and Kootenai Tribes, the novel explores the agency of inquiry that old man Bull offers to his grandson Antoine after their painful impotence, their seeming lack of agency, in facing the new dam that "killed the water" at the story's opening: "Grandson, when a man goes anyplace, whether to hunt or to visit relatives, he should think about the things he sees, or maybe the words somebody speaks to him. He asks himself, What did I learn from this? What should I remember? Now, I will ask, What did you see today? We will sit here, and you tell me what you saw" (8). The question "What did I learn from this?" is essentially a question of translation. However harsh the circumstances, a sense of surviving through this question, of ongoing authenticity translating experience into understanding, drives young Antoine's quest and Bull's question. That authentic ability to learn from experience, the authority to translate any encounter into terms that carry personal and cultural meaning, informs the main characters in McNickle's severe tales.

Indeed McNickle saw that form of authenticity as translation at the core of Native societies. We find his considered view on this subject in detailed professional correspondence from the year of his death in 1977, as he was finishing *Wind from an Enemy Sky*. Here McNickle is consulting on and disagreeing with a young writer's manuscript that he has reviewed for the University of California Press. In his critique we glimpse a broad and positive anthropological perspective driving his sense of his own and others' Native narratives: "The argument here [that McNickle proposes] starts from the premise that the Native American race was highly adaptive, as witnessed by the extremes of climate and terrain to which the people shaped their lives." The aging scholar and novelist then applies that "highly adaptive" cultural quality to colonial history: "After four hundred years, a brief span in the history of a race, the native Americans are still making adjustments—and surviving." While he underlines the ability to adapt and survive, McNickle offers a deeper cultural "confidence" that grows from the land itself: "To live in harmony with nature is to trust nature, in the confidence that good times would always follow bad times" (cited in Purdy, *Word Ways* 108). McNickle argues that a culture moving in exchange with the land and other cultures, one that translates its experiences of contact into its own terms, will survive with the assurance of an authentic people, however excruciating their losses.

To focus McNickle's argument through the lens of our five principles is to read his sense of tentative assurance for both the Native America he worked to rescue and the America he worked to build. If assurance arises from reciprocity, dialogue, and the authentic translation of mutual exchange, the underlying issue is communication, and that, in its deterioration, is another term for McNickle's central subject. Communication is the foundation not only of translation in authenticity, as we have been exploring, but of community as complementary animism. Everyone gets to talk—because everyone knows how to listen. As Owens comments in his afterword to the 1988 edition of *Wind from an Enemy Sky*, "Ironically, it is communication that fails repeatedly and inevitably in D'Arcy McNickle's novels, and it is communication that McNickle devoted his life to realizing. No one—Indian or white—has contributed more to understanding between the two worlds than McNickle with his novels and such nonfiction works as *They Came Here First, Indians and Other Americans,* and *Native American Tribalism*" (264). Along with *communication,* the operative word in Owens's characterization is *ironically:* how ironic that a champion of communication should be remembered for so forcefully recounting its failures. Yet his memorable fictions play exactly on that kind of contrary power. Through ironic reversal with precise positioning of characters and social forces in dramatic tragedies, McNickle chose to make his positive points about building communication and "understanding between the two worlds" by negative examples. Moreover, while his fiction marks the pitfalls, his nonfiction also maps some potential escapes.

Tragedy and Translation

In McNickle's characterization of a well-intentioned but cross-culturally ignorant patrician, Adam Pell observes of the Little Elk nation, a fictional stand-in for the author's Salish, in *Wind from an Enemy Sky,* "They are a solemn people, and solemn people are likely to be unpredictable" (211). Pell senses that survivors of tragedy may make claims. The balance of tragedy and trust, of loss and survivance in McNickle remains a matter of debate, and that debate provides the context of authenticity as translation. Owens and John Purdy, for example, take nearly opposite positions on this question, quite usefully laying out the polarities for this study to find a middle road. On the one hand, as we saw, Owens characterizes McNickle's fictions as focused on a failure to communicate. Here he enlarges that failure to an existential condition: "McNickle develops the theme of misunderstanding in *Wind from an Enemy Sky* in the barrier of silence between Indian brothers, in the miscommunication between Indian and white, and in the seeming impossibility of dialogue between all men" (Afterword 259). The harsh and painful realities of difference resonate in Owens's analysis.

On the other hand, unraveling Owens, Purdy teases out the threads of survivance woven through McNickle's cloth: "For Owens and others, *Wind* is a conventional protest novel about the demise of Native cultures. It is not. To see the distinction, one must consider the text's tribal point of view, which is not as fatalistic as some critics would have us believe; protest serves two audiences, and in different ways" (*Word Ways* 113). I'm not sure that Owens would have agreed that McNickle writes merely about "the demise of Native cultures" as much as about miscommunication and imbalanced power between cultures. Yet Purdy does a convincing job of explicating McNickle's novel in the light of surviving tribal values, illuminating "the main structural device of the book—the progression of Antoine's journey and education" (132) as assurance that the people carry on, that is, that they can translate their experience into terms meaningful to themselves. Again he points out that, at the end of *Wind*, the next generation continues: "Antoine witnesses the final scene, but, like Archilde at the end of *The Surrounded*, takes no physical action. Instead, he participates in an act of understanding" (133). Such an act reinforces the authentic response to the fundamental question, laid out at the beginning of the story: "What have you learned today?"

Thus Purdy reads survivance in the finale: "To respond to the final scene, readers need to recognize the innate strengths and durability of Native cultures and realize that, perhaps, their unique, long-standing relationship with the landscapes of this continent possesses a logic of endurance that we would all be well advised to understand" (*Word Ways* 132). Purdy traces how "the songs sung earlier by Henry Jim and Antoine remain as well." Yet if the songs remain, so do the echoes of gunfire.

The useful reading lies somewhere in between Purdy and Owens. The issue is authenticity: what survives? The trick, again, in invoking a comic view, a view of survivance, is not to forget the real losses that a tragic view, a view of lamentation, remembers and honors. Because McNickle resided on the pivot point in American Indian history between annihilation and self-determination, his work tips back and forth on that scale between tragedy and comedy, between assimilation and cultural continuity. That ambiguous reality is the moment his stories tell. They remind us also how uncertain and incomplete the resurgence of Native cultures remains, how steady the sacrifice required for authentic tribal sovereignty both to reaffirm itself and to weave into and change American society.

Ultimately we cannot know why an author made the rhetorical choices she or he decided upon, but in McNickle's case there are some clear explanations for the solemn design in his own fiction and nonfiction, as well as in the scholarship. Let's look at the rationale from the texts themselves to understand his take on the survival and translation of authenticity after the turn of the century. A year before his death, McNickle was explicit about his literary purposes in a letter written in 1976 to an editor at Harper & Row during the preparation of the manuscript of *Wind from an Enemy Sky* for publication: "I guess the most general thing I can say is that I wanted to write about the Indian experience as objectively as possible; not just the usual story of the wronged Indian, but the greater tragedy of two cultures trying to accommodate each other.... I would like the reader to see the Little Elk episode not as an isolated tragedy, about which one need not get too concerned, but as a critical statement about the quality of human behavior when people of different cultures meet" (cited in Owens, Afterword 258). Here the operative word is *tragedy*, as McNickle clearly saw tragic polarities in history in "the quality of human behavior when people of different cultures meet." The Salish had been forced to move, between 1855 and the turn of the century, from their Bitterroot River homeland north to the Flathead Reservation, in confederation with the Kootenais and the Pend d'Oreilles. His generation was the first born on the reservation, following the more violent history of his mother's people as Métis in Canada during that Salish diaspora.

McNickle experienced his own personal and literary share of this tragic narrative. For this we have his and others' perspectives to consider. In Dorothy Parker's biography of McNickle, she cites a letter written in 1974, when he was seventy, to the historian Robert Bigart, describing the reservation setting of his major novels as "a hell of a society to grow up in" (*Singing an Indian Song* 16). As Parker explains, "Frontier Montana at the turn of the century may well have been a 'hell of a society' for a sensitive young boy. The Flathead country was unusually chaotic at that time because of its impending allotment and the opening of the reservation to white homesteaders" (16). Senator Dixon, with interests in the Missoula Mercantile that would soon supply the settlers, pushed through legislation in 1910 opening "surplus" lands to white homesteaders after tribal allotment on the Flathead Reservation. The young McNickle witnessed the fencing of the open range and even the brutal final roundup of the local buffalo herd. It indeed traumatized him: "As a child of five or six I stood watching, amazed and terror-stricken, through the heavy timbers of the corral. One buffalo cow had been gored and her insides were pouring out. I either saw or was told about the great bull who went charging up the ramp and right through the other side of the stock car" (16). These kinds of images—of evisceration and of enraged natural power fenced and tricked into death—form a foundation for his fiction, for Archilde's final shackles and for Bull's final sacrifice.

Yet the losses were driven home even more poignantly by the institutional violence of his own boarding school experience, a common twisting of the colonial knife in the heart of his family. McNickle's mother, Philomene, fought unsuccessfully against the bureaucracy to fend off loss of her children to a distant school. Her grief permeates McNickle's narratives. For instance, Purdy compares Philomene to the protagonist's mother in *The Surrounded*: "Like Philomene, McNickle's mother, Catharine was born at a time of radical change. Philomene saw her people, the Métis, move from a powerful force on the northern plains to a race of homeless refugees, powerless and at the mercy of forces beyond their control. They had fought for their lands—and lost. McNickle recognized that the story of his family was similar to the story of the Salish and of Native peoples in general" (*Word Ways* 41). The mind of a refugee must be in a state of steady stress and apprehension. Comfortable whites in McNickle's novels, like those he associated with in his adulthood, have no idea of the tensions tearing at the psyches of Indians in his narratives. Educating whites to those cultural pressures is one of his literary methods toward redressing the inequities. Yet, as Purdy suggests of Catharine in *The Surrounded*, "She also demonstrates the ability of Native traditions to prevail over adversity, including the ill effects of European colonization. She is not a flat character" (41). Those ill effects ran directly through McNickle's family as his mixed-blood mother and white father divorced and fought over custody of the three children.

Thus McNickle's logic of tragedy flowers from his family garden. As an outcome of the divorce, his Métis mother had to endure seeing the children exported as tribal members, when McNickle was nine years old, to the federal boarding school in Chemawa, Oregon. Many accounts of Indian boarding schools describe the intertribal support and friendship among students, as well as suicide and desperate, sometimes fatal escape to which traumatized children turned in such oppressive predicaments.[13] Autobiographical echoes as well as literary details of these feelings animate McNickle's fictions. We read his recollections directly in Archilde's and his brother's brutal memories of the Ursuline School in *The Surrounded*. Similarly McNickle speaks in *Wind from an Enemy Sky* through Antoine's more distant Chemawa boarding school episode and the resulting grief, delirium, and death of Antoine's mother, Celeste, again a dramatization of his own mother's sorrows.

In his literary map of authentic Salish experience, McNickle further connects the personal dread in boarding school with the inexorable political tribulations unfolding at home: "There had been nights at the government's school when he lay in bed holding his knees and listening to his heart pound, knowing that trouble in some indefinable form would come" (*Wind* 203). Economic and social torment, built on miscommunication, takes specific, personal form in the motivations of each of the Indian characters in *Wind*, as we see with Antoine's family: "Celeste, his mother, was Bull's first girl child, as he, Antoine, was her first child, and everyone told him she had never gotten over his going away. When the government men came to the camp and took him, without even saying where he would go, she told everybody, 'He is dead,' and soon she was dead. All this he learned when he returned" (110). In this vortex of grief, McNickle links community with mother love. A sense of maternal power is broken off by official government acts of abduction.

Yet that maternal, sheltering force is not gendered, not ascribed to Salish women alone in the novel, as Bull's efforts to protect his daughter and his grandson are denied by colonial compulsions working into the veins of the Indian camp. As Celeste moves into delirium, Bull laments: "Holding her, he knew the deep and helpless feeling of not being able to carry his child away from a time of trouble to let her start over again" (*Wind* 202). These emotional limitations of historical circumstances even restrict Bull's grandfatherly responses, another plot feature that McNickle employs to dramatize Indian losses on a personal scale. When Antoine first returns, Bull is hardened toward his grandson by his own grief at the loss of his beloved daughter, after she died of grief over the abduction of her son at the hands of the boarding school recruiters. Eventually Bull tries to start over again with Antoine. Bull's efforts speak to a sense of continuity, of peoplehood and sovereignty also working through the camp.

McNickle the storyteller eases that personal narrative into a more positive trajectory (of course, only to tantalize the reader before the ferocious finale, where the songs do continue): "Deep within, Bull still carried the remembrance of the boy's mother, of the hurt that came to her. He would start to explain to the boy how such a thing could happen and how the people could no longer protect themselves or their own children, then he would stop short. A boy should not grow up feeling that his life would be worthless. Bad times would come soon enough, of their own accord, without a grandfather telling how nothing good could be expected. A people needed young ones who would put the sun back in the sky" (*Wind* 203-4). Thus a grim sense of doom permeates McNickle's landscapes, a harsh reality of facing an enemy wind, of being surrounded by "bad times" that "would come soon enough, of their own accord," with so little room for Indian choices for authenticity, for individual or community agency, for sovereignty.

The worst that the well-intentioned Agent Rafferty fears, when he advises Adam Pell to keep silent about the destruction of the sacred Feather Bundle, does indeed unfold: "These people have come to the end of the road. After what you tell us, it would be better if you told them nothing. That's what I mean when I say it is nonsense. This gift will not give back what they lost. It will only expose them to a terrible truth, destroy hope. Whatever nasty things we did to them in the past, this will be the most devastating. I am sorry" (*Wind* 235). In McNickle's tragic view, Rafferty's regret is as ineffective as his good intentions. The fact that he, the Indian agent, is finally shot by Bull, along with Pell, the elite financier, land developer, and Indian curio collector, is clearly an indication that the plot requires more than cross-cultural sympathy within a patriarchal colonial construct. McNickle's logic drives to the only real remedy: authentic restoration of tribal sovereignty, a retranslation of political and cultural power, of Indian agency on the land, not another federal agency. Such a remedy would translate both American and Native American sovereignty.

"Keep Him Alive by Singing"

Perhaps because translation is a most challenging form of communication, McNickle is explicit in *Wind from an Enemy Sky* about the issue as it bears on authentic experience and expression. On the plot level of the text there are numerous scenes, each a microcosm of centuries of treaty councils, in which Indian and white leaders attempt to communicate through a translator. The first attempt at a council that occurs in the novel is, tellingly, rebuffed. When Henry Jim, so close to death that his people's songs are keeping him alive, rides down to the Agency, he vaguely recalls a time when he himself was a translator for the U.S. marshal: "In a time that he could now scarcely remember, he had interpreted for this man" (57). Now such exchange is impossible, as the marshal shouts, "There's been a killing, that's what's wrong! . . . So just tell your boys to go on home" (57).

Many ensuing councils and conversations, at various levels of formality, weave through the narrative, with specific reference to translation. For example, when Iron Child says to Agent Rafferty, "I talk here for Henry Jim," the text highlights the distance bridged through translation: "He explained through The Boy" (84). There is also the distance not bridged, as when The Boy tries to explain to Rafferty that the songs are keeping old Henry Jim alive. "Do they really think they can keep him alive by singing—?" Rafferty asks, and the text maps the divide: "The Boy seemed to speak from a great distance. 'I guess they'll try'" (*Wind* 85). When Rafferty visits Henry Jim's death bed, old man Two Sleeps "addressed himself to The Boy" as translator. His words are bracketed by the linguistic and cultural separation: "Tell this man: We are camped here at the old man's place so he will feel our power and not be discouraged" (123). When Henry Jim responds to Rafferty's visit, McNickle focuses on the language barrier as though it divides life and death itself in the old man: "He had started to speak in English, as he could do around white men, but he kept slipping back into his own language, then into English, like a man following a vanishing trail" (124). As the old man takes his last breaths, "The Boy moved up beside him, across from the doctor, and translated" (127). Yet at the end of the scene, as the question turns away from the dead to face conflicts among the living, translation explicitly ceases when Bull says one of his few relatively conciliatory statements in the text, here about the agent: "The Boy did not translate Bull's soft reply: 'Maybe this one is different, as you said. He doesn't push'" (128). Similarly in the meeting with the parents of the murdered young man, Bull's commanding presence is again bracketed by the need for a translator: "He turned to The Boy: 'Tell this woman I am sorry about her son'" (160), and again he addresses the agent through that filter: "Now, say to the government man that I came because he asked" (161). In these and many other scenes, McNickle chooses to foreground the necessity for the translator. Language is not transparent. The opacity of linguistic difference is as thick as the narrative's ethnic and political differences.

Even within the Indian camp, there are issues of translation, as when old Henry Jim first walks unannounced into his brother Bull's camp to try to make peace. Appropriate to his lifelong choices of exchange, Henry Jim assumes his motives and words will translate across the years of estrangement from Bull, as McNickle writes, "Under the wide-brimmed black hat, it was impossible to see the visitor's face, now that he was seated, but the voice came strong and calm. He talked without hurrying, as if he never doubted that he would be heard" (*Wind* 17). Yet Bull, identifying his brother with white men's ways, is not so willing to pretend that translating across the gap of miscommunication comes easily. In his first response to Henry Jim, "after some minutes," before he softens somewhat, Bull speaks to that gap both among their people and between them and the whites: "You gave our power to a white man. I never learned how to talk to a white man. So why do you come to me and to my camp? Just bring it back here; then maybe we can talk" (19). Translation and communication here depend upon temporal authenticity, on the return of the Feather Boy Bundle. Communication, according to Bull's clear logic, cannot be built on miscommunication. Retrieving the bundle would translate into authentic exchange.

Yet for all these dramatized attempts at translation in the novel, authentic culture and language in McNickle remain ultimately untranslatable. The author is explicit about this central theme. "The words men speak never pass from one language to another without some loss of flavor and ultimate meaning" (*Wind* 2), he writes of Bull's name. That abyss, that aporia, that difference in language becomes tragic opposition, ending in eventual violence for Bull and others. Authenticity in McNickle thus stands as that which cannot be translated.

Yet in McNickle's deeply oppositional and tragic narratives, that impossibility extends not only in the gap between cultures but also in the gaps within cultures, families, and individuals themselves. His tragedy is more than colonial conflict; it is the human condition, aggravated by colonialism. It is both political and existential. One thinks again of Bull's inability to access his delirious daughter, Celeste, in her mother-grief over her son's seizure by boarding school officials. Or the thirty-year failure of language between Henry Jim and Bull. Or the stark either/or, Indian-versus-white choices on Archilde's and his mother's mental and spiritual horizons. Or the sophisticated ignorance and destructive good intentions of Adam Pell. The tragic paradigm in McNickle's fiction is not the fact of these oppositions, internal or external, psychological or social. Instead his tragedy resides in the failure of narratives, characters, and social forces to find alternative ways to elude or to blend and dissolve those oppositions. The closure of the narrative line drawn with these oppositions renders them absolute. McNickle's severe insistence on such linguistic, psychological, and cultural gaps and distances amounts to a semiotics of suffering, ground into language and psyche by the weight of colonial history. Cultivated on the River Thames and La Loire, as well as the Flathead River, his early twentieth-century reading of his family's and his culture's calamitous inheritance anticipates the isolation and existential angst of his contemporaries Sartre and Camus, as he echoes the structural distance between signifier and signified in Saussure. His own youthful years in Paris may have personalized some of that French theory, and he indeed stands between the worlds, just as his work presages Vizenor's "ruins of representation," which are a failure of translation as authenticity recedes to the ruins of the past.

The effect of denying translation is that authenticity recedes painfully into either a past or a parallel opposition. For instance, chapter 3 of *Wind* launches with explicit theorizing on interpersonal linguistic barriers, here between the brothers Bull and Henry Jim, who have held pivotal leadership positions among their people, thus divided by alliance with one or the other:

> How to translate from one man's life to another's—that is difficult. It is more difficult than translating a man's name into another man's language....
>
> Henry Jim from the first had tried to discover what white men were saying, and what they meant beyond the words they used—and that had been the difference between him and his brother. He had studied these strange men from beyond the mountains and the words of their discourse ever since they came among his people. (26)

This difference between brothers lies at the bottom of the crevasse that splits the entire narrative. One tries to translate; the other knows better. In fact Henry Jim's choice at the end to die in a tipi instead of in his own white-man house is again a hint on McNickle's part that any solution lies in cultural vigilance, not accommodation, precisely because translation "is difficult": "At first it did not seem strange that 'the old one'—the elder brother—should be lying on a buffalo robe in the tepee—only later, after he had been there awhile, did Antoine wonder why he had left his big house to make a bed on the ground" (*Wind* 115). Henry Jim's death-bed explanation only reaffirms his authentic Indian selfhood as untranslatable: "I want to die in my own house" (118), not the big wooden house he has been living in for decades, where he raised his family, but a traditional skin tipi, as Doc Edwards observes: "'See the big tepee, with the pointed things on it—that's a real old-timer. Henry Jim is in there. He moved out of his big house two days ago.' He said it with a kind of wonder in his voice" (122).

Yet moving away from tragic oppositions in his later nonfiction, McNickle directly affirms that peculiar Native, land-based certainty as survival, as something other than tragic, notably at the conclusion of *Native American Tribalism: Indian Survivals and Renewals*, published in 1973, when he was finishing *Wind*. He writes of the emerging Native American literary renaissance following N. Scott Momaday's 1969 Pulitzer Prize for fiction and links it to the political, economic, and cultural resurgence in Indian Country toward the end of the twentieth century: "All through North America, from the Arctic to the Florida peninsula, the long submerged Indian minority has been discovering the value of the published word, and this may prove to be the decisive force in bringing into being an enduring policy of *self-determined* cultural pluralism" (169, emphasis added). A faith in his own literary project is evident here, but his terminology is especially remarkable, marking his insider functions and presaging the Indian Self-Determination Act of 1975. What is even more significant, as he writes of "Indian nationalism, pan-Indianism, Red power" (170), is how he predicates this Native resurgence on that authentic value, a "certainty of self" underlying a growing sense of solidarity among Indian peoples across tribal lines. This nonfiction certainty contrasts with the tragic certainties of his fiction: "It is this certainty of self which the young proclaim, sometimes loudly. There is no such certainty for them in the white man's affluent society" (170). McNickle's insistence on difference, on the certainty of Indian identity and authenticity apart from "the white man's affluent society" articulates and promotes the very "self-determined pluralism" that would not bow to assimilation.

While he clearly presents an alternative future for American society, we may also read an echo here in another of his phrases, "the elders . . . are not confused about who they are" (*Native American Tribalism* 170), with the Mashpee elders of that same decade, whom James Clifford described. Wampanoag Supreme Sachem Elsworth Oakley insisted in 1978, after the Mashpees' loss in court of their tribal status, "How can a white majority decide on whether we are a tribe? We know who we are" (*The Predicament of Culture* 344). That fundamental and authentic self-certainty both in McNickle's Indian characterizations and in Mashpee voices suggests how these very different moments of Indian history may operate in similar ways. The dichotomies of McNickle's narratives seem to eclipse what Clifford described in Mashpee identity as a nexus on a field of exchange. Instead Clifford's phrase, "a dichotomy of absorption and resistance" drives McNickle's story lines. Yet the effect in *Wind* and *The Surrounded* is rather to more firmly, with more certainty, gauge the difference, the distinctness of each nexus of Indian identity that Clifford describes. Both within Indian society and within a larger pluralistic American model, McNickle affirms the paradox of communal identity, of the individual both within and against the group. According to McNickle, Indian cultures, if they are to survive in America, if they are to avoid assimilation, must insist on their differences, on the untranslatable as well as the translatable authentic. That would translate into a more authentic America.

"Rude and Arrogant": Authenticity in Alexie

Finally, we may see the play of authenticity in two of Alexie's novels, *Indian Killer* and *The Absolutely True Diary of a Part-Time Indian*, which occupy opposite poles of his work thus far. *Indian Killer* was Alexie's first novel-length experiment in "serious fiction" for adults. Because it is written in the tragic mode, with a certain mystery-thriller element to the plot, it will provide useful context not only for this discussion of authenticity, but for his humor as well. In the tear of the clown, comedy is never fundamentally separate from tragedy, especially in Indian writers like Alexie. *Diary* was his National Book Award–winning first experiment in young adult fiction, and it continues his prevalent mode of comic poignancy. (It won eighteen other national awards as well.)

There are two opening points to the discussion of authenticity in Alexie: alterity and agency. First, explicitly in interviews and both implicitly and explicitly in his writing, he disavows precisely the static, stoic version of authenticity that my discussion jettisons as well. He waves off the drums-and-feathers stereotypes as inauthentic or unreal, "that whole 'corn pollen, four directions, Mother Earth, Father Sky' Indian thing" (Mabrey, "The

Toughest Indian"). Alexie's criticism of these "generic cultural touchstones" indeed echoes the radical critique of "cosmopolitanism" by the Dakota scholar Elizabeth Cook-Lynn. Her insistence on tribal specificity and the local rather than universal meaning and force of Native narratives provides a theoretical underpinning that paradoxically supports Alexie's innovative approaches. Alexie's breakfast cereal becomes Cook-Lynn's frybread. His affirmation of pop cultural influences like *The Brady Bunch* becomes her reappropriated story of tribal resilience. To elude dominant and limiting assumptions, both Cook-Lynn and Alexie link daily Native lives to daily Native concerns, but Alexie is also explicit about linking Indigenous concerns to the American mainstream. Here we find the human and the humane in his humor.

The effect of this Native specificity is that Alexie offers more alterity than authenticity; that is, he provides "mutual selfhood" by eluding or playing against common images of Indian authenticity. This dynamic of alterity in Alexie is useful because it again clarifies the paradoxical processes of authenticity and identity formation. Especially for young Indian readers—a target audience for Alexie—retranslated authentic Indian identities play on the page in ways that affirm their contemporary lives. For non-Indian readers, necessarily implicated in the history of colonial selfhood, vivid Native characterizations, precisely because of shared, quotidian imagery in common breakfast cereals and TV programs, let them identify with and therefore recognize alterity. Thus instead of narrating an Indigenous Other to continue as a screen on which American selfhood may project itself and its assumptions about authenticity, Alexie presents an Indigenous self, an alterity, that exposes and evaporates those projections.

Further, instead of romantic assumptions, his formula of Poetry = Anger x Imagination becomes itself a blueprint for authenticity as translation that neatly parallels the translation dynamic in Ortiz's version of authenticity as nationalism. It affirms the "creative power" of Indian lives. Combining Alexie's equation with that of Ortiz, we can map the authentic process: poetry, as artistic expression and especially as expression of the heart of America, emerges from America's oppressed narrating their experience. In that expression, anger is transformed, that is, *translated* by imagination into terms that are meaningful for Indian people. That storytelling engine rewrites America itself.

Thus the authenticity of translation in Ortiz becomes the agency of imagination in Alexie. Alexie's work carries a sense of authenticity by the act of translating contemporary Indian experience into compelling, thus meaningful narrative form. Let's look at examples of such authenticity and agency in *Indian Killer* and *Diary*.

Studies of the grotesque in American literature from Poe to Stephen King have pointed to sources of horror imagery in the repressed memory of American institutional violence. Slavery, Indian wars, the Civil War, and uncountable dead in the war-ravaged twentieth century have provided plenty of blood for the grotesque imagination.[14] In *Indian Killer* Alexie makes explicit that link between repressed history and the repressed psyche of American violence by setting grotesque violence as an outcome of colonial history. As he says in an interview, "It's also a novel about, not just physical murder, but the spiritual, cultural and physical murder of Indians" (Highway, "Spokane Words" 40). Authenticity must face that history.

In this disturbing thriller, he thus translates deracinated urban Indian experience into a set of contemporary questions, continuing mysteries. By linking murder to imagery of Indian blood rituals, the novel plays in nuanced ways against white guilt, trapping the non-Indian reader into assuming the worst about Indian protagonists in a mystery murder plot. Alexie keeps the ending ambiguous, reflecting innuendoes in the novel's title: a killer who's Indian? or a killer of Indians? Alexie has said, "The title, *Indian Killer*, is a palindrome, really, it's 'Indians who kill' and it's also 'people who kill Indians.' It's about how the dominant culture is killing the First Nations people of this country to this day, still" (Highway, "Spokane Words" 40). With that ambiguity he sets up the Anglo reader to scapegoat the Indian and then appropriately, authentically experience white guilt yet again, "still."

Further, it's an energetic meditation on authentic contemporary Indian identity, or, as Richard Nicholls put it in the *New York Times Book Review*, Alexie's "vigorous prose, his haunted, surprising characters and his meditative exploration of the sources of human identity transform into a resonant tragedy what might have been a melodrama in less assured hands."[15] We are discovering through this study that "the sources of human identity" lie in authentic links to community and sovereignty, as this novel sets those links out of reach.

Thus the protagonist, John Smith, an Indian adopted in infancy and entirely alienated from any tribal identity, wanders through the novel, wondering at "the sources of human identity," until those sources become clearer in the negative while he quietly turns psychotic under mainstream pressures. As Smith's identity is unraveling, other plot lines foreground the very question of authentic representation. A pompous professor of anthropology, Dr. Clarence Mather, tries to invent himself as more Indian than Indians. A "faux Indian" white author, Jack Wilson, with his own pitiful aspirations to being Indian, profits from his "Indian novels" with the cross-cultural protagonist as his Indian detective, Aristotle Little Hawk. In parallel, downward trajectories, two young, brilliant college students, cousins from the Spokane reservation, Marie Polatkin and Reggie Polatkin, come up against the violence of white-Indian relations as well. Alexie's allusions to the seventeenth-century colonial Mather family and to the nineteenth-century American name Jack Wilson, of Wovoka, the Paiute prophet of the Ghost Dance, are typically dripping with historical ironies, as is, of course, the name of John Smith. The professor objectifies and reduces Indians to artifacts, while the novelist profits by maintaining Indian stereotypes, and the Indian characters strive with mixed success and failure to affirm their humanity against centuries of such pressures. The plots and characterizations set up authenticity as the reverse reflection of all their various failures.

As he thinks about the two Indian students in the novel, "Dr. Clarence Mather sat at a disorganized desk in the bowels of the Anthropology Building. . . . Though fairly intelligent and physically attractive, [Marie Polatkin] was rude and arrogant, thought Mather, hardly the qualities of a true Spokane. As if it ran in the family like some disease, Reggie Polatkin had also failed to behave like a true Spokane. Mather knew he could teach both of them a thing or two about being Indian if they would listen to him, but it seemed all of the Spokanes were destined to misunderstand his intentions" (*Indian Killer* 135). Mather's clear colonial hubris, assuming that he knows more about being Indian than Indians do—and can train them to become themselves—turns out to be a mask for his own desire as "the white man who wanted to be so completely Indian" (136). We shall look at Vine Deloria Jr.'s "American Fantasy" and the national desire to replace the Indian on the land, here "so completely." This echo becomes the question of authenticity. Who's the real Indian? The real American?

For Alexie the novelist, a resonance of ambiguity is enough for the plot to venture as an answer. Yet it's clear in the plot that Reggie, "a half-Indian who wanted to be completely white, or failing that, to earn the respect of white men" (*Indian Killer* 136), has a claim beyond the wannabe professor. The comparison becomes explicit in the text as soon as Reggie revolts against Mather's appropriation of audiotapes of Spokane elders whose stories belong to their families, not to Mather and his career. Reggie's spontaneous *respect* underlines his connection to Indian values, as we glimpse that traditional, respectful dynamic of community, identity, and authenticity.

Yet the characterization is, as usual, more complex. Reggie wants to destroy the tapes, not return them to his people, because he himself lacks those connections: "The professor had wanted to make them public and publish an article about them, but Reggie had heard the recorded voice of that old Spokane woman and had been suddenly ashamed of himself. He'd heard that ancient voice and wanted to destroy it. He'd wanted to erase the tapes because he had not wanted anybody else, especially a white man like Mather, to have them. He'd wanted to erase them because they'd never be his stories" (*Indian Killer* 137). Reggie covers his own shame of alienation from his people's stories with anger at the white man who claims those stories now. No one is pure. No one is authentic in the static sense. "Stories die because they're supposed to die" (137), Reggie proclaims, in defense of his own cultural insecurity. And because this novel is more tragic than comic, the plot does not adapt and blend that harsh reality with mitigating promise. Authenticity resides here mainly in the authority of an author, behind the text, who translates reality into fiction.

Thus in the final short chapter, ironically entitled "A Creation Story" yet only hinting at ongoing prospects, the omniscient narrator-author gets the final word, delivered obliquely and thus perpetuating the mystery and ambiguity. He does not name the Indian killer, but points to the ongoing fact of Indian deaths: "The killer dances and will not tire. The killer knows this dance is over five hundred years old. . . . With this mask, with this mystery, the killer can dance forever. The killer plans on dancing forever. The killer never falls. The moon never falls. The tree grows heavy with owls" (*Indian Killer* 420). In this remarkable concluding passage, the poetic rhythm of short, parallel sentences pronounces the colonial sentence of death "over five hundred years old." All of the futile or semifutile struggles by the characters, both Indian and non-Indian, to affirm or invent their authentic Indian identity are submerged in this authentic authorial translation of a relentless history in which "the killer never falls."

Authenticity certainly does not reside in the central character, John Smith. He gradually spirals through his adoption as a newborn by a white couple into suicidal psychosis precisely because of his crisis of authenticity and identity: "When John imagines his birth, his mother is sometimes Navajo. Other times she is Lakota. Often, she is from the same tribe as the last Indian woman he has seen on television" (*Indian Killer* 4). In contrast, Marie sums it up in court testimony, defending the late John Smith against suspicion that he was "the Indian killer," in the penultimate chapter of the book: "Listen to me. John Smith was screwed up. He was hurting. He didn't know up from down. He got screwed at birth. He had no chance. I don't care how nice his white parents were. John was dead from the start. And now you're killing him all over again. Can't you just leave him alone? . . . John never hurt anybody. And this isn't over" (417). Marie, as the strongest character in the novel, forecasts the dark authorial perspective of the final passage, quoted above.

However, Marie's presence rescues the novel from unmitigated doom. As Nicholls points out, "Marie . . . has a firm grip on her identity" and "is a complex and memorable presence, the most original female character Mr. Alexie has yet invented." As such, she is in a position of authority, and thus authenticity, to translate mystery into certainty, like the author: "And this isn't over." We are reminded of McNickle's tragic endings, where grim futures are leavened by intergenerational Indian survivance. Further, Marie's strong-Indian-woman role, an understated affirmation of maternal power, gives the dark finale precisely that cathartic potential which is the Aristotelian purpose of tragedy and which links the death in tragedy—through the audience's catharsis—to the life-giving purposes of comedy. Here again we arrive at the dynamics of authenticity, translating "over five hundred years" of killing into a dim hint of hope.

The ending of *The Absolutely True Diary of a Part-Time Indian* offers a suitable retrospective on this discussion of authenticity as translation in Alexie's work. In the last scene of this semi-autobiographical work, when the first-person protagonist, Junior, or Arnold Spirit Jr., is reconciling with his lifelong friend, Rowdy, on a rez basketball court, the friend performs a remarkable act of translation that concisely affirms Junior's—and Alexie's—authenticity. Amid forceful echoes from Alexie's earlier fiction of relations between Thomas Builds-the-Fire and his violent friend, Victor, and echoes of Alexie's own experiences, Rowdy's dialogue resolves, or at least explains the key question of authenticity, identity, and community from *Reservation Blues*: Can you leave the rez and remain Indian? In *Diary*, Junior, like Alexie himself, has left the rez to attend a better high school in the actual town where Alexie had gone: "So what was I doing in racist Reardan, where more than half of every graduating class went to college? Nobody in my family had ever gone near a college. Reardan was the opposite of the rez. It was the opposite of my family. It was the opposite of me. I didn't deserve to be there. I knew it; all of those kids [in the Reardan high school classroom] knew it. Indians don't deserve shit" (56).

At that early point in the novel, Rowdy's violent temper had overwhelmed his feelings for his friend, and Junior sported "a purple, blue, yellow, and black eye. It looked like modern art." In the white high school, he was "the Indian boy with the black eye and swollen nose, my going-away gifts from Rowdy" (*Diary* 56). After the full progress of the novel through Junior's struggling but successful first year at Reardon, Rowdy reconnects with his friend amid appropriately obscene joking and teasing. By way of refusing Junior's renewed invitation to join him next year in Reardon, Rowdy comes out of his tough shell to explain the authentic key to the novel—and to much of Alexie's work. Here is Rowdy's explication, minus the increasingly emotional repartee of Junior in the text:

> "I was reading this book about old-time Indians, about how we used to be nomadic. . . . So I looked up nomadic in the dictionary, and it means people who move around, who keep moving, in search of food and water and grazing land. . . . Hardly anybody on this rez is nomadic. Except for you. You're the nomadic one. . . . I always knew you were going to leave. I always knew you were going to leave us behind and travel the world. I had this dream about you a few months ago. You were standing on the Great Wall of China. You looked happy. And I was happy for you. . . . You're an old-time nomad," Rowdy said. "You're going to keep moving all over the world in search of food and water and grazing land. That's pretty cool. (*Diary* 229–30)

By translating Junior's, and Alexie's, search for educational fulfillment into the adaptive strength, resilience, and survivance of the "old-time nomad" in their ancient tradition, Rowdy and the novel adopt the comic mode to affirm an authenticity in modern Indian choices.

As a summary glance at this key term in Alexie, let's briefly translate his representations of authenticity into the language of citizenship. As you will recall, the question of American citizenship, bearing on each of these issues of identity, community, sovereignty, and humor or humanity, is essentially a question of authenticity as well. A citizen of a nation is an authentic member; a noncitizen is inauthentic. It is a specifically legal and generally political category that Alexie invoked in his emphasis on political rather than cultural identity for American Indians. Apess, Winnemucca, McNickle, and Silko critique the peculiar American disjunction between citizen and Indian in various nuanced ways, within a common pattern. We have seen that they translate "Indian" and "citizen" into broader questions of the individual and community. By representing Indian communities as the matrix of a communal Indian individualism, these writers establish an *Indian* context for citizenship. Similarly Alexie's question of artistic agency translates, in a political context, into this question of citizenship, where political agency becomes dual citizenship. When he states that Indian identity "is much less cultural now and much more political" ("A Dialogue on Race"), he is invoking the practical agency of simultaneous American and Indigenous citizenship for American Indians.

"Sunrise / Accept this Offering"

If functioning Indigenous authenticity is not merely rooted in "old days" but derives from a chosen Native American authority to translate the present into "their own—Indian—terms," as Ortiz suggested, we have seen how these writers and their characters exercise such choices on American ground. Apess translated colonial Christian discourse into an argument for Indian rights. He translated Metacomet, King Philip of the Wampanoags, into an authentic American patriot. He translated the story of his own wife, an obscure, mixed-blood New Englander, into one of the saintly "five Christian Indians," even as he translated his passion for her into an affirmation of racial equality: "*I am not looking for a wife, having one of the finest cast*" (*On Our Own Ground* 160). Above all, as a "son of the forest," he translated himself into both a proud Pequot and an authentic American.

Winnemucca's life and writing showed us the delicate and often distressing balancing act required in the role of the authentic translator. As she compared her Paiute "life and customs" with Victorian domestic virtues, as she literally translated documents and messages between U.S. forces and her communities, and as she translated silence into resistance by transforming covert oppression into overt corruption in the Indian Ring, she gained celebrity status from a national audience of sympathizers even as she lost the confidence of many in her own Indigenous nation.

McNickle, in choosing the tragic narrative mode, translated manifest destiny into manifest inequity. Yet he not only showed his white readership the errors of the American ethos of conquest and white supremacy; he also showed his Native readers the strength of survivance through authentic sacrifice. In Bull and Catherine, as well as in Antoine and Archilde, he depicted the story of translation and transformation, whereby elders exercise authority and youth discover it in the authentic, nationalist process of translating their pain into promise, their sacrifice into survivance for their people. By the time Bull sacrifices others' and his own life—when Antoine could again be "proud for him"—the ambiguous shackles that had bound Archilde at the end of the earlier novel are translated into Antoine's clear consciousness and commitment to his people.

In a similar direction, Silko further translates history into prophecy, shifting the power of narration from the destroyers back to the people on the land. In her "mythification of lived experience," she weaves and translates reality into myth and myth into reality to charge both with authenticity and gravitas. This process of authentic translation, of translation as authenticity, affirms the potency of storytelling. The act of authorship, both oral and literary, becomes the crucible of an ongoing, ever-emerging authenticity in Betonie and Tayo, in Lecha and Zeta, in Hattie and Indigo. By the time she begins to cultivate *Gardens in the Dunes*, Silko is translating America itself into an authentic reconnection with the ancient stones, even as she reconnects Native people with the life of their homelands.

Alexie, as always, mixes it up. In a semi-autobiographical, young adult novel, he translates himself, his own search for education and self-expression into the old-time values of nomadic Indian life. Nomadism and "moving, in search of food and water and grazing land," as Rowdy describes it, works as a metaphor for translation and authenticity in Alexie and the other authors in this study. Authenticity is able to find its sustenance in change, to adapt and translate its changing environment into meaningful nourishment, into expression of self. Alexie's harsher, grimmer novel of John Smith does the same work, through the interrogative, like McNickle's tragic mode. The question of authentic Indian identity grows so loud that Smith's humanity, his self-expression simply translates into fact by the fact of his pained existence and by the presence of observers like Marie Polatkin affirming his existence to the court of public opinion: "Can't you just leave him alone? . . . John never hurt anybody. And this isn't over." Her mixed message stands as another metaphor for Indian authenticity across the centuries.

5

THE LAST LAUGH

Humor and Humanity in Native American Pluralism

Let's start with universals and move quickly to the particulars of Native American humor.

1. Generally, and mysteriously, humor "happens" through a structural reversal, a surprise. The unexpected quip or act or juxtaposition sets up irony, the incommensurability of language and reality, a mismatch of what is said and what is meant. A pun links incongruous categories. A vertical man slips on a banana peel and becomes horizontal. Then laughter "happens."

2. Humor humanizes by bringing us down to earth, where we discover the ground of our humility. A ground theory must account for this factor. Etymological linkages are useful here: *humor, human, humus, humility*. Thus grounded humor is humane, yet Indigenous humor extends to and grows from the ground of a more-than-human world.

3. As in most ethnicities, Native American humor divides into the in-group and the out-group tease, but the particulars are crucial:
   a. In-group tease = Can you shed your ego to identify with the community? = *unshika* (pitiful/humble in Lakota terminology).
   b. Out-group tease = America, can you shed your story to identify with reality? = historical humility.

4. Thus, linking 1, 2, and 3, the biggest joke on America is the survivance of Indians because that's a reversal of America's originary, founda-

tional, constitutive story of the vanishing Indian. The vanishing Indian stereotype and narrative function as the rationale to cover up the reality not only of ongoing Native nations but equally of stolen land as the foundation of America; thus the fact that Indians never vanished means that America is and was always already a failure in its own values of freedom and justice for all. How ironic! Ha! Ha!

It is not unique to Native American humor that there is a dark side to the comedy, but the historical circumstances of Indian survivance, and the power of humor in that many-generational act, are unique. As Low Man Smith, the protagonist of Sherman Alexie's short story "Indian Country," bitterly and ironically contemplates the bigoted, homophobic, self-righteous Native American Christian sneering at him across a dinner table (an absent father alienated from his lesbian daughter), "Low knew for a fact that everything was funny. Homophobia? Funny! Genocide? Hilarious! Political assassination? Side-splitting! Love? Ha, Ha, Ha!" (*The Toughest Indian in the World* 144). Being able to laugh in the face of history is both humbling and empowering.

Political Postindians: The Biggest Joke on America

Carol Juneau, a member of the Hidatsa and Mandan tribes, has been a Democratic Party member of the Montana House of Representatives and later the Montana Senate. Her roots lie in both the Ft. Berthold Reservation of North Dakota and the Blackfeet Reservation in her longtime state of residence. For more than a decade she has been a leader in the Montana capital among a fresh handful of Indigenous senators and representatives in promoting and passing, with the necessary support of the broad majority of non-Indian legislators, the 1999 legislation Indian Education for All, MCA 20-1-501. This measure implements and funds the unique provision, included in Montana's revised 1972 Constitution, to honor and foster the state's Indigenous cultures. Article 10, Section 1(2) of the Montana Constitution declares, "The state recognizes the distinct and unique cultural heritage of American Indians and is committed in its educational goals to the preservation of their cultural integrity." The constitution and the legislation recognize that Indian cultures are relevant not only to reservations but statewide to all Montana residents. Now, after decades of neglect, that recognition is emerging through this legislation in the schools. Five hundred years after Columbus, these political actions indeed carry millennial resonance. Carol Juneau's niece, Denise Juneau, a lawyer, is currently the elected superintendent of schools for the state of Montana.

If such news seems like a joke on America's story of manifest destiny, Indians and their allies are more than laughing. They are still fighting the Indian wars, now in the courts, the legislative halls, and the classrooms. As Silko writes, "Deep down the issue is simple: the so-called Indian Wars from the days of Sitting Bull and Red Cloud have never really ended in the Americas" (*Yellow Woman* 123). The ironic dynamics of retelling the story of America as *not conquest* come to light via two words in contemporary Indigenous discourse that open us to ancient and twenty-first-century perspectives on humor in Native American literatures. One is an original, the other a familiar term in a fresh form, and both are generated by "trickster" personas in American Indian literary circles. As ever in this field of study, both terms are simultaneously new and timeless; they both apply to the current moment and to centuries of Native literary and oral expression. The first, a neologism articulated by Gerald Vizenor, is *postindian*. The other, as rearticulated by Sherman Alexie, is *political*. As we look at their take on these concepts, we shall see further how these terms express a concluding and originary dynamic of this study: the crucial connection between humor and humanity in American Indian arts.

Vizenor coined the term *postindian* precisely to elude "the white man's Indian," that morass of colonial and Western identity questions and projections, mapped by Robert Berkhofer, Roy Harvey Pearce, and others whom I discussed in the introduction. "The white man's Indian" obscures Native nations and individuals behind Euro-American desire and fear. By bending language, Vizenor strives to step outside that colonial "Indian" mask: "The Indian was an occidental invention that became a bankable simulation; the word has no referent in tribal languages or cultures. The postindian is the absence of the invention, and the end of representation in literature; the closure of that evasive melancholy of dominance" (*Manifest Manners* 11). If *Indian* has "no referent in tribal languages or cultures," then a Native *presence* in literature, which would be "the end of representation in literature," an insistence instead on tribal "presence" in language, would have to be "postindian." Since Euro-Americans invented their own "Indian" both to conquer and to desire in dispossessing them of their lands, then the presence of Native expression would be "the absence of the invention." The lowercase *indian* resists Columbus's originary misrepresentation in *los Indios*. No longer would Native voices necessarily reflect the colonizer.

Thus Vizenor's "postindian" concept encapsulates the redefinitions of our key terms that we have been mapping in this study. The struggles of Indigenous authors to elude colonial representation, to reclaim authenticity, identity, and community in the name of Native sovereignty, have been precisely an effort to move beyond "Indian" inventions and projections of Euro-America.

Parallel to other Indigenous artists and social thinkers, particularly like William Apess in the nineteenth century and Vine Deloria Jr. in the twentieth, Vizenor, now spanning the "treeline" of the twenty-first century, builds on a resonant insight through his notion of intuitive thought in haiku. In the minimalist Japanese form, Vizenor recognized that just as nature remains paradoxically inside and outside the poem, the presence of Native America remains ironically both inside and outside American representations of Indians.[1] Like Apess and Deloria, Vizenor has initiated new discursive forms on the foundation of a key idea. All three share a polemic that is sharply critical and a tone that is both visionary and ironic. Apess focused his intellectual lights on the ironies of American Christian hypocrisy against Native humanity. Deloria focused on the ironies of American legal history against Native sovereignty. Vizenor focuses on language games in the ironies of American ideology against Native reality. Writing, "The postindian is an ironist" (*Manifest Manners* 68), he mounts another unique and original, fundamental critique of American discourse. These three public intellectuals focus on language and its misuses in Native and American history so that the ramifications of their works intricately overlap among religion, law, history, and politics in dominant and alternative discourses.

Vizenor's insights are central to a discussion of Native American humor. He elaborates on the ironies of "manifest manners" and the ways that "trickster discourse" can speak to the shadows of the real, the "shadow survivance" beneath, beyond, and before domination. Trickster discourse speaks to and from shadow survivance by eluding the binaries of dominant and dominating modern history. For instance, in Vizenor's novel *The Heirs of Columbus*, he imagines political deconstruction at even the level of biogenetic codes of DNA. Here the oppositions become complements: "Those who can imagine their antinomies and mutations are able to heal with humor" (134). Referring to the four amino acids that make up deoxyribonucleic acid, the text explains, with an understated mix of discursive irony and ecstasy, "These four letters are held together in a signature by their opposites, the biochemical codes are held by their own opposites, and here is where the shaman and the trickster touch that primal source of humor, imagination, and the stories that heal right in the antinomies of the genetic code" (134). Where history would reify antagonisms as racial and racist antinomies, Vizenor's tricksters find healing by crossing to the heart of the oppositions. His text invokes the "agonistic humor of tricksters" (135), who explain how that healing humor works against the loneliness and separation brought by Columbus (184) to the psyche of the Western Hemisphere: "We heal with opposition [via humor], not separation" (176).

Although Vizenor is impatient with what he sees as "Indian" nostalgia in some Native American critics and writers who claim a "nationalist" or, especially, "separatist" approach, and although those same critics dispute Vizenor's approach as "cosmopolitan" (or international), the concept of postindian is indeed one that both camps value and perform. Insofar as *postindian* signals an attempt to express and examine Native lives in ways that elude the pervasive historical power of the colonial gaze, both the innovative nationalists and the master of trickster discourse are on the same page. On the one hand, nationalists elude colonial co-optation by finding a field larger than and sometimes separate from dominant history: their unique, ancient, and sovereign relations to and in the land. Instead of domination, they find self-determination. On the other hand, a cosmopolitan trickster eludes colonial co-optation by finding a deconstructive line into the antinomies, the belly of the beast: the universal, ancient, and sacred life pulse itself. Instead of death he finds life in modern Indian experience. Thus Vizenor's compassionate trickster reverses and neutralizes the historical power of the dialectic, while Robert Warrior's, Jace Weaver's, and Craig Womack's communal conversations and celebrations decenter that same historical power. From different angles, both approaches, nationalist and cosmopolitan, evidently reaffirm the primary dynamic of tribal sovereignty. That is what could be called an inside joke.

Similarly Alexie's way of wielding the political dimensions of Native

American reality returns us to sovereignty, the beginning and ending of this discussion. Echoing the claims and musings of some of his fictional characters, Alexie affirmed a "new" political principle in a conversation with President Clinton during the 1998 "Dialogue on Race," televised on the Public Broadcasting Service: "I think the primary thing that people need to know about Indians is that our identity is much less cultural now and much more political. That we really do exist as political entities and sovereign political nations. That's the most important thing for people to understand, that we are separate politically and economically. And should be." Beyond "the personal is political" ethos of contemporary social movements,[2] Alexie's statement suggests how his own intense characterizations of Native and non-Native individuals pack a peculiar political purpose. Personal Indians are political Indians by the dynamics of sovereignty. His emphasis on the political and legal status of tribal sovereignty rather than the cultural dynamics of tribal life reflects his own mixed engagement with both mainstream and Native cultures. He has said that he avoids the "drums and feathers" or "sacred" aspects of Indian life in his work partly because that realm simply is not the business of outsiders. In an interview with *60 Minutes*, he uses his pop persona to deflect stereotypes of Indian spirituality and to get more mileage out of some of the same lines:

> It's that whole "corn pollen, four directions, Mother Earth, Father Sky" Indian thing where everybody starts speaking slowly, and their vocabulary shrinks down until they sound like Dick and Jane. And it's all about spirituality, and it's all about politics. . . . So I just try to write about everyday Indians, the kind of Indian I am who is just as influenced by the *Brady Bunch* as I am by my tribal traditions, who spends as much time going to the movies as I do going to ceremonies. . . . That's so tiring. Who wants to be wise, you know? You get carpal tunnel syndrome from carrying the burden of your race. . . . I'd like to have villains. I'd like to have goofballs. (Mabrey, "The Toughest Indian in the World")

Steering clear of stereotypical imagery certainly is a postindian strategy. Alexie's own "business of fancydancing" necessarily echoes through all the dimensions of Indian life because, as we have seen, the political and the spiritual are not separable. Constructing characterizations of "villains" and "goofballs" becomes in this context another linkage to common humanity in Native stories. Representing pop culture, "going to the movies," becomes a strategic reappropriation.

Yet Alexie goes further than simply reversing the power to claim common, everyday experience as a Native right to rewrite American definitions. Like other Native writers, he is not only critical of popular representations of Indians. James H. Cox points out, in a discussion of "the popular culture invasion in Alexie's fiction," that Alexie is direct about fatal effects, that he dramatizes ways "non-Native storytellers who participate in storytelling traditions that either romanticize or villainize Indians are directly responsible for violence committed against Native people" (*Muting White Noise* 147). Not only is Alexie influenced by the *Brady Bunch* culture, but he critiques its imperial values in "films, television programs, pop songs, New Age books, radio talk shows, and mystery novels—and the many forms of violence perpetrated against contemporary Native people" (146). In an incisive comment that forecasts my discussion of the mirror image of tragedy in Native comedy, Cox states that Alexie's political aesthetic insists "stories that obscure the difficulties of contemporary reservation life can be as destructive, and as much an assertion of dominance, as stories that obscure the strengths of Native communities" (146-47). Alexie wants the full spectrum of Native community for literary and political purposes. As a realist, he tries in his writing to push down on the activist lever by pressuring the solid fulcrum of social despair. In that way, "the difficulties of contemporary reservation life" at the low end of that lever might be raised and eased.

What is unique about any political agenda in Alexie's approach is the extent to which he foregrounds humor and, through that comic mask, the common humanity of Native America. As a sort of punk trickster, Alexie performs the role of an Indigenous bard profoundly, swaggeringly, at ease in the halls of media power and the cultural mainstream. In addition to conversing directly with the president of the United States, he appears a decade later as a repeat guest on television's popular comic news program *The Colbert Report*, among others, while on his international lecture circuit he fetches speaking fees in the tens of thousands of dollars. Whether such sums are a measure of mastery or of co-optation is a controversy that continues to follow his texts as well. As Joseph L. Coulombe writes, "To many critics his playfulness may demonstrate skill as a writer, but it betrays Indian people by presenting them as clichés who deserve to be laughed at" ("The Approximate Size of His Favorite Humor" 94). Coulombe, however, finds the political edge in Alexie's dramatizations of "a national disgrace," the external and internalized oppression in Indian Country. According to Coulombe, Alexie's unsentimental portrayals actually focus on the political as "the inevitable result of centuries of abuse and neglect. . . . [He] shrewdly presents this socio-political reality with humor to soften its initial impact" (108). This view reflects the frequent claim that humor helps survivance. Coulombe explains, "Alexie's humor is central to a constructive social and moral purpose evident throughout his fiction. . . . He uses humor—or his characters use humor—to reveal injustice, protect self-esteem, heal wounds, and create bonds" (94). Alexie's humor, like that of other Native writers, does more than soften the impact of social critique; it does the work of authenticating and humanizing, nudging the Indigenous "other" toward selfhood in popular representation, healing both sides of the racial divide.

Like Vizenor wielding the term *postindian*, Alexie's focus on political identity shrugs off the weight of colonial history that would de-politicize Indian affairs in favor of Euro-American "inventions" of the plight of the vanishing Indian. By returning to political terms—"That we really do exist as political entities and sovereign political nations"—Alexie sounds a clear message that the tired, oppositional conversations about authenticity, identity, and community need to fall away in favor of what is sometimes called tribal sovereignty. The extent to which he ironizes those issues in his work opens a new chapter in Native American literature and calls for some focus here on Alexie in this summary chapter on the humane dimensions of Indian literary humor. Vizenor's postindian peels away the stereotypes, and Alexie's political Indian fills that void with the humor of humanity.

"Old Jokes"

In M. L. Smoker's prose poem "The Feed," she writes, "Our aunties are in the kitchen, preparing the boiled meat and chokecherry soup and laughing about old jokes they still hang onto because these things are a matter of survival" (*Another Attempt at Rescue* 47). Such a line from this contemporary Assiniboine poet spans the spectrum of our first four key terms in Native American literature, yet she gets at something else. We have discussed significant epistemologies and politics of authenticity, identity, community, and sovereignty, but now we return to the conversation on the ground, in that kitchen, through that belly laughter that speaks to the vitality at the core of Native narratives.

Indeed energies of the daily miracles of subsistence breathe through Indigenous pages. Continuing questions of honor and shame, of gender balance, of ethical value, of existential and philosophical inquiry, of poverty and economic development, of internecine political rivalry, of neocolonial bureaucracy, of racism, addiction, suicide, violence, abuse, and the individual and social energies of healing—such issues and more are the politics of postindians. One particular aspect, laughter, especially remains alive, although it often remains hidden by race relations. In the poem "Backwaters," the Chippewa and Assiniboine writer Joe McGeshick describes those complex relations through the compression of poetry: "They laugh showing bleeding smiles" (*The Indian in the Liquor Cabinet* 45). The line alludes to one by another Montana writer, the Blackfeet and Gros Ventre author James Welch, in his poem, "Plea to Those Who Matter": "And I—I come to you, head down, bleeding from my smile, / happy for the snow clean hands of you, my friends" (*Riding the Earthboy* 34). Complex and violent emotions negotiate the domination of Indian lives by whites, "who matter." Yet in Welch's and McGeshick's ironic bitterness, there is still room for genuine laughter beyond the spilling blood in such imagery.

Because of the pain of history, laughter in Native literature and communities often is described as a survival mechanism, but as humor it is more. If authenticity is translation, Native humor is translation of tragedy into the comic mode. Any clown knows this. If the authentic act, as we have seen in Simon Ortiz, is one of remaining open, of taking experience and translating it into one's own terms, and thereby affirming one's own existence through language, then humor is a special version of authenticity. A good joke feels real because it rewrites reality. Always surprising, it claims the sudden authority of a different perspective, a revision, a rereading. One of my favorite Native cartoons was published in the *Char-Koosta* newspaper on the Flathead Reservation in the 1980s. The first comic box shows an unhappy vendor at a powwow, with a sign over his stand that reads, "BEST FRYBREAD IN THE USA." No one is standing in line at his booth. The next box shows a pair of vendors under a sign that reads, "WORLD'S GREATEST FRYBREAD," and no customers stand there either. The third box shows a similar lack of customers under a sign that says, "THE VERY FINEST FRY-

BREAD IN THE UNIVERSE." The fourth and final box shows another vendor serving a long line of eager customers, with a sign over the booth that reads, "PRETTY-GOOD FRYBREAD." Whenever I tell this joke in Indian Country, folks laugh out loud. Here the cartoonist has translated the capitalist culture of vending sales into an Indigenous group ethos of honest humility, the opposite of self-promotion, expressed in the value of understatement. Humor and humility here begin to link to human, and even humus, the land itself. Things are not "the best," the "greatest," nor "the very finest," but they are "pretty-good." Through humor we get a radical rereading, a different perspective on the hyperbole of modern advertising—and in the process we get an affirmation of Indigenous experience and discourse.

Native humor takes the experiences of colonialism and traditional cultures, the genocidal losses, the now silent but resonant trauma of massive waves of death to disease, the dislocation from and isolation on sacred lands, the daily violence and poverty, the survivance and vitality of new generations, the modern tensions of identity, the continuing group values and struggles to maintain community, and it translates all of that and more into laughter. As a narrator says darkly in Alexie's short story "The Sin Eaters," "Indians will love anything if given the chance" (*Toughest* 78). Good humor is open-hearted, and thereby strong.

One delightful and incisive collection of essays on Native humor, entitled *Me Funny*, edited by the Canadian Ojibwa playwright, writer, and humorist Drew Hayden Taylor, goes further than I ever can in offering readers both explanations and experiences of Indian humor. The six-line subtitle, full of sepia-archaic, nineteenth-century echoes of emphasis in italics and bold fonts, hints at the ironies in both the form and content of the book: "A far-reaching exploration of the humour, wittiness and repartee dominant among the First Nations people of North America, as witnessed, experienced and created directly by themselves, and with the inclusion of outside but reputable sources necessarily familiar with the Indigenous sense of humour as seen from an objective perspective." The jokes on the publishing world, on white scholars, and on Indians proliferate. Making no claims to "an objective perspective," I will link some of the issues in this study to "the humour, wittiness and repartee" that Taylor displays "directly." That trail of laughter will lead us back to Native ground.

Philosophical Irony and Community Humor

In this discussion of humor, the dynamics of irony frequently arises, so it will be useful to briefly distinguish these two terms. Irony and humor are not synonymous. Irony is the larger category, and humor one form of irony, a broad one, an almost unclassifiable phenomenon, that inexplicably brings laughter. Another discussion might explore how there are two kinds of irony, comic and tragic.

Although irony and humor do not mean the same thing, humor, as a subset of irony, relies on ironic reversals, and it is that fundamental rhetorical strategy of historical or postcolonial reversal that animates much of Indian writing, whether funny or not. While ironic reversals may also be tragic, it is crucial for reading Native literatures to recognize that by such reversals the comic—the laughter of a trickster god—resides in tragedy as well. Thus the comic embraces the tragic, and thus Native voices survive genocide.

For our purposes, irony generally is a rhetorical position or perspective that employs a turn or reversal of direction between representation and reality, or, alternatively, between expression and meaning. A simplified definition of irony is "to say one thing and mean another." For example, on a gray, cloudy day, it might be an unhumorous ironic statement to say, glumly, "Another beautiful day!" Irony rhetorically points to the intentional reversal of the speaker, with no room for straightforward earnestness. Similarly in the old joke, when the Lone Ranger urgently demands Tonto's advice to avoid an Indian attack from all sides, "What'll we do?" is an ironic reversal of expectations, as we shall discuss further below, for Tonto to say, in the stereotyped lingo, "What you mean 'we,' white man!?"[3]

The structure of humor as reversal indeed illuminates the irony built into the other four terms of Native literary expression. For instance, authenticity as dynamic translation may be seen as an ironic reversal of expectations of static authenticity. Similarly identity as change marks a reversal of expectations of identity as fixed. Community as animate self to self becomes a reversal of the dominating colonial paradigm of self to other. Sovereignty as sacrifice reverses sovereignty as domination. Whether Native authors choose narrative structures identifiable as tragic or comic, they tend toward the ironic in these fundamental structural reversals of national narrative.

How any such irony transforms into humor, and thence into laughter, is still a mystery to both humanists and scientists. Perhaps evolutionary biologists and neuropsychologists will learn to factor the social and chemical formulae that constitute laughter. They are hard at the task. It may remain moot whether the functions of a smile, as it flows with internal endorphins and externally pleasurable strategies for survival and bonding, are cause or effect of its own symptoms.

Whatever the case, humor clearly fulfills purposes that make us human in ways that are not separate from the rest of creation. To be human and humane in this sense is to be good-humored. As William James puts it, "Common sense and a sense of humor are the same thing, moving at different speeds. A sense of humor is just common sense, dancing." The good sense that recognizes what makes us common can take deliberate, logical form, or it can speed up for a dancing sense of humorous, seemingly illogical surprise, exposing our common humanity underneath our vaunted individuality and hierarchy.

Thus if a dancing leap of imagination is somehow the mechanism of comedy, irony is one level of comedy available even to the suffering, as Alexie comments—ironically through the voice of a dogmatic white anthropologist in the short story "Dear John Wayne": "Irony, a hallmark of the contemporary Indigenous American" (*Toughest* 190).

Patently, Indigenous irony is a voice for historical ground. Ironic narrative structures echo the long history of treaty negotiations across North America, where Euro-American envoys invariably sought, and sometimes unilaterally appointed, a "chief" with whom to negotiate treaties for land acquisitions, a "leader" whose authority often did not speak for his own, less hierarchical Native nation. The further irony of those treaties is how nonbinding their language proved to be in political and economic reality. No treaty in the modern history of North America was honored by the Euro-Americans. A broken treaty is an ironic treaty. As Alexie suggests in his poem "The American Artificial Limb Company," Indians learned irony from the white man: "You have to understand that white people invented / irony," says the first-person narrative voice (*One Stick Song* 33). He is referring to treaty writing and treaty breaking as ironic by definition, where irony is saying one thing and meaning another.

Slippery signifiers in treaty language shape the context for the humorist Gerald Vizenor as well and his postmodern take on "the ruins of representation." Reflecting precisely the practice of treaty breaking, Euro-America's "terminal creeds" would kill off their own "white man's Indian." They thus have ruined the language of dominant history, indeed the law of the land, by making it only ironic. Thus the need for a postindian to rewrite the stories.

"A Constant"

In never-ending variations, Native humor plays around two primary jokes, one aimed at the out-group and the other at the in-group. One is historical, the other existential, both playing on fundamental ironies of American and Native American experience. Out-group humor strikes the ultimate joke on America: You never recognized that "the vanishing Indian" never vanished and never will? This is the joke on American history. In-group humor strikes the ultimate tease on any selfishness in identity, more in the form of a question, as a tease always embodies an interrogative, a dare: Can you let go of your separateness, your hubris, and recognize your pitiful yet sustaining connections to community? Can you translate your self-referentiality into group terms? The in-group joke is rough play of the communal self against selfishness. Ultimately, can you sacrifice for the group?

It is possible to identify a third generalized joke that may be considered a combination of the out-group and in-group modes of humor. This is the joke on American hypocrisy: Indians are more American (and "civilized" and Christian) than you brutal white savages. Intriguingly this third ironic strategy fundamentally folds the out-group and the in-group into one contested definition of *American*.

White and Indian, everybody's pretensions to greatness are brought down by each of these ironies: the tease is all about how low you can go; the "return of the vanishing Indian" is all about how high you cannot go, how the white man's lofty manifest destiny is neither destined nor manifest. Further overlaps between these two questions of in-group and out-group reversals provide endless fodder for play, such as when colonizing hubris pushes against its own human contradictions and when colonized hubris forgets its own connections with humanity.

One of the most explicit articulations of this necessary humility, and its constitutive, animistic interconnections, is a "philosophy of insignificance" of the Meskwaki author Ray A. Young Bear: "The philosophy that espouses cosmic insignificance, a belief that humans are but a minute part of world order, has shaped my words" (*Black Eagle Child* 256). Honest recognition of one's place in the world, as both "minute" and "part" of a "world order" of the cosmos, leads to a lifetime of decisions, large and small, to remain in touch with a sentient universe. Young Bear sees his grounded philosophy that does not make grand claims as the substratum of his Meskwaki ways, and it underlies his explicit sense of animism. It fosters an existential sense of irony, being simultaneously both insignificant and part of a world order. Thus Young Bear's philosophy of insignificance becomes a structural dynamic of both in-group and out-group jokes. Humility drives Native humor, where in-group teasing demands members' humility and out-group humor derides non-Indian hubris, its reflex of superiority.

Toward that out-group humor, Kimberly Blaeser lists various methods by which Native writers have responded to "the representations and mis-representations of history." Her catalogue is useful for approaches we have been reading in these five writers: "The tacks Native authors have taken also run the gamut of possibility and have included revisionist accounts, pre-emptive interpretations of contemporary historical events, 'eye-for-an-eye' propagandistic distortions, attempts at completely autonomous repre-sentations, and multiple combinations of all the above" ("The New 'Fron-tier'" 38–39). Each of these "tacks" attempts not only to navigate but to change the prevailing winds of history. As a primary impetus for Native expression, the work of revisionary history has been steady and long. Blae-ser describes Native efforts at literary laughter within that larger project as "those which, by their humor, work to disarm history, to expose the hidden agendas of historiography and, thereby, remove it from the grasp of the political panderers and return it to the realm of story" (39). Her invocation of "the realm of story" that would "disarm history" seems to envision an authentic narrative, a reality, apart from propagandistic distortions of cul-turally biased historiography.

Blaeser echoes Elizabeth Cook-Lynn's "reality-based historical contexts" and registers Native humor as a door to that clarity. Like Simon Ortiz call-ing for authentic history to heal America, Blaeser describes that realm of reality as a place of healing, as she observes "this re-forming of history into healing story" ("The New 'Frontier'" 49) among Native literary humorists. Indeed, echoing Vizenor, she applies the word *liberation* to this process: "Key to the ability of these writers to undertake such a liberation is their keen awareness of the contested visions of history and their imaginative rendering of the places (both physical and intellectual) of cultural historical contact" (39). These "contested visions of history" remain the first function of "their imaginative rendering." According to Blaeser, Native literature, whether humorous or deadly serious, critiques history.

Vizenor similarly describes "critical responses" that laugh. He affirms a peculiar form of humor as the third of "four postmodern conditions in the critical responses to Native American literatures": "The third is trickster liberation, the uncertain humor of survivance that denies the obscure maneuvers of manifest manners, tragic transvaluations, and the incoherence of cultural representations" ("Ruins of Representation"). In other words, the liberating energy of trickster humor frees Native narratives to showcase survivance against American mainstream narratives of manifest destiny, projected tragedy, and stereotypical fatalism, "the end of the trail." The vanishing Indian has not vanished, ha ha! (In addition to "trickster liberation," Vizenor's other three postmodern strategies are "aural performances," "translations," and "narrative chance.") Vizenor explains, in his original and uniquely compressured language, that these four conditions "are an invitation to tribal survivance. The traces of natural reason and the shadows of coherence have endured over science in the humor of cotribal stories" ("Ruins"). The science of which Vizenor speaks is primarily the peculiar objectifying social science, especially anthropology, emerging out of the nineteenth century into the twentieth, that would measure Indigenous skulls while erasing Indigenous humanity.

The arrogation of universal authority by which early anthropology assumed itself capable of defining and "salvaging the savage" in Native cultures has been shown to be an ideological vanguard of the colonizing project.[4] As numerous studies and his own self-reflections have suggested, trickster humor in Vizenor does the work of undermining the false assumptions of scientism and its pretensions to objectivity.[5] Instead trickster offers diverse ways of knowing that open up, through laughter and surprise, the compassionate heart of the reader. Scholars have often explored the trickster dynamics in the prose and poetry of James Welch, Louise Erdrich, Thomas King, and other contemporary Native writers. As Wayne Stein (Chippewa), professor and former director of Native American Studies at Montana State University, said at a memorial for Welch, "Indian humor is about celebrat-

ing life, even at its quirkiest."[6] The comment speaks to the links—the trickster boundary crossings—that connect literature and life in Native communities and individuals.

Vizenor's statement on "trickster liberation" also targets the larger historical narrative forces that would reify manifest destiny in the politely sinister discourse that he dismisses as "manifest manners." Of course that
historical discourse is predicated on Turner's frontier thesis, a decidedly
unhumorous presumption from a Native point of view, because it attributes
civilization to one side and savage "free land" to the other. From the "other
side of the frontier," this tragic paradigm of American national identity, a
frontier mentality, derives from the primitive yet dominant idea that civilization and wilderness are discrete realities rather than complex systems of
interaction. As Native humor translates that tragic paradigm of separation
into a complex comedy of interconnection, it rejects the reductive dualisms
of the frontier.

It may have taken centuries of colonialism to reflect clearly on this simple phenomenon of historiography, but the contemporary British philosopher Mary Midgley points out that the most common logical error is the
reductive fallacy, oversimplifying explanations of complex reality to a facile formula, such as the triple abstractions of a frontier between civilization
and wilderness. In *Myths We Live By*, Midgley critiques the "megalomania"
of a reductive social science to describe the psychology of this political tendency and the politics of this psychological tendency (45). Such reductionism certainly resonates with Vizenor's "terminal creeds" and with Daniel
Heath Justice's equation, "Simplification is just another word for genocide"
(*Our Fire Survives the Storm* 157).

Jon Turney offers the term *pragmatic pluralism* as a useful, alternative
ethical philosophy.[7] Evidently the reductive megalomania so alluring to
historians, and so pervasive in their textbooks, has missed the realities of
America's pragmatic pluralism. Similarly Ken Egan Jr. offers a valuable and
parallel term, *pragmatic comedy*, in a context of Western literature in general and Montana literature in particular, as he critiques the allure of "apocalypse" in telling America's western story. Egan describes this as a siren
call, an "immature" "attraction to a Manichean sensibility that teaches the
conflict between the light and the dark, the virtuous and the sinful, the saved
and the damned . . . the apocalyptic story of paradise lost" ("*The Big Sky* and

the Siren Song of Apocalypse" 14, 15). Egan is deconstructing the familiar frontier mentality, the apocalyptic underbelly of manifest destiny. As he explains, instead of the abstractions of western apocalypse, "the term 'pragmatic' suggests an engagement with immediate issues, concrete dilemmas, practical needs. Here 'comedy' is not meant to suggest humor. . . . Instead, 'comedy' names a narrative structure that pulls toward the resolution of tension, of difficulty, of despair" (15–16). He points the general reader of western fiction toward the aesthetics and ethos of Native American literature, which, as I am reading these authors, has by both necessity and propensity "pulled toward the resolution of tension, of difficulty, of despair" as a mode of survivance against the frontier narrative of modern history. The frontier remains the same mental divide that always blocked America from the human realities of American land and, if Simon Ortiz is correct, from America's own humane principles. The joke is that the frontier never existed. Native writers find endlessly amusing ways, as well as sad and poignant ones, to expose that mental obstacle of the frontier. They often see through the "solid" ideology of frontier thinking in practical ways of remaining rooted to the ground on which that ideology has been laid.

Humor is pluralistic; the possibilities are endless. Yet ironic strategies do more than celebrate uncertainties. They play on the tensions. They tug on the interconnections. As the spider of laughter spins its web, it surrounds the victim's sense of separation. The Cherokee scholar Clint Carroll traces "promising contradictions" ("Articulating Indigenous Statehood" 21) for Indigenous pluralism in the third space of sovereignty, between federal and state jurisdictions. Similarly the anthropologist Anna L. Tsing, in a piece entitled "Indigenous Voice," writes of "a global politics in which inconsistency and contradiction become our greatest assets" (57). A spectrum of "promising contradictions" offers a reenergized, global Indigenous movement a new set of strategies: "unity based on plurality: diversity without assimilation . . . authenticity *and* invention, subsistence *and* wealth, traditional knowledge *and* new technologies, territory *and* diaspora" (33). The serious historical dichotomies that would antagonize each set in Tsing's catalogue become complements, extensions, expansions of possibility via *and* instead of *or*.

This revised, ironic geography of ideology insists on the grounded nature of Indigenous humor that plays along reified borders. Thus Blaeser acutely describes Native humorists' play along the edges of the frontier: "They do not proceed from the illusion of any pristine historical territory, untouched by the accounts of the opposition. Instead they draw their humor and power from an awareness of the reality of the place where the diverse accounts of history come into contact with one another. They take for granted and force recognition of the already embattled visions all readers bring to the text" ("The New 'Frontier'" 38). Blaeser neatly links "humor and power" to a different geography, a larger and more diverse "place" than the old frontier. She further explicates how processes of Indian humor are grounded in the land itself rather than in oppositional dynamics of white versus Indian:

> These authors expend little of their wit and energy to advance either of the opposing sides of these arguments; instead, they flesh out the frontier in all its immense complexity. They shift and reshift their story's perspectives, turn the tables of historical events, unmask stereotypes and racial poses, challenge the status of history's heroes and emerge somewhere in a new frontier of Indian literature, somewhere between fact and fiction, somewhere between the probable and the possible, in some border area of narrative which seems more true than the previous accounts of history. (39)

Rather than taking sides, these authors "flesh out the frontier in all of its immense complexity." They erase the reductive line of the frontier in favor of a larger, more multifarious field. Against colonial historiography, Native humor writers, such as Carter Revard, Vizenor, and Gordon Henry in Blaeser's study, playfully "shift and reshift" perspectives on history. We have seen how our five writers "flesh out the frontier in all its immense complexity." Because the frontier is reductively dualistic, a complex frontier is no longer a frontier. That's another joke.

In addition to the reductive frontier, or rather because of the pervasive power of frontier mentality, many readers of Native American literatures in the out-group and in-group have yet another stubborn obstacle to overcome: "the stoic Indian" or "the wooden Indian."[8] The image has persisted for centuries, yet of course it has little reality beyond colonial projections. It *is* the white man's Indian. It serves those projections by providing a static antagonist for the dynamic pioneer protagonist of the frontier. The stoic Indian is a sitting duck on the carnival target range of frontier mentality.

Instead of this easy target, the Shoshone Bannock journalist Mark Trahant affirms that other liberating aspects of Indian humor are deeply embedded in Indian communities and literary traditions:

> I have a hard time even imagining American Indians as stoics—humorless, resigned, reverent—no matter the tribe involved. Ancient legends are filled with humor. Whether it's about a coyote, spider or a raven, there are hundreds of stories with jokes hidden in the morality tale.
>
> I grew up in a reservation community where humor was a constant. As I began to travel and experience places and cultures far from my own, I heard that same laughter echoed wherever I went.
>
> I began to wonder how the non-Indian world came to believe the story of the wooden Indian.
>
> Native writers and storytellers have chipped away at that wooden image for a long time. Creek poet and journalist Alexander Posey wrote the hard-hitting satire, the "Fus Fixico Letters," about corruption in what was then the Indian Territory, now Oklahoma. He poked fun at political characters, such as Teddy Roosevelt—he called him President Rooster Feather—and Secretary of the Interior Ethan Allen Hitchcock. Posey renamed the secretary "It's Cocked," because he hated making difficult decisions. These days, Northwest poet and author Sherman Alexie loads his writing with outrageous wit and humor—not to mention comedic genius on stage. ("Indian Humor")

Certainly Posey's caricatures and Alexie's wit, the outrageousness of their comic gestures, are joined to outrage. Simon Ortiz lists rage as one of his universal themes. The scholar Lois Welch describes her training in Native humor as "finding the hilarious entwined with the hair-raising, watching outrage vanquished by the outrageous" ("Wild but Not Savage"). If everything is political, certainly Native humor is that, but what is remarkable is the multigenerational span of outrage that refines itself in the absurdities of Indian joking. There is no doubt a fatalism that speaks out of centuries of seeming powerlessness to change the big picture. Yet the ways that humor, as Trahant says, remains "a constant" in Indian life work not to soften but to survive narratives of tragedy.

Despite its pervasiveness, Native humor, as Trahant observes, is even less visible to the mainstream than the literature that it enlivens. In spite of efforts by Native writers and in spite of twenty-first-century cosmopolitanism, or perhaps because of it, that stoic image remains in film and other media. Clearly the stoic Indian is merely another rendering on the settlers' palimpsest of the noble savage. It keeps the Indian individual rather than communal, and therefore defeatable. A community on and of the land is basically unbeatable. The colonial project, now the American dream, still must write its own stories on the bodies of the land. By depriving Natives of humor, colonial projection makes them less human. Beneath that fantasized stoicism is a deeper fantasy of violence and forced subjugation of the Indian body in the colonial enterprise. The stoic Indian is a silent Indian, and the silent Indian is a silenced one. This is the silence of death in a vanishing body, a body always allowed to perform only its silence, thus its death, as a testament to the fantasy of a people's disappearance.

Indian stoicism is a metonym for white supremacy. The shellac of bravery and fortitude on the wooden Indian paints the face of death itself, a peculiar death imposed by assumptions of white supremacy. This syndrome serves America and its need to ennoble its conquest of a continent. As Gordon M. Sayre explains of King Philip, Pontiac, Tecumseh, and other leaders of anticolonial wars of resistance in *The Indian Chief as Tragic Hero*, the image of the defeated, even martyred Indian chief became an icon for American national identity in the eighteenth and early nineteenth centuries. America needed catharsis to purge the complexities of freedom and dispossession. "The dynamic of the Indian chief as tragic hero was consistent with the social functions of tragedy as established by Aristotle," Sayre writes. "The ethos of the Indian tragic hero was articulated not only in stage tragedies, but also in gothic novels, verse romances, travel narratives, and ethnographic texts by famous, obscure, and anonymous authors writing in English, French, and Spanish" (3). We may add to his list the wooden, cigar-store Indian.

Indian tragedy is America's success, so if Indians laugh, that entire narrative implodes. America's tragedy of Indian losses operates by Indians' heroic resistance to what must be the equally heroic imperial enterprise of America. By the pure oppositionality of Hegel's dialectical model of tragedy, both sides have matched value, but the winning side absorbs the sacrificed value of the loser, the martyr. Thus the tragic mode of American history finds its ultimate antagonist in the stoic Indian. These are Vizenor's "terminal creeds." The model amplifies the nobility of American expansion while it reifies racial exclusions. Yet such exclusions erode in the liquid flow of historical complexity. American realities may not be tragic after all. That's why Indians keep laughing.

The Comic Mode

A seminal essay published in 1972 by Joseph W. Meeker, "The Comic Mode," which generated his book *The Comedy of Survival: Studies in Literary Ecology*, helps to clarify Trahant's "constant" even as it begins to explain the ground of Indigenous laughter. Following this logic, we may further understand Indigenous rewriting of American reality. If one of the keys to survival is humor, how specifically does it function beyond lightening the mood? Is humor merely an opiate of the masses, a relief valve, or dust in the oppressor's eyes? Or does humor offer a different set of insights into what it means— and does not mean—to be human, to suffer and to survive? If humor is one key to survival, what kind of world does humor build to survive in? Or the inverse: What kind of world builds humor? As Vizenor summons "trickster liberation, the uncertain humor of survivance," Native humor suggests a different perception of history itself. Humor offers a different way of writing the story.

Although Meeker writes of cultural traditions very different from Native literatures, citing *Lysistrata* and *Catch-22*, he elucidates the narrative logic that links humor and survival. His study is an early example of the emerging literary practice of ecocriticism, looking at literature through the lens of the land, and the eco-logic that he describes becomes a comic narrative structure for people and literatures of the land. Not only is the "bicultural play" or "bicultural intelligence" that Kenneth Lincoln described (*Indi'n Humor* 310) part of this humanizing link, but we may follow Meeker's perspective to arrive at the linkage between the comic and the pluralist, as we return to the ground.

Connecting the comic mode with evolutionary ecology, Meeker writes of "the comedy of biology," or the ecological balance evolved in nature, as parallel to the narrative structures of comic storytelling. He lays out the contrast: "Tragedy demands that choices be made among alternatives; comedy assumes that all choice is likely to be in error and that survival depends upon finding accommodations that will permit all parties to endure" ("The

Comic Mode" 164). Meeker is not mapping a "nice" nature but a balanced system, a story of equilibrium, and he enlarges the revisionary map to the entire theory of evolution: "Evolution itself is a gigantic comic drama, not the bloody tragic spectacle imagined by the sentimental humanists of early Darwinism. Nature is not 'red in tooth and claw' as the nineteenth-century English poet, Alfred, Lord Tennyson characterized it, for evolution does not proceed through battles fought among animals to see who is fit enough to survive and who is not" (164). As he deconstructs social Darwinism, Meeker is unraveling the narrative of colonialism itself: "Rather, the evolutionary process is one of adaptation and accommodation, with the various species exploring opportunistically their environments in search of a means to maintain their existence. Like comedy, evolution is a matter of muddling through" (164). Where literary tragedy is the story of oppositional aggression and death, comedy is the story of interactive survival and life.

Meeker describes comic structure as a narrative ecology of interrelationships that generates stories and character structures other than tragic binaries. One thinks of Gregory Schrempp's description of traditional Native notions of "distributed power": "Although all life depends upon some degree of self-interested utilization of the natural environment . . . reciprocity is required by the fact that the powers of the natural world are distributed throughout all of its forms" ("Distributed Power" 26). Hierarchy requires tragedy; reciprocity requires comedy.

Although Meeker's discussion itself suffers from the Platonic dualisms on which tragedy is built, as between physical and metaphysical—one might say between death and life—his notion is useful in marking the links between the comic and communal aspects of survival. His polarized dialectic limits Meeker to see comedy throwing off morals and values in favor of survival at any cost, yet he comes around to the possibility of a different ethic of mutuality, one that approximates tough decisions that colonized people have had to make many times over. Contrasting the pretensions of tragedy and its absolutes of right and wrong, he advocates for the reciprocal pragmatics of ecologic thought: "More appropriate to our time are the relatively modest assumptions made by the comic spirit. Man is a part of nature and subject to all natural limitations and flaws. Morality is a matter of getting along with one's fellow creatures as well as possible. All beliefs are provisional, subject to change when they fail to produce harmonious consequences. Life itself is the most important force there is: the proper study of mankind is survival" ("The Comic Mode" 167). "Getting along with one's fellow creatures" as a principle in nature as well as in culture must include predators and prey, colonizers and colonized in a balance that does not eliminate loss.

An emergent logic of pluralism begins to come clear, ultimately in mutual mortality, where Meeker's comic universe is not a prelapsarian dream: "Necessity, of course, is real. All must eat and in turn be eaten, storms must come and go, and injustices must occur when so many rightful claimants contend. But that is just the point: comedy and ecology are systems designed to accommodate necessity and to encourage acceptance of it, while tragedy is concerned with avoiding or transcending the necessary in order to accomplish the impossible" ("The Comic Mode" 163). Comedy is *necessary* as the "real" rather than secondary to tragedy as the "impossible." This is not mere optimism, but realism. The very harshness that pulls down the corners of the mouth on the tragic mask makes necessary the reverse side's comic smile.

For our purposes, Meeker's "rightful claimants" are both Indian communities and non-Indian settlers, not by transcendent principles of right and justice but by pragmatic necessity, according to a comic rather than tragic story. The necessity faced by Indian humor is indeed the pitiful position into which history has forced the jokester. As Simon Ortiz explains, "the themes of family, community, religion, humor, and rage are the most common" among not only Indian people but the working people of America ("Towards a National Indian Literature" 12). Kathryn W. Shanley characterizes the work of Ortiz, partially, as "a sorrow, a joy, and a raging grief" ("Prairie Songs" 102). The modern universality of oppressed and repressed rage makes the comic mode not only more remarkable but more intense and complex, while more comprehensible as well.

To reclaim authority from a tragic and denigrating history, Native ironists undercut non-Indians' "rightful claim" in many ways. Here we see the foundation of out-group humor in Native communities and literary expressions. Generally the settlers' arbitrary claims to two sources of power, civilization *and* wilderness, become the twin targets of Native humor. The intruders, from conquistadors to missionaries, from Puritans to pioneers, claimed that they themselves had the power to define civilization and that their definition gave them power over the wilderness. Native Americans have responded by disagreeing in manifold ways, asserting broader definitions of civilized culture and prior, broader rights to the land. This fundamental reversal, jokingly exposing the whites' lack of civilization and lack of land right, is an originary move of Indian humor that reduces the white man from the tragic heroic to the comic human level. He is no longer lord of the realm. His delusion of overcoming and civilizing the wilderness is just that: a delusion.

The irony is both logical and historical, indeed ethical. Logically there was no wilderness and no civilization, in contrast to the Euro-American episteme. Historically, ethically, and legally, aboriginal land rights precede the fifteenth-century papal Doctrine of Discovery. If reassertions of aboriginal land rights stand at the center of Native American politics and literatures, it is now by Indian joking and persuasion as well as legal proceedings rather than by battle that the white man discovers he is no longer the only "rightful claimant." Manifest destiny insisted precisely that whites were the only rightful claimant to America. Indian humor pulls away that right. No longer the big man at the top of a racial autocracy, the white man is resettled on the real ground of plurality.

The theoretical junctions and disjunctions between Meeker's ecology of survival and Bakhtin's discursive heteroglossia are useful to note here. As Native ironists reappropriate the English language to their own subversive purposes, they evoke multiple and complex fields of discourse whose ideological and historical weight intensifies the focused impact of their jokes, barbs, and ironies. Joy Harjo and Gloria Bird's resonant book title "Reinventing the Enemy's Language" encapsulates this dynamic. Not only does the comic mode—in English or other languages—sustain an ecology of survival, but it also strengthens a strategy of ridicule. Polyglossia authorizes irony just as pluralism authorizes difference.

As Bakhtin explains of the unconscious discursive formation of the individual, linguistic structures may shape identities. In a (post)colonial context, Indigenous authors who manipulate colonial languages may wield the master's tool to critique and reshape colonial cultures from both inside and outside. Bakhtin makes a useful distinction: "Another's discourse performs here no longer as information, directions, rules, models and so forth—but strives rather to determine the very bases of our ideological interrelations with the world, the very basis of our behavior; it performs here as *authoritative discourse*, and an *internally persuasive discourse*" ("Discourse in the

Novel" 342). Language as the established discourse of a society carries authority, and it thereby structures "an individual's ideological becoming." Language use invokes various historical, political, and ideological authorities. Thus the external authority of social power structures, as they shape discourse, persuades internal structures, expressed in an individual's language, to match dominant "ideological interrelations with the world."

However, the manipulation by Native writers of what Bakhtin calls external "authoritative discourse" and "internally persuasive discourse" reverses discursive power relations. Colonial Euro-American language, the bifurcated discourse of the frontier and manifest destiny, arrogates to itself external authority to be *the* discourse of history. When a Native author uses English for an aesthetic statement with ethical ramifications in a colonized world, she summons the authoritative imprimatur of the colonizer on her descriptions and on her implicit or explicit demands. The very fact of her language use, built on the presence of polyglossia in her readership's mental linguistic synapses, acts to de-authorize the reductive binaries of that still pervasive colonial mind-set of endless dualisms (civilization/wilderness, mind/matter, noble/savage, man/woman, good/bad). A Native voice in English trades the frontier for a larger field. The joke begins in the Native body itself as the mouth and mind express the English language.

A caveat: it is speculative by necessity, but I must observe that Indian humor and irony are not merely postcolonial responses to historical invasion and trauma, although certainly humor helps to navigate that trauma. Humor and irony are not mere survival techniques, although they help communities survive. They are not desperate glee, nor generational denial of genocidal losses, although they rise through such losses. Indians laughed before the white man arrived here. Then they laughed at the white man. More than that history, via Meeker's comic mode we may understand generally how Indian humor is an aspect of a worldview, a validated sense of kinship and interconnection, wherein human foibles and hubris tickle a whole web of relations, including colonial ones. Diverse cultural and historical preferences may tend more or less toward tragic or comic modes of telling one's own stories. Native humor comes out of a varied set of unique human contexts that precede the colonial era.

Toward this perspective, the Northern Arapaho scholar Angelica Lawson addresses humor as an integral part of the oral tradition, as do Smoker and

Trahant. Her perspective offers some insight on in-group humor as well: "Literatures that utilize information contained within the oral tradition addressing ceremonies and ritual, humor, and family demonstrate cultural resilience and the resilience of those concepts. Perhaps that is why Native American writers have adopted and adapted both the aesthetics and ethics embedded in these songs, stories, and prayers, and continue them in their contemporary writing" ("Resistance and Resilience" 21). Lawson contextualizes humor as one key part of oral traditions that Native writers employ today in what she calls "resilience literature," complementing "resistance literature": "Resilience literature incorporates Native American aesthetics and ethics from the oral tradition" (30). The more familiar resistance literature that takes an overtly political stand might also employ humor. Her elaboration of these two literary approaches makes for an intriguing view of survivance that offers important perspectives beyond my earlier discussion about the complementary dynamics of dialectics and dialogics in Native literatures, where resistance literature tends toward the dialectic and resilience literature toward the dialogic. Lawson incorporates humor as an originary feature of Native cultures that serves Native communities through both forms of literary expression.

With these strategies writers in this study go about the work of reanimating America's stoic Indian. Every characterization, every narration, every argument is a complication of mainstream stereotypes, a humanizing toward what Alfonzo Ortiz calls "fully sentient and multi-dimensional beings." Instead of stoic we simply get realistic Indians, who certainly might exemplify bravery and fortitude, even taciturnity, but who also display doubt, humor, fear, sorrow, joy, cleverness, pettiness, deviousness, even silliness—an open field of human qualities.

Clowns of Diversity

Readers today who generally recognize the limitations of stereotypes might no longer be surprised by the fact that Indian boys coming of age like McNickle's Antoine are teased as much as honored, nor that Winnemucca's first-contact Paiutes saw their invaders as "white brothers," nor that there was a Sioux "peace movement" in the nineteenth century, nor even that Lakota warriors had beloved male friends, *kolas*. Indeed the Fool Soldiers might have the last laugh now that their radical reciprocity can seem commonplace in a world of infinite global exchange. The logic of *pluribus* has become both clearer and more confused as American generations begin to recognize the historical logic of a multicultural, then pluralistic nation against the ahistorical illogic of racial and ethnic exclusions. Even "tragic" ironies such as Truckee's rebuked embrace of belligerent settlers or a Dakota's murder of a Lakota can be transformed in the context of a long-running comic, at times comedic tradition in Native writing. In Ishmael Reed's essay "What's American about America?" he cites the *New York Times* of June 23, 1983: "At the annual Lower East Side Jewish Festival yesterday, a Chinese woman ate a pizza slice in front of Ty Thuan Duc's Vietnamese grocery store. Beside her a Spanish-speaking family patronized a cart with two signs: 'Italian ices' and 'Kosher by Rabbi Alper.' And after the pastrami ran out, everybody ate knishes" (4). It is hardly surprising anymore that global and local circumstances are forcing changes in historical categories and ways of thinking that never did fit events on the ground.

What remains less obvious, however, and what this study attempts to make visible, is how certain Native insights into the potentials of *pluribus*, such as the kinds of boundary crossings the Fool Soldiers envisioned, have driven writings by American Indians since the beginnings of colonization, and especially since the founding of the United States. Meeker's "comic spirit," wherein "morality is a matter of getting along with one's fellow creatures as well as possible," becomes the politics of pluralism in Native writers' responses to colonial domination. Getting along with one's fellows may be a practical outcome of animism, suggesting further that pluralism is a political expression of Indigenous animism, a topic worthy of a separate study.

Throughout the Western Hemisphere, in writing and oratory, Native voices have suggested pluralistic interaction in various ways with Europeans and other settlers or invaders. In contrast to both annihilation and assimilation, pluralism is a logical, one might even say natural challenge to colonialism and then to exclusive and imperialistic nationalism. Native efforts at cross-cultural communication and equity required by pluralism began with the shoreline Taino greetings that Columbus saw only as naïve and have remained invisible to colonial eyes since the admiral labeled *los Indios* as potential slaves.

Although it has its own discursive history, *pluralism* is a useful word for the leveling equilibrium of cultures that Indigenous voices have reasonably suggested to reverse colonialism, to elude slavery and conquest. I suggest that pluralism is a central component of Native humor. Philosophically, pluralism in European tradition has been set against monism, a multiplicity of causes against a single cause. This juxtaposition in principle has then lined up on each side of the colonial binaries, where Indigenous animism is set against Euro-Christian theism, where Indigenous racial difference is set against colonial racial dominance, and where Indigenous political and economic diversity is set against centralized colonial and now corporate power.

Pluralism may be distinguished from multiculturalism by the tendency of the latter to homogenize difference. Multiculturalism, once an ethos of equality, has been co-opted as a term by corporate capital for entrée into diverse markets. Multiculturalism has become multicapitalism, the absorption of difference and resistance into hierarchies of revenue stream, that is, multiple markets. A classic example of such co-optation is torn and faded denim pants: in the 1950s and 1960s they were a sign of resistance, of nonconformity, of noncommercial, noncorporate identity on the part of those "countercultural" renegades who refused to wear gray suits. Very soon, however, Levi Strauss, Wranglers, and a host of new brands cashed in on the growing market for worn blue denim as hippy chic. The corporations began manufacturing them as "stone-washed," faded, and even pretorn. By the turn of the century, they even perfected a yellowed grunge technique to sell new denims that simply look dirty. Counterculture becomes multiculture becomes capital culture. Yet a less cynical reading of multiculturalism recognizes that it still holds within it the seeds of what might more usefully be called pluralism. Instead of the hierarchical conformities of multicultural assimilation, instead of the melting pot, pluralism has always suggested a radically democratic social dynamic. Pluralism includes a social ethos of difference as the robust energy of community. Yet even progressives in American politics tend to see in difference only a threat to solidarity, as people of color and women in activist communities know too well. The underlying concept, often held by both the right and the left, is that utopian community must be homogeneous. The result again may be dominance of the normative.

For contrast, Anna Marie Smith explains the notion of radical democratic pluralism promoted by the theorists Ernesto Laclau and Chantal Mouffe. She describes their social map: "The diversity among democratic differences must be affirmed as a good in itself; minority groups should never be asked to pay the price of cultural self-destruction through assimilation and disciplinary neutralization in exchange for inclusion, legitimacy and recognition" (*Laclau and Mouffe* 33). In language that forecasts the United Nations Declaration on the Rights of Indigenous Peoples, Smith clarifies the alternative postcolonial society: "Genuine 'tolerance' must mean that minority groups are granted access to the material resources that they need to preserve their rights and to promote their distinct democratic differences" (33). There is a reason such theory is termed "radical." It goes to the root of modern, that is, American social questions. If "minority groups should never be asked to pay the price of cultural self-destruction," then American history should never have happened. Diversity as a good in itself is the precise opposite of America's predominant imaginary, where *unum* trumps *pluribus*. The ironies of Native American literary humor constitute a chorus of "democratic critiques" of "the values held by the majority." A pluralistic society would be seen as a horrifying hall of mirrors only by those who insist on seeing themselves in every other face. The hall of mirrors appears chaotic to those who would deny difference.

New conversations about pluralism around the turn of the twenty-first century have clarified in retrospect some of the ideas that colonized peoples have put forth over the past five hundred years to offset the paradigm of a dominating center and exploited or neglected margins. Under various names, such as feminism, Négritude, Black Power, Red Power, and tribal sovereignty, various social margins have invoked pluralism as a principle to resist being homogenized by the commodification processes of capitalism. Pluralism would maintain differences of culture against such economic forces, and that would be a joke on the American model of the melting pot.

Ironies of Blind Power

Although it frequently has blinded them to subtler dynamics of history, the hierarchical position of colonizing populations "naturally" has allowed them to desire and assume that their power is a one-way street by which they can control the colonized: initially toward the mercantile center and gradually toward the dominant normative economy. Under ensuing oppression, the colonized populations have desired to see that exchange of power in reverse, as a two-way street, or even a roundabout on a more reciprocal field of exchange. Moving beneath the advocacy of political and cultural pluralism versus monism lies the question of who has the power to change or control the other. In the dialectic of history, claiming such power to alter, assimilate, even annihilate the subordinated population has backfired when the claim is based on the assumption that the dominating self will remain "the same," that the thesis itself will not be synthesized with the antithesis.

This field of reversals is ripe for humor's harvest. Reciprocity rather than marginalization, isolation, or domination thus becomes a power strategy of pluralism as a form of irony, and irony can fuel laughter. To survive, the powerless must recognize these dialectical implications for the powerful, and then complicate the mutual transformations by drawing on a larger field, a set of other dialectical vectors. This is a logic of jesters, tricksters, and clowns: the imaginative invocation of surprising factors by the seemingly foolish and powerless that undercuts and alters the powers that be. A power strategy of pluralism thus tends toward a wider field of reciprocity, rather than marginalization, domination, or isolation. A more complex view of power relations on the part of the powerless means generally that Indigenous voices have recognized more clearly than their colonizers how the colonizers and their cultures may have been changed—acculturated—by Native contact.[9] Thus the Lone Ranger and Tonto fistfight in heaven. What looked to the mainstream media like a clean hierarchy of white cowboy over Indian sidekick is shown by a Native author to be a spiritual battle to reclaim history. The irony of this change in perspective, this invisible reversal becomes the historical ground, a *terra comica*, of Native humor.

Against the violent realities of history, this contrary conception of Native transformations of Euro-American culture is so intensely idealistic, however invisibly actual and operable, that it regularly needs irony to sustain it. The ironic notion of reverse acculturation indeed motivates and animates much of Native American—as well as some Euro-American—literature and social commentary from colonial times to the present. In this narrative, Europeans are not "going Native" and not replacing Natives, as in James Fenimore Cooper; rather they are learning, often in unconscious ways, democratic, humanistic, and pluralistic values through long-term cultural interaction with Native Americans, as in Leanne Howe or Vizenor. It is a profoundly "civilizing" process. Thus Native humor is not only about hilarities of "the human condition" but more specifically about this reverse acculturation, or even reverse colonization—the inadmissible fact that European immigrants, not only Indigenous inhabitants, have been transformed by the American experience. These are the "invisible ironies" of history, not only that American Indians contributed to the "modern" world by way of social values such as democratic principles in constitutional law, or the equality of men and women, or scientific advancements in metallurgy, horticulture, architecture, and artistic and cultural contributions, but further that the American nation itself is built around the absent presence of sovereignty of Indian nations. Tribal sovereignty of Native nations has always been the negative space, the terra incognita on the map of the American enterprise.

The scholar Juan Bruce-Novoa traces this inverse history to the earliest colonial records of the sixteenth-century atypical conquistador Cabeza de Vaca, who tried to protect Indian communities from marauding Spanish Christians in his years of shipwrecked wanderings from the Mississippi River to Mexico City. Advocating that the Indians be "won by kindness" instead of by military coercion, Cabeza de Vaca's earnest sense of mutuality, while maintaining his colonial purpose, contrasts with the voracious opportunism of dominant colonial corporate history. His voice may indeed be an early instance not only of ethics but of reverse acculturation at the start of the colonial project. Bruce-Novoa's characterization of that mestizo quality as foundational for American literature suggests how deeply such nondualistic perspectives might be reshaping our history. In a "process of continuous displacements" between "civilization" and "nature," Cabeza de Vaca's text represents "the American culture" itself (*Reconstructing a Chicano/a Literary Heritage* 4, 9, 8): "How do we formulate a name for a being who does not belong on one side or the other of the binary oppositions of 'we' and 'the other?'" (11). He is "a being whose essence is alterability" (11), and the syncretic America he traces becomes, unlike the ostensibly stable colonial centers, forever a "process." He becomes "the intermediary between two exclusive codes" (13) of the Christian Spaniards and the Indians, while he leaves the Indians with the "utopic illusion" of achieving "the ideal of living among different cultures and enjoying the best aspects of each" (15). Yet he and his text embody "the possibility of otherness within sameness itself" (16). As a first mestizo, Cabeza de Vaca becomes "a malleable point of syncretism without a firm base in any solid pole, a being capable of transforming any binary order into a field of plurivalent points in a continuous flux" (17). Bruce-Novoa is describing a process of Americanization from the European side that mirrors James Clifford's description of a nexus of identity from the Mashpee side. Cabeza de Vaca "was forever marked with the sign of Americanness: continual alterability as neither native nor foreigner, but a mixture of the two" (17). The ironic point here is that in the midst of colonial domination, a European is reshaped by American Indian cultures, as the acculturation process moves both ways. Something "American" emerges in and as the process itself, from the start.

Yet Native voices, instead of adopting that culpable and conciliatory tone of Cabeza de Vaca, more often have needed to switch the dominant power relations by tilting the crown of the monarch or by protecting the pompous Puritan from his own ignorance. These transformations generate an undercurrent of irony that sparks humor, what we might call utopian humor, the joke that rebalances history. Humor erupts out of the ironic surprises of pluralism. Humor melts hierarchies when arrogations of colonial power have the literal ground pulled out from under them, only to find themselves flattened and humbled on a field of humanity.

These ironies of reversed colonialism were not lost on European writers early in the colonial period, whose works in this genre compose a literary historical context for later Native American critics such as Samson Occom and William Apess in the late eighteenth and early nineteenth centuries. Indeed, as Robert Berkhofer points out in *The White Man's Indian: Images of the American Indian from Columbus to the Present*, the ongoing European tradition of ironic self-critique by negative comparison with admired "savages" began in the sixteenth century with Michel de Montaigne and his "polemical and satirical use . . . of the noble American Indian": "The transition from description of the American Indian as Noble Savage to the use of the Noble American Indian as a critic of European society and culture is difficult to date, but scholars generally agree that most of the chief milestones occurred in France from the late sixteenth century to the late seventeenth century" (74–75). In his 1580 *essai* "On Cannibals," reflecting on explorers' accounts of Brazil, Montaigne writes ironically, "I do not find that there is anything barbaric or savage about this nation, according to what I've been told, unless we are to call barbarism whatever differs from our own customs. . . . In them the most natural virtues and abilities are alive and vigorous, whereas we have bastardized them and adopted them solely to our corrupt taste." In his early colonial moment, Montaigne goes to the heart of the issue that has plagued centuries following his own: "unless we are to call barbarism whatever differs from our own customs." He defines the reflex to denigrate difference, and he traces ways that reflex not only oppresses but also represses virtue "at home" under pretenses of "the perfect." When Native writers attack this reflex, they emphasize further the ironies of unacknowledged exchange and mutual modification.

Nearly two centuries after Montaigne, Jean-Jacques Rousseau enshrined that ironic pattern in what was then and perhaps remains the world's most unfortunate, and approved, oxymoron: "the noble savage." Rousseau himself applied the term more to re-enlightened Europeans, transformed by visions of wild nature, than to indigenes in the colonies, precisely in this ironic mode of reversed colonialism and transformation.

"Good Government"

One of the earliest written Native articulations of the ironic potential in colonial contact for balanced exchange rather than domination is by the Peruvian Felipe Guaman Poma de Ayala. His 1,200-page bilingual illustrated letter to King Philip III of Spain, entitled *The First New Chronicle and Good Government*, written in Spanish and Quechua over more than four decades up to 1615, lectured the king on colonial reform to transform both cultures. It is a study in colonial irony. Guaman Poma advises the Spanish monarch that "good government," unlike the current system, would equalize colonizer and colonized, combining European and Incan aspects of technology and theology in the administration by Indians of Andean society. The ironies are pointed as well as generalized. For instance, speaking of Pizarro's invasion of 1514, Guaman Poma writes, "Each day they did nothing but think of the gold and silver and riches of the Indies of Peru. They were like a desperate man, foolish, crazy, out of their minds with their greed for gold and silver. . . . Thus were the first men; they did not fear death with their interest for gold and silver. Worse are the ones of this life [Guaman Pomo's later generation], the Spanish corregidores [overseers], priests, and encomenderos. With their greed for gold and silver they go to hell" (374). Although himself an Incan elite, here is an aging peon on the margins of the known world adroitly claiming the authority of a clear vision of hell by which to instruct the imperial head of Catholic Spain at the colonial center. Like

Apess and Winnemucca, he directly reverses the Christian racial hierarchy by pointing out Christian racist hypocrisy.

One of the paradigmatic ironies of this paradigmatic piece is that although it was taken by courier from Lima to Madrid, it was never delivered to the Crown, yet it is being read more today than four hundred years ago. A Peruvian colleague tells me that in his homeland it is regarded merely as a picture-book. However, its resonance with Indigenous literary discourse over centuries registers its significance for revisionary history from the earliest moments of the colonial era. Mary Louise Pratt, in her seminal piece, "Arts of the Contact Zone," describes Guaman Poma's monumental work as "a revisionist account of the Spanish conquest, which, he argues, should have been a peaceful encounter of equals with the potential for benefiting both, but for the mindless greed of the Spanish." Pratt identifies the nonhierarchical Indigenous perspective that enters the "contact zone" with expectations of equality and mutuality rather than superiority or inferiority. We may call this a pluralistic expectation. Yet the brutal absurdity of colonial arrogance leads Guaman Poma into the ironic mode of reversal, as Pratt observes: "The Indies, he argues, should be administered through a collaboration of Inca and Spanish elites. The epistle ends with an imaginary question-and-answer session in which, in a reversal of hierarchy, the king is depicted asking Guaman Poma questions about how to reform the empire." Pratt describes the Q&A in which the Native is the authority and the king of Spain is the petitioner, highlighting the ironic reversals of an Indigenous worldview that discursively manipulates and rebalances colonial relations. Guaman Poma's rhetorical strategy here presages precisely the dynamics we have examined of an Indigenous nationalist authenticity that Simon Ortiz describes as reappropriating colonial language forms to make them "meaningful in their own terms" ("Towards a National Indian Literature" 8).

Guaman Poma's original letter was delivered by a Danish ambassador to Spain in the seventeenth century, apparently never received, but then archived in the Danish national museum and "undiscovered" for three hundred years. The editors of the digital online edition at the University of Copenhagen describe it notably as "a complex and unique mixture of historiography and utopianism. On one hand, it contains an entirely original framework for Andean historical self-understanding, as an alternative to the colonial viewpoint. . . . Guaman Poma formulates far-reaching proposals for reform aimed at turning the chaotic viceroyalty into a dynamic self-governed kingdom within the Spanish empire."[10] His syncretic vision makes room for Native autonomy as it forecasts the work of centuries of native writers, thinkers, and leaders to follow.[11]

The irony of difference in historical perspective continues across the centuries of colonialism. In eighteenth-century New England, the Mohegan preacher Samson Occom writes in *A Short Narrative of My Life* (1768) of continuing Mohegan hospitality, "As our Custom is, we freely Entertain all Visitors." Yet he does not hesitate to name the injustice of white prejudice that pays him a fraction of what white ministers and missionaries receive for the same services: "So I am *ready* to Say, they have used me thus, because ... I am a poor Indian." In context, it may be argued that Occom's strategy was not reciprocity but acceptance of assimilation, as he attempted to become more Christian than the whites themselves in a "twice as good" ethos to outdo his oppressors at their own game. Yet his interpellated critique of white racial and class prejudice sets him apart as the Indian he is, invoking justice against the way "they have used me thus." Like Apess's similar dynamics a generation later, Occom's use of Christian discourse remains an ironic tool not for erasing Indian identity, but for the reverse, for altering Euro-American society in its relations with Native Americans, for a continuing irony of insistence on pluralism within the Church and the nation.

Pluralism seems to reflect inwardly as well as outwardly. A published anecdote about an Occom sermon delivered around 1776 affirms all five of the key terms of this study, where the Mohegan Presbyterian minister narrates the irony of transformation in authenticity and identity, with echoes for community and sovereignty. Discussing "traditionary religion" of his people, Occom suggests that an inward openness to transformation allows an outward openness to pluralism. The concluding passage of Harold Blodgett's biography of Occom features this account from the Reverend Daniel Waldo, written in 1853, seventy-seven years after Occom preached "in an old meeting-house, in the part of Franklin, Conn., then known as Pettipaug": "His voice was pleasant, but not very loud—sufficiently so, however, to accommodate his text, but I recollect that his subject led him to speak somewhat at length of what he called a traditionary religion; and he told an anecdote by way of illustration. An old Indian, he said, had a knife which he kept till he wore the blade out; and then his son took it and put a new blade to the handle, and kept it till he had worn the handle out; and this process went on till the knife had had half a dozen blades, and as many handles; but still it was all the time the same knife" (Blodgett, *Samson Occom* 217). With no shortage of irony, that "same knife" might remain the best metaphor for an authenticity that translates itself across so many identities on the ground of change that it becomes its own sovereign community!

If such adaptability or resilience is a key to survivance, it evidently has social, ethical resonances in tolerance of change and difference. In early nineteenth-century New England, Apess's retrospective narrative of the seventeenth century envisions a pluralistic Native inclusiveness in response to colonial intrusions. According to Apess, the leadership of Native communities struggled to maintain good humor and hospitality against the mendacity and darker motives of the settlers. Summoning evidence to contrast Indigenous strategies with white colonial acquisitiveness, he describes the "benevolent chief" Mascononomo, who "bid the Pilgrims [the Puritans of the Massachusetts Bay Colony] welcome to his shores and, in June 28, 1630, ceded his land to them for the small sum of eighty dollars, now Ipswich, Rowley, and a part of Essex" (*Eulogy* in *On Our Own Ground* 285). The forbearance that Mascononomo and other chiefs of the area showed must have been exercised from positions of power over the far-outnumbered Puritans in Massachusetts, yet it remained a pattern of conciliation if not reconciliation as the power shifted. Speaking of King Philip in the 1660s, Apess writes, "When he came into office it appears that he knew there was great responsibility resting upon himself and country, that it was likely to be ruined by those rude intruders around him, though he appears friendly and is willing to sell them lands for almost nothing, as we shall learn from dates [of land sales] of the Plymouth colony, which commence June 23, 1664" (290). Apess's point is not simply that Indians were the good guys and settlers were bad, but that the complexities of colonial relations do not obscure Native leaders' efforts at reciprocity, of a nonhierarchical vision for social relations.

Indeed writing of his own time, Apess claimed that the majority of white citizens of Massachusetts in the 1830s wanted to grant Mashpee Indians their rights and freedom, but they were obstructed by a small group of demagogues: "We believe the wish to relieve us from bondage is general throughout the state, and we earnestly hope that a few designing men will not be able to accomplish their selfish ends, contrary to the will of a majority of the people" (*Nullification* in *On Our Own Ground* 203). Further, he was grateful that the Massachusetts legislature reflected those numbers: "We thank the majority of the controllers of public affairs, that they had more sense than to think of holding the rightful lords of the soil in bondage any longer, for the gratification of selfish and unjust men. Honorable is it to Massachusetts that there are enough good and upright men in authority to counteract the measures of those of a different character and remedy the evils they may occasion" (205). In his discussion of the Massachusetts legislature appropriating funds for Indian education, Apess even sees a rallying of support: "A number of gentlemen spoke in favor of this allowance, and all showed that a spirit of kindness, as well as justice toward the long-oppressed red men, begins to warm the hearts of those who make our laws, and rule over us. We trust we are thankful to God for so turning the hearts of men toward us" (249). Rather than drawing lines of simplistic oppositions here, Apess the activist tried to apply a more complicated, more pluralistic mapping to all sides of the historical divide by which America may tell its story.

Among many twentieth-century examples of Native Americans' ironic writing or rewriting of American identity as pluralistic, we have seen what we might call a compassionate irony in the Acoma poet Simon Ortiz's 1981 essay "Towards a National Indian Literature," addressing America on its fear of its own "deepest and most honest emotions of love and compassion." Similarly with ironic compassion for the admiral, the Ojibwa Gerald Vizenor's 1991 novel for the bicentennial, *The Heirs of Columbus*, reimagines Columbus as a descendent of ancient Mayan explorers to the Mediterranean, jokingly suggesting a broader humanity in a circular history.[12]

"We Are All Clowns"

The earnestness and seriousness of such historic reversals do not, however, dictate the tone of their expression. As the ironies of Vizenor, Alexie, and so many writers before them suggest, a Native American sense of humor is one of the most productive ways to view these different cultural approaches to colonial relations. Simon Ortiz's serious invocation of American compassion in *from Sand Creek*, tracing roots of Native alcoholism from an 1864 Colorado massacre to a twentieth-century veterans hospital, differs sharply from Alexie's and Vizenor's ironies in tone, and by its poetic potency forges a form neither comic nor tragic. Yet all three writers employ direct reversal, whether humorous or grave, to rewrite history. We could say that Native joking has an undercurrent of ethical importunity, or that tragic contexts echo in the humorous texts.

The reversals of humor may certainly sting in nonsubversive ways, as in racist or sexist jokes that dehumanize, casually denying the humanity of the "other" in gestures that maintain established oppositions. Juxtaposed against the racist background, Indian humor is essentially humanizing. Echoing Lincoln's term "bicultural intelligence," Lois Welch locates Indian humor, like any pun, as a "bisociation" between the two quite separate worlds of Native America and Euro-America, drawing on the term from Arthur Koestler, who describes "the simultaneous correlation of an experience to two otherwise independent operative fields" (Welch, "Wild But Not Savage"). The double irony is that Native irony tends to link humanistically rather than to separate the "independent operative fields" of Euro-American and Native American experience. Whether wit, humor, sarcasm, or irony, reversals of binaries and hierarchies play in most jokes. Indeed the inverse poetics of humor closely parallels the inverse logic of Native literary politics that subverts dominant perceptions by humanizing the "other side of the frontier" (A. Ortiz, "Indian/White Relations). Laughter generated by verbal reversals opens mental doors to political and historical reversals, and Native storytellers harness humor to reverse both external and internalized oppression, laughing at both the invaders and themselves. Ultimately the vulnerabilities exposed in humor point toward an ethics of mortality and thus compose a soft plea for empathy instead of brutality.

One step short of—or beyond—mortality, laughing at oneself amounts to a kind of reappropriation of foolishness for its positive, boundary-breaking dynamics. Across many cultures, this claim to celebrate the fool underlies various clowning and scapegoat traditions.[13] The restraining or even repressive social imaginary often needs the release valve of humor, but when those restrictions carry the additional pressures of colonialism, clowning functions further to undercut and redistribute power. It then pushes to change the status quo permanently, not just temporarily to appease the people to accept their precarious social or cosmological position. The fundamentally pluralistic insight that can imagine such reversals functions internally as well as externally in Native humor.

As the Hopi scholar Emory Sekaquaptewa describes some ritual functions of laughter, "Clowns make fun of life and thereby cause people to look at themselves" ("One More Smile" 152). Laughter in Indian families and communities, with echoes in the literature, is unique in its relentless teasing qualities, pushing on an ethics of humility and even humiliation in order to test the "victim" to own the existential condition of *unshika*, as the Sioux and Assiniboine say, "pitiful" before the Great Mystery. If you can survive those taunts, you can survive anything. Shanley, invoking the *unshika* value, writes of "truth and fierce beauty" in the poetry of Simon Ortiz, who reaches a position beyond words "when our pitiful selves know keenly how pitiful we are" ("Prairie Songs" 102). When you own your very common humanity, you are both vulnerable and invincible. At the bottom of the barrel, you're beyond reproach.

As Sekaquaptewa explains, "The heart of the Hopi concept of clowning is that we are all clowns. This was established at the very beginning when people first emerged from the lower world" ("One More Smile" 150). The visionary leader of the clowns "chose this way of reminding his people that they have only their worldly ambition and aspirations by which to gain a spiritual world of eternity. He was showing them that we cannot be perfect in this world after all and if we are reminded that we are clowns, maybe we can have, from time to time, introspection as a guide to lead us right. From this beginning when we have been resembled to clowns we know that this is to be a trying life and that we will try to fulfill our destiny by mimicry, by mockery, by copying, by whatever" (151). The heart of this humor is recognition of imperfection, that is, the incongruous disparity between our fantasy and our reality in this "trying life." We have to use our imperfect tools, our "worldly ambition and aspirations," to approach "a spiritual world of eternity." Here we return to a paradigm different from domination, to another kind of *unshika*. In various Native communities and cultures, such a recognition is both enacted in daily teasing and ritualized in seasonal ceremonies. Describing the Hopi practice, Sekaquaptewa continues, "This whole idea of clowning is re-enacted at the time of the *katsina* dances. When they are dancing in the plaza the *katsinas* represent the spiritual life toward which Hopi destiny is bent. . . . When the clowns come they represent man today who is trying to reach this place of paradise" (151).

Precisely at this most sacred moment, when *katsinas* offer eternal life in the town plaza, the dancing clowns bring it all down to earth, and perhaps bring earth up to eternity, by their coarseness and selfishness. Thinking "they can finally have eternal life like the *katsinas*," the clowns grope and grab and poke even the *katsinas*: "Finally, one of the clowns touches a *katsina* and upon his discovery of these beautiful beings, the clowns immediately try to take possession of them. 'This is mine!' 'This is mine!' They even fight each other over the possession of the *katsinas* and over the food and things they find" ("One More Smile" 152). This shameful comic drama makes the participants and the people "look at themselves" through that "introspection" that might indeed help us "try to fulfill our destiny." This language does not claim mastery, but ongoing, pitiful effort, the comic ability to adapt and survive.

For all its other functions, then, humor retains an explicit goal of survivance, even for Native stand-up comedians. For example, Don Burnstick, a Cree from Alexander First Nation in Alberta, Canada, offers this affirmation in promotional material for his comedy tour: "After all that we have gone through, we have never lost our sense of humour, and it's time to share that. This is the spirit of healing and the essence of my performance." "It's time to share that," perhaps partly because he feels it's time for the settler cultures to recognize Indian humanity through Indian humor.

From the start, ridicule and humor, by reimagining power relations, authorize and reinforce a Native alterity that threatens the puritanical and hierarchical structures of colonizing European cultures. A Native comic approach to history and to the American story has always been deeply subversive to the militaristic and legalistic power struggles triggered by European desire for land. Lincoln refers to "a new image of the surviving Indian as comic artist more than tragic victim, seriously humorous to the native core" (*Indi'n Humor* 5), though that "new" image has been expressed in Native communities and writings for generations across centuries. The strength of that humor casts off the crushing weight of past and present with reference to some alternative, different future. With that dynamic, the buoyancy of Indian humor is deeply forward-looking, if not optimistic.

"You Survived?"

A classic moment of popular humor in the name of Native survival can subvert the project of manifest destiny. Is there anyone who has not heard this joke, a parody of Hollywood's image of the wooden Indian in its most famous TV version? The Lone Ranger and Tonto are out riding the range. Suddenly they are surrounded by hostile Indians charging over the horizon. The Lone Ranger says, "Tonto! A thousand Indians to the north of us! A thousand Indians to the east! A thousand Indians to the south! A thousand Indians to the west! What are we gonna do!?" And Tonto answers, unperturbed, "What you mean 'we,' white man?"

Multiple layers of surprise spark this comic reversal, now a part of America's cultural mainstream. The popularity of this anonymous joke actually speaks to Apess's trust in the support of a Massachusetts majority and to Simon Ortiz's "compassionate" heart of America. Humor reflects pathos. Tonto's reaffirmation of his racial and cultural ties as deeper than his individual ties spring the tensions between these inseparable companions. He claims radical difference—"I'm not a part of your 'we,' white man!"—against the homogenizing effects of oppressively conformist, pistol-packing Americanization.

Part of the surprise erupts from the combined restraint and outrage in Tonto's words and tone. His calm retort replays the stilted, stereotyped half-English of the movie Indian, echoing the taciturnity if not the silence of the frontier trading post's preferred wooden Indian. Yet while he maintains the outer demeanor of the Native as tabula rasa on which the dominator may write the script of subjection, he subverts that colonial fantasy by speaking his pent-up anger, by claiming his difference against dominant authority. The joke is funny also because of its more general subtext of Indian reversals, an affirmation that Indians can indeed win, that they can turn the so-called tide of history. The joke makes manifest an unmanifest destiny. (Alexie's famous short story title, "The Lone Ranger and Tonto Fistfight in Heaven," draws on that same dynamic.)

Tonto's anger, especially in the context of their fictional friendship, hones the barb of humor further by breaking the boundary of betrayal.[14] Against the whole radio and TV serial history of dramatic reciprocity, of mutual rescues and escapes, of "I'll cover you!" and "Thanks, Tonto!," here finally the Indian turns his back on the white man—precisely when the white man subsumes the Indian in his "we, white man" identity. Tonto's insistence on difference undercuts the assimilationist assumptions of the white project. This betrayal of expectations is the spike of humor in the reversal:

Tonto is willing not only to point out the politics of manifest destiny but also to show that those politics are so egregious as to justify a personal betrayal.

Further, the poignancy of this moment, sparking humor by the surprise of difference, derives notably from Leslie Fiedler's famous point of the manly bonding in American frontier narratives.[15] The default homoeroticism of their friendship is harshly spurned by Tonto's insistence on his separate identity—and his life. Indeed by denying that homoerotic bond, Tonto triangulates his relations beyond his dialectic with Kemosabe, reengaging not only his Indian community but his Indian land as well.

This psychological dimension of betrayal thus suggests influential ways that Indian-white relations operate in popular culture by a dialectic and a dialogic different from the paradigm of slave and master on which Hegel defined the dialectic.[16] Especially in the ideological freedom of the West, racial relations between the Lone Ranger and Tonto suggest that there has been room for genuine affirmation of cross-racial friendship on the land. This may apply to Natty Bumpo's, the Lone Ranger's, or Thoreau's West, and even to Winnemucca's or Silko's. If that friendship negotiates the fragile ethics of colonial relations, how is that mutual affirmation different from Hegel's dialectic, wherein the lordsman needs the bondsman to affirm his identity as master just as much as the slave needs a master in order to be a slave? Certainly, as the Tonto joke suggests, one fundamental difference is in power relations. In the ahistorical dreams of ideology, Indian-white identities do not operate solely by Hegel's mutual dialectical interpenetration expressly because of the wider, dialogical field of land rights that enables both Indians and whites to generate the power of their identity *without* the other. On the "frontier" there seems to be a place, the West, to escape dialectical history and mutuality. The bodies of Indians and cowboys appear to remain separate. On the plantation, however, there is no such room to roam. The bodies of slaves and masters become a contested family. The Indian's *land* is the currency of Indian-white relations, whereas the slave's *labor* is the currency of master-slave relations. Thus the power is external in the former and internal in the latter. Of course, black bodies are tied by sweat and blood and generations to the land. And of course, Indian bodies are internal to and interpenetrate the land: "My land is where my people lie buried." Indians in American ideology always—and precipitously in the moment of this joke—threaten to reverse manifest destiny and retain their aboriginal power of connection to the land.

Aboriginal land rights thus remain the literal and legal ground not only of Indian humor but of the sovereign power of Native nations. Cross-racial friendship among whites and Indians then requires, as the Tonto joke ironically points out by its absence, a respect on the part of whites for Indian land rights, politically and legally in the form of tribal sovereignty. Prior to Tonto's betrayal came the Lone Ranger's betrayal of such respect for Indian land, a classic cowboy's self-identifying disrespect for Indian rights and values. If the Lone Ranger is the ultimate cowboy, he needs Tonto's land in order to become his own invented, immigrant identity, but Tonto does not need him.

Thus that larger dialogic field of the land itself distinguishes Indian-white relations from master-slave dynamics, and ultimately the reaffirmation of Tonto's originary linkage to the land animates his betrayal of the Lone Ranger. Tonto's betrayal is not first a betrayal of friendship; instead it is a denial of the Lone Ranger's first betrayal and disrespect of Tonto's land rights—Tonto's Indigenous identity. The exposure of disrespect and betrayal as the substratum of their friendship is too true. Thus the joke. Thus the laughter. Tonto names a colonizing disrespect that betrayed their friendship from the start. The laughter of surprise erupts in the discovery that quiet Tonto knows all of this and is willing to speak truth to power. He invokes the biggest joke on history: mutual respect. Thus the surprise. When Tonto rejects a colonized "we," he prompts a recognition of tribal sovereignty, of who "we" all are in relation to land rights in America.

Thus an Indigenous sense of humor, working through such ironic reversals, generates rhetorical and historical force by reimagining the "inevitable," even denying the "plight of the Indian." Through humor's generic strategies of surprise, boundary breaking, and iconoclasm, Native joking reflects social strategies of resistance and reappropriation. It manifests simply in "We laugh to survive," or it marks the deep cultural difference in the white man's image of a stoic, dehumanized wooden Indian as an ignorant and wishful projection of a Euro-American psyche, or it articulates the complex politico-literary theory of Vizenor's "trickster discourse" that would elude and deconstruct those "terminal creeds" of the vanishing Indian. The great leveler, humor invokes life and death, beginning and end, the equality of mortality. Humor is antihierarchical because humorless formality is built by power relations to maintain hierarchies.

Through word play, irony, satire, farce, burlesque, absurdity, or scatology, an Indian sense of humor further opens doors for cultural exchange that undercut the paradigm of dominance. It is worth emphasizing how many of the Native writers we look at play on the biggest utopian joke of all: in the long run, Indians may prevail. As Silko suggests in her novel *Almanac of the Dead*, all things European will "disappear" as Indigenous reality slowly erodes European projections to the painful point where America may discover itself. In the opening critical salvo on Indian humor in his 1969 classic, *Custer Died for Your Sins*, Vine Deloria Jr. lays out the stakes: "Humor, all Indians will agree, is the cement by which the coming Indian movement is held together. When a people can laugh at themselves and laugh at others and hold all aspects of life together without letting anybody drive them to extremes, then it seems to me that that people can survive" (168). Survival succeeds "when a people can laugh at themselves." The Tonto joke tries to get Americans to laugh at themselves, reflected in the Lone Ranger. He's doomed, but if we can laugh at ourselves, America might survive to become America. Reversals in the joke gesture to the absurd possibility of a different story, a story of surviving.

Outrageous or not, absurd or sensible, Native American ironists point implicitly and explicitly to a community of radical pluralism in America. They navigate issues of a different authenticity, a different identity, and a different community in ways that America still is barely able to conceive, precisely because America can barely imagine the tribal sovereignty underlying those differences.

Native artists of diverse mediums play on this ignorance. The renowned contemporary artist George Longfish (Haudenosaunee), for instance, aimed at this big target during a recent showing of his work at the Montana Museum of Art and Culture:

> One of his works of art depicts a photo of Longfish standing below Chicago skyscrapers. The black-and-white image is imprinted with stacked red-lettered words that read: "Tribal. Seneca. Warrior. Artist. Healer."

The image is meant to remind people that Natives are very much a part of contemporary culture. Too often, he said, people look at an Indian and fall into a stereotypical greeting. They want to call him "chief," he said. "It's hard for them to say hello to you in the present time. It's like the only way they can connect to you is to go into the past."

They grapple with reality: "You survived?"[17]

Standard American history makes Indian survival—and therefore contemporary Indians—invisible. As Longfish explains, "It's hard for them to say hello to you in the present time."

Thus average Indians simply know more about history than do average Americans raised on the same history textbooks. Native Americans know the distinction between the receiving end of history and the myth, promulgated by that history, that their history must come to an end. Because they know they have not vanished, they can make fun of Americans still living in that fog of vanishment. This ironic setup is the foundation of a comic epistemology that is by definition more valuable to Indians than any overblown rumors of their tragic demise. It is invaluable to the rest of America as well, if it means clarity on the historical present. Euro-America's tragic, heroic, and genocidal imagination wants to wreak fulfillment of its own apocalyptic dreams. Native stories and Native storytellers keep trying to rescue themselves and America from that tragic tale.

If the heart of humor is a metaphorical leap of imagination, then surprise, reversal, and laughter rise out of the gaps that humor leaps across. Native humorists make that leap to outpace imperial nostalgia and historical tragedy. Further, humor makes the leap for its own sake, not merely out of repugnance or to escape from the closure of tragedy, but in affirmation of its own expansive energies. Certainly Native humor is often self-effacement in the face of suffering, toward a kind of Keatsian negative capability that can imagine itself into other lives and possibilities, other histories. Even though this desperate feature of humor may function frequently, the comic does not factor down to the serious. Aristotle remains current: cathartic resolution of tragedy is not the purpose of comedy, but it is the de facto purpose of tragedy. (Alexie has much to say about jettisoning "resolution.") Comedy has other purposes, less self-preserving ones. Comedy makes light of working hard to make a different world, an alternative, a bigger picture than the bloody stage. Tragedy slays the actors for the audience's benefit, denying the past in favor of a better future, selecting and excluding along the measured timeline of history. Comedy embraces the past, the present, the future, the actors, and the audience, adapting all to an infinite mutual potential. The point of Native comedy is to make sure that tragedy is not the normative measure. Again, Vizenor's trickster discourse rewrites the "terminal creeds" that finish off America's tragedy of the Indian. This assurance is crucial for Native survivance, because comedy means survival.

Finally, this process itself of juxtaposing and separating comedy from tragedy is parallel to the process of juxtaposing the Indigenous "other" to the colonists' normative dominant "self" precisely because the juxtaposition insists that the Indigenous is just as much a "self" as the colonist is an "other." Comedy may stand separate from and equal to tragedy, just as the colonized may stand separate from and equal to the colonizer—and it is so often through comedy that the colonized make this claim.

In this context of the comedy of survival, let's look first at Alexie's recharged comic mode, then at Apess's slashing ironies, Winnemucca's bemused jokes on frontier soldiers, McNickle's somber novels, and Silko's reversals of Euro-American arrogance.

Irony and Agency: Humor in Alexie

As we have seen in the broader discussion of Indigenous humor, the paramount example of these energetic claims of humor is the voice of the Spokane Indian writer Sherman Alexie. In a 1995 interview, Alexie quipped that he was "the Indian *du jour*," and he certainly holds that dubious title nearly two decades later. Indeed he most radically and pointedly confronts non-Indian audiences with the ongoing presence of Indian Americans, an artistic assault on American national identity. If Alexie claims, "I'm just as much a product of *The Brady Bunch* as I am of my grandmother" (qtd. in Keillor, *Writer's Almanac*), then an Indian raised on TV is not a vanishing Indian—or is he? It's a river of questions about authenticity, identity, community, and ultimately sovereignty, as humor plunges us into that stream.

Alexie's is a populist voice, uniquely situated for both modern tribal changes and ancient tribal sovereignty. That paradoxical duality is another source of his irony. As Garrison Keillor intimated, the fact that Alexie and his Indian characters eat the same breakfast cereal as everyone else plays havoc with American identity via the comic mode in general, and via Indian humor in particular, as it twists the ironies of American history.

Unlike many Indigenous writers, Alexie rarely points toward the redemptive power of Native community as a direction for his protagonists' struggles, though he keeps the question alive. The neocolonial politics and internalized oppression of reservation life seem to have made him wary of such hope, and, further, he is strategic in representing what Cox refers to as "the difficulties of contemporary reservation life" (*Muting White Noise* 146). Instead his bold, sometimes campy style tends to affirm a more individual agency unique to Native identities, by a distinct artistic pattern of personal affirmation and reconnection. One reviewer marks an ironic balance, claiming that Alexie's "dry sincerity leavens the sentiment" of his Indian tales.[18] He is sincere, though always ironic, in his social critique of historical legacies. For all his humor, indeed in the heart of his humor, Alexie circulates the grave themes of ongoing colonial history and its personal effects in Indian Country. As 118-year-old Etta explains in Alexie's short story "Dear John Wayne," "Having fun is very serious" (*The Toughest Indian*, 193).

There is something startling about Sherman Alexie. It's like the difference between modernists recovering the myth and postmodernists abandoning the myth of meaning. His style tends toward the latter, the iconoclastic. Commandingly postindian, he rages against even the need for an (old) order, if that former pattern is the oppression and repression of Indians. Like Emerson naming "the Poet" of America into being, and then like Whitman stepping into that role, Vizenor named America's postindian, and Alexie stepped up. Where the white man's Indian is rural, Alexie is urban. Instead of spiritual, he's skeptical. Instead of cultural, he's political. Instead of stoic, he's humorous. Instead of past, he's present, though of course none of these binaries represents the real complexity that is the point. I'd suggest that Alexie marks a profound moment for American letters, on the order of initiating a new American discourse for the next millennium. He seems to be more intent on "reinventing the enemy's language," to use Harjo and Bird's title, than on recovering an Indian past. As the Transcendentalists offered the sum of two thousand years of neo-Platonic cosmology ("I am a transparent eyeball"), America's postindians open a key set of notions for the next era ("Poetry = Anger x Imagination"). What links American Transcendentalists and Native American voices across the millennial divide is the persistence of pragmatism, here a kind of practical pluralism that authorizes itself to act in a field of possibilities. Thus authenticity claims its identity as part of a multivalent community in the sovereign name of freedom. Thus Alexie can laugh.

Part of the profound attraction of Alexie as a successful writer of celebrity status (among most of his non-Indian readers and among many, but not all, of his Indian readers) is his exercise of the etymological linkage between comedy and the commons. He appeals to community in the mode of a global-village bard. The *Oxford English Dictionary* neatly factors *comedy* into Greek roots denoting "village singer," through the roots of "revel, merry-making" in its homonymal source "village," plus "singer" (a. F. *comédie* (14th c. in Littré), ad. L. *comoedia*, a. Gr. *komedia*, n. of practice f. *komedos* comedian; a compound, either of *komos* revel, merry-making, or of its probable source, *komé* village + *aidos* singer, minstrel, f. *aidein* to sing (cf. ODE). The *komedos* was thus originally either the bard of the revels or the village bard. Thus Alexie, moving with eloquent and ironic facility between Indigenous and post-postmodern expression, seems to welcome readers into a world of celebratory connections underneath the historical tragedies. The cross-cultural commons becomes comic.

Further, by identifying Indians with everyday objects of modern American pop culture like electric guitars, skyscrapers, and television, Alexie normalizes Indian lives. That simple literary strategy is a radical act. As Keillor put it on public radio's *The Writer's Almanac* of Alexie's collection *The Lone Ranger and Tonto Fistfight in Heaven*, "It was one of the first works of fiction to portray Indians as Americans who watch all the same TV programs as everybody else and eat the same breakfast cereal." Keillor's combination is subtly significant. The spectrum of human experience that spans TV programs and breakfast cereal embraces the ranks of modern, persistently hierarchical binaries: art and life, mind and body, culture and nature, civilization and wilderness, whites and Indians. Alexie's radical embrace of these oppositions is evidently the reason Keillor made such a point on his nationally syndicated radio daily. Alexie humorously reworks the foundational history of modern America.

The danger in normalization, of course, is homogenization. If Alexie depicts American Indian lives as concerned with the same mainstream issues as *The Brady Bunch*, doesn't that strategy remarginalize real Indigenous issues, especially tribal sovereignty? Co-optation remains a risk, and it certainly echoes the problems of multiculturalism confronting any group or individual that claims both recognition and difference in America's so-called melting pot. Our discussions of dialogics address such dangers, but those difficulties will persist as long as the founding dialectics continue to play out in American history. Alexie's work must negotiate those historical crevasses, so let's look more closely at how he expresses the political in the personal postindian. Indeed as the leading voice of the second generation of the Native American literary revival begun in the 1960s,[19] Alexie's persona as a punk trickster provides this study with its final turn.

In a separate piece (Moore, "Sherman Alexie"), I analyzed a recurring pattern in Alexie's pained portraits of Indian individuals, a pattern that links agency or limited power to dramatic intimacy, ever saturated in irony. It is a practice in his work that will help here to clarify the humane dynamics of humor. By imbuing often sexual bodies with a vitalizing sense of humor and the friction of irony, Alexie affirms a sense of subjective will and humanity in his Native characters that helps set them free in their colonial contexts.

This dynamic pattern fits one of Alexie's aesthetic proclamations that we touched on earlier. In *Old Shirts and New Skins*, a peripatetic character, Lester FallsApart, pronounces the crucial equation: "Poetry = Anger x Imagination" (xi). It is a complex idea woven through Alexie's texts, repeated in some of his other works, for instance in the multigenre piece "The Unauthorized Autobiography of Me," published seven years later in *One Stick Song*. Each of the factors in the equation affirms an ability to *do something*, to act, a calculus of creative strength suitably blurred and ironized by Lester's last name. Alexie offers here an axiom linking aesthetics to ethics, evidently a dynamic of his own on the order of $E = mc^2$ linking energy to matter, connecting art to life.

Thus Poetry in the formula, or storytelling for Alexie's characters, resonates with creative expression as power, a fulfillment of will, a proficiency in surviving, an assertion of agency. As one of his most entrapped characters broods in "The Sin Eaters," "With my voice, I suddenly believed, I could explode the walls of that room and escape" (*Toughest* 112). Anger as a positive force for Alexie resonates with passion, authenticity, and the bodily intimacy of sweat and contact. Anger intimately affirms subjective freedom, though Alexie frequently ironizes anger with poignancy by gesturing to oppressive limits: "I pull out my wallet and give them a buck each. I don't feel generous or guilty, just half-empty and all lonely in this city which would kill me as slowly as it is killing these three cousins of mine" ("Freaks," in *First Indian On the Moon* 49). "So much has been taken from us that we hold onto the smallest things left with all the strength that we have" ("Unauthorized . . ." in *One Stick Song* 13). Authentic emotions of anger, desire, fear, grief, whether gentle or violent, open an intimate door. Imagination resonates in Alexie's formula with the ability to leap mentally across paradoxes and traps of existence, the pathos of American history. Comedy is an imaginative strategy that both transcends and deconstructs, and thus survives, pain. The liberating value of imagination is amplified by its absence in a brutal opposite, as a character says of his own warrior nature in the short story "Saint Junior": "When you resort to violence to prove a point, you've just experienced a profound failure of imagination" (*Toughest* 175; echoing Martin Luther King Jr.).

This spiraling pattern of intimacy, irony, and agency can be sexual or political, personal or public in Alexie's work. Language plus the body equals purpose; that is, when the body communicates, when it achieves expression across the intimate borders of bodily difference, then it spirals out of the vortex of both existential and political alienation. His comedy sparks the surprise of reconnections, and his irony refocuses connections by their lack. The affirmation is tough, facing harsh realities, but it is ultimately enlivening and empowering. As he maps the intimate psychological and social violence of Indian-white relations, he not only humanizes that history of grief, but he minimizes it by showing how humor can survive even death. The narration of "Saint Junior" says of six "ghosts" of the Cold Spring Singers drum group, "They understood what it meant to be Indian and dead and alive and still bright with faith and hope" (*Toughest* 153). As Alexie explains in an interview, "These aren't happy stories necessarily. But I think they are positive stories" (Spencer, "What It Means to Be Sherman Alexie" 36).

In this affirmative mode, and similar to the compassionate irony of Simon Ortiz and Vizenor in the previous generation, Alexie displays a certain powerful, ironic compassion in his novel *Reservation Blues*. He imagines the Indian medicine woman Big Mom mystically shaping contemporary American culture through pop music:

There were stories about Big Mom that stretched back more than a hundred years. . . . Indians all over the country would play a scratched record of Elvis, Diana Ross, Chuck Berry, and strain to hear the name *Big Mom* hidden in the mix. . . . Big Mom was a musical genius. She was the teacher of all those great musicians who shaped the twentieth century. There were photographs, they said, of Les Paul leaving Big Mom's house with the original blueprint for the electric guitar. There were home movies, they said, of Big Mom choreographing the Andrews Sisters' latest dance steps. There were even cheap recordings, they said, of Big Mom teaching Paul McCartney how to sing "Yesterday." . . . Musicians from all over the world traveled to Big Mom's house in the hope she would teach them how to play. Like any good teacher, Big Mom was very selective with her students. (200–201)

Alexie's absurdities here reflect the seriousness of the allegory: colonialism works both ways. American Indian influences on America and the modern world are real. American Indians, like everyone else, exist in a global history of exchange, not in some separate prelapsarian or satanic enclave of colonial dreams or nightmares, to be neither idealized nor feared. Native ironists envision utopian circumstances, both mythological and historical, in which Euro-Americans are transformed by Native cultures in narratives of exchange rather than domination.

Another one of many cross-cultural spoofs in *Reservation Blues* is particularly illustrative of Alexie's reversals of mainstream hierarchies. The running joke in the novel, an ironic and humorous leitmotif, is the question repeatedly posed to the reservation Indian rock band by audiences and the news media: "Who's the lead singer?" Because the band operates democratically, by informal, mutual understanding, the question turns on itself, unanswered, to point toward a common sense of teamwork in the band, a sense of community or group identity, even among all the competition and contention. The ironic reversal of group versus individual identity is silent but effective. Further, we laugh at the latent historical critique in the humor because whites in the novel want a leader, just as they desire the noble savage to stand and be recognized. He makes a better target that way, and we have seen that Alexie prefers to remain a moving target.

Alexie's conscious aesthetic connection between irony and agency provides a lens into his humorous approach to the other four terms of this study. Indeed the incisive humor and resulting sense of humanity that animates his work becomes his focus without polemical positions on sovereignty, identity, community, or authenticity. His publications speak to these core issues, as ironic imagination strikes poetry into politics.

"Heigh-ho!" Humor in Apess

Apess's fundamentally ironic stance places him near the source of a long tradition of Indian humor. While his exhortations stand on the earnest self-assertion of humanity, his eloquence in *Nullification*, for instance, frequently breaks into his default tone of irony that flips the social hierarchy on its head, contrasting white inhumanity with Native vulnerability, and Native vulner-ability with their claim to equality. As Maureen Konkle explains, "Apess's deployment of irony is a means of calling attention to the discrepancy between white knowledge [structures of racist hierarchy] and Native expe-rience, and it dramatizes the frustration of being in an absurd position on a daily basis, mocks the discrepancy between what's known about him and how he and other Native peoples perceive themselves" (*Writing Indian Nations* 106). Fundamentally they perceive themselves as autonomous human beings with political interests.

Thus irony becomes another argument for sovereignty. The contrast of Indigenous against white racist perceptions ultimately highlights Native qualities that emerge as sovereignty. Several examples of Apess's rhetorical reversals to highlight sovereignty have emerged in our discussions thus far. Here he waxes ironic through hyperbole at the reactionary hubbub over the Mashpees' claim of rights, especially at the governor's hysterical effort to consider rallying a posse comitatus in response to their nonviolent actions to reclaim their woodlot:

This letter [of the governor's concerns] was read to the [Mashpee] peo-ple, and was to them as a provocation and a stimulus. They thought it grievous that the governor should think they had put him in mind of his oath of office, to secure the Commonwealth from danger, and given him cause to call out perhaps fifty or sixty thousand militia; especially when the great strength and power of the Marshpee tribe was considered. To this supposed great demonstration of military power they might, possibly, have opposed a hundred fighting men and fifteen or twenty rusty guns. But it is written, "One shall chase a thousand, and two shall put ten thousand to flight"; so there might have been some reason for persons who believe the Bible to fear us. Who can say that little Marshpee might not have discomforted great Massachusetts? Nevertheless, the birthplace of American freedom was spared so great a disgrace; for the governor, very wisely, remained at home. (*On Our Own Ground* 183)

Irony in the humorous mode—and certain laughter among his supporters—both melts and forges the polarities of Apess's joke, as "the great strength and power of the Marshpee tribe" becomes also "that little Marshpee." This passage of mocking mastery twists many loose threads of logic in the half-woven minds of his oppressors. For "persons who believe in the Bible to fear us"—but who are in the biblical role of the oppressive unbelievers—they would have to recognize that the Mashpee are the "one" and "two" favored by God over a "thousand" or "ten thousand" of His enemies, who must be the citizens who would side with the governor against the Mashpee. Ridicule shreds sanctimonious power.

Instead of ad hominem attacks on individuals, derision in Apess focuses primarily on institutions and social systems that enforce the second-class status of Indians. This rhetorical strategy is notable as another indication that his focus is tribal sovereignty, not self-promotion or individual status. For example, describing a Mashpee gathering in the meetinghouse, Apess parenthetically exploits the no-man's-land between Mashpees as Americans and as noncitizens:

Toward the close of the day Mr. Fiske desired the Hon. Mr. Reed to explain to the Indians the laws, as they then stood, and the consequences of violating them. He told us that merely declaring a law to be oppressive could not abrogate it; and that it would become us, as good citizens whom the government was disposed to treat well, to wait for the session of the Legislature and then apply for relief. (Surely it was either insult or wrong to call the Marshpees citizens, for such they never were, from the Declaration of Independence up to the session of the Legislature in 1834.) (*On Our Own Ground* 183)

Apess flags the white shame of Mashpee disenfranchisement to contrast the Indians' status against American ideals through the nation's first five decades. Yet he still calls for relief through legislative action. Thus he accepts, we might say comically lives with or adapts to, the ironic positioning of Indians in a society that encourages them to act as "good citizens" while depriving them of citizenship.

In *Nullification*, a treatise triggered by the irony of a "pretended riot explained," there is another lively example of Apess's ironic sense of humor relevant here. After carefully calculating the economic contributions of the Mashpee to the Commonwealth of Massachusetts over more than a century, he proposes that the Commonwealth repay the interest, if not the principal of $56,000, on the annual $400 paid to indifferent missionaries who resided among but never served the Mashpee people over 140 years. Those monies were intended for the Mashpee. An initiating irony structures the statement of his pecuniary concern because he knows full well that such monies will never be paid back. Yet almost giddy with the incontrovertible logic of irony, he turns the screws and pushes it further still: "Thus, though it is manifest that we have cost the government absolutely much less than nothing, we have been called state paupers, and as such treated. Those are strange paupers who maintain themselves, and pay large sums to others into the bargain. Heigh-ho! It is a fine thing to be an Indian. One might almost as well be a slave" (*On Our Own Ground* 188). In an antebellum Massachusetts that prides itself on not being a slave state, Apess's suggestion that the Commonwealth enslaves its Indigenous population exposes the charade of liberty and good citizenship. Yet even here he chooses ironic laughter over grim recrimination: "Heigh-ho!"

Before we leave his examples, we must refer again to Apess's intimations of sexual inadequacy, where he identifies racial prejudice with sexual inadequacy. Apess points directly to an erotic interest beneath racism, as when he criticizes a Massachusetts law against miscegenation between whites and Indians: "I do not wonder that you blush, many of you, while you read; for many have broken the ill-fated laws made by man to hedge up the laws of God and nature. I would ask if they who have made the law have not broken it" ("Looking-Glass" in *On Our Own Ground* 159–60). This level of irony overturns power and powerlessness, undermining political power in the public sphere by exposing its personal vulnerability in desire in the private sphere. Rhetorically he designs this disrobing of power for laughter.

We have seen how Apess calls on his readers to manage such ironic contradictions by the earnest appeal to a wider sense of humanity as common creatures of one God. Thus in what at first may seem contradictory in his thinking, the ironic principle of shared humanity becomes a principle of sovereignty. Applying to Native rights both an Enlightenment ethos of universal rights and an antebellum discourse of Christian transcendentalism for which he was a preeminent orator, Apess affirms recognition of the humanity in another as the recognition of inherent sovereignty. He does so by describing each as a child of the Lord, "that God who is the maker and preserver both of the white man and the Indian" ("Looking-Glass" in *On Our Own Ground* 155). Such individual sovereignty translates into social rights. The irony of humane social values translates into material political values.

Apess's 1836 oration, "An Indian's Looking-Glass for the White Man," as we have seen, drives home the ironies. He invokes the biblical God as a universal creator Who would bless both Indians and whites, if the whites would let Him and if they would listen to an Indian voice instruct them in the ways of brotherhood: "I will refer you to St. Peter's precepts (Acts 10): 'God is no respecter of persons,' etc. Now if this is the case, my white brother, what better are you than God? . . . Let me ask why the men of a different skin are so despised. Why are not they educated and placed in your pulpits?" (*On Our Own Ground* 159). As we have seen, he concludes his remarks with a utopian vision of American pluralism: "The Lord will reward you, and pray you stop not till this tree of distinction shall be leveled to the earth, and the mantle of prejudice torn from every American heart—then shall peace pervade the union" (160–61). Apess could conceive of one nation under God that not only included Indians but that learned its deepest lessons of Christian charity and forbearance from its Indian citizens and former enemies. Leveling divine irony on their hypocrisy, he insists on the fundamental Christian tenet, that they love their enemies as themselves, a founding principle of pluralism.

"Merrymaking": Humor in Winnemucca

With an earnestness more saturated with pathos than the unyielding ironies of Apess, Winnemucca's account of her "life among the Piutes" expresses very little direct humor beyond the fundamental ironies of the frontier.

Instead she generally takes the rhetorical position of ethnographically describing her people's humor and "merrymaking" in ironic juxtaposition to "their wrongs and claims." However, she does offer a few moments of levity in her text.

We saw in the discussion of authenticity how Winnemucca, echoing Apess, rhetorically structured her appeal to her white audiences and readers: Indian *solidarity* and *irony* calling on *pity* in an outraged appeal to universal *humanity*. Again, each of these terms overlaps the others. Further, they reflect aspects of our five key terms, as humanity becomes linked to authenticity and identity, solidarity to community, and so on. Winnemucca's reciprocal rhetorical strategy speaks to central concerns of national identity in Native nations and in the American populations whom she addressed.

A paradigmatic example of her ironic juxtaposition between "merrymaking" and "wars and their causes" arises early in her account: "Just about noon, while we were on the way, a great many of our men came to meet us, all on their horses. Oh, what a beautiful song they sang for my father as they came near us" (*Life Among the Piutes* 13). She is describing a springtime scene from her very young childhood, probably 1847, when Old Winnemucca was gathering the people in the mountains for protection, "for there would be a great emigration that summer" of settlers from the East. Winnemucca recalls this moment both literally and metaphorically as "the end of our merrymaking" (14). First there were five days of festivities, celebrating community culture: "Oh, how happy everybody was! One could hear laughter everywhere, and songs were sung by happy women and children" as the people danced at night, hunted, fished, played football games, and "ran races on foot and on horses." Then Old Winnemucca lowered the boom of both myth and history, introducing his painful dream to his people: "My father got up very early one morning, and told his people the time had come,—that we could no longer be happy as of old, as the white people we called our brothers had brought a great trouble and sorrow among us already" (14). The idyll is invaded. A prelapsarian nostalgia aches through the ensuing history. If the serpent in the Garden of Eden is an ironic presence, the white man in Paiute Country is Winnemucca's fundamental irony as well.

Yet *Life Among the Piutes: Their Wrongs and Claims* is not entirely without humor. Of course, it surfaces at the expense of whites. For example, when the captain of the volunteer scouts warns General Howard, for whom Winnemucca is working as interpreter, of an ambush from "a high hill" ahead, she writes that she and her sister "knew what it was but we did not say anything for we wanted to see what they would do." The fleeing Indians whom the scouts are trailing had set on a hilltop a decoy of rocks stacked to look like warriors standing to fight. Previously she had been contradicting the misinformation of the scouts, accusing them in fact of telling lies to Howard. When she says, "I will show you that there are no Indians there" and the general sends the troops up, "They found everything just as I had told them. How they did laugh that evening when we camped for the night. It is a way by which we Indians do deceive the white people by piling rocks on each other and putting round ones on the top to make them look like men. In this way we get time to get away from our enemy" (171). While her pronouns here place her within an Indian role—"we Indians," "we get time to get away"—her reference to the American troops with whom she is working and traveling as "our enemy" is loaded with ironies and ambiguities. The laughter here clearly defuses her difficult position. It does so on many levels, including the larger appeal to her white audiences who may see more clearly her humanity in her humor.

"The Room Exploded with Laughter": Humor in McNickle

Examples from *Wind from an Enemy Sky* will suffice to convey McNickle's sense of humor. Few novels are more serious, but these passages offer more than comic relief. They do all the complex work of revising historical misrepresentations and specifying tribal lives. And they are funny. Early on, when the tribal elders are discussing what to do about the immense wrong of the white men's dam on their mountain river, Old Louis, known for his "bitter mouth," expresses his disgust and distrust of the BIA agent through dismissive humor. The force of his statement stands in narrative contrast to the earlier impotence of Bull's futile rifle shot at the massive concrete wall of the dam. Old Louis sneers at the prospect of more talk with the agent: "For my part, I won't have anything to do with men who despise my blood. If we have to go to this man and ask his help, we might as well relieve ourselves in the bushes and walk away" (23). Like Coyote consulting and then disregarding the advice of his own turds, the reductive becomes the honest story. The scatological becomes eschatological. The bitterness of Old Louis, sprinkled throughout the novel, gains further dimensionality of character toward the end, when the reader discovers the sorrow that he carries as the victim of oppressive brutality. His wry humor twists against violence.

As the novel progresses in its inexorable logic of tragedy, McNickle does employ a small dose of farcical comic relief. Yet again this glimpse of human foibles does more thematic work by personalizing and humanizing the resistant politics of Bull's camp in the mountains. At the expense of the women, who indeed play a background role to the male protagonists in this novel, we see big Marie Louise trying to get on a horse: "The horse snorted, then reared. But instead of leaping ahead, it merely sat on its haunches. Marie Louise rolled to the ground, a bundle of skirts. Relieved of that burden, the beast reared again, then vaulted high into the air, came down on stiff legs and was off" (*Wind* 99). We have seen how horses function with realistic detail in McNickle to animate the world and the characters themselves. Here a spirited horse masters one of the leading women of the camp, and the scene both vivifies and amplifies the plot. The pratfall sets up the characters Bull and Henry Jim, with their serious work, as more vertical and dramatic in contrast.

Serious moments are infused with humor as well. At one of the most dramatic expressions of self-sacrifice in *Wind from an Enemy Sky*, when old Two Sleeps offers to take the rap for the younger Pock Face's murder of the white man at the dam, McNickle humanizes the old man's nobility by a timely insertion of humor through humility, a certain self-tease. As Two Sleeps offers his own aged life in substitute for the impulsive, young—and guilty— Pock Face, he relieves his stunned kinsmen of their astonishment by another extraordinary sacrifice. He gives up his own serious pitifulness by getting them to laugh at him as he offers to sacrifice himself to white law enforcement: "When he said, 'Even if they decide to cut off the things that make a man, mine are all dried up anyhow and no use to me,' the room exploded with laughter. They all looked at the old man" (92). Under the laughter, they look at him in quiet awe. Mastering the moment of expression, McNickle lets Two Sleeps's humorous self-mockery eclipse the heroic stature of his own selflessness.

Such reversing layers of irony are woven into a kind of catechism of humor that McNickle depicts as the curriculum for the next generation who must survive these desperate times. Before the tragic climax of the novel, just after a portentous scene in which young Antoine is all but crowned the heir apparent to his grandfather Bull's leadership role, he endures teasing by old Iron Child, whose "powerful voice could always be heard above all others when people sat in council, but when he wanted to tease, his voice became a song full of laughter": "Our grandson will remember this day. When we are gone and he is the leader of our people, he can tell his children that he put the sun back where it belongs and made the stars come out at night. . . . Our grandson will thank everybody and then he will go home and his wife will scold him for believing everything people tell him. You be careful, grandson. Pick a wife who doesn't talk too much" (*Wind* 240). The twisting ironic reversals are elegant: the boy is honored, but he should not take himself too seriously, and his future wife should bring him down to size, but he should protect himself from the pitiful truth by finding a wife who is not so forward. Again the humor flows partly at the expense of the women, except that they are shown to be the ones to bring the men into realistic perspective, down to their real stature as pitiful humans.

This reductive function of humor echoes Ray A. Young Bear's "philosophy of insignificance." Such complex characterizations and thematic twists in humor are able to move McNickle's narratives far beyond the "stoic Indian" stereotype. The racial exclusions built into that stereotype erode in the flow of historical and cultural complexity, in the plurality of humanity.

"Fierce Wit": Humor in Silko

To read the wide-ranging, earnest, mythopoetic, even prophetic writings of Leslie Marmon Silko in search of humor is to enter further into a redefinition of the term. Silko's political urgency pushes her prose and poetry against the heaviness of history, so that any lightness of humor can often feel remote. Her driving conviction, instilled in her from childhood by the matriarchs of her family, that "these United States were founded on stolen land" (*Yellow Woman* 81) grows out of her prior certainty that "the People and the Land ARE Inseparable" (85–91). History is inseparable from the story Silko tells, and history is not humorous. She herself is a keeper of the almanac. An embodied sense of injustice permeates her words, as it suffuses the work of each Indian writer in this study. An irony in injustice, a daily reality of ethical and legal imbalance across the weave of time and space, fires her expression. At times it glows warm, as in the characters of Betonie in *Cer-*

emony, Calabazas in *Almanac*, and Indigo in *Gardens*; most times it burns fiercely hot across her narratives.

I will borrow her own nonfiction term for her Auntie Kie's "fierce wit" to describe the tenor of humor in Silko. She learned her lessons well. Conveniently for this analysis of humor, Silko wields that descriptive phrase as she introduces an actual joke in her essay "Auntie Kie Talks about U.S. Presidents and U.S. Indian Policy," set during the first Reagan administration, just prior to his reelection. Here's the punning family gag, plus context, as Silko weaves it into the characterization:

> Although she is in her late sixties, Auntie Kie has lost none of her fierce wit. She is always ready to "air her views," as she so delicately puts it. (One of my cousins says what really gets aired are her opponents' views—Auntie Kie shoots them full of holes.) I tell her I have a magazine article to write: what another four years of Ronald Reagan will mean to Native American Indians.
>
> "Oh, *that's* a good one!" Auntie Kie says, laughing so much she nearly spills the soda. But she gets a serious expression on her face, and she says, "That question is different for us Indians than it is for other Americans. It's complicated." I nod my head. That's why I've come to get her answer. (*Yellow Woman* 81)

Silko's writing echoes her aunt's answer in medium as well as message. Not only does she herself, like her aunt, shoot her opponents, the world's "destroyers," full of holes with her alternative histories, and not only does she find moments of levity in the ironic mode along the way, but in her work Silko consistently returns to "a serious expression," precisely as she illustrates how "that question is different for us Indians." It is Auntie Kie who asserts that there is no legal basis for the United States of America, founded as it is on "stolen land." That originary irony permeates Silko's oeuvre. Until the United States faces that "complicated" shadow in its own constitution, "another four years" of any governmental administration will be yet another joke: "*That's* a good one."

Silko's irony can function as an assumption of agency, as it indicates critical insight and thus authorizes a position at least theoretically outside the system of domination. For the finale of her 1994 essay, "Border Patrol State," she sums up her critique of the "murderous" and racist policies of the Immigration and Naturalization Service against dehumanized "illegal aliens" with this layered ironic vision:

> One evening at sundown, we were stopped in traffic at a railroad cross-
> ing in downtown Tucson while a freight train passed us, slowly gaining
> speed as it headed north to Phoenix. In the twilight I saw the most
> amazing sight: dozens of human beings, mostly young men, were rid-
> ing the train; everywhere, on flatcars, inside open boxcars, perched on
> top of boxcars, hanging off ladders on tank cars and between boxcars.
> I couldn't count fast enough, but I saw 50 or 60 people headed north.
> They were dark young men, Indian and mestizo; they were smiling and
> a few of them waved at us in our cars. I was reminded of the ancient
> story of Aztlán, told by the Aztecs but known in other Uto-Aztecan
> communities as well. Aztlán is the beautiful land to the north, the ori-
> gin place of the Aztec people. I don't remember how or why the people
> left Aztlán to journey farther south, but the old story says that one day,
> they will return. (*Yellow Woman* 123)

The passage finishes a brief nightmare of fascist domination, steel border fences, and full-body searches by the U.S. Border Patrol with poignancy: "They were smiling." The classic Native American out-group joke on Amer-ica—that "the vanishing Indian" has not and never will vanish—turns from the brutal past and present toward a quietly promising future. The good humor of "dozens of human beings" appears through the twilight of centu-ries of oppression.

As Silko describes the irresistible current of mostly "dark young men, Indian and mestizo; they were smiling and a few of them waved at us in our cars," she affirms the comic mode of mutual survival, as ordinary as any bal-anced ecosystem. Earlier in the essay she affirms this natural law: "The great human migration within the Americas cannot be stopped; human beings are natural forces of the earth, just as rivers and winds are natural forces" (*Yellow Woman* 123). The mythic forces that she invokes throughout her work are indeed these "natural forces" that "cannot be stopped," and, further, these natural forces are cultural, "the great human migration," as well.

On the basis of that epistemological erasure of a nature-culture divide, Silko then rewrites history as the essay continues. At the start of this chap-ter, we read her clear statement: "Deep down the issue is simple: the so-called Indian Wars from the days of Sitting Bull and Red Cloud have never really ended in the Americas." Here she explains further: "The Indian people of southern Mexico, of Guatemala, and those left in El Salvador, too, are still fighting for their lives and for their land against the cavalry patrols sent out by the governments of those lands. The Americas are Indian Country, and the 'Indian problem' is not about to go away" (*Yellow Woman* 123). The "natural forces of the earth" suggest that in Silko's cosmogony "the so-called Indian Wars" and the "Indian problem" will come to balance through strength grown from the land. If Silko is rarely funny, her vision is ultimately as good-humored as those young men waving from the boxcars, playing out the ultimate ironies of history.

In her grim novel *Almanac of the Dead*, Silko, like McNickle, offers some genuine comic relief. Deep in the narrative weave of international trafficking in drugs, guns, and body parts, as some—not all—of the Indigenous characters hold on to their connections with the land and its values, she concocts a joke on the whites in a revisionist history of Geronimo. Old Pancakes, one of three or four old men playing the trick on the whites, manipulated the vision of white onlookers to reflect their own projections of Geronimo back to them: "Shrewd Pancakes had made the best of the situation. And if the whites wanted to pay him to ride spotted ponies in Wild West shows and wave an unloaded rifle over his head as the character the white journalists called Geronimo, then that was okay with the old man" (235). Because the whites needed a noble enemy to ennoble their own shabby history of domination of a continent and their own betrayal of their own higher values, they needed a Geronimo to mourn. Because America is founded on the vanishing of the Indian, they needed an Indian ghost to shoot blanks in their Wild West show. Old Pancakes is willing to go along with the pretense "because he had seen a lot of changes throughout those years of struggle" (235), and his grounded identity maintains faith in Indigenous survivance through those changes. All the historical hype around Geronimo becomes a four-layered joke on the whites. The confidential chuckle rides on Silko's long-range view of generational change.

In Silko's first novel, *Ceremony*, the pivotal figure, Betonie, exemplifies the full spectrum from humus to human to humor. His grounded hogan, his sand painting, his shamanistic embrace of the protagonist, Tayo, and his laughter all combine to generate a life-giving infusion, that good humor that is the healing vitality at the heart of Indian survivance, the center of the other four terms. Betonie laughs as he discusses with Tayo the Gallup dump, overseen by his hogan. He is comfortable as he describes his position in time and space prior to the arrival of the whites, sitting in his center, "where none of them want to live" above the dump. Betonie is comfortable because he possesses authentic knowledge that he belongs "with the land." His life is at peace here, where he has translated all his worldly travels into "these hills." Throughout his exchanges with Tayo, there are references to Betonie's healing by example, laughing and smiling. The effect is to offset not only the threatening presence of "the destroyers" in the novel but also to erase the destructive image of a stoic Indian in the minds of Silko's readers. Indeed Tayo's own grim, humorless demeanor of repression and trauma, which underlie a history of the white man's stoic Indian, is the face and character of colonial disease that Betonie's good-humored nature heals.

One of the key flashbacks in *Ceremony* sets Tayo and Rocky in front of the army recruiter, as we saw, and here the irony is empowering. Ignorant of his own white supremacy, the military man thinks he is effectively propagandizing as a way to round up these Indian youth through platitudes: "'Anyone can fight for America,' he began, giving special emphasis to 'America,' 'even you boys. In a time of need, anyone can fight for her. . . . Now I know you boys love America as much as we do, but this is your big chance to *show* it!'" (66). It is only because they were already intent on signing up that Tayo and Rocky ignore the multiple ironies of condescending ignorance in "even you boys." Instead of being "anyone," a warrior culture of first Americans might indeed feel they have a peculiar right, prior to the recruiter and his claims, to "fight for America." The joke remains between Silko and her readers.

The Joke on History

Imagine the laughter that carries through tipi walls in a camp circle at Crow Fair. Imagine the laughter that drifts through the cigarette smoke around a kitchen table on the Ft. Peck Reservation. Imagine the laughter among community health researchers who promote antidiabetes diets on the reservation and who make the point that frybread is not real Indian food. Imagine the laughter that lifts off the pages of any of these writers, comedians, and artists we have reviewed. Among the laments and claims, the irony of their strength to survive echoes with laughter.

Because daily survivance cannot be reversed, expressing, even celebrating life, even after a holocaust, seems inevitable. Ironic humor allows both the massive losses of death and the massive energies of life. Ironic reversals become more sophisticated and more convincing when more of a knowledge base is inverted, when more of America's story is told and retold.

Humor as a mechanism for healing works not just by reversing and undoing history. It needs to know how to put history back together, beyond laughter as a distancing mechanism. It is precisely the comic mode, as Meeker suggested, that weaves life into history, that learns to collect and coordinate, to adapt and adopt rather than tragically to cut off possibilities for survival. Humor is healing because it embraces the whole, even by negative gestures. The significance of Simon Ortiz's healing vision cannot be overestimated.

If a political postindian may step off the page, the ultimate ironic reversal would be a "good government" that respectfully enlists the governed in a genuinely democratic system, as Guaman Poma prescribed in the sixteenth century, presaging America's Declaration of Independence and Lincoln's Gettysburg Address. If Indians are stoic, they are so only to the extent of their "constant" humor that reminds us we are all clowns. Vine Deloria Jr. and David Wilkins also remind us that this is no joke. They suggest quite practically that the federal government should "return tribes to their political status as it existed prior to the prohibition against treaty making in 1871" (*Tribes* 158–59), when both sides held the status of equal signatories. Out of five hundred years of subjugation, it is an ironic view that liberates the realities of pluralism on American ground. "Heigh-ho!"

CONCLUSION

America's Struggle with Authenticity

Will Simon Ortiz's vision ever happen? Will America ever "be America again," as Langston Hughes asked? Will America even approximate its own ideals? Will the joke on history play out? Few writers allow themselves to prophesy. To find America's own "compassionate heart," as Ortiz describes it, would amount to the rewriting of history as Native writers have inscribed it for centuries. I spoke of Native American ironic literary transformations as utopian humor. However, with ironic reversals in Alexie's courageous Junior, or in Vizenor's portrait of Columbus as a descendant of Mayan explorers, we might describe them as fantastic, if not utopian. With political resonance Vizenor, Alexie, Thomas King, Craig Womack, and many others build intriguing fantasies to contrast an imbalanced world. Humor does indeed erupt out of these surprises of pluralism, but such jokes rarely convey utopian ideals as directly as in Ortiz. "And it will rise / in this heart / which is our America." Ortiz carries the historical reversals further than most writers to target America's hidden but compassionate heart.

He is able to do so precisely because he does not pretend to answer the big, unanswerable question: Will there be an end, or at least a purpose, to suffering? Whether revising history is or is not possible, the historic losses cannot be reversed. Yet they can be reworked in expression, in art: "This perception and meaningfulness has to happen; otherwise, the hard experience of the Euroamerican colonization of the lands and people of the Western Hemisphere would be driven into the dark recesses of the Indigenous mind and psyche. And this kind of repression is always poison and detriment to creative growth and expression" (Ortiz, "Towards a National Indian Literature" 9). Ortiz's essay on literary nationalism focuses this process of translating pain into expressive purpose. He carries that emotional logic to political dimensions of transformation, retelling the story of America itself.

We may thus turn the multifaceted lens of ground theory on America's frontier mentality and focus further the question of authenticity on American national identity. If the external behavior and effects of frontier mentality are relatively easy to see on the land, its internal effects are less so. The issue of Native authenticity lies at the heart of America's own national anxiety. Repeatedly the colonists and their descendants have cloaked themselves in the mantle of nativism, essentially a national longing for authenticity. In *Playing Indian*, Philip Deloria describes what he calls "an antimodern quest for authentic truth":

> For all the transmutations that have come with two hundred and fifty years of Indian play, certain threads have held continuing power in the weave of American life. Indians *were* first and original Americans, and taking on Indian identity *was* in fact a moment of no return for rebellious colonists. Notions such as these have guided the actions of Tea Party Indians, fraternalists, Camp Fire Girls, hobbyists, and Deadheads alike. And yet, Indian play was hardly clear-cut, for if Indianness was critical to American identities, it necessarily went hand in hand with the dispossession and conquest of actual Indian people. (182)

Deloria connects this contradiction between admiration and dispossession of Indians with other contradictions "undergirding the nation's history and sense of collective identity," including the disjunction between America's "rhetoric of egalitarianism and the reality of slavery and class struggle" (182). Although it is arguable that the quest for authenticity is layered deep in "modernist" aesthetics, as a rebuilding of myth after the Enlightenment, the ethical reality of American exclusions has given the lie to aesthetic dreams of American inclusions. Slavery and conquest have trumped equality and freedom. They also have blinded Euro-American readers to Native American literary expression, with its political significance. In this study I, like others, have been suggesting that an originary American contradiction, an epistemological structure that shapes a history of conflict lies between the European mind-set of polarities and the American experience of multiplicities, and, further, that Indigenous storytelling makes that contradiction crystal clear. Anxieties of confluence, of the material fact that humans exist on the ground and flow together from all sides of the ideological divide, continually befuddle America's frontier mentality.

When the eighteenth-century tax protestors, playing on the doubly distanced images of the British Mohawks club, disguised themselves as Mohawks tossing crates of tea into Boston Harbor, were they being themselves in drag? The dualisms of cross-dressing can never resolve the anxieties of cross-cultural exchange. Similarly the nineteenth-century Euro-American Native American parties movement both invoked and negated authenticity in its self-contradictory logic of anti-immigration politics. The twentieth-century New Age movement was not only an affirmation and an appropriation of things Native; it was tied to the political denial of things American. In the twenty-first-century a Minuteman vigilante movement along the Mexican border against illegal immigration continues to deny history in favor of racial exclusions. America's binary self-constructions lead inevitably to contradictions on the larger ground of the natural and cultural continent. The wave of manifest destiny surges back and engulfs the nation in its own imperial flood.

Philip Deloria explains that in these varied moments of cultural cross-dressing, American citizens seized the ultimate mask: "While its citizens created the United States around such dissonances [as Indigenous dispossession and African slavery], many of them found that playing Indian offered a powerful tool for holding their contradictions in abeyance. Indianness gave the nation a bedrock, for it fully engaged the contradiction most central to a range of American identities—that between an unchanging, essential Americanness and the equally American liberty to make oneself into something new" (*Playing Indian* 182). The performance of "Indianness" coupled with the erasure of actual Indians became yet another "bedrock" of contradictions in American national identity. The performance was and is inauthentic because it denies actual Indians. Because of dispossession itself, because of the ethical contradictions, the "bedrock" Deloria describes is not the actual ground. It is John Marshall's "actual state of things," a history that denies the land by denying its human inhabitants that cannot be separated from it.

The adolescent dream of inauthentic American exceptionalism that could hold "their contradictions in abeyance," as Philip Deloria describes it, recalls us to the need for a particular "maturity" of which his scholarly father, Vine Deloria Jr., speaks as well. According to the elder Deloria's essay "The American Fantasy" (the foreword to an anthology on Indian images in film), seekers after authenticity—Americans—must always find it beyond their grasp because they are looking outside and behind themselves, at their own projections of Indians. The claim to authenticity is its own denial because it is based on preemptive time, prior to the ideological "actual state of things." The past must be past, and it must be kept there. The immigrant doth protest too much. Authenticity must remain elusive by this temporal formulation. In spite of all claims and denials, the "real American" remains the "real Indian." Authenticity projects onto the American other. So the white-racialized American self can never be that. The southwestern Minutemen's logic of "we were here first" must so clearly bow to the American Indian that the internal cost to the illogic of these projections is alienation of both the colonizer and the colonized. The result is that fundamental anxiety of confluence, an alienation from oneself and from the land that feeds us all.

So how can America reconnect with the land? This study of authenticity, identity, community, sovereignty, and irony listens to ways that Native voices listen to that ground. Louis Owens offers a compelling discussion of the process of colonizers' alienation from their very conquest. First citing Leela Gandhi, "In order for Europe to emerge as the site of civilizational plenitude, the colonized world had to be emptied of meaning," Owens explains the "strange dance of repulsion and desire that has given rise to both one of the longest sustained histories of genocide and ethnocide in the world as well as a fascinating drama in which the colonizer attempts to empty out and reoccupy not merely the geographical terrain but the constructed space of the Indigenous Other" ("As If" 175–76). The moral substructure of colonization requires a denial of "meaning" as humanity in "the Indigenous Other." But here is where the ground speaks. Conquest is ethically and legally acceptable if those conquered are subhuman. (This question was explicit in the debate between Las Casas and Sepulveda in the sixteenth-century Spanish court of Charles V, over the question of whether Native Americans have souls.)

Yet that erasure takes its toll. By depriving their victims of humanity—in order to victimize them—the colonizers, as Owens paints them, suffer "the ultimate, haunting emptiness the colonizing consciousness faces at last once it is forced to confront a world emptied of meaning outside of itself. Because there is no way back to that infinitely retreating moment of origin—and no explorer's route to a gold Uramerica—the green breast of this new world remains forever distant as it draws the Euramerican psyche onward" ("As If" 175). The colonizer's dream becomes a nightmare.

That nightmare of course has material and psychological consequences for those "others." As Owens writes, "If a fear of inauthenticity is the burden of postmodernity, as has been suggested by David Harvey in *The Condition of Postmodernity*, among others, it is particularly the burden not only of the Euramerican seeking merely his self-reflection, but even more so that of the Indigenous American in the face of this hyperreal 'Indian,'" constructed by the colonizer ("As If" 176). Authenticity becomes the issue when power relations are based on denying the humanity of human beings.

Yet Ortiz offers a direction beyond Owens's "hyperreal 'Indian.'" The phrase we have seen in Ortiz's discussion of authenticity, "to make those forms meaningful in their own terms" ("Towards a National Indian Literature" 8), concisely reverses the colonial process that would empty the world of meaning. It translates the meaningless "socio-political-colonizing force" into "forms meaningful in their own terms." Perhaps the "authentic" part is not only "their own terms" but the energy, the spirit to *act* in such a way. Thus, again, authenticity becomes a verb rather than a static noun of a past condition.

To map the elusiveness of that verb Vine Deloria Jr. describes the "American fantasy" of the noble savage in its various guises as a "subconscious drive for authenticity" ("Foreword" xiv). He contrasts Native authenticity with what he sees as a structural alienation in American identity. Americans on this land still operate by a colonial inheritance, a legacy of conquest, that alienates them from this land. To pinpoint a persistent American mentality of colonialism, Deloria refers all the way back to the sixteenth-century conquistadors' frustrated attempts to find the Seven Cities of Gold, a frustration they expressed desperately by torturing Indians in hopes of extracting fulfillment of their own fantasies. Equating cultural expropriations in the late twentieth century to the depredations of conquistadors in the sixteenth,

Deloria offers a sweeping critique: "As long as the white suspects that he does not know the whole story and that we are trying to keep our secrets—whether gold, history, religion, or lands—from him, he will find one torture or another to plague us with until we tell him something. The obvious solution to the whole thing would be for the white to achieve some kind of psychological and/or religious maturity" (xv). He goes on to express doubt about that "obvious solution": "Underneath all the conflicting images of the Indian one fundamental truth emerges—the white man *knows* that he is an alien and he *knows* that North America is Indian—and he will never let go of the Indian image because he thinks that by some clever manipulation he can achieve an authenticity that cannot ever be his" (xvi). Deloria suggests that by dehumanizing "the Indian" as a vanishing noble savage, a Euro-American mind strikes upon an image sufficiently reductive to manipulate and co-opt entirely into its own acquisitive terms.

"The Indian" can both remain conquered and continue to provide a fantasy image of rugged, nature-rooted American individualism, a tragic image stretching from James Fenimore Cooper's *Last of the Mohicans* to Kevin Costner's *Dances with Wolves*. Imperialist nostalgia in that image eclipses the conscience that would guard against dehumanizing Indians, while a hallucination of national roots in that image can send its tendrils deep into American lands as the psychological energy to justify dispossession.

In *The Ethics of Authenticity*, the Canadian philosopher Charles Taylor studies modern American alienation and the culture of self-fulfillment, or the culture of narcissism, as a struggle for authenticity, in ways that might reflect or amplify Vine Deloria Jr.'s provocative claim. Taylor sets his study in the context of "sweeping away the old orders" (5) and a "loss of purpose" (4) among the "malaises of modernity" (1), which he lists as individualism, instrumental reason, and loss of freedom in a technocratic world. His is a philosophical analysis of the politics and social psychology of what we might call the inheritance of colonial-capitalist history, a world that oppresses the dispossessed while it represses de facto interconnectivity of those who possess power.

Probing the depths of modern angst, Taylor sketches directions for that "psychological and/or religious maturity" Deloria calls for. In his analysis of narcissism, Taylor argues that there is some potential in the mainstream's selfish impulse for a sort of enlightened self-interest. It is a "tension and struggle" that "can go either way" (*The Ethics of Authenticity* 77)—toward "its most self-centred forms" (77) or toward "the sense of an ideal [of authenticity] that is not being fully met in reality" (76). The "inherent thrust and requirements of this ideal" (77) and the "moral force of this ideal of authenticity" do battle with selfishness, toward the potential that "the ethic of practical benevolence" (106) may reconnect the self to a wider world of interrelationships. "If authenticity is being true to ourselves, is recovering our own 'sentiment de l'existence,' then perhaps we can only achieve it integrally if we recognize that this sentiment connects us to a wider whole" (91). Echoes of Winnemucca's and Verney's traditional Indigenous "respect" might reverberate in Taylor's "ethic of practical benevolence." He invokes the environmental crisis (8) and other modern enigmas such as Tocqueville's "soft despotism" (9) of an immensely powerful yet mild and paternalistic government as the staging grounds of this battle for authenticity.

Intriguingly Taylor's proposed healing for "the sense of powerlessness" engendered by being "governed by large-scale, centralized, bureaucratic states" is "decentralization of power, as Tocqueville saw. And so in general devolution, or a division of power, as in a federal system, particularly one based on the principle of subsidiarity, can be good for democratic empowerment. And this is the more so if the units to which power is devolved already figure as communities in the lives of their members" (*The Ethics of Authenticity* 119). Decentering is both a postmodern strategy and a five-hundred-year-old anticolonial, Indigenous strategy. We thus return to ground theory. In Taylor, individual authenticity discovers communal authenticity through this dynamic. Here are echoes of our chapter on community where Owens notes, "The recovering or rearticulation of an identity [is] dependent upon a rediscovered sense of place as well as community" (*Other Destinies* 5). Further, thanks to Tocqueville, Taylor's analysis supports Ortiz's linkage between authenticity and nationalism, or decentralized sovereignty, and we find in Taylor's psychosocial map of "devolution, or a division of power," another conceptual space for tribal sovereignty, perhaps eventually Tocqueville's and others' "democracy of nationalities," or even John O'Sullivan's "nation of many nations," minus the "manifest destiny"!

When I was a doctoral student, one of my professors, Russell Barsh, a legal scholar of Indigenous rights, stated in a graduate seminar that this matter of decentralization, specifically involving ethnic difference within nation states, will be the millennial question of the twenty-first century. It is a vigorous tension between nationalism and pluralism. The devolution of which Taylor speaks is developing in the United Kingdom, where the Parliament of Scotland has been reinstated and where Wales stands in line. He points out that Canada's federal system has been fortunate in preventing "greater centralization on the model of the United States" (*The Ethics of Authenticity* 119). Recently, in parallel, the Zapatero government in Spain passed a "statute of autonomy" for Catalonia as a "nation," with Barcelona as its capitol city. There are other examples worldwide—too many of them bloody ones—of a tendency toward gradual recognition of pluralism rather than uniformity in the body politic.

In Taylor's newly refederated vision for the United States we also see reflections of the Iroquois Confederacy and indeed of tribal sovereignty, that is, decentralized power in legal, treaty-validated communities. The politics and legal evolution of tribal sovereignty, in that battle for authenticity that Taylor describes, may be mapping a revised American democracy, and that story, told by Native writers, may be the long road toward Deloria's "maturity."

In the chapter on sovereignty, I explored this Indigenous process of decentering as a strategic aspect of modern and postmodern theory and politics, partly through the analysis of Philip Harper, who explains that so-called postmodern issues of decentering and recentering power "have always concerned marginalized constituencies" (*Framing the Margins* 4). Toward a conclusion it will be useful to return briefly to this aspect of a ground theory in conversations about postmodernism.[1]

Such decentering in these five writers is quite different from, or is rather the inverse of, what the scholar Robert M. Nelson describes of "postmodernism" in a different context of Native American literature: "Underlying the postmodern temperament is this recurrent conviction that alienation *is* the human condition and that consequently *all* statements of meaningful relationship between the individual and anything/everything else are, necessarily, fictions" (*Place and Vision* 4). Nelson posits that some major Native novels begin with such alienation, which is then cured by the narratives' "rather old-fashioned-looking but still potent vaccine: geographical realism" (6). The protagonists he examines in Silko, N. Scott Momaday, and

James Welch all find healing on the land. He affirms, as we have seen, that such (re)connection to the land provides a larger, healing context than the toxic, linear history of opposition that is manifest destiny.[2]

Thus many Native writers directly resist what recently may be called postmodern alienation, but they do so, I'd suggest, as William Apess codified the technique in the 1820s and 1830s, by decentering, by finding a different center, or a larger set of centers, in Indian and cross-cultural communities on the land. Nelson describes this process slightly differently: "The land as a place provides them with a referential framework that lies ... 'outside' the postmodern temperament but, as things develop in each of these fictions, as the basis for recentering self-consciousness as well" (*Place and Vision* 6). The "place" of the fiction becomes the "vision" of healing.

However, that shift to the outside is itself a move of difference, a reappropriation of distributed power. Nelson's "outside" is thus quite useful as a positive postmodern strategy. As the dialogics of ground theory clarifies, the larger field of more complex triangulations finds positions and interconnections "outside" the binary structures of self and other that have been so alienating to both the dispossessed and the privileged in the modern colonial capitalist system. The ground itself is that "outside" where reconnection becomes visible. (Thus Nelson's own book title, *Place and Vision: The Function of Landscape in Native American Fiction*.) As a "son of the forest," Apess grounds his vision in the spirit of those Native villages of New England and Ontario where he found community, and his project was to affirm the "outside" place of those communities "inside" the vision of America. Winnemucca pleads for community across the racial divide, on the land "outside" the terms of the frontier. McNickle's harsh prose paints the shackles that entrap Indigenous actors who would seek to step "outside" those terms and remain on their land. Silko develops a mythos of the "outside" on the land and across time on a scale that eventually trumps colonial history. Similarly Alexie repopulates American geography with American Indians "outside" the terms of historical erasure.[3]

In Indigenous narratives the "inside" and "outside" are so often blurred, and so much of the natural is cultural and the cultural is natural. That is the point. As we saw in the chapter on community, animism blurs the human and nonhuman worlds. A dualistic structure might miss some of the dynamics in Silko and other writers where land and language overlap in nonlinear, atemporal place, as she writes, "because after all, the stories grow out of this land" (*The Delicacy and Strength of Lace* 25-26).

The ideological magnetism of binaries remains, however, deeply entrenched. As we have seen, America's alienation from authenticity begins in its conceptual divide between nature and culture, precisely as that divide enables conquest by erasing the Indigenous cultures of that nature. A ground theory makes alternatives visible, disclosing where nature and culture coalesce in Indigenous community and throughout the five terms.

Recent ecocriticism also can help us understand the continuing ideologies of Euro-American dispossession of Indian land, as the ecocritique analyzes specifically the divide between nature and culture. Moving beyond psychological and philosophical aspects of deep ecology and its account of Americans' destructive alienation from the land, ecocriticism provides some terms that might clarify Vine Deloria Jr.'s decades-old contention about American authenticity.

We may say that ecocriticism is a literary application of complexity or connectionist theory, complicating the nature-culture divide. For instance, Nick Selby, in an essay entitled "'Coming back to oneself/coming back to the land': Gary Snyder's Poetics," writes usefully of "a self-division lying at the heart of the American psyche" (180). Critiquing Ralph Waldo Emerson's assertion that "America is a poem in our eyes" ("The Poet" in *Selected Essays, Lectures, and Poems* 222), and contrasting Snyder, Selby points out a deconstructive dynamic by which the American self becomes separated from the land as other, even when expressing appreciation or celebration of that land. Selby suggests that "Emerson's bringing together of 'America' and 'poem' keeps the two terms separate" in a founding American syntax. Emerson's formulation then "indicates the way in which 'self' is privileged over 'land,' even while their inseparability is being asserted" (179) in American ideology. Thus a privileged self assumes and subsumes, even consumes a deprivileged other; this is another formula for American alienation.

Considering Deloria's view of America's fantasy overcoming that alienation, the privilege to subsume the other is especially and precisely the claim to write the Native American out of history and the Euro-American self of manifest destiny into the heart of the American narrative on the land. By erasing the Native, America asserts privilege, but in so doing sacrifices and deprivileges nature itself, the very land that America feels privileged to claim.

Thus, again, it is the ethics of our imbalanced history that alienates us from the land, and a revised history, revised by Native American voices in dialogue with other Americans, is what may connect us with America's own dream of itself.

National alienation projects alienation. In *from Sand Creek*, Ortiz writes of the quandary of Native Americans having to see themselves as part of this country and its history: "But were we a part of the history of something atrocious like that?" If it is difficult for Indigenous peoples to identify themselves as targets of "mass destruction," "thievery and genocidal killing" that meant the "'winning' of the West," Ortiz points out that it seems at least as difficult for non-Indians to face it too: "Most people prefer not to face it and deal with it. In fact, U.S. society really doesn't face it or deal with it. Instead, the United States insulates itself within an amnesia that doesn't acknowledge that kind of history" (6). Such a state of denial institutionalizes alienation, from the classroom to the courtroom. If the story of America is its identity, American history textbooks and the elaborate governmental and corporate structures of the textbook publishing industry refuse its citizens the right to self-knowledge. We have become ungrounded. That process was necessary to the colonial project.

Although Deloria and Ortiz both have challenged America to its own ethics of authenticity, to come to grips with its violent history of exclusions, they have been virtually ignored precisely because of what it would mean to face that history. The stakes are vast. These two writers map two steps familiar to those suggested by many other Native American authors. Deloria calls attention to the process by which a history of inhumanity leads to alienation, and he stops there, with the need to register that history as a first step, unalloyed with alternative futures. Ortiz suggests a next step, an affirmation in the recognition of flouted humanity of other and self. Like Apess, he invokes an America true to "justice and humanity." Because the land itself remains the ultimate issue, the realignment of Indigenous nationhood on the land becomes part of many very specific conversations, from dam removals to the Great Sioux National Park in the Black Hills of South Dakota.

One trick in Ortiz's suggestion is that American history's "burden / of steel and mad / death" (*from Sand Creek* 9) is a record of oppression that denies not only the humanity of the oppressed but equally and previously the humanity of the oppressor. To return to Deloria's terms, merely confronting a history of alienation will only confirm how alien Euro-Americans remain in this hemisphere, because "the white man *knows* that he is an alien" ("Foreword" xvi). That authenticity "cannot ever be his" to the extent that standard American history textbooks continue to exclude the humanity of others.

The Fool Soldiers, who knew those exclusions from all sides, traced a different story in their footsteps in the snow, as Native writers trace a different story in ink on paper. The history that Indigenous writers have been plotting for generations does not replay the alienation and the facile erasures inherent in the narrative of manifest destiny. Instead a grounded, "authentic" history, what Cook-Lynn refers to as "reality-based historical contexts" ("The American Indian Fiction Writer" 31), recognizes the tragedies and survivals of "fully sentient and multidimensional beings," again as Alfonso Ortiz ("Indian/White Relations" 10) suggested. Further, a key aspect of multidimensional Indigenous beings remains their political struggle, or tribal sovereignty. As Maureen Konkle argues, "To the extent that scholars refuse to recognize Native political autonomy as a category for analysis, they continue to participate in a colonial epistemology" (*Writing Indian Nations* 291). Indigenous writers have been striving to change that epistemology for centuries.

Thus this study does not disagree with Vine Deloria Jr. on his crucial point of Euro-American fantasies of authenticity, except to point out that the corrosive alienation of which he speaks is not the end of the story that Native writers have been telling to those alienated audiences. Deloria's work recognizes this additional point, as his own efforts to provoke American readers into maturity testify to his ironic faith in this vague possibility. Native writers and storytellers across five hundred years have made it part of their project not only to affirm their Native communities and authentic identities against the alienating forces of colonialism but also to help heal or wake up their largely white audiences, to foster that essentially ethical maturity that Deloria calls for in the psychology of the settler nation. Maturity must involve authenticity, an honest, grounded recognition of the stories that make us who we are, and authenticity involves community, a recognition of our interrelated humanity.

In reaffirming lost interrelationships, Native narrative retellings of history do not hide past and present tragedies. If America faced its past as plunderer and deceiver as well as designer and dreamer, what would America become? Such questions may seem far away, but they move in the soil and soul of Native narratives. For speaking to such visions and nightmares, some writers have been called fools.

> This America
> has been a burden
> of steel and mad
> death,
> but, look now,
> there are flowers
> and new grass
> and a spring wind
> rising
> from Sand Creek.

—Simon Ortiz, *from Sand Creek*

BIOGRAPHICAL APPENDIX

For fuller critical biographies, refer to Kenneth M. Roemer, ed., *The Dictionary of Literary Biography*, vol. 175: *Native American Writers of the United States* (Farmington Hills MI: Gale, 1997) and Joy Porter and Kenneth M. Roemer, eds., *The Cambridge Companion to Native American Literature* (New York: Cambridge University Press, 2005).

William Apess 1798–1839

Born into an American Indian community but indentured as a child into white families of Jeffersonian Connecticut, William Apess had a best-seller in 1829, *Son of the Forest*, a tale of Christian conversion that set a pattern for Native American autobiography.[1] For less than a decade, from 1829 to 1836, Apess published, preached, and organized across New England on behalf of Indian rights, speaking more than once at Boston's famed Odeon Theater, until he disappeared into reputedly drunken poverty and died of "apoplexy" at age forty-one in New York City in 1839. His brilliant and sad life has been studied increasingly, especially due to the invaluable bibliographical and biographical services of Barry O'Connell, the scholar largely responsible for bringing Apess's extraordinary voice to the attention of modern America. Now Apess has garnered the critical interest of Arnold Krupat, Maureen Konkle, Robert Warrior, and many others. To map his varying rhetorical approaches is to follow a remarkably modern, perhaps anachronistically postmodern and decentering mind, whose ethical critique of early nineteenth-century America has yet to be answered. His inclusive vision of American identities has barely come clear after the bicentenary of his birth.

Sarah Winnemucca 1844–1891

Historically Sarah Winnemucca is a crucial figure in the development of the Great Basin, of the Northwest, and of U.S. Indian policy. Born in 1844 in Nevada, just as the juggernaut of California-bound settlers and gold-seekers was gaining momentum, she was the granddaughter and daughter of two major figures of the Northern Paiutes, Truckee and Old Winnemucca. Her grandfather, active with the U.S. Army in the Mexican-American War under General John C. Frémont, was careful to arrange an education in English for his bright granddaughter. That cross-cultural training defined her life, leading not only to stage acting in Virginia City and San Francisco but to a position as interpreter for the U.S. Army in the frontier wars of Oregon and Nevada, during which she performed numerous acts of daring-do, recounted in her 1883 autobiography, *Life Among the Piutes: Their Wrongs and Claims*. Through her articulate, openly subversive, and resistant correspondence in the newspapers of Nevada and San Francisco, exposing agents of the "Indian Ring," she waged a seemingly futile war of words. Her pieces were picked up by *Harper's Weekly* and gained her national notoriety in the 1870s and 1880s. Struggling to rescue her Nevada people, the Northern Paiutes, from neglect and frontier abuses by the Bureau of Indian Affairs, she gave lecture tours from Baltimore to Boston. Her one book grew from transcripts of those East Coast lectures. She was dramatically successful in winning over her immediate audiences but was unsuccessful in her larger goal of changing specific governmental policies toward the Paiutes.

D'Arcy McNickle 1904–1977

D'Arcy McNickle, born in 1904 of a Canadian Métis mother and an Irish American father, was enrolled in the Confederated Salish and Kootenai Tribes on the Flathead Reservation in Montana. After growing through the emotional privations of boarding school, he sold his land allotment to attend Oxford University, then traveled throughout Europe and gained a broadly educated perspective. Eventually he worked for decades in the U.S. Department of the Interior's Bureau of Indian Affairs as a maverick community developer in the Southwest and other regions. He ended his career as a university scholar. His two major novels, *The Surrounded* and *Wind from an Enemy Sky*, the latter published posthumously, fictionalize his younger years on the reservation in the early century before and after the 1934 Indian Reorganization Act. Like his nonfiction, the trajectory of his fiction in the two novels, in poems and numerous short stories, and in his book-length tale, *Runner in the Sun*, written for the juvenile market, blazes the narrative trail of "homing in," as mapped by the scholar William Bevis.[2] In this pattern the Indigenous individual is first drawn away but eventually returns to the land and Indigenous culture.

Leslie Marmon Silko 1948–

Born in 1948 into a mixed-blood family in the Laguna Pueblo community in New Mexico, Silko is among the most influential Native American writers of the twentieth and early twenty-first centuries. In the flowering of Native writing since the 1960s, she shares the canonized leadership of the so-called Native American Renaissance with Louise Erdrich, Joy Harjo, N. Scott Momaday, James Welch, Simon Ortiz, and Gerald Vizenor.[3] Her storytelling strengths are mythopoetic yet graphic, lyrical yet historical, in now more than a dozen works of fiction, poetry, essay, photography, and film. The conceptual geography of her work is fundamental to the dialogic nucleus and structure of this study. Winner of numerous arts and humanities grants, she was awarded a prestigious MacArthur Foundation Fellowship in 1983, which helped to support her while writing the novel *Almanac of the Dead*. Her work has been widely anthologized since her first published short story, "The Man to Send Rain Clouds," and her first novel, *Ceremony*, has been among the most widely taught in American undergraduate literature courses. Maintaining a very private writing life beyond her public venues on author tours and as a professor of creative writing at the University of New Mexico, the University of Arizona, and Navajo Community College (now Diné College), Silko is explicit about her mixed-blood upbringing on the edges of Laguna pueblo culture and about her own dedication to the Native storytelling tradition. Nearly every biography quotes her saying, "I am of mixed-breed ancestry, but what I know is Laguna" (Velie, *Four American Indian Literary Masters* 106). Her grandmother and aunt raised her on stories, "passing down an entire culture by word of mouth" (106). With her own dual consciousness on the margins of both Indigenous and mainstream cultures, like each of the other writers in this study she remains both distant and deeply engaged in her people's struggles. Hers is the fitting position for "witness," for the storyteller's craft, and she is quite explicit about her own function in the traditional role of Arrowboy, Estoy-eh-muut, who watches and records the evil in the world in order to witness, distract, and disempower its force: "Something is wrong,' he said./'Ck'o'yo magic won't work/if someone is watching us" (*Ceremony* 259). Standing on the ground of witness, Silko's work combines an unflinching eye for detail and despair with a mythic vision cutting through oppositional mentalities that deny Indigenous survivance on the land.

Sherman Alexie 1966–

Raised on the Spokane Indian Reservation in eastern Washington, Sherman Alexie chose to pursue education in an off-reservation high school, went on to try premed and prelaw at Gonzaga University, and then discovered his writing gift at Washington State University. Starting with his first book, published in 1992, *The Business of Fancydancing: Stories and Poems,* he has been prolific in various genres. His popular persona as comedian, slam poetry champ, experimental writer, filmmaker, and social pundit has itself become a work of art. (Alexie "retired" as the reigning "world heavyweight poetry bout champion" after winning four years in a row, 1998–2001.) I focus on him in the chapter on humor as a "punk trickster." His work shares with that of many American Indian writers a central motif reaffirming Native lives and Native nationhood, though his direct comedic style and ironic attitude set him apart from the earnest lyricism of many of the now canonized elder Native writers such as N. Scott Momaday, Louise Erdrich, and Silko. As he echoes the comedic writers Alexander Posey, Thomas King, Thomson Highway, Drew Hayden Taylor, and other Indigenous masters of ironic critique, Alexie pushes a mask of humor to the front of the literature.

NOTES

Introduction

1. In Lewis's journal entry of August 19, 1805, written in what is now Montana, as he was describing the Shoshones he reflected back on the Corps' sexual experiences among the Sioux during the previous travels of 1804. Other archival material suggests ambiguity in Martin Charger's patrimony. There was a nineteenth-century St. Louis trader, Reuben Lewis, whose name might have become confused with the more famous Lewis in this story. See correspondence dated November 20 and December 6, 1915, between Samuel Charger of LaPlant, South Dakota, son of Martin, and Doane Robinson, secretary of the South Dakota Historical Association in Pierre (Doane Robinson Collection, Alphabetical Correspondence, folder 58: "Charger, Martin," South Dakota State Historical Society). Sam indicates that his grandfather, who would be the son of a "Lewis," traveled to St. Louis in 1824 to receive a horse from his father there. Meriwether Lewis died in 1809, so the later trader is the more likely the father of Zomie and grandfather of Charger.

2. Sources for the Fool Soldiers story include the University of South Dakota Indian Oral History Collection; Britain, *Return to Shetek*; Derounian-Stodola, *The War in Words*; Sneve, *Betrayed*; Ketcham et al., *The Fool Soldiers*; King, "The Fool Soldiers."

3. Although such terms invoke impossible generalizations that miss specific histories, I am somewhat more comfortable using the term

colonial than *postcolonial* to describe aspects of past and present Euro-American relations with Indigenous peoples of the Americas. Certainly the Euro-American enterprise was a colonizing one, and certainly that enterprise is neither past nor post-.

4. See Jace Weaver's discussion of "communitism," in *That the People Might Live*, as the value of advocacy driving Native American literature.

5. Prior to critical questions of authenticity, identity, community, sovereignty, and irony there remains the bibliographic work of scholarship in bringing to light Native texts from across the centuries. A. LaVonne Brown Ruoff has been a leader of this foundational scholarship, and a number of scholars, critics, editors, and writers such as Daniel F. Littlefield, Arnold Krupat, Brian Swann, H. David Brumble, Joseph Bruchac, Duane Niatum, Joy Harjo, Gloria Bird, Maurice Kenny, and others have contributed by editing and publishing autobiography, nonfiction, fiction, and poetry.

   At the outset, I also want to recommend a different form of literary criticism emerging in the field. Scholarship and criticism have developed over the past generation from literary ethnography through literary separatism and linguistic nationalism, while archival bibliography remains core. I note especially three 2008 publications as models of methodology in Native American literary studies: Brooks, *The Common Pot*; Kelsey, *Tribal Theory in Native American Literature*; and Wilson, *Writing Home*. Since I possess neither the linguistic knowledge, the nationalist identity, nor the concomitant skills and perspectives of such accomplished and innovative scholars, I develop a different approach. Avoiding what Maureen Konkle refers to as "culturalist" critique, I overlap with Brooks, Kelsey, and Wilson by following Sherman Alexie's (and William Apess's) focus on "the political," in its many layers.

6. Gordon Henry Jr. marks an important set of questions about the applicability to American Indian literatures of "the historical associations with the words *nationalism* and *nationalist*" and indeed the term *nation* itself: "For some readers those terms may bring to mind, in thought and ideology, in some parts of the world, ways in which nationalism bears traces (at some ends of theories) of colonial

resistance, postcolonial theory, legal and political theory, and (at other ends) oppressive nationalist states" (Henry et al., *North American Indian Writing* 22). Add the complex histories of "domestic dependent nations," plus the current discourse of "tribal sovereignty," and the terminology clearly needs refining and refreshing.

7. A recent article by the Cherokee scholar Clint Carroll usefully discusses the differences between *nations*, *states*, and *nation-states*. Toward a rebalanced future, Carroll observes, "Indigenous peoples can form (and are forming) state-like governments that do not necessarily carry all the philosophical and ideological baggage of their imperial counterparts" ("Articulating Indigenous Statehood" 4).

8. Alfonso Ortiz discusses his objections to the following eight "standard historical concepts and categories" as "self-serving": Western civilization, the frontier, wilderness, the civilization/savagism dichotomy, Christianity as "an unquestionable good," Indians as "without any law or government," Manifest Destiny, and colonial and national labels for the periods of American history. Ortiz then proceeds to offer specific historiographic positions and perspectives to offset the damaging legacy of these corrupting notions.

9. Perhaps it is because of this historical force of the "frontier" mentality that two major scholars of Native American literature, Arnold Krupat and Louis Owens, both have upheld the term as still useful. Acknowledging the ideological baggage associated with the term *frontier*, Krupat writes in *Ethnocriticism*, "Central to ethnohistorical work is the concept of the *frontier*" (4). He describes the term as a subjective position: "Ethnocritical discourse, in its self-positioning at the frontier, seeks to traverse rather than occupy a great variety of 'middle grounds,' both at home and abroad" (25). "Rather, in a more relativist manner, the frontier is understood as simply that shifting space in which two *cultures* encounter one another" (5). As I discuss further, it remains unclear to me where the critical value lies in recycling a binary term to describe more complex systems, especially a term laden with dramatic, and indeed violent dualisms of erasure. It tends to serve precisely the reductive dualisms that would retain the "two cultures" in dialectic stasis when the cultural nexus is more dynamic than "frontier" positions or perspectives allow.

10. For a convenient text of Turner's eloquent essay, see http://national humanitiescenter.org/pds/gilded/empire/text1/turner.pdf *(accessed October 20, 2009)*.

11. Recent generations of historians, literary and otherwise, have addressed some blind spots in the Turner thesis, for instance, Smith, *Virgin Land*; Limerick, *Legacy of Conquest*; and White, *Middle Ground*. For a broad intellectual history of the conversation around the frontier thesis, see Klein, *Frontiers of Historical Imagination*.

12. See, for instance, Berlant, *The Anatomy of National Fantasy*.

13. In the spirit of dialogic clarity and complexity, it is important to explain that colonial and American voices of conscience have raised alarms against the brutal effects of this oppositional ideology from the start. Las Casas defended Native human rights in the sixteenth-century Spanish royal court. The relatively progressive Puritan Roger Williams in the seventeenth century and the Quaker John Woolman in the eighteenth century worked radically to represent colonized people of color as human rather than subhuman, based on humane interpretations of theological affirmations of the soul. From within their missionizing Christian perspectives, Williams's *Key into the Language of America* (1643) and Woolman's "Some Considerations on the Keeping of Negroes" (1754), an early abolitionist text, assumed the humanity of Natives and African Americans. Ralph Waldo Emerson's 1838 "Cherokee Letter" to President Martin Van Buren denounced the inhumanity of the 1830 Indian Removal Act as it was about to be carried out, against the directives of the Supreme Court. From the sixteenth century onward, progressive (though often patronizing) voices were raised "in defense of the Indian."

14. See, in chronological order, Pearce, *Savagism and Civilization*; Fiedler, *Return of the Vanishing American*; Vine Deloria, *Custer Died for Your Sins*; Berkhofer, *The White Man's Indian*; Drinnon, *Facing West*; Walker, *Indian Nation*; Philip Deloria, *Playing Indian*; Scheckel, *The Insistence of the Indian*.

15. The neologism *survivance* was invented by Gerald Vizenor to connote both survival and resistance, a continuity of strength through the vicissitudes of cultural and historical change. It has become standard terminology in Native American literary studies.

16. After various procedural gymnastics, the Senate, almost completely uninformed of the content or process of the standards, swayed by inflammatory rhetoric, and in the midst of other voting negotiations, recorded a 99–1 vote for a resolution on January 18, 1995, against the revised history standards. "Historian Eric Foner wrote to the *New York Times* that behind the congressional action lay 'an ominous precedent—the Senate manipulating Federal funds to promote an official interpretation of American history'" (Nash et al., *History on Trial* 236).

17. Gail Collins published an update on the textbook controversy, "How Texas Inflicts Bad Textbooks on Us," in the *New York Review of Books*: "Ever since the 1960s, the selection of schoolbooks in Texas has been a target for the religious right, which worried that schoolchildren were being indoctrinated in godless secularism, and political conservatives who felt that their kids were being given way too much propaganda about the positive aspects of the federal government" (18). The article traces conservative activism especially in the sciences and social studies curricula, with repercussions on a national level through publishers' unique attention to the Texas textbook market.

18. Although a central journal in the field, *American Indian Quarterly*, recently chose to accept no more articles rehashing "Indian identity," the necessary step, clearly, is to reposition identity (and authenticity, etc.) in context of the other terms.

19. This too-familiar dynamic of imperial aspirations and national self-definitions, a dialectic of identity between the colonies and the imperial center, gets careful treatment in Burton, *After the Imperial Turn*.

20. I am indebted for the concision of these definitions to conversations with Franklin W. Knight. See his study *Race, Ethnicity, and Class* for further discussion and context.

21. See joint press release dated December 15, 2004, "U.S. Fish and Wildlife Service and the Confederated Salish and Kootenai Tribes Negotiate Annual Funding Agreement for National Bison Range Complex."

22. See, for example, Paula Gunn Allen, Joanne Barker, Kimberly Blaeser, Susan Berry Brill de Ramirez, Lisa Tanya Brooks, Philip Deloria, Vine Deloria Jr., Larry Evers, Daniel Heath Justice, Penelope Myrtle

Kelsey, Maureen Konkle, Scott Lyons, Felipe Molina, Alfonso Ortiz, Simon Ortiz, Louis Owens, Robert Dale Parker, Malea Powell, John Purdy, A. LaVonne Brown Ruoff, James Ruppert, Kathryn W. Shanley, Scott Stevens, Mark Trahant, Gerald Vizenor, Robert Warrior, Jace Weaver, Michael D. Wilson, and Craig Womack.

23. Witness the continuing controversy in revisionary history over Thomas Jefferson's legacy of mutuality with his slave Sally Hemings and her progeny. Some celebrate the miscegenation, some deny it. The question is who is "we" in "our" forefathers' "We, the people."

24. Ground theory is similar in some ways to the "grounded theory" of the social scientists Barney Glaser and Anselm Strauss, outlined in their 1967 book *The Discovery of Grounded Theory*. Their reversal of scientific method—to start with data and thereby generate hypotheses and categories—describes some of my process of deriving analytical terms from Indigenous texts. However, the label *ground theory* is not metaphorical or adjectival, like *grounded*. It does not gesture toward an abstract analysis of or relation to the land and its lives. The term *theory* does that work of abstraction. Rather, the nominal *ground* names the foundation and presence of the land, the ecology of culture and nature in every aspect of Indigeneity. The five terms that analyze the spectrum of Indigenous representation build on that ground.

25. Native scholars have mapped the ethical pitfalls of what the Creek intellectual Craig Womack calls "theorizing American Indian experience," and I appreciate both the warnings and the welcome to enter such a sensitive yet crucial conversation. Gordon Henry Jr. summarizes the circumstances: "No doubt culturally rooted American Indian ways of knowing and of receiving and transmitting knowledge should inform interpretative discourse on American Indian literature and culture" (Henry et al., *North American Indian Writing* 15). Henry is referring especially to "the critical discourse produced by Native scholars," while others in the past generation of scholarship by Native and non-Native academics have concurred with this fundamental principle. It fosters an ethics of criticism linked to cultural ways of knowing on the ground of Indian community. The challenge to theoretical principle, of course, is in the practice.

26. The Taos scholar P. Jane Hafen underlines the ironic complexity of criticism and scholarship of Native American literatures, a point that evolves the terms of my 1994 essay. In conversation with the Mohave scholar Michael Tsosie, Hafen explains, "Even using the term 'decolonization' acknowledges the success of the conquerors when, in fact, Indigenous peoples have survived and resisted systematic and institutionalized colonization" ("Living to Tell Stories" 27). Such vexed co-optations across the historical dialectic are the reductive oscillation that dialogics, and a more specific ground theory, defuses, especially as that historiography is locked in oppositional discursive terms. The purpose and function of such a theory are precisely to make visible how "Indigenous people have survived and resisted," and how that revised story bears on relations between the so-called colonized and colonizers.

27. As I explained in "Decolonializing Criticism," the critical ethnography of James Clifford in *The Predicament of Culture* was important to my work, especially where Clifford described narratives of identity among the Mashpee tribe of Massachusetts as they navigated legal and political recognition in the 1970s: "Yet what if identity is conceived not as a boundary to be maintained but as a nexus of relations and transactions actively engaging a subject?" (344).

28. In *Shifting Boundaries*, Schouls elaborates "three contemporary faces of pluralism, which may be distinguished by the labels, 'communitarian,' 'individualist,' and 'relational'" (x). He prefers the relational form, which he characterizes as "identification with, and political commitment to, an Aboriginal community" (x–xi). His analysis echoes usefully the five terms of this study, where community is a focus of the other four.

29. André Droogers and Sidney M. Greenfield, in "Recovering and Reconstructing Syncretism," write of the "notion of connectionism." The word describes "the complexity of human thinking, which is viewed not only as open to the (so-called) sentential logic of serially organized verbal propositions [but] also—and much more importantly—is able simultaneously to consult parallel schemas as 'collections of interconnected neuronlike units'" (34). This distinction between linear and systems thinking suggests the familiar verbal ver-

sus visual modes of knowing in the human brain. It moves from biological to ecological analysis, where modes of knowing become
modes of seeing and interacting in the natural and social world. Here
again we map relationships on a field of transactions, a complex set of
dialectical polarities crisscrossing in a wider, dialogical conversation.

30. I especially value the theoretical force Brill gives to "co-" in her conversive terminology, and I pick up that crucial lens via the *co*mic
mode, which plays on and pragmatically resolves the tensions of the
commons, the ground that gives life and takes death. Indeed as my
chapter on humor and irony claims, the commonality in the comic
stands at the center, the ground, of the other four themes of this
study. In my choice to retain dialogic frameworks for ground theory,
I am pushing Mikhail Bakhtin's terms beyond his technical limits on
linguistic agency in heteroglossia, limits that Brill measures well. I
cast my "di-" with dialogics precisely because that prefix accounts
for the historical force of dichotomies, even while bringing those
forces into conversation with each other.

31. *Morning Edition*, National Public Radio, Wednesday, August 22,
2001. And see related Associated Press stories on the Klamath River
water controversies: Don Thompson, "Ways of Life Rise and Fall
with Klamath River" and Pauline Arrillaga, "Water Fight" www
.missoulian.com (accessed September 2, 2002).

32. Jodi Rave, "Natives Join Inauguration Ceremonies," *Missoulian*
(MT), January 4, 2005.

33. As I discuss further, John Marshall's 1832 Supreme Court decision in
Worcester v. Georgia acknowledges that the usurpation of Indian
lands was not in accordance with civilized modern behavior by the
rule of law but by right of "power, war, conquest." Marshall con-
cluded that because conquest was historical fact, "the actual state of
things," such illegal usurpation would become the legal foundation
of the new nation's relations with those who held aboriginal land
rights. That false relation of domination then became the law of the
land, on which the United States is built.

34. See Vine Deloria Jr.'s classic chapter "The Red and the Black" in
Custer Died for Your Sins for a discussion of Native politics of tribal
sovereignty in contrast to African American politics of integration,

as he makes a distinction between legal rights and civil rights, respectively.

35. See, for instance, Weaver et al., *American Indian Literary Nationalism* (2006); and Womack and Acoose, *Reasoning Together: The Native Critics Collective* (2008).

36. See Graff, "Co-optation."

37. For further examples of Indigenous transformations of Europeans, see the discussion of constitutional contributions in Barreiro, *Indian Roots of American Democracy*.

38. For dialogue within Native academic circles see, again, Weaver et al., *American Indian Literary Nationalism*; Womack and Acoose, *Reasoning Together*.

1. Knowing It Was to Come

1. Ruppert's discussion proceeds in dialogue with Paula Gunn Allen, Leslie Silko, Geary Hobson, and Jack D. Forbes (*Mediation* 28).

2. See Gerald Vizenor's use of this phrase, for instance, in *Heirs of Columbus*, 29, 39; and see Krupat's discussion of Vizenor's usage in his *The Turn to the Native*, circa p. 64. The critical question suggested in the phrase "stories in the blood" is one of racial essentialism, and Krupat attends to that issue. Ground theory clarifies fields of relations, especially in Native strategies that can invoke change yet retain "essential" connections as deep as "stories in the blood."

3. Jodi Rave, "Burns, Tester Wooing Native Vote in Campaigns' Final Weeks," *Missoulian* (MT), October 22, 2006.

4. One of the most nuanced discussions of this legendary moment in American history is in Strickland, "The Eagle's Empire."

5. For contemporary perspectives on reactionary movements against the resurgence of tribal sovereignty, see, for instance, Bordewich, *Killing the White Man's Indian*; Dudas, *The Cultivation of Resentment*.

6. Gretchen Ruethling, "Honoring Warriors from Both the Past and the Present," *New York Times*, June 10, 2006, http://www.nytimes.com/ 2006/06/10/us/10horses.html?_r=0 (accessed August 8, 2007).

7. See DeMallie, *The Sixth Grandfather*, 97, 135-37.

8. See Gerald Graff's nuanced discussion of "teaching the conflicts" as a pedagogical principle in *Professing Literature*, 2, 8, 14, 252, for example.

9. See Elmer, *On Lingering and Being Last*, for a broad discussion of the issues: "Sovereignty seems to be everywhere these days, and no one is very happy about it" (1), especially because many see the term as "an expression of Eurocentrism" (2). Elmer points usefully to "the trope of personification" and the interweaving of individual and national identities, where "the modern problem of sovereignty, as that unfolds in the new world, exemplifies a racialized logic of personification that conjoins individual and collective identities" (7), among various New World ethnicities. My own interweaving of Indigenous identity and sovereignty in this study, along with community, authenticity, and irony, analyzes a different slice of that "individual and collective" dynamic.

10. For another provocative perspective, I am indebted to Professor Michael D. Wilson in conversations on preferring the term *freedom* to *sovereignty*, a perspective linked to Alfred's point that for Indigenous nations, the term *sovereignty* has been co-opted in the ongoing colonization process.

11. See, for instance, Alfred's *Peace, Power, Righteousness*, 56, in the section entitled "'Sovereignty': An Inappropriate Concept."

12. See, for instance, Deloria's "Self-Determination and the Concept of Sovereignty"; Barker, *Sovereignty Matters*.

13. For context of federal Indian policy, and on termination in particular, see Wilkins, *American Indian Politics and the American Political System*; Wilkinson, *Blood Struggle*.

14. See Miller, *Native Americans, Discovered and Conquered*, as well as his commentary on Russia's contemporary applications of the doctrine at http://lawlib.lclark.edu/blog/native_america/?cat=7.

15. Following Anne Waters's essay "The Myth of 'Tribalism' and U.S. Colonialism" in the special issue of *Hypatia*, M. A. Jaimes-Guerrero offers the following perspective on the term in her essay "'Patriarchal Colonialism' and Indigenism: Implications for Native Feminist Spirituality and Native Womanism": "The meaning of 'tribalism' is often connoted with conformity and the subservience of the individual to the group, because each individual group member must follow group culture and rules, with little or no independent thinking—an almost 'infantile' behavior posture. On the more positive side,

tribalism connotes kinship and protection, meeting group members' needs for community and acceptance. This is the case among Native tribes, other ethnic groups, and other extended family traditions— including even gangs and athletic teams. Other terms attributed to the 'tribal order' include magic, rituals, mysticism, animism, protection of ancestral or cultural traditions, myths, rights of kinship, and sacred places. . . . Generally speaking, tribalism is not considered to reflect a high level of maturity or civilization within the Euroamerican hegemony; indeed, it is often considered to be primitive or savage, and therefore backward and uncivilized" (59)

16. For a theory of vertical binaries, see Deleuze, "The Simulacrum and Ancient Philosophy."

17. There are, again, vast historical contexts for the concept in addition to contemporary contests. See, for instance, in addition to other texts already cited, Wilkins, *American Indian Sovereignty and the U.S. Supreme Court*; Anaya, *Indigenous Peoples in International Law*; Williams, *The American Indian in Western Legal Thought*.

18. Barreiro, *Indian Roots of American Democracy*; Lyons and Mohawk, *Exiled in the Land of the Free*.

19. We read in Bailey, "Blackstone in America," "Jefferson said that Blackstone and David Hume's *History of England* 'have done more towards the suppression of the liberties of man, than all the millions of men in arms of Bonaparte,' because both books glorified the systems Jefferson had devoted his life to fighting. Yet on two occasions Jefferson listed the Commentaries as required reading for law students. . . . Jefferson's core disagreement with Blackstone, however, was Jefferson's opposition to adopting English common law in America. He was not alone in this view. Many advocated adopting a civil code along ancient Roman and contemporary European lines, and saw it as a final break away from England."

20. Again see Barreiro, *Indian Roots of American Democracy*.

21. These events helped establish the discourse analyzed in Bruyneel's *The Third Space of Sovereignty*.

22. Testimony on S.2111, The Honorable John A. Kitzhaber, M.D., Governor of the State of Oregon, Senate Energy and Natural Resources Committee, Water and Power Subcommittee, July 14, 1998.

23. Governor John Kitzhaber, comments to the Seattle City Club, September 17, 1999.

24. ATNI Resolution 98–07, "Three Sovereigns Governance of the Columbia River Basin Ecosystem," http://atni.org/~tribes/98winresolutions.htm#98–07.

25. Jim Luce, "Land of the Three Sovereigns" *Seattle Times*, May 3, 1998, http://seattletimes.nwsource.com (accessed May 4, 1998).

26. Kitzhaber comments, September 17, 1999; Bob Fick, "Batt Lashes Out against Salmon Proposal," idahonews.com, http://news.google.com/newspapers.

27. House Committee on Agriculture, February 27, 1998, http://agriculture.house.gov.

28. Bill Crampton, Opinion/Editorials, December 10, 1997, http://archives.seattletimes.com/cgi-bin . . . /display?storyID=36d4adeb5f&query=Bill+Crampton.

29. A similar Three Sovereigns approach is being considered for the Colorado River Basin, but it is telling that a gathering in 2008, the Colorado River Basin Science and Resource Management Symposium—Coming Together: Coordination of Science and Restoration Activities for the Colorado River Ecosystem, included minimal involvement from regional Native nations, even though the symposium made a claim to inclusion: "This basin-wide symposium will provide scientists, stakeholders, land and resource managers, and decision-makers the opportunity to learn about these various programs and exchange ideas and data enhancing the effectiveness of these programs—and their success in restoring and conserving the river's ecosystem." Native participation consisted of a very small percentage of papers and poster presentations among other speakers and panelists. Water Education Foundation, http://www.watereducation.org/doc.asp?id=1072&parentID=849 (accessed February 13, 2009).

30. Governor John Kitzhaber, "American Fisheries Society Speech," February 18, 2000, http://www.ccrh.org.

31. Other relevant cases include the highly influential 1974 Boldt Decision on northwest Native fishing rights and the ongoing issues of Native fishing in Wisconsin. See the Northwest Indian Fisheries

Commission website, http://www.nwifc.wa.gov; the Center for Columbia River History website, http://www.ccrh.org; Alex Tizon, "25 Years after the Boldt Decision: The Fish Tale That Changed History," *Seattle Times*, February 7, 1999, http://kohary.com/env/bill_020799.html (accessed August 9, 2007); Blumm, "Native Fishing Rights."

32. All citations to Apess are from his collected works, *On Our Own Ground*.

33. See Indian Law Resource Center, *Indian Rights—Human Rights*.

34. Buell, *New England Literary Culture*, 201.

35. Early nineteenth-century usage inserted an "r" in "Marshpee."

36. Consult Richard Slotkin, *Regeneration through Violence*, for the brutal edge of an ideology of erasure that Apess confronted.

37. In this context, comparisons of Apess's texts to King's are irresistible, especially to King's equanimity and nonviolence in his 1963 Letter from the Birmingham Jail. In part of that letter, the treatise "Why We Can't Wait," King wrote, after reciting a litany of brutal moments of segregation, "When you are forever fighting a degenerating sense of 'nobodiness' . . . then you will understand why we find it difficult to wait" (293).

38. See Trexler's *Sex and Conquest* for erotic domination in colonialism.

39. I discuss the "postindian" further in the chapter on humor.

40. Lyle Denniston, "Separation of Powers: Supreme Court Again Looking at How to Define Jurisdictions of Feds, States." *Missoulian* MT, May 22, 2000.

2. A Plethora of Animistic Factors

1. Moore, "Decolonializing Criticism."

2. "Reciprocal participatory perception" is a useful term from David Abram's *The Spell of the Sensuous*.

3. See my discussion of Young Bear's philosophy of insignificance in "Ray A. Young Bear."

4. Jodi Rave, "Natives Striving for Status in Tribes," *Missoulian* (MT), May 20, 2007, http://missoulian.com (accessed October 20, 2009).

5. See Robert W. Venables, "The Founding Fathers: Choosing to Be the Romans," in Barreiro. *Indian Roots of American Democracy*, 67–106.

6. See, for instance, DeMallie, "Kinship."

7. See, for instance, Red Eagle, *Red Earth*; Kipp, *Viet Cong at Wounded Knee.*

8. See Bigart, "Warriors in the Blackboard Jungle."

9. Again see Trexler's *Sex and Conquest* regarding erotic domination in colonialism.

10. Another study might explore further contradictions, where early American white projections onto Indians in captivity narratives and dime novels of sexual promiscuity or even dominance find their real-life mirror-image in these sexual depredations by white settlers on Indian women.

11. I look more closely at Winnemucca's representations of her family role as leaders in the chapter on authenticity.

12. See also Shanley's essay "Blood Ties and Blasphemy" for further discussion of "race," class, and gender in Native communities.

13. See O'Connell, introduction xix–xx.

14. It is noteworthy that this passage supplied the title for Simon Ortiz's 1983 edited volume, *Earth Power Coming: Short Fiction in Native American Literature.*

15. We should note again the painfully parallel theme of African American males in the civil rights movement, carrying signs that read, "I am a man."

16. See my related discussion of "radical patience" in "Silko's Blood Sacrifice."

17. Ecocriticism is the study of how literature and other arts represent relations between nature and culture. It offers a useful lens for further study of Native literatures, where those fundamental categories may break down. See, for instance, Glotfelty and Fromm, *The Ecocriticism Reader*; Adamson et al., *The Environmental Justice Reader.*

3. The Soul of the Indian Is Immortal

1. Joseph McDonald, remarks accepting on behalf of D'Arcy McNickle the H. G. Merriam Award for Montana Literature at the posthumous presentation by the Friends of the Maureen and Mike Mansfield Library, April 12, 2006, University of Montana.

2. See, for example, William Cronon's classic 1983 study, *Changes in*

the Land: Indians, Colonists and the Ecology of New England, for a detailed analysis of ecological changes in New England with the advent of European settlement, as well as for Indigenous effects.

3. Although it is set among prehistoric southwest cave dwellers, we might recognize McNickle's other novel, *Runner in the Sun*, written for a young adult readership and published in 1954—halfway between the publications of *Surrounded* and *Wind*—in a transitional position as a tipping point or fulcrum of McNickle's fictional trajectory toward affirmation of cultural regeneration.

4. For historical perspective, see Salish and Pend d'Oreille Culture Committee, *The Swan Valley Massacre of 1908: A Brief History*.

5. See O'Connell, introduction, xxiv–xxix, lxvii.

6. See especially Warrior, "Eulogy on William Apess"; Konkle, *Writing Indian Nations*.

7. Further, we must add to her textual persona the influence of her editor, Mary Peabody Mann. Mary Mann was the wife of Horace Mann, the famous education reformer; sister to Elizabeth Peabody, the activist publisher of the Transcendentalists; and sister-in-law to Nathaniel Hawthorne. The question of Mary Mann's involvement in Winnemucca's manuscript begs for archival investigation.

8. See *Indian Country Today*, March 22, 2005, http://www.indiancountry todaymedianetwork.com.

9. See Silko, *Almanac of the Dead* 472, 496, 503.

10. See Moore, "Rough Knowledge and Radical Understanding."

11. See "The Priest of the Sun" section in Momaday, *House Made of Dawn* and Momaday's seminal essay, "Man Made of Words."

12. See my discussion of Alexie's short story, "Dear John Wayne," and others of his works, in "Sherman Alexie."

13. See Bloom, *The Anxiety of Influence*.

14. See Whorf, "An American Indian Model of the Universe."

4. The Creative Ability of Indian People

1. Critical studies of Indian literature often begin with a discussion of the history and controversy of the term *authenticity*, usually as it revolves inside the term *Indian* or *Native American*. For instance, Owens begins *Other Destinies* with this view: "To begin to write

about something called 'the American Indian novel' is to enter a
slippery and uncertain terrain. Take one step into this region and we
are confronted with difficult questions of authority and ethnicity:
What is an Indian?" (3). He proceeds to discuss identity issues of
blood quantum, legal definitions, popular prejudices, and more.
Similarly, early in *That the People Might Live* Weaver states, "To discuss something labeled 'Native American literature' is to enter a
thicket that would make Brer Rabbit . . . envious. Almost immediately, briarlike questions arise. Who or what is a Native American?"
(4). Weaver cites other Native writers and concludes, "Ultimately,
racially based definitions are insufficient; what matters is one's
social and cultural milieu, one's way of life" (6). In *Reading the Fire*,
Ramsey suggests "literary ethnography" as a rubric for Native literary studies but cautions, "The danger lies in the way ethnographic
literary study tends tacitly to deny the imaginative freedom of the
writer" (182). Ramsey further discusses the dynamics of individualistic versus group identities toward the location of an authentic
Native voice. The issue in these ruminations is authenticity. In parallel studies of autobiography, Krupat and Brumble pursue the authenticity question. Krupat carefully analyzes what he labels the "original, bicultural composite compositions" of Indian autobiography to
delineate precisely what is and what is not "Indian" about a text in
an analysis that locates criteria of Indianness in an ethnographic
past (*For Those Who Come After* 31). Brumble explores constructions
of the self in Native autobiography, comparing, like Krupat's analytical category, the real with the less real, less authentically Indian subjectivity in the text, again as group-oriented rather than individualistic. Brumble suggests that "self-written autobiography is at least the
subject's *own* fiction, the subject's own conception of the self, and so
it must always be authentic in this sense at least" (*American Indian
Autobiography* 11). The critical goal of discovering authenticity is evident in the focus of such analyses, looking for an "authentic in this
sense at least." Weaver has coined a dismissive phrase for this kind
of analysis, calling it a "gymnastics of authenticity" (*That the People
Might Live* 9) because of its "essentializing" tendencies. Purism still
haunts the search for authenticity. Bernardin points out that Native

writers as well as critics, Native and non-Native, have all too frequently been embroiled in what she calls "the authenticity game." The reason for dismissing or ridiculing the question of authenticity, as I suggest, is that it eclipses other compelling questions and dynamics. A focus on authenticity tends to remain caught in a colonial relation to Native texts, at times because of the positionality of the critic as much as of the text. The Native voice in the text too often is relegated to a static, "authentic" past, solidifying the critic's own position in a specular, retrospective present, in the winning future of that lost past. Insofar as authenticity—which remains a premium—is defined only as pure or precolonial, such a focus excludes that quality from postcontact Indigenous cultures and voices.

2. I must call attention to a sadly relevant contemporary context. An article by John Stromnes, "Sociologist: Indian Women in Prison Need Respect," *Missoulian* (MT), June 28, 2006) included this passage: "Offering advice on how better to rehabilitate American Indians, who make up a disproportionate share of the burgeoning women's prison population . . . Luana Ross, a professor at the University of Washington, offered this main prescription [to the state Department of Corrections of Advisory Council]: 'Respect the Indian women as human beings, and honor their culture, traditions and family values. . . . Eliminate the repression of Native culture that goes on in the women's prison,' she said, referring to it as 'racism.'" Such elementary advice echoes a central point of Native writers across the centuries, but it highlights by contrast fundamental issues in authenticity as an affirmation of humanity deserving respect. In *Inventing the Savage*, Ross analyzes both implicit and explicit ways that disrespect is institutionalized.

3. Note the nineteenth-century usage of "Native American" parties to identify Euro-American "Nativist" settlers opposed to further immigration by French, Irish, Asian, and other nationalities. See, for instance, Gitlin's discussion of the nineteenth-century "Native American" anti-immigration movement in *The Twilight of Common Dreams*.

4. Resonance with Martin Buber's communicative goals in *I and Thou* is evident in Heidegger and others in this conversation.

5. See West, *Race Matters*.

6. See Duran and Duran, *Native American Postcolonial Psychology*; and O'Nell, *Disciplined Hearts* on the intriguingly painful concept of an "empty center" (56) of American Indian cultures. Temporal authenticity, the real as past, commands this view.

7. For some of the scholarly conversation around the Iroquois influence through Ben Franklin and others on the U.S. Constitution, as well as Haudenosaunee influence on the American women's rights movement and other cultural exchanges, again see Barreiro, *Indian Roots of American Democracy*.

8. See more discussion of Black Elk's vision of the circle in the sovereignty chapter.

9. See, for instance, Gort et al., *Dialogue and Syncretism*; Greenfield and Droogers, *Reinventing Religions*; Stewart and Shaw, *Syncretism/Anti-Syncretism*.

10. Any discussion of authenticity in Winnemucca must note her possibly inauthentic or exaggerated claims, especially concerning the chiefdom of her family over all Paiutes and her status as a princess. As we saw in the chapter on community, traditional Paiute society was organized as a loose confederation of clans, and her language of leadership must be seen through multiple filters, cultural and historical (see Zanjani, *Sarah Winnemucca* 8–9). If Winnemucca downplayed Paiute headmen outside her family's lineage, the jury is still out on how influential were her grandfather Truckee and her father Old Winnemucca. What is especially relevant here is Winnemucca's effort, like that of so many other intermediaries, to shape authenticity as translation into the terms of the invaders. She translated her patrilineal line of chiefs who consulted with their people into perhaps a more Euro-American model of her grandfather as "chief of the entire Piute nation," who eventually appointed her father as "head chief of the Piute nation" (*Life Among the Piutes* 67). This was authenticity as the authority to invent or rework a reality for literary and political purchase. It worked to fulfill the expectations of her primarily white readership and to rally support for her people's cause.

11. It is relevant to compare the rhetorical sexual politics of Winnemucca and her editor, Mary Peabody Mann, in her chapter 2 to the strategy

of Harriet Jacobs and her similar white activist editor, Lydia Maria Child, in *Incidents in the Life of a Slave Girl* (1861). In Jacobs the rhetorical tactic was to paint slavery as sexually immoral and corrosive to the virtue of Woman, and thereby to enlist white womanhood in the abolitionist cause. Cruelty in slavery and on the Indian frontier was generally recognized in American public discourse, but sexual corruption was not as openly acknowledged. The "monstrous features" that Child and Jacobs sought to expose were parallel with the sexual depredations of the settler culture in Paiute Country that it was Winnemucca's and Mann's purpose to expose as well.

12. See Vizenor on the "tribal striptease" (e.g., *Trickster of Liberty* 44).

13. See, for example, La Flesche, *The Middle Five*; Lomawaima and McCarty, *To Remain an Indian*; Child, *Boarding School Seasons*.

14. See Harpham, *On the Grotesque*; Di Renzo, *American Gargoyles*; O'Connor, *The Grotesque*; Brogan, *Cultural Haunting*; Berglund, *The National Uncanny*.

15. Richard E. Nicholls, "Skin Games," review of *Indian Killer*, *New York Times Book Review*, November 24, 1996.

5. The Last Laugh

1. For discussion of this dynamic in Vizenor, see Moore, "Moon Vines among the Ruins." Note that "treeline" is a frequent image and theme throughout Vizenor's work.

2. For a useful discussion of the untraceable roots of the phrase "the personal is political" in mid-twentieth-century circles of social philosophy and activist feminist and labor movements, see the Women Studies listserv page at http://userpages.umbc.edu/~korenman/wmst/pisp.html.

3. See Tuleja, "What Do You Mean We, White Man?"

4. See Vine Deloria Jr., *Custer Died for Your Sins*, chapter 4, "Anthropologists and Other Friends." And see Fabian: "Anthropology's alliance with the forces of oppression is neither a simple nor a recent one" (*Time and the Other* 2; also 18–19, 46–49, 149).

5. Many studies and creative works, large and small, have explored the dynamics of the trickster trope in Native American literatures, and I refer the reader to critical works, starting with Ballinger's *Living Side-*

ways and Ballinger's eighteen-page bibliography. Instead of focusing on that widespread trickster form and instead of repeating the work of those studies, this chapter looks at an underlying aesthetic and ethic of pluralism that animates trickster and other comic modes. Validating the communal nature of Native humor that I am reading in this study, many trickster tales hold Coyote or Raven or Fox or Iktomi accountable for his and/or her own grandiose selfishness.

For what Vizenor calls "trickster hermeneutics," see, for instance, Babcock-Abrahams, "'A Tolerated Margin of Mess'"; Moore, "Myth, History, and Identity in Silko and Young Bear"; Blaeser, *Gerald Vizenor*; Kroeber, "Deconstructionist Criticism and American Indian Literatures" and "An Introduction to the Art of Traditional American Indian Narration"; Krupat, "Post-structuralism and Oral Literature"; Lincoln, *Indi'n Humor*; Linscott, "The North American Indian Trickster"; Murray, *Forked Tongues*; A. Ortiz, "The Sacred Clown"; Radin, *The Trickster*; Roberts, "The African American Animal Trickster as Hero"; Ruoff, "Oral Traditions and New Forms" and "Woodland Word Warrior"; Vizenor, introduction, "The Ruins of Representation,"; "Trickster Discourse," and *The Trickster of Liberty*; Wiget, "His Life in His Tail."

6. Wayne Stein, comments at memorial for James Welch, Wilma Theater, Missoula, Montana, August 28, 2003.

7. Jon Turney, "Against Simplicity," review of Mary Midgley's *The Myths We Live By*, *Guardian* (London), August 15, 2003, http://www .guardian.co.uk/books/2003/aug/16/highereducation.news1 (accessed October 20, 2009).

8. Driving on Interstate 84 in northeastern Oregon during the summer of 2005, travelers could see a full-size billboard image of a cigar-store wooden Indian with the inscription, "Close, but no cigar." That pun is followed by an invitation to visit a new Umatilla tribal museum (funded by casino money), where tourists can see beyond the wooden Indian imagery to a new tribal self-representation.

9. See, for instance, Barreiro, *Indian Roots of American Democracy*; Lyons and Mohawk, *Exiled in the Land of the Free*; Weatherford, *Native Roots*.

10. "El sitio de Guaman Poma," Det Kongelige Bibliotek, www.kb.dk/ elib/mss/poma/.

11. Mapping the historical dialogues, it is important to point out that early voices for reciprocity were not confined entirely to the colonized. In varying degrees, at least three of the earliest names in the Spanish colonies were calling for more humane respect across the racial lines. Bartolomé de las Casas, Bernardino de Sahagun, and Cabeza de Vaca each recognized the efficacy and perhaps the ethics of mutuality instead of domination, even if for purposes of conversion. Similarly in early New England, we can contrast both Thomas Morton and Roger Williams, the apostates, with William Bradford and John Endecott, the more orthodox Puritans, in parallel ways to the differences south of the border between the benign Las Casas and the imperial Hernando Cortés. Although it is abundantly clear that even the more humane approaches and the "good intentions" of missionaries and others served the imperial purposes of the colonial project, the point is that opportunities for dialogue did exist from the beginning and the dialectical history that erased dialogue was not inevitable.

12. See the research into pre-Columbian Native American voyages to Europe by the late Jack Forbes, emeritus professor of Native American Studies at University of California-Davis, *The American Discovery of Europe*.

13. See, for instance, Girard, *Violence and the Sacred* and *The Scapegoat*.

14. I'm grateful to Kathryn W. Shanley for comments sparking this direction of the discussion.

15. See Fiedler's *Love and Death in the American Novel* and *Return of the Vanishing American*.

16. See paragraphs 178–96, entitled "Independence and Dependence of Self-Consciousness: Lordship and Bondage," in Hegel's *The Phenomenology of Spirit*.

17. Jodi Rave, "Defining Culture: George Longfish," *Missoulian* (MT), April 4, 2007.

18. Elvis Mitchell, "A Poet Finds His Past Is Just Where He Left It," film review, *New York Times*, October 18, 2002, http://www.nytimes.com/2002/10/18/movies/film-review-a-poet-finds-his-past-is-just-where -he-left-it.html (accessed October 20, 2009).

19. See Kenneth Lincoln, *Native American Renaissance*.

Conclusion

1. This process across the centuries of decentering power and difference has been questioned lately by white male liberals as the Balkanization of the left into a politically ineffective morass of identity politics. See Rorty, *Achieving Our Country*; Gitlin, *The Twilight of Common Dreams*. In my piece "The Twilight of White Liberalism," I recognize this lamentation as partly a backlash, but there is certainly more to the conversation. For instance, Gitlin describes the democratization and the "postmodernization of history" as a slippery slope "to multiply boundlessly. The result is vertigo" (197). It is difficult even for progressive liberals to conceive of a community of difference.

2. Among many studies of the healing power of Indigenous stories, see, for instance, the recent Canadian publication by the Métis scholar Jo-Ann Episkenew, with the instructive title *Taking Back Our Spirits: Indigenous Literature, Public Policy, and Healing*. Episkenew writes concisely, "Not only does Indigenous literature respond to and critique the policies of the Government of Canada; it also functions as 'medicine' to help cure the colonial contagion by healing the communities that these policies have injured. It accomplishes this by challenging the 'master narrative,' that is, a summary of the stories that embody the settlers' 'socially shared understanding'" (2). Because of such strategies of Indigenous voices on both sides of the Canada-U.S. border, it is important to keep in mind the continental, indeed hemispheric, indeed global resonances of such healing practices of Indigenous narratives. For more perspective on global Indigenous dynamics, see, for example, Chadwick Allen's *Blood Narrative*.

3. Affirming the "ground," Nelson shows further how Silko's and other Native narratives convey "landscapes that function as pre-verbal, pre-conceptual, pre-cultural frames of reference, frames that shape the creative vision and language of these texts" (*Place and Vision* 9). With this lens on the land as presence in Indigenous writing, Nelson shows "that the land has a life of its own" (8) and that such geographic vitality imposes itself actively on the human imagination rather than only vice versa. Critiquing a literary humanism that assumes a "preemption of significance, or privileging of human

imagination" (8), Nelson foregrounds "the *pre*-human context of the human condition in these stories" (8). Drawing on his actual travels in those places, Nelson's analysis does the literal groundwork to show how "a physical landscape . . . comes to exist (the way referents can be said to 'exist') within the fiction as well" (6). In Nelson's work on the living presence of the land in Native fiction, where "referents can be said to 'exist,'" we may read also a critique of Derrida's skepticism about a "metaphysics of presence." Unlike a Derridean world of signification where nothing is grounded, in Nelson's view of Silko's landscape the land remains a presence, perhaps like the ineffable "excess"—another "outside"—to a Derridean universe of slippery signification. Yet the terms of Nelson's analysis are indeed vulnerable to deconstruction, especially where he might depend on the linear binary of natural and cultural, that is, his "pre-human" and "human." The structuralism must deconstruct where those oppositions contain each other, where nature and landscape are "pre-human" or "pre-verbal, pre-conceptual, pre-cultural," against culture as "human."

Biographical Appendix

1. Ruoff, *American Indian Literatures*, 53.
2. See Bevis's chapter 6, "McNickle: Homing In," in *Ten Tough Trips: Montana Writers and the West*.
3. See Kenneth Lincoln's influential 1983 book, *Native American Renaissance*. Also note James Ruppert's summation of the controversy over the label and the historical category: "Scholars hesitate to use the phrase because it might imply that Native writers were not producing significant work before that time, or that these writers sprang up without longstanding community and tribal roots. Indeed, if this was a rebirth, what was the original birth?" ("Fiction" 173).

BIBLIOGRAPHY

Abram, David. *The Spell of the Sensuous: Perception and Language in a More-than-Human World*. New York: Vintage, 1996.

Abrams, M. H. *The Mirror and the Lamp: Romantic Theory and the Critical Tradition*. New York: Oxford University Press, 1971.

Adamson, Joni, Mei Mei Evans, and Rachel Stein, eds. *The Environmental Justice Reader: Politics, Poetics, and Pedagogy*. Tucson: University of Arizona Press, 2002.

Alcoff, Linda. "Cultural Feminism versus Post-structuralism: The Identity Crisis in Feminist Theory." *Signs: Journal of Women in Culture and Society* 13.3 (1988): 405–36.

Alexie, *The Absolutely True Diary of a Part-Time Indian*. New York: Little, Brown, 2007.

Alexie, Sherman. *The Business of Fancydancing: Stories and Poems*. Brooklyn: Hanging Loose Press, 1992.

———. *The Business of Fancydancing: The Screenplay*. Brooklyn: Hanging Loose Press, 2003.

———. *Dangerous Astronomy*. Boise ID: Limberlost Press, 2005.

———. "A Dialogue on Race with President Clinton." Transcript. Public Broadcasting System, July 9, 1998. http://www.pbs.org/newshour/bb/race_relations/OneAmerica/transcript.html (accessed October 20, 2009).

———. *First Indian on the Moon*. Brooklyn: Hanging Loose Press, 1993.

———. *Flight: A Novel*. New York: Black Cat, 2007.

———. "Ghost Dance." In *McSweeney's Mammoth Treasury of Thrilling Tales*, ed. Michael Chabon. New York: Vintage, 2002. 341–53.

———. *I Would Steal Horses*. Niagara Falls NY: Slipstream, 1992.

———. *Indian Killer*. New York: Atlantic Monthly Press, 1996.

———. *The Lone Ranger and Tonto Fistfight in Heaven*. New York: Atlantic Monthly Press, 1993.

———. *Old Shirts and New Skins*. Los Angeles: American Indian Studies Center, University of California, 1993.

———. *One Stick Song*. Brooklyn: Hanging Loose Press, 2000.

———. "Relevant Contradictions." theStranger.com 12.24 (February 27– March 5, 2003) (accessed October 20, 2009).

———. *Reservation Blues*. New York: Atlantic Monthly Press, 1995.

———. *Seven Mourning Songs for the Cedar Flute I Have Yet to Learn to Play*. Walla Walla WA: Whitman College Book Arts Lab, 1994.

———. *Smoke Signals: A Screenplay*. New York: Hyperion, 1998.

———. *The Summer of Black Widows*. Brooklyn: Hanging Loose Press, 1996.

———. *Ten Little Indians: Stories*. New York: Grove Press, 2003.

———. *The Toughest Indian in the World*. New York: Grove Press, 2000.

———. "The Unauthorized Autobiography of Me." In *One Stick Song*. Brooklyn: Hanging Loose Press, 2000. 13–25.

———. *Water Flowing Home*. Boise ID: Limberlost, 1995.

———. "What I've Learned as a Filmmaker." In *The Business of Fancydancing: The Screenplay*. Brooklyn: Hanging Loose Press, 2003.

Alfred, Taiaiake. *Heeding the Voices of Our Ancestors: Kahnawake Mohawk Politics and the Rise of Native Nationalism*. Toronto: Oxford University Press, 1995.

———. *Peace, Power, Righteousness: An Indigenous Manifesto*. Toronto: Oxford University Press, 1999.

Allen, Chadwick. *Blood Narrative: Indigenous Identity in American Indian and Maori Literary and Activist Texts*. Durham NC: Duke University Press, 2002.

Allen, Paula Gunn. "The Sacred Hoop: A Contemporary Perspective." In Studies in *American Indian Literature: Critical Essays and Course Designs*, ed. Paula Gunn Allen. New York: MLA, 1983. 3–22.

———. "Teaching American Indian Oral Literatures." In *Studies in American Indian Literature: Critical Essays and Course Designs*, ed. Paula Gunn Allen. New York: MLA, 1983. 33–51.

Anaya, S. James. *Indigenous Peoples in International Law*. New York: Oxford University Press, 1996.

Anderson, Benedict. *Imagined Communities: Reflections on the Origin and Spread of Nationalism*. 1983. New York: Verso, 2006.

Apess, William. *On Our Own Ground: The Complete Writings of William Apess, a Pequot*. Ed. Barry O'Connell. Amherst: University of Massachusetts Press, 1992.

Aristotle. *De Poetica (Poetics): The Basic Works of Aristotle*. Ed. Richard McKeon. New York: Random House, 1941.

Babcock-Abrahams, Barbara. "'A Tolerated Margin of Mess': The Trickster and His Tales Reconsidered." In *Critical Essays on Native American Literature*, ed. Andrew Wiget. New York: Hall, 1985. 153–85.

Bailey, Greg. "Blackstone in America: Lectures by an English Lawyer Become the Blueprint for a New Nation's Laws and Leaders." *Archiving Early America*. http://www.earlyamerica.com/review/spring97/black stone.html (accessed October 20, 2009).

Baker, Robert. *The Extravagant: Crossings of Modern Poetry and Modern Philosophy*. Notre Dame IN: University of Notre Dame Press, 2005.

Bakhtin, M. M. "Discourse in the Novel." In *The Dialogic Imagination: Four Essays*, ed. Michael Holmquist. Austin: University of Texas Press, 1981. 259–422.

Ballinger, Franchot. *Living Sideways: Trickster in American Indian Oral Traditions*. Norman: University of Oklahoma Press, 2004.

Banks, James A. *Educating Citizens in a Multicultural Society*. New York: Teachers College Press, 1997.

———, ed. *Multicultural Education, Transformative Knowledge, and Action*. New York: Teachers College Press, 1996.

Banks, James A., and Cherry A. McGee Banks, eds. *Multicultural Education: Issues and Perspectives*. 4th ed. New York: Wiley, 2001.

Barker, Joanne, ed. *Sovereignty Matters: Locations of Contestation and Possibility in Indigenous Struggles for Self-Determination*. Lincoln: University of Nebraska Press, 2005.

Barnes, Kim. "Leslie Marmon Silko Interview." *Journal of Ethnic Studies* 3 (Winter 1986): 83–105.

Barreiro, Jose, ed. *Indian Roots of American Democracy*. Ithaca NY: Akwe:Kon Press, Cornell University, 1992.

Barsh, Russell Lawrence, and James Youngblood Henderson. *The Road: Indian Tribes and Political Liberty*. Berkeley: University of California Press, 1980.

Basso, Keith. *Wisdom Sits in Places: Landscape and Language among the Western Apache*. Albuquerque: University of New Mexico Press, 1996.

Bataille, Gretchen M., and Charles L. P. Silet, eds. *The Pretend Indians: Images of Native Americans in the Movies*. Ames: Iowa State University Press, 1980.

Bates, Sarah, curator. *Indian Humor*. San Francisco: American Indian Contemporary Arts, 1995.

Beard, Laura J. "A Society Based on Names: Ray Young Bear's *Black Eagle Child: The Facepaint Narratives*." *Wicazo Sa Review* 21.2 (2006): 127–45.

Beck, Nicholas. "The Vanishing Californians: The Education of Indians in the Nineteenth Century." *Southern California Quarterly* 69.1 (1987): 33–50.

Bellin, Joshua David. *Demon of the Continent: Indians and the Shaping of America*. Philadelphia: University of Pennsylvania Press, 2001.

Berglund, Renee L. *The National Uncanny: Indian Ghosts and American Subjects*. Hanover NH: University of New England Press, 1999.

Berkhofer, Robert F., Jr. *The White Man's Indian: Images of the American Indian from Columbus to the Present*. New York: Knopf, 1978.

Berlant, Lauren. *The Anatomy of National Fantasy: Hawthorne, Utopia and Everyday Life*. Chicago: University of Chicago Press, 1991.

Bernardin, Susan. "The Authenticity Game: 'Getting Real' in Contemporary American Indian Literature." In *True West: Authenticity and the American West*, ed. William R. Handley and Nathaniel Lewis. Lincoln: University of Nebraska Press, 2004. 155–75.

Berry, Philippa, and Andrew Wernick, eds. *Shadow of Spirit: Postmodernism and Religion*. London: Routledge, 1992.

Bevis, William W. *Ten Tough Trips: Montana Writers and the West*. Seattle: University of Washington Press, 1990.

Biolsi, Thomas, and Larry J. Zimmerman, eds. *Indians and Anthropolo-*

gists: *Vine Deloria, Jr., and the Critique of Anthropology.* Tucson: University of Arizona Press, 1997.

Bigart, Robert. "Warriors in the Blackboard Jungle." *Elementary School Journal* 74.7 (1974): 408-21.

Bird, Gloria. "The Exaggeration of Despair in Sherman Alexie's *Reservation Blues.*" *Wicazo Sa Review* 11.2 (1995): 47-52.

Blaeser, Kimberly M. *Gerald Vizenor: Writing in the Oral Tradition.* Norman: University of Oklahoma Press, 1996.

——. "The New 'Frontier' of Native American Literature: Dis-arming History with Tribal Humor." In *Native American Perspectives on Literature and History*, ed. Alan R. Velie. Norman: University of Oklahoma Press, 1994. 37-50.

Bloch, Maurice. "Language, Anthropology and Cognitive Science." *Man* 26.2 (1991): 183-98.

Blodgett, Harold. *Samson Occom.* Hanover NH: Dartmouth College, 1935.

Bloom, Harold. *The Anxiety of Influence.* 1973. New York: Oxford University Press, 1997.

Blumm, Michael C. "Native Fishing Rights and Environmental Protection in North America and New Zealand: A Comparative Analysis of Profits a Prendre and Habitat Servitudes." *Wisconsin International Law Journal* 8.1 (1989): 1-50.

Bordewich, Fergus M. *Killing the White Man's Indian: Reinventing Native Americans at the End of the Twentieth Century.* New York: Doubleday, 1996.

Bradford, William. *Of Plymouth Plantation: Bradford's History of the Plymouth Settlement, 1608-1650.* 1909. San Antonio TX: Vision Forum, 2003.

Brant, Beth (Degonwadonti), ed. *A Gathering Of Spirit: A Collection by North American Indian Women.* Ithaca NY: Firebrand Books, 1988.

Brill de Ramírez, Susan Berry. *Contemporary American Indian Literatures and the Oral Tradition.* Tucson: University of Arizona Press, 1999.

Brimlow, George F. "The Life of Sarah Winnemucca: The Formative Years." *Oregon Historical Quarterly*, June 2, 1952, 103-34.

Britain, Barbara, producer. *Return to Shetek: The Courage of the Fool Soldiers.* DVD. Sioux Falls SD, 2007.

Brogan, Kathleen. *Cultural Haunting: Ghosts and Ethnicity in Recent American Literature.* Charlottesville: University of Virginia Press, 1998.

Brooks, Lisa Tanya. *The Common Pot: The Recovery of Native Space in the Northeast*. Minneapolis: University of Minnesota Press, 2008.

Bross, Kristina, and Hilary E. Wyss, eds. *Early Native Literacies in New England: A Documentary and Critical Anthology*. Amherst: University of Massachusetts Press, 2008.

Brown, Dee. *Bury My Heart at Wounded Knee: An Indian History of the American West*. New York: Holt, Rinehart, & Winston, 1971.

Bruce-Novoa, Juan. *Reconstructing a Chicano/a Literary Heritage: Hispanic Colonial Literature of the Southwest*. Tucson: University of Arizona Press, 1993.

Brumble, H. David. *American Indian Autobiography*. Berkeley: University of California Press, 1988.

Bruyneel, Kevin. *The Third Space of Sovereignty: The Postcolonial Politics of U.S.-Indigenous Relations*. Minneapolis: University of Minnesota Press, 2001.

Buell, Lawrence. *New England Literary Culture: From Revolution through Renaissance*. New York: Cambridge University Press, 1989.

Burnstick, Don. Promotional flyer. University of Montana. September 2005.

Burton, Antoinette, ed. *After the Imperial Turn: Thinking with and through the Nation*. Durham NC: Duke University Press, 2003.

Butler, Judith. *Gender Trouble: Feminism and the Subversion of Identity*. New York : Routledge, 1990.

Cabeza de Vaca. *La Relación*. 1555. Southwestern Writer's Collection at Texas State University. www.library.txstate.edu/swwc/cdv/index.html (accessed October 20, 2009).

Canfield, Gae Whitney. *Sarah Winnemucca of the Northern Paiutes*. Norman: University of Oklahoma Press, 1983.

Carlson, David J. *Sovereign Selves: American Indian Autobiography and the Law*. Urbana: University of Illinois Press, 2006.

Carroll, Clint. "Articulating Indigenous Statehood: Cherokee State Formation and Implications for the U.N. Declaration on the Rights of Indigenous Peoples." In *Indigenous Rights in the Age of the UN Declaration*, ed. Elvira Pulitano. Minneapolis: University of Minnesota Press, 2012. 143–71.

Chatwin, Bruce. *The Songlines*. New York: Penguin, 1987.

Child, Brenda J. *Boarding School Seasons: American Indian Families, 1900–1940*. Lincoln: University of Nebraska Press, 2000.

Christie, Stuart. "Renaissance Man: The Tribal 'Schizophrenic' in Sherman Alexie's *Indian Killer*." *American Indian Culture and Research Journal* 25.4 (2001) 1–19.

Clifford, James. *The Predicament of Culture*. Cambridge MA: Harvard University Press, 1988.

Cohen, Felix S. *Handbook of Federal Indian Law*. Washington DC: USGPO 1945.

Cole, David. "Lost in Translation." *Nation* 282.19 (2006): 6.

Collins, Gail. "How Texas Inflicts Bad Textbooks on Us." *New York Review of Books* 59.11 (2012) 18–20.

Conrad, Susan P. *Perish the Thought: Intellectual Women in Romantic America, 1830–1860*. Secaucus NJ: Citadel Press, 1978.

Cook-Lynn, Elizabeth. "The American Indian Fiction Writer: Cosmopolitanism, Nationalism, the Third World, and First Nation Sovereignty." *Wicazo Sa Review*. 9.2 (1993): 26–36.

Coulombe, Joseph L. "The Approximate Size of His Favorite Humor: Sherman Alexie's Comic Connections and Disconnections in *The Lone Ranger and Tonto Fistfight in Heaven*." *American Indian Quarterly* 26.1 (2002): 94–115.

Cox, James H. "Introducing Gerald Vizenor to Sherman Alexie: A Consideration of the Contemporary Indian Spectrum." Paper presented at American Literature Association Symposium on Native American Literature, Puerto Vallarta, Mexico, November 1999.

——. *Muting White Noise: Native American and European American Novel Traditions*. Norman: University of Oklahoma Press, 2006.

Cronon, William. *Changes in the Land: Indians, Colonists and the Ecology of New England*. New York: Hill and Wang, 1983.

——. "Frederick Jackson Turner." In *A Companion to American Thought*, ed. Richard Wightman Fox and James T. Kloppenberg. Cambridge, England: Blackwell, 1995. 691–92.

Cross, Raymond. "Tribes as Rich Nations: An Inquiry into Tribal Self-Determination as a Means for Restoring Tribal Life-Worlds." *Oregon Law Review* 79.4 (2000). http://law.uoregon.edu/org/olrold/archives/79/79olr893.pdf (accessed October 20, 2009).

Cutter, Martha J. *Lost and Found in Translation: Contemporary Ethnic American Writing and the Politics of Language Diversity*. Chapel Hill: University of North Carolina Press, 2005.

D'Andrade, Roy. *The Development of Cognitive Anthropology*. Cambridge, England: Cambridge University Press, 1995.

de la Cadena, Marisol, and Orin Starn, eds. *Indigenous Experience Today*. New York: Berg, 2007.

Deleuze, Gilles. "The Simulacrum and Ancient Philosophy: Plato and the Simulacrum." In *The Logic of Sense*. New York: Columbia University Press, 1990. 253–65.

Deloria, Ella. "Kinship Was the All-Important Matter." 1944. In *Native Heritage: Personal Accounts by American Indians, 1790 to the Present*, ed. Arlene Hirschfeler. New York: Macmillan, 1995. 9–11.

Deloria, Philip J. *Playing Indian*. New Haven CT: Yale University Press, 1998.

Deloria, Vine, Jr. *Custer Died for Your Sins*. New York: Macmillan, 1969.

———. *Destroying Dogma: Vine Deloria Jr. and His Influence on American Society*. Ed. Steve Pavlik and Daniel R. Wildcat. Golden CO: Fulcrum, 2006.

———. "Foreword: The American Fantasy." In *The Pretend Indians: Images of Native Americans in the Movies*, ed. Gretchen M. Bataille and Charles L. P. Silet. Ames: Iowa State University Press, 1980. ix–xvi.

———. *God Is Red: A Native View of Religion*. 1972. Golden CO: Fulcrum, 1992.

———. "Religion and Revolution among American Indians." *Worldview* 17 (January 1, 1974). Reprinted in *For This Land: Writings on Religion in America*, by Vine Deloria Jr. and James Treat. New York: Routledge, 1999. 36–43.

———. "Self-Determination and the Concept of Sovereignty." In *Economic Development in American Indian Reservation*, ed. Roxanne Dunbar Ortiz. Albuquerque: University of New Mexico Native American Studies, 1979. 22–28.

Deloria, Vine, Jr., and Suzan Shown Harjo. *We Talk, You Listen: New Tribes, New Turf*. Lincoln: University of Nebraska Press, 1970.

Deloria, Vine, Jr., and Clifford M. Lytle. *American Indian, American Justice*. Austin: University of Texas Press, 1983.

Deloria, Vine, Jr., and Clifford M. Lytle. *The Nations Within: The Past and Future of American Indian Sovereignty*. Austin: University of Texas Press, 1984.

Deloria, Vine, Jr., and James Treat. *For This Land: Writings on Religion in America*. New York: Routledge, 1999.

Deloria, Vine, Jr., and David E. Wilkins. *Tribes, Treaties, and Constitutional Tribulations*. Austin: University of Texas Press, 1999.

DeMallie, Raymond J. "Kinship: The Foundation for Native American Society." In *Studying Native America: Problems and Prospects*, ed. Russell Thornton. Madison: University of Wisconsin Press, 1998. 306–56.

———, ed. *The Sixth Grandfather: Black Elk's Teachings Given to John G. Neihardt*. Lincoln: University of Nebraska Press, 1984.

Denning, Michael. *The Cultural Front: The Laboring of American Culture in the Twentieth Century*. New York: Verso, 1998.

DeRosa, Robin, ed. *Assimilation and Subversion in Earlier American Literature*. Newcastle, England: Cambridge Scholars Press, 2006.

Derounian-Stodola, Kathryn Zabelle. *The War in Words: Reading the Dakota Conflict through the Captivity Literature*. Lincoln: University of Nebraska Press, 2009.

DiNova, Joanne R. *Spiraling Webs of Relation: Movements toward an Indigenist Criticism*. New York: Routledge, 2005.

Di Renzo, Anthony. *American Gargoyles: Flannery O'Connor and the Medieval Grotesque*. Carbondale: Southern Illinois University Press, 1993.

Dirlik, Arif. *Postmodernity's Histories: The Past as Legacy and Project*. Lanham MD: Rowman & Littlefield, 1999.

Dobyns, Henry F. *Their Number Become Thinned: Native American Population Dynamics in Eastern North America*. Knoxville: University of Tennessee Press, 1983.

Douglass, Frederick. *Narrative of the Life of Frederick Douglass, an American Slave*. 1845. New York: Penguin. 1986.

Drinnon, Richard. *Facing West: The Metaphysics of Indian-Hating and Empire-Building*. Minneapolis: University of Minnesota Press, 1980.

Droogers, André. "Syncretism: The Problem of Definition, and the Definition of the Problem." In *Dialogue and Syncretism: An Interdisciplinary Approach*, ed. J. D. Gort et al. Grand Rapids MI: Wm. B. Eerdmans, 1989. 7.

Droogers, André, and Sidney M. Greenfield. "Recovering and Reconstructing Syncretism." In *Reinventing Religions: Syncretism and Transformation in Africa and the Americas*, ed. Sydney M. Greenfield and
André Droogers. New York: Rowman & Littlefield, 2001. 21–42.

Du Bois, W. E. B. *The Souls of Black Folk*. 1903. New York: Oxford University Press, 2007.

Dudas, Jeffrey R. *The Cultivation of Resentment: Treaty Rights and the New
Right*. Stanford: Stanford University Press, 2008.

Duran, Eduardo, and Bonnie Duran. *Native American Postcolonial Psychology*. Albany: State University of New York Press, 1995.

Duran, Eduardo, Bonnie Duran, and Maria Yellow Horse Brave Heart.
"Native Americans and the Trauma of History." In *Studying Native
America: Problems and Prospects*, ed. Russell Thornton. Madison: Uni-
versity of Wisconsin Press, 1998. 60–76.

Ebersole, Gary L. *Captured by Text: Puritan to Postmodern Images of Indian
Captivity*. Charlottesville: University of Virginia Press, 1995.

Egan, Ken, Jr. "*The Big Sky* and the Siren Song of Apocalypse." In *Fifty
Years after* The Big Sky: *New Perspectives on the Fiction and Films of A. B.
Guthrie, Jr.*, ed. William E. Farr and William W. Bevis. Helena: Mon-
tana Historical Society, 2001. 9–19.

Elmer, Jonathan. *On Lingering and Being Last: Race and Sovereignty in the
New World*. New York: Fordham University Press, 2008.

Emerson, Ralph Waldo. "Letter to Martin Van Buren, President of the
United States." In *Ralph Waldo Emerson: Selected Essays, Lectures, and
Poems*, ed. Robert D. Richardson Jr. New York: Bantam, 1990. 101–5.

———. *Ralph Waldo Emerson Selected Essays, Lectures, and Poems*. Ed. Robert D. Richardson Jr. New York: Bantam, 1990.

Emerson, Ralph Waldo, and Henry David Thoreau. *Nature/Walking*. Boston: Beacon Press, 1991.

Episkenew, Jo-Ann. *Taking Back Our Spirits: Indigenous Literature, Public
Policy, and Healing*. Winnipeg: University of Manitoba Press, 2009.

Evernden, Neil. "Beyond Ecology: Self, Place, and the Pathetic Fallacy."
In *The Ecocriticism Reader: Landmarks in Literary Ecology*, ed. Cheryll
Glotfelty and Harold Fromm. Athens: University of Georgia Press,
1996. 92–104.

Fabian, Johannes. *Time and the Other: How Anthropology Makes Its Object.* New York: Columbia University Press, 1983.

Farr, William E., and William W. Bevis, eds. *Fifty Years after* The Big Sky: *New Perspectives on the Fiction and Films of A. B. Guthrie, Jr.* Helena: Montana Historical Society, 2001.

Fernandez, James. *Persuasions and Performances: The Play of Tropes in Culture.* Bloomington: Indiana University Press, 1986.

Fiedler, Leslie. *Love and Death in the American Novel.* New York: Dell, 1966.

——. *Return of the Vanishing American.* New York: Stein and Day, 1968.

Fisher, Philip. "Democratic Social Space: Whitman, Melville, and the Promise of American Transparency." *Representations* 24 (Fall 1988): 60–101.

Flanagan, Kieran, and Peter C. Jupp, eds. *Postmodernity, Sociology and Religion.* London: Macmillan and St. Martin's Press, 1996.

Forbes, Jack D. *The American Discovery of Europe.* Champaign: University of Illinois Press, 2007.

Fowler, Catharine S. "Sarah Winnemucca." In *American Indian Intellectuals,* ed. Margot Liberty. 1976 Proceedings of the American Ethnological Society. St. Paul: West, 1978. 33–42.

Frazier, Sandra LeBeau. "New York." Unpublished manuscript.

Fried, Morton H. *The Notion of Tribe.* San Francisco: Cummings, 1975.

Gandhi, M. K. *Non-violent Resistance (Satyagraha).* 1961. New York: Dover, 2001.

Geer, Emily Apt. "Lucy W. Hayes and the New Women of the 1880's." *Hayes Historical Journal* 3.1–2 (1980) 18–26.

Geertz, Armin W. *The Invention of Prophecy: Continuity and Meaning in Hopi Indian Religion.* Berkeley: University of California Press, 1994.

Gehm, Katherine. *Sarah Winnemucca: Most Extraordinary Woman of the Paiute Nation.* Phoenix AZ: O'Sullivan Woodside, 1975.

Georgi-Findlay, Brigitte. "The Frontiers of Native American Women's Writing: Sarah Winnemucca's *Life Among the Piutes.*" In *New Voices in Native American Literary Criticism,* ed. Arnold Krupat. Washington DC: Smithsonian Press, 1993. 222–52.

Girard, René. *The Scapegoat.* Baltimore: Johns Hopkins University Press, 1986.

———. *Violence and the Sacred*. Trans. Patrick Gregory. Baltimore: Johns Hopkins University Press, 1977.

Gitlin, Todd. *The Twilight of Common Dreams: Why America Is Wracked by Culture Wars*. New York: Metropolitan Books, 1995.

Glaser, Barney, and Anselm Strauss. *The Discovery of Grounded Theory: Strategies for Qualitative Research*. Piscataway NJ: Aldine Transaction, 1967.

Glotfelty, Cheryll, and Harold Fromm, eds. *The Ecocriticism Reader: Landmarks in Literary Ecology*. Athens: University of Georgia Press, 1996.

Godfrey, Joyzelle, Bill Iron Moccasin, and Joseph M. White. "American Indian Fathering in the Dakota Nation: Use of Akicita as a Fatherhood Standard." *Fathering*, January 1, 2006. http://mensstudies.metapress .com (accessed August 17, 2007).

Gort, J. D., et al., eds. *Dialogue and Syncretism: An Interdisciplinary Approach. Currents of Encounter: Studies on the Contact between Christianity and Other Religions, Beliefs, and Cultures*. Grand Rapids MI: Wm. B. Eerdmans, 1989.

Gould, Janice. "American Indian Women's Poetry: Strategies of Rage and Hope." *Signs*. 20.4 (1995): 797–817.

Graff, Gerald. "Co-optation." In *The New Historicism*, ed. H. Aram Veeser. New York: Routledge, 1989. 168–81.

———. *Professing Literature: An Institutional History*. Chicago: University of Chicago Press, 1987.

Green, Rayna. "Native American Women." *Signs*, Winter 1980, 248–67.

———. *Native American Women: A Contextual Bibliography*. Bloomington: Indiana University Press, 1983.

———. "The Pocahontas Perplex: The Image of Indian Women in American Culture." *Massachusetts Review*, Autumn 1975, 698–714.

Greenfield, Sydney M., and André Droogers, eds. *Reinventing Religions: Syncretism and Transformation in Africa and the Americas*. New York: Rowman & Littlefield, 2001.

Guaman Poma de Ayala, Felipe. *The First New Chronicle and Good Government*. http://www-personal.umich.edu/~dfrye/guaman.htm (accessed October 20, 2009).

Gussman, Deborah. "'O Savage, Where Art Thou?' Rhetorics of Reform in William Apess's *Eulogy on King Philip*." *New England Quarterly*. 77.3 (2004). http://www.jstor.org/discover/10.2307/1559826?uid=2129$uid =2&uid=70&uid=4&sid=21102272978097 (accessed March 20, 2006).

Hafen, P. Jane. "Living to Tell Stories." In *North American Indian Writing, Storytelling, and Critique: Stories through Theories, Theories through Stories*, ed. Gordon D. Henry Jr., Nieves Pascual Soler, and Silvia Martínez-Falquina. East Lansing: Michigan State University Press, 2009. 27–41.

Hallowell, Irving A. "Ojibwa Ontology, Behavior and World View." In *Culture in History: Essays in Remembrance of Paul Radin*, ed. Stanley Diamond. New York: Columbia University Press, 1960. 25–61.

Harjo, Joy. *She Had Some Horses*. New York: Thunder's Mouth Press, 1983.

Harjo, Joy, and Gloria Bird. *This I Believe*. National Public Radio, July 8, 2007.

Harjo, Joy, and Gloria Bird, eds. Introduction to *Reinventing the Enemy's Language: Contemporary Native Women's Writings of North America*. New York: Norton, 1998. 19–31.

Harper, Philip Brian. *Framing the Margins: The Social Logic of Postmodern Culture*. New York: Oxford University Press, 1994.

Harpham, Geoffrey. *On the Grotesque: Strategies Of Contradiction in Art and Literature*. Princeton NJ: Princeton University Press, 1982.

Hegel, G. W. F. *The Phenomenology of Spirit*. New York: Oxford University Press, 1979.

Heelas, Paul, ed. *Religion, Modernity and Postmodernity*. Oxford: Blackwell, 1998.

Henry, Gordon D., Jr., Nieves Pascual Soler, and Silvia Martínez-Falquina, eds. *North American Indian Writing, Storytelling, and Critique: Stories through Theories, Theories through Stories*. East Lansing: Michigan State University Press, 2009.

Hester, Thurman Lee, Jr. *Political Principles and Indian Sovereignty*. New York: Routledge, 2001.

Highway, Tomson. "Spokane Words: Thomson Highway Raps with Sherman Alexie." *Aboriginal Voices* 4.1 (1997) 36–40.

Hogan, Linda. "Who Puts Together." In *Studies in American Indian Literature: Critical Essays and Course Designs*, ed. Paula Gunn Allen. New York: MLA, 1983. 169–77.

Howe, Leanne. "The Story of America: A Tribalography." In *Clearing a Path: Theorizing the Past in Native American Studies*, ed. Nancy Solomon. New York: Routledge, 2002. 29–49.

Huhndorf, Shari M. *Mapping the Americas: The Transnational Politics of Contemporary Native Culture*. Ithaca NY: Cornell University Press, 2009.

Indian Law Resource Center. *Indian Rights—Human Rights: Handbook for Indians on International Human Rights Complaint Procedures*. Washington DC: Indian Law Resource Center, 1984.

Irmer, Thomas. "An Interview with Leslie Marmon Silko." The Write Stuff. http://www.altx.com/interviews/silko.html (accessed May 16, 2007).

Ivison, Duncan, Paul Patton, and Will Sanders, eds. *Political Theory and the Rights of Indigenous Peoples*. New York: Cambridge University Press, 2000.

Jacobs, Harriet A., and John S. Jacobs. *Incidents in the Life of a Slave Girl* (1861) and *A True Tale of Slavery* (1861). Ed. George Hendrick and Willene Hendrick. St. James NY: Brandywine Press, 1999.

Jaimes-Guerrero, M. A. "'Patriarchal Colonialism' and Indigenism: Implications for Native Feminist Spirituality and Native Womanism." In "Indigenous Women of the Americas." Special issue, *Hypatia* 18.2 (2003): 58–69.

Jespersen, Thora Christine. "Engendering Adventure: Men, Women and the American 'Frontier,' 1880–1927." PhD diss., Rutgers University, 1997.

Josephy, Alvin. *Now That the Buffalo's Gone: A Study of Today's American Indians*. New York: Knopf, 1982.

Justice, Daniel Heath. *Our Fire Survives the Storm: A Cherokee Literary History*. Minneapolis: University of Minnesota Press, 2006.

Kalt, Joseph P., and Joseph W. Singer. *Myths and Realities of Tribal Sovereignty: The Law and Economics of Indian Self-Rule*. Cambridge MA: Harvard Project on American Indian Economic Development, 2004.

Karttunen, Frances. *Between Worlds: Interpreters, Guides, and Survivors*. New Brunswick NJ: Rutgers University Press, 1994.

Keillor, Garrison. *Writer's Almanac*. National Public Radio, October 10, 2005. http://writersalmanac.publicradio.org/programs/2005/10/03/index.html#friday (accessed October 10, 2005).

Kelsey, Penelope Myrtle. *Tribal Theory in Native American Literature: Dakota and Haudenosaunee Writing and Indigenous Worldviews*. Lincoln: University of Nebraska Press, 2008.

Ketcham, Jim. *The Fool Soldiers: A Tale of Courage and Compassion*. 4th ed. N.p.: Jim Ketcham, 2006.

Ketcham, Jim, Jim Nelson, Alan Woolworth, Barbara Britain, and Marcella LeBeau. *The Fool Soldiers*. *Minnesota's Heritage* 4 (2008).

King, Martin Luther, Jr. "Letter from Birmingham City Jail." In *A Testament of Hope: The Essential Writings of Martin Luther King, Jr.*, ed. James Melvin Washington. San Francisco: Harper & Row, 1986. 289–302.

King, Thomas J., Jr. "The Fool Soldiers: A Tale of the Sioux." *Red Man* 3.8 (1912): 319–22.

Kipp, Woody. *Viet Cong at Wounded Knee: The Trail of a Blackfeet Activist*. Lincoln NE: Bison Books, 2008.

Klauss, Morton. "Seeking Syncretism: The Case of Sathya Sai Baba." In *Reinventing Religions: Syncretism and Transformation in Africa and the Americas*, ed. Sydney M. Greenfield and André Droogers. New York: Rowman & Littlefield, 2001. 201–12.

Klein, Kerwin Lee. *Frontiers of Historical Imagination: Narrating the European Conquest of Native America, 1890–1990*. Berkeley: University of California Press, 1997.

Knight, Franklin W. *Race, Ethnicity, and Class: Forging the Plural Society in Latin America and the Caribbean*. Waco TX: Baylor University Press, 1996.

Kolodny, Annette. *The Land Before Her: Fantasy and Experience of the American Frontiers, 1630–1860*. Chapel Hill: University of North Carolina Press, 1984.

Konkle, Maureen. *Writing Indian Nations: Native Intellectuals and the Politics of Historiography, 1827–1863*. Chapel Hill: University of North Carolina Press, 2004.

Kroeber, Karl. "Deconstructionist Criticism and American Indian Literatures." *Boundary 2* 7 (1979): 73–89.

———. "An Introduction to the Art of Traditional American Indian Narration." In *Traditional American Indian Literatures: Texts and Interpretations*. Lincoln: University of Nebraska Press, 1981.

Krupat, Arnold. *Ethnocriticism: Ethnography, History, Literature.* Berkeley: University of California Press, 1992.

———. *For Those Who Come After: A Study of Native American Autobiography.* Berkeley: University of California Press, 1985.

———. "Monologue and Dialogue in Native American Autobiography." In *The Voice in the Margin: Native American Literature and the Canon.* Berkeley: University of California Press, 1989. 132–201.

———. "Post-structuralism and Oral Literature." In *Recovering the Word: Essays on Native American Literature,* ed. Brian Swann and Arnold Krupat. Berkeley: University of California Press, 1987. 113–28.

———. *The Turn to the Native: Studies in Criticism and Culture.* Lincoln: University of Nebraska Press, 1996.

———. *The Voice in the Margin: Native American Literature and the Canon.* Berkeley: University of California Press, 1989.

Kucich, John J. "Sons of the Forest: Environment and Transculturation in Jonathan Edwards, Samson Occom and William Apess." In *Assimilation and Subversion in Earlier American Literature,* ed. Robin DeRosa. Newcastle, England: Cambridge Scholars Press, 2006. 5–23.

La Flesche, Francis. *The Middle Five: Indian Schoolboys of the Omaha Tribe.* 1900. Lincoln: University of Nebraska Press, 1963.

Larson, Sidner. *Captured in the Middle: Tradition and Experience in Contemporary Native American Writing.* Seattle: University of Washington Press, 2000.

Lawson, Angelica Marie. "Resistance and Resilience in the Work of Four Native American Authors." PhD diss., University of Arizona, 2006.

Lewis, Meriwhether, et al. *Journals of the Lewis and Clark Expedition.* Ed. Gary Moulton. Lincoln: University of Nebraska Press, 2002.

Liberty, Margot, ed. *American Indian Intellectuals.* Proceedings of the American Ethnological Society, 1976. St. Paul MN: West, 1978.

Limerick, Patricia. "Frontier." In *A Companion to American Thought,* ed. Richard Wightman Fox and James T. Kloppenberg. Cambridge, England: Blackwell, 1995. 255–59.

———. *Legacy of Conquest: The Unbroken Past of the American West.* New York: Norton, 1987.

Lincoln, Kenneth. *Indi'n Humor: Bicultural Play in Native America.* New York: Oxford University Press, 1993.

————. *Native American Renaissance.* Berkeley: University of California Press, 1983.

Linderman, Frank B. *Plenty-Coups, Chief of the Crows.* 1930. Lincoln: University of Nebraska Press, 2002.

Linscott, Mac. "The North American Indian Trickster." *History of Religions* 5 (1966): 327–50.

Lomawaima, K. Tsianina. *They Called It Prairie Light: The Story of Chilocco Indian School.* Lincoln: University of Nebraska Press, 1995.

Lomawaima, K. Tsianina, and Teresa L. McCarty. *To Remain an Indian: Lessons in Democracy from a Century of Native American Education.* New York: Teachers College Press, 2006.

Lourde, Audre. *Sister Outsider: Essays and Speeches.* Berkeley: Crossing Press, 1984.

Lukens, Margaret Austin. "Creating Cultural Spaces: The Pluralist Project of American Women Writers, 1843–1902 (Margaret Fuller, Harriet Jacobs, Sarah Winnemucca, and Zitkala-Sa)." PhD diss., University of Colorado, Boulder, 1991.

————. "Her 'Wrongs and Claims': Sarah Winnemucca's Strategic Narratives of Abuse." *Wicaso Sa Review,* Spring 1998, 93–108.

Lyons, Oren, and John Mohawk, eds. *Exiled in the Land of the Free: Democracy, Indian Nations, and the U.S. Constitution.* Santa Fe NM: Clear Light, 1992.

Lyons, Scott Richard. "Rhetorical Sovereignty: What Do American Indians Want from Writing?" *College Composition and Communication* 51.3 (2000): 447–68.

————. *X-Marks: Native Signatures of Assent.* Minneapolis: University of Minnesota Press, 2010.

Lyotard, Jean-François. *Le Différend: Phrases in Dispute.* 1983. Trans. Georges Van Den Abbeele. Minneapolis: University of Minnesota Press, 1988.

————. *The Postmodern Condition: A Report on Knowledge.* 1979. Trans. Geoff Bennington and Brian Massumi. Manchester, UK: Manchester University Press, 1984.

Maaka, Roger, and Augie Fleras. "Engaging with Indigeneity: Tino Rangatiratanga in Aotearoa." In *Political Theory and the Rights of Indigenous Peoples,* ed. Duncan Ivison, Paul Patton, and Will Sanders. New York: Cambridge University Press, 2000. 89–112.

Mabrey, Vicki. "The Toughest Indian in the World." Interview, *CBS News 60 Minutes II*, March 20, 2001, http://www.cbsnews.com/60-minutes/ (accessed October 20, 2009).

Madsen, Deborah L., ed. *Native Authenticity: Transnational Perspectives on Native American Literary Studies*. Albany: State University of New York Press, 2010.

Mandel, Ernest. *Late Capitalism*. 1972. Trans. Joris De Bres. London: NLB, 1975.

Mann, Charles C. *1491: New Revelations of the Americas Before Columbus*. New York: Knopf, 2005.

Marable, Manning. *How Capitalism Underdeveloped Black America*. 1983. Updated ed. London: Pluto Press, 2000.

Martin, Joel W. *The Land Looks After Us: A History of Native American Religion*. New York: Oxford University Press, 1999.

McGeshick, Joseph R. *The Indian in the Liquor Cabinet and Other Poems*. Baltimore: Publish America, 2006.

McNickle, D'Arcy. *Native American Tribalism: Indian Survivals and Renewals*. (Rev. ed. of *The Indian Tribes of the United States*.) New York: Oxford University Press, 1973.

———. *Runner in the Sun: A Story of Indian Maize*. 1954. Albuquerque: University of New Mexico Press, 1987.

———. *The Surrounded*. 1936. Albuquerque: University of New Mexico Press, 1978.

———. *They Came Here First: The Epic of the American Indian*. Revised ed. New York: Harper & Row, 1975.

———. *Wind from an Enemy Sky*. Albuquerque: University of New Mexico Press, 1978.

Meeker, Joseph W. *The Comedy of Survival: Literary Ecology and a Play Ethic*. 3rd ed. Tucson: University of Arizona Press, 1997.

———. "The Comic Mode." 1972. In *The Ecocriticism Reader: Landmarks in Literary Ecology*, ed. Cheryll Glotfelty and Harold Fromm. Athens: University of Georgia Press, 1996. 155–69.

Midgley, Mary. *The Myths We Live By*. New York: Routledge, 2003.

Mihesuah, Devon A. *American Indians: Stereotypes and Realities*. Atlanta GA: Clarity Press, 1996.

————, ed. *Natives and Academics: Researching and Writing about American Indians*. Lincoln: University of Nebraska Press, 1998.

Miller, Robert J. *Native Americans, Discovered and Conquered: Thomas Jefferson, Lewis and Clark, and Manifest Destiny*. Westport CT: Praeger, 2006.

Momaday, N. Scott. *House Made of Dawn*. New York: Harper & Row, 1977.

————. "Man Made of Words." In *Indian Voices: The First Convocation of American Indian Scholars*, ed. Rupert Costo. San Francisco: Indian Historian, 1970. 49–84.

Montaigne, Michel de. "On Cannibals." http://www.gutenberg.org/files/3600/3600-h/3600-h.htm (accessed April 21, 2004).

Moore, David L. "Cycles of Selfhood, Cycles of Nationhood: Authenticity, Identity, Community, Sovereignty." In *Native Authenticity: Transnational Perspectives on Native American Literary Studies*, ed. Deborah L. Madsen. Albany: State University of New York Press, 2010. 39–67.

————. "Decolonializing Criticism: Reading Dialectics and Dialogics in Native American Literatures." *Studies in American Indian Literatures*, Winter 1994, 7–33.

————. Introduction to "Cultural Property in American Indian Literatures: Representation and Interpretation," ed. David L. Moore. Special issue, *American Indian Quarterly* 21.4 (1997): 545–54.

————. "Moon Vines among the Ruins: Gerald Vizenor's Poetics of Presence." In *Gerald Vizenor: Texts and Contexts*, ed. Deborah Madsen and A. Robert Lee. Albuquerque: University of New Mexico Press, 2010. 106–28.

————. "Myth, History, and Identity in Silko and Young Bear: Postcolonial Praxis." In *New Voices: Critical Essays on Native American Literatures*, ed. Arnold Krupat. Washington DC: Smithsonian Press, 1993. 370–95.

————. "Ray A. Young Bear." In *Dictionary of Literary Biography*. Vol. 175: *Native American Writers of the United States*, ed. Kenneth M. Roemer. Detroit: Gale Research, 1997. 322–30.

————. "Rough Knowledge and Radical Understanding." In "Cultural Property in American Indian Literatures: Representation and Interpretation," ed. David L. Moore. Special issue, *American Indian Quarterly* 21.4 (1997): 633–62.

———. "Sherman Alexie." In *Cambridge Companion to Native American Literature*, ed. Kenneth Roemer and Joy Porter. Cambridge, England: Cambridge University Press, 2005. 297–310.

———. "Silko's Blood Sacrifice: The Circulating Witness in *Almanac of the Dead*." In *Leslie Marmon Silko: A Collection of Critical Essays*, ed. James Thorson and Louise Barnett. Albuquerque: University of New Mexico Press, 1999. 149–83.

———. "The Twilight of White Liberalism." WBAI-FM, April 2002. www .wbai.org.

Morrison, Dorothy Nafus. *Chief Sarah: Sarah Winnemucca's Fight for Indian Rights*. New York: Atheneum, 1980.

Murray, David. *Forked Tongues: Speech, Writing and Representation in North American Indian Texts*. Bloomington: Indiana University Press, 1991.

Myers, Kelly. "Reservation Stories with Author Sherman Alexie." *Tonic* 1 (May 11, 1995): 8–9.

Nash, Gregory B., Charlotte Antoinette Crabtree, and Ross E. Dunn. *History on Trial: Culture Wars and the Teaching of the Past*. New York: Vintage, 2000.

Neihardt, John G. *Black Elk Speaks*. 1932. New York: Pocket Books, 1972.

Nelson, Robert M. *Place and Vision: The Function of Landscape in Native American Fiction*. New York: Lang, 1993.

Niezen, Ronald. *The Origins of Indigenism: Human Rights and the Politics of Identity*. Berkeley: University of California Press, 2003.

Norton-Smith, Thomas M. *The Dance of Person and Place: One Interpretation of American Indian Philosophy*. Albany: State University of New York Press, 2010.

Nygren, Ase. "A World of Story-Smoke: A Conversation with Sherman Alexie." *MELUS* 30.4 (2005): 150–69.

O'Brien, Sharon. "Tribes and Indians: With Whom Does the United States Maintain a Relationship?" *Notre Dame Law Review* 66.5 (1991): 1461–1502.

Occom, Samson. *The Collected Writings of Samson Occom, Mohegan: Leadership and Literature in Eighteenth-Century Native America*. Ed. Joanna Brooks. New York: Oxford University Press, 2006.

———. *A Short Narrative of My Life*. 1768. History Matters. http://history matters.gmu.edu/ (accessed July 30, 2010).

O'Connell, Barry. Introductions to *On Our Own Ground: The Complete Writings of William Apess, A Pequot*, ed. Barry O'Connell. Amherst: University of Massachusetts Press, 1992. xiii–lxxvii, and interspersed.

O'Connor, William Van. *The Grotesque: An American Genre, and Other Essays*. Carbondale: Southern Illinois University Press, 1962.

O'Nell, Theresa DeLeane. *Disciplined Hearts: History, Identity, and Depression in an American Indian Community*. Berkeley: University of California Press, 1996.

Ong, Walter. *Orality and Literacy: The Technologizing of the Word*. New York: Routledge, 1991.

Ortiz, Alfonso. "Indian/White Relations: A View from the Other Side of the 'Frontier.'" In *Indians in American History: An Introduction*, ed. Frederick E. Hoxie. Arlington Heights IL: Harlan Davidson, 1988. 1–16.

———. Obituary for D'Arcy McNickle. *American Anthropologist* 81.3 (1979): 632–36.

———. "The Sacred Clown." In *Symposium of the Whole: A Range of Discourse toward an Ethnopoetics*, ed. Jerome Rothenberg and Diane Rothenberg. Berkeley: University of California Press, 1983, 270–73.

Ortiz, Simon, J., ed. *Earth Power Coming: Short Fiction in Native American Literature*. Tsaile AZ: Navajo Community College Press, 1983.

———. *from Sand Creek*. Oak Park NY: Thunder's Mouth Press, 1981.

———. *from Sand Creek*. 1981. Tucson: University of Arizona Press, 1999.

———. "Towards a National Indian Literature: Cultural Authenticity in Nationalism." *MELUS* 8.2 (1981): 7–12.

Owens, Louis. Afterword in D'Arcy McNickle, *Wind from an Enemy Sky*. Albuquerque: University of New Mexico Press, 1978. 257–65.

———. "As If an Indian Were Really an Indian: Uramericans, Euramericans, and Postcolonial Theory." In "Native American Literature: Boundaries and Sovereignties," ed. Kathryn W. Shanley. Special issue, *Paradoxa*, no. 15 (2001): 170–83.

———. *Dark River*. Norman: University of Oklahoma Press, 1999.

———. *Mixedblood Messages: Literature, Film, Family, Place*. Norman: University of Oklahoma Press, 1998.

———. *Other Destinies: Understanding the American Indian Novel*. Norman: University of Oklahoma Press, 1992.

Parker, Dorothy R. *Singing an Indian Song: A Biography of D'Arcy McNickle.* Lincoln: University of Nebraska Press, 1992.

Parker, Robert Dale. *The Invention of Native American Literature.* Ithaca NY: Cornell University Press, 2003.

Patterson, Orlando. *Freedom in the Making of Western Culture.* New York: Basic Books, 1991.

Pavlik, Steve, and Daniel R. Wildcat, eds. *Destroying Dogma: Vine Deloria, Jr. and His Influence on American Society.* Golden CO: Fulcrum, 2006.

Peabody, Elizabeth P. *Sarah Winnemucca's Practical Solution of the Indian Problem: A Letter to Dr. Lyman Abbot of the "Christian Union."* Cambridge MA: John Wilson and Son, 1886.

Pearce, Roy Harvey. *Savagism and Civilization: A Study of the Indian and the American Mind.* 1953. Berkeley: University of California Press, 1988.

Peroff, Nicholas C. "A Window on the Past: Complexity Theory in American Indian Studies." In *Destroying Dogma: Vine Deloria, Jr. and His Influence on American Society,* ed. Steve Pavlik and Daniel R. Wildcat. Golden CO: Fulcrum, 2006. 93–104.

Personal Narratives Group, ed. *Interpreting Women's Lives: Feminist Theory and Personal Narratives.* Bloomington: Indiana University Press, 1989.

Peyer, Bernd C. *The Tutor'd Mind: Indian Missionary-Writers in Antebellum America.* Amherst: University of Massachusetts Press, 1997.

Phelan, Peggy. *Unmarked: The Politics of Performance.* New York: Routledge, 1993.

Porter, Joy, and Kenneth M. Roemer, eds. *The Cambridge Companion to Native American Literature.* New York: Cambridge University Press, 2005.

Powell, Malea. "Rhetorics of Survivance: How American Indians *Use* Writing." CCC (*College Composition and Communication*) 53.3 (2002): 396–434.

Pratt, M. L. "Arts of the Contact Zone." *Profession* (1991). Modern Language Association. http://www.jstor.org/discover/10.2307/25595469?uid=2&uid=4&sid=21102273077867 (accessed April 21, 2004).

———. *Imperial Eyes: Travel Writing and Transculturation.* New York: Routledge, 1992.

Preston, Christopher J. "Environment and Belief: The Importance of Place in the Construction of Knowledge." *Ethics & the Environment* 4.2 (1999): 211.

―――. *Grounding Knowledge: Environmental Philosophy, Epistemology, and Place*. Athens: University of Georgia Press, 2003.

Purdy, John Lloyd, ed. *The Legacy of D'Arcy McNickle: Writer, Historian, Activist*. Norman: University of Oklahoma Press, 1996.

―――. *Word Ways: The Novels of D'Arcy McNickle*. Tucson: University of Arizona Press, 1990.

Purdy, John Lloyd, and Blake Hausman. "A Conversation with Simon Ortiz." *Studies in American Indian Literatures* 12.4 (2000): 1–14.

Radin, Paul. *The Trickster: A Study in American Indian Mythology*. New York: Schocken Books, 1972.

Ramsey, Jerald. *Reading the Fire: Essays in the Traditional Indian Literatures of the Far West*. Lincoln: University of Nebraska Press, 1983.

Ranco, Darren, and Dean Suagee. "Tribal Sovereignty and the Problem of Difference in Environmental Regulation: Observations on 'Measured Separatism' in Indian Country." *Antipode* 39.4 (2007): 691–707.

Red Eagle, Philip H. *Red Earth: A Vietnam Warrior's Journey*. Duluth MN: Holy Cow! Press, 1997.

Reed, Ishmael. "What's American about America?" In *Ourselves Among Others: Cross-Cultural Readings for Writers*, ed. Carol J. Verburg. 2nd ed. Boston: St. Martin's Press, 1991. 4–7.

Resaldo, Renato. "Imperialist Nostalgia." *Representations* 26 (1989): 107–22.

Richey, Elinor. "Sagebrush Princess with a Cause: Sarah Winnemucca." *American West* 12.6 (1975): 30–33, 57–63.

Ridge, Martin. "Turner, Frederick Jackson." In *The Reader's Companion to American History*, ed. Eric Foner and John A. Garraty. Boston: Houghton Mifflin, 1991. 1089–90.

Roberts, John W. "The African American Animal Trickster as Hero." In *Redefining American Literary History*, ed. A. LaVonne Brown Ruoff and Jerry W. Ward. New York: MLA, 1990. 97–114.

Roemer, Kenneth M., ed. *The Dictionary of Literary Biography*. Vol. 175: *Native American Writers of the United States*. Farmington Hills MI: Gale, 1997.

Ronda, Bruce A., ed. *Letters of Elizabeth Palmer Peabody: American Renaissance Woman*. Middletown CT: Wesleyan University Press, 1884.

Rorty, Richard. *Achieving Our Country: Leftist Thought in Twentieth-Century America*. Cambridge MA: Harvard University Press, 1998.

Rosenau, Pauline Marie. *Post-modernism and the Social Sciences: Insights, Inroads and Intrusions*. Princeton NJ: Princeton University Press, 1992.

Ross, Luana. *Inventing the Savage: The Social Construction of Native American Criminality*. Austin: University of Texas Press, 1998.

Rowlandson, Mary White. *A Narrative of the Captivity and Restauration of Mrs. Mary Rowlandson*. 1682. http://www.library.csi.cuny.edu/dept/history/lavender/rownarr.html (accessed October 20, 2009).

Ruoff, A. LaVonne Brown. *American Indian Literatures: An Introduction, Bibliographic Review, and Selected Bibliography*. New York: MLA, 1990.

———. "Oral Traditions and New Forms." In *Studies in American Indian Literature: Critical Essays and Course Designs*, ed. Paula Gunn Allen. New York: MLA, 1983, 147–68.

———. "Three Nineteenth-Century American Indian Autobiographers." In *Redefining American Literary History*, ed. A LaVonne Brown Ruoff and Jerry Ward. New York: MLA, 1990. 251–59.

———. "Woodland Word Warrior: An Introduction to the Works of Gerald Vizenor." *MELUS* 13: 1–2 (1986): 13–43.

Ruppert, James. "Fiction: 1968–Present." In *The Cambridge Companion to Native American Literature*, ed. Kenneth M. Roemer and Joy Porter. New York: Cambridge University Press, 2005.

———. *Mediation in Contemporary Native American Fiction*. Norman: University of Oklahoma Press, 1995.

Said, Edward. "The Politics of Knowledge." 1991. In *Falling into Theory: Conflicting Views on Reading Literature*, ed. David S. Richter. Boston: Bedford, St. Martin's Press, 2000. 189–98.

———. *The Question of Palestine*. London: Vintage, 1980.

Salish and Pend d'Oreille Culture Committee. *The Salish People and the Lewis and Clark Expedition*. Lincoln: University of Nebraska Press, 2005.

———. *The Swan Valley Massacre of 1908: A Brief History*. St. Ignatius MT. Pamphlet.

Sands, Kathleen Mullen. "Indian Women's Personal Narrative: Voices Past and Present." In *American Women's Autobiography*, ed. Margo Culley. Madison: University of Wisconsin Press, 1992. 268–94.

Sayre, Gordon M. *The Indian Chief as Tragic Hero: Native Resistance and the Literatures of America, from Moctezuma to Tecumseh*. Chapel Hill: University of North Carolina Press, 2005.

Scheckel, Susan. *The Insistence of the Indian: Race and Nationalism in Nine-teenth-Century American Culture.* Princeton NJ: Princeton University Press, 1998.

Schouls, Tim. *Shifting Boundaries: Aboriginal Identity, Pluralist Theory, and the Politics of Self-Government.* Vancouver: University of British Columbia Press, 2003.

Schrempp, Gregory. "Distributed Power: An Overview. A Theme in American Indian Origin Stories." In *Stars Above, Earth Below: American Indians and Nature,* ed. Marsha C. Bol. Pittsburgh: Carnegie Museum of Natural History, 1998. 15–27.

Scordato, Ellen. *Sarah Winnemucca: Northern Paiute Writer and Diplomat.* New York: Chelsea House, 1992.

Scott-Childress, Reynolds J., ed. *Race and the Production of Modern American Nationalism.* New York: Routledge, 1999.

Sekaquaptewa, Emory. "One More Smile for a Hopi Clown." In *I Become Part of It: Sacred Dimensions in Native American Life,* ed. D. M. Dooling and Paul Jordan-Smith. New York: Parabola, 1989. 150–57.

Selby, Nick. "'Coming back to oneself/coming back to the land': Gary Snyder's Poetics." In *Reading under the Sign of Nature: New Essays in Ecocriticism,* ed. John Tallmadge and Henry Harrington. Salt Lake City: University of Utah Press, 2000. 179–97.

Senier, Siobhan. "'That Is What I Said to Him': American Women's Narratives about Indians, 1879–1934." PhD diss., University of Illinois, Urbana-Champaign, 1997.

———. *Voices of American Indian Assimilation and Resistance.* Norman: University of Oklahoma Press, 2001.

Shanley, Kathryn W. "Blood Ties and Blasphemy: American Indian Women and the Problem of History." In *Is Academic Feminism Dead? Theory in Practice,* ed. Social Justice Group at the Center for Advanced Feminist Studies, University of Minnesota. New York: New York University Press, 2000. 204–32.

———. "Prairie Songs and Poor Prayers." *Studies in American Indian Literatures* 16.4 (2004): 101–2.

———. "Thoughts on Indian Feminism." In *A Gathering of Spirit: A Collection by North American Indian Women,* ed. Beth Brant (Degonwadonti). Ithaca NY: Firebrand Books, 1988. 213–15.

Shoemaker, Nancy. *American Indian Population Recovery in the Twentieth Century*. Albuquerque: University of New Mexico Press, 1999.

Siemerling, Winfried, and Katrin Schwenk, eds. *Cultural Difference and the Literary Text: Pluralism and the Limits of Authenticity in North American Literatures*. Iowa City: University of Iowa Press, 1996.

Silko, Leslie Marmon. *Almanac of the Dead*. 1991. New York: Penguin, 1992.

———. *Ceremony*. New York: New American Library, 1977.

———. *Gardens in the Dunes: A Novel*. New York: Scribner, 1999.

———. *Laguna Woman*. Tucson AZ: Flood Plain Press, 1993.

———. *Sacred Water: Narratives and Pictures*. 2nd ed. Tucson AZ: Flood Plain Press, 1993.

———. *Storyteller*. Boston: Little, Brown, 1981.

———. *Yellow Woman and a Beauty of the Spirit*. New York: Simon & Schuster, 1997.

———. *The Turquoise Ledge*. New York: Viking, 2010.

Silko, Leslie Marmon, and James Wright. *The Delicacy and Strength of Lace: Letters between Leslie Marmon Silko and James Wright*. St. Paul MN: Graywolf Press, 1986.

Simon, Bruce. "Hybridity in the Americas: Reading, Mukherjee, and Hawthorne." In *Postcolonial Theory in the United States*, ed. Amritjit Singh and Peter Schmidt. Jackson: University of Mississippi Press, 2000. 412–13.

Slotkin, Richard. *Regeneration through Violence: The Mythology of the American Frontier, 1600–1860*. Middletown CT: Wesleyan University Press, 1973.

Smith, Anna Marie. *Laclau and Mouffe: The Radical Democratic Imaginary*. New York: Routledge, 1998.

Smith, Henry Nash. *Virgin Land: The American West as Symbol and Myth*. 1950. Cambridge MA: Harvard University Press, 1970.

Smith, Robert Charles. *We Have No Leaders: African Americans in the Post-Civil Rights Era*. Albany: State University of New York Press, 1996.

Smoker, M. L. *Another Attempt at Rescue*. Brooklyn: Hanging Loose Press, 2005.

Sneve, Virginia Driving Hawk. *Betrayed*. New York: Holiday House, 1974.

———. *Grandpa Was a Cowboy and an Indian and Other Stories*. Lincoln: University of Nebraska Press, 2000.

Sollors, Werner. *Beyond Ethnicity: Consent and Descent in American Culture.* New York: Oxford University Press, 1986.

———. "A Critique of Pure Pluralism." In *Reconstructing American Literary History*, ed. Sacvan Bercovitch. Cambridge MA: Harvard University Press, 1986. 250-79.

———, ed. *The Invention of Ethnicity.* New York: Oxford University Press, 1989.

Spence, Mark. "Let's Play Lewis and Clark! Strange Visions of Nature and History at the Bicentennial." In *Lewis and Clark: Legacies, Memories, and New Perspectives*, ed. Kris Fresonke and Mark Spence. Berkeley: University of California Press, 2004. 219-38.

Spencer, Russ. "What It Means to Be Sherman Alexie." *Book* (July–August 2000): 32-36.

Stevens, Scott Manning. "William Apess's Historical Self." *Northwest Review* 35.3 (1997): 67-84.

Stewart, Charles, and Rosalind Shaw, eds. *Syncretism/Anti-Syncretism: The Politics of Religious Synthesis.* London: Routledge, 1994.

Stewart, Patricia. "Sarah Winnemucca." *Nevada Historical Society Quarterly* 14.4 (1971): 23-38.

Strauss, Claudia, and Naomi Quinn. *A Cognitive Theory of Cultural Meaning.* Cambridge, England: Cambridge University Press, 1997.

Strickland, Rennard. "The Eagle's Empire: Sovereignty, Survival, and Self-Governance in Native American Law and Constitutionalism." In *Studying Native America: Problems and Prospects*, ed. Russell Thornton. Madison: University of Wisconsin Press, 1998. 247-70.

Stromberg, Ernest, ed. *American Indian Rhetorics of Survivance: Word Medicine, Word Magic.* Pittsburgh: University of Pittsburgh Press, 2006.

Swagerty, William R., ed. *Indian Sovereignty: Proceedings of the Second Annual Conference on Problems and Issues Concerning American Indians Today.* No. 2. Chicago: Newberry Library, 1979.

Swann, Brian, and Arnold Krupat, eds. *Recovering the Word: Essays on Native American Literature.* Berkeley: University of California Press, 1987.

Taylor, Charles. *The Ethics of Authenticity.* Cambridge MA: Harvard University Press, 1992.

Taylor, Drew Hayden. *Me Funny*. Vancouver: Douglas & McIntyre, 2005.

Taylor, Mark C. *Altarity*. Chicago: University of Chicago Press, 1987.

Thoreau, Henry David. *Walking*. In Ralph Waldo Emerson and Henry David Thoreau, *Nature/Walking*. Boston: Beacon Press, 1991.

Thornton, Russell, ed. *Studying Native America: Problems and Prospects*. Madison: University of Wisconsin Press, 1998.

Trachtenberg, Alan. *Shades of Hiawatha: Staging Indians, Making Americans, 1880–1930*. New York: Hill & Wang, 2004.

Trahant, Mark. "Indian Humor Belies the Stoic Stereotype." *The Herald* of Everett, Washington. *Canku Ota (Many Paths)*, an Online Newsletter Celebrating Native America, no. 28, January 27, 2001. http://www .turtletrack.org (accessed October 20, 2009).

Trejo, Judy. "Coyote Tales: A Paiute Commentary." *Journal of American Folklore* 87 (1974): 66–81.

Trexler, Richard C. *Sex and Conquest: Gendered Violence, Political Order, and the European Conquest of the Americas*. Ithaca NY: Cornell University Press, 1995.

Tsing, Anna Lowenhaupt. *Friction: An Ethnography of Global Connection*. Princeton NJ: Princeton University Press, 2005.

——. "Indigenous Voice." In *Indigenous Experience Today*, ed. Marisol de la Cadena and Orin Starn. New York: Berg, 2007. 33–67.

Tuleja, Tad. "What Do You Mean We, White Man?" in *The New York Public Library Book of Popular Americana*. New York: Macmillan, 1994. *http://www.highbeam.com/Search.aspx?q=new+york+public+library +book+of+popular+americana* (accessed March 3, 2010).

Turner, Frederick Jackson. "The Significance of the Frontier in American History." 1893. http://nationalhumanitiescenter.org/pds/gilded/ empire/text1/turner.pdf (accessed October 20, 2009).

University of South Dakota Indian Oral History Collection. "Field Notes from an Interview with Frank Flying Boy on the Fool Soldiers." Steve Plummer, Frank F. Boy. University of South Dakota Indian Oral History Collection. Part 2, no. 207.

——. "Field Notes from an Interview with Jason Holy Bull on the Fool Soldiers." C. E. R. Francois Mauriac, Jason H. Bull. University of South Dakota Indian Oral History Collection. Part 2, no. 208.

"U.S. Fish and Wildlife Service and the Confederated Salish and Kootenai Tribes Negotiate Annual Funding Agreement for National Bison Range Complex." U.S. Fish and Wildlife Service, December 15, 2004. http://mountain-prairie.fws.gov/cskt-fws-negotiation/ (accessed October 20, 2009).

Utter, Jack. *American Indians: Answers to Today's Questions.* 2nd ed. Norman: University of Oklahoma Press, 2001.

Velie, Alan R. *Four American Indian Literary Masters.* Norman: University of Oklahoma Press, 1982.

Venuto, Rochelle R. "Indian Authorities: Race, Gender and Empire in Mid-Nineteenth Century U.S.-Indian Narratives." PhD diss., University of of California, Santa Cruz, 1998.

Verney, Marilyn Notah. "On Authenticity." In *American Indian Thought,* ed. Anne Waters. Oxford: Blackwell, 2004. 133-39.

Vizenor, Gerald. *Bearheart: The Heirship Chronicles.* Minneapolis: University of Minnesota Press, 1990.

———. *The Heirs of Columbus.* Hanover NH: University Press of New England, 1991.

———. Introduction to *Narrative Chance: Postmodern Discourse on Native American Literatures,* ed. Gerald Vizenor. Albuquerque: University of New Mexico Press, 1989. 3-16.

———. *Manifest Manners: Postindian Warriors of Survivance.* Hanover NH: Wesleyan University Press, 1994.

———. "The Ruins of Representation: Shadow Survivance and the Literature of Dominance." *American Indian Quarterly* 17.1 (1993): 7-30. http://muse.jhu.edu/journals/aiq (accessed October 20, 2009).

———. "Trickster Discourse: Comic Holotropes and Language Games." In *Narrative Chance: Postmodern Discourse on Native American Literatures,* ed. Gerald Vizenor. Albuquerque: University of New Mexico Press, 1989. 187-211.

———. *The Trickster of Liberty: Tribal Heirs to a Wild Baronage.* Minneapolis: University of Minnesota Press, 1988.

Walker, Cheryl. *Indian Nation: Native American Literature and Nineteenth-Century Nationalisms.* Durham NC: Duke University Press, 1997.

Warrior, Robert Allen. "Eulogy on William Apess: Speculations on His New York Death." *SAIL* 16.2 (2004): 1-13.

———. "'Temporary Visibility': Deloria on Sovereignty and AIM." In *Native American Perspectives on Literature and History*, ed. Alan R. Velie. Norman: University of Oklahoma Press, 1994. 51–62.

———. *Tribal Secrets: Recovering American Indian Intellectual Traditions.* Minneapolis: University of Minnesota Press, 1995.

Washburn, Wilcomb E. "A Fifty-Year Perspective on the Indian Reorganization Act." *American Anthropologist*, new series, 86.2 (1984): 279–89.

Waters, Anne. "The Myth of 'Tribalism' and U.S. Colonialism." In "Indigenous Women of the Americas." Special issue, *Hypatia* 18.2 (2003): ix–xx.

Waters, Frank. *The Man Who Killed the Deer.* 1942. New York: Pocket Books, 1971.

Weatherford, Jack. *Native Roots: How the Indians Enriched America.* New York: Ballantine, 1991.

Weaver, Jace. *That the People Might Live: Native American Literatures and Native American Community.* New York: Oxford University Press, 1997.

Weaver, Jace, Craig S. Womack, and Robert Warrior. *American Indian Literary Nationalism.* Albuquerque: University of New Mexico Press, 2006.

Welch, James. *Riding the Earthboy 40.* New York: Harper & Row, 1971.

———, panelist. "Writing and Writers in Two Cultures." Montana Festival of the Book, Missoula, Montana, September 8, 2001.

Welch, James, and Paul Stekler. *Killing Custer: The Battle of the Little Bighorn and the Fate of the Plains Indians.* New York: Norton, 1994.

Welch, Lois M. "Wild but Not Savage: Eudora Welty and Humor in Native American Writers, Principally Louise Erdrich with Passing Mention of Thomas King." Paper presented at American Literature Association, Boston, May 2005.

West, Cornel. *Democracy Matters: Winning the Fight against Imperialism.* New York: Penguin, 2004.

———. *Race Matters.* New York: Vintage, 1994.

White, Hayden. *Tropics of Discourse: Essays in Cultural Criticism.* Baltimore: Johns Hopkins University Press, 1986.

White, Richard. *The Middle Ground: Indians, Empires, and Republics in the Great Lakes Region, 1650–1815.* Cambridge England: Cambridge University Press, 1991.

Whorf, Benjamin Lee. "An American Indian Model of the Universe." *International Journal of American Linguistics* 16.2 (1950): 67–72.

———. *Language, Thought, and Reality: Selected Writings of Benjamin Lee Whorf.* Ed. John B. Carroll. Cambridge: Technology Press of Massachusetts Institute of Technology, 1956.

Wiget, Andrew. "His Life in His Tail: The Native American Trickster and the Literature of Possibility." In *Redefining American Literary History*, ed. A. LaVonne Brown Ruoff and Jerry W. Ward. New York: MLA, 1990. 83–96.

Wilkins, David E. *American Indian Politics and the American Political System.* 2nd ed. Lanham MD: Rowman & Littlefield, 2006.

———. *American Indian Sovereignty and the U.S. Supreme Court: The Masking of Justice.* Austin: University of Texas Press, 1997.

Wilkins, David E., and K. Tsianina Lomawaima. *Uneven Ground: American Indian Sovereignty and Federal Law.* Norman: University of Oklahoma Press, 2002.

Wilkinson, Charles F. *American Indians, Time, and the Law.* New Haven CT: Yale University Press, 1987.

———. *Blood Struggle: The Rise of Modern Indian Nations.* New York: Norton, 2005.

Williams, Robert A., Jr. *The American Indian in Western Legal Thought: The Discourses of Conquest.* New York: Oxford University Press, 1990.

Williams, Roger. *Key into the Language of America.* 1643. Bedford MA: Applewood Books, 1997.

Wilson, Angela Cavender. "Grandmother to Granddaughter: Generations of Oral History in a Dakota Family." In *Natives and Academics: Researching and Writing about American Indians*, ed. Devon A. Mihesuah. Lincoln: University of Nebraska Press, 1998. 27–36.

Wilson, Michael D. *Writing Home: Indigenous Narratives of Resistance.* East Lansing: Michigan State University Press, 2008.

Winnemucca, Sarah. *Life Among the Piutes: Their Wrongs and Claims.* 1883. Facsimile ed. New York: Putnam, 1969.

Winthrop, John. "A Modell of Christian Charitie." 1630. http://religiousfreedom.lib.virginia.edu/sacred/charity.html (accessed October 20, 2009).

Womack, Craig S. "The Integrity of American Indian Claims (Or, How I Learned to Stop Worrying and Love My Hybridity)." In *American Indian Literary Nationalism*, ed. Jace Weaver, Craig S. Womack, and

Robert Warrior. Albuquerque: University of New Mexico Press, 2006. 91–177.

———. *Red on Red: Native American Literary Separatism*. Minneapolis: University of Minnesota Press, 1999.

———. "Theorizing Native American Experience." In *Reasoning Together: The Native Critics Collective*, ed. Craig S. Womack and Janice Acoose. Norman: University of Oklahoma Press, 2008. 353–410.

Womack, Craig S., and Janice Acoose, eds. *Reasoning Together: The Native Critics Collective*. Norman: University of Oklahoma Press, 2008.

Woody, Elizabeth. *Seven Hands, Seven Hearts*. Portland OR: Eighth Mountain Press, 1994.

Woolman, John. "Some Considerations on the Keeping of Negroes." 1754. http://www.archive.org/stream/considerationsonoowool/ considerationsonoowool_djvu.txt (accessed April 25, 2013).

Young Bear, Ray A. *Black Eagle Child: The Facepaint Narratives*. Singular Lives: The Iowa Series in North American Autobiography. Albert E. Stone, series editor. Iowa City: University of Iowa Press, 1992.

———. *Remnants of the First Earth*. New York: Grove Press, 1996.

Zanjani, Sally. *Sarah Winnemucca*. Lincoln: University of Nebraska Press, 2001.

Zinn, Howard. *A People's History of the United States: 1492–Present*. 1980. New York: HarperCollins, 2010.

Zumthor, Paul. *Oral Poetry: An Introduction*. Trans. Kathryn Murphy-Judy. Minneapolis: University of Minnesota Press, 1990.

INDEX

248, 269, 272, 277, 303, 331, 333–36,
340, 345, 355, 373, 375, 380, 384n5,
395n32, 395n36, 397n6; and animism, 132; and authenticity, 261–
68; and community, 93, 95, 105,
108–9, 130–39; and humor, 351–
53; and identity, 189–98; lineage
linked to King Philip, 133, 193; and
nonviolence, 63, 69–71, 72, 351,
395n37; and sovereignty, 60–74,
77, 78, 90
—Works: *Eulogy on King Philip*,
60–61, 63, 67, 68, 130–34, 161,
189, 191, 224, 265, 268, 335, 397n6;
*The Experiences of Five Christian
Indians*, 64, 190, 197, 262, 268,
297; *Increase of the Kingdom of
Christ*, 131, 132, 137; "An Indian's
Looking-Glass for the White
Man," 62, 65, 68, 131, 135, 137,
190–91, 193, 194–98, 236, 272,
353–54; *Indian Nullification of the
Unconstitutional Laws*, 63–73, 136–
37, 190, 267–68, 336, 351, 353;
"Petition of the Marshpee Tribe
of Indians," 64, 70–72, 263; *Son of
the Forest*, 131, 189, 191, 193, 266,
268, 297, 379
the Apocalypse, 132, 315–16
Apocalypto (film), 21
Archilde (character), 78, 80, 82,
142, 163, 175, 183–88, 223, 281, 282,
283, 287, 298. *See also* McNickle,
D'Arcy—Works: *The Surrounded*
Aristotle, 221, 319, 344
army (U.S.), 2–3, 123, 162, 199–201,

206–7, 261, 270, 362, 380
Arrowboy (Estoy-eh-muut, character), 382. *See also* Silko, Leslie
Marmon—Works: *Ceremony*
"Articulating Indigenous Statehood" (Carroll), 316, 385n7
"Arts of the Contact Zone" (Pratt),
169, 333
"As If" (Owens), 368
assimilation, xii, 21–22, 28–29, 33,
47, 65, 79, 82, 90, 101, 106, 109,
124, 137, 147, 184, 186, 212, 230,
263–65, 281, 289–90, 316, 326–29,
334, 340
Assiniboines, 154, 307, 308, 338
authenticity, 13–16, 41, 50, 225–27;
and Alexie, 227, 237, 290–99; and
Apess, 261–68; and authority,
24–25, 232, 234, 237, 239, 248, 251–
53, 254, 267, 271–72, 278, 294, 295,
297, 298, 308; etymology of, 236;
and McNickle, 279–90; and narration, 232–33, 268, 270, 275; and
Silko, 234, 248–61; as translation,
15, 43, 225–99, 308, 310, 400n10;
and Winnemucca, 268–77,
400nn10–11
"The Authenticity Game" (Bernardin), 236, 237, 398

Baker, Robert: *The Extravagant*, 173
Bakhtin, Mikhail, 169, 242, 390n30;
"Discourse in the Novel," 323–24
Banks, James A.: *Educating Citizens
in a Multicultural Society*, 24–25;
Multicultural Education, 20

Bannock Tribe. *See* Shoshone-
Bannock Tribes

Bannock War, 75, 119, 206, 270

Barker, Joanne: *Sovereignty Matters*,
51–52, 392n12

Barreiro, Jose: *Indian Roots of
American Democracy*, 391n37

Bataan Death March, 254

Batt, Phil, 59

Beard, Laura: "A Society Based on
Names," 233

Bearheart (Vizenor), 173, 227

Bellin, Joshua David: *The Demon of
the Continent*, 8–9

Berkhofer, Robert: *The White Man's
Indian*, 20–21, 23, 104, 302, 331,
386n14

Berlant, Lauren: *The Anatomy of
National Fantasy*, 17, 230, 386n12

Bernardin, Susan: "The Authenticity Game," 236, 237, 398

Betonie (character), 83, 215, 248–
59, 264, 298, 358, 361–62. *See also*
Silko, Leslie Marmon—Works:
Ceremony

Bevis, William W.: *Ten Tough Trips*,
405n2

"Beyond Ecology" (Evernden),
95–96, 98

the Bible, 65, 117, 192, 352

Bigart, Robert: "Warriors in the
Blackboard Jungle," 396n8

Big Mom (character), 88, 158–59,
349–50. *See also* Alexie, Sherman—Works: *Reservation Blues*

Big Paul (character), 139–42. *See*

also McNickle, D'Arcy—Works:
The Surrounded

Bird, Gloria: "The Exaggeration of
Despair in Sherman Alexie's *Reservation Blues*," 12, 222, 384n5;
Reinventing the Enemy's Language,
323, 346

Black Eagle Child (Young Bear), 54,
312–13

Black Elk, 40, 105, 248, 400n8

Black Elk Speaks (Neihardt), 40–41,
105

Blackfeet Reservation, 241, 301

Blackhawk, 31

Black Lodge Singers, 241–42

Black Power, 328

Black Robes. *See* missionaries

Blackstone, William: *Commentaries
on English Law*, 57, 393n19

Blaeser, Kim, 10, 313–14, 316–17
—Works: "The New 'Frontier,'" 10,
313, 317; *Gerald Vizenor*, 402n5

Blood Struggle (Wilkinson), 89–90,
392n13

Boldt Decision (1974), 43, 394n31

"Border Patrol State" (Silko), 359

Bordewich, Fergus: *Killing the
White Man's Indian*, 391n5

Boston MA, 114, 198, 276, 367, 379,
380

The Boy (character), 143, 150, 187,
261, 286. *See also* McNickle,
D'Arcy—Works: *Wind From an
Enemy Sky*

Bradford, William, 403n11

The Brady Bunch, 291, 305, 306, 345

Char-Koosta News, 308

Cherokee Nation v. Georgia, 38–39, 47

Cherokees, xiv, 6, 9, 17, 25, 29, 37, 39, 44, 47–48, 93, 101, 166, 170, 316, 385n7, 386n13

Cheyenne River Sioux Reservation, 4, 112

Cheyennes, 25, 44, 52, 171

Child, Lydia Marie: *Boarding School Seasons*, 401n13; *Incidents in the Life of a Slave Girl*, 401n11

Chippewa Crees, 101

Chippewas, 101, 308, 314. *See also* Ojibwas

Choctaws, 17, 29, 37, 166, 227, 244, 270

Christ, 64, 69, 192, 268

Christianity, 6, 29, 53, 244, 259, 276, 301, 303, 312, 327, 330, 385n8, 386n13; and Apess, 64–68, 130–38, 162, 190–97, 262–69, 379; and messianism, 87, 141, 213, 261; and race, 68, 131, 333–34; and Winnemucca, 114, 117, 123–24, 269

Christian Transcendentalism, 50, 68, 269, 346, 354, 397n7

Civil War (U.S.), 6–7, 292

Clarence Mather (character), 293–94. *See also* Alexie, Sherman—Works: *Indian Killer*

Clifford, James, 92, 95, 107, 180, 195, 198, 200, 331; *The Predicament of Culture*, 100, 147, 170–72, 289–90, 389n27

Clinton, William J. (Bill), 297, 305

The Colbert Report, 306

Cold Spring Singers (fictional drum group), 349. *See also* Alexie, Sherman—Works: *The Toughest Indian in the World*

Cole, David: "Lost in Translation," 233

Collier, John, 176. *See also* Indian New Deal

colonialism, 11, 15, 25, 93, 133, 148, 178, 182–83, 185, 212, 213, 221, 238, 309, 315, 321, 350, 369–70, 376, 392n15, 395n38, 396n9; and dialogism and dialectics, 41, 106, 167, 170, 231, 326; internalized, 86, 123, 267, 287; and its projections, 31, 62, 186, 369; reversed acculturation, 327, 331–32; and sexual violence, 137, 186

Colorado River Basin, 394n29

Columbia River Basin, 58, 203, 394n24, 395n31

Columbus, Christopher, 31, 302–4, 326, 336, 365

"comedy," etymology of, 347

The Comedy of Survival (Meeker), 320–24, 326, 363

"The Comic Mode" (Meeker), 320–21, 322, 324, 363

community, 13–16, 32, 41, 50; and Alexie, 93, 101, 157–61, 164; as animism, 92, 94, 96–100, 102, 105–7, 110–13, 132–56, 241; and Apess, 93, 95, 105, 108–9, 130–39; communal identity, 37, 50, 171,

The Delicacy and Strength of Lace
  (Silko), 255–56, 373–74
Deloria, Ella: "Kinship Was the All-
  Important Matter," 104
Deloria, Philip, 236, 259; Playing
  Indian, 293, 366, 367–68
Deloria, Vine, Jr., 39, 55–56, 96,
  107, 236, 259, 293, 363, 366–70,
  372–76, 392n12, 401n4; and inher-
  ent powers, 49–51, 83; and oral
  traditions, 245–46, 303; and peo-
  plehood, 42–44, 53, 76
—Works: "American Fantasy," 293,
  368, 369; Custer Died for Your Sins,
  20, 343, 386n14, 390n34, 401n4;
  God Is Red, 40, 53, 96, 111, 148;
  The Nations Within, 43, 49–50, 83
DeMallie, Raymond: "Kinship,"
  105–6, 396n6; The Sixth Grandfather, 391n7
Denniston, Lyle: "Separation of
  Powers," 89, 395n40
Department of the Interior (U.S.),
  47, 50, 228, 273, 318, 380
DeRosa, Robin: Assimilation and
  Subversion in Earlier American Literature, 28–29
Derrida, Jacques, 235, 405n3
dialectics and dialogics, xiv, 27–31,
  34, 57, 66, 70, 73, 100, 106–8, 111,
  171–72, 231, 239, 240, 242, 325, 341–
  42, 348, 373, 381, 386n13, 389n26,
  390nn29–30, 403n11; and animism, 90, 93–95, 98; and Apess,
  130, 131, 193, 195–96, 198, 262;
  and Manicheism, 170, 315; and

Marxism, 98, 120, 157, 167; and
  McNickle, 179, 185, 278, 279; and
  Owens, 166, 169–70; and
  Winnemucca, 202, 204, 207
"A Dialogue on Race" (Alexie), 297,
  305
Dinés, 174, 227–28, 381. See also
  Navajos
Doc Edwards (character), 146, 187,
  277, 289. See also McNickle,
  D'Arcy—Works: Wind from an
  Enemy Sky
Doctrine of Discovery, 6, 47, 323
domestic dependent nations, 22,
  38, 47–48, 56, 57, 89, 385n6
Donner Party, 118
Douglass, Frederick: Narrative of
  the Life of Frederick Douglass, an
  American Slave, 72, 263
Drinnon, Richard: Facing West,
  20–21, 23, 386n14
Droogers, André: "Recovering and
  Reconstructing Syncretism,"
  389n29; Reinventing Religions,
  400n9
Dudas, Jeffery R.: The Cultivation
  of Resentment, 391n5
Duran, Eduardo: Native American
  Postcolonial Psychology, 400n6

Eastman, Charles, 106
ecocriticism, 98, 320, 374, 396n17
Edwards, Jonathan, 64
Egan, Ken, Jr.: "The Big Sky and
  the Siren Song of Apocalypse,"
  315–16

Indian Gaming Act (1988), 110

Indian Killer (Alexie), 290, 292–95, 401n15

Indian Law Resource Center, 395n33

Indian liberalism (coined by Carlson), 60

Indian New Deal, 54, 82, 176–77

Indian Nullification of the Unconstitutional Laws (Apess), 63–73, 136–37, 190, 267–68, 336, 351, 353

Indian Removal Act (1830), 6, 39, 72, 108, 386n13

Indian Reorganization Act (1934), 46, 49, 54, 109, 381

"Indian Ring" (Winnemucca), 162, 199, 224, 228, 269

Indians and Other Americans (McNickle), 280

Indian Self-Determination and Education Assistance Act (1975), 45–46, 49, 59, 82, 95, 109–10, 175, 289

"An Indian's Looking-Glass for the White Man" (Apess), 62, 65, 68, 131, 135, 137, 190–91, 193, 194–98, 236, 272, 353–54

"Indian Town," Plymouth MA, 63–64

Indian wars, 72, 158, 159, 163, 178, 246, 248, 276, 292, 302, 341

"Indian/White Relations" (A. Ortiz), 7, 85, 337, 376

Indigenous Holocaust, 94, 363

Indigenous nationalism, 7, 22, 29, 32–33, 55, 189, 212, 221, 289, 384n6; and authenticity, 8, 238, 239, 240–41, 291, 366, 371. *See also* nationhood

Indi'n Humor (Lincoln), 320, 337, 339, 402n5

individualism, 160, 162, 199–200, 297, 389n28, 398n1

"Introduction to Native American Literature" (Alexie), 219, 223

Iron Child (character), 80, 143, 286, 358. *See also* McNickle, D'Arcy—Works: *Wind from an Enemy Sky*

irony, 5–6, 14, 66–67, 112, 139, 219, 245, 261, 269, 271, 276, 300–364; as distinguished from humor, 310. *See also* humor

Iroquois Confederacy (Haudenosaunee), 31, 54, 56–57; and "covenant chain," 102; and influence on U.S. Constitution, 11, 400n7; language of, xii; as model democracy, 11, 54, 245, 372

Israelites (Hebrews), 132, 138, 190, 266

I Would Steal Horses (Alexie), 219

Jackson, Andrew, 6, 39, 48, 60, 63, 132, 189, 268

Jack Wilson (character), 293. *See also* Alexie, Sherman—Works: *Indian Killer*

Jacobs, Harriet, 401n11

Jaimes-Guerrero, M. A., "'Patriarchal Colonialism' and Indigenism," 392n15

James, William, 311

Methodist Church, 64, 135, 191–92, 262

Métis, 108, 282–83, 380, 404n2

Midgley, Mary: *The Myths We Live By*, 315, 402n7

Miller, Robert J.: *Native Americans, Discovered and Conquered*, 392n14

Minnesota Territory, 2

Minnesota War ("Minnesota Uprising"), 2–3

missionaries, 44, 65–66, 69, 73, 102–3, 124, 139, 141, 265, 269, 322, 334, 353, 403, 428

Missoula Mercantile, 282

Mixedblood Messages (Owens), 167, 169, 212, 231, 240

"A Modell of Christian Charitie" (Winthrop), 130, 132, 136

modernism, 139, 172–74, 196, 248, 346, 366

Mohawk, John: *Exiled in the Land of the Free*, 393n18

Mohawks, 42, 55–57, 77, 376

Momaday, N. Scott, 221, 289, 372, 381–82

—Works: *House Made of Dawn*, 20, 397n11; "Man Made of Words," 397n11

Montaigne, Michel de: "On Cannibals," 331–32

Montana Legislature, 301

Montana Museum of Art and Culture, 343

"Moon Vines among the Ruins" (Moore), 401n1

Moore, David L.: "Decolonializing Criticism," 28, 95, 389nn26–27, 395n1; "Moon Vines among the Ruins," 401n1; "Myth, History, and Identity in Silko and Young Bear," 402n5; "Ray A. Young Bear," 395n3; "Rough Knowledge and Radical Understanding," 397n10; "Sherman Alexie," 348; "Silko's Blood Sacrifice," 396n16; "The Twilight of White Liberalism," 4004n1

Morton, Thomas, 403n11

Mouffe, Chantal, 327

Muddy Lake NV, 119

Murray, David: *Forked Tongues*, 402n5

Muting White Noise (Cox), 306, 346

"Myth, History, and Identity in Silko and Young Bear" (Moore), 402n5

"mythification of lived experience" (Zumthor), 232, 267, 298

Myths and Realities of Tribal Sovereignty (Kalt and Singer), 44–46, 52

The Myths We Live By (Midgley), 315, 402n7

names, significance of, 87, 113–14, 180, 182, 198–200, 204, 233, 288, 348

"narrate," etymology of, 232

narration, 87–88, 94, 142, 162, 164, 177, 179, 194, 207, 210, 325, 402n5; and authenticity, 41, 93, 111, 170, 232–33, 257, 268, 270, 275, 298, 349. *See also* storytelling

Narrative Chance (Vizenor), 314

nationhood, 5–13, 12, 17–18, 22, 24, 27, 39, 43–44, 61, 82–83, 240, 242,

Ortiz, Alfonso, 385n8
—Works: "Indian/White Relations," 7, 85, 337, 376; obituary for D'Arcy McNickle, 176; "The Sacred Clown," 402n5
Ortiz, Simon, 95, 108, 297, 308, 316, 318; and authenticity, 8, 226, 291–92, 308, 313, 338
—Works: *from Sand Creek*, vii, 24, 26, 35, 238, 247, 336, 375, 377; "Towards a National Indian Literature," 232, 234, 238–40, 247, 322, 333, 336, 366, 369
Osages, 9, 42, 44, 103
O'Sullivan, John, 371. *See also* manifest destiny
Other Destinies (Owens), 37, 92, 166, 168–69, 183, 211, 229, 371, 397n1
Our Fire Survives the Storm (Justice), xiv, 6, 18, 25, 27, 44, 170, 315
Owens, Louis, 17, 174, 183–85, 189, 218–19, 228–31, 279–82, 368–70, 385n9
—Works: "As If," 368; ; *Mixedblood Messages*, 167, 169, 212, 231, 240; *Other Destinies*, 37, 92, 166, 168–69, 183, 211, 229, 371, 397n1
Oytes (Piute subchief), 203–4

Paiutes, 54, 75–79, 99, 103–4, 108–9, 116, 121–29, 149, 162, 198–206, 223, 269, 275, 293, 325, 355, 380, 400nn10–11; and Victorian moral codes, 114–15, 224, 271–73, 298; and "white brothers," 117–20
pan-Indianism, 128, 189, 289

paracolonial (term), 173, 213
Parker, Dorothy R.: *Singing an Indian Song*, 176, 282
Parker, Robert Dale: 388n22; *The Invention of Native American Literature*, 23
Parrish, Samuel, 79, 124–26, 162, 203
paternalism, 54, 98–99, 117, 124–27, 203–4, 371
Pattee, John, 3, 31, 90–91
Peabody, Elizabeth, 114, 273–74, 276, 397n7
Peace, Power, Righteousness (Alfred), 42–43, 55–57
Pearce, Roy Harvey, 23, 302; *Savagism and Civilization*, 12, 20–21, 386n14
Pell, Adam (character), 186, 187, 280, 285, 287. *See also* McNickle, D'Arcy—Works: *Wind from an Enemy Sky*
Pend d'Oreilles, 282
peoplehood, 43–44, 76–80, 82–85, 144, 213, 256. *See also* sovereignty
Pequots, 63, 134, 193, 197, 262, 266, 268, 297
performance theory, 127–28, 129, 199–200, 367. *See also* Winnemucca, Sarah: role as princess
"Petition of the Marshpee Tribe of Indians" (Apess), 64, 70–72, 263
Philip. *See* "King Philip" (Metacomet)
"philosophy of insignificance" (Young Bear), 98, 312–13, 358

U.S. Supreme Court. *See* Supreme Court (U.S.)

Utter, Jack: *American Indians*, 226

Venables, Robert W.: "The Founding Fathers," 395n5

Verney, Marilyn Notah: "On Authenticity," 174, 227–28, 247, 371

veterans (American Indian), 106, 254

Victorian morality: and domesticity, 114–15, 224; and Paiute moral codes, 272–74, 298

Vizenor, Gerald, 31, 88, 92–93, 195–96, 213, 227, 288, 307, 311, 313–17, 329, 336, 346, 349, 365, 381, 386n15, 391n2, 401n1, 401n12; and "terminal creeds," 172–73, 222, 315, 319–20, 342, 345; and "trickster discourse," 169, 173, 302–4, 314, 342, 345, 402n5
—Works: *Bearheart*, 173, 227; *The Heirs of Columbus*, 89, 303, 336, 391n2; *Manifest Manners*, 213, 302, 303, 314–15; *Narrative Chance*, 314; "Ruins of Representation," 92, 173, 195–96, 288, 314, 402n5; *The Trickster of Liberty*, 401n12, 402n5; *The Voice in the Margin* (with Krupat), 171, 262–63, 379, 384n5, 385n9, 391n2, 398n1, 402n5

Walking (Thoreau), 39, 229

Wampanoags, 19, 289–90, 297

Warrior, Robert Allen, 32, 42, 100, 265, 304, 379, 397n6

—Works: "Eulogy on William Apess," 397n6; "Temporary Visibility," 42; *Tribal Secrets*, 42, 55, 100

"Wars and Their Causes" (Winnemucca), 116, 122, 124, 132–33, 272, 355. *See also* sexual violence

Washington DC, 127, 199, 201

Washington State, 43, 75, 201, 273, 382

Washington State University, 220

Water Education Foundation, 394n29

Waters, Anne: "The Myth of Tribalism," 392n15

Waters, Frank: *The Man Who Killed the Deer*, 110–11

Weatherford, Jack: *Native Roots*, 402n9

Weaver, Jace, 29, 32, 100, 198, 304, 391n38
—Works: *American Indian Literary Nationalism*, 212, 391n35; *That the People Might Live*, 92–93, 384n4, 398n1

Webster, Daniel, 61

Welch, James, 373, 381, 402n6
—Works: *Fools Crow*, 167; *Riding the Earthboy*, 40, 308, 314–15

Welch, Lois: "Wild but Not Savage," 318, 337

West, Cornel: *Democracy Matters*, 247; *Race Matters*, 400n5

Wheatley, Phyllis, 29

white brothers, 76, 104, 108, 116, 129, 162, 190, 194, 199, 203–4, 275, 325; "Paiute legend," 117–20

White Lodge, 2–3, 90–91

The White Man's Indian (Berkhofer), 20–21, 23, 104, 302, 331, 386n14

White, Richard: *The Middle Ground*, 386n11

The White Roots of Peace (Iroquois), 245

Whorf, Benjamin Lee: "An American Indian Model of the Universe," 397n14

Wild West show, 208, 361

Wilkins, David: *American Indian Politics and the American Political System*, 363; *Tribes, Treaties, and Constitutional Tribulations*, 392n13, 393n17

Wilkinson, Charles: *Blood Struggle*, 89–90, 392n13

Williams, Robert A., Jr.: *The American Indian in Western Legal Thought*, 393n17

Wilson, Jack (character), 293. *See also* Alexie, Sherman—Works: *Indian Killer*

Wilson, Michael D.: *Writing Home*, 227, 384n5, 392n10

Wind from an Enemy Sky (McNickle), 37, 40, 78–82, 142–50, 163, 174–75, 178–88, 248–49, 277–90, 356–58, 381, 397n3

Winnemucca, Mattie, 120, 201–2, 206

Winnemucca, Sarah, 5, 16–17, 43, 70, 78–79, 90, 95, 99, 101, 104–9, 130–31, 137, 149–50, 162–64, 171, 175, 178–79, 222–23, 228, 238–39, 248, 261, 297–98, 325, 333, 341, 345, 371, 373, 380; and animism, 114–17; and authenticity, 268–77, 400n10, 400n11; and community, 114–30; and humor 354–56; and identity, 198–207; and role as princess, 121, 128–29, 199, 201–7, 274, 276, 400n10; and sovereignty, 74–77; and Victorian morality, 122, 204, 272

—Works: *Life Among the Piutes*, 54, 74, 75–77, 103, 114, 115–26, 129–30, 199–207, 269, 271–76, 354–56, 380, 400n10; "Wars and Their Causes," 116, 122, 124, 132–33, 272, 355; "The Yakima Affair," 201–2

Winthrop, John: "A Modell of Christian Charitie," 130, 132, 136

Womack, Craig, 32, 304, 365, 388n25

—Works: *American Indian Literary Nationalism*, 212; *Reasoning Together*, 391n35; *Red on Red*, 42

Woody, Elizabeth: *Seven Hands, Seven Hearts*, 59–60

Worcester v. Georgia, 39, 47, 390n33

Word Ways (Purdy), 142, 145, 178, 184, 188, 242, 279, 280–81, 283

Wounded Knee Massacre (1890), 7, 261

Wounded Knee Occupation (1973), 4

The Writer's Almanac (Keillor), 345, 347

CPSIA information can be obtained at www.ICGtesting.com
Printed in the USA
BVOW02s0452300415

398341BV00001B/16/P